RUNNING THE RACE

RUNNING THE RACE

The "Public Face" of
CHARLTON HESTON

BRIAN STEEL
WILLS

SB

Savas Beatie
California

Library of Congress Cataloging-in-Publication Data

Names: Wills, Brian Steel, 1959- author.
Title: Running the Race: The "Public Face" of Charlton Heston / by Brian Steel Wills.
Description: El Dorado Hills, CA: Savas Beatie, [2022] | Includes
    bibliographical references and index. | Summary: "Brian Steel Wills'
    captures for the first time a comprehensive view of the actor's climb to
    fame, his search for the perfect performance, and the meaningful roles
    he played in support of the causes he embraced in *Running the Race: The
    "Public Face" of Charlton Heston*, the first full-length biography of the
    actor in many years. Award-winning historian Brian Steel Wills dug deep
    to paint a rich portrait of Heston's extraordinary life–a mix of
    complications and complexities that touched film, television, theater,
    politics, and society. His carefully crafted "public face" was impactful
    in more ways than the ordinarily shy and private family man could have
    ever imagined."– Provided by publisher.
Identifiers: LCCN 2022006876 | ISBN 9781611216288 (hardcover) |
    ISBN 9781954547469 (ebook)
Subjects: LCSH: Heston, Charlton. | Motion picture actors and actresses–
    United States–Biography. | LCGFT: Biographies.
Classification: LCC PN2287.H47 W55 2022 | DDC 791.4302/8092
    [B]–dc23/eng/20220519
LC record available at https://lccn.loc.gov/2022006876

First edition, first printing

SB
Savas Beatie
989 Governor Drive, Suite 102
El Dorado Hills, CA 95762
916-941-6896 / sales@savasbeatie.com

Savas Beatie titles are available at special discounts for bulk purchases in the United States. Contact us for more details.

Proudly published, printed, and warehoused in the United States of America.

To our youngest grandchildren,

Reid, Vivian Briana, Mikayla, William, and James, Jr.,

in the hope they will enjoy the movies as much
as their "Grandpa"/"PawPaw" has through the years.

Charlton Heston in the movie *Ben-Hur*.

Author's Collection

Contents

A gallery of photos and illustrations can be found following page 206.

Abbreviations

AC/AJC: Atlanta Constitution/Journal-Constitution

ALJ: Charlton Heston, Actor's Life Journals

BD: Charlton Heston Beijing Diary

BG/BDG/BSG: Boston Globe/Boston Daily Globe/Boston Sunday Globe:

BHC: Bristol Herald-Courier

GBPL: George H. W. Bush Presidential Library and Museum, College Station, TX

CHA: In The Arena

CHCF: Charlton Heston Clipping Files

GH: Good Housekeeping

LAT : Los Angeles Times

LJPL: Lyndon Johnson Presidential Library, Austin, TX

HL: Margaret Herrick Library, Beverly Hills, CA

NYT: New York Times

RNPL: Richard Nixon Presidential Library, Yorba Linda, CA

RTD: Richmond Times-Dispatch

RRPL: Ronald Reagan Presidential Library, Simi Valley, CA

SEP: Saturday Evening Post

UCLA: University of California, Los Angeles

VP/VPLS: Virginian-Pilot/Virginian-Pilot and Ledger-Star

WHORM: White House Office of Records Management

Wills: Brian Steel Wills, Charlton Heston Collection

PREFACE

As far back as I can remember the movies have been a part of my life. They represented both special family time on given Sundays after services and social outlets throughout my teenaged years. Most often, I preferred historical dramas, or at least those with context from the past, and few actors seemed to embody that connection as clearly as Charlton Heston. One of the earliest volumes in my possession was a compendium of Heston films by Jeff Rovin.[1]

The actor's most well-known roles came as Moses in *The Ten Commandments* and as the principal protagonist in *Ben-Hur*. Likewise, Heston's engagement with British troops threatening New Orleans, in the Sudan against the forces of the Mahdi, defending the legations in Peking from the Boxers, holding the Moors out of Spain, or painting the ceiling of the Sistine Chapel, evoked a fascination that remained long after the screen, large or small, went dark. In addition to these portrayals, several Heston motion pictures have remained memorable for me. The Western *Will Penny*, in which a hard-boiled cowboy views life's opportunities through eyes wizened by age and experience, is one. Another, with a particularly well-crafted opening sequence, is *The Mountain Men*, heightened by the presence of another favorite actor, Brian Keith, and the chemistry between the principal performers. Heston's jaded police officer Thorn and his resource with a memory, Edward G. Robinson's Sol Roth, in *Soylent Green*, as well as astronaut Taylor's visit to the *Planet of the Apes*, or the apparently "sole" survivor in the streets of Los Angeles in *The Omega Man*, demonstrated that he could fit into the science fiction genre, too. I made sure that whenever *Ben-Hur*, *The Ten Commandments*, *Khartoum*, *El Cid*, or virtually any other Heston movie came on television I tried to watch, even if he would have winced at the depiction of these big motion pictures

---

1 Jeff Rovin, *The Films of Charlton Heston* (New York, 1976).

on small screens. I also really enjoyed the actor's successful foray into comedy in *The Private War of Major Benson*, in which his hard-nosed professional soldier runs into formidable challenges from the cadets, Julie Adams's Lammy, William Demarest's caretaker, and the "ladies" of the convent. Heston demonstrated that he could make his serious persona work against these lovable foils in an endearing way.

Framed as a race, this volume pays homage to the depiction of the intensely personal contest between Judah Ben-Hur and his long-time friend Messala. For those desirous of examining the whole *Ben-Hur* story in minute detail, Jon Solomon has written a thorough treatment of it in *Ben-Hur: The Original Blockbuster*. That work allows the reader to examine the impact of the novel as well as the 1925 and 1959 films. Elements of Solomon's work appear here as they pertain to Heston and his image/persona but interested persons should read his fascinating account in full.

Readers of this volume should note that it is not intended to be strictly biographical, although there are significant biographical elements about it. The book is also not meant to serve as a primer for creating, developing, or maintaining a "brand," although that, too, is present. It contains many of the details of the creative process Heston pursued, so that readers can follow his journey and understand better the nature and demands it exacted of him and his loved ones. The subject is unique, following Heston as he generates his own "public face" and finds ways to utilize it for multiple purposes. Just as someone studying coaching or gridiron leadership can learn from and quote the legendary Green Bay Packers coach Vince Lombardi, or specific political and military figures, so can one follow the life and career of Charlton Heston with benefit. He strove for perfection in his craft and, like all humanity, fell short. He knew better than most what it meant to be frustrated or disappointed, especially when he began directing and casting others rather than worrying about being selected himself. His desire and effort to do his best and keep his promises remain inspiring.

A family man who nevertheless put strains on the loved ones he cherished as his focus turned repeatedly to his work and its tremendous demands on his time, attention, and energies, Charlton Heston managed to keep a marriage intact while serving his industry and the public causes he embraced. He became a celebrity and international superstar in an era in which he thought it was just as important to be responsible and accountable as a member of his profession and a representative of the performing arts. His service in World War II and his many endeavors on behalf of the various agencies of the United States government and charities demonstrated a sense of devotion to America. While he considered the stage his home, the cinema brought him international fame; it has continued to be richer for the presence of the powerful physical force with the resonant voice whose roles ranged from Moses and Judah Ben-Hur to the ordinary individuals so often confronted by extraordinary circumstances.

As anyone will say who has engaged in such a project, this one would not have been possible without the help of others. Many individuals and institutions have assisted with the research for this work. My colleagues in the Department of History and Philosophy and the Dean's Office in the College of Humanities and Social Sciences at Kennesaw State University have been supportive. The Center for the Study of the Civil War Era at KSU, of which I have had the privilege of serving as director since 2010, has allowed me the freedom to engage in research and writing when not involved with activities in support of the Civil War Center's programming and operations. In Wise, Virginia, my wife, Elizabeth Wills, has remained a necessary foundation of support for all the projects I have undertaken, be it this one or those connected with the Civil War Center.

Thanks also go to Theodore P. Savas of Savas Beatie for standing by this volume when the Coronavirus pandemic threw enormous challenges into the process. Its publication depended upon his perseverance, for which the author is appreciative. Thanks also to the team at Savas-Beatie that saw the project through to fruition. Special appreciation goes to Joel Manuel for his meticulous and attentive copy-editing of the manuscript. It was a pleasure to work with him.

I have dedicated this volume to the next generation of our collective families. We who have preceded them now stand on their shoulders.

Filmography and Characters
of Charlton Heston

Peer Gynt (1941) (Peer Gynt)

Julius Caesar (1950) (Mark Antony)

Dark City (1950) (Danny Haley)

The Savage (1952) (Warbonnet/Jim Aherne, Jr.)

Ruby Gentry (1952) (Boake Tackman)

The Greatest Show on Earth (1952) (Brad Braeden)

The President's Lady (1953) (Andrew Jackson)

Pony Express (1953) (Buffalo Bill Cody)

Arrowhead (1953) (Ed Bannon)

Bad for Each Other (1953) (Dr. Tom Owen)

The Secret of the Incas (1954) (Harry Steele)

The Naked Jungle (1954) (Christopher Leiningen)

The Private War of Major Benson (1955) (Major Bernard "Barney" Benson)

Lucy Gallant (1955) (Casey Cole)

The Far Horizons (1955) (William Clark)

Three Violent People (1956) (Colt Saunders)

The Ten Commandments (1956) (Moses)

The Buccaneer (1958) (Andrew Jackson)

The Big Country (1958) (Steve Leech)

Touch of Evil (1958) (Ramon Miguel "Mike" Vargas)

The Wreck of the Mary Deare (1959) (John Sands)

Ben-Hur (1959) (Judah Ben-Hur)

El Cid (1961) (Rodrigo Díaz de Vivar (Bivar)/El Cid)

Diamond Head (1962) (Richard "King" Howland)

The Pigeon that Took Rome (1962) (Captain Paul MacDougall)

55 Days at Peking (1963) (Major Matt Lewis)

The Patriots (1963) (Thomas Jefferson)

The Agony and the Ecstasy (1965) (Michelangelo)

The Greatest Story Ever Told (1965) (John the Baptist)

Major Dundee (1965) (Major Amos Charles Dundee)

The War Lord (1965) (Chrysagon)

Khartoum (1966) (General Charles "Chinese" Gordon)

Planet of the Apes (1968) (George Taylor)

Counterpoint (1968) (Lionel Evans)

Will Penny (1968) (Will Penny)

Elizabeth the Queen (1968) (Robert Devereaux, Earl of Essex)

Number One (1969) (Ron "Cat" Catlan)

Julius Caesar (1970) (Mark Antony)

The Hawaiians (1970) (Whip Hoxworth)

Beneath the Planet of the Apes (1970) (George Taylor)

The Omega Man (1971) (Robert Neville)

Skyjacked (1972) (Captain Henry "Hank" O'Hara)

Antony and Cleopatra (1973) (Mark Antony); also director

The Call of the Wild (1973) (John Thornton)

Soylent Green (1973) (Detective Robert Thorn)

The Three Musketeers (1973) (Cardinal Richelieu)

Earthquake (1974) (Stuart Graff)

Airport 1975 (1974) (Alan Murdock)

The Four Musketeers (1975) (Cardinal Richelieu)

Two-Minute Warning (1976) (Captain Peter Holly)

Midway (1976) (Captain Matt Garth)

The Last Hard Men (1976) (Sam Burgade)

Gray Lady Down (1978) (Captain Paul Blanchard)

Crossed Swords (1978) (King Henry VIII)

The Awakening (1980) (Matthew Corbeck)

The Mountain Men (1980) (Bill Tyler)

Mother Lode (1982) (Silas McGee/Ian McGee); also director

Chiefs (1983) (Hugh Holmes)

Nairobi Affair (1984) (Lee Cahill)

Proud Men (1987) (Charley MacLeod, Sr.)

A Man for All Seasons (1988) (Sir Thomas More); also director

Original Sin (1989) (Louis Mancini)

Treasure Island (1990) (Long John Silver)

Solar Crisis (1990) (Admiral "Skeet" Kelso)

The Little Kidnappers (1990) (James MacKenzie)

Almost An Angel (1990) (God) (uncredited)

The Crucifer of Blood (1991) (Sherlock Holmes)

Crash Landing: The Rescue of Flight 232 (1992) (Captain Al Haynes)

Wayne's World 2 (1993) (Good Actor)

Tombstone (1993) (Henry Hooker)

True Lies (1994) (Spencer Trilby)

In the Mouth of Madness (1994) (Jackson Harglow)

The Avenging Angel (1995) (Brigham Young)

Alaska (1996) (Perry)

Hamlet (1996) (The Player King)

Gideon (1998) (Addison Sinclair)

Any Given Sunday (1999) (AFFA Football Commissioner)

Town & Country (2001) (Eugenie's Father)

Planet of the Apes (2001) (Zaius) (uncredited)

The Order (2001) (Professor Finley)

My Father, Rua Alguem 5555 (2001) (Josef Mengele)

Genghis Khan: The Story of a Lifetime (2010) (Trogul)

INTRODUCTION

A Public Life for a Private Person: "The Look of Eagles"

"What's in a name?"

—William Shakespeare, *Romeo and Juliet* (II, ii)

"The Look of Eagles."

—Description for a confident racehorse

Charlton Heston's path in life required that he undergo multiple identifications. Born John Charles Carter, he became "Chuck" to his friends and close associates. To his wife, Lydia Clarke Heston, he occasionally became "CH" or "Charlie," although he professed to find little joy in the application of the latter version of his identity. In his autobiography, *In the Arena*, Heston noted pointedly, "I *hate* the nickname 'Charlie.' No one ever calls me that more than once except Lydia." Even her use of this version of his name prompted a visceral response. "When she says it, my heart shivers. To this day."[1]

For so much of his life, however, "Charlton Heston" was the name and "face" instantly recognizable to the public and fans of his work. Writer Helen Van Slyke of *The Saturday Evening Post*, which a young Heston had once sold "from a canvas bag when it cost five cents," captured the essence of this phenomenon: "Charlton

---

1 Charlton Heston, *In the Arena* (New York, 1995), 47. Lydia referred to him as "old CH" in a 1981 "This is Your Life" episode. "This is Your Life (TV) transcript," 17, Charlton Heston Papers, f.369, HL.

Heston. Even the name rolls like thunder on the tongue, evoking images of the mighty characters with whom he's identified."[2]

Supplementing a name that could distinguish him, Heston also grew into a distinctive physical frame as an adult. His early associate and director David Bradley later jested about a scouting expedition to New Trier High School in search of prospective talent for his projects. "I was looking for a tall, good-looking Nordic type guy. I had to settle for Chuck Heston." Bradley remembered, "I looked and he's towering above anyone else and I said this guy will do." This striking characteristic became crucial to establishing a lasting film persona. Writer Donald Spoto observed, "Heston's large form is magnified more, indeed, on the big screen," where this quality became "extended," embodying "the pure form of [a] man of power." Film critic Robert Osborne explained, "Timing and facial structure pushed him into the big-time."[3]

As an adult, Charlton Heston was always appreciative of the raw materials with which nature and heredity blessed him. He recognized the advantages of his physical attributes and worked diligently to maintain them. In addition to a 6'3" frame and a camera-friendly visage, he benefitted enormously from a rich resonating voice, which he labelled a "useful bequest to me" from his father. Heston recalled later that in Michigan, "they used to call me 'Moose.'"[4]

The actor refused to rely on his physical attributes alone. He never lost the desire to achieve perfection in any role he undertook and employed stringent means to accomplish that standard. This level of commitment ensured that he thrived in every arena he entered. "Charlton Heston is stimulated by a hard day's work and carries his job home with him, where he primes and polishes the next day's schedule," one writer explained in 1958. John Henry Steele quoted Heston

2 Helen Van Slyke, "From 'Moses' to 'Midway,' Charlton Heston is Larger Than Life," *SEP* (Jan./Feb.1976), 46.

3 "This is Your Life transcript," 13, HL; Quoted in Steven Cohan, *Masked Men: Masculinity and the Movies in the Fifties* (Bloomington, IN, 1997), 155; Donald Spoto, *Camerado: Hollywood and the American Man* (New York, 1978), 214; Robert Osborne, *Academy Awards Illustrated: A Complete History of Hollywood's Academy Awards in Words and Pictures* (LaHabra, CA, 1966), 245.

4 *CHA*, 18, 37. This physical description was published in 1950: "For those who cherish such information, he is 6 feet and 3 inches tall, weighs 205 pounds, has gray-blue eyes and blondish hair, wears size 12 shoes and a 7½ hat." Morton Elliott Freedgood, "Big Man, What Now?" *NYT*, Oct. 15, 1950, Heston Clipping Files, HL.

as saying, "I don't see how a perfectionist can automatically shut out his work at a given hour."[5]

"Mr. Heston" carried his weight beneath a sturdy and studied persona that, while seemingly stiff and distant, covered a man of integrity and humor. His professionalism and perfectionism often meant that he suffered fools less than fulsomely, and they as well as others, some of whom recognized the fact, expressed themselves accordingly. Even so, any reading of his private correspondence and interactions readily reveals a sophisticated, thoughtful, and generous individual. Heston's devotion to his wife and family became legendary in a Hollywood world in which long-term marriages and strong nuclear families were uncommon.

A man of both contradictions and consistencies, Heston could be satisfied and disappointed with equal fervor. This complicated quality exhibited itself in an often-busy public life. As a writer observed of one aspect of that active existence, "He enjoyed being a political independent who made up his mind on an issue-by-issue basis."[6] Heston wanted to project himself as thoughtful and inquisitive, in addition to being creative and artistic, in all his pursuits.

In a free flowing, stream-of-consciousness piece that appeared in *Photoplay* magazine in 1958, Heston exposed these complexities. Labeling himself a shy individual who "dislikes large parties, prefers entertaining small groups of friends, and has a congenital distrust of flattery," he offered a contradictory possibility as a career, should acting fail him. "When the day comes that I'm no longer working at my trade, don't be surprised to see me try for the diplomatic service or even politics. I like talking to people." This same private person understood that his public life required transformation and sacrifice that he had to be prepared to make. "The day when an actor 'wants to be alone' is over," he observed. "Fans like to feel they know you personally, and I must confess I get a big kick out of making friends with people I'd never have the opportunity to meet if I shut myself up."[7]

Heston recognized the contradictory forces at work in his life and career. "I suppose the primary difference between the public's perception of who and what I am and my own perception of me is that I remain a shy person," he told an interviewer. "I have learned to be a public actor because I have been doing it for so

---

5 Joseph Henry Steele, "Unmasking Charlton Heston," *Photoplay* (Jan. 1958), 52.

6 Steven J. Ross, *Hollywood Left and Right: How Movie Stars Shaped American Politics* (New York, 2011), 288.

7 Steele, "Unmasking Charlton Heston," 74. On another occasion, he suggested "Carpenter" as a possible choice of career. "Front Row Center," *Atlanta Weekly*, Aug. 11, 1985.

long." Yet even as Heston touted a latent desire to create new friendships easily, he acknowledged the on-going struggle this level of contact with others required. "I've got self-confidence, true," he explained. "You can't succeed as an actor without that." Still, the exposure he allowed to occur through his work did not entirely mask the struggle within. "The image so many of the parts I've played has created in the public mind can serve as a refuge for a shy man."[8]

Through much of his life, the game of tennis provided Chuck Heston with an essential outlet, one that could be a source of fitness and a refuge from outside intrusions at the same time. "I think I used it as a cover-up when someone invited me to dinner—to change the subject you know," he explained to an interviewer.[9] He battled constantly with the need to build and maintain an audience while also keeping anyone outside a few select family and friends from getting too close.

Writer Ed Leibowitz captured the complicated nature of the private man as public figure after witnessing a Heston appearance at a National Rifle Association gathering. "If only Heston were the ideological parody political opponents would like him to be," he insisted. "Instead, he's as wildly divergent as the sober NRA set and the architectural triumph on the ridge," he noted of the Heston family home in California. "Yes, he is an implacable conservative, but almost all his closest friends are liberal Democrats, and he counts his participation in the 1963 March on Washington, where he led the artists' contingent, among the proudest moments of his life." From the writer's perspective, the actor was "a pious scourge in public, but at home he's the well-traveled connoisseur with not a trace of ill temper, who's prone to profanity and tears."[10]

Charlton Heston seemed to be happiest when ensconced in the refuge he had built after *Ben-Hur* on "my ridge" above Coldwater Canyon overlooking Beverly Hills. As he noted, "Most of the people I want to see, the things I want to do, happen right here." He craved the sense of privacy the property offered him and enjoyed "time alone, all by myself." Heston understood that the source of this desire arose from within him, dating back to his earliest years. "As a guy brought up in the Michigan woods," he explained, "I *really* need it."

At the beginning of his Hollywood career, he acquired his Michigan home place and the deep woods that surrounded it. "I own one of those lakes now, Russell Lake," he told an interviewer. "It was one of the first things I bought with

---

8 Roberta Plutzik, "Last of the Epic Heroes," *Horizon* (Mar. 1980), 33.

9 "Keeping in Trim," MGM Pressbook for *Skyjacked*, 1972, Wills.

10 Ed Leibowitz, "Charlton Heston's Last Stand," *Los Angeles* (Feb. 2001), 63.

my movie money." After the success of *The Ten Commandments*, another writer observed, "Moses Hides Out in the Woods Instead." Describing the purchase as occurring, in Heston's words, "with the first dough I made in pictures," Earl Wilson added that he "sells Christmas trees off the timberland, leases hunting and fishing rights, and rides and skis when he is there—meanwhile reading scripts . . . and remembering his boyhood." Another article reiterated the fact that "he does a lucrative Christmas tree business," and also referenced his aspirations to "build a 300-seat repertory theater" on the land as well. Through the years, Heston remained connected to the region, with a Christmas tree brought down annually for the holiday celebration in Beverly Hills. Co-star Donald Pleasance captured several layers of this symbolism when he described the role he played as Heston's nemesis in one of their films. "In 'Will Penny' I was *really* wicked. You can't do anything worse than burn Charlton Heston's Christmas tree."[11]

The creation of the Russell Lake Corporation was another manifestation of this phenomenon. In 1956, Heston unveiled his plans. "While the Charlton Heston company, which he calls Russell Lake Corp., was formed to control his timberland interests in Michigan," a description of the project noted, "he intends also to use its facilities for picturemaking as well as summer stage undertakings." The design was ambitious. "He plans to maintain a footlight establishment at St. Helen's, Mich., and undertake a picture next summer. Heston has one more film to do under contract at Paramount. He may add TV to the other activities of his own organization."[12]

Heston intended the Russell Lake Corporation to serve both as homage to his past and as a hedge for the future. His vision, boldly touted in a 1959 *Los Angeles Times* report, was supposed to begin independent film production after he had fulfilled his contractual commitments, but the dream of a fully functioning entity failed to transpire. Heston ultimately dissolved the company in order to avoid the appearance of conflicts when he took a leadership position in the Screen Actors Guild.[13]

---

11 Maynard Good Stoddard and Cory SerVaas, "Charlton Heston: He'd Rather Pretend Than Be President," *SEP* (Sept. 1984), 44; Earl Wilson, "Moses Hides Out in the Woods Instead," Scrapbooks, Heston Papers, HL; Steele, "Unmasking Charlton Heston," 74; *CHA*, 322; See also Charlton Heston, *The Actor's Life: Journals, 1956–1976* (New York, 1976), 187, 421, 481, hereafter cited as *ALJ*; Mary Blume, "Donald Pleasance—Proud of His Wicked Film Ways," *LAT*, July 21, 1968.

12 Edwin Schallert, "Charlton Heston Plans Varied Activities," *LAT*, Oct. 11, 1956.

13 "Heston to Form His Own Company," *LAT*, Feb. 18, 1959.

In addition to his Midwestern roots, Heston took enormous pride in his Scottish background and heritage. Noting in his autobiography his connection to "Clan Fraser of Inverness," he labeled the link "a blood strain I'm very proud of," and thought the clan motto (*"Je suis prest*—I am Ready") particularly appropriate. He took considerable pleasure in a trip to Scotland in the summer of 1972 that allowed him to connect to that past. He experienced "the very different delights of the Fraser country," on July 19; on the following day, he hiked "across the moors" and reveled that it was "[m]arvelous to do it in a kilt . . . it made all the difference, somehow." This "very full Fraser day" led the actor to conclude, "I'm prouder than ever of my Fraser blood."[14]

From the youth growing up in the isolated woodlands of the Midwest to the man who made good in his career through the sweat and toil of his own brow, Charlton Heston took many of these elements of his heritage to himself almost literally. Long before his involvement with the National Rifle Association, he saw guns and hunting as a way of life rather than simply a fascinating diversion or sport. Likewise, he looked at family in an idyllic sense. Heston boasted that he was anachronistic in a world of Hollywood royalty and Washington connections, yet he appreciated the benefits of his profession and recognized the flexibility that the elevated status he had attained allowed him to enjoy. "I didn't go after fame," Heston once insisted; "I wanted to be an actor." He explained, "I don't think stardom is what any serious actor has in mind. What they have in mind is acting, getting good parts." As such, he maintained that "[s]tardom is not something you seek; it's something you accept." "The material rewards are considerable—certainly out of all proportion to merit," but this status allowed "what the artist wants above all else: *control.*"[15]

Whatever role he might take in public affairs, Heston's appearances in epic films provided important context for his most recognizable roles. One scholar observed that "Charlton Heston is arguably the über-epic actor, famous for his lead roles in some of the biggest mid-century epics." Director Carol Reed's biographer assessed the actor's suitability for these larger-than-life portrayals, writing that Heston's "sculpted looks and dominant presence were ideal for the scale of monumental acting needed on a wide-screen, and his muscularity meant he wore armour and togas of epics with conviction." In 1972, a writer for the *Los Angeles Times* called

---

14 *CHA*, 15–16; *ALJ*, 391–392.

15 Dotson Rader, "If I Ran & Won, I'd Never Be Able to Act Again," *Parade Magazine* (Mar. 9, 1986), 4–5, 7.

him simply "Chuck Heston: A Toga Man in the Jeans Era." Another noted that Heston's "presence in many epics of the 1950s and 1960s has made him a virtually integral feature of the genre."[16]

Cinematically, Heston will always be associated with the dramatic chariot race that marked the culmination of the complex relationship between the Roman Messala (Stephen Boyd) and the Jewish Judah Ben-Hur. In film history, the contest presented in the 1959 version has become iconic. As one scholar has observed, "indeed, *Ben-Hur*'s chariot race is arguably among the most famous episodes not only in the Hollywood epic corpus, but in the entire history of film-making." The effect for one young viewer was unforgettable. "I remembered as a 12-year-old sitting in the Cinerama Theater, watching Heston defeat Stephen Boyd in the famous chariot race," news correspondent Michael Blowen explained. "His hands gripped the reins, his powerful shoulders controlled six white horses, his eyes glared with the grim determination of a man possessed—he played a hero to a 12-year-old."[17]

Purportedly, Heston disdained labeling the massive project as an "epic" motion picture. "Don't call it an epic," he told one interviewer. "That's a dirty word in my vocabulary. Films labelled epics are invariably bad ones." The sheer spectacle of much of what comprised *Ben-Hur* for audiences who flocked to see it and for the awards that came its way, however, suggested that few considered the term to apply negatively in this instance. A British reviewer noted that "although everyone connected with this . . . enterprise—including Charlton Heston . . . and William Wyler—disclaims with horror the idea that *Ben-Hur* is anything so vulgar as an epic, this useful four-letter word will do to convey to most people the nature and scope of this enormous 3½-hour film." Heston insisted that Wyler's ability to remain focused on "keeping the people in them the important thing" meant that a "colossal" picture like *Ben-Hur* could have a personal quality, too, allowing it to become what he termed "Hollywood's first intimate spectacle."[18]

---

16 Joanna Paul, *Film and the Classical Epic Tradition* (Oxford, 2013), 155; Nicholas Wapshott, *The Man Between: A Biography of Carol Reed* (London, 1990), 319; Joyce Haber, "Chuck Heston: A Toga Man in the Jeans Era," *LAT*, Dec. 3, 1972; James Russell, *The Historical Epic and Contemporary Hollywood: From Dances with Wolves to Gladiator* (New York, 2007), 7.

17 Paul, *Film and the Classical Epic Tradition*, 213; Michael Blowen, "For Heston the Key is Resilience," *BG*, July 21, 1980.

18 Paul, *Film and the Classical Epic Tradition*, 230; Pete Martin, "I Call on Ben-Hur," *SEP*, Aug. 20, 1960, 40.

Through the years and in various manners, Heston delighted in retelling the story of his intense preparations and his concern that he not only look like a creditable charioteer, but succeed in crossing the finish line ahead of his competitors. "Chuck, you just make sure y'stay in the chariot," his trainer Yakima Canutt explained. "I guarantee yuh gonna win the damn race."[19] Some versions of this exchange, which remained part of Heston's storytelling repertoire, became a defining element of his public persona, even employed as a tale told to fellow partygoers in an Anheuser Busch commercial for a much later generation of viewers, and ostensibly, beer drinkers.

Heston's long career obviously encompassed much more than the biblical epic that emanated from the pen of former Union general Lew Wallace, subtitled "A Tale of the Christ." The sturdy Midwesterner was also Moses, compelled by a divine hand and the direction of Cecil B. DeMille to spring to screen superstardom while leading his people from bondage in ancient Egypt. Indeed, the characters of Judah Ben-Hur and Moses defined and influenced much of the essence of Charlton Heston's public persona for the rest of his life.

Heston was fortunate to be among the rare actors who embodied at least two distinctive and memorable screen figures, but this also required him to balance his subsequent choices in order to avoid becoming typecast. One writer suggested that for Heston, films such as *Ben-Hur* and *The Ten Commandments* created the dynamics for the actor's increased stature. "It's been said that a performer never achieves true stardom until he's typed." Michael Druxman did not indicate the source for the comment but recognized the degree to which it applied to Heston and, although he contested the point, offered a reason as to why the matter bore significance. "Actually, he appeared in a wide variety of film roles following *Ben-Hur*, but it is the memory of the sweeping epics—biblical, medieval, and otherwise—which has remained most vivid with the public." Actor Rex Harrison, with whom Heston worked in *The Agony and the Ecstasy*, explained the nature of their shared profession. "The kind of style you develop as an actor has, of course, a lot to do with the kind of material you choose to act, and this is something on which an actor must bring all his intelligence to bear because it's very difficult to get it right."[20] Any performer risked limitation by audiences that demanded to see that individual only in the roles they had come to expect.

---

19 *CHA*, 186; see also *ALJ*, 48.

20 Michael B. Druxman, *Charlton Heston: A Pyramid Illustrated History of the Movies* (New York, 1976), 80; Rex Harrison, *A Damned Serious Business* (New York, 1991), 43.

Whatever parts he accepted, Heston was prepared to bring with him a serious and thorough approach to portraying them. A meticulous student of history and literature, he valued learning as much as he could of each character or the world and time period in which that person had lived. "If you're playing a biographical character, there's the additional element of research involved, and exploring, as deeply as you can, into what the character actually was; what kind of man he really was." To achieve this level of investigation, the actor was willing to go to extraordinary lengths. "His preparation is intense," one interviewer noted. "For example, to portray Michelangelo, he read six hundred letters written by the artist." Heston found such primary sources "the most valuable research of all. Letters are usually the best material for finding out the true character of a person. Better than biographies."[21]

These practices took root in his days in college and manifested themselves in his work. One writer noted, "There were those who were inclined to ridicule him for his intense dedication to the role he was to play because he was never seen on the Paramount lot, during his year of preparation, without a stack of books under his arm." For Heston, these were not theatrical elements. "Books, to him, are not mere props."[22] Heston's endeavor to learn about each of the historically based figures became almost legendary among his industry peers.

The actor also felt that for any role to be as believable as possible for moviegoers, he had to buy into it himself. "Whenever I play someone it doesn't matter who it is or whether he actually lived or not," he noted; "I like to find the outside of the man first, what he looks like, what he wears, what he sounds like, the way he walks." Heston felt that by considering these aspects, he could explore deeper, but the external assessment had to occur first. "I can't find the middle of the man before I find the outside."[23]

Even where biographies were the best sources available, the actor recognized the importance of drawing upon multiple interpretations in order to arrive at the point of view that made the most sense to him. "If you do your homework right, you read biographies that reflect the different views. But still, you have to arrive at one view that you decide is the one you're going to use." Noting that no performance allowed for "a compendium" of all of the possible interpretations, an actor had to decide which one felt right "intellectually, but also with the equipment you can

21 Rovin, *Films*, 18; Van Slyke, "From 'Moses' to 'Midway,'" 47.

22 Hyatt Downing, "Hollywood's Moses," 3, Heston Papers, HL.

23 Michael Munn, *Charlton Heston: A Biography* (New York, 1986), 191.

bring to bear on him." In that final analysis, Heston asserted, "[y]ou obviously choose a view of the man that will lend itself most readily to your own equipment. Not simply physical equipment, but emotional equipment as well."[24]

As he suggested, the actor supplemented his voracious appetite for written sources with other tangible connections to the figures he portrayed. For this process to occur, setting and imagination could be useful, but wardrobe was essential. As Heston explained in an interview, "I feel at home in 'wardrobe'—but it's important to get used to it." These elements were not superficial, but rather meant to uncover parts of the character he wanted to absorb. "I think many actors wearing complicated or unfamiliar period 'wardrobe' make a great mistake in taking as much of it off as quickly as they can." Such distinctions were not trivial. "If 'wardrobe' cannot become clothing—if it remains 'costume'—then you fail with it in your work," he said. Heston believed that inhabiting some portion of the clothing was critical to finding the person inside, but his insistence on doing whatever was required to identify with a given character could prove daunting. "I think it's very important to wake up in the morning and see the clothes lying in the corner where you kicked them off the night before," he explained. He understood that this method was key for him to employ as much because of its psychological significance as anything else. "The trap most actors fall into is to regard the 'wardrobe' as a costume—dress-up clothes. And if they think that way, it's liable to look that way." Through the repetition of this pattern on his part, wife Lydia grew used to the incongruity of seeing her husband in their modern home while clad in period wardrobe and surrounded by relics and reading material. "I remember having the Dead Sea Scrolls discussed at breakfast the way other men might discuss baseball. And it's still a bit unnerving to see him tramp into the kitchen in chain mail or a suit of armor or dressed like Michelangelo." In an interview conducted in connection with the release of *El Cid* in 1961, Lydia Heston noted that her husband could be more "serious" with some roles. She added, however, that over time she "learned to live" with "these various characters at home."[25]

The search for Charlton Heston's characters took many forms and evolutions. He believed that he could "find" them in wardrobe or their surroundings, but

---

24 Rovin, *Films*, 18.

25 Jay Leyda, ed., *Voices of Film Experience: 1894 to the Present* (New York, 1977), 202; Hamill, "Heston: Larger Than Life," 90; "1961 Vintage Radio Interviews with Charlton Heston and Lydia Heston," *El Cid*, The Weinstein Corporation, 2008.

he identified most when he saw a characteristic in them that he recognized in himself: "a remote, obsessed drive that motivates most of the great men I've played," both historical and fictional. He felt this as he struggled mightily "to find each one, and somehow stay true to him." Whatever Lydia might think about Charlton's obsessions, he saw them as critical to his performances. "I find the character from the specifics about him in the way he looks, the clothes he wears, the watch he carries." He also took pains to present the appropriate accents, studying language patterns when necessary to obtain authenticity for each role. "I resonate enormously on these external things," he observed of these techniques. One writer agreed, calling Heston "[m]ethodically thorough in preparing for a role." Lydia concluded, "He is, after all, an actor, and there are times when he gets too tied up in his work for his own good."[26]

Heston knew that if a performance lacked authenticity, it would have a negative effect on the audience's receptivity of the part, the actor in it, and the credibility of the film itself. As a consummate professional, aware of the importance of box office as well as the technical aspects of his craft, he wanted the people sitting before him in theaters to invest themselves in what they were seeing as much as he did himself.

Though Heston might cringe at many of the formal trappings and note privately his impatience with the elements that marked his public existence, he recognized the fact that the external world he had chosen to inhabit made his internalized one possible. The balance that defined the public and the private, or "the inner and the outer me," as he called them, represented the irrepressible battle he fought throughout his life. "Over the years I've learned well how to be a public person, a celebrity," he observed, although he admitted, "Christ, how I hate that word!" Biographer Michael Munn noted that "in an interview, the curtain may go up but so too do the invisible barriers," adding that Heston did "his best to give the single interviewer or the viewing audience what they have, as it were, paid to see: the *public* person." His public "face," as he termed it, became a crucial part of who he was. Heston also understood the bargain into which he had entered; "If you make your living as a star (I hate that word, too), you have a responsibility to your public identity."[27] Nevertheless, he felt a similar obligation to remain as true as possible to his "inner self" and the family and close friends he cherished.

---

26 *CHA*, 334; Donald Chase, "Between Scenes with Charlton Heston," *SEP* (Nov. 1983), 42; Hamill, "Heston: Larger Than Life," 90.

27 Munn, *Charlton Heston*, 10; *CHA*, 116.

Heston remained aware of the energy offered him by the authoritative figures he had embodied in his most recognizable cinematic endeavors. Indeed, he worked hard to maintain the aura that surrounded them, and him. After over a decade as an established star, a writer noted, "on-screen and off, Heston has a powerful presence." Another observer explained that the desire for a significant off-screen impact stretched across a wide range of public service causes, leaving Heston free to employ "as much time as I want to put into them."[28]

Certainly, his highly recognizable public "face" was crucial for his career and informed the choices he made and the causes he supported. Whatever the response to his efforts, Heston's franchise became a carefully crafted one. The relationship between the celebrity figure that others witnessed and accepted and his audience itself remained of paramount importance: "You offer not only your talent . . . you have to risk *yourself*."[29]

As a performer, Heston understood the signal imperative: he required an audience. Michael Munn explained that in a group setting, the actor engaged readily. "But what has struck me more than anything else is that when he has an audience—even if it's a gaggle of journalists at a press call—he performs in a totally different manner in comparison to the private interview." The writer felt that under those circumstances Heston "literally plays to the crowd and on these occasions, as when he has a television audience, he enjoys himself immensely. What he puts over is to all intents a *performance*, and he responds to the number of listeners, to the environment, and to his enthusiasm for the subject under discussion accordingly."[30]

Despite the strong and persistent desire for privacy that remained with him, Heston recognized that he led a very public life. He remarked, "I don't think I've ever been a really satisfactory movie star, the persona that, unavoidably, has defined my life and most of my work." Aspects of the profession simply did not fit his approach to it or to life. Even so, he accepted that many public activities were "part of the work," and he practiced and prepared those aspects as much as he would lines from a script or marks on a stage. "Fortunately, people go to my films and plays in sufficient numbers to keep the franchise valid," he observed, and maintained he was grateful for that, as he truly appeared to be.[31]

---

28 George McKinnon, "Movies/Heston as 'Failure,'" *BG*, June 21, 1970; Plutzik, "Last of the Epic Heroes," 33.

29 *CHA*, 234–236.

30 Munn, *Charlton Heston*, 9–10.

31 Ibid., 235–236.

At the same time, Heston was genuinely appreciative for his career and the living it gave him. "I've been extremely fortunate doing it because I've been able to support my family and send my children to school," he explained; acting also presented him with a platform for "people to take down all my opinions and print them." Indeed, the range of the subjects and vehemence of those views could be impressive, with one scholar noting Heston's "penchant for dramatic rhetoric."[32] Given his education, profession, and passions, it would have been surprising for him to express himself, when he chose to do so, in any other way.

Much of what Charlton Heston admired and aspired to be in the public realm of performance fit into what he viewed as the broad definition of tradition in his profession. He knew that motion pictures gave him star power and television provided access to larger-scale audiences, but first and foremost he thought of himself as an actor. "I do a play every other year," he observed. "It is a very important part of my life, and my life is my work." The stage was the place where he felt he could hone his craft. Because of his screen success, theater was a privilege he could afford whenever he desired it. As one author observed of the big-budget screen projects Heston accepted, "Apart from needing the money to live on, it was also a variation upon the long-running theme of his career in which he used movie money to subsidize his work in the theatre."[33]

Under any circumstances, only one playwright held the greatest sway for him. "In my trade, the real test is can you play a Shakespearean role?" Heston was just entering his place in film when he made clear the degree to which he intended Shakespearean roles to dictate his career choices. He mapped out a scheme to tackle key roles at different stages of his life. "I don't think I am ready for Brutus yet," he explained in 1954, "but I feel that Antony still is within my range, as is Petruchio, and that I will be ready for Brutus about five or 10 years from now, and Macbeth 10 to 16 years hence." King Lear could come later. For Heston, "Shakespeare spells completeness to me in the opportunities that he affords an actor through his lifetime, and I will never be happy, I am sure, without essaying one play or another from time to time. What is more, I like to work on the stage."[34]

---

32 Druxman, *Charlton Heston*, 140; Emilie Raymond, *From My Cold, Dead Hands: Charlton Heston and American Politics* (Lexington, KY, 2006), 63.

33 Stoddard and SerVaas, "Charlton Heston," 103; Bruce Crowther, *Charlton Heston: The Epic Presence* (London, 1986), 126.

34 Martin, "I Call on Ben-Hur," 40; "Heston Maps Career as Shakespearean Actor," *LAT*, Jan. 17, 1954.

Scholar Mike Jancovich thought Heston's affinity for theater generally and British connections in particular was an effort to obtain status as a "legitimate theatrical actor," which could buffer him against criticism for his work in commercial films. Heston always insisted that his appearance on any stage meant a return to "actor's country" and that there was no better representation of that artistic endeavor and the craft he had embraced for himself than Shakespeare's native land.[35]

Indeed, Heston took great pride in any connection with the United Kingdom and its most celebrated practitioners of the stage and screen. When visiting London in 1965, he wrote passionately of its theatrical venues. "Well, they ARE marvelous, except that the places other people go to play, I go to work." He elaborated on London particularly: "I've been here I don't know how many times; my roots on both sides are British. As an American I was raised on Anglo-Saxon history and suckled on Shakespeare and the rest." When asked in a popular television newspaper supplement what he would take to the moon, the actor responded, "The Collected Works of William Shakespeare and my wife."[36]

Heston gravitated to American figures as well. He held Gary Cooper in high esteem and enjoyed the opportunity to act with him. He did not have the same chance with John Wayne, although the "Duke" had wanted him in *The Alamo*, either as Jim Bowie or Col. William Travis. Heston turned down both roles, but respected Wayne's star power. "He created a permanent niche for himself as *the* American actor," Heston explained in an interview. "Beyond any question, beyond any doubt, John Wayne is the *absolute* all-time movie star."[37]

Heston's competitive sense did not give way easily, especially if Wayne nudged him out of a role, but he thought his friend's marketing capability was inspiring. "Wayne's greatest achievement may have been creating John Wayne. The character he played, the character he invented, was the American persona of the man who is hard and believes in doing right and will do it against all odds." Heston knew,

35 Mark Jancovich, "'Charlton Heston is an Axiom': Spectacle and Performance in the Development of the Blockbuster," in Andy Willis, ed., *Film Stars: Hollywood and Beyond* (New York, 2004), 67; Charlton Heston Newsletter, Mar. 30, 1966, Heston Papers, HL. This designation remained vital to him throughout his life and career. See also Haber, "Chuck Heston: A Toga Man in the Jeans Era," and "Dialogue on Film, 1980," UCLA.

36 Newsletter, "London, England," Aug. 28, 1965, HL; "Front Row Center."

37 Michael Munn, *John Wayne: The Man Behind the Myth* (London, 2003), 348. Munn noted Wayne's preference for either Bowie or Travis in *The Alamo*, roles which went to Richard Widmark and Laurence Harvey, respectively; ibid., 204–205. On another occasion, Heston noted that Charles Lindbergh was a figure he admired, in addition to Cooper.

however, that every persona had its limitations. "There are actors who can do period parts," he noted without referencing himself, "and there are actors who can't." Then, specifically addressing Wayne's performance as a Roman centurion in the crucifixion scene in *The Greatest Story Ever Told*, he observed candidly, but without malice, "God knows Duke Wayne couldn't play a first-century Roman."[38]

Like a professional athlete, Heston quickly learned that at the highest levels, everyone else was talented and capable, too, and that he must work to set himself apart from his colleagues. Similarly, he recognized that while a successful product was a wonderful accomplishment, what usually followed was pressure to repeat or exceed the earlier work for an audience that constantly demanded more. In a retrospective moment he experienced while directing an all-Chinese cast in a Beijing production of *The Caine Mutiny Court-Martial*, Heston expressed what he saw as the essence of motivation in his craft. "Acting is not supposed to be a competitive undertaking," he observed; but "[i]t is though . . . unavoidably." Then, in a manner of assessment born of long experience, he explained that a sense of competitiveness had existed for him from his earliest years, and it grew over time: "Later on, you can't help but keep track of the other guys." Internally, the assessment became, "Christ, I should've done that part after all . . . look at the grosses. I would've been better in it, too." Of course, there was no way to know the degree to which one person could embody a role in a similar manner or with the same degree of box-office response as another. In the end, Heston decided there was something more fundamental at work. "In truth," he concluded, "actors compete only with themselves, and the part."[39]

He seemed to admire most those individuals who had demonstrated the capacity to make a difference in something greater than themselves. "If one examines carefully every one of my forty films," he observed, "a central theme runs through the majority of them. Almost all the characters I've played are men with an individual sense of total dedication and responsibility which motivates their triumphs." When pressed in an interview about his argument that some individuals had the capacity to make an enormous impact, Heston responded, "An *extraordinary* man can effect change. Jackson, Jefferson, and a number of other

38 Ibid., 134, 249.

39 "October 18th [1988] Tuesday, Opening Night, Beijing," *BD*, 133.

men I've played could do it." Then in a moment of introspection, he added with humility, "I don't put myself in the same category."[40]

In the modern era, Heston found Winston Churchill enormously compelling. Another contemporary figure, Ronald Reagan, symbolized leadership in different settings, ranging from their shared proximity via Screen Actors Guild activities to Reagan's terms as governor of California and president of the United States. Even so, Heston had no enduring aspirations of public political office for himself, preferring instead to portray such figures through his artistic endeavors; he pronounced himself sufficiently satisfied by undertaking those portrayals. One modern student of the connection between actors and politicians observed, "Heston's political career was both typical of film star activism in the post 1960s era—in that he spoke out in favor of causes but avoided running for public office—and an atypical instance of an actor striving for a quasi-presidential role."[41] As these public manifestations suggested, Heston also appreciated the various platforms available to him.

In all facets, from a theater stage to a sound stage, on and off location, Heston enjoyed his trade, but recognized the demands it made on those he loved. "Of course my work intrudes enormously on my personal life," he admitted, "and takes time from my wife and from my children that I wish it didn't have to take. But they react with understanding." Then, without appearing to realize the point he was making, he insisted, "My work is the center of my life, and they understand that. We're quite cohesive about it."[42]

Chuck Heston enjoyed other indulgences, too. Although his schedule demanded that he take care of himself, often through a strict regimen of exercise, he appreciated good food and drink. One assessment of the rising star offered glimpses of these more private aspects to an eager public. In addition to being "overly fond of oysters and clams," Heston consumed "four pounds of steak daily, plus two pounds of tomatoes." When moments of unwinding allowed, he enjoyed a libation in addition to his ubiquitous cups of coffee. "His favorite drink is a straight shot of Bell's twelve-year-old Scotch," the writer noted.[43]

---

40 Rovin, *Films*, 213; Lawrence Linderman, "Charlton Heston Interview," *Penthouse Magazine* (August 1980), 110–112.

41 Burton W. Peretti, *The Leading Man: Hollywood and the Presidential Image* (New Brunswick, NJ, 2012), 311, n. 40.

42 Rovin, *Films*, 21.

43 Steele, "Unmasking Charlton Heston," 51, 74.

Although he lived in an environment of performance, Charlton Heston operated under few illusions. He knew what critics thought of him and his work and labored diligently to protect himself by embodying standards of perfection and professionalism in all facets of his life. His sense of humor served as a ready safety valve for dealing with the public. Beneath the surface simmered a potentially volcanic temper that he kept largely controlled, but which occasionally found articulation in some of his more piercing personal expressions. The actor's journals became the means by which his most critical evaluations found release.

To those outside his immediate circle of friends and family, Heston often appeared to be studied and separated. Michael Munn considered the performer careful in his responses during interviews, seemingly drawing upon an internalized script for anecdotes as illustrations. Characterizing his subject as "deviously clever at it," the writer concluded, "you begin to realize that you're hearing the same answers you've heard before, almost word for word." He noted, "But what I have since discovered through personal experience is that Heston doesn't just give an interview—he *performs*. Sometimes flawlessly, sometimes poorly." Yet the actor seemed more guarded in one-on-one situations, careful not to expose too much of himself. In these settings he appeared to accept the role "dutifully," as "part of the job of acting." The shift in demeanor left Munn puzzled. "It's as though *he* is in control of the interview and you can be sure that he'll tell you exactly what he wants you to know." At another point in 1980, Heston asserted, "I spend a great deal of time in public and can do it very well—but it's a professional skill."[44]

Heston understood the necessity for promotion. He recognized that there was a process to be followed and accepted the role he was required to play as essential in any product's successful marketing. Heston's name, face, and voice often proved indispensable to such campaigns. Yet, as writer Michael Druxman suggested, "His impressive list of credits notwithstanding, Heston has never been considered by his industry to be truly viable when it comes to attracting patrons to the box office." He argued that other factors associated with the historical/biblical spectacles and colorful science fiction films brought individuals into the seats, whereas his "best performance to date—*Will Penny* (1968)—died in the theaters, despite, in several instances, above average and even superior critical reviews." Writer Ed Leibowitz took a different tack, calling ventures such as *Will Penny* "the best" of "some smaller films that cast him in an unfamiliar light, where he's liberated from being Charlton Heston." Even so, the writer explained, "this was not the Heston his fans were

44 Munn, *Charlton Heston*, 9–10; Plutzik, "Last of the Epic Heroes," 33.

prepared to accept," preferring instead his "enduring film persona—mighty and outsize."[45]

In any event, Charlton Heston's motion picture presence carried over into the realm of celebrity influence in the political arena. Indeed, scholar Steven Ross proclaimed him "the first prominent practitioner of image politics." Ross noted that such identifiable roles "allowed him to forge a cinematic person of such gravitas that he repeatedly used it to lend authority to his off-screen role as [a] political spokesperson." In the aftermath of the 2000 presidential election, another writer labeled the veteran actor "Hollywood's most effective activist" and its "preeminent public citizen."[46]

Heston explained, "Well, I think I play my part in the public process. Heaven knows, I shout my mouth off all the time and have, as all performers and actors, an unusual, if you like unfair access to the public forum. If I want to talk about some public issue I get on television." Until later in his life, the actor argued that most of his positions were largely not political ones, even when he spoke in favor of candidates who supported them. He added, "I have taken a very public part in the political process on behalf of candidates from both parties all the way back to Adlai Stevenson back in 1952 which was about the first time I had enough public identity to make it worth my while, and I have served in appointive offices for Kennedy, Johnson, Nixon, and Reagan."[47]

Regardless of the setting, Charlton Heston remained focused on the persona he was creating and developing. If he could not separate himself from his screen presence, however, he did not really wish to do so. "I wanted the arena," he explained, maintaining that it was "sweat, sand, and blood, where it really counts." He always expected to "take the test, and give your best . . . and then somehow be better."[48] Heston saw aspects that some might find overwhelming, discouraging, or intimidating, as challenges to overcome rather than endure or avoid. His achievements established his worthiness of entering in the acting arena and his satisfaction at emerging victorious from it. Such accomplishments also solidified his name and reputation among his peers and his public.

---

45 Druxman, *Charlton Heston*, 12; Leibowitz, "Last Stand," 64.

46 Mark Harvey, *Celebrity Influence: Politics, Persuasion, and Issue-Based Advocacy* (Lawrence, KS, 2017), 29; Ross, *Hollywood Left and Right*, 9; Leibowitz, "Last Stand," 61, 65.

47 Stoddard and SerVaas, "Charlton Heston,"42.

48 Ibid., 73.

At the same time, Heston sought to live and reflect the values he held closest as a responsible professional, husband, and father. When asked what advice he would give his children, the answer was unequivocal: "Do your best, keep your promises, and be on time." He believed firmly that these were essential ingredients for success. Tellingly, when asked "You knew you were grown-up when you _____," he offered another insight into his character by answering when he "[l]earned to accept the blame for what happens to me." As Heston explained in one interview, he took pride in being able to "keep" his public and private lives "separate on the one hand and live them both at the same time on the other."[49] Yet both spheres defined him. Beneath the exterior of the "public" figure lay an individual who wanted others to perceive him as fair and honest, and prepared to act in the interests of others.

At the same time, the "public" and "private" dichotomies could not easily be untangled. While filming *55 Days at Peking* on location, he learned that his personal driver, Ricardo Perez, had not been paid for five weeks. Heston intervened to correct the matter, only to find out that nothing had changed. At this point, more than a lack of payment for a worker was at play, for the star had inserted himself into the situation and could not avoid feeling personally affected. He returned to the office, dressed in the dingy uniform of the Marine officer he played in the film, and announced that he had covered the sum out of his own pocket. The production company now owed him instead. Professional clout had allowed Charlton Heston to fulfill an obligation that Chuck Heston insisted must be met.

Each of these qualities translated into a successful public career and the subsequent exposure that Heston sustained through thorough preparation and dedication. From his earliest time on stage, buttressed by a consistent professionalism, a solid work ethic, and a commitment to what he saw as the values expressed through his career and beyond it, Charlton Heston exhibited "the look of eagles."[50]

---

49 "Front Row Center"; "1961 Vintage Radio Interviews with Charlton Heston and Lydia Heston."

50 Commonly known in the racing world as reflective of a confident thoroughbred, this term appears, for example, in Linda Carroll and David Rosner, *Duel for the Crown: Affirmed, Alydar, and Racing's Greatest Rivalry* (New York, 2014), 9.

Chapter One

TO THE POST
1920s-1940s

"It was a fine place to be a boy in."
—Charlton Heston on growing up in Michigan

"In those days I wasn't satisfied being me."
—Heston, on his childhood

Performances:
Peer Gynt, August 25, 1941

Charlton Heston was always a product of the Midwest. Born October 4, 1923, in Evanston, Illinois, to a dynamic mother from Chicago, Lilla Charlton, and a charming father, Russell Whitford Carter, the child grew up in a middle-class family. Lilla was the force that engulfed it, long after they had left their home outside of Chicago and moved to the woods of Michigan in his earliest years. She was determined that rather than be known by his birth name, John Charles, the firstborn son would be Charlton. This name was emblematic of the firmness of their bond and the connection to the Scottish roots that Charlton Heston maintained throughout both of their lives.[1]

---

1 Marc Eliot, *Charlton Heston: Hollywood's Last Icon* (New York, 2017), 4-5. Eliot interviewed Holly Heston Rochell for comments about her father's early life.

Although Charlton Heston remained largely reserved about his private or family life, he was often frank and open about what he did share. His expressions of affection for his parents were forged in the crucible of circumstances that surrounded his youth. He later noted that Lilla's recollection of his early years differed from his own, particularly regarding the pastime of hunting. For Heston, the guns he remembered taking into the woods offered him a sense of freedom and independence that he cherished. His Scots heritage gave him a sense of frugality and stubborn pride as well. Throughout his career, a staunch professionalism and desire for perfection were the part of the inner core that both drove him to focus so intently on his craft and provided him with the means for success and financial independence.

The degree to which Chuck Heston really was the little boy wandering the Michigan woods with his imagination ablaze was less relevant than his need to believe that image in order to fit this conception of himself. In any case, the depictions he offered of his youth remained consistent over the years. The adventurous figures of his mind provided both a comforting memory and motivation as he wound his way through his professional life. Heston always seemed to prefer looking back even as he strove to move his life and career forward.

Heston's *An Actor's Life*, published in 1976, opened with a section biblically titled "At the Beginning," in which he described his youth. Employing an allusion to the mythical Paul Bunyan, he recalled an idyllic world before declaring, "it was a fine place to be a boy in." He also observed that he "had a very happy boyhood."[2]

In the quieter world away from the environs of Chicago, the young man learned to entertain himself, developing the creative imagination he would bring to his life and career years hence. Heston found that he enjoyed taking on other personas. Although often professing to a happy youth, he admitted that he occasionally preferred to be someone else. "What acting offered me was the chance to be many other people." He also acted because no other outlet appeared to hold as much satisfaction for him. Eventually, the desire to perform prevailed. "I couldn't conceive of doing anything except acting," he observed. "Acting is pretending. But I *like* it."[3]

2 *ALJ*, xii; HARDtalk, BBC Interview with Tim Sebastian, 1997, part 3, www.youtube.com/watch?v=LkhLjPnjyYQ, accessed June 11, 2018.

3 Radar, "If I Ran & Won," 5; Belmont Interview, Aug. 1967, Heston Papers, 11, HL; Druxman, *Charlton Heston*, 140.

The youth's traditional education came in a one-room schoolhouse populated mostly by extended kin. The presence of cousins and close neighbors supplemented the sense of comfort in a relatively quiet, communal, and isolated existence. The Michigan woods he walked through to reach the school also provided a buffer from outside intrusion and an opportunity to enrich a youthful imagination.

Early in life, Chuck Heston developed many traits that remained with him. He learned to be creative and resourceful. Years later, when a reader inquired for the segment, "Ask them Yourself," "What's the cutest Mother's Day story you know?" the answer featured "one about Charlton Heston." "When he was 14, he bought his mother a big box of chocolates several days before Mother's Day." Wanting to keep the special present a surprise, he neglected to refrigerate it. Opening the box to check on the contents, he was broken-hearted to see they had melted. He reacted creatively, however, by adding the note: "Mom, you melt my heart, too."[4]

Several passions emerged during these early years. Heston realized that he loved the outdoors and enjoyed books, combining these pursuits with a desire to perform. "I used to read books," he observed, "and then go outside and act them out by myself. I'd act all the parts in turn." Expanding on an important source for this inspiration, he noted, "At seven I read Ernest Thompson Seton's 'Lives of the Hunted' about animals, and acted out all the parts myself," describing Seton's work as "the greatest single influence on his life." Later, when asked why Americans like Ernest Hemingway seemed to be so attracted to Europe, Heston observed, "Hemingway, like all complete artists, was attracted by the world." Naming the works of Hemingway and Shakespeare as some of his favorites, he answered a query about his plans to come: "To go on acting."[5]

Heston pursued these interests in that tiny schoolhouse, whose numbers were too small and age ranges too great to allow for team sports or larger group activities. "I learned a lot in that school," he recalled, "most importantly, how to read." He was fascinated by the transition from having a parent read to him as a child to discovering the joys of reading for himself. "I've never gotten over the infinite wonder of that," he observed in his autobiography. Classics such as Jack London's *Call of the Wild* and Robert Louis Stevenson's *Treasure Island* opened new worlds to a fertile mind and eventually re-emerged as film projects. Indeed, his love of reading formed the central part of Heston's preparation for many future roles as

---

4 "Ask Them Yourself," clipping, circa 1977.

5 Munn, *Charlton Heston*, 23-24; Steele, "Unmasking Charlton Heston," 51, 74; "Interview with Charlton Heston, 11-9-64," "The Agony and the Ecstasy publicity," f.2, Heston Papers, HL.

well as the foundation for fostering his active imagination and providing a source of personal entertainment and education, which he passed along to his children and grandchildren. Although he insisted that he never developed "excellent research discipline," Heston passed along a dedication to understanding the past that he embraced sincerely. "I was finished with school before I figured out that history is not only the most important subject, it's the *only* subject," he recalled telling his son Fraser. "You'll find that out, sooner or later."[6]

Though Charlton Heston found pleasure and release in volumes of literature and history, the works of others could not contain his love of words. He might deny a desire to set his thoughts to paper, but numerous instances related the opposite. In 1958, he maintained that had he not succeeded in acting as a profession, "he would like to have become a writer." The young student also enjoyed developing other artistic talents. "I liked to draw cowboys in my geography book," he noted, illuminating a tendency to occupy himself in a manner that remained with him. He found other outlets in mechanical drawing and art courses. One observer noted, "When Charlton Heston sits at a table and has nothing particular to do the artistic comes out in him. He's forever 'doodling,' his bent being largely toward drawing persons."[7] Together, these habits stood him in good stead as he researched roles and recorded his life on movie sets and in theaters across the globe.

As a student, young Heston was also learning about the world of acting. He later told columnist Hedda Hopper, "No, I'm the only one," when asked if any other members of his family were actors, but he may have been thinking of immediate relations. The degree to which family connections imparted any influence over an impressionable youth existed primarily through a more distant one. "A portrait of the actor as a young boy (age 5) would show him sitting at the knee of an uncle, Percy Charlton, himself an actor of some distinction," a writer of a piece on Heston's emerging talent explained, "eagerly drinking in the secrets of the trade which made Chuck a stand-out in the school Christmas pageant."[8]

Although he had an important role, "stand-out" was a bit of an exaggeration with respect to this first theatrical production; he spent the better part of the

---

6 *CHA*, 21; Munn, *Charlton Heston*, 22, 24; Plutzik, "Last of the Epic Heroes," 32.

7 Steele, "Unmasking Charlton Heston," 74; Eliot, *Charlton Heston*, 6; A. S. Kay, "Let's Go Places," Scrapbooks, HL.

8 Charlton Heston, Feb. 1952, 6, Hedda Hopper Papers, f.1665, HL. According to Heston, "I started acting in grammar school. I played Santa Claus in a Christmas pageant." Ibid.; Freedgood, "Big Man, What Now?", HL. See also Crowther, *Charlton Heston*, 10, and Plutzik, "Last of the Epic Heroes," 34.

performance waiting to make his appearance. Still, Heston maintained that his involvement in the play was instrumental in stoking the fires that burned within him. Responding to an observation that he had participated "in every class play at the Stolp public school in Wilmette," Heston added, "Sometimes I think my ambition to become an actor dates back farther than that. When I was 5 I starred in a Christmas pageant in Evanston—that was the real beginning." Elsewhere, Heston recalled that despite his normally quiet demeanor, "I guess I was always hamming things up. . . . I appeared in every school entertainment at the grammar school I attended." Some of this critical foundation included presenting "his own puppet show" to classmates.[9]

Heston remembered this as the time when a stage and an audience first inspired him. "I played Santa Claus. . . . It wasn't a big part and I had to stay cooped up in a chimney until my entrance at the end of Act II." The role required a lesson in patience and discipline, as he remained in close confinement while the play proceeded until he could finally spring forth and utter the critical line, "Merry Christmas!" Even so, great-uncle Percy Charlton, who was among the family members in attendance, seemed to be impressed. Of the performance, he concluded, "Another actor in the family." And so it was.[10]

The young fellow's world expanded in other ways as well. The birth of a sister, Lilla Ann, redefined Heston's family circle, but he continued to derive comfort through his jaunts into the woodlands. The rich diversity of seasons that brought shifts from the lush of spring and the heat of summer to the colors of autumn and the snows of winter defined his wider universe.

If rabbit hunts were part of the fertile imagination of frontier life with Davy Crockett more than a routine activity, such forays represented a meaningful sense of independence for the youth. Heston did not mind being alone, since he often was not; he took along a German shepherd dog named "Lobo" as a welcome and trusted companion.[11] Together, these mental images of the wandering boy,

9 Freida Zylstra, "Young Wilmette Actor's Star Rises in Hollywood, Goes Directly to Films After Success in TV," *Chicago Daily Tribune*, Feb. 22, 1951, Heston Clipping Files, HL; Hyatt Downing, "Hollywood's Moses," 9, HL; Marjory Adams, "Film Producers Want Actors Not Charmers, 'Hot' Star Says," *BDG*, Aug. 8, 1950.

10 Hedda Hopper, "Hollywood Life Too Easy, Says Heston," 1952. See also Hopper, "No Restin' For Heston," *Chicago Sunday Tribune*, Apr. 6, 1952, and *ALJ*, xii; Druxman, *Charlton Heston*, 15. See also "Biography of Charlton Heston," Paramount—Hal Wallis Productions, March 1950, Heston Clippings File, HL, and Steele, "Unmasking Charlton Heston," 74.

11 *CHA*, 20, 22-23. Heston continued to stress the importance of this historic figure in later interviews as well. See Vernon Scott, "Charlton Heston's Life Story," *GH* (May 1986), 128, 130.

the faithful dog, the ever-present guns, the traditional Christmas tree, and the freedom and sense of security became fixtures of his existence and foundations for his well-being.

Not all the elements of his childhood were reflections of a happy existence, however. One of the most memorable of these occurred when a neighbor killed his dog in a fit of rage. Heston recalled that Lobo's death "was the first loss of my life. I still think of him." His affection for dogs remained another tangible connection to his past as he grew older. "I've owned dogs all my life, mostly shepherds," he said of his family's beloved "Arthur Pendragon," known commonly as "Drago."[12]

Unfortunately, this was not the only trauma he confronted over a short time frame. The next year, at age 10, Heston suffered a greater, equally lasting shock. He noted repeatedly in subsequent years the deep degree to which his parents' separation and divorce affected him. Lilla determined that the marriage was not salvageable and abruptly uprooted her children from their secure existence. The family headed for Columbus, Georgia, where mother, eldest son, daughter, and newborn baby brother, Alan, lived with an aunt. Thrust into an unfamiliar world, Heston remembered this brief period as a mixture of relative opulence and Southern charm, with the uncomfortable challenges of fitting into a new school and community. He found that he could make only one friend, a fellow named Josh, who was the son of the family's African American maid. In a similar fashion to the way in which Georgian Jimmy Carter described such associations, the future actor observed, "I only knew him as my friend."[13]

Still, brief glimpses of happiness punctuated his time in Georgia. When Heston returned later to explore a dark side of the Civil War in a production on the trial of Henry Wirz, commandant of the infamous Andersonville Prison, Heston reflected on his childhood memories of the area. "He did remember 'vividly' one thing about Dr. [William F.] Jenkins' home where he lived—the big pecan tree in the front yard," a newspaper writer who interviewed him explained. "He said he was always overwhelmed with the fact that I could just go out in the yard and stuff my pockets full of them." Jenkins also recognized a fondness for "big eating" in his young visitor, telling writer Herschel Cribb, "I used to have a lot of fun trying to fill Charlton up." Heston's mother summed up the twin elements of her growing

---

12 *CHA* 22, 286. Heston employed such terms as "sainted," "faithful," and "devoted" to describe the cherished pet, which also accompanied the family on several overseas location shoots. Heston introduced "Arthur Pendragon" in his June 6, 1961, entry; *ALJ*, 120-121.

13 Jimmy Carter, *An Hour Before Daylight: Memories of a Rural Boyhood* (New York, 2001), 73. Carter's friend was Alonzo "A. D." Davis.

son by noting, "Oh, I never remember a time when Charlton didn't love books and didn't love food."[14]

Even with such pleasant diversions, the forced break from his father and the outdoor environment the boy had known were particularly difficult. "It was an extremely traumatic experience," he attested as he looked back at a youth interrupted; "It colored my whole adolescence." Heston was certain that he somehow bore responsibility for his parents' breakup, and "felt a deep sense of personal guilt." In his adult years, Heston retained this perspective. "This was then and still remains the most traumatic experience of my life, including [my participation] in World War II."[15]

Young Heston had to learn to channel such feelings into the best possible course, and the demand for such flexibility offered him additional incentive to improvise when it came to maintaining a sense of personal equilibrium. "In those days I wasn't satisfied being me," he noted candidly. "You see, I always thought of myself as inadequate."[16] As anyone caught up in challenging circumstances, he could choose to go in different directions. Turning inward, he might retreat into isolation or depression, which exacerbated his tendencies toward shyness and withdrawal, or he might become antisocial in an extreme, even violent manner, as an expression of his feelings of anger and self-loathing. Fortunately, other factors and a strong resolve cast Heston on a path that allowed him to compensate for absence and disappointment in a constructive way. His memories of this period also became an essential part of his personal and professional narrative.

In the meantime, a new male figure emerged in Heston's life. The Southern sojourn proved short-lived, and Lilla took her family back to St. Helen. John Charles returned to a changed world that included a new stepfather, Chester Lucien "Chet" Heston, who had worked with Russell Carter for a time. With his marriage to Lilla, Chet stepped into the gap that resulted from Russ's departure. Perhaps the most important development from the standpoint of future identity was the fact that John Charles Carter became Charlton Heston, a hybrid of his mother's family name and his new surname. Lilla's determination to remove any overt connection to the past brought an indelible element into her son's life. Heston insisted that

14 Herschel Cribb, "Charlton Heston Cast in Andersonville Role," in Scrapbooks, HL; "This is Your Life transcript," 10, HL; Bill King, "Chiefs: An Unusual Portrayal of the South and an Unusual Role for Heston," *AJC*, Nov. 11, 1983, 4.

15 *CHA*, 30.

16 Rader, "If I Ran & Won," 5.

although he respected Chet for his stepfather's determination during those difficult days, he accepted the change not so much due to affection than from a desire to avoid drawing attention to the family's circumstances.[17]

Disruption continued to be the norm in a challenging economy as Chet tried to find work. For a brief time, Alliance, Ohio, was home, then Wisconsin, and finally Wilmette, where the new patriarch secured a position as a welder. This move into the Chicago suburbs gave the family a real home and Heston an important refuge. A converted third floor became his bedroom. "I had the whole floor to myself," he remembered. "That meant a lot to me."[18] As he had once done in the Michigan woods, in this valuable new space, he escaped from unwelcome intrusions.

When not ensconced in his third-floor abode, Heston eventually discovered a fascinating world outside his home. The Chicago suburbs offered interesting diversions, and he found outlets for his imagination in the images that blazoned forth from movie screens in local cinema houses. "I could be Gary Cooper and Errol Flynn," he explained, "which was fine with me."[19]

Heston adapted to his universe, but new circumstances could not sunder old relationships entirely. In the first year in Wilmette, Russell Carter came back to see his son. Heston was playing softball with friends when his father drove up and caught his attention. Russ remained in the vehicle while they talked, and the awkward moments passed before his father drove away again for another indefinite separation from the boy. The reunion had only reaffirmed the void that Heston felt and the awkwardness and sense of guilt that he had imposed upon himself.[20]

Newly resettled and renamed, young Charlton Heston entered New Trier High School. His experiences there later assumed vital meaning—"I can't emphasize enough how important New Trier turned out to be for me."[21] Initially at least, the new environment exacerbated his feelings of being an outsider. Heston tried to adapt in ways that his background and awkwardness at fifteen permitted. His name brought additional unsettlement when a teacher misidentified him as "Charlotte" and compounded the error by insisting that the "Heston girl" identify herself.

---

17 *CHA*, 33, 38.

18 Ibid., 34.

19 *ALJ*, xiii.

20 *CHA*, 34.

21 Eliot, *Charlton Heston*, 13.

Joining the rifle team and the chess club offered him some opportunities for involvement and acceptance. Like so many others, however, the worst moments of his teenaged years came with the awkwardness wrought by sudden physical changes. Heston found that his frame shot upward before the rest of his body could catch up with it. The actor liked to tell how friends at the time remarked, "Every family has a skeleton in its closet, but the Hestons have let theirs out and are educating him."[22]

His awkwardness exacerbated his tendency toward shyness. When he and actor Bruce Dern worked together, Dern told him that they had attended the same high school. "Oddly enough," he recalled, "Heston never knew I went to New Trier until I told him one day on *Will Penny*." The star replied by listing some of the Hollywood figures with whom he had attended the school, at the same time illustrating the isolated circumstances that prevailed at the time. "Hugh O'Brian, Rock Hudson, and Heston were all in the same class," Dern noted, "and none of them knew each other until they came to Hollywood."[23]

High school could be traumatic, but it also proved transitional and helped Heston to identify his own creative path. "At New Trier we not only began to find our way into Shakespeare," he recalled, "but I discovered [Thomas] Wolfe and [Ernest] Hemingway and [Robert] Frost as well." New vistas opened that built upon his earlier interests. Drama classes, plays, and radio productions proved crucial to his progress from childhood affectation to the pursuit of practiced art. In this new setting, he found additional affirmation of his inclination toward acting when he saw a production of *Twelfth Night* in Chicago and realized that adults pretending to be others was a legitimate and accepted practice. As a whole, he explained, "They gave me the center of my life: my work." He added tellingly, "It began my life."[24]

In addition to whatever inspiration and direction his teachers might provide the prospective thespian, New Trier High School also gave him a dose of reality when it came to the pitfalls of a career in performance. As an essay theme in his junior year, Heston selected "Acting as a Profession." In looking back on the information he gathered for the paper, the now-successful performer observed,

---

22 Martin, "I Call on Ben-Hur," 42.

23 Bruce Dern, with Christopher Fryer and Robert Crane, *Things I've Said, but Probably Shouldn't Have* (Hoboken, NJ, 2007), 47.

24 Munn, *Charlton Heston*, 28-29; *CHA*, 37.

"The statistics indicate what any actor knows that you really can't [expect to] make a living acting, which did not daunt me at all."[25]

The earnest pupil was certainly not lacking in determination. He recalled, "From a one-eyed pirate in that first play through every part I could get in every production till I graduated, I soaked up different people to be, and some idea of what acting was." Heston also found his way into other areas of performance, as when he lent his voice to a production of *Macbeth* adapted to radio for the school's English classes.

As Heston moved into his final two years of study, he shelved experiments with the rifle, chess, and football as he found expanded opportunities with the local Winnetka Community Theatre. This training both nurtured his desire to perform and opened a way for him to continue his pursuit of acting as a career when he was awarded a $300.00 scholarship to the School of Speech at Northwestern University.[26]

Still, the road to Hollywood did not open in some traditional fashion for him, with discovery by an established mogul or a professional talent scout. Instead, young Heston was acting in a high school play when he caught the eye of a visitor who was in something of desperate straits himself. David Bradley was a student at Northwestern University, anxious to produce and direct a version of Henrik Ibsen's *Peer Gynt*. Unfortunately, his Peer had wrangled a summer stock gig and was no longer available.

Bradley watched as one of the actors on that small stage, a "gangling, six-foot, startling creature named Heston," radiated a presence he thought could be adapted for his purposes. Bradley determined to convince the young man to join in his enterprise, and Heston assumed that an agent from "Tinsel Town" had come to offer him his big break. "Never mind Hollywood," the visitor asserted, "Would you like to play Peer Gynt?"[27] Heston was unsure where this opportunity would lead or of the exact nature of the role, but was shrewd enough to know that any work in his chosen craft would be beneficial. A certain amount of naiveté did not hurt in this instance either.

The budding actor had other options as well, but they were hardly as attractive. He had an opportunity for summer employment in a steel mill working for his stepfather. Even with a potential paycheck from that job, the choice was not

---

25 "Screen Actors Guild Interview—Legacy, June 1994," UCLA.

26 *CHA*, 39.

27 Munn, *Charlton Heston*, 30.

difficult for him to make. "Playing Peer Gynt in a movie, free, still looked better than handling hot steel for eighty-five cents an hour," he remembered.[28] Indeed, Heston approached the role of a self-centered youth with gusto. His screen debut had elements of the actor to come, with a figure that dominated the screen and the occasional "Heston stance," with arms akimbo and head thrown back.

As his high school career wound down, Heston knew he felt most comfortable in the guise of others in a theatrical performance, but he remained a part of a very real world from which he could not always escape. His attendance at the senior prom provided new challenges to overcome. Heston recalled that he "solved the problem of neither having a date nor knowing how to dance by walking the beach until three o'clock in the morning. That way I would seem to be out for an appropriate length of time." Despite the isolation of these circumstances, he claimed, "you survive those things."[29] Such moments allowed Heston to develop the kind of imperturbability that would be useful in the years ahead.

After graduating from New Trier, his admission to Northwestern became pivotal to his journey, although initially he struggled to find his place there as well. Charlton Heston was a long way from Hollywood at this point. He was not even particularly clear on his own identity. Lilla's insistence upon naming her child Charlton in preference to John Charles had cost the young man a middle name. For a brief time, he tried "Lance," although the new moniker slipped away, except as stenciled on his luggage chest.[30] Validation would have to come in other forms.

In his quest for acceptance, Heston tried football. "I was an end on the freshman squad at Northwestern the year Otto Graham was the varsity quarterback. They used to run over us in scrimmages during the week." Unlike his celebrated teammate, Heston's efforts did not result in gridiron success. He insisted, "After I'd had my nose banged a few times I decided I'd better quit football if I ever hoped to have an acting career."[31]

A decade later, as he prepared for a role that brought him to the cinematic gridiron, he recalled lightheartedly of his brief Northwestern football career, "I had everything an end needed except speed and good hands." Certainly, lacking these salient features proved problematic at the time. "My career was spectacularly

28 *CHA*, 41.

29 Scott, "Charlton Heston's Life Story," *GH*, 130.

30 Eliot, *Charlton Heston*, 12, 16.

31 Jerry Nason, "Graham Makes Actor of Heston," *BG*, Nov. 4, 1959.

unremarkable," he noted. "I was strictly cannon fodder for the varsity." When he held a special screening of the film *Number One* at his home, Heston remembered battling the senior star, Otto Graham. "It didn't take too much intelligence to realize I didn't have it." Even so, the situation provided him with another crucial element of his future screen prominence. A broken nose from a hard tackle became an unmistakable asset as his life progressed. "It's gotten me a lot of parts," he quipped frequently.[32]

As his focus turned to acting, Charlton Heston found little time for football, anyway. Near the end of his life, a retrospective noted that as a "student of the School of Speech, Heston dove into the theater world right away, participating in six university productions." Many of these initial roles were small, but they built his confidence and seasoning. He remained determined to learn all he could, but never failed to help when others in these productions requested it. One fellow student recalled that he helped her overcome a severe bout of stage fright by reading A. A. Milne poems to divert her attention and by offering his assuring presence at subsequent performances. Heston insisted that he never endured the malady himself. "I always thought I could do it," he maintained. "You have to believe you can do it."[33]

Heston's college acting career also benefitted from working under an able instructor: Alvina Krause. Scholar Emilie Raymond concluded that this mentorship provided the young man perhaps his best lesson, observing, "it was through her that Heston acquired the thick skin needed for the acting business." As he progressed, he demonstrated that an innate sensitivity remained, but Krause hardened him to the realities of all types of criticism. After achieving success, he reminded his professor that he did not recall receiving any plaudits from her at the time. "People who have to be encouraged to act," Krause retorted, "have no business doing it."[34]

If Professor Krause proved demanding of her students and unrelenting in her expectations, this only drove the fledgling actor to improve himself and work hard to develop the skills necessary for later success. She recalled, "At the tryouts, Chuck Heston, a freshman, tries out for the lead of the show, the 2nd lead, the third lead,

---

32 "Charlton Heston: Old Pro to Play 'The Pro,'" *LAT*, May 24, 1968; John Hall, "Welcome to the NFL," *LAT*, July 17, 1969; *CHA*, 126; Rader, "If I Ran & Won," 5; Scott, "Charlton Heston's Life Story," *GH* (May 1986), 130.

33 Karen Werling, "Appreciation: Charlton Heston's Life as a Wildcat," *North by Northwestern* (Apr. 16, 2008), www.northbynorthwestern.com/story/heston-at-northwestern, accessed Mar. 25, 2019; John H. Richardson, "Heston," *Esquire* (July 2001), 66.

34 Raymond, *Cold, Dead Hands*, 12; *CHA*, 48-49.

the servant, anything!" This persistence marked his desire to perform and allowed Krause to shape his early course. "Unmistakably, [she was] one of the greatest teachers in the world," he maintained afterward. "Every, every person should have in his life the experience of a great teacher. Alvina Krause was a great teacher."[35]

As a student, Heston already had a notion of advancing through practical methods rather than charisma or physical attributes. "Most of the film actors of the period I was in college—1941 and 1942—were chosen for personalities and photogenic charm," he observed after his first Hollywood production. "Some of us who studied drama seriously," he added pointedly, did so with the objective of "acting for a living [and] were not interested in motion pictures for that reason."[36] Heston was determined to make his way forward in his profession through hard work, dedicated study, and stage experience rather than by means of the superficial aspects that could prove temporal.

Proximity to a great urban center provided the student with additional theatrical opportunities. Later, a writer for the *Chicago Daily Tribune* noted these connections. "Wilmette's Charlton Heston, named by Hollywood columnist Hedda Hopper as one of the year's most promising screen finds, made unprecedented use of Chicago stepping stones on his way to Hollywood: Speech classes at Northwestern university, a unique Chicago-made movie, and Chicago radio broadcasting." The latter allowed him to employ his distinctive voice. "While in college he also acted on a number of Chicago radio shows, including 'Terry and the Pirates.'"[37]

When not exercising his acting talents, he remained busy in other endeavors. At night, he worked as an elevator operator so that he could keep food on his plate, but he also found time for reading and studying when that work slowed down. His mother recalled that her son "really liked the job . . . because it gave him time to study." She explained that occasionally, the exasperated manager of the facility would call her. "Mrs. Heston, Charlton has hung a sign in the elevator, 'I have laryngitis and cannot talk.'" Heston attributed a great deal to his college employment. "All that I am—or almost all—I owe to the co-op apartment building at 5510 Sheridan Rd. When I was in college I was the midnight to 8 a.m. elevator operator there. This gave me a good share of the night to read Shakespeare and the Old Testament. I read for voice and diction." Writer Ruth Waterbury observed of

35 "This is Your Life transcript," 14, HL.

36 Adams, "Film Producers Want Actors Not Charmers, 'Hot' Star Says," *BDG*, Aug. 8, 1950.

37 Zylstra, "Young Wilmette Actor's Star Rises in Hollywood, Goes Directly to Films After Success in TV," *Chicago Daily Tribune*, February 22, 1951, Heston Clipping Files, HL.

the restless student, "He got little sleep, of course, but that was all right; he was determined to become great in the theatre."[38] The aspiring actor was absorbed by the desire to learn and determined to achieve the highest standard of performance possible.

In 1941, however, Charlton Heston also made the decision that would have the most significant impact upon his personal life and, ultimately, his public persona: he sat behind an attractive classmate in "Fundamental Theatre." He insisted that he had experienced "love at first sight" with the lovely Lydia Clarke. "It can happen and it did for me." The love affair that ultimately resulted was personally and professionally transformative. "I would not be here without her," he told one interviewer.[39]

Even so, making the transition from head and heart to actual contact was no easy accomplishment. Unfortunately, Heston had little practical preparation to assist him. A writer observed of the student's love interests, "He'd been too busy concentrating on becoming an actor to think of them."[40] Yet the dark-haired beauty seated so tantalizingly close transfixed him. Heston apparently could not resist the chance to interact with her. Lydia remembered the sensation of someone pulling on her hair; he insisted he had only touched, perhaps even caressed it gently. In either case, for him, the connection was already irresistible.

The bond began to develop when Lydia unexpectedly turned to ask his opinion as to how she might deliver an innocuous opening line in a class performance. "I wonder if I could ask your advice, Mr. Heston?" she queried. "In this production of 'The Madras House' which our class is doing, I have an entrance line that is bothering me. I have to come in and say, 'My frog is dead.' Now, how do you think I should say that line?"[41]

Heston was in the half of the class preparing for another play at the same time, but he did not let this stymie him. "For reasons I cannot explain, she felt I might be able to advise her on this," he recalled. "And I offered—there are four possible

38 "This is Your Life transcript," 11, HL; Larry Wolters, "TV Leads to Heston's Moses Role," Scrapbooks, Heston Papers, HL; Ruth Waterbury, "Charlton Loves Lydia," *Photoplay* (June 1953), 60, Heston Clipping Files, HL.

39 Ibid.; HARDtalk, BBC Interview with Tim Sebastian, 1997, part 3, www.youtube.com/watch?v=LkhLjPnjyYQ, accessed June 11, 2018.

40 Helen Limke, "Bringing Up Baby," *Photoplay* (Oct. 1955), 113.

41 Waterbury, "Charlton Loves Lydia," 100.

readings, of course."[42] He added, "I wanted to come up with a shattering reading for Miss Clarke," hoping to impress her with his sincerity and creativity while also taking advantage of the chance to further their acquaintance. "But I did recognize a golden opportunity when I saw it, and I suggested to Miss Clarke that we go to the malt shop and discuss the matter over a cup of coffee."

Elated when she agreed, he realized that her consent created another challenge: He had no money. "Then, as she accepted," he noted, "I was in another panic, and I had to make an excuse to leave her for a moment, while I negotiated the delicate matter of a loan of a dime from another student." Thus, Charlton's pursuit of Lydia began in earnest, although she largely rebuffed him for a time. Her own desires for a career did not involve sacrificing those plans for even the most appealing union, and this one did not seem to hold much promise. "The truth is," Lydia observed of her determined suitor, "I thought Chuck was impossible." Most importantly, it also proved "impossible" for her to avoid him indefinitely. Lydia had not been too impressed at the outset. "Oh I thought he was quite an arrogant young man at first," she recalled, "but he did grow on me."[43]

Describing the couple's relationship in 1953, writer Ruth Waterbury noted the significance of the initial encounter and the budding romance. "Shy, awkward, insecure, there couldn't have been any better corrective for him in college than to fall in love with a spirited, brainy girl like Lydia Clarke." Yet, her "spirited" character could not dim his ardor. "When I first dated Lydia," Heston explained, "she had a spitfire temper." Indeed, these emotions complemented their more cerebral interactions. "She forced him to think," Waterbury posited, "because she argued every point with him."[44]

Heston's prospective companion had to overcome many obstacles before their relationship could flourish. "Lydia frankly admits now she thought the big, lanky fellow from Michigan looked as wild as the woods he'd come from." Undeterred by her hesitations, he kept his focus on establishing a long-term relationship with someone who wanted to be an actor as much as he did. "Chuck persisted," writer Helen Limke observed. "Lydia resisted. Chuck persisted. They married."[45] This progression ensured that Charlton Heston would never be the same.

---

42 Lydia said the line was "Minnie, my frog is dead." "This is Your Life transcript," 15, HL.

43 Waterbury, "Charlton Loves Lydia," 100; "This is Your Life transcript," 15, HL.

44 Waterbury, "Charlton Loves Lydia," 100.

45 Limke, "Bringing Up Baby," 113.

Other challenges arose, however. In the aftermath of the Japanese attack on Pearl Harbor on December 7, 1941, the United States entered the Second World War. As it did for so many others like them, the war intruded on the young couple's future. Two years later, in the middle of his sophomore year, Heston abruptly enlisted in the Army Air Corps. When he was issued jungle fatigues, Heston thought he likely would be deployed to the China-Burma-India Theater. All the while, the soldier hoped romance would blossom before he was sent overseas.

Since he had begun courting Lydia in earnest, Heston's entreaties had proven unsuccessful. This continued to be the case when he headed off to basic training and his initial stateside postings, but an unexpected telegram offered him the prize he had sought: Lydia's hand. The couple married at Grace Methodist Church in Greensboro, North Carolina, on March 17, 1944, when they managed to locate a pastor and witnesses who could perform and validate the ceremony.[46]

Wrangling a pass to get married was one thing, but the young soldier realized that imperatives other than his own shaped their immediate future. Fortunately, his theatrical interests proved useful even in the service. For Lydia to have some sense of his current whereabouts, and without revealing vital secrets or running afoul of military censors, he devised an ingenious method of encryption. She would retain one of two identical maps covered with grids; Heston planned to use William Shakespeare's plays as the keys on his copy. He could identify a passage and, using that reference for coordinates, she would know where he was at any given time, if the communications themselves arrived.

Heston also managed to find ways of blending his artistic interests with his service obligations. When asked later if the sketches for which he was becoming known had brought him any income, he noted, "Well, when I was in the army I got involved in a project to do 25 or 30 illustrations for a slide lecture on Macbeth. But, to the best of my memory that's the only money I've ever received for my art and I think that's probably the best way to do it because I am not required to do it well. I just do it to please myself and have to meet no professional standards."[47]

The couple found that some military priorities was useful as well. Stationed for a time at Selfridge Field near Detroit, Charlton and Lydia enjoyed the opportunity to see each other and created the chance for an unexpected reunion of another type. They were preparing to spend a special weekend together that would include a performance of Paul Robeson in *Othello*. In the course of arranging tickets,

---

46 *CHA*, 53.

47 "Heston Taped Interview – August 16, 1955," 26, Heston Papers, HL.

Heston thumbed through a phone book and stumbled on a familiar name. "Carter, Russell W." caught his eye and he stammered to Lydia, "I think I found my father." She encouraged him to reach out and a quick telephone call turned into a visit between son and daughter-in-law with the estranged father, his new wife, Velda, and their daughter, Katy. Charlton would not lose contact again and Lydia now had additional family to support her during her husband's military deployment.[48]

By mid-1944, Charlton Heston was still in the United States, although a summons to Seattle portended a transfer to an active front. By way of a commandeered civilian vessel, Heston's bomber squadron was soon on course for Alaska's Aleutian Islands. American forces had subdued the Japanese occupiers of outlying Attu and a combined effort compelled the evacuation of Kiska, the two islands invading troops had reached. Sergeant Heston was among the personnel hastening to the region as part of the 77th Bombardment Squadron. Although further Japanese incursion was unlikely, air support might prove useful for other military operations.

The circumstances at the new posting were far from ideal, with often uncertain and dangerous weather, as well as isolation. The men in his squadron adapted themselves as best they could to the climate and conditions, but Heston found that enemy fire would not be his greatest danger. Icy conditions frequently made movement treacherous and when Sergeant Heston raced to reach a plane, he fell beneath an ambulance and awakened in a hospital in a cast. His active service over, the airman returned to support duty at Elmendorf Air Force Base in Anchorage as operations in the Pacific wound to a close. In March 1946, he received orders to proceed home to await his discharge from the service. Although the usual military bureaucracy posed a final, exasperating delay, and engine trouble over Canada provided additional drama, Charlton Heston arrived at Great Falls, Montana intact and reentered civilian life.[49]

Heston later said he thought he was going to take part in "Operation Olympic," the invasion of the Japanese home islands that was expected to produce heavy casualties on both sides. Planned for late 1945, it was rendered unnecessary by the atomic bursts over Hiroshima and Nagasaki. "If we had to go through that

---

48 Eliot, *Charlton Heston*, 36-38. Russell had remarried in 1935. Their daughter Katy was six years old when Charlton and Lydia met her in 1941.

49 *CHA*, 56-60; James E. Wise, Jr., and Paul W. Wilderson, III, *Stars in Khaki: Movie Actors in the Army and the Air Services* (Annapolis, MD, 2000), 130-133.

invasion," he noted to one writer, "I'm not sure I'd be standing here."[50] Despite the relatively brief time he spent in uniform, his military service became one of the fundamental pillars upon which he built his future public service and identity.

The other essential pillar was Lydia. The couple had waited a long time and endured many challenges before entering a union that would achieve legendary status among his peers and fans for its longevity. Heston well understood what had drawn him to her but was less sure of why she had finally chosen him. Although there was undoubtedly more to lure her affections, she insisted that one quality attracted her. "Words, Charlie . . . words. I loved the way you talked about things."[51]

His words had forged his most important personal relationship, one that would stamp his professional career with the most significant support system he could ever have imagined. "Charlie's" and Lydia's bond extended to the end of his life and bolstered his public persona through a marriage that defied the odds in the glitz and glamor of Hollywood. He often made light of the ingredients for marital success, saying how important it was to be "a superb husband," or to remember the most important words for sustaining a stable marriage: "I was wrong." Significantly, he recognized and forthrightly acknowledged that Lydia was the cement of their union.

Later in life, he had an unusual dream in which he seemed to be returning to the days of the Second World War, albeit with service in Europe rather than his actual assignment in the Aleutians. Heston explained his enthusiasm for doing it all again, only improving matters this time. This sentiment reflected the sense of perfectionism that marked all his connections and served as the basic tenet for his life and career. "I'm never content with any of my films," he explained to one interviewer, but would repeat for others. "I always feel I could do it better if I could do it again."[52] The love affair between these two creative and dynamic individuals demonstrated that for all the glitches and obstacles in any relationship, Charlton and Lydia Heston surely could not have done much better for each other. Ever anxious to achieve as close to perfection as he could come in every endeavor, "Charlie" understood that he had reached a pinnacle in this most important arena.

Heston always admitted his shyness, attributing it to the isolation and disruption of his early years. The former came from the same environment that

---

50 Susan Bickelhaupt, "Before he was Moses," Names & Faces, *BG*, Feb. 13, 1995.

51 Charlton Heston and Jean-Pierre Isbouts, *Charlton Heston's Hollywood: 50 Years in American Film* (New York, 1998), 16.

52 Susan Karlin, "Guest Shot," *Playboy* (May 1993), 28.

allowed childhood fantasy to flourish and from which he never detached himself. The latter came from the sudden dissolution of his parent's marriage. The Michigan woods were at once a refuge that remained forever real and vital to him, the symbol of a deep, penetrating world through which he traversed with the benefit of his wits and Scots determination. During this formative period, education and performance had become essential lodestones, as was his marriage to Lydia Clarke. Charlton Heston was on his way along a track that could take him, and her, toward a finish line whose heights were as yet unimaginable to either of them.

Chapter Two

THE CLUBHOUSE TURN
1940s-1950s

"What are the parts?"
—Charlton Heston

"I was off to a good start."
—Heston after *Dark City*

Performances:

State of the Union, Asheville, NC, 1947

The Glass Menagerie, Asheville, NC, 1947

Kiss and Tell, Asheville, NC, 1947

Antony and Cleopatra, New York, Nov. 26, 1947-May 13, 1948 (Proculeius)

Leaf and Bough, Boston, New York, Jan. 21, 1949-Jan. 22, 1949 (Glenn Campbell)

The Outward Room, CBS Studio One, Jan. 9, 1949; Sept. 26, 1949

Julius Caesar, CBS Studio One, May 1, 1949

Smoke, CBS Studio One, June 15, 1949

Battleship Bismarck, CBS Studio One, Oct. 24, 1949

Suspicion, Suspense Series, Nov. 8, 1949

Of Human Bondage, CBS Studio One, Nov. 21, 1949

Jane Eyre, CBS Studio One, Dec. 12, 1949

Design for a Stained Glass Window, New York, Jan. 23-28, 1950 (John Clithrow)

The Willow Cabin, CBS Studio One, Feb. 27, 1950

The Hypnotist, *The Clock Series*, Mar. 22, 1950

Hear My Heart Speak, *The Philco-Goodyear Television Playhouse*, June 25, 1950

Wuthering Heights, CBS Studio One, Oct. 30, 1950

The Taming of the Shrew, CBS Studio One, June 5, 1950

Julius Caesar, 1950

Dark City, Oct. 6, 1950 (Kansas City and Seattle)

Letter from Cairo, CBS Studio One, Dec. 4, 1950

Macbeth, CBS Studio One, June 5, 1951

The Petrified Forest, La Jolla Playhouse, Aug. 21, 1951
Santa Fe Flight, Suspense Series, Oct. 2, 1951
Route 19, Lux Video Theatre, Oct. 8, 1951
Your Show of Shows, Oct. 13, 1951; Dec. 22, 1951
A Bolt of Lightning, Nov. 12, 1951
One is a Lonesome Number, Schlitz Playhouse, Nov. 23, 1951

Not many forces exerted greater influences on Charlton Heston than his wife, Lydia, and his mother, Lilla. One had made the decision to stand by him from their early days at Northwestern and the other steered his life through the dramatic force of her personality. Heston strove to please both of them and each had a profound impact on who he was personally and who he sought to be professionally. Knowing his education and interests, Lilla helped to direct the course of the young actor's life with a simple query: "Well, my son, do you intend to teach acting?" The reply came without hesitation: "Of course not." Hers was just as clear. "Well then, catch the next plane to New York and put your foot in the door."[1]

The option certainly made sense to Chuck Heston. Service in distant outposts had not instilled in him a desire to follow a career path in the military, although it left him with a lifelong sense of appreciation for those who wore the uniform. If his career trajectory were to send him along another course, his earlier experiences offered context and created in him a desire to support the armed services.[2] For himself, a course was now set that would carry him to venues across the globe in the years to come. Heston insisted that his chief goal was always to come as close as possible to the perfect performance. While this ideal remained elusive, he felt that the effort allowed him to improve continually as an actor.

In the meantime, the Hestons returned to New York, where the couple struggled to make ends meet. Sounding like a character he would play many years later, Heston described the period as a "shining time," before noting that memory is not always the most dependable guide. The budding actor's status as a veteran

---

1 Quoted in Werling, "Appreciation," *North by Northwestern*.

2 *CHA*, 60, 61, 372, 374-376.

proved helpful in finding a place to live, but "Hell's Kitchen" became an interesting metaphor for Charlton and Lydia. They learned quickly that neither of them was much of a cook, and the "cold water" flat they inhabited required any hot water they wanted to use to be heated on the stove. These conditions led to illness that required Lydia's hospitalization and dissipated the family savings. Adapting to this new setting in the big city was going to present an on-going, if surmountable, obstacle.[3]

Another writer described the couple's humble abode more creatively as belonging to "Hell's Pantry," although one resident explained of the apartment, "You can't miss it. It's all decorated up." Salvation Army furniture made the space livable, with homemade additions and improvements to spruce it up. Even as things began to improve for them financially, Heston insisted, "I see no reason for leaving this apartment. Our friends are used to it."[4]

Lydia joined her husband in seeking whatever employment she could find. "There was nothing, nothing, nothing," Heston insisted later. The actor found the nature of the disappointment in obtaining work for himself even more challenging than might ordinarily be the case. "No one who hasn't been an actor can know how ego-shattering that is," he explained of reading or auditioning unsuccessfully. "In ordinary work, you are just turned down, impersonally. But in theatrical work, you are told you are too big or too short, your eyes aren't the right color, your voice is terrible." In each case, he observed tellingly, "The rejection is a total rejection of you as an individual."[5]

The main chance seemed never to develop for the young couple. Both modeled to make ends meet, with Heston wearing little except a modified jock strap for work in an art student studio. "Listen, that wasn't a bad job," he observed, adding, "you got a dollar and a half an hour and every fifty minutes they gave you a break, a cup of coffee and a cookie." He also remembered, "It was fairly tough work holding a pose, also boring. I used to run over Shakespearean soliloquies in my head."[6] The long hours taught patience and allowed him to hone his memory skills, but were obviously not helping his long-term prospects.

---

3 *ALJ*, xiii; Waterbury, "Charlton Loves Lydia," 100-101.

4 Earl Wilson, *L.A. Daily News*, June 16, 1951, Heston Clipping Files, HL.

5 Waterbury, "Charlton Loves Lydia," 100-101.

6 "This is Your Life (TV) transcript," 17, HL; *CHA*, 66.

These appeared to brighten when the Asheville Community Theater in the mountains of North Carolina, seeking a seasoned director, found two performer/directors. The Hestons spent a productive time in the region, staging plays and adding valuable elements to their repertoires. "My first real money in the theater profession was made there," he recalled later. The salary of $100 a week represented a significant windfall for the struggling couple. They also had the chance to gain experience on multiple levels. "We both directed and acted," he explained in one interview. "When she did a play, I directed it. When I was the star, she directed. We did 'The Glass Menagerie', 'State of the Union', things like that."[7]

Elsewhere, Heston noted that as they remained past the initial run, he and Lydia "eventually saved $1,000, which was the most I had had at one time." Nostalgically, he added, "Asheville was a beautiful place, and oriented to the arts. I was almost trapped by security." He had fond memories of the community. "It would have been a wonderful life, building our own theater, a home, and a family in the lovely town of Asheville. But somehow it wasn't what Lydia and I wanted."[8]

Obviously, a sense of security was not enough. When the company attempted to lure the couple into a longer-term arrangement, they considered and rejected the offer jointly. According to one writer, their desire was to "do fine things in the theatre," which meant they had to leave the more isolated Asheville for a place that gave them a better chance at that big break. Besides, as Heston recalled, "Another thing was that I didn't particularly like directing. I wanted to play the scenes myself, not tell other actors how." Lydia added, "We directed one another, but we both knew that directing was mental, where acting was emotional. We both missed the release of acting." He noted of the pivotal decision, "We talked it through, and decided to go back to [New York City] and give Broadway one more try."[9] Sacrificing a concrete position for the uncertainties of other chances was exactly the type of decision that separated Charlton Heston from those who would have followed the safer course. Already having had trouble obtaining meaningful employment in his field, he accepted the challenge and anticipated that the gamble would pay off for him this time.

---

7 Mal Vincent, "Security, Asheville Almost Got Him," *VP*; Scott, "Charlton Heston's Life Story," *GH*, 248; Charlton Heston, Feb. 1952, 8, Hedda Hopper Papers, HL.

8 Vincent, "Security, Asheville Almost Got Him"; Heston and Isbouts, *Hollywood*, 20; Copies of Playbills for *The Male Animal* for Feb. 13-15, 1947, and *Guest in the House*, for Mar. 28-29, 1947, directed by Heston, are located in Family Scrapbooks, HL.

9 Waterbury, "Charlton Loves Lydia," 101; Heston and Isbouts, *Hollywood*, 20.

Popular stage personality Katharine Cornell had decided to appear on Broadway as Cleopatra in a version of the Shakespeare classic. Heston determined to audition for a part, with the calculation that any role in this project would open the way for others. Of course, first he had to *get* a part. In a hall crowded with aspirants, Heston inserted himself, knowing he had no appointment. A shift into a closer seat opened when the occupant went inside for his turn. Yet, the time passed as everyone else auditioned. At the end of the day, still sitting in the empty hallway, Heston finally got his opportunity when the secretary inquired as to who he might be, given that no other names remained on her list. Insisting that there must have been a mistake, the actor offered what may have been his most important performance. "'What?! That can't be! Maynard Morris made the appointment," he recalled, admitting that he was "treading water now, since I'd never met the distinguished MCA (Music Corporation of America) agent, let alone set foot inside the MCA office." Heston's bluff worked and he learned that he could enter the inner sanctum, since a "little time" remained.

Doubling as Katharine Cornell's husband and the producer/director for this production, Guthrie McClintic turned his attentions to this last supplicant of the busy day. The tall figure made an immediate impression. A "cold reading" from the play followed and the actor summarized the initial reaction the executive expressed. "Not bad," Heston remembered Guthrie saying. "Come back tomorrow at ten."[10]

The actor never forgot the feeling of triumph at having won a place on a Broadway stage. "One of the supremely happy memories of my life is that of me walking up Sixth Avenue a few days later on a brilliant autumn morning," he recalled, "on the way to my first rehearsal in my first engagement in an honest-to-God Broadway play." He could not help but swell at the prospect. "That's pretty heady stuff when you've been pointing to it for so long." Heston also remembered the warmth of the "September sun on my shoulders" as he contemplated the impact this moment could have on his life. "A kid actor with a sixty-five-dollar-a-week bit part, I felt like God—or Laurence Olivier, which comes to about the same thing."[11]

Charlton Heston had found his Broadway debut and although the supporting role of Proculeius was not Marc Antony and Heston had not reached the point that he merited inclusion in "Who's who in the cast," the vehicle could not have been more satisfying. He was also able to display the qualities that would mark

10 Ibid., 22-23.

11 *CHA*, 78.

his career and establish his reputation among his peers. "The clear instruction was in the old, iron rule: Don't be late, don't be sick, don't screw up."[12] Each of these carried the imprint of self-awareness and insecurity masked by self-confidence. The rules were "iron" and not meant to be bent, much less broken. Furthermore, the most important was avoiding anything less than his best. "Don't screw up" remained the one commandment that could not be broken, since failing to appear on time or using illness as an excuse, however plausible, might mean a sudden end to a hard-won role.

As a newcomer, Heston was smart enough to observe how others conducted themselves to take cues for himself while also determining how to fit into this new milieu in a manner that indicated he belonged there. Interestingly, this desire to conform manifested itself in an innocuous detail. When the troupe gathered, he noted, "There's a sense of—portent, even ritual. In 1947, everyone wore jacket and tie," apart from "Ms. Cornell" in her fur coat. The men quickly shed their jackets and loosened their ties, allowing Heston to see another feature. "I remember noticing that the principal actors wore French cuffs and links. 'Hah!' I thought. 'That's what real actors wear . . . cuff links.' Ever since, so have I."

Those long hours of rehearsing Shakespeare in his head at modeling stints or in his efforts to woo Lydia were at last producing significant dividends for his career, although not without moments of sheer terror, as when Cornell summoned him to her dressing room. Fearful of what might be awaiting him, Heston proceeded to the meeting. His initial trepidation at the prospect of being reprimanded or fired gave way to more sinister concerns when he found Cornell sitting before him in a robe. But her intentions became clear as she explained that the sword Heston wore in one of their scenes together had produced severe bruising on her leg. Might he not wear the weapon differently so that this could be avoided in future performances? A relieved Heston stammered his appreciation of the situation and promised to accede to the request as she ushered him to the door. The production continued its successful run without further incident for, or from, him.[13] Even so, when the performances ended, Heston knew he had to find other work. Fortunately for the aspiring performer, new opportunities awaited.

Heston emerged from his stage debut on the "Great White Way" anxious to continue to hone his skills and chart a course in acting. A chance for residential summer stock work came with the admonition that while the locals enjoyed seeing

---

12 "Antony and Cleopatra," *Playbill*, Martin Breck Theatre, 1948, 27, 36, 38, 40, 42, 44; *CHA*, 80.

13 Heston and Isbouts, *Hollywood*, 23-24.

the plays, they did not care much for mingling with the actors involved in them. "If this bothers you, you'd better tell me now," the person making the offer advised. "Hell, I don't care," Heston replied. "What are the parts?"[14]

Just as had been the case in Asheville, working in Mt. Gretna, Pennsylvania, provided plenty of those parts. According to Heston, "We had a great summer; worked our asses off and had a marvelous time." Indeed, Charlton and Lydia immersed themselves in a stunning slate of shows—"ten plays in eleven weeks"— that offered little respite. "It was hell, but it was heaven for a kid with acting ants in his pants," he recalled. "I worked like a hungry dog that summer, which is good, and learned a lot as well, also good. What you learn is facility and flexibility, which are key skills." He knew that he had to adapt to changing conditions and unexpected situations with equanimity, a trait he had not yet acquired at this early point in his career.[15]

The Hestons returned to New York City when the summer residency closed. Lydia had the most success, finding an agent and landing an important role. Charlton was happy for his "girl," but anxious for his own next chance. She paved the way for an introduction to her agent, Maynard Morris, the same name he had dropped earlier to secure an audition. Morris found him work, "but it was for the second lead," and despite the possibility of another Broadway credit, Heston's appreciation remained muted. "That's the only time I've ever understudied, and I didn't enjoy it," he recalled. "The understudy has to sit and watch—very closely." He did not like sitting and watching when others were tramping the boards. "I felt like a caged bear," he admitted. Ironically, the situation forced more introspection and required building additional patience into his arsenal for future use. "Theoretically, you can learn by watching, but the main thing I learned, with growing conviction, was that I could do the part better."[16] The same drive infused his desire to improve each performance, but beneath lurked a powerful combination of self-confidence and self-doubt, along with a healthy dose of ego, to prod him along.

Still, in 1962, he reflected on this dismal period, wracked by a loneliness that tempered the holiday season in those early years. "Christmas hasn't passed for me so little marked since '48 when I was in Boston about to take over the lead in Leaf and Bough, and sat alone on the bed of the rooming house, methodically

---

14 *CHA*, 84.

15 Stuart Kaminsky Interview, Part I, 25, Heston Papers, HL; *CHA*, 83-84; Material for "Gretna Playhouse, Mt. Gretna, Pa., Summer Season 1948," are in Family Scrapbooks, HL.

16 *CHA*, 85.

opening my gifts early Christmas morning before going to rehearse."[17] Then, he had needed the companionship that Lydia provided, but it would be some time before circumstances granted that boon.

In the meantime, Heston prepared for work. He knew that an understudy had to be ready to step in on short notice, and such a moment arose as rehearsals proceeded. He accepted the challenge with enormous satisfaction—"they'd let me out of the cage"—but cold reality set in when the play struggled for enough positive notices to sustain a longer run. Heston's humor allowed him to recall that *Leaf and Bough* "was not a success," with a particularly caustic critic noting the production might be known more accurately as *Bow and Leave*. Nevertheless, the actor received "decent notices," by his own reckoning. In any case, five performances were not enough to allow Heston to develop his part, but they offered valuable training.[18]

Like New York, Boston served as sort of an Eastern touchstone for Heston. He stayed in contact with various individuals through phone calls or correspondence that kept his name in the newspapers or before radio listeners. Writer Joseph Finnigan reported on the circumstances of the actor's life. "Charlton Heston is Proud of Being a Working Actor," he explained, noting that his "success in a gigantic motion picture like 'Ben-Hur' has not yet wiped away the memories of lean days when he couldn't find a job in pictures." Heston was blunt about his primary motivation. "I still can remember chronic unemployment," then added, "I've only recently reached the eminence of having two jobs at once."

A sense of professionalism buttressed him throughout. "Somebody once told me the difference between a professional and an amateur," Heston explained. "The difference is that the pro does something even when he doesn't want to." His concern was laudatory: "I don't want to take a break." Already he had gotten into the habit of jotting his views into notebooks, not so much as a reflection of his activities as a method of assessing his work and as a buffer to the barbs of negative reviews. "I leave these notes for myself and they're a lot worse than those anybody else could leave. I'd better be my own worst critic. Who else could be?" he observed rhetorically. "Sometimes I'd like for my performance to finish the way I envisioned it in my mind."[19]

Another short production provided an additional credit and a means for Heston to move into a historical setting. *Design for a Stained Glass Window*

17 *ALJ*, 162.

18 *CHA*, 86, Rovin, *Films*, 13.

19 Joseph Finnigan, "Charlton Heston is Proud of Being a Working Actor," *BSG*, July 1, 1962.

took audiences to sixteenth-century England. Enthusiastically, Heston began to cultivate a beard for the part, but found, as he later observed, "It took me longer to grow it than the play ran on Broadway." Still, such plays were important in that they offered him the chance to work with and learn from acting veterans like Martha Scott. Additionally, as Heston observed, "It gave me a Broadway credit in a leading role."[20]

Television personality Robin Leach later asserted, "Soon Charlton . . . had turned his stepfather's name into that of the hot new Broadway star." A struggling actor, with "decent notices" and the occasional "Broadway credit," however, still required luck and stamina to survive. Charlton Heston had both. The fortune came with the advent of television as a dramatic option and the determination to keep working, wherever that work might be available. With television attempting to branch out into territory some purists thought reserved to the stage and other critics felt belonged to Hollywood, CBS launched a serious venture called *Studio One* in 1948. He remembered, "I was just struggling along on the Broadway stage, when I got a big part on the TV show, 'Studio One,' that paid $15."[21] Meager as it was, this windfall meant that the leanest aspects of their lives could be deferred, if not left behind entirely.

Heston consumed the parts with the voracious appetite of an actor who had found steady employment and an aspiring professional who wanted to build his credits. In the heady year of 1949, *The Outward Room* came first on January 9, followed by *Julius Caesar* (May 1), *Smoke* (June 15), *Battleship Bismarck* (Oct. 24), *Of Human Bondage* (Nov. 21), and *Jane Eyre* (Dec. 12). Columnist Hedda Hopper latched onto the rising talent from live television she described as "a solid click" as part of the "stolen talent." She boasted, "The list of stars we've taken from radio, and now TV, would fill this column." As Heston transitioned to the new medium, Hopper observed, "Hal [Wallis] thinks he'll be another Burt Lancaster."[22]

Live television productions offered Heston another venue in which to hone his skills, make important connections with other practitioners in his craft, and begin to create a presence outside the smaller framework that had thus far marked his professional world. "For us as actors," he recalled, "the key advantage was that we were learning a new technology and establishing an audience identity before

---

20 *CHA*, 91, Kaminsky Interview, Part I, 128.

21 Robin Leach, "Fame, Fortune and Romance," UCLA; Earl Wilson, *L.A. Daily News*, June 16, 1951, Heston Clipping Files, HL.

22 Hedda Hopper, "Glenn Ford, Eleanor Film Globe-Trotters," *LAT*, Mar. 10, 1950.

we ever made movies. We were already known by the time we got to Hollywood." When a writer argued that Heston should avoid television like the "bubonic plague," as other stars had chosen to do, the actor retorted that he planned to continue to do so regardless. "I can't explain why other actors don't do it . . . I do it because I enjoy doing it, because I think an actor should keep working, because I can reach an audience that I wouldn't be able to reach with a movie."[23]

Heston felt this television work gave him a distinct advantage once his chance to enter motion pictures occurred. "When the cameras started to roll," he explained about appearing in his first major film, "I realized how invaluable my television experience had been." In both forms of production, the performer has "to hit your marks, you have to match your movements, remember the angles, and watch the shadows." Although Heston was, in his candid admission, "as green as grass" when it came to motion picture requirements, "unlike those actors who came to Hollywood fresh from the stage, I had learned to do that."[24]

The convergence of a new system with individuals not already locked into the pre-existing one on Broadway or in Hollywood also allowed Charlton Heston to emerge. "Live television was the big break," he remembered. Then, with his usual self-deprecating humor, he added, "I wasn't very smart, but I did realize that something very important was about to happen." Without a studio contract or a lengthy Broadway commitment to tie him down, he could explore the medium for its value to his still-budding career. His earlier contacts and experience with Katherine Cornell and Guthrie McClintic facilitated a part in CBS's *Julius Caesar*. "Somewhat to my disappointment," he observed, "I got cast as Cinna, a minor role. I was secretly hoping my Cornell-McClintic credit would get me a more respectable part." Then, when another performer became ill, Heston got a chance to be seen in a bigger role. The fill-in so impressed director Franklin Schaffner that he asked Heston, "Stick around a minute, will you?" A subsequent reading of Marc Antony's funeral oration for producer Worthington "Tony" Miner allowed the young actor's progression to continue. He returned to the part of Cinna, but within a week landed a lead role in *Jane Eyre*.[25]

Opportunities for other such roles followed in quick succession. "It was a marvelous time," Heston remembered. He remained busy and contentedly

---

23 Heston and Isbouts, *Hollywood*, 26; Bob Thomas, "Charlton Heston Should Avoid TV, It Says Here," Scrapbooks, HL.

24 Heston and Isbouts, *Hollywood*, 36.

25 Ibid., 26; *CHA*, 87-88.

discontented. Always angling for another project, Heston had moved from part to part in the world of live television drama. "In the space of 16 months as a kid of 23 I played 'Jane Eyre,' and 'Macbeth' and 'Of Human Bondage,' and 'Taming of the Shrew' and 'Julius Caesar' and Henry James and Turgenev." It was like residential summer stock all over again, except this time for broad audiences rather than local ones. "Live TV lasted less than ten years, then it was over," he recalled. "But it was a wonderful, shining time for all of us." More importantly, Heston's decisions continued to open other opportunities to him. "Of all the choices I made, as well as the things that just happened to me, this was the most valuable," he assessed later.[26]

Heston's collaboration with Tony Minor and Franklin Schaffner as well as his ability and desire to tackle William Shakespeare in any medium continued to bear fruit. When Minor considered bringing *Macbeth* into the *Studio One* orbit, he turned to the other two men to gauge his options. "Listen guys, could you do a 90-minute version of *Macbeth*," he inquired. Schaffner's affirmative response and Heston's willingness to work on a tight ten-day rehearsal schedule clinched the deal. Schaffner came up with the device of employing an Irish wolfhound to serve as Macbeth's "companion" in order to give the portrayal a new look that audiences might find appealing. "It turned out to be a wonderful idea," Heston recalled. So did putting the play on live television in the CBS network's "first nation-wide broadcast."[27]

Charlton Heston's personal loyalty and incessant desire to keep working led him back to his *Peer Gynt* colleague, David Bradley. Bradley wanted to film *Julius Caesar* and naturally thought of his Northwestern friend for a key part. He tried to appeal to Heston's vanity by insisting that the recent television version had been unsatisfactory and that together they could do better. Best of all, the actor could play Marc Antony. "That's fine, David. I'd like to do it," Heston explained when Bradley broached the subject with him. "But I act for a living now. I have to have some kind of salary, even for a great part." He remembered being one of only two persons who were paid for taking part in the production. "I told them I had a new wife, Lydia Clarke, who was at Northwestern with me, and I needed a salary. The cameraman held out for a salary, too. We each got $35 a week."[28]

26 Haber, "Chuck Heston: A Toga Man in the Jeans Era"; *CHA*, 89.

27 Heston and Isbouts, *Hollywood*, 29.

28 Heston recalled making $50 per week, *CHA*, 89; Marjory Adams, "Charlton Heston/A Hero for all Roles," *BG*, Oct. 20, 1970.

Certainly, the timing could not have been more fortuitous. Having forsaken the certainty of Asheville for the greater risks and intermittent chances of Broadway, Heston obtained a critical opportunity when his television work fell under the notice of Harold Brent "Hal" Wallis, a successful director who, as such individuals tend to be, was constantly in search of new talent. The two men exhibited interesting traits that might have created an irreconcilable gap between them. Instead, the strong stubborn streak of one who did not intend to abandon the boards of Broadway met with the independent and fiercely determined nature of the other, who wanted to try the young actor in a role for which he thought he was well suited. A Heston-Wallis contractual arrangement that worked for both parties resulted.[29]

Heston was also the beneficiary of an extraordinary moment in motion picture history. Dynamic agent Lew Wasserman of MCA had negotiated an arrangement for actor James Stewart that provided for a percentage of the profits from two of Stewart's films; this would pave the way for actors like Heston. "Thus, for the first time," one scholar noted, "the fact that stars were largely responsible for the success of a movie was reflected in the bottom line." This was certainly an arrangement Heston found both appealing and potentially profitable.[30]

Nevertheless, Heston was determined not to lock himself into a contract that would preclude any real options to do stage or live television work. The Wallis deal gave him the freedom, as he remembered it, "to do what I wanted most: the chance to choose what I did." Studio head Jack Warner had expected to sign the rising star to a contractual arrangement of his own and was none too pleased to have someone else take him away. The angry mogul ordered the studio to ban MCA from its sets in a power struggle designed to punish such transgressors and their representatives.[31]

From as far away as New York, the city that Heston refused to take himself away from entirely, news spread of the brewing feud. "Another Warners fight," the *New York Times* informed its readers, "against a more doughty opponent, the Music Corporation of America, Hollywood's largest talent agency—began to look

---

29 The early contract summaries can be found in the Heston Papers, f.1138, HL. The Wallis-Hazen agreement is dated "1-11-50." For *Dark City*, the contract called for "1 photoplay during the period of one year commencing 3-1-50" and compensation of "$1,000. per week 10 weeks and $1,000. per week for services in excess of 10 weeks." Ibid.

30 Connie Bruck, *When Hollywood had a King: The Reign of Lew Wasserman, Who Leveraged Talent into Power and Influence* (New York, 2003), 114.

31 *CHA*, 93.

like a war of attrition." It came about because of "a dispute over the services of Charlton Heston, a newcomer to the screen, who derived immense publicity from the controversy he engendered." The imbroglio barely lasted long enough for the ink in the newsprint to dry, ending after only two days when Warner realized that his studio stood to lose more than either Wallis or Heston, given MCA's sizeable client list and the desire to keep those actors employed.[32]

In addition to securing an unusual degree of freedom, Heston had experienced the satisfying result from a power struggle with one of the most important figures in Hollywood. Despite the internal doubts that drove him, as a young actor he could not fail to recognize that he had achieved a demonstrable public indication of name recognition in his profession. Instead of squelching the young actor's Hollywood career, Jack Warner had helped to start it.

Even so, Heston was reluctant to go to California, forcing Wallis to use his charm to convince the young man to hear his proposition. Agent Maynard Morris had helped both Charlton and Lydia out before and now worked to persuade him to listen. Perhaps Morris's most important service was to pass Heston's name to agent Herman Citron, who could handle affairs on that side of the country. Citron would be responsible for inking the actor to a potential five-picture deal, which permitted Wallis the flexibility to continue to work with Heston if things went well or to cut ties with him if they did not. The actor attributed much of his success to the individual known as "the Iceman." In his autobiography, Heston noted, "Fortunately, he was my shark, absolutely determined to see that I got more than my share of the good parts," and that the client was compensated well for his work. He saw their partnership as straightforward. "Our arrangement was simple: I chose the scripts, he made the deals." As in any dynamic relationship, there were instances in which the principles disagreed and occasionally clashed. "His asking money *is* damned high," Heston confided in his journal in 1956, "but I wish he'd arrive at *something* for me."[33] Still, he trusted Citron's judgment and recognized his importance to his career, employing both Lydia and "the Iceman" as sounding boards.

Nevertheless, at this stage of his career Heston cherished flexibility above all else. He wanted to be sure that no contractual arrangement prevented him from undertaking the work in the theater that he deemed essential for his growth and

---

32 "Warners vs. M.C.A.," *NYT*, May 21, 1950; *CHA*, 93.

33 *CHA*, 160. Heston explained that it was not until much later that he learned of Citron's reputation and distinctive nickname. *ALJ*, 5. In looking back, Heston maintained, "So far, his record is better than mine."

development as a performer. The actor would be set either way, as a potential star in the Hollywood firmament or as a theatrical performer returning to the stage in New York. Of course, the whole journey might have ended had Lydia exhibited any negative reaction. She had been absent for months with her role in *Detective Story*, when she returned to New York to find Charlton waiting with his suitcase in hand. "I'm sorry, darling," he recalled later telling her, "but in an hour I'm taking off for California." Although he had kept her informed of his progress as much as pen and paper allowed, the suddenness of another separation was powerful. Yet, as a writer noted a few years later, the moment also reflected the strength of their affection. "And all you have to know about the happiness of their marriage is illustrated by the fact that on this occasion they stayed right there at the airport, hand in hand, for that hour," Ruth Waterbury explained.[34]

Wallis's publicity director met the new arrival as he deplaned in California. "We signed a young actor out of New York called Charlton Heston," Walter Seltzer recalled. Carrying a still to aid in identifying the traveler, Seltzer noted, "I remember he was wearing a very tired blue suit, which I guessed was his only suit at the time, and the pants were very thin." The fellow was unprepared for the world he was entering, and Seltzer was equally unsure of his suitability for it. "I was a bit hesitant to invite him to come to lunch with me at Romanoff's, but I did," Seltzer remembered. With Wallis already waiting at the restaurant, the duo proceeded, and Heston found himself in the company of Hollywood star-power. One of his personal idols, Spencer Tracy, was sitting only one table over. If Wallis and Seltzer had been uncertain of the reception they would receive from the performer who seemed incapable of loosening his Eastern ties, a pointed question settled matters. "How do you like everything so far?" Seltzer wanted to know. "This must be heaven," Heston responded with genuine charm.[35]

The men soon embarked on a project based upon a crime novel called *No Escape*. Heston was to play one of the men who swindled another out of his money in a crooked card game that led to the victim's suicide. The opening occurred when Burt Lancaster's commitments elsewhere made him unavailable, giving "a real opportunity to a new Hal Wallis find, Charlton Heston," according to one writer. "There are two important male assignments," Edwin Schallert explained, "but Heston does the Lancaster part."[36]

---

34 Waterbury, "Charlton Loves Lydia," 99, HL.

35 Cecil Smith, "Charlton Heston: For All Seasons," *LAT*, Feb. 27, 1966.

36 Edwin Schallert, "Lupino Again to Star Tod Andrews; 'Cities' Features Ann Vernon," *LAT*, Apr. 1, 1950.

Heston was less sure of the nature of the project. "I'd never heard of film noir," the actor remarked years later; but if he was unfamiliar with the genre, he was confident of his ability to embody the role. "I felt at home there," he explained.[37] Even so, the new style and performance environment were not the only elements Heston had to overcome. He could not help but miss his wife, who had remained behind to continue work in *Detective Story*, and knew he could not flourish in any situation without her blessing. With her assurance, Heston placed his name on a Wallis contract for a part in the renamed *Dark City*.

The commitment allowed Wallis to promote his new film personality, with Heston set to work with Lizabeth Scott and veteran stars Ed Begley, Dean Jagger, Don DeFore, Harry Morgan, Jack Webb, and Viveca Lindfors. When the cameras rolled on April 5, 1950, the newcomer had his initiation into life at Paramount Studios and on shoots at such notable locations as the Griffith Observatory planetarium, the Santa Monica pier, Union Station, and several prominent hotels. The subject might not allow Heston to demonstrate his full range as a leading man, but the work gave him critical motion picture experience and important exposure.

Wallis was determined to keep the momentum going for his budding film star. He considered Heston's placement in a project based on the notorious activities of William Quantrill and his raiders in Civil War Kansas. "He will be teamed with Burt Lancaster," Edwin Schallert speculated, "whom he replaced in his first film." The writer added, "Whether Heston will play in 'Ethan Frome' at Warners may still be in doubt, but I won't be surprised if he does that picture." Wallis also demonstrated evidence of his commitment by picking up Heston's "options . . . long before [they] were due," according to Hedda Hopper, who declared the actor had "gone over big with exhibitors on a recent tour."[38] The transplanted New York stage talent was clearly making a mark in Hollywood circles.

As another *Los Angeles Times* headline informed readers, "Television Pushes Actor to Top in Movie World." "Television is making its force felt in more ways than one in the motion picture domain," the writer observed. "The most striking evidence, I believe, is the stir created over an actor, Charlton Heston, who has never been seen in a picture, but who has unquestionably been observed by millions in the video medium as a player in Studio One shows out of New York." Noting

37 *CHA*, 95-96, 98.

38 Edwin Schallert, "Hal Wallis to Spend $19,500,000 on Pictures; Marlowe Joins 'Mister,'" *LAT*, June 9, 1950; Hedda Hopper, "Second Story Bought for Robert Merrill," *LAT*, Sept. 27, 1950.

the studio imbroglio over the actor's independent signing, the writer nevertheless concluded, "TV has thus pushed him to the front with lightning speed."[39]

Publicity continued to build for Heston. Formerly relegated to the body of columns, he now found his name in headlines and his face in featured photographs. In November, Walter Ames highlighted the actor's transition. "Don't look now but television might have given Hollywood its next big star in husky Charlton Heston," he exclaimed, noting comparisons he believed were favorable to *Gone with the Wind*'s Leslie Howard. "I asked him which was the tougher, movies or television," and Heston indicated he thought the former, for its schedules and physicality. The actor suggested that in television, he also had an unusual advantage "because he has an ear for TV lines the same as some musicians have an ear for music." He concluded, however, that "the flickers are harder because of his closing scenes in 'Dark City,'" fighting with a powerful Mike Mazurki, "not one day but two days in a row."[40]

While in California, the actor's actual residence, for the time being, was "a furnished apartment up behind Grauman's Chinese." He remembered having Merv Griffith as a neighbor, but believed "a high proportion of the other tenants seemed to be hookers." Yet this setting did not disturb Heston, who preferred to find his challenges in developing his character and technique before the camera. "When you're a kid," he explained in looking back at this formative period, "things seem easy because you don't know they're hard."[41]

Heston was anxious to return to New York and Lydia when his responsibilities with the film ended. They were able to spend time with Louis Jolyon "Jolly" and Kathryn West, an instance of the way the Hestons maintained a circle of close friends throughout their lives. The couples were able to "sneak" a viewing of *Dark City* and the screen novice recalled coming away "enormously impressed, but then, it was my first film and I was still learning." The actor was not the only one pleased with the end product, and understood the publicity required to make the picture successful. Heston explained that the director had "immediately" turned Walter Seltzer to the task, and the promoter "set up a tour for me."[42]

---

39 "Television Pushes Actor to Top in Movie World," *LAT*, June 25, 1950.

40 Walter Ames, "Bergen, Charlie McCarthy in TV Debut Today; Heston Says Movies Tougher Than Video," *LAT*, Nov. 23, 1950.

41 *ALJ*, xvi.

42 Louis Jolyon "Jolly" West was a psychiatrist whom the actor had gotten to know while they both worked in New York City. Heston recalled that they played chess together while Lydia was appearing in *Detective Story*. *CHA*, 100.

Interestingly, his film debut was not highest in the mind of the emerging actor. "You should think that a young man (giant type) who had just signed one of the most flattering Hollywood contracts ever given might stop dreaming for a while," columnist Jay Carmody asserted. "After all, Hollywood's money is real." The writer suspected that Heston, whom he described as "bitter about Communism and thinks that as a former B-25 pilot he may have to interrupt his movie contract," was concerned that the Cold War might heat up. Still, Heston seemed most anxious to assume a role as a brutal Soviet interrogator in an upcoming project. "It is a horrible character," the actor noted, "in fact I can't think of a more offensive one, but what an opportunity for an actor!" He also remained consumed with his "12-city tour" to promote *Dark City* and thought the traditional "new actor build-up" beneficial in other ways. "After all," he concluded, "a man gets to new places, meets new acquaintances, and in the case of Washington, gets his first chance to see the Folger Shakespeare Library." The stage and screen actor who still aspired to meet his mentor, Laurence Olivier, was ready to take on any challenge.[43]

The publicity junket's schedule proved grueling and repetitive, but necessary for the young man who was absorbing every aspect of his craft. "It was rough," Heston remembered. "We did fourteen cities in twenty-three days, always staying just ahead of the film's opening." More importantly, he explained, "I learned something that is crucial to an actor—how to do interviews. No doubt that was reflected in the good press we got out of it." He always appreciated the other benefits this early lesson brought to his career. "[I]t's a popular position for public figures to take that interviews are a great bore—and they can be of course," he remarked more than a decade later, "but it's pleasant to have somebody paid to listen to you talk about yourself." The connection of a budding star to his public was taking shape as well, with television and radio spots, as well as lunches with press personnel and others who could help to make audiences aware of the coming feature and its star. Heston was pleased with the degree to which this part of his career was beginning to take shape. "I was off to a good start."[44]

The actor was already demonstrating staying power in his profession, tempered by his willingness to learn and his desire to promote his work wherever the publicity demands might send him. Although she did not yet feature the rising star, columnist Hedda Hopper could barely disguise her feelings when she gushed,

43 Jay Carmody, "Newest of Male Film Stars Dreams of a Stage Role," *Evening Star* [Washington, DC], Aug. 14, 1950.

44 Heston and Isbouts, *Hollywood*, 36; "M" Interview, July 1967, Heston Papers, HL; *CHA*, 100.

"Charlton Heston, a huge, talented fellow, caused considerable commotion when he came here to make his first picture, 'Dark City,' last summer." Hopper said "Charlton, in addition to being a very good actor, also has a great personality. In one picture he registered impact and authority."[45] Likewise, Los Angeles critic Philip K. Scheuer offered kudos to Heston with a headline that read "'Dark City' Introduces Charlton Heston, Promising Rugged Type." Boston columnist Marjory Adams reflected upon his budding career. "Charlton Heston has spent just seven weeks of his whole life in Hollywood," she informed her readers. "He has made only one picture, 'Dark City,' which won't be seen in Boston or most other cities in America before October." Yet the "handsome, boyish young man" was already in demand "by three different film organizations," including the likes of Hal Wallis, Warner Brothers, and Howard Hawks. Adams marveled at the way in which the young actor skirted the traditional grooming process usually required of others. "Wallis wanted to test Heston for the films—but Heston said he could not shave off his beard which he had grown so carefully" for his role in a production of *Design for a Stained Glass Window*. Consequently, she explained, "there was no test and Heston signed his contract without a painful audition before the cameras." If, as one colleague wrote, "he was the hottest new boy on any film lot," Adams was appreciative of Heston's brief stopover in "a sort of 'get-acquainted' visit" that represented the first opportunity since his theater days to be back in Boston. Heston insisted that it had been his willingness to work that helped him get started in Hollywood. "I can safely say the young man who wants a picture career these days," he explained to the writer, "will be better off if he spends a few years getting ahead on Broadway." He considered theater seasoning imperative, concluding, "there isn't a single newcomer among the men who hasn't already had quite a little experience on the stage. Gregory Peck, Kirk Douglas, Wendell Corey, Marlon Brando, Montgomery Clift, to name a few."[46]

Heston knew he was becoming educated in many aspects of his profession but found that he mainly wanted to work and was willing to do what it took to position himself for the longer race to come. Hollywood did not have to wait long for the gangling kid from the Midwestern woods who had begun to make a pivotal turn on the track of his burgeoning career. Among the routine requirements for

45 Hedda Hopper, "Local and Imported Discoveries Project Elusive 'Movie Presence,'" *LAT*, Dec. 31, 1950.

46 Philip K. Scheuer, "'Dark City' Introduces Charlton Heston, Promising Rugged Type," *LAT*, Feb. 5, 1951; Marjory Adams, "Film Producers Want Actors Not Charmers, 'Hot' Star Says," *BDG*, Aug. 8, 1950.

his entrance into the world of cinema was membership in the Screen Actors Guild. Heston later recalled that this involved "Equity Junior membership then Senior membership." But he was adamant in remembering that he "didn't pay much attention to it. Once I started working I was working."[47]

Dark City provided a useful foundation for a new "face" in Hollywood, but Heston's performance did not open doors for him immediately, thereby offering a different kind of lesson for the young man. He badly wanted to play the lead in a film version of the successful stage production of *Detective Story*. "I was elated to hear that William Wyler wanted to test me for the lead," Heston noted of the famed director. The actor realized that he should follow the "modest success" of his first major picture "with something more substantial to keep the momentum in Hollywood going." Unfortunately, his "need" to continue his progress in motion pictures and his confidence that he would win the role—"I told myself there was no question I'd get the part. Mind you, I always think that about any part."—did not translate into work on this occasion. Wyler chose another actor for the role, and the way Heston learned the news proved particularly troubling. "Then, one day, I heard on Louella Parson's radio show that Willy had cast Kirk Douglas. Just like that. It was a tough thing to take—a shot right between the eyes."[48]

Although he was not seeking it directly, Heston had a measure of revenge in a competition with Douglas when it came to one of the most important roles he would ever play. Both men sought the lead in a remake of a 1927 film. Douglas had finished his work in *The Vikings* with no desire to make costumers again, but a new script emerged that changed his mind. "The leading role was perfect for me— Ben Hur!" Wyler thought he might be suited for the role of the nemesis Messala, but as Douglas observed, the director "wanted Charlton Heston for Ben Hur, and he got him. I was disappointed."[49]

In the meantime, Chuck Heston's disappointment at losing out on the feature role in *Detective Story* was very real. He could not be sure of what might lie ahead for him, but columnist Hedda Hopper had less concern over his future. Noting his failure to secure "even . . . a meeting" with William Wyler, she deemed the circumstance "a lucky thing." The void left him free to get work on a different

---

47 "Screen Actors Guild Interview—Legacy, June 1994," UCLA.

48 Heston and Isbouts, *Hollywood*, 37.

49 Kirk Douglas, *The Ragman's Son: An Autobiography* (New York, 1988), 303.

production with another famed director. "He couldn't get a greater break," she concluded.[50]

Much later in his career, Heston allowed himself the freedom to accept that another actor was better poised for a role he had assumed was his for the taking. Noting that Douglas gave a "very good" performance in *Detective Story*, he did not concede that he would have loved to have given the role his best shot. Still, the timing of the unhappy circumstance was significant. "And, as it turned out," Heston remembered with the benefit of hindsight, "not getting the part was the best thing that could ever have happened to me." His greatest opportunity was set to come as he packed his bags and made ready to return to the East Coast, disappointed but unbowed by the setback. Bidding farewell to his new associates at Paramount Studios, the actor "got in my car and headed for the gate."[51]

---

50 Hedda Hopper, "Pidgeon Winning Good Role of Legal Eagle," *LAT*, Dec. 1, 1950.

51 Heston and Isbouts, *Hollywood*, 37.

Chapter Three

THUNDERING TO THE FRONT
1950s

"But once you learn my name, you're not likely to forget it."
—Heston on Hal Wallis's attempt to change his name.

'I think it's amazing the way the circus manager fitted in with these professional actors."
—A viewer's take on Heston's role as a circus boss

Performances:
The Greatest Show on Earth, Jan. 10, 1952 (New York)
Cashel Byron's Profession, Robert Montgomery Presents, Jan. 14, 1952
The Wings of the Dove, Mar. 10, 1952
The Liar, Curtain Call, Aug. 22, 1952
The Savage, Sept. 1952
Ruby Gentry, Dec. 25, 1952 (New York)
Macbeth, Bermuda, 1952
The Closed Door, Robert Montgomery Presents, Dec. 29, 1952
Elegy, The Philco-Goodyear Television Playhouse, Jan. 25, 1953
The President's Lady, May 21, 1953
Pony Express, May 1953
Arrowhead, Aug. 3, 1953
"A Day in the Town," *Medallion Theatre*, Dec. 12, 1953
Bad for Each Other, Dec. 24, 1953
Your Show of Shows, Jan. 16, 1954
Freedom to Get Lost, Danger Series, Feb. 2, 1954
The Naked Jungle, Mar. 4, 1954
The Secret of the Incas, June 6, 1954
Mr. Roberts, Palm Beach, 1954
The George Gobel Show, Mar. 3, 1955
The Far Horizons, May 20, 1955

The Colgate Comedy Hour, June 12, 1955; June 26, 1955;
Aug. 7, 1955; Aug. 28, 1955; Sept. 4, 1955
The Private War of Major Benson, Aug. 2, 1955 (United States)
Along Came Jones, *Robert Montgomery Presents*, Sept. 26, 1955
The Birth of Modern Times, *Omnibus*, Oct. 9, 1955
Person to Person, Oct. 14, 1955
Lucy Gallant, Oct. 20, 1955 (New York)
The Seeds of Hate, *General Electric Theater*, Dec. 11, 1955
Bailout at 43,000 Feet, *Climax!*, Dec. 29, 1955

Almost everything that would shape Charlton Heston's career and public life truly began with Cecil B. DeMille. The giant of Hollywood could direct or deflect the trajectory of any potential star. DeMille knew what he wanted and was constantly looking for strong material and the actors that would breathe screen life into it. On April 24, 1950, he was having lunch at the studio commissary when he spotted an actor and took mental note of his potential. DeMille recognized that Heston might be a fit for his future projects and on the following day resolved to speak to *Dark City* director William Dieterle about the young man. His homework included screening the film for himself and viewing other screen tests that involved Heston. DeMille's assertion to a colleague, "I think he's awfully good," did not reveal his misgiving that for all the actor's efforts there remained concern about his dimensions on screen. "He is not quite right for our picture," he observed a short time later, worried that Heston's screen persona had "a sinister quality" that might overshadow his performance. On the positive side of the ledger, the director assessed, "He's sincere—you believe him— has some power." Heston, however, seemed to be missing a key characteristic for building empathy with an audience. "Find out if he has any humor," DeMille demanded of a member of his entourage. "Everything I've seen him in he's dour."

It did not help that *Dark City* fell into the film noir genre or that Heston was still building the presence that would allow him to grow as an actor and, later, as a star. Even so, he was never quite able to shake the popular notion that he lacked a sense of humor or a lighter side. One early assessment noted Heston's "obvious inclination to take himself seriously."[1] In a subsequent interview, he exhibited

1 "Moses from Michigan," *Coronet* (Oct. 1956), 8.

a raw sensitivity to the matter. "There's another element in *Will Penny* which is not in many of my films," he observed to Stuart Kaminsky, "somewhat to my annoyance because I don't think of myself as a humorless person. But most of my parts are quite humorless parts." He thought the roles themselves were limiting in this fashion. "Now some of this is intentional, as with *Naked Jungle*, as with Michelangelo. But still the bottom line, and this is something I think about a great deal because I think it's responsible for the fact that I don't really enjoy a very generous critical press, by and large."

Heston remained sensitive on the subject. "But I'll tell you this: if I am trapped in any way in terms of my public image which is something people are always telling me, it's not in terms of playing epics or heroes. I have found more elbow room in that area than any other actor in America because I have far more costumes to choose from." Certainly, his record of success with period pieces both indicated his bankability to film executives and comported to audience expectations. Still, Heston could not help feeling restricted in the range of roles he was offered. "But if I am trapped in any way, and I think you'd have to say this, it's I seem to be caught in playing very serious bastards." His own tendency toward professionalism and perfectionism led to perceptions among colleagues of his seriousness. One fellow actor observed, "If he asks you to pass the salt at dinner, he sounds as if he might be going into Hamlet's soliloquy."[2]

The transplanted Midwesterner knew he could come across as overly serious, but his inveterate sense of positive energy lent a critical hand at an important moment. He had first met Cecil B. DeMille in the same way that others usually did, over a private lunch. That session had not seemed particularly productive except to give Heston a connection with the legendary director he might exploit if the opportunity arose. He recalled that this meeting occurred inadvertently, although another account suggested more deliberateness. "Heston met the director through calculated maneuvering," a writer for a short *Coronet* piece observed.[3] At any rate, the actor was on his way off the studio lot in a new convertible when he happened to glance in DeMille's direction; Heston instinctively waved at him, and more importantly, smiled, as he passed by. That affable gesture caught the director's eye and DeMille waved back automatically, and then revisited the possibilities for the otherwise serious young man.

2 Stuart Kaminisky Interview, Part II, Heston Papers, 98-99, HL; Hyatt Downing, "Hollywood's Moses," 3, HL.

3 "Moses from Michigan," 8.

Additional viewings of Heston's work led DeMille to reassess the young actor's potential. "Heston has a funny way of speaking—it's an artificial way . . . like James Mason," DeMille observed. Most importantly, he concluded, "Am inclined to give him the part." A three-film contract followed, which Heston signed on November 28, 1950. The agreement took into consideration Heston's pre-existing connection with "Wallis-Hazen Productions" and ranged in salary from $2,000 a week for ten weeks to $3,000 per week for the third DeMille project. The contract's most important element for the young working actor was its series of ten-week guarantees.[4]

The first of these was a circus picture, *The Greatest Show on Earth*, in which DeMille cast Heston as the tough manager of a big top roadshow. The director hoped to tap into the popularity of the traveling circuses that had entertained "children of all ages" for decades and was determined to be authentic with respect to props, settings, and the many wardrobe details. Heston received a valuable lesson on this point when he answered a summons to DeMille's office, where he found almost every surface covered by a range of fedoras. "It is very important that you wear the right hat," the director insisted. "Shoes I don't care about, but your hat is in every shot, even more so in close-ups." Heston recalled that he tried each of them on until they arrived at the one that appeared to be "right."[5]

In only his second major motion picture, Heston had the opportunity to watch a master craftsman at work. He observed DeMille's habits and techniques and received reinforcement about the intangibles he had already embraced. When an actor was late for a scene, he witnessed DeMille take the crew to task for allowing the discrepancy to occur, sparing the performer's ego, but making the point so that a repetition of such behavior was less likely.[6] Author Phil Koury noted that the director could be a demanding taskmaster, as demonstrated in a speech he made before a line of individuals when a train scene in the movie bogged down:

Ladies and gentlemen, the men you see before me are assistants. It is their job to assist. Assist means to help. We are here in an important picture and this is an important scene. It takes a lot of time and money to bring people and equipment all the way from Hollywood. Maybe these gentlemen don't realize this. Now, unless I can do this scene we will have no picture. These

4 Robert S. Birchard, *Cecil B. DeMille's Hollywood* (Lexington, KY, 2004), 346.

5 Heston and Isbouts, *Hollywood*, 41.

6 *CHA*, 108-109.

gentlemen know this but they either don't have the ability or they don't care. In either case they are useless to me. I should encourage them to pack up their bags and return to Hollywood, as a favor to me, to the cast and the cameramen. Errors in judgment I can forgive, stupidity never. If you can't do the job please have the courage to tell me, so I can get someone else.[7]

Though Heston needed no such prodding to do his best, he took note of DeMille's exacting standards. Additionally, the chance to work with the director and a veteran performer of the stature of Jimmy Stewart, who played Buttons the clown, was for him "a marvelous basic course in professionalism."[8]

Working with DeMille also meant a tremendous advantage for any rising actor in more important ways than simply learning one's craft. Heston was gaining exposure in his industry. Just as he had once hoped that his Cornell-McClintic Broadway credit would prove useful in the theater, now he recognized that association with the award-winning Cecil B. DeMille was likely to produce dividends in his film career. "I have been going ever since," Heston explained later as he looked back at the opportunity.[9]

In February, Hollywood reporter Darr Smith of the *Los Angeles Daily News* detailed his "frantic interview" with a young man "we confidently predict will soon be one of Hollywood's top stars." Writing from the film set in Florida, Heston concluded, "Having the lead in this picture is certainly the luckiest thing that could have happened to me in this or in any year." He had appeared on Smith's radio show, *In Hollywood*, for KFWB, before he and Lydia left California. "If you can crawl out from under the mass of copy I saw you buried under when we left, drop us a line and tell us how the radio show is coming along. We were so damned rushed the day I did it with you, I didn't get a chance to go into it much. See you soon. CHUCK."[10]

Then, in May, the buildup continued with Smith observing, "Now you take the case of actor Charlton Heston—he plays the tough circus boss, and the word is that this job of acting is going to make him one of Hollywood's biggest stars."[11]

7 Phil A. Koury, *Yes, Mr. DeMille* (New York, 1959), 145.

8 *CHA*, 108-109.

9 Pete Hamill, "Heston: Larger Than Life," *SEP* (July 3, 1965), 91.

10 Darr Smith, *L.A. Daily News*, Feb. 26, 1951, Heston Clipping File, HL.

11 Darr Smith, *L.A. Daily News*, May 10, 1951, HL.

Indeed, his role in *The Greatest Show on Earth* secured Heston's place in the acting firmament. Like any performer, he was aware of his rising status as reflected in his billing or placement on the marquee or the cast list. Achieving placement above the title or at the top of the playbill was a clear indication that the film or the stage production the audience was about to see would largely be considered yours.

The picture also presented Lydia Heston with the chance to develop an interest that would sustain her long after she made the decision to shift away from a full-time acting career of her own. As a subsequent press release for her husband illustrated, "When Heston was in Florida, for instance, with 'The Greatest Show on Earth,' Lydia was on hand with her camera to shoot stills." Lydia's work became an essential part of developing her husband's public "face." As this report indicated, "Later these were used by Chuck's agent for 'planting.'"[12]

Hollywood columnist Sheilah Graham held Heston's prospects high. "Better start reading your Bible and mythology," she observed, "Charlton Heston, now touring with 'The Greatest Show on Earth' is the greatest hit with the gals since Frank Sinatra's press agent zoomed him to the top."[13]

Even as he tried to forge a viable pathway to a career in Hollywood, both Charlton and Lydia remained committed to the theater. Actors Gregory Peck, José Ferrer, and Dorothy McGuire had established a company in La Jolla in 1947 that offered summer performances.[14] In the late summer of 1951, the Hestons enjoyed "a footlight reunion" as one writer termed it, appearing in *The Petrified Forest*, which ran from August 21-26.[15]

In the meantime, additional movie projects kept Heston's name and image before the public. On August 11, Darr Smith announced, "Charlton Heston, the Hal Wallis star whom we predict is going to be one of the biggest things in Hollywood, sends in the following note from the depths of South Dakota where he has just finished making 'Warbonnet' for Paramount studios."[16]

Renamed *The Savage*, the motion picture offered two matters of importance to Heston: the chance to be in a Western and another opportunity to hone his craft.

---

12 "Charlton Heston—A Success Story," Press Release, Heston Clipping File, HL.

13 Sheilah Graham, "Hollywood Diary," *Evening Star*, Feb. 20, 1952.

14 Gary Fishgall, *Gregory Peck: A Biography* (New York, 2002), 122-123.

15 Edwin Schallert, "Wechsler Will Produce 'Anne;' Heston and Wife Named Play Principals," *LAT*, June 23, 1951; "Stellar Quartet Scores in 'Petrified Forest,'" *LAT*, Aug. 25, 1951. For the listing of early productions, see, www.lajollaplayhouse.org/who-we-are/about-the-playhouse/production-history/.

16 Darr Smith, *L.A. Daily News*, Aug. 11, 1951, HL.

In the first instance, Heston recalled, "From the day I signed to make movies, I'd been aching to play in one," but admitted that the film was not particularly good. Nevertheless, he kept learning his trade, as well as enjoying the work in a visually stunning location in South Dakota's Black Hills. He gained another useful lesson on this set. Anxious to understand his character, Heston sought from director George Marshall a "motivation" for a scene. "Look, kid," he recalled Marshall's response. "In movies, it isn't always can you act, it's can you run a horse to a mark. In this shot, that's your motivation; just hit the damn mark. OK?" Heston remembered, "I got the message. I hit the mark. Acting is partly a question of focus."[17]

Charlton Heston was getting work in a steady and consistent fashion, but like all performers, he found that some coveted roles eluded him. Though speculation held that he would portray prisoner of war Sgt. J. J. Sefton in a film version of *Stalag 17*, the memorable role went to William Holden. Yet even as Heston accepted other parts, reports making the rounds indicated a significant challenge that had faced the actor when Hal Wallis initially signed him. The promoter wanted a catchier name for his rising star. Hollywood critic Hedda Hopper noted that Heston "put up a battle and wouldn't do it." Heston understood the usefulness of promoting a memorable brand and admitted that he might "be wrong" to have refused, before adding, "But once you learn my name, you're not likely to forget it. It's mine, and it seemed kind of a phoney thing to do to change it."[18]

In the same extensive interview with Hopper, the young actor demonstrated maturity and insight. She noted bluntly of *Dark City*, "I liked you in your first picture, but I didn't like the picture. It was a helluva way to introduce a new star." Nonplussed, Heston replied, "I guess people thought that. But I'm not complaining. For an actor to get a lead in his first picture is really something." He was incredulous when she insisted that he was now "wanted all over town by every studio." To her assertion that he was being talked up for the sort of parts screen idol Clark Gable might ordinarily get, Heston observed, "That is very encouraging. I haven't had a real nibble since finishing 'War Bonnet'. So I'm glad to hear that from you." Hopper assured him that he was "going to be a big star."

Heston was certain that being in a DeMille production was as responsible as any other factor for the sudden attention to his career. He and Lydia would do their best to promote the film overseas, while also taking some time as tourists.

---

17 *CHA*, 118-119.

18 Hedda Hopper, "Charlton Heston Set for Billy Wilder Film," *LAT*, Oct. 11, 1951; Charlton Heston, Feb. 1952, 5, Hopper Papers, HL.

"Lydia and I have never been to Europe," he explained. "It's our first trip, and we're going to try to take it in. We're tremendously excited about it." On the business side, he had promised DeMille "if he wanted me to go any where and do anything for the picture, I would go." He had already exhibited this quality to a high level. "As a matter of fact," he told Hopper, "I've worked harder the past two weeks than I did when we were making the picture."

Heston also wanted to prevent typecasting if he could help it. "The main thing I want to avoid is doing the same thing over and over," he explained. A recent script offering had featured the "part of a guy who runs a circus." Heston said he "sent it back. I want to avoid working in any circus play or picture for a long time. If my next part could be different from 'War Bonnet' and 'Greatest Show,' I'd be in clover." He also did not want to take too much time off between projects. "I don't have time. I have too much to learn." He knew the extremes. "Actors don't have a chance to learn. They're either pounding the pavements looking for a job, or they become a star." And when the latter occurred, "Then someone decides they shouldn't do this or they shouldn't do that, so there's no chance to learn their trade."

Although time would expand and alter the list to a degree, Charlton Heston identified the individuals he found most commendable as role models in the profession. "My favorite stage actor is [Laurence] Olivier. I admired him very much, and my favorite screen actor is Gregory Peck. I admire him more than any other actor in this country." Among his female colleagues, there were Katharine Cornell and Judith Anderson as "my favorites on the stage; and on the screen, Claudette Colbert and Barbara Stanwyck." He did not divulge the reasons he had arrived at any of these examples or the ways in which he deemed them influential on his own artistic endeavors and interpretations, but the choices illustrated his appreciation for the work and skills of other performers.[19]

Heston knew his contacts with columnists like Hedda Hopper offered him exposure to large numbers of readers, who in turn could become part of the audiences that would sustain his career. In July, she again devoted a portion of her column to him. "No Holidays for Heston," it began. "Charlton Heston, when I first met him, said that he didn't think it wise for a movie actor to sit around Hollywood waiting for another job between films. And he certainly practices his theory." She noted the proliferation of his work, including "a week of summer stock at the Princeton Theater" with Lydia, as well as "a show" in New York, for 'Curtain

19 Ibid., 1-2.

Call,' the TV program on which he was discovered for movies." The Hestons also planned to return to the West Coast to begin filming *The President's Lady* and to help Cecil B. DeMille celebrate his golden anniversary.[20]

The DeMille magic had one practical function for the studious Heston, who signed on to portray Andrew Jackson. In addition to screening the 1938 version of *The Buccaneer* and offering use of his library resources, the director lent the actor what Heston came to view as "a combination research item and good luck piece, a lovely little wax statuette of Jackson, about ten inches high, which I kept in my dressing room while we were shooting *The President's Lady*." Heston recalled that when the picture wrapped, he returned the talisman, but later received it as "additional recompense" when his role as Jackson in a remake of *The Buccaneer* stretched beyond the level of a cameo as the filming progressed.[21]

Another lasting piece of advice that emerged from the film came from director Henry Levin. Heston was sure that he had captured what he could of his subject when Levin insisted he could find more. "Just remember," he explained, "you don't know you're going to be President yet." Heston found the observation significant at the time and critical later. "Every time I play one of these major great men," he noted subsequently, "I try to remember that."[22]

His work in the early part of the decade neither typecast Heston entirely nor took his career where he wanted it to go. Three of the films, *Ruby Gentry* (1952), *Bad for Each Other* (1953), and *Lucy Gallant* (1955) were no more than contemporary dramas that did little to build his career. Three were Western-style actioners, *The Savage* (1952), *Pony Express* (1953), and *Arrowhead* (1953), which satisfied his craving for the genre but did not generate much of the same for moviegoers. Heston could be brutally honest in assessing his performance, although less sure of the reason for it. "I think I was coasting on chemistry there," he observed about *Arrowhead*. "I was working almost constantly and loving all of it, but maybe I was absorbing more than I was giving the camera."[23] Contemporary accounts, on the other hand, detected a more salutary effect. A snippet in the *Los Angeles Times* noted, "Charlton Heston, who portrays Buffalo Bill Cody in Nat Holt's

20 Hedda Hopper, "Phyllis Kirk to Star in 'Come on, Texas,'" *LAT*, July 29, 1952.

21 Heston noted that he took the role to fulfill his obligation to Paramount Studios on the contract purchased from Hal Wallis. See Rovin, *Films*, 37.

22 *CHA*, 125.

23 Ibid., 119.

'Pony Express,' is rapidly proving himself to be one of Hollywood's most versatile players."[24]

Two of his films in this period were exotic adventures, *The Naked Jungle* (1953) and *Secret of the Incas* (1954), which took Heston and his fans to new locations. Two others were the type of historical drama that frequently defined Heston's career: *The President's Lady* (1953) and *The Far Horizons* (1955). Though these allowed him to explore characters with biographical heft in Andrew Jackson and William Clark, they provided him with little professional lift. In each instance, Heston seemed to be working diligently, if struggling in the process, to establish a film persona that would reach the widest audience.

He was learning the hard lessons of his profession, especially the fickle nature of timing and the struggle to retain and maintain audience attention. While *Hollywood Reporter* indicated that the actor had "shown commendable progress since coming to Hollywood," it also pointed out that he had "yet to learn that the camera is his friend and that he does not need to act quite so hard to get over his effects." Heston had always been a serious student of his craft and this blunt assessment captured his desire to bring gravitas to each role. He might be "doing fine" in that publication's view, and prepared to move from "about mid-channel in a career that should land him among such powerful (and relaxed) giants of movie box-office as Gary Cooper, Cary Grant and John Wayne," all of whom had gone through "(very painfully) what he's going through now."[25] Still, he knew as well as anyone that his continued progress would depend upon the next role he accepted and the degree to which it generated ticket sales.

Whatever the box office appeal of this run of features, Heston was obtaining valuable experience in front of the cameras while working with actors who added to his circle of Hollywood contacts, acquaintances, and, in some cases, friends. His list of co-stars was impressive, ranging from Karl Malden, Brian Keith, Jack Palance, and Thomas Mitchell to Eleanor Parker, Donna Reed, and Julie Adams. In addition, Milburn Stone, Forrest Tucker, Robert Young, William Conrad, and William Demarest were among the performers who went on to exhibit a presence in popular television series as well as film work.

Working with stars on stage and screen was expected; taking a public position in the political arena was another matter. Heston later insisted that his national political interest and engagement began around this time, with the 1952

24 "Actor in Buffalo Bill Part Proves Versatile," *LAT*, Apr. 26, 1953.

25 Quoted in Eliot, *Charlton Heston*, 76.

presidential campaign of Adlai Stevenson. While the election "broke no new ground for Hollywood," according to one scholar of the relationship between Tinsel Town and Washington politics, that year "nonetheless marked a fundamental departure in the film community's political participation." Because of a very full calendar of work that left him little time for other activities, Heston would yet not play the role undertaken by Lauren Bacall, Humphrey Bogart, or Robert Ryan in Stevenson's campaign, but he was interested in the state of the nation and those the voters could tap to lead it.[26]

Heston also found time for an extraordinary event associated with one of his recent motion pictures. In December, a report surfaced that during his work on *The Savage*, he had been inducted "into the Sioux tribe during location filming of the outdoor drama in South Dakota." Receiving the name "Iron Shell" from the leader of the Sioux during a ceremony that marked the occasion, Charlton Heston could boast of another unique milestone that moviemaking had given him.[27]

Hedda Hopper subsequently lamented missing the chance to see Heston in California when he had to sprint back to New York to meet other commitments. "He's one actor who believes in working constantly, and not sitting around waiting for glory to be handed to him on a silver platter," she observed. Although not impressed with *Dark City*, as she had remarked to him earlier, Hopper thought his work in *The Greatest Show on Earth* was noteworthy and "convinced me we had a new star on our hands."[28]

Though Charlton's Hollywood star was in the ascendant, the Hestons were still trying to maintain a presence on both coasts. In the flat they had occupied since he returned from the service, the couple shared the tight spaces and limited furnishings happily. A feature on the "thirty-dollar-a-month unheated" apartment noted the spartan quarters, with furniture obtained from the local Salvation Army or constructed by Heston himself. "The desk cost two dollars and fifty cents," Lydia offered, and "the end tables less than that." As work became available, the couple put away what they could, although Lydia indulged by purchasing an ivory chess set for her husband. "The Hestons don't have to be practical these days," writer Beverly Linet observed. "Chuck makes over a thousand dollars a TV show

---

26 Ronald Brownstein, *The Power and the Glitter: The Hollywood-Washington Connection* (New York, 1990), 129-131.

27 "Star of 'The Savage' Accepted Into Tribe," *LAT*, Dec. 21, 1952.

28 Hedda Hopper, "Heston Believes in Hard Work," *This World San Francisco Chronicle* (Apr. 6, 1953), 14.

and has a generous yearly guarantee from his movie contracts with Paramount and producer Hal Wallis." Yet when she broached the notion that they might move to better accommodations, Heston balked. "Why should we? We're comfortable enough—and convenient to the heart of the theatrical district." Additional savings allowed them to purchase other items, including an "original Toulouse-Lautrec sketch that hangs over our bed, my new Packard convertible, and our acreage and old hunting lodge in Michigan." Of course, he was beginning to be noticed more in the neighborhood, even as he agreed to referee the occasional ball game for the local kids and answer queries from them: "Ain't you the actor in that circus movie?"[29]

As the children in his New York City neighborhood indicated, Heston's appearance in a Cecil B. DeMille film meant his career and subsequent public recognition were advancing. The success of the picture itself added to the famed director's prestige and insured that Charlton Heston did not disappear. Indeed, he often acknowledged the role's importance. "When I got it," he noted later in a *Saturday Evening Post* article, "my agent said happily, 'More people will see you in this film than in your next five pictures put together.' I thought that statement rashly optimistic then; now it seems conservative." He concluded, "Certainly, 'The Greatest Show on Earth' lived up to its name at the box office."

Of course, solid box office receipts were critical to all parties, but Heston took special pleasure in a different type of feedback that had filtered to him, which had special satisfaction to his inner performer. "The nicest comment I've heard about this part came from a woman letter writer. After praising the performance of Betty Hutton, Jimmy Stewart and Cornel Wilde, she added; 'I think it's amazing the way the circus manager fitted in with these professional actors.'" He remained appreciative of such expressions, noting several years later, "I still get letters from [the] tour I did in 1951 for 'Greatest Show on Earth'—letters from Wales, Paris, Rome. It is difficult to conceive of the impact of DeMille's films on audiences. That's why any actor would play in a DeMille film for free."[30]

Heston's pride in making his role believable to moviegoers was only one of the benefits he felt that the picture provided. "An interesting thing about film acting," he explained, was that "you pick up a lot of curious physical skills." For

29 Beverly Linet, "I Was There," *Photoplay* (June 1952), 50, 77.

30 Charlton Heston, "The Role I Liked Best . . ." *SEP* (July 18, 1953), Heston Clipping File, HL; "Interview, Oct. 23, 1956," Heston Papers, HL; Crowther, *Charlton Heston*, 22. In his autobiography, Heston shifted the gender of the correspondent to "man," *CHA*, 113.

The Greatest Show on Earth, he "had to learn how to load animal cages on a flat car with a 10-ton deisal [sic] cat which is a task I don't expect to undertake again in the near future." He found such instances reinforced the sense that "an actor has to learn how to do everything just well enough to have his picture made doing it."[31]

In December, *Macbeth* beckoned Heston to the stage in Bermuda. His love of Shakespeare and his desire to improve as an actor made the chance irresistible. In trying to describe the feeling he had gotten while playing Moses, he harkened back to the play. "I don't think I can really convey to you what a genuinely moving experience it was to take part in this," he told an interviewer. "The only comparable thing I've ever done was playing Macbeth, the last time in Bermuda." He recalled fondly "buckling on the chain mail and furs of Macbeth in the dark guts of that ancient fort in Bermuda last year, and then pacing the sea wall in the wet wind, waiting to go on."[32]

Forays onto the stage provided growth and creative excitement, but roles in film paid the bills. One writer assessed Heston's progress positively at this point in his career. "His association with a lengthy list of screen successes has, undeniably, made him a 'prestige' star in both Hollywood and the world, and if his name cannot 'make' a marquee, it can certainly enhance it."[33] Indeed, as the 1950s progressed, Charlton Heston's name took position at or near the top of the films in which he appeared. For a time, this meant following an established individual whom producers thought would have box office draw or appeal, such as Eleanor Parker in *The Naked Jungle* (1954), Fred MacMurray in *The Far Horizons* (1955), Gregory Peck in *The Big Country* (1958), or Gary Cooper in *The Wreck of the Mary Deare* (1959). This was especially the case if the actor played the title role, such as Jennifer Jones in *Ruby Gentry* (1952), Susan Hayward in *The President's Lady* (1953), Jane Wyman in *Lucy Gallant* (1955), or Yul Brynner in *The Buccaneer* (1959).

Heston remembered the period with mixed emotions. "In the next three years," he wrote in his autobiography, "I made ten films, which was probably too many." The fickle nature of acting meant doing as much as possible, while such possibilities existed. His phrase for the phenomenon was apt: "Dancing as fast as I can." Another student of Charlton Heston and his work concluded that the fault for this creatively lean period lay in other areas. "In many ways this misuse of Heston's talents since his early impact in *The Greatest Show on Earth*

---

31 "Heston Taped Interview—August 16, 1955," 16, HL.

32 "Paramount Pictures Corp.—The Ten Commandments," Heston Papers, HL.

33 Druxman, *Charlton Heston*, 14.

was typical of Hollywood," writer Bruce Crowther observed, "and an actor with less determination to success might well have allowed himself to be buried by the weight of ten or more indifferent movies." Crowther believed Heston's ability to avoid the fate of obscurity came as a result of his being "as tough as his on-screen image," and argued that as a result "he managed to weather these patchy years," all the while "learning his trade and proving himself to be at all times prepared and reliable."[34]

He certainly took nothing for granted. Writer Sheilah Graham observed a habit that was both commendable and admirable for a motion picture celebrity. "When he isn't working or flying, Charlton is entertaining the myriad members of Heston fan clubs. They visit him at the studio where he wines and dines them, as if they were visiting diplomats. He employs two full-time secretaries to help answer fan mail, and has a reputation in Hollywood that not many other stars have—of never brushing off a fan or a fan letter."[35]

Even so, he felt that his first performance for DeMille remained paramount to his success. While in New Orleans promoting *The President's Lady*, Heston found a writer more interested in his reaction to the recognition *The Greatest Show on Earth* had received at the Academy Awards. The actor struck a tone of modesty and pragmatism. "In Hollywood," he noted, "serious workers do not undertake a picture with the idea of winning an award." He felt that the greatest desire was to "do a good job," with the implication that any recognition would take care of itself. As for himself, "I would be both delighted and dumbfounded to be nominated for an award," he explained, adding, "I would be even more flabbergasted if I ever won one." As in so many other instances, he observed, exposing his bias toward the theater, "I'm working to be a good actor, which isn't necessarily synonymous with being in films. I still hope to be one some day."[36]

Heston also watched as his compensation grew to include percentages of sales that would build on his base salaries. For *Scalpel*, eventually released as *Bad for Each Other*, the terms included "$30,000, payable, $3,000 per week for 10 weeks," and "7½% of gross receipts not exceeding $1,000,000.00. 8% of gross receipts in excess of $1,000,000,00."[37] These figures certainly represented a turn from the

---

34 *CHA*, 114; Crowther, *Epic Presence*, 38-39.

35 Sheilah Graham, "'One Night I was on TV, and the Next Day I Signed a Movie Contract,'" *BSG*, July 17, 1955.

36 "Star of Award Winner Is Delighted at Selection," *New Orleans Times-Picayune*, Mar. 21, 1953, Heston Clipping Files, HL.

37 "Paramount Pictures contract summaries," Heston Papers, f.1138, HL.

difficult days of pounding the pavement for work and accepting roles that brought in much less remuneration.

At the same time, Heston launched a full-fledged advertising campaign for numerous commercial products, with each of his films serving as the foundation upon which to present them. In conjunction with *Pony Express*, he served as a spokesperson for "Jeris Antiseptic Hair Tonic." The actor's image and signature appeared as a "rave" for a product that promised to lead to "greaseless good grooming and healthier, handsome hair." Displayed in popular magazines, Heston's photograph appeared with the item, serving as endorsement of both the product and his latest motion picture.[38]

Other work in promotion brought the Heston image before potential customers of products that the actor was willing to endorse. As his profile grew, he added to the wide range of activities built upon his movie roles. Camel Cigarettes employed numerous celebrities to draw attention to its brand, with Charlton Heston appearing in his movie garb as Buffalo Bill Cody from the film *Pony Express*. "Why did *you* change to Camels, Charlton Heston?" the ad queried. "I've smoked most of the leading brands and found that *Camels* suit me the best. I can count on them for *Mildness* and *Flavor* every time!" A series of inset photos depicted scenes from the motion picture and captions designed to connect the audience with the actor and pitchman, including: "Like so many stars, Charlton Heston is a Camel smoker."[39]

Whatever the makers of Camels cigarettes wanted potential consumers to believe, Heston himself did not smoke cigarettes. In a *Photoplay* essay that promised to "unmask" the star, he described the habit as "nasty," although he professed to smoking a pipe on rare occasions. Several decades later, another feature labeled him a "lifelong non-smoker" and attributed his position to the death of his father from the effects of the habit. "He doesn't smoke," a similar exploration into his life revealed the next year. "Smoking just never appealed to him." More to the point came the assertion, "In fact, he has always been repelled by it."[40]

Heston also became involved in a campaign for Van Heusen Century Shirts. One ad depicted the star smiling in a central panel with the legend: "Charlton Heston starring in Paramount Pictures' 'Legend of the Incas.'" That the authors

---

38 An example of the Heston Jervis advertisement in *Look* (Apr. 7, 1953), 6.

39 An example of the Heston Camel advertisement on the back cover of *Popular Mechanics Magazine* (Apr. 1953).

40 Steele, "Unmasking Charlton Heston," 74; Chase, "Between Scenes with Charlton Heston," 45; Stoddard and SerVaas, "Charlton Heston," 45, 101.

of the advertisement had substituted "Legend" for "Secret" in the title of the forthcoming film did not appear to phase the performer any more than wearing a shirt that "won't wrinkle ever," even if you were to "twist," "twirl," "bend," or "curl it." As the ultimate in celebrity endorsement, the text ensured readers, "'This feature rates 4 stars,' says Charlton Heston."[41] Another touted a "Moulin Rouge" version, with the caption noting the actor's appearance in *Secret of the Incas*. The Van Heusen campaign carried into the following year with Heston now listed as "starring in Paramount Pictures' 'The Naked Jungle.'" The ad also featured wife Lydia adjusting her husband's shirt collar to ensure that he would always look his best.

Quality shirts might keep the actor in good wardrobe order, but his equilibrium, as well as his apparel, underwent a physical challenge during rehearsals for a stage production of *Macbeth* in the Caribbean in August 1953. *The Royal Gazette* announced to its readership, "Heston Hurt in Accident." The accompanying article took on a dramatic element. "In the best tradition of the theater, Charlton Heston, star of 'Macbeth,' has said that 'the show will go on,' tonight at Fort St. Catherine, despite painful injuries he received on Saturday evening when he was thrown from a motor bike on his way to dinner following rehearsal."[42]

In addition to the spate of advertising ventures with which Heston affiliated himself, his profile increased in other ways. "Charlton Heston's theory seems to be join Paramount and see the world," writers Reba and Bonnie Churchill observed. "So far, each of his eight films has called for a location trip. His 1954 schedule follows the same pattern." Interestingly, the "same pattern" also meant that the Hestons remained ensconced in multiple worlds, even as to their living arrangements. "To keep up their whirligig of activities," the writers explained, "the Hestons maintain three residences—one in Beverly, a farm in Michigan and an apartment in New York." The couple adapted to the circumstances creatively. "This also calls for the most unique stationery we've ever seen. All three addresses are listed with a small square opposite each in which to check at which residence they are."[43]

For now, the Michigan woodlands remained Heston's most sacred refuge. He later insisted that he hoped his son would be able to grow up there. "Of course,

---

41 An example of the Heston Van Heusen Century Shirt advertisement found in *Life* (Sept. 7, 1953), 115.

42 "Heston Hurt in Accident," *The Royal Gazette*, Aug. 17, 1953, Family Scrapbook, HL.

43 Reba and Bonnie Churchill, "Charlton Heston Is Seeing World," *Newslife*, Oct. 26, 1953, Heston Clippings File, HL. Biographer Marc Eliot noted that for their primary residences the Hestons were now paying $135.00 a month; see Eliot, *Charlton Heston*, 72.

there are problems to living in the woods, just as there are problems anywhere," he noted. "There is the problem of aloneness, but I think this is more likely to prove an asset than a detriment. It teaches self-reliance." Whatever the lessons, these beginnings were part of who Heston was and how he presented himself publicly. "I wouldn't give up my home in Michigan for anything," he maintained.[44]

Charlton Heston was working diligently to promote his name and build his career. Film work came in multiples during the mid-fifties, although the vehicles were not always those likely to carry him to the most dizzying heights of his profession. He wanted to ensure that the films that followed *The Greatest Show on Earth*, would demonstrate his diversity as well as his marketability.

As it turned out, a very big break was about to come for him; Cecil B. DeMille was contemplating a remake of *The Ten Commandments*. The famed director knew he needed someone who could breathe life into the principal character and bring box office heft to the project. That person did not immediately appear to be Charlton Heston, but circumstances pushed Victor Mature out of the role and opened the way for someone else. Fellow actor and DeMille associate Henry Wilcoxon recalled Heston stating his case at a dinner: "I'd like a crack at Moses," but he felt that more groundwork was required before presenting the idea to DeMille. The opening came when Wilcoxon compared a photograph of Michelangelo's Moses and a publicity still of Heston. He recalled drawing a beard on the still and laying it before the director, but was set back momentarily when DeMille thought the actor in the photo was Victor Mature. Wilcoxon offered a little more prodding with another unbearded Heston image. "Why that's Chuck Heston . . . (the light dawned) that's Chuck, too?! That's remarkable!" and DeMille called immediately for a makeup test so they could "see this for real." The director recalled never having "any doubt about who should play the part of Moses, and my choice was strikingly confirmed when I had a sketch made of Charlton Heston in a white beard and happened to set it beside a photograph of Michelangelo's famous statue of Moses."[45]

Heston's look worked to his advantage in this case, but other factors were involved. DeMille knew the performer's work ethic and acting capability from *The Greatest Show on Earth*. As DeMille explained in an interview, Heston had demonstrated "the mental and spiritual qualities to play Moses—he has great

---

44 Helen Limke, "Bringing Up Baby," *Photoplay*, 113-114.

45 Katherine Orrison, *Written in Stone: Making Cecil B. DeMille's Epic, The Ten Commandments* (Lanham, MD, 1999), 15; Donald Haynie, ed., *The Autobiography of Cecil B. DeMille* (Englewood Cliffs, NJ, 1959), 415.

honesty, respect for truth, spiritual integrity, and personal courage. In fact, I like him."[46] Public perceptions of the actor's stable personal life and unsullied reputation could not hurt, given the moral authority of the character and the tone of the film the director wanted to set.

Charlton Heston understood as well as anyone what working on another DeMille production would mean. He was even more appreciative that this time it would be in a lead role rather than a supporting one, and that extraordinary talent would surround him. "If you can't make a career out of two DeMilles, *The Greatest Show on Earth* and *The Ten Commandments*, you'll never make it," he observed. The opportunity ensured the actor a chance at cinematic significance and more. As one writer remarked, "With this role he could hardly help but become an international star of the first magnitude." Of course, Heston also recognized that the risk was DeMille's as much as his. "I was the greenest of them all, but I had the best part."[47]

Even with the news on the part of Moses, Heston occasionally received reminders of the degree of work left to do to achieve greater personal recognition. When a very young Clint Eastwood strolled through the Universal Studios gym with a friend they "noticed Charlton Heston, with a towel wrapped around him, relaxing after a work-out," as Floyd Simmons related. Both spoke to the actor, but when Simmons noticed that Eastwood did not follow, he returned. "He was back there speaking to Heston," Simmons explained. "I turned around and heard him say, "Are you Chuck Connors?" "No, I'm Charlton Heston." "Oh, I thought you were Chuck Connors." Simmons did not note how the actor responded to the misidentification, or even if Eastwood had failed to recognize Heston or was "maybe trying to level him off."[48]

Regardless of his prospects, Heston committed to return to the stage whenever possible, and in January 1954 did so in the play *Mister Roberts* in winter stock at the Palm Beach Playhouse in Florida." It was during this run that he learned of being chosen for the coveted role of Moses; even so, he wanted confirmation from DeMille himself. "And I, of course, called him long-distance at once to make certain it wasn't a cruel hoax on the part of some of my more humorously inclined

---

46 "Interview with Cecil B. DeMille Via Shirley Thomas, NBC Program 14 April 1954," 2, Heston Papers, HL.

47 Rovin, *Films*, 70. Heston gave a variation of this observation in the introduction to his journals; *ALJ*, xvi; Crowther, *Epic Presence*, 42; Heston and Isbouts, *Hollywood*, 58.

48 The Heston-Connors resemblance was uncanny, and Eastwood and Connors were both in popular television Westerns as Rowdy Yates in *Rawhide* (1959-65) and Lucas McCain in *The Rifleman* (1958-63), respectively. Patrick McGilligan, *Clint: The Life and Legend* (New York, 1999), 78.

friends." When he learned the casting was in earnest, Heston recalled that he "waxed incoherent and told him how delighted and pleased I was."[49]

When not on the stage or working out to remain in shape, the actor undertook his other public duties seriously. In March 1954, he agreed to appear at a Boston theater that was showing the thriller *The Naked Jungle*, in which a massive infestation of soldier ants devours the estate of Heston's character. An announcement not only promised a "Personal Appearance by Charlton Heston," but also insured fans that he would be in the lobby for an hour "and present orchids to the first 100 women to greet him." Subsequent coverage indicated that the actor fulfilled this obligation, assuring the recipients that there "were no ants on the orchids," and offering interviews about his recent work and career to the *Boston Daily Globe* and radio station WORL.[50]

As he often indicated and the Boston appearance confirmed, Heston was not about to loll into idleness or allow his career's momentum to be lost. The *Los Angeles Times*, noted simply, "Heston Travels," before elaborating, "Charlton Heston has left on an 11-city personal appearance tour in connection with his latest starring role—Paramount's 'The Naked Jungle.'" He was slated to return "late in April to discuss with Cecil B. DeMille his forthcoming starring role in 'The Ten Commandments.'"[51]

The actor had hoped recent movies like *Bad for Each Other* and *Lucy Gallant* could do more than just give him the opportunity to sell merchandise or build a box office presence with a wider audience, particularly as he contemplated the lead in a DeMille picture with a biblical context. On his collaboration with Jane Wyman, he maintained, "It seemed a good modern romance to get under my belt before I disappeared into the Old Testament."[52]

Charlton Heston continued to lend his name and growing film persona to popular products as a celebrity endorser. One in particular reflected the increasing amount of travel his work required. "For once, give a man something he can really use—good luggage," he explained while touting Amelia Earhart Luggage. Tapping into his appearance in the soap-opera style *Lucy Gallant* in this instance, audiences

49 "Heston to Be Star in 'Mr. Roberts' Play, *LAT*, Nov. 22, 1953; "Charlton Heston Interview," Cecil B. DeMille Collection, *The Ten Commandments*—Interviews, f.9, HL.

50 "Personal Appearance by Charlton Heston," *BDG*, Mar. 23, 1954; Marjory Adams, "Charlton Heston Visits Boston, Gives Lucky Girls Orchids," *BDG*, Mar. 26, 1954. The radio station later became WROL.

51 "Heston Travels," *LAT*, Apr. 6, 1954.

52 *CHA*, 128-129.

also knew the actor's penchant for flying to film locations and on promotional tours.[53] Sturdy luggage would come in handy on such junkets.

Heston also spent time culling through offers and screenplays, but not all of these panned out as he wished. Seeking to maintain a vigorous work schedule even as he prepared for one of his most significant roles with C. B. DeMille, he dedicated a portion of 1954 to negotiating potential projects with James Woolf and Romulus Productions. At least one of these efforts focused on the British explorer James Cook, but hesitation existed over the cultural appropriation. Columnist Edwin Schallert observed "the only doubt concerned the Heston impersonation of an Englishman, especially one so famous, in a British picture." Even so, the writer remained optimistic: "even that may well be overcome."[54] The degree to which this issue served as the reason that the American actor never took up the role would have been especially galling to him as a student of history, an Anglophile, and an actor. Certainly, any cultural differences did not prevent him from subsequently portraying a popular British figure when he played Charles "Chinese" Gordon in *Khartoum*.

November 1954 presented the actor with two satisfying experiences. The first came with rehearsals for *Mister Roberts*. "God, what a pleasure to be rehearsing a play again in New York City," he noted on the 19th. "I think back to the first New York rehearsal for 'Antony and Cleopatra' in the fall of '47, when I was so impressed with Kent Smith's French cuffs, and the whole idea of being a working actor . . . and today I felt the same." The second occurred ten days later in what the actor termed "the most elaborately produced TV interview I've ever been a part of," in connection with Arlene Francis's *The Home Show*.[55]

Heston remained inordinately busy in 1955, engaging in activities that ranged from feature films to television appearances. He undertook public roles with fresh verve, especially when he considered the mission important. One such effort represented what a scholar described as "his first political statement" when he championed suitable recognition in Los Angeles for inventor Thomas Edison that February.[56] Offering a cash contribution to "start the ball rolling," Heston

---

53 Advertisement, Wills.

54 Edwin Schallert, "Charlton Heston Eager for Capt. Cook Break; Cooper Forms Company," *LAT*, Sept. 22, 1954. From earlier, see also, Edwin Schallert, "Heston-Romulus Deal in Negotiation; Noah Beery Stirs Up Indians," *LAT*, Mar. 6, 1954.

55 *ALJ*, 141.

56 Raymond, *Cold, Dead Hands*, 63.

hoped to find some means of recognizing this seminal figure in his business. "It is appalling," he maintained in his correspondence with the mayor of the city, "that nowhere in all Los Angeles—the world capital of the motion picture industry—is there a single lasting memorial to the man who invented the motion picture camera and projector." Emilie Raymond wondered at his "zeal over a rather trivial issue," but thought the situation allowed him to express "his willingness to use his name to influence government and his penchant for dramatic rhetoric." Heston certainly hoped to employ his skills at persuasion in promoting a cause. In so doing, however, he demonstrated less a desire to engage in activism than an appreciation for the unique and creative figures he deemed to be of importance to the development of motion pictures. A few days later, the *Los Angeles Times* reiterated the main point for its readers.[57]

At the same time, Heston continued to seek out the means of feeding both his creative needs and his financial security, although these could lead him in different directions. "I get $85 a week for the play," he told one interviewer. "My agent was furious and said—why the head usher gets more than that." He was aware of the circumstances, but insisted, "I'm afraid if I acquire so much in material possessions I can't afford to work for $85 a week in a play when I want to." He recognized that his position was not common among performers. "It isn't that I scorn material possessions. But I want to work and travel. There are lots of places I want to work that can't pay much money." He also valued his independence. "Not only do I want to be able to take jobs at $85 a week, but I want to be able to turn down the $10,000 offers if they're not right for me." As stubbornly determined to control his career as he was proud of being free to follow his muse, Heston concluded, "So far I've never taken a job because I needed the money."[58]

As Heston wrapped up his work on *Lucy Gallant*, he prepared for DeMille's biblical epic. He planned to spend considerable time in Egypt getting ready for his performance well before the first camera rolled, as he liked to say. He expected the shoot to be demanding, but approached it as he did every role, by trying to inhabit the character. When asked about his technique, Heston explained, "The first thing that occurs to any actor preparing for a role, of course, especially the role of a real man, is to do as much reading as you can." In this case, as biographer Bruce Crowther explained, "He threw himself into the part with a degree of enthusiasm.

57 "Edison Memorial Proposed by Actor," *LAT*, Feb. 10, 1955; Raymond, *Cold, Dead Hands*, 63; "A Memorial to Edison," *LAT*, Feb. 14, 1955.

58 "Interview, Oct. 23, 1956," HL.

. . . Already noted for the care with which he prepared for his roles, especially any which called upon a measure of historical verisimilitude, Heston studied the Old Testament and the work of biblical scholars."[59]

The collaboration guaranteed that DeMille would do everything he could to allow his leading man to find his Moses. "My personal preproduction was extensive," Heston recalled. "I had to undergo fittings for some fifteen or twenty costumes, from the intricate platelet armor I wore in my first scene as an Egyptian prince through the burlap rag of the brick pits and the Levite mantle of the Exodus." He also had to develop skillsets that might seem ordinary outside of the character, but were essential to it. Heston recalled that he had to learn how to "walk with a staff which is a somewhat more complicated skill than you might imagine." He added, a bit mischievously, "I might say that I learned how to part the Red Sea but I had considerable assistance from Paramount for that."[60]

Certainly, *The Ten Commandments* offered Heston a platform for stretching his talents and carving a public persona from which he never departed. Most gratifying for the legendary figure who directed him was the degree to which the actor grew in the role for which his physical attributes appeared initially so well suited. "Charlton Heston brought to the role a rapidly maturing skill as an actor and an earnest understanding of the human and spiritual quality of Moses," DeMille explained.[61]

In addition to the assistance DeMille offered, Heston appreciated other factors that existed between the legendary figure and himself. "I think DeMille understood the dimensions of the task," he recalled, "he surely did his best to help me, not so much with specific direction of the performance of each scene but by creating a kind of climate where I could find the man." For the actor, this indirect intervention meant a great deal. "He kept me insulated from the casual, jokey camaraderie of a movie company. Once I was in the makeup and wearing the Levite robe, I kept pretty much apart. Between setups, I stayed in a little trailer on the set."[62]

Though Heston's preference for immersing himself in a role made sense to him, it rendered him less approachable than those who chose to interact with their

59 "Heston Taped Interview – August 16, 1955," 2, HL; Crowther, *Epic Presence*, 42.

60 Heston and Isbouts, *Hollywood*, 58; "Heston Taped Interview – August 16, 1955," 16, HL.

61 Haynie, ed., *The Autobiography of Cecil B. DeMille*, 415.

62 *CHA*, 139.

colleagues. One writer observed, "On a set he is austere, separate. Between takes he retreats to a corner of a field or soundstage, head in hand, alone. Rather than banter with technicians, he seeks refuge in his dressing room." Such seeming aloofness did not ingratiate the principal actor with the rest of the cast, and his propensity for remaining focused on the character's motivations did not help, either. "Heston wanted to talk about Moses' id," one member of the crew complained, "but we were only trying to find out how the hell to get cold beer in Egypt." When deep in the role, even his wife had difficulty jarring him back to modern reality. After a visit to the set for lunch with her husband, Lydia's departing kiss elicited no response. "I'm your wife. Remember?" she chided, and Chuck became himself again with a laugh and a hug before returning to the world Moses inhabited.[63]

Heston recognized that in order to embody a figure of this import, he could not approach the role as just another performance; he had to take on the persona of a man inspired by God to lead his people out of their bondage in Egypt. As one account of the buildup to the filming of the exodus recorded, "for weeks—until the scene was finally shot—Heston never allowed himself to sit, take phone calls, drink coffee from paper cups or behave like a relaxed human being between takes." The effort to remain in character benefitted him on multiple levels as a performer and enhanced the ways in which others embraced his portrayal.[64]

Heston himself was definitely aware of this situation. As he explained, "Mr. DeMille, and I must say that I am in complete agreement with him, both here in Hollywood and in Egypt took great pains to see that I either appeared in public as myself, as Chuck Heston in civilian clothes or in the character of Moses, never half in and out." On the set, the separation served as "the reason I ate in the dressing room." Out on the shoot, "I wouldn't sit down in a modern camp chair [and only] ate and drank in front of the company if it was part of the scene." For the actor, this situation did not prove to be an imposition. "It wasn't an unusual chore."[65]

In the exodus scene, Heston remembered that DeMille supplied the appropriate gravitas by noting, "When you lift your staff to signal the start of the Exodus, twenty thousand hearts will be beating in front of you." The performer's pause as the director called for the action to begin reflected Heston's anxiety in undertaking "the biggest shot *I'd* ever tried," but he "turned and led them, and never saw them

63 Plutzik, "Last of the Epic Heroes," 34; Rovin, *Films*, 70.

64 "Moses from Michigan," 8.

65 "Heston Taped Interview – August 16, 1955," 6, 15, HL.

follow, so I don't know what they looked like. But I know what it felt like. It felt magnificent."[66]

As a performer, he also understood the practical elements of his work. Walking barefoot on the rocky terrain of Mount Sinai, he observed, "I think you can persuade an actor to do almost anything if you convince him that he will look effective and photograph well while doing it." Yet Heston had thought that having taken off his shoes before God, Moses would not be focused on retrieving them as he departed. Then, when he initially broached the possibility of supplying the voice of God in his interactions with Moses, DeMille replied pleasantly, "We'll have to think about that. You already have a pretty good part, you know."[67]

DeMille's gentle jest reflected Heston's demanding role as Moses through the range of years that took him from triumphant son of Sethi to the old man who survived the time in the wilderness to bring the Lord's Commandments to his people, but would never set foot in the Promised Land. Ultimately, to settle the matter of God's voice in interactions with Moses, DeMille observed that he drew upon the Biblical text in which the voice from the Burning Bush would be that of "Moses' father, Amram, so as not to frighten him. That lovely courtesy of God suggested that our audience too might accept a not unfamiliar voice, a little slowed and deepened: so the Voice of God at the Burning Bush is Charlton Heston's voice."[68]

Despite reaching this important decision, Heston's experience with the Mt. Sinai scenes also illustrated the complexities of the shoot. He received the dubious nickname "Tanglefoot" when he slipped and dropped one of the sacred tablets and endured good-natured ribbing for the incident. The actor also had to return in May 1956 to take "another crack at the voice of God this morning." He declared the effort "Better, I think. I'm glad de Mille decided to use my voice for this." The subsequent film confrontation between an incensed Moses and his wanton followers before the Golden Calf also supplied humorous, if occasionally ribald stories that Heston liked to relate and insisted "really did happen" on the set.[69]

Innovations in motion picture technology also enhanced Heston's natural features on film. As writer Steven Cohan insisted, "size counts even more" in

---

66 "Paramount Pictures Corp.—The Ten Commandments," 1-2, Heston Papers, f.159, HL.

67 Ibid., 16; *CHA*, 132.

68 Haynie, ed., *The Autobiography of Cecil B. DeMille*, 431. DeMille did not use Heston's voice again with the creation of the Ten Commandments, so as to give that incarnation a "unique, powerful, fatherly" quality with "a touch of austerity and even anger." He chose not to identify the source; ibid., 431-432.

69 Eliot, *Charlton Heston*, 110; *ALJ*, 3; *CHA*, 140.

describing his screen relationship with co-star Yul Brynner. He noted that the VistaVision technique allowed the actor to occupy the screen with "a vertical perspective of the human body" that produced a powerful visual effect. In numerous scenes, Heston's Moses stood out and above all others. "The composition calls attention not just to the straight line of the actor's massive body," Cohan explained, "but to his spatial command over other, more visibly diminutive bodies as well because of his size."[70]

But elements outside of the actor's attributes and the quality of filmmaking threatened the production of the massive endeavor. DeMille's health became a crucial factor when a heart attack sidelined him and halted filming. There was always the chance that the legendary director would not pull through and that, even with extensive celluloid already exposed on the project, the studio might back away from it. Herman Citron, Heston's "Iceman," was pragmatic. His client needed to work regardless of DeMille's fate. A visit with the ailing director suggested that Citron was right, for the time being at least, and that another project could fit in until the circumstances plaguing *The Ten Commandments* sorted themselves out.[71]

Heston continued to be a proud spokesperson for the film. "Heston says he can't help sounding like a press agent as he writes of the 500 chariots (Pharaoh Yul Brynner in pursuit of the Israelites), the massiveness of the largest set ever filmed (gates of Tanis and sphinxes) and 'the color of 7000 extras on the sands of Sinai,'" writer Philip Scheuer related. Impressed by the sheer scope of his surroundings, Heston professed that he found the work simultaneously grueling and exhilarating. DeMille had been determined to have the performers walk where Moses and his followers had trod. Heston thought the terrain "the toughest to get to, the toughest to work in and the longest hours when we got there. It was terrible—and magnificent."[72]

Even with the success the DeMille epic appeared likely to provide him, Heston still held strong views regarding the roles he intended to pursue going forward. "I'll never make another Biblical picture as long as I live," he insisted to a writer who sought to learn "Charlton Heston's Success Secret." "After I finish this picture, that is," he clarified. "As Moses, I have reached the top in Biblical moviemaking. How can I go higher—even in the Bible?" Hyperbole aside from "one of the more likeable actors in Hollywood and the lad with the most loyal fans and fan clubs,"

---

70 Steven Cohan, *Masked Men: Masculinity and the Movies in the Fifties* (Bloomington, IN, 1997), 157.

71 Eliot, *Charlton Heston*, 102.

72 Philip K. Scheuer, "Brando's Neither 'Slob' Nor Best Actor, Critic Argues," *LAT*, Dec. 5, 1954.

Heston was determined to be realistic about his options. Still, he felt that timing was working against him. "There's only one thing bad about this film. It should come at the end of an actor's career. Everything that follows is an anti-climax."

Consistently anxious to avoid being typecast, Charlton Heston sought to move into areas that would challenge his carefully crafted screen persona. With his portrayal of Moses, he was convinced that at least one genre was closed to him. "I think for example that it would be difficult for me to do a comedy," he observed with conviction. "I believe that." He was determined to make the effort, however. "I've got my agent looking for comedy scripts on a top priority basis," he maintained a few years later. "I must have it for a change of pace." With serious roles behind him and an offer to portray Charlemagne on the big screen, Heston realized the window to avoid locking himself into specific roles was narrowing. "I will probably do it," he noted of the medieval warrior king, "but I must have something light in between."[73]

A comedy seemed to offer the best opportunity for exhibiting a different type of performance, and with that thinking in place, he accepted the role as a crusty army officer given responsibility for resurrecting a moribund parochial military school. *The Private War of Major Benson* permitted Heston to indulge in lighter-hearted fare. Even so, he realized he would serve as the straight man foil for the precocious children and the other actors with whom he would share the screen. "But the comedy depends on my being serious. Major Benson is serious as hell," he admitted in a later interview.[74]

Heston thought the script showed promise, as did the chance to move away from the work he had put in as Moses. He was adamant about doing the film. "Look, I *have* to do that picture," he told his agent Citron. "Just get me the damn picture." He recalled observing, "I wanted to make it so much I said to M.C.A., 'Pitch Universal an offer they can't turn down.' So M.C.A. told Universal, 'You can have Chuck Heston free. All we ask is a percentage of the possible net, not the gross.'" The deal might easily have turned sour for the actor. "For a while," he explained, "I was even in the hole for the restaurant lunch charges run up while we were shooting. But it worked out." The percentage rose with the film's popularity and put Heston on a par with other stars, turning the comedy into "one of the most successful films I've ever made."[75]

---

73 "Heston Taped Interview – August 16, 1955," 24, HL; James Bacon, "Heroic Heston Wants to Do Comic Next," *BDG*, Apr. 19, 1960.

74 Kaminsky Interview, Part II, Heston Papers, 100, HL.

75 *CHA*, 136; Martin, "I Call on Ben-Hur," 43.

Some of the accounting edginess and the concern about Lydia's pregnancy may have crept into the film. He participated in classes for expectant parents sponsored by the Beverly Hills Red Cross, demonstrating such capability in feeding and diapering a doll that his classmates dubbed him "the most dexterous baby handler in the group." Still, on the set, a young Sal Mineo, one of the students Maj. Barney Benson was supposed to whip into shape, reportedly considered Heston "brittle and self-possessed." According to a Mineo biographer, during the filming, the older performer "did not interact with the children off camera."[76]

Mineo's assessment reflected some of the less laudatory ways other performers saw him. Heston's focus on his characters meant he often related more to those figures than to his co-stars. This distance allowed the actor to become Moses, as he and DeMille needed that screen portrayal to be, but others saw unintended stiffness and aloofness. Ironically, on the *Major Benson* shoot his focus on work nearly cost him the most important appearance he wanted to make. As Heston remembered it, "By February, I was finishing up *Major Benson* on location at a military school some forty miles from Los Angeles. At the end of a long day, I drove wearily back to Universal to look at the dailies before going home." He approached the gate of the facility only to find a message that Lydia had gone to the hospital. The message had remained undelivered on the premise that he was not to be disturbed while on set. Heston hastened to his wife's side. "I got there before Fraser did, but not by a hell of a lot," he observed. February 12, 1955, found them the proud parents of a child cast almost immediately, via telegram, by Cecil B. DeMille as the baby Moses when shooting on *The Ten Commandments* resumed.[77]

Like all new fathers, Heston learned that his life had changed from that moment. A sense that he and Lydia could survive whatever occurred now involved someone else. He denied the rumor that in a frenzied state of mind he had returned to the *Major Benson* set with his shoes on the wrong feet. This would have been an unlikely feat, since he had left the set before he learned of his wife's labor and his son's impending birth. The story nevertheless served to humanize the actor in a colorful spread in *Photoplay* in October 1955.[78]

With DeMille's recovery, Heston returned to *The Ten Commandments* and brought Fraser along to play the infant Moses being released amidst the bulrushes

---

76 Scott, "Charlton Heston's Life Story," *GH*, 248; Michael Gregg Michaud, *Sal Mineo: A Biography* (New York, 2010), 37.

77 The telegram read: "CONGRATULATIONS. HE'S CAST IN THE PART. CECIL B. DEMILLE," *CHA*, 138.

78 Limke, "Bringing Up Baby," 52.

to prevent Pharaoh's men from finding and killing him. Heston was the doting father during these scenes, carefully watching the proceedings and insisting that he would be the only person to handle the child between takes. At least two complications arose. One was a nurse who tried to prevent the anxious father from retrieving his son. He dispensed that matter with a cold stare. The other was a wetness that Heston assumed was the natural course of things for a baby until the issue persisted and a careful inspection revealed a leak in the basket. Heston's co-star Henry Wilcoxon responded wryly, "That's the first time I ever heard of a bed wetting the baby." Lydia remained stoic throughout, having expected their son to express himself more often than he did. "Fray's a born trouper," she concluded.[79]

Heston did not expect this cameo to open an acting career for his son. Despite his own rise to stardom, the actor remained adamant about not encouraging younger people to go into the profession that was finally taking him to the top. "The odds against any actor being able to make a living are so long," he insisted as far back as 1955. When asked if he thought baby Fraser should pursue an acting career when he grew up, he replied, "I would wish him well in some other profession." Heston did not plan to prevent the decision if Fray made it, but he was wary. "I would feel differently if there were a chance of every good actor succeeding eventually, but this is not the case—too often it's a matter of chance." Chance had been kind to him, but the writer speculated, "Chuck must have been thinking over those long years of struggling to get his break, the months of pounding the pavements after he'd returned from the war." Success had certainly remained elusive until he finally found the work he had been seeking. "Things began to go easily then, but Chuck Heston has never been able to forget those long years."[80]

He was understandably proud of the part he played in the DeMille spectacular. "As a man, Moses is a towering figure, surely one of the best roles in the history of film," he assessed later. He also argued that he would love to do the part again, "when I'd need less makeup and could provide a more deeply honed native gift."[81]

Friend and fellow actor Milburn Stone thought Heston's portrayal of Moses had an enduring effect on all who saw it. "It's never left him," Stone explained. "The aura's still there, all around him."[82] Heston's ability to carry his character from the esteemed ranks of Egyptian royalty through the desert as an exile and a return

79 Ibid., 114.

80 Ibid.

81 *CHA*, 145.

82 Druxman, *Charlton Heston*, 59.

to free his people from bondage imbued this Moses with an impressive range and quality.

Circumstances were indeed fortuitous for Heston at this time. He had finished *The Private War of Major Benson*, which had proven to be a successful foray into comedy, and completed his famous role in *The Ten Commandments*. Each of the performances had an impact, the iconic one of Moses indelibly so. Yet as he had expressed before, Heston was determined not to let even the best role limit or restrict him in any way. When asked how he thought people would accept him in other roles after Moses, he observed, "That of course, is impossible to predict. I don't think anyone could quarrel with the fact that in Moses I have already played the most important role I or, I really believe, any actor will ever play. But this is not to say that I do not hope that audiences will accept me in other roles. . . . I think though it will still be possible to play a variety of roles. I intend to do my best to."

Heston thought he would remain viable even for roles diametrically opposite from that sainted figure. "But if what you're getting at is do you think that the fact that I have played Moses should prevent me from accepting the role of Judas Iscariot or Iago I strongly disagree. I don't for a moment hold with this. I think that an actor should play the role that attracts him." Even so, he was realistic. "Now as I said I do think there are roles that audiences will be dis-inclined to accept me in. If I therefore refused such a role it would mean merely because of the economic facts of life and not that I felt that I was in some way debasing the role of Moses which I had played some years before." In any case, worrying about this aspect would be problematic on many levels. "It's difficult to assess the effect a role that will be seen by so many millions more people than have ever seen any actor play any other role on that actor's future career."

Even with an intervening comedy to his credit, Heston felt that his best course as a performer was to move away from the type of figure he had just portrayed when *The Ten Commandments* wrapped. "I want to play immediately parts as different as I can from Moses but this has always been something I've tried to do," he argued. "I always try to avoid repeating a kind of role." He understood the significance of his identification with the character. "There are qualities in the personality of Moses which therefore to whatever degree we later discover, audiences may identify me with those qualities. They are also qualities that are . . . found in many, in the major characters, in many plays and films and thus you wouldn't be going counter to what an audience would expect of you."[83]

---

83 "Heston Taped Interview – August 16, 1955," 23-24, HL.

As he surveyed his career, this awareness forced the admission that "what I'm beginning to come to realize is that audiences, which includes critics, come to see a film with a certain idea which is formed by the shadow of the man that makes the film and has not a lot to do with what's really there." With a measure of resignation for the professional who fought so diligently for as much control over his craft as he could exert, Heston observed, "It's what they've decided is going to be there." Indeed, the shadow of Moses could have proven intimidating, but it did not eclipse the stature Charlton Heston was achieving in his profession. A visit to the Paramount Studios by Shah Reza Pahlavi of Iran underscored the ways in which the performer was beginning to serve other public functions as his own profile grew.[84]

Although a strong physical presence characterized many of Heston's roles, scholar Emilie Raymond concluded that DeMille's classic had supplied the foundation for the actor's future film work. "*The Ten Commandments* allowed Heston to establish a public persona that emphasized an independence strongly influenced by morality and masculinity," she maintained. Raymond also recognized that this element "became another permanent feature of Heston's newly prominent public persona."[85]

Heston reflected the same attitude in a contemporary interview. "This is a point of view I've arrived at gradually in the few years I've been in pictures. I now believe that most actors are much too careless about the physical shape they are in. When you consider that an actor's body is one of the main tools of his craft why it certainly behooves him to get in the best shape he possibly can." One of Heston's trainers, James Davies, observed that he "slaved ferociously" and explained that to stay in proper trim, "he labored seven days a week with the exception of three Sundays." The results also provided a window into the complexities that came with this strict regimen. "He grew grumpy toward the end of his ordeal, of course, as all athletes do when approaching peak condition," Davies noted before adding admiringly, "but when he got through he was an awful lot of man."[86]

The payoff came when viewers and critics saw Heston's physicality as essential to his roles. "Charlton Heston is an axiom," one writer noted. "The pent-up violence expressed by the somber phosphorescence of his eyes, his eagle's profile,

---

84 Kaminsky, 101; "Shah of Iran and Queen Feted by Film Industry," *LAT*, Dec. 30, 1954.

85 Raymond, *Cold, Dead Hands*, 23.

86 "Heston Taped Interview—August 16, 1955," 18, and "The Ten Commandments Publicity," f.159, Heston Papers, HL; Hyatt Downing, "Hollywood's Moses," 8, HL.

the imperious arch of his eyebrows, the hard, bitter curve of his lips, the stupendous strength of his torso—this is what he has given and not even the worst of directors can debase," French critic Michel Mourlet observed. Young Heston definitely exuded a unique charm through his portrayals and in person. An office worker watching him stride past for a film session commented not so quietly, "Lord, he's pretty."[87]

Aside from his work in front of the cameras, Heston understood well the need to continue his obligation to the films he completed. With *The Ten Commandments*, however, the director had unique feelings about what course would best serve the purpose of promotion. "A two-month p.a. tour by Charlton Heston, covering 14 key cities for 'The Ten Commandments' will be devoted mainly to speeches before civic, educational and religious organizations, the actor said yesterday," according to one article. "On instructions from Cecil B. DeMille, Heston will make no stage appearances at theatres where the Paramount release will play. Press interviews and TV guestings will be set."[88] For a motion picture with a runtime of over 200 minutes it was clear that DeMille did not want to overtax an audience's patience or take away from the primacy of the showing itself by inserting unnecessary commentary.

On the other hand, the famed director did not wish to overlook any promotional method that might contribute to the film's success. Among the more creative of these was the manufacturing of "faux tablets" that were widely distributed. One account noted the presence of over "2,000 monuments" to draw attention to the film. Both Heston and Yul Brynner were among the stars and dignitaries who made appearances, with the film's Moses in attendance as one of the speakers at an unveiling of the replica tablets in Dunseith, North Dakota.[89]

Of course, as Heston and his family knew well, work did not occur in a vacuum. Whatever his status, Heston could not avoid the personal developments that complicated anyone's life. In 1955, his stepfather, Chet Heston, died suddenly, leaving Lilla once more without a spouse, although her eldest child would continue to provide support for her. "I was proud to pay off the last of the mortgage and

87 Quoted in Garry Wills, *John Wayne's America* (New York, 1998), 22; Don Young, "Commanding Star Visitor Charlton Heston Makes Handsome Impression," Scrapbooks, HL.

88 "Theatre P.A.'s Excluded from Heston 14-City Tour," Scrapbooks, HL.

89 Tomas Alex Tizon, "Suit Pans Director's Publicity Stunt," *LAT*, July 27, 2003; See also, "F.O.E. Ten Commandment Monuments in North Dakota (6)," www.eaglesmonuments.com/states/North_Dakota.html, accessed Mar. 25, 2019.

give my mother the deed to the house he'd worked so hard to provide," Heston remembered later.[90] This personal gesture, as well as many of his public ones, demonstrated the kind of character DeMille had recognized in the man who became his Moses. Now, Charlton Heston would have to determine how his race, professionally and personally, would continue.

90 *CHA*, 33.

Chapter Four

RUNNING STRONG
1950s

"As usual, out of work, I begin to itch. More than a week without something definite
ahead and I'll start to sweat."
—Heston after *The Ten Commandments*

"I don't see how I could be surer, seeing a film I'd made, that it's good work."
—Heston on screening *Ben-Hur*

"This year may have done it."
—Heston, December 31, 1959

Performances:
Forbidden Area, Playhouse 90, Oct. 4, 1956
The Ten Commandments, Oct. 5, 1956
What's My Line? Oct. 28, 1956
Three Violent People, Dec. 1956
The Steve Allen Show, Dec. 2, 1956; Mar. 15, 1959
Mister Roberts, Newport, 1956
Mister Roberts, New York, 1956
Detective Story, various, 1956
Switch Station, Schlitz Playhouse, May 17, 1957
The Trial of Capt. Wirz, Climax!, June 27, 1957
The Ed Sullivan Show, Nov. 17, 1957; Jan. 25, 1959; July 26, 1959; Dec. 27, 1959
This is Your Life, Dec. 11, 1957
Beauty and the Beast, Shirley Temple's Storybook, Jan. 12, 1958
The Eddie Fisher Show, Jan. 21, 1958
Point of No Return, Playhouse 90, Feb. 20, 1958
Touch of Evil, Feb. 1958
The Big Country, Aug. 13, 1958 (Atlantic City)
The Buccaneer, Dec. 1, 1958

Perry Como's Kraft Music Hall, Feb. 7, 1959
The 31st Annual Academy Awards, Apr. 6, 1959
The Wreck of the Mary Deare, Nov. 6, 1959
Ben-Hur, Nov. 18, 1959 (New York)
Macbeth, Ann Arbor, 1959

In the wake of *The Ten Commandments*, the years seemed to be kinder to Charlton and Lydia Heston. They retained an address in New York City and an apartment at Park La Brea Towers in Los Angeles and settled, for the moment, into raising their son. The routine was enormously satisfying after the grueling schedule of film work and associated travel, but Heston quickly became restless, as he always did when another project was not immediately pending. He described this phenomenon as driven by "my Scots blood and Depression boyhood," which left him "uneasy when unemployed."[1]

The actor reflected this attitude in a May 21, 1956, journal entry. "As usual, out of work, I begin to itch," he noted. "More than a week without something definite ahead and I'll start to sweat." He had seen lean patches occur before where shoe leather on street pavement seemed to happen more regularly than time on the stage or screen. He tried to direct his MCA agent, Edie Van Cleve, toward a production of *Detective Story* with Lydia in New York, still feeling the urge to take on the role he had lost to Kirk Douglas, one he "always wanted to [do]." But work of any kind was now high on the agenda. "I'm not constituted for a life of leisure, I guess," he concluded; "I'd rather drop dead in a dressing room."[2]

Happily, work came to fill the professional void with a Western ultimately released as *Three Violent People*. Set in the immediate aftermath of the Civil War, it featured Heston as a former Confederate officer named Colt Saunders returning to a feuding family and entering an unhappy marriage. On March 26, he declared, "Well, I'm making a living again." The requirement to lie unconscious in an early scene in the film was hardly challenging, but he was pleased to announce, "It's good to be back at it."[3]

---

1 Eliot, *Charlton Heston*, 115; *CHA*, 147.

2 *ALJ*, 4.

3 Ibid., 3.

Heston was already striving to generate measures that would both ensure his future financial stability and provide wider artistic opportunities. He met with legal advisers to launch a venture that would allow him to turn to film production if he wished. "The stage is now set for Russell Lake Corporation to dip any kind of finger in the production pie it chooses," he noted in the summer of 1956. Named for the area that retained an almost mystic quality for him, he came to realize that even promising prospects were not always the best ones. "This was the production company I set up before I learned that actors, if they can get it, are better off with a percentage of the gross than with any part, including all, of an independent production company."[4]

Meanwhile, in order to accentuate his appearances on the big screen and establish his "face" and name to the public he was courting, Heston continued to take part in as many projects as possible. On October 28, 1956, he strode onto the set of *What's My Line?* as the mystery celebrity guest. In the segment, the panelists donned blindfolds and had the opportunity to ask questions in round-robin fashion that would enable one or more of them to identify the individual seated before them alongside moderator John Daly. Heston had greater difficulty than other participants in disguising his voice, already identifiable through his earlier work and especially because of his portrayal of Moses. Columnist Bennett Cerf inquired if he was "a member of the show business fraternity," and the actor noted revealingly, "Well, there are several schools of thought on that. I'd like to believe so." Actor Arlene Francis was enamored with the voice she was hearing. "Oh, he's a deep one," she observed, before querying, "Are you in pictures?" Heston felt less constrained, replying, "Frequently." Cerf asked if he might be "in one of those endurance pictures" that was making the rounds and Francis narrowed the choices to *The Ten Commandments*. "Oh, you're heaven in it," writer Dorothy Kilgallen gushed. It had taken the group relatively few questions to make the proper identification. "I thought I was being very clever you know," the actor quipped, but his trademark delivery had been his undoing. "There aren't many voices like that," Kilgallen offered. Of course, Heston hoped that the viewers and the studio audience would know readily what the panelists had not initially: exactly who he was.[5]

Charlton Heston also enjoyed public support from an individual who established a dedicated fan club for him. He used the opportunity to connect with

---

4 Ibid., 6.

5 Charlton Heston, "What's My Line?" Oct. 28, 1956, www.youtube.com/watch?v=ZavJcwBIlrU, accessed Oct. 23, 2018. Other celebrity "challengers" from *The Ten Commandments* who appeared on the show included Yul Brynner, Edward G. Robinson, and Vincent Price.

fans in something of a systematic fashion, but the arrangement ended abruptly with the founder's death. In a newsletter in 1956, Heston noted the transition and the way he preferred to proceed. "In the months since it occurred, I imagine you've been having as much trouble as I have adjusting to Iona's shockingly sudden death," he explained. "I have never, I think, known a woman so dedicated as she was to a single purpose that the club should be the best of its kind." Heston took pride in this aspiration, but felt that with her passing he had reached, "the reluctant conclusion that the CHARLTON HESTON FAN CLUB should end with Iona." Despite a busy schedule "travelling around the country a great deal this fall, on behalf of THE TEN COMMANDMENTS," he hoped to "get much of your reaction in person, but I wish you'd write me about it, too." Heston intended to fill the void with a periodic newsletter that he typed himself, and he would employ a staff member from Paramount Studios to assist in mailing it out. With his usual sense of determination, he added, "because if we're going to do this, I'd like to start." He closed with his appreciation "for all you've done in the past for the club, and for me," beginning another odyssey that would last for another decade. In addition to its practical purposes, the newsletter served to humanize him and connect him to his fan base through updates and photographic inserts from numerous film and family settings. Heston was usually diligent in working on these forms of communication. While traveling to Chicago by train in the summer of 1956, he "managed to get the fan club journal letter finished in the club car this morning and got off the train with the gratifying sense of a man who hasn't loafed his time away."[6]

Heston was also developing a greater understanding of the importance and scale of promotion for the most monumental projects. He recalled, "The advance drumbeat of publicity on *Commandments* was building week by week." By the time he appeared at the premieres for the film, there was no doubt that DeMille's epic production was resonating with moviegoers. Describing the New York event as "the blazing success everyone expected," Heston noted the ticket sales and box office longevity with understandable pride. "Every actor should have a really blow-away hit every so often," he recalled; "it's very warming to the ego."[7]

He could not dispute that *The Ten Commandments* had been important to his career, but he was more circumspect concerning just how far he believed the film and his role had elevated it. This sentiment was as much a holdover from the

6 Newsletter, "1956," Heston Papers, HL; *ALJ*, 6.

7 *CHA*, 150.

period in which he was waiting for the film's release and doing the publicity work that it required. "So far the only concrete advantage the film has gotten me was a pass into the Criterion tonight to see *Moby Dick*," he noted with exasperation in early September. Heston referred to such parts as "man-killers," but recognized that despite the demands they made on performers, the rewards could be enduring. "In the long perspective," he observed, "the only thing that counts is how you did on the big parts. Not the ones for this year, or last year, but the ones they play every century."[8]

Indeed, Moses was such a part and it promised to help build upon and sustain a career in show business. In January 1957, the *Rocky Mountain News* asserted for its readers, "Charlton Heston Can Expect to be a Big Hit for 50 Years."[9] The additional time for reflection since the motion picture's release allowed another writer to note that not only had the film become "the largest-grossing movie of all time, but that it "was also the making of Charlton Heston." In any case, as his profile rose, the actor boasted receiving "seven thousand fan letters monthly."[10]

Heston certainly wanted to present the impression of a man on the move. The March 1957 edition of the actor's typewritten record opened with the "[s]ound of heavy breathing as Charlton Heston enters late and running." The situation allowed the performer to connect with fans as an ordinary person. "The only virtue I can distill out of starting this letter as late as I am is that it makes a wonderful demonstration of how fully actors share the human failings of everybody else; and procrastination is certainly the worst of mine." Lest anyone think that this malady affected the most important areas of his life, he hastened to add, "about the only events for which I am unfailingly prompt are getting to work, and taking my son pony riding." The first reference underscored Heston's dedication to professionalism in his work and the second his devotion to his family. On the latter, he observed with a touch of Heston humor, "Lydia tells me that anyone who's ever tried to change diapers on a two-year old boy wearing spurs will understand the complications this can cause." He remained focused on promoting his work and recognized, as he wanted fans to know, that he valued the place to which it had brought him. "The

8 Heston liked Gregory Peck very much in the role of Ahab; *ALJ*, 9-10. He particularly associated the term with *Macbeth*, colorfully describing his latest effort at the part in 1973: "I've climbed the bloody mountain, I've seen the goddam elephant. Every one of these mother-loving parts is a man-killer, and I've only barely escaped alive from this one each time." *ALJ*, 445.

9 "Charlton Heston Can Expect to be a Big Hit for 50 Years," *Rocky Mountain News* [Denver, CO], Jan. 19, 1957, Scrapbooks, HL.

10 Hamill, "Heston: Larger Than Life," 88; Steele, "Unmasking Charlton Heston," 74.

film itself," he observed of *The Ten Commandments*, "and my role as Moses, will always remain one of the creative peaks of my career." He recognized how special the role and the film were for him and shared this understanding with his readers. "I'm a fairly happy guy," he asserted, "and I can usually find something to be glad about in every part . . . but Moses had more to offer than any of them."[11]

These communications allowed him to build fan loyalty, but Heston realized his work in public relations could not rely solely on occasional newsletters. He had to continue to make himself available to the writers who could tell his story. Nevertheless, the effort required attention he preferred to leave for stage and screen performances. "The publicity calls are getting almost as tough as the acting calls," he observed in late October. "I had to start at six this morning, having breakfast with a lady writer for *Esquire*, giving her my most considered and unique opinions on the hows and wherefores of the movie business."[12]

On the personal side, the Hestons remained close to Jolly and Kathryn West. In late November 1957, Heston recorded, "I got up early for breakfast with Jolly West, whom I see too infrequently." Subsequently, he called the doctor "one of my oldest and closest friends." They were also busy preparing to build something else that both he and Lydia wanted desperately: a home of their own design in Beverly Hills. The effort had to begin with land and the Hestons were fortunate in that regard. "Well, we found it!" he exclaimed, with appreciation to his father for his assistance. "Thanks to Russ's expert guidance, the same day we determined to look for land, we found what I'm sure is the best piece left in town, at a fantastic price. Just under three acres in Coldwater Canyon looking over the most compelling view I've *ever* seen out here, bar none." It would be some time before the landscaping and construction permitted them to move into the new home, but there was no doubt when he proclaimed, "We're all delighted."[13]

Additional public exposure allowed Heston to increase the number of fans and potential viewers of his work that made building and maintaining such a home possible. Occasionally, these efforts also gave him the opportunity to demonstrate his humor in more open fashion, with the Coldwater Canyon property providing material. Heston later revealed that a hurried arrival by an inspector might have halted matters before they got started over the assertion that there was not enough slope to the site. "While he was talking," Heston explained, "his car started rolling

---

11 Newsletter, "The first day of Spring, March 20 [1957]," HL.

12 *ALJ*, 33.

13 Ibid., 36, 32.

and disappeared over the edge of the cliff." Completely wrecked in the area below, the inspector turned and observed, "Well, I guess the slope here is adequate."[14]

Both the progress of his house and his tennis game brought Heston pleasure away from work and routines associated with his profession. "The new house looks as though it'll be everything I'd hoped for," he noted in early March 1959, then capped off the time with special family adventure on the ridge. "This afternoon we entertained for the first time in Coldwater, with a picnic lunch." He prepared the feast "over a fire I built in my own hearth." The work that remained did not dampen the family's spirits, or his. "The walls aren't up and there's no roof, but the kites flew, soaring in the light breeze lifting over the ridge, and the sun was warm."[15]

In all his work, Heston established a reputation for professionalism that made him impatient with those (including himself) who fell short of the standard he expected. He was especially hard on colleagues he felt were more concerned with their perceived status than in hitting their marks, learning their lines, or arriving at work on time. In this period, one person who earned his ire was a co-star in two productions, *The Ten Commandments* and *Three Violent People*. Even in the latter stages of life, when he reflected on his association with Anne Baxter, Heston felt bound to offer strained views regarding her professionalism before concluding, "Never mind . . . nobody can play everything."[16] Of course, Heston knew he could not "play everything" either; but if perfect performances were impossible, self-improvement in one's craft was not.

He continued to be active in several spheres. As part of the campaign to promote *Three Violent People* and bring the Heston brand to as wide-ranging an audience as possible, the actor undertook the role as spokesperson for the Mayflower moving company. Heston's campaign stressed the symbiotic connection between the nation's past, a company made famous for helping customers relocate to new homes, and the desire to bring his latest project to the attention of potential moviegoers. "You'll be pleased with Mayflower's better local moving methods . . . I was!" noted Heston, who was listed as "Co-starring in Paramount Pictures' 'Three Violent People' in VistaVision and Technicolor." Wearing contemporary clothing rather than period garb suitable to the film, the first line of the advertisement touted, "Charlton Heston knows why people today prefer Mayflower moving

14 Jim Liston, "At Home with Charlton Heston," *The American Home* (May 1962), 16.

15 *ALJ*, 67.

16 Heston, *To Be a Man*, 47-50.

and storage." Then, in an interesting trait in common with this spokesperson, the writer of the piece added, "He knows that Mayflower improves its service through constant research!"[17]

For the July 1957 edition of his newsletter, Heston also let fans know that he had taken a guest stint as a questioner on *The $64,000 Question* television program. Likewise, he was slated to appear in a televised dramatization of the trial of Henry Wirz, Confederate commandant of Andersonville Prison. The production featured a historically based presentation of the effort to hold Wirz accountable at trial for the deaths of Union prisoners of war at the notorious Georgia facility. Both projects meant that Heston remained on television screens, expanding his audience reach. [18]

Even as he added to the types of parts he undertook in motion pictures, Heston's role in the CBS depiction of *The Trial of Capt. Wirz*, allowed him to delve into a topic and era of personal interest: the Civil War. Newspaper writer and editor William S. Kirkpatrick authored a piece on the program entitled, "A Dark Corner of U.S. History," that opened with a photograph and the words of the U.S. prosecutor played by Heston. "Then the orders of Gen. Winder [Wirz's superior] outweighed the orders of your conscience!" In echoes of a defense raised by individuals from the Second World War (and later Vietnam) came the haunting reply, "I tell you I could not—I could not—disobey!"[19]

Heston considered potential fan reaction as he weighed his projects. "As long as you think I should be on [television] OFTENER than I am," he suggested, "I have no problem." Then, demonstrating an awareness of how the pace and nature of his work mattered, he added, "The other way around, and I'm in trouble. Besides, it's time I did another movie, I think." The actor explained that the production he was undertaking next, *The Big Country*, would offer several opportunities. "It would be my first work for [William] Wyler, and my first heavy, in film anyway," he maintained, apparently neglecting the inadvertently dark gambler he had played in *Dark City*, "and I'm very attracted by both these prospects. Wyler is one of the finest directors in the world and I'd give a lot to work for him. I think Greg [Peck] and I would make an interesting combination, too."

He also felt it necessary to continue to convey personal connections with fans by including information about his family in his newsletter. Lydia had the unique

---

17 An example of the Heston Mayflower advertisement found in *SEP*, Sept. 8, 1956, 108.

18 Newsletter, July 1957, HL.

19 William S. Kirkpatrick, "A Dark Corner of U.S. History," 1957, 17.

experience of understanding the profession as both a performer and from her perspective as a wife and mother in an actor's family. In a note she appended to this edition, she described their anticipation for a vacation in Puerto Rico. "Some of you imagine that an actor loafs between pictures," Lydia surmised, "believe me, mine doesn't! Endless conferences, interviews, photographic sessions, and piles of scripts to be read keep Chuck jumping, though he does find time for tennis." Even this latter element, as a "tennis widow," she felt was preferable to other types of athletic or sporting endeavors that could affect negatively upon family time on the rare occasions when it was available.[20]

Heston understood the imperatives of his profession. "I'd been at it long enough to figure that out," he recalled concerning negotiating ploys for billing placement when it came to securing parts, "but I was still very preoccupied with the size and centrality of my part." Remembering his lean early years, the actor was determined to maintain the forward progression of his career. "Is it better to have a good part in an important film, or the best part in an OK film?" he recalled asking his agent. "I know the answer to that now. I did not then."[21]

In his fall newsletter, Heston drew once more on his established reputation as well as prospective acting opportunities. Regarding the inclusion of Carroll Baker as a possible love interest for Heston's character in *The Big Country*, he observed slyly of his co-star's identification with another film, "somebody said the picture should be re-titled MOSES MEETS BABY DOLL." Heston also anticipated returning to the role of Andrew Jackson, albeit a different one than he had played opposite Susan Hayward in *The President's Lady*. "I realized then that it was a part I hadn't nearly squeezed all the juice out of," he remarked, "and I've been looking ever since for another chance to play the man I consider to be one of the most significant in our history."

He considered his options in other media platforms as well. "I think I've stayed off the tube long enough to take another crack at it," he commented of his time away from live television. While he worked on those prospects, the father enjoyed the pleasant roles assigned in playtime with Fraser to occupy his attentions. In every case, he concluded, "Give me almost any kind of part to play . . . a lunging cougar ambushing Jim Bowie," with Fray, "chasing Greg Peck around on a horse," in *The Big Country*, "Andrew Jackson at New Orleans" in *The Buccaneer*, [then] convince me it's got a couple of good scenes, and I'll grab my makeup kit and be

20 Newsletter, July 1957, HL.

21 *CHA*, 163-164.

there." An itinerate thespian at heart, he observed, "As long as some of you come and see the results, I've got it made."[22]

As he had revealed in his newsletter, in *The Big Country* Heston got to work with an individual he had long admired. In considering a role in an ensemble cast, however, he nearly missed his chance to do so. As still the "foolish boy that I was," he recalled, he had gone home to consider the offer for the part of cowboy Steve Leech and told his agent, Herman Citron, "I think I'll pass on this one, I mean it really isn't that good a part, there are six better parts in it." Heston noted in his journal on June 30, "I spent an inconclusive and not too effective half hour explaining to Wyler and Peck why I didn't think the part in *The Big Country* was good enough. It's a hell of an opportunity to pass up, though." The campaign to win him over continued into the next week, with the actor admitting that he was not "in love with" the part, feeling it would "require an ego-bruising drop in billing." Still, Heston came around to appreciating good work. "All actors get preoccupied with billing order, but I've learned it doesn't matter a damn as long as your name's in the same size type."[23] If time eventually allayed such concerns, the still-maturing actor felt he had to be cognizant of such matters.

Citron, who also represented Wyler, chided his acting charge for taking such a short-sighted position. "You have an offer to work with Gregory Peck for maybe the best director in film, and you're worrying the *part* isn't good enough for you?" Arguing that most actors would relish the opportunity, the agent insisted, "I'm telling you, you *have* to do this picture!" Heston remembered that the vehemence was not lost on him; he "finally . . . saw the light" and joined the project.[24]

Author Bruce Crowther saw Heston's decision as particularly noteworthy given that a supporting role in a star-laden cast could appear problematic. The choice seemed better reserved for "very young actors on the way up, or older ones on the way out" rather than for "an established leading man" in a role "far removed from the heroes with whom he was becoming associated in moviegoers' minds." Yet Crowther decided that Heston's risk and rewards were reasonable, given the prospective benefits. "What mattered," Crowther maintained, "was that he could observe the work of a great director at close range" and in the process establish a

---

22 Newsletter, October 1957, HL.

23 Scott Berg, Charlton Heston, Interviewed, Mar. 1983, William Wyler Collection, compiled by Jan Herman, *Ben-Hur*—interviews, Heston, Charlton, f.3, HL; *ALJ*, 27.

24 Berg, Heston Interviewed, HL; *CHA*, 164.

good rapport with Wyler, something which was to prove enormously beneficial to his career in the very near future."[25]

Once cast in the picture, Heston set aside any hesitations and turned his full devotion to the role. In the film's iconic fistfight scene, Heston's Leech tangled with Peck's character in a futile struggle the director set against the vast expanse of the surrounding countryside. "Heston and Peck sustained many real bumps and bruises," author Gene Reese noted of their screen clash. "Heston missed a mark and landed on a rock, injuring his back."[26] But the scene effectively emphasized the futility of fighting to resolve disputes and the contrast of humans lost against the immense backdrop of the landscape that framed them.

Some of the film's elements were painful in other ways, as reflected in the Heston-authored "What I Want, and Don't Want, From My Director." Despite the title, the actor's intentions were not meant to be dictatorial. The document was less a statement of demands than an exercise in self-evaluation. "One thing I don't think a director has to do—and there are a lot of actors who get a lot of money who don't agree with me on this—is create an atmosphere or a mood particularly comfortable for me." He believed that growth was the essential element for him as a performer. "What I need is to make me be as good as I can be," he explained. If Heston was prepared to assert "a loud voice and strong opinions" on his part, he felt it incumbent on the director to convince him otherwise or to insist that this was how the shot needed to be done. "Then I'll do it."[27]

Of course, for an individual of Wyler's stature and background, this attitude was seen as an unnecessary and ingratiating indulgence. Even Heston appeared to recognize this point when he grabbed the director's script binder to locate a scene he wanted to discuss and saw the long list of screen credits etched there in gold-embossed lettering. He wisely concluded that Wyler knew what he was about and would make the actor better without his prodding. In the desire to better understand the situation with a director who shot multiple takes yet offered so little feedback—"Chuck, if I don't say anything, that means it's good"—Heston contacted Gary Cooper, who had worked with Wyler on *Friendly Persuasion*. He remembered Cooper telling him, "an actor never feels like a worse actor than when he's being directed by Wyler. But he never feels like a better actor than when he

---

25 Crowther, *Charlton Heston*, 55.

26 Gene Freese, *Classic Movie Fight Scenes: 75 Years of Bare Knuckle Brawls, 1914-1989* (Jefferson, NC, 2017), 133.

27 Charlton Heston, "What I Want, and Don't Want, From My Director," 19, Wyler Collection, HL.

sees the final film." As things turned out, Wyler did just fine by Heston. "Doing a scene for Willie is like getting the works in a Turkish bath," he observed colorfully. "You darn near drown but you come out smelling like a rose."[28]

Despite his rewarding experiences with Cecil B. DeMille and William Wyler, Heston recognized that no single film or director would be enough to sustain a career. "I wanted to find something special for my next picture," he remembered. "Happily, I did," he explained of a script entitled *Badge of Evil*, which became the film *Touch of Evil*. He also understood that his work in film or television depended on many others to be successful. He could always give a better performance, yet his best effort required appropriate direction, technical support, and artistic collaboration. If other actors provided powerful impressions through their work, they could help him improve his. This was one reason that he preferred working with outstanding directors, dedicated, professional actors, and expert technical practitioners. In the case of his next director, Orson Welles, some of the best advice involved technique. "You know Chuck," he recalled Welles telling him, "you should work on your tenor range." The actor/director explained the benefit of developing these skills. "The tenor range has a knife edge. Your bass is a velvet hammer. Use them both."[29]

When Universal sent the crime drama's script for Heston's consideration, he insisted that only good direction could prevent the resultant work from becoming pedestrian. Heston remembered suggesting Orson Welles after he learned the latter had already signed as "the heavy" in the film. "It genuinely seemed to strike them as a radical suggestion, as though I'd asked my mother to direct the picture." Welles maintained that Heston had misunderstood that he was going to direct from the beginning: "Well, any picture that Welles directs, I'll make." Only then did the studio executives consider the matter, and despite Welles's reputation for overspending on his projects, they thought the choice acceptable.[30]

The production proceeded with Welles selling Heston on the idea that his character should be a Mexican detective rather than an American one. The director's greatest contribution, as far as his co-star was concerned, was keeping the work fresh. "Film acting is not often very interesting," he admitted as he pondered his past roles. "Orson has the capacity as a director to somehow persuade you that each time is *indeed* the most important day in the picture, and that's kind of marvelous,

---

28 Berg, Heston Interviewed, HL; Eliot, *Charlton Heston*, 142; "Working for William Wyler," *Action*, 20.

29 *CHA*, 152, 160.

30 *ALJ*, 18; Orson Welles and Peter Bogdanovich, *This is Orson Welles* (New York, 1998), 297.

and I applaud it." Heston certainly enjoyed working with his mercurial colleague. "Orson *seduces* you in a marvelous way. You know he's one of the most charming men in the world, if it's important to him to be charming. He is, at *minimum*, interesting—but if it's important to him to enlist your support and cooperation, he is as charming a man as I have ever seen."[31]

For his part, Welles conveyed a mutual esteem. "He's the nicest man to work with that ever lived in the movies," he observed. "I suppose the two nicest actors I've ever worked with in my life are [John] Gielgud and Heston." Welles recalled one scene in particular. "I'll never forget Chuck Heston, one night, at the end of those seven weeks. He was on the far side of the bridge, and I told him to quickly cross over in a shot." Heston wanted to understand the reason for the bit. "And he said, without irony or anger, very sweetly, 'Do you mind telling me *why* I'm crossing the bridge?'" Welles urged him to finish the scene and "when you get over here I'll tell you!" Heston subsequently learned that the director was afraid of losing his "light" with the coming of dawn and was hurrying to wrap the scene.

Welles thought highly of Heston's work. He was "[w]onderful in it. We rehearsed for two weeks before we shot, and he was an absolute soldier all the way through." Welles elaborated, "I think he has the makings of a great heroic actor. And I don't know what movies may lead him into doing, but he has all the equipment—the voice, the physique, the intelligence, and everything—he's a big American heroic actor." As far as the director was concerned, Heston's performance could not have been better. "All you have to do is point and Chuck can go in any direction."[32]

By November, with Heston deep in other work on *The Big Country*, Universal Studios was still wrangling with Welles over the final touches on *Touch of Evil*, hoping to shove the troublesome figure aside without alienating performers like Heston, who would have to participate in possible reshoots. Nevertheless, the tug-of-war put the actor in an awkward position as he tried to fulfill his contractual obligations while remaining true to his director. Heston's assurances from Welles that he would cooperate at no additional cost to the production appeared to ease the situation. "This settles it for me," he recorded. "If he doesn't do it, I don't."[33]

---

31 James Delson, "Heston on Welles," *Take One* (Vol. 3:5), 8. See also Terry Comito, ed., *Touch of Evil, Orson Welles, Director* (New Brunswick, NJ, 1985), 213-222.

32 Welles and Bogdanovich, *This is Orson Welles*, 305.

33 *ALJ*, 34.

Instead, the impasse remained, with Heston anxious to resolve the dilemma to everyone's satisfaction if possible. An impassioned letter from Welles arrived as the reshoots loomed: "If you are tempted to think of yourself as the helpless victim of sinister Hollywood forces over which you have no control, I must tell you that you're wrong. You aren't helpless at all." He concluded decisively, "You can do this by getting a little tough now."[34]

Heston received the message and embraced it, canceling his appearance for work the next day at a personal cost of $8,000 for lost time, which he absorbed out of his own pocket. Further discussions led to his return to the studio for retakes and another emotional appeal from Welles:

> There's this character—(known and loved by all)—he might be called "Cooperative Chuck" . . . he is not merely well disciplined in his work, but positively eager—even wildly eager—to make things easy for his fellows on the set and for all the executives in their offices . . . In a word, he's the Eagle Scout of the Screen Actors' Guild.
>
> The purpose of this communiqué is to beg him to leave his uniform and flag in the dressing room.[35]

When discussions continued—"A damn difficult day, on the whole" as Heston described it—and at the continued insistence of Universal production chief Ed Muhl that the work must proceed without Welles, Heston relented. He later recalled, "I didn't handle this too well. My reluctance to do the retakes without Orson was reasonable; postponing my decision not to do them until Sunday evening was not." Still, going back to work was not without internal cost: "I have done worse work in the movies than this day of retakes, but I don't remember feeling worse." Everyone tried to be "pleasant enough, but in a hell of a tough position."[36]

In quieter moments of reflection, particularly with his acting colleagues, Charlton Heston revealed his thoughts on the directors under whom he had labored. In 1975, Bruce Dern was working with the legendary Alfred Hitchcock in *Family Plot* when he shared with Heston his sense that with certain directors, he felt that "just maybe we might do something nobody had ever done before."

---

34 Ibid.; Welles and Bogdanovich, *This is Orson Welles*, 306.

35 Welles and Bogdanovich, *This is Orson Welles*, 307.

36 *ALJ*, 35-36.

The observation resonated immediately with Heston. "I know exactly what you mean," he said. "I only had it once in my life. As much as I adored Willy Wyler on *Ben-Hur*, I only had it once. And that was on *Touch of Evil*." Heston nostalgically explained, "Every day I went to work with Orson. I thought, just maybe." Then he wistfully added, "Did we do it every day? No. But there was always that chance."[37]

On *Touch of Evil*, Heston knew he was watching a master at work and was determined to learn as much from him as possible. "Orson probably taught me more about acting than any film director I've worked for," he explained afterward. "Which is not to say I necessarily did my best film performance for him, but he taught me a great deal about acting—the whole, acting generically." For Heston the work was educational and, most important for him personally, both "stimulating" and "as satisfying creatively as anything I've ever done." Indeed, many aspects of the project were fulfilling, but to the studio Welles's direction was not one of them. Welles reflected that while he was temporarily sidelined, "Heston kept phoning me to say what he was doing and to ask if it was all right, because if I didn't approve he would walk off."[38]

According to writer Jean-Pierre Isbouts, "1958 was the year in which Charlton Heston became a superstar. Before that, he was respectable Hollywood actor who had already appeared in fifteen films, achieved considerable screen recognition, and received favorable notices." He might balk at the label—"I prefer the idea of a successful actor." Heston disapproved of the term "star"—"I don't like the label"—and found "superstar" to be "even worse." Yet he accepted that he could not truly complain. "It built my house, put my kids through school, and gave me the key choices in my work, usually what part I play and with whom." Nevertheless, there were tradeoffs of privacy, and time, energy, and attention that might have gone elsewhere. The "ego massage" of seeing one's name on the marquee and having many others be responsible for the logistics of your life considerably eased any burdens, but he certainly meant what he said when he observed, "I would be glad to have a little more elbow room. For an actor, that's hard to find. . . . As a guy brought up in the Michigan woods, I *really* need it." In the wake of his on-camera success, there was no departing from the reality of being a "movie star, the persona that, unavoidably has defined my life and most of my work."[39]

---

37 Dern, *Things I've Said*, 144.

38 Delson, "Heston on Welles," 9; Welles and Bogdanovich, *This is Orson Welles*, 307. See also Gene D. Phillips, *Out of the Shadows: Expanding the Canon of Classic Film Noir* (Lanham, MD, 2012), 214.

39 Heston and Isbouts, *Hollywood*, 73; *CHA*, 234-235.

Heston's career as a "movie star" was about to become even more complicated. Director William Wyler was prepared to follow *The Big Country* with an even bigger film: *Ben-Hur*. His gigantic set-piece presentation would take the central character, Judah Ben-Hur, from the pinnacle of power in Jerusalem to the depths of exile aboard a Roman galley as a slave and a subsequent return to prestige as an adopted son of a Roman commander. His restoration also meant a reunion with his nemesis Messala, a boyhood friend who had become an implacable enemy, and a chariot race between the rivals that paved the way for ultimate redemption.

As usual, speculation filled the Hollywood grapevine as to who would assume the title role, with names ranging from Robert Taylor and Stewart Granger to Marlon Brando and Burt Lancaster. Wyler presented the possibility of portraying Messala to Heston, who later insisted, "I was frankly more interested in doing another picture for him than *in which* of the two marvelous parts I did in it." Then, in early January 1958, Heston met with agent Herman Citron to discuss another script, but found his focus lacking. "It's interesting," he admitted, "but my main concern currently is settling 'Ben Hur'; very hard to weigh seriously other projects until this goes one way or another."[40]

While waiting for word on *Ben-Hur*, Heston found solace in his tennis game and a television program that appeared to have attracted both a good audience and positive reviews. "As for *Beauty and the Beast*," he noted in his journal, "I seem to have hit the jackpot with a TV show. We had a huge rating, and all the notices I've heard anything about were excellent." Heston was happy the positive reviews were universal among those who expressed any opinion to him.[41]

As work on a role as Andrew Jackson in *The Buccaneer* got started, the actor got a call to meet Cecil B. DeMille for lunch. The director wanted to share some Madeira that dated to the year 1815, when the historical Andy Jackson had stopped the British advance toward New Orleans at Chalmette Plantation. DeMille slipped an inquiry into the conversation. "So, I understand William Wyler wants you for *Ben-Hur*." Heston remained coy as to which part, if any, he might get. "Well, Ben-Hur's the part of course," the veteran observed. "You can always get good actors to play bad men. Heroes are harder." He demurred on DeMille's offer to

---

40 Newsletter, June 3, 1958, HL. For the early speculation in casting for the 1959 version of *Ben-Hur*, see Jon Solomon, *Ben-Hur: The Original Blockbuster* (Edinburgh, UK, 2016), 731; "Monday, Jan. 6, 1958," "Charlton Heston 'Ben Hur' Diaries," *Cinema* (July 1964) 10. For a Wyler-centric perspective, see Madsen, *William Wyler*. Some discrepancies exist between the *Cinema* version of the diaries, those Heston published as his *Journals*, and a 2011 release by Fraser C. Heston of copies of the originals.

41 *ALJ*, 40.

call his colleague on the matter as they ended the visit. Nevertheless, the legendary director offered, "If I were you, I wouldn't worry."[42]

With no "final word" on the *Ben-Hur* casting, Heston tried to endure the waiting. "Very damaging to the ego," he admitted. He was tackling his make-up for *The Buccaneer*, as well as retakes DeMille wanted for *The Ten Commandments*, in addition to contemplating other choices. "With unemployment looming, necessity making decision on various offers more pressing." Another television presentation, *Point of No Return* for *Playhouse 90*, promised to supply both the necessary "work" and a chance for his "first modern role in Lord knows how long."[43] The actor remained quite conscious of varying his characters in order to remain fresh for himself as well as his audience.

A few days later, he was still mulling his options. At a lunch meeting, with still no word on *Ben-Hur*, Heston decided to accept *Point of No Return*, which would alleviate the restlessness he always felt when not acting and provide a wage-earning job that would pay the bills. Yet it all became moot when Citron and Edd Henry of MCA informed him that Wyler had made up his mind and they had reached a deal. Heston recognized the opportunity before him, noting succinctly, "God, what a thing!"[44] After an excruciating period in limbo, with *Ben-Hur*, Charlton Heston now had landed his highest profile role since Moses.

Even so, the celebration could not break on a larger scale until he catered to some Hollywood conventions. "It was terribly hard to carry such big news as mine around all day in silence," Heston asserted. "According to an agreement," he observed, "I gave it to [Hedda] Hopper this morning, but no-one else had it till tonight, when we told the people at the party, to some very warm talk." Enjoying the development with Lydia, his friends, and champagne eased the tension; the relieved actor recorded, "I guess I'm not out of the business quite yet, no matter how bad things are."[45]

---

42 Heston and Isbouts, *Hollywood*, 100-101.

43 *ALJ*, 40; "Fri., Jan. 17th," "'Ben-Hur' Diaries," 10.

44 "January 1958, 21 Tuesday," *Ben-Hur Diaries*, Fraser C. Heston. See also *ALJ*, 41. The *Cinema* edition included a colorful telephone exchange between Citron and Heston in which the former conveyed the news. In the published version of the journals, Heston made no mention of the earlier conversation and noted that it was in the evening when he saw the agent in person that he learned of the casting decision. "Tues. Jan. 21st," "'Ben-Hur' Diaries," *Cinema*, 10.

45 "January 1958, 22 Wednesday," Fraser Heston ed., "Wed. Jan. 22nd," "'Ben-Hur' Diaries," 10. In his published journals, Heston downplayed the role Hopper played; *ALJ*, 41.

The contractual paperwork that solidified the details of the new project also illustrated a new kind of reality for the star. His salary stood at "two hundred fifty thousand dollars for thirty weeks and prorated after that. Plus travel and expenses for all." The trajectory for Charlton Heston's career was certainly on the rise, as he recorded in his work journal. "Not bad compared to the sixty-five dollars a week I got from [Katharine Cornell] ten years ago."[46]

Heston understood that long work awaited, but he enjoyed the special treatment afforded him as the principal in a major studio production. "Metro is unquestionably the studio to go if you want to be treated like a big fat star." Basking in the moment, he declared, "Lunch in the executive dining room was all it would be imagined . . . court jesters and all." An epic Wyler picture certainly promised to be "pretty staggering." Even with an actor's superstition to contain him, he could not help but be excited at the prospects. "I hesitate to go out on record about another mammoth undertaking, after *Ten* [*Commandments*] failed to catapult me to the heights, but this sure Lord won't hurt me."[47] Although Heston found it difficult to grasp the degree to which his portrayal of Moses for DeMille had been life and career transforming, he knew the role he was undertaking could be very special.

In the meantime, the Hollywood routine continued. Business lunches, blocking, and rehearsals for the upcoming CBS drama marked the time. Heston also remained focused, as he usually was, with workouts that were taking on renewed urgency. "The Ben Hur costumes are proceeding in good shape," he explained. "If I can control my weight, I'll look the way I should."[48]

As preparations continued for the trip that would eventually take the Heston family across the Atlantic for *Ben-Hur*'s filming, the actor completed his live television work with the telecast of *Point of No Return*. "I think the show came off well," he opined, appreciating the opportunity to take a character across a span of years and "playing a man whose situation let me use my own experiences . . . something I rarely do with a part."[49]

Once in New York City, time slipped by in a flurry of activities before the Hestons raced for the ocean liner *United States*, which would bring them to the

---

46 *ALJ*, 41.

47 "Thurs., Jan. 23rd," "'Ben Hur' Diaries," 10. Interestingly, in his published journals, Heston colored his predictions on the film and the casting in stronger terms; *ALJ*, 41.

48 "February 1958, 10 Monday," Fraser Heston, ed.

49 *ALJ*, 41.

Old World. Friends and well-wishers waved them off as the actor enjoyed the moment "from the warmish vintage champagne to the streamers hanging wet in the spray as we passed Ambrose light." He savored the voyage; "I'll never forget it." London, Dublin, and Paris provided additional stops for the entourage in March and early April before it finally arrived in Rome to a crush of journalists and "a train of Cadillacs," which whisked them off to the lavish villa that would become home for the duration of the shoot.[50]

Of course, Heston would find little time outside of his work to enjoy the amenities in the months to come. The demands *Ben-Hur* required proved grueling long before any cameras began to roll. He travelled the next day to Cinecittá Studios to meet highly regarded stuntman, Yakima Canutt, charged with making Heston's Judah Ben-Hur into a successful chariot racer. Afterward, there was time for a birthday dinner with Lydia, "with echoes of 1952, the same day. So far we've come, since then."[51]

Shortly after their introduction, Heston and Canutt settled into work with a team of horses. "I managed to get a half hour in a chariot with Canutt, delighted to discover that the four horse team gave me less trouble than I remember in Egypt with two. Perhaps it's like a lot of other things . . . the first two are the hardest!" Indeed, among the rare skills he had touted when work had begun on *The Ten Commandments* was learning "how to drive [a] chariot."[52]

He later insisted that he had never driven a chariot before Canutt taught him how to do so for *Ben-Hur*, but as he alluded in his journal, a scene in *The Ten Commandments* showed the young prince of Egypt returning to adoring crowds from his conquest of Ethiopia guiding a two-horse version of the vehicle. A scholar of the novel and film versions of *Ben-Hur* noted that Heston was not completely "a novice," but "he still had trepidations."[53]

A degree of reticence appeared in the actor's work journal as well. When sloppy conditions on the track provided "a good excuse not to let the teams [run]

---

50 "March 1958, 11 Tuesday," Charlton Heston, *On the Set of Ben-Hur: The Personal Journal of Charlton Heston* (Turner Entertainment and Warner Bros., 2011, DVD); *ALJ*, 41, 44-45.

51 "April 1958, 14 Monday," *On the Set*.

52 "April 1958, 15 Tuesday," *On the Set*; *ALJ*, 45 offered a slightly different version; "Heston Taped Interview – August 16, 1955," 16, HL.

53 Heston may have been thinking about the four-horse version when he replied to a question about being in a chariot before: "Never had, no," although the scene in *The Ten Commandments* was brief and certainly nothing on the scale of the later chariot race. See *This Is Your Life*, February 26, 1981, 36, HL; Solomon, *Ben-Hur*, 759-760.

full out anyway," Heston confessed that this "relieved me . . . I'm not up to that yet anyway." He also seemed perplexed when "*Newsweek* shot a few things, for what use I can't imagine, but we shall see."[54] If he did not comprehend fully the degree of interest the project was already drawing, that situation would change quickly.

Heston was prepared to spend a prodigious amount of time attempting to achieve competence with the chariot and horses that would allow him to look authentic on film. "Life falling into routine patter," he wrote on April 18, noting "days spent on practice track working with Yak, *not* with whites . . . several docile teams, bays and chesnuts, [sic] more my speed." Slowly gaining confidence, Heston noted, "With luck, may solo next week. So far, just holding on, white knuckled, while Yak drives."[55]

Each day seemed to bring new challenges and milestones as he progressed. "I am working with more and more confidence with the chariots now," he wrote on April 19, "though still a long way from real skill of course. Under Yak's eye, however, I feel perfectly able to do more in the scene than is expected of me." Fraser offered a special bonus in his first chariot ride, demonstrating what the proud father declared "commendable grit." Heston wanted to assist his director and provide continuity for the camera. He noted that under Canutt's tutelage he had arrived at a point where he could assure that he would "be able to shoot most of my stuff without doubling." On the same day he noted, "I also managed to solo in the chariot today, with the prospect of working alone in it from here out."[56]

As the actor recalled, the key moment in his training occurred when Canutt stepped off unnoticed as Heston focused on the task of handling the horses. April 30 found him progressing still further. "Yak is moving me up through some of the tougher teams with the chariots, and I'm gradually gaining a gratifying modicum of ease with a team." With an eye to the technical qualities this could offer, in addition to less reliance on stunt doubling, he noted, "At least I'll always be able to drive in and out of a shot in pictures now." Then, on May 3, he recorded, "Chariot somewhat better; at least able drive around track without shaking visibly." At the same time, he discarded the experiment for protecting his eyes as a failure, if not a hindrance. "Finally decided work chariot without [contact] lenses, and risk sand."[57]

---

54 "April 1958, 17 Thursday," *On the Set.*

55 "Fri., April 18th," "'Ben-Hur' Diaries," 11.

56 "April 1958, 19 Saturday," *On the Set*; *ALJ*, 46; "April 1958, 26 Saturday," *On the Set.*

57 *ALJ*, 46. The *Cinema* version was off by a few days and included a colorful scene of a "very big event, cheers from stable boys, etc." "Tues., April 29th," "'Ben-Hur' Diaries," 11; "April 1958, 30 Wednesday," *On the Set*; *ALJ*, 47; "Sat., May 3rd," "'Ben-Hur' Diaries," 11.

Each time now, either Canutt or Wyler seemed to be adding components to build toward the climax of putting the race before the cameras. "Couldn't call it all-out race by any means," Heston noted on May 10, "but there were several teams running hell-for-Wyler." In the exercise, the actor was transitioning from working the team to establishing some level of comfort with the other performers in the setting of the scene. "I managed to finish in front (that's what it says in the script)," but it was just as pleasant for him to see son Fraser watching his father amidst all the activity "from sidelines."[58]

Though Heston usually embraced the public relations aspect of his work, an unpleasant lunch with an English journalist led the actor to label the experience the "toughest part of the day" as he sought to "skirt his more obvious pitfalls." Later, Heston proudly noted that he had "since learned to do a flawless defensive interview. They can't lay a glove on me."[59]

While the script continued to undergo extensive revision and the preparations drew to a close, Heston could focus on the work he had been anticipating: actually acting when the cameras finally rolled. "Well, the first day is behind me," he wrote on May 20. "It lifted off my chest like a weight that had been growing there imperceptibly, I suppose, since the day I knew most of this year would be spent Benhurring with WW."[60]

Heston's time with Wyler on *The Big Country* had familiarized him with the director's style, but he had been part of an ensemble cast, not the principal expected to carry the picture. *Ben-Hur* would test, and occasionally strain, their relationship. The actor's initial impressions were positive. Wyler seemed "to be succeeding in what I feel is the vitally necessary task of injecting details of tiny reality into the huge canvas he must color before we're done," Heston assessed at the outset. When filming finally began on the racing scene, Heston recorded, "Today was a long day of shooting what should be the very spectacular (there's that word creeping in) shots of chariots lining up to enter the arena. Rather tough driving, but little dialogue." He was reaching a level with his director that he had not known in their earlier picture together. "I am surer this year than last, I think, of the way to use the best of WW's method, in terms of playing a scene."[61]

---

58 Ibid.

59 *ALJ*, 48.

60 "May 1958, 20 Tuesday," *On the Set*; *ALJ*, 49.

61 "May 1958, 21 Wednesday," "May 1958, 22 Thursday," *On the Set*.

Undeniably, the race was the most visually stirring element of the movie, and Heston understood this early in the filming. "Although it will only be a single sequence in the finished film, I think the high point of the shooting so far for most people has been the chariot race," Heston explained to his newsletter readers from Italy in the late summer of 1958. Visitors flocked to the gigantic set, "competing with the Colosseum and the Roman Forum" as attractions that indicated the power of film illusion over historical reality. A volume dedicated to the making of the motion picture included a list of "more than a score of famous show-business personalities" who came to see a portion of the filming, while some "25,500 tourists from all over the world" also flocked to the scene of the spectacle.[62]

As the publicity volume indicated, many of these "tourists" were celebrities themselves. The "endless stream of VIPS," as historian Jon Solomon described it, included politicians, members of the press, and fellow actors. Photographers captured Hedda Hopper stepping onto the chariot alongside the star. Airlines and game shows offered special tours and prizes to highlight the opportunity to participate in the unique experience. Indeed, everyone seemed to want to get into the act. Even television personality Ed Sullivan hoisted himself onto a chariot for his popular show to help build anticipation.[63]

Heston continued to put in long hours, especially with the chariot race scenes. As it turned out, experiments with contacts in his eyes were the least of his concerns. "If I don't win this race soon, my hands are going to give out. Calluses well built up now, but after five straight days fingers get awfully stiff."[64] Controlling the team that would take him to victory in the arena was only part of the physical exertion in the filming; scenes depicting the rowing required from a slave consigned to a Roman galley were still to come.

He was also pursuing his time-honored tradition of researching a part, but on this occasion the exercise had an unexpectedly deleterious effect. "I remember I got in terrible trouble with Willy on Ben-Hur because as part of my preparation, having done a lot of research on first century Rome and all that, and Judea at the time of Christ, I did about twenty pages of typing on Ben-Hur's life before the

---

62 Newsletter, August 15th, 1958, Ferragosto, HL; "Random Revelations," *The Story of the Making of Ben-Hur: A Tale of the Christ* (New York, 1959), np.

63 Solomon, *Ben-Hur*, 766-767; Axel Madsen, *William Wyler: An Authorized Biography* (New York: Thomas Y. Crowell, 1973), 349. Solomon noted the show aired the clip on July 26 and Dec. 27, 1959 (*Ben-Hur*, 769).

64 "Sat., Aug. 9th," ibid.

story began." He felt strongly that this had been beneficial, noting, "it's the kind of thing we use[d] to do in school, and I've done that kind of thing on other parts." Yet, for this director, the reaction came swiftly. "Willy was appalled and deeply offended by it. He thought I was trying to con him, and I think if we hadn't already shot a couple of weeks, he would have fired me." Heston was concerned that the innocent gesture had set back his relationship with the director and believed, "it took me a long time to get even [square] with Willy, [be]cause he had no patience for that kind of approach to a scene."[65]

Controversy aside, Heston continued to immerse himself in the many physical challenges that lay ahead. "Considering we are not shooting, workday is certainly full—three hours chariot practice, one hour javelin practice," he recorded, adding with a touch of Heston humor, "I'll never make the Olympics." Still, it was not these aspects of the work that he considered the most daunting. "I was very cowardly at doctor's office," he confessed, sitting for "the fourth fitting for contact lenses designed to protect [my] eyes from flying stones during the race sequence. Frankly, they hurt like hell!" He concluded, "Inclined to think I'd prefer stones."[66]

Despite the intense realism and the tremendous scope of the sets and the action, the entire production rested on Charlton Heston's ability to demonstrate the fortitude of his character in the face of adversity. "His ideas on making Judah Ben-Hur more than a lay figure in a costume picture are becoming clearer and clearer," Heston seemed relieved to note of Wyler's direction. "Main areas of work here seem to lie in the beginning when we must make him an untried, uncommitted man, thus allowing room for change at slave galley and on Calvary." Heston recognized that strong writing as well as rehearsal were essential. "This is crucial scene of whole first half of the story since it motivates everything that follows," he observed of his "quarrel" with his friend and future antagonist, the Roman Messala. "Christopher [Fry]'s version a vast improvement," he explained of the new writer's changes in the script, "and Willy brought out its virtues in his usual manner as we worked." That "usual manner" consisted of "picking, carping, nagging, fiddling; a reading here and a gesture there until you are trammeled and fenced in by his concept."[67]

65 Berg, Heston Interviewed, 8, HL.

66 "Mon., April 21st," ibid. Ironically, Stephen Boyd lost time before the cameras while suffering with the contacts he wore. See for example, "Mon., June 16th," "Wed., June 18th," "Sat., June 21st," and "Sat., Aug. 9th," ibid., 12-13.

67 "Sat., May 17th," "'Ben-Hur' Diaries," 12; Leyda, *Voices of Film Experience*, 200.

In his zeal to find his character and extract his own best performance, Heston made another critical miscalculation that further strained his relationship with the director. He and Wyler had struggled to strike the right tone in a scene where Judah and Messala first quarrel. "We talked after rehearsal," Heston recorded, "and he thinks I'm too flat through the opening scenes we've been working on." The criticism nagged at the actor. Carrying the creative tension back to the villa, he laid out his views in "a long Selznick-type memo" he planned to offer Wyler as his contribution to the effort. Heston remembered years later just how badly the plan backfired. "This was an absolutely terrible idea, one of the worst mistakes I ever made."[68]

A gesture undertaken in good faith threatened to undo the connection the work in two films had created between Wyler and Heston. If other directors accepting suggestions in written form was valuable, William Wyler was not among their number. He explained the matter succinctly. "They've been writing on this script for two years, most of it no good. What I need you to do is act, not write about it!" The actor never seemed quite to understand why his director had been so offended. Indeed, he may have caught Wyler at a bad moment, rather than exhibiting any real animus toward him personally; Wyler's later comments on Heston's performance were glowing. At any rate, under the circumstances as he interpreted them, Heston recalled, "It took me a long time to get back in his good graces after this blunder."[69]

With all that was going on in the shoot, or perhaps because of it, Heston paused to continue his fan newsletter. On June 3, he related, "This year, which I've already cut into so deeply before filming has even begun, I suppose I will still always remember as the year I made BEN HUR!" Heston had known that the filming would lock him up for a long time, limiting the other areas of his work he had held open to himself since the days of Hal Wallis. "Both the stage and live television are mediums I enjoy," he explained, "and to some extent I feel they offer me both parts and audiences the movies cannot. But Wyler and BEN HUR together were too much to pass up." In any case, with all the work he had done and was committed to doing, Charlton Heston felt secure in making one promise. "So in case any of you were wondering, there won't be any shortage of Heston on your neighborhood screens while I'm here chasing Romans around." He also acknowledged the cinematic magic possible with a team of horses in a chariot race.

68 *ALJ*, 50.

69 *CHA*, 194; *ALJ*, 50.

"It's very exciting, though, and I have learned in two months to be a little more than a white-faced passenger as they tear around the track. Besides, I've read the end of the script and I know I win." Heston was thrilled to be where he was in his career. In the meantime, he explained, "No time for writing more. I have to go make a movie."[70]

Whatever he may say or feel, to deliver a great performance, Heston was smart enough to know he needed strong direction. On June 5, he noted, "Today was one of the toughest days I've ever had professionally. Willy really opened up to me, and it was not an ego-boosting experience." The director wanted his actor's best, even if he had to wrest it from him. "He does not like, not so much with what I have done so far on the part . . . there he seems satisfied . . . but in his view, what my potential for the part is with my present attitude on acting and life." Heston quoted Wyler as telling him, "this could be the most important day of my career" and that he "held out high hope and much promise," but the critique struck hard and the actor concluded, "It ain't gonna be fun, for awhile [sic], though."[71]

Even so, Heston had difficulty understanding everything the director was asking of him. "He could be very tough, very relentless," he observed. "And you think, I'm never going to get it, I never in my career, and by that time [I] was well along as a successful young actor, but I never felt so close to failure." The best illustration of the situation came "quite early in the shooting . . . he called me in and he said, 'Chuck, you have to be better in this part.'" Taken aback, Heston sought clarification, but when the director was not specific, he replied, "Well, that's kind of hard to deal with, Willy." Wyler acknowledged the point, but a frustrated Heston could only say that he thought the director had liked what he had done in *The Big Country*, "and he said, 'yeh, that was an easier part, though . . . this is a harder part.'" The actor could get no more, except the admonition that "'it's just got to be better.'" Heston recalled leaving his dressing room and carrying "my wound home to Lydia, who stopped the bleeding. Still, for one of the few times in my life, I didn't sleep well that night." Fortunately, the challenge to improve was exactly what Heston needed. "I think I tend myself as an actor to settle too easily," he admitted later. "I think that's one of the things I learned from Willy, that you can do it better."[72]

70 Newsletter, June 3, 1958, HL.

71 "June 1958, 5 Thursday," *On the Set; ALJ*, 50.

72 Berg, Heston Interviewed, 7, 17, HL; Heston and Isbouts, *Hollywood*, 112.

Heston's response was to pour himself even further into the role. "I worked my ass off this morning," he observed a few days after Wyler's difficult evaluation he had endured. Even then, the pressure to achieve the best performance remained. "I had very few lines in the scene," he recorded on June 10, "but that's when Willy's tough. He's harder to please when you're listening than when you're talking." The actor preferred to work out a scene involving his character, just as might happen on stage, but Wyler had other ideas. "He doesn't like at ALL, I've decided, to discuss character in broad terms . . . or even in terms of a given scene," Heston concluded. Still, the benefit of not forcing some aspect of a scene because of "a previous notion" about it appeared to be sound.[73]

Gradually, Heston started to think his performance was improving. On June 14, he noted, "I'm regaining my confidence, I think, without losing any of the salutary effects of the dose of cold water WW threw." "WW is beyond question the toughest director I've ever worked for," he insisted on June 19, "and I still think the best." By July, Heston believed he had reached a positive position at last, observing, "Well, WW has either changed (and softened) his tune, or I've improved my craft. My earnest hope that the last is the correct answer is reinforced by the applause that greeted my final effort on the scene where Judah pleads for his family's innocence." The performer thought this exhibition of approval outmatched even "Willy's thrice-repeated praise," and felt understandably vindicated by his effort.[74]

Wyler's demands for the best from his cast and crew meant exacting the greatest exertion from everyone involved. After a grueling day filming an attempt to escape from prison he termed "the most demanding physically I've had yet," Heston observed, "I left a lot of sweat, not to mention a drop or two o[f] blood, on floor of that cell." The director was not prepared to settle for anything less than he thought possible, however, telling his actors at one point, "I'm not going to throw out this one till you get it right." Even so, he revealed a rare side of himself when sharing a beer with his star at the hotel bar. "You know," Heston recalled him saying, "I really like to be a nice guy. It's easier to be nice, actually. . . . The problem is, you can't make good pictures that way." The actor tried to be sympathetic, deciding to defuse the moment with a humorous aside. "I know that, too. . . . Don't worry, I'm okay. Remember, I'm only an imitation Jew." The comment left Wyler laughing, according to Heston, "harder than I've ever seen him laugh."[75]

73 *ALJ*, 50; "June 1958, 12 Thursday," *On the Set*.

74 "June 1958, 14 Thursday," "June 1958, 19 Thursday," "July 1958, 4, Friday," *On the Set*; *ALJ*, 51.

75 "June 1958, 26, Thursday," *On the Set*; "Sat., July 12th," "'Ben Hur' Diaries," 13; Heston and Isbouts, *Hollywood*, 112.

When an interviewer for *The Saturday Evening Post* asked about the possibility of on-set injuries, Heston mentioned "the ridiculous lengths to protect you off set." He noted, "There I was doing a chariot race, using no doubles for most of it, and I was jumping from a burning galley with falling timbers all around me." On his day off, however, studio executives rejected the notion of riding horses on a private course or even playing tennis at the risk of spraining an ankle. He recalled asking, "What do you think I'm doing out there with those chariots every day, playing hopscotch?"

The same interviewer brought up the doubts others had raised as to whether Heston even piloted the chariot himself, causing the actor to retort, "Tell your nasty, suspicious friends, that I drove my own chariot through eighty-five per cent of that race." He had worked on this aspect of his performance to achieve the appearance of authenticity as much as to demonstrate his skill, but he had done it himself. "All I had to do was learn to stay on board so they could film me there." Of course, as Yakima Canutt had told him and a reading of the novel confirmed, the outcome was pre-ordained. "That race was rigged back in 1880 by General Lew Wallace."[76]

Naturally, Heston's personal involvement in so much of the filming meant he was routinely exposed to danger. Tasked with filming the action, second unit director Andrew Marton said the race "required the kind of director worry can't paralyze." Still, he had received strict instructions to do everything in his power to keep the principals safe. "If you curl one hair on their heads," producer Sam Zimbalist admonished Marton, before giving him *carte blanche* to put the important sequence on celluloid. Fortunately, the nature of the work did not deter any of the other actors. "Heston and Boyd did all the chariot driving they seem to be doing except for two stunts," Marton explained.[77]

The intricate work also required creativity, skill, and courage from the individuals tasked with the trickier elements of the filming. In one of the most exciting elements of the race, Yakima's son Joe Canutt flew into the air as his chariot careened over a wreck, producing jangled nerves and a four-stitch gash on the chin. Heston recalled watching as Joe hurtled over the chariot, "I thought he was a dead man." The dailies of the scene certainly overwhelmed Wyler. "We have to use that!" Yak knew that the script did not call for such a moment, and expressed his doubts before observing, "I promised Chuck he'd win this race. I don't believe

---

76 Martin, "I Call on Ben-Hur," 43.

77 Andrew Marton, "Ben-Hur's Chariot Race," *Films in Review* (Jan. 1960), 27-32, 48.

he can catch that chariot on foot." Then, in the Hollywood tradition, a fortuitous image became a reality on celluloid with footage of Heston climbing back into the chariot while the horses and the vehicle careened ahead to victory. "A scary shot," he concluded, "it scared me, anyway."[78] That shot became an indispensable part of one of the most dramatic races ever captured on film.

Marton's other task was to render the final showdown between Messala and Ben-Hur as realistically as possible. "In order to show the immediate danger in which they were," he explained, "I decided to pan from the interlocking and splintering wheels to the two antagonists in vicious combat." The effort required that "we had to chain the camera car to the two chariots." Marton insisted that he did not realize at the time "that if one horse stumbled, the whole contraption—horses, chariots, stars, camera-car—would crash and pile up in disaster."[79]

Though the finished sequence still had to be shaped by the cutting and editing process, Heston was exhilarated to have been part of staging the great race on celluloid. "A very exciting day today," he remarked on July 2, "racing past those screaming extras over the finish line was as thrilling a thing as I've done in pictures, I think." Lydia, Fraser, and others were on hand to view the scene as well to capture the occasion personally.[80]

Heston continued putting pieces together for the race, noting on July 7 that he "spent most of it roaring by Steve's bloody and twitching form on the sand and then turning off to go back for my victory wreath while he's carried limply off." On the same day, miles away in California, Heston's father Russ was proceeding with work on the site of the Coldwater Canyon home. The actor could not help but contemplate, "When, I wonder, will we finish?"[81]

In the meantime, there was yet more chariot work to complete. "If I come out of this picture with nothing else," Heston thought, "I'll at least be able to drive a wagon in and out of the scene in the next western I do." He had put enormous effort into mastering the task in order to look creditable on film. "Charioteering is a fairly hardwon [sic] and largely useless skill," he observed, "but one I take some pride in." The next day, he pronounced that, outside of unexpected requirements,

78 Heston and Isbouts, *Hollywood*, 110.

79 Marton, "Ben-Hur's Chariot Race," 27-32, 48.

80 "July 1958, 2 Wednesday," *On the Set*.

81 "July 1958," 7 Monday," ibid.

"I finally won the race, and conceivably drove my last chariot. All I can say is that it's been quite a race!"[82]

As the summer of the shoot reached a boiling point, MGM executives were thrilled to learn that a survey indicated that over half of the respondents already "knew about" *Ben-Hur*, which according to one scholar represented "the highest percentage ever recorded for an upcoming film." Billboards splashed the news to drivers on the New Jersey Turnpike and MGM operators greeted callers with "*Ben-Hur* is coming." Displays and supplemental materials ranging from casual consumers to schools and church congregations brought still more attention to the public. Because of the Lew Wallace connection, publicity for the movie even tied into coverage of the impending centennial of the Civil War.[83]

Besides concluding the race, August brought another dimension to the picture. "A whole new set, whole new sequence, new costumes, and with Jack Hawkins beginning work, even a new character," Heston explained on the 25th. Yet, the freshness of the shift in focus to this part of the storyline offered a sobering moment as well. While working through the scene where Quintus Arrius adopted Ben-Hur as a son for saving his life at sea, Heston noticed an odd detail. "Wandering through the garden, I caught sight of Leo Genn's costume from *Quo Vadis* on the back of an elderly extra. I wonder what future epic will find a place in the background for the fancy gold and green getup I'm wearing?"[84]

Extremes of heat and cold on location added to the demands on cast and crew. The discomfort evident in the galley hold did not extend to performers alone, as the technicians had to fit into tightly cramped spaces scorched by lights. "This damned slave galley is exactly that," Heston remarked. "Hottest set I've ever worked in and those damned oars are *heavy*, especially at six P.M." Of course, if the actor could retire to better conditions for the evening, his character could not, and the melding of fact and fiction continued when Heston's Ben-Hur and Jack Hawkins's Arrius later spent uncomfortable time on a cold, wet set awaiting their screen rescue after their naval battle. At the end of the month he declared, "Today was, in terms of pure physical effort, probably as hard as I've ever worked in any part. We spent the morning doing shots of the rowing, including the change of speeds Arrius tests

82 "August 1958, 8 Friday," "August 1958, 9 Saturday," ibid.

83 Solomon, *Ben-Hur*, 768-770.

84 *ALJ*, 55, 56.

Judah with. A real bone-breaker." One solace was the family members watching, "ensconced on a side bench."[85]

According to Heston, the difficult work belied the common perception of a coddled film star. "For an epic you struggle across some of the most exotic and uncomfortable landscapes of the earth for month after month of sixty hour weeks, wondering whoever called acting a glamorous way to make a living." In the case of *Ben-Hur*, an exhausted Heston observed to his director, "We've been shooting in Rome all year, and I'm anxious to go home . . . but I'm damned if I expected to row all the way!"[86]

The script had been a point of contention from the beginning, with Wyler accepting the project based on one version and other contributors entering to improve the original or subsequent drafts. Complications arose as various interpretations entered the writing process. Writer Gore Vidal always maintained that he saw the Judah Ben-Hur and Messala relationship as latently homosexual in nature. Heston was as adamant in insisting that Vidal's version never made it past the earliest stages. He and the next writer, Christopher Fry, lamented a Hollywood-style complexity. "If I were writing an original screenplay instead of adapting a semiclassic novel, I wouldn't have the girl's role in the story at all," Fry explained at the time. "The significant emotional relationship is the love/hate between Messala and Ben-Hur. The audience knows this, and they're not interested in the Ben-Hur/Esther story." Heston agreed. "There really is no *place* for the love story here." Generally appearing less confident in such situations, Heston's interpretations of his characters worked best when they were engaged in more wide-ranging pursuits than in the intimate moments of love and passion.

Vidal later insisted that he broached the subject of a latent sexual attraction between the one-time friends and future antagonists, only to have the director insist that nothing be said to Heston lest the matter distress him. Interestingly, in 1961, Heston considered an opportunity to work with Otto Preminger on *Advise & Consent*, with that director offering him the role of Brig Anderson. At the time, Heston recorded his view of the character and the role. "I'm not put off by the homosexual angle," he noted, "but the part isn't very interesting. Anderson is acted upon rather than acting." For the performer who balked at taking an ensemble part in *The Big Country*, even with the certainty of working with Gregory Peck and William Wyler, this reasoning should not have surprised anyone. In this case,

85 "Tues., Sept. 9th," "Mon., Sept. 15th," "'Ben Hur' Diaries"; "September '58, 30 Tuesday," *On the Set*.

86 "Mammoth Movies I Have Known," 5, Heston Papers, Writings and Papers, f.485, HL.

rather than accept "essentially a static character," regardless of his sexual orientation, Heston saw another part as more compelling. "The role of Senator Cooley," he added enthusiastically, "would be a plum . . . I'll try to buck for that."[87]

Subsequently, when Herman Citron asserted his client's case, Preminger indicated a preference for Spencer Tracy, causing Heston to remark, "[W]ho can blame him?" Neither he nor the "Iceman" could overcome the impasse, "so we walked away." For Heston, the breaking point was the part itself, not the nature of the character he might portray. Years later he observed of the casting of Senator Cooley, which finally went to Charles Laughton, "It was the part to play."[88]

Work found no abatement on Oct. 4, although "for a wonder, quit work by five thirty," which he declared was "WW's birthday present for me." Leaving the set to enjoy time with Lydia and a small contingent of friends, Heston recorded, "So here I am thirty five." After the gathering, he wrote, "I guess I could hardly hope to have come farther, halfway through my three score and ten." Additional work with the horses remained, and he said the animals turned in good performances. "I've played with many actors who didn't do as well." As the location work wound down, he could see the end more clearly. "Unless we do those added chariot shots I've seen the last of those white horses . . . till the premiere."[89]

Yet even as the actor strove to satisfy the demands of his career, sobering moments of another sort came for him and his colleagues when word arrived that Sam Zimbalist had died suddenly. "We were shocked with surprise to find, not an hour after I'd spoken with him on the set, that Sam Z. had died in his hotel. God!! You really'd better do it good, because when you're done . . . you're done!!" The next day, Wyler made a brief statement. "I'd settle for that myself, I think," Heston asserted, "to have men I'd worked with stop the cameras for a moment and think about me, while the work waited at hand."[90]

Only a short time later, Heston learned that Tyrone Power, who was just 44, had died from a massive heart attack while filming *Solomon and Sheba* near Madrid. "Ty Power's shockingly sudden death on set in Spain yesterday made me suddenly aware of my mortality," Heston admitted. "Appropriate time to think of it since we were shooting on our day off to take advantage of continuing fine

---

87 *ALJ*, 120.

88 Ibid.

89 "October 1958, 4 Saturday," "October 1958, 9 Thursday," *On the Set*.

90 "November 1958, 4 Tuesday," "November 1958, 5 Wednesday," *On the Set*.

weather." Heston then suffered two accidents in the course of what should have been routine scenes. "Neither blow disabling," he noted, "but both gave me pause, thinking of Ty."[91]

If thoughts of mortality crowded the production as it proceeded toward its close, numerous visitors graced the set, seeking to enjoy the experience before it ended. Heston was particularly delighted to see at least one such individual. "A face from the past appeared in the endless train of VIPs on our sets . . . Susan Hayward, very impressive and very welloff [sic] as a transplanted Georgian." He thought his former co-star looked "happy, but pressing a little."[92]

The pressure for a superior finished product continued to build on all involved. Production costs were adding up; the chariot race alone had drained one million dollars from studio coffers. Ticket sales would have to be virtually unprecedented to recoup the picture's budget. Heston was determined not to falter, even as the small injuries mounted. "This racket [is] sure not [the] padded refuge for idle boozehounds Hollywood novels make it out," he insisted. "Have been shooting ten and twelve hour days, six days every damn week, not to mention a few Sundays since May."[93]

In his November newsletter, he offered an assessment that displayed a reticence for prediction, but also a sense of excitement stirring in him from the material he had put on film. "I don't like to speak too early," he explained, "but this one looks like something VERY special." Dimensions alone were sure to make *Ben-Hur* very special indeed. Movie audiences would see the results from the enormous resources expended to create scenes meant to reflect the majesty and splendor of Rome and the protracted journey of Judah Ben-Hur. Heston later observed, "Metro has so many pictures with emphasis on huge dimensions that their publicists really drip superlatives." He concluded, "Anyhow, publicity departments can't help beating their drums about such things." Outside of these elements, there was another significant factor to consider: "Anyway, you can be sure that they'll be showing *Ben-Hur* somewhere for a long, long time to come. When you add that to *The Ten Commandments*—which passed the fifty-million-dollar admissions mark last January—before those two pictures have completed their merry-go-round, I'll have been seen by more people than any other actor in the history of the world."[94]

---

91 "Sun., Nov. 16th," "'Ben Hur' Diaries," 34. In his published journals, Heston noted that carrying a lighter stand-in for the actress playing Tirzah was part of this consideration; *ALJ*, 60-61.

92 *ALJ*, 61.

93 "Sun., Nov. 16th," "'Ben Hur' Diaries," 34.

94 Newsletter, November 11, 1958, HL; Martin, "I Call on Ben-Hur," 40.

Heston had been quite aware of what the film could mean for him. As he closed his journal for 1958, he tried to capture the essence of the completed work and the reception that awaited. "I suppose this is a pivotal year," he began, "half my three score and ten. In it I made the picture that may or may not be the best I'll ever make, but it'll certainly either finally press me into the thin, airless reaches where the supernovas drift or demonstrate conclusively that my orbit is a different one." Wyler had pushed him toward that higher trajectory as a performer, but the actor also carried within him the desire to excel. Hedging, he also revealed that inner source of propulsion. "Eaten though I am by the drive to that further space, I'm not sure I'd be unhappy with either end. That's probably because so much more happiness stems for me now from my family." Heston had much to celebrate at the end of a busy and productive year. "Whether the film I made turns out to be memorable or not, I know the year we spent making it will be . . . and Rome will mark us all forever."[95]

Indeed, 1959 would an important transition year for Charlton Heston. The final shooting and a quick flight to London for a premiere of *The Big Country* heralded the passage of two Wyler-Heston pictures into new phases. The Hestons were at sea heading back to the United States when word reached them of the passing of another legendary force in their lives: Cecil B. DeMille. "The death of a man of seventy-seven can hardly be surprising," he recorded in his journal, "but it shook me." He had no real opportunity to mourn in the traditional way, as DeMille's funeral took place before they landed, but the director's influence on his life and career was unmistakable.[96]

When he got back to Hollywood, Heston sat at the typewriter to record his reaction to DeMille's death. The legendary director had meant everything to the rising star, and had helped assure his place in the cinematic firmament. Heston appreciated what his role as Brad in *The Greatest Show on Earth* had meant, but the next DeMille assignment would surpass any other he had played. "As for the second part he gave me, who can measure how much a role like Moses means to an actor?"[97]

A flurry of travel across country by train and then in a new Corvette and a new Ford station wagon, including a stop in Detroit for an event "the Ford Motor people set up," kept the Hestons occupied until they reached Chicago for a brief

95 *ALJ*, 61.

96 Ibid., 65.

97 Newsletter, April 13, 1959, HL.

visit with his family. From there the caravan headed for California, with a stop in Oklahoma City to spend a little time with Jolly and Katherine West. Finally, the bedraggled travelers arrived in Los Angeles, where the new house and local chores awaited. "Falling back into the routine of this town was painless," Heston noted. A picture with Gary Cooper and the chance to play Macbeth did not seem possible at the same time, until a delay in one allowed an opportunity for the other. As usual, Citron worked his magic. Heston would get his deal for *Wreck of the Mary Deare*, with "a piece of the gross" and the chance to do *Macbeth* in Ann Arbor, Michigan. An evening dining with Laurence Olivier—"Now if I can meet Hemingway, I'll have it made"—and a lunch with Gary Cooper—"whom I've admired fervently clear back to when I could do it for ten cents"—represented a whirlwind of meaningful moments for him.

Heston was immersed in *Mary Deare* and glorying in his "Macbething," as well as carrying out a brief stint with *The State of the Union*, while awaiting the final work on *Ben-Hur*. Working tennis in when he could, the actor also fit in parties with Aristotle Onassis and a dinner and reception with Soviet Premier Nikita Khrushchev. Meanwhile, work slowed on the Coldwater house until his financial circumstances could improve, and the Hestons were interviewed as prospective adoptive parents.

Heston's money worries centered on tax issues with the Internal Revenue Service. With prodding from Herman Citron, he turned to Paul Ziffren to handle such matters. The accountant convinced his client that creating three corporations was necessary. "I trust all will be well," Heston observed, "but it's staggering to contemplate the commercial complexity of my career, suddenly." As biographer Marc Eliot described the transition, "Now he was big business."[98]

The most important domestic development was the completion of the Coldwater Canyon home. Heston took special pride in the role that his father, Russell, had played in supervising the project, and later sent him a note explaining the connection he felt and the importance it had in his life. "The mark of your hand will be on that whole ridge, and the house you built there . . . long after we're both dead and Fraser is living there as happily, I hope, as I know we will."[99] Russell's return to his son's life had meant everything to him, and the "House that Hur Built" would be the salient feature of the personal life that Charlton Heston allowed Chuck Heston to embrace.

---

98 *ALJ*, 77; Eliot, *Charlton Heston*, 187.

99 Ibid., 184.

Amid all this activity, and only a few days after his thirty-sixth birthday, Heston screened *Ben-Hur* at MGM Studios. He was delighted by what he saw. "I don't see how I could be surer, seeing a film I'd made, that it's good work," he concluded. Even so, he tried to temper his reaction. "My best frame of reference is my initial enthusiasm for *Ten Commandments* and this seems better. It's surely worth all the aching effort and painful months. This one should do it; this one should surely do it."[100]

Heston's sense of what the film could be was accurate. In a London press conference, he said he had not cared whether he played a villain or a hero. "Change is healthy," he observed, and "an actor thrives on diversity." Besides, a film was bound to be only as good as the director's ability to put his or her vision on celluloid, and, as Heston noted, "Willy's poorest film is good by any other standard." Even so, he noted that when the filming wrapped on January 7, 1959, Wyler had paused before dashing to catch a flight to London to observe to his star, "I hope I can give you a better part next time." His response, as captured in a journal entry, reflected his sentiments: "I hope we all gave him the masterpiece it should be." Heston later insisted, "*Ben-Hur* is not my favorite performance. I have *never* given a performance with which I was totally pleased."[101] He always maintained that the search for perfection was the elusive goal that spurred him on, but there was no doubt that *Ben-Hur* brought him to a higher level of respectability in his profession.

Perhaps the most profound critique of Heston's performance came in an open letter Wyler issued after filming. While some might view this correspondence as a publicity device, it nevertheless had an aura of sincerity:

> *Dear Chuck*: It is an old story among actors that in a film like *Ben-Hur* individual performances are swallowed up by the enormous size of everything else. As you know, I am not given to easy compliments, but I feel that your portrayal of Judah Ben-Hur is an acting achievement of the highest order.

With Wyler, compliments had not come lightly; they had tended not to come at all.

---

100 *ALJ*, 77.

101 Madsen, *William Wyler*, 333; "January 1959, 7 Wednesday," *On the Set*; David Resin, "20 Questions: Charlton Heston," *Playboy* (May 1983), 206.

The fact that audiences everywhere become deeply and emotionally involved in the story of Ben-Hur proves that you have succeeded in bringing him to life. Much gratifying praise has been showered on the film for its handling of the figure of Christ. I wonder how many people realize that they saw Him only mirrored in your face and felt His presence through your emotions. . . . It was a demanding role both physically and emotionally, and you approached it with intelligence and humility.[102]

Of course, the marketing wizards at MGM would do all they could to help to ensure the film's success. Their promotional campaign matched the epic/spectacle nature of the movie itself. As a result, in the words of one source, "*Ben-Hur* mania swept the nation." One student of the *Ben-Hur* phenomenon noted that the studio "wanted to make it clear to the industry that they intended to exploit this film thoroughly," including a soundtrack sold separately, and "a full schedule of pre-publicity more than eighteen months before the film was to be released and before principle photography had commenced." A volume devoted to the making of the picture published by Random House stoked additional interest through short essays, photographs, and removable end-pieces of the chariot race and the film's featured storylines. Newsreels also kept the film before the public, including one in which the actor greeted advance ticket buyers, signed autographs and shared coffee.[103]

Merchandizing offered the chance to place *Ben-Hur* in the formative minds of young people through coloring books, comics, and toys, all designed to capitalize on the film's popularity. Interest in the extravaganza continued decades later. Rusty Kern featured *Ben-Hur* products in the Christmas edition of *Playset Magazine* in 2006. "As a boy, I saw Ben-Hur many times when it first came out in Christmas, 1959," he recalled, noting that he had chosen the themed playset for his "big gift" that year. In the "Center Spread Story," he observed, "That Christmas, the spectacle of Ben-Hur carried right over to the pages of the Sears catalog," but was not buried in the traditional toy section. "This time, as if to make an unmistakable statement of greatness, there was a Ben-Hur playset in the front, spread over two huge pages and in full color." Children, or their parents, could select between three sizes, but key among the figures was the protagonist. "Ben-Hur is an exact likeness of Charlton Heston," the magazine's readership learned, "portrayed as

---

102 Martin, "I Call on Ben-Hur," 21.

103 Heston and Isbouts, *Hollywood*, 114; Solomon, *Ben-Hur*, 766; *The Story of the Making of Ben-Hur*; Peter Roberts, "Costliest Film Makes Screen History," "News of the Day," featured in the *Ben-Hur* Collector's Edition's bonus materials.

[the] avenging charioteer with arms outstretched holding unseen reins." Building on earlier concepts, Frank Rice at Louis Marx & Co. obtained licensing rights for the toy figures from the motion picture. "They wanted to promote it bigger and better than any film in history, and an offer was made for Louis Marx & Co. to get involved." Crafty promoting to the manufacturer, including tickets to an exclusive premiere of the movie, sealed the deal and development got underway for production of a playset of which few could "claim to be its equal."[104]

Ben-Hur's premiers became spectacles in themselves. Torrid advance ticket sales and star appearances, including by Heston, meant ample coverage in New York and Los Angeles as the film became box office bonanza. MGM's publicists continued to hype the picture as it moved into reissues. There was one constant, as Heston observed ten years later: "As most everyone knows, a chariot race is the highlight of the story." Noting the grueling practice and preparation, nothing outshone the last day of filming for the dramatic scene. "I've acted in some spectacular films since 'Ben-Hur,'" Heston closed, "but that race and that final day will remain in my memory forever."[105]

The time had flashed by as the kid from Michigan, Chicago, and Northwestern went from a struggling actor to a steadily working Hollywood personality and cinematic star. He juggled reading scripts and weighing offers to returning to the stage, particularly when this allowed both he and Lydia to tread the boards. "We wrapped up a deal to do State of the Union in Santa Barbara with Lydia," he noted in July. "We've come a long way since doing that play in North Carolina in '47."[106]

He remained gripped by nostalgia later in the month while in Chicago. "It's good to be back in the settling, Midwestern frame house, reeking with reminiscence," he observed. "That wide, summer-green veranda is still the essence of adolescence for me, as the dusty St. Helen trail roads are the essence of my boyhood."[107]

Lydia did some exploring of her own when the Hestons returned to Los Angeles. "We arrived before sunset and stopped at Coldwater, luxuriating in the growing feeling of home about the place," Heston noted in his journal. "A lovely evening with Lydia, searching out the house where I first stayed in Hollywood, when I came

104 *Playset Magazine* (Nov./Dec. 2006), 5, 15, 16, 17, 25.

105 Michael Fitzmaurice, "West Coast Welcomes Ben-Hur," *News of the Day*; Peter Roberts, "The Night Ben-Hur Came to Broadway," *News of the Day*; and Peter Roberts, "'VIP' Opening: Capital Welcome for Ben-Hur," *News of the Day*, *Ben-Hur* Collector's Edition DVD. See also Solomon, *Ben-Hur*, 778-779; Charlton Heston, "What it was Like to Drive that Famed 'Ben-Hur' Chariot," in "Exhibitor's Campaign Book from MGM" for *Ben-Hur*, 1969, 5.

106 *ALJ*, 73.

107 Ibid.

out alone for *Dark City*." Like so many things in a fast-transitioning world, however, changes had already occurred in the short intervening years. "It's gone now."[108]

The Hestons were in almost constant flux, with a busy schedule and the new house not yet ready to be occupied. One diversion offered myriad benefits, including a degree of normalcy, in the meantime. "I play a lot at the court at Park LaBrea," Charlton wrote, referencing tennis at their temporary abode. "[T]hey have a very great pro. I think it's a wonderful sport—no matter at what level you play the game, it can absorb you completely." He realized that another sport offered the chance for greater social interaction, but found it unsuitable to his circumstances. "Golf takes so much time—the greens always away out—it takes a half day just to drive there and back without playing."[109] His shyness also remained a factor. Heston knew concentrating on golf would have meant sacrificing some of the buffer to outsiders that he felt tennis provided.

In the midst of all his film work, Heston's public persona continued to flourish. In December 1959, *Look* magazine captured the imagery of the dramatic confrontation of the chariot race in a spread entitled "Ben-Hur Rides Again," and declared the remake "an expensive burst of confidence in the public's taste for lavish spectacles." The brief publicity piece offered tidbits to entice moviegoers that emphasized the complexity and enormity of the process for just this portion of the film: "Chariot race took three months to film," and "Nine chariots compete over 2½-mile course."[110]

A decade of persistent work had placed Charlton Heston in an incredible position. He was ending it in London, a city he loved, with Laurence Olivier, an actor and mentor he admired. "Today I lunched with Larry, which I've not yet been able to call him, of course," Heston professed in his journal. Warning signs of the stage production of *The Tumbler* were already there, despite Olivier's direction. "I'm still convinced I'll learn from this, however it turns out," Heston maintained.[111]

The London premiere of *Ben-Hur* came two days after the lunch with Olivier. Rave reviews for the film "included [the] sort of personal notices I'd been hoping for, fruitlessly, from [the] beginning," leaving Heston in a state of near euphoria. Mixing with "a sprinkling of royals" while indulging in a champagne party courtesy

---

108 Ibid., 74.

109 "Interview, Sept. 1, 1959," 7, Heston Papers, HL.

110 "Ben-Hur Rides Again," *Look* (Dec. 8, 1959), 62-63.

111 *ALJ*, 81.

of the director who had driven him to the performance of a lifetime, Heston wrote, "we all basked in [the] high tide of glory." He concluded, "I think we all earned it."[112]

A difficult moment arose at the end of the decade that had established him; it would have seemed insurmountable had it happened earlier. "Hedda doesn't love me anymore," he wrote just a few days after Christmas. Of his break with one of Hollywood's publicity power brokers, he wrote, "I'll survive without too many bruises, though certainly low on Hedda's list for life." The actor had initially agreed to be a guest on the columnist's televised special, *Hedda Hooper's Hollywood*, but chose to withdraw in favor of appearing with Ed Sullivan instead. Hopper, who had hoped to bring the current stars of *Ben-Hur*, Heston and Boyd, together with earlier ones, now insisted of the taping, "we played the scene without him, and we didn't miss him." When Sullivan predicted retaliation from the scorned party, Hopper responded that while she had no such intentions, she no longer considered the actor "a man of his word."[113]

Heston later recalled that what once would have been a career-threatening fiasco was not by this point. "As it was," he noted in comments in his published journals, "it was a two-day wonder and not worth that." Of course, at the time, he was not so sure. "L'affaire Hopper is growing into a major item," he worried on December 30, but his publicist, Bill Blowitz, "thinks it's all really working out OK." His answer was to write a letter explaining the matter from his perspective. He professed that "it's a silly thing to waste time over."[114]

All the while, plaudits came in for past performances and opportunities occurred for future ones, with Heston continuing to strive to perfect his craft. Still, he knew that the end of the decade brought a special sense of accomplishment to his career: "This year may have done it. *Ben* turned out to be everything we hoped for it, and very nearly everything *I* hoped for as well, though not utterly. During the year I became a better actor, and a happier man." Yet a strong urging and uncertainty remained: He wanted another chance to perform on the stage, which "might just make me the more-than-ordinarily-good actor I hunger to be."[115] As such assessments illustrated, there was always the internal demand for perfection, but with *Ben-Hur* he "may have done it," indeed.

112 "December 1959, 16 Wednesday," *On the Set*; *ALJ*, 81.

113 *ALJ*, 82; "Hopper vs. Sullivan, Heston Quits Hedda's Show as Feud Flares," *LAT*, Dec. 30, 1959; "Hopper and Sullivan Swap More Insults," *LAT*, Dec. 31, 1959.

114 *ALJ*, 82; Ibid.

115 "December 1959, 31 Thursday," *On the Set*; *ALJ*, 82.

Chapter Five

THE JOYS OF SETTING THE PACE
1960s

"I made it."

—Heston on his Academy Award, April 4, 1960

"It was a very stirring day. I'll never forget it, and I'm proud to have been part of it."

—Heston on the "March on Washington," August 28, 1963

Performances:

The Tumbler, New York, Feb. 24-27, 1960 (Kell)

The Annual Academy Awards, Apr. 4, 1960 (32nd); Apr. 5, 1965 (37th); Apr. 10, 1967 (39th)

The Steve Allen Show, April 11, 1960

The Ed Sullivan Show, May 1, 1960; Nov. 6, 1960; Mar. 31, 1968; June 9, 1968

Tiptoe Through TV, *The Revlon Revue*, May 5, 1960

The 12th Annual Primetime Emmy Awards, June 20, 1960

The Fugitive Eye, *Alcoa Premiere*, Oct. 17, 1961

An Old-Fashioned Thanksgiving, Nov. 21, 1961

El Cid, Dec. 6, 1961 (London); Dec. 14, 1961

The Milton Berle Spectacular, Mar. 9, 1962

At This Very Moment, Apr. 1, 1962

Diamond Head, Dec. 27, 1962 (Japan); Feb. 13, 1963 (Los Angeles)

The Pigeon that Took Rome, June 20, 1962

Perry Como's Kraft Music Hall, Jan. 30, 1963

The Merv Griffith Show, Feb. 18, 1963; Feb. 28, 1968; Dec. 29, 1969

The 20th Annual Golden Globe Awards, Mar. 5, 1963

55 Days at Peking, May 6, 1963 (United Kingdom); May 29, 1963 (New York)

The Fugitive Eye, *Kraft Mystery Theater*, July 17, 1963

The Patriots, *Hallmark Hall of Fame*, Nov. 15, 1963

A Tribute to John F. Kennedy from the Arts, Nov. 24, 1963

The World's Greatest Showman: The Legend of Cecil B. DeMille, Dec. 1, 1963

The Mike Douglas Show, Sept. 24, 1964, Sept. 25, 1964, Feb. 28, 1968

F.D.R., Jan. 8, 1965
The Greatest Story Ever Told, Feb. 15, 1965 (New York)
Major Dundee, Mar. 16, 1965 (New York)
The Jack Paar Program, Apr. 16, 1965
The Agony and the Ecstasy, Oct. 7, 1965
The War Lord, Nov. 17, 1965
The Eamonn Andrews Show, Dec. 12, 1965
A Man for All Seasons, Los Angeles; Miami, 1965, 1966
Cinema, Feb. 4, 1966
A Whole Scene Going, June 8, 1966
Khartoum, June 9, 1966 (London); June 15, 1966
The Linkletter Show, June 29, 1966
Jimmy, July 7, 1966
The Hollywood Stars of Tomorrow Awards, Jan. 28, 1967
Bogart, Apr. 23, 1967
Will Penny, Dec. 14, 1967 (London); Apr. 10, 1968
Elizabeth the Queen, Hallmark Hall of Fame, Jan. 31, 1968
Planet of the Apes, Feb. 8, 1968 (New York)
Counterpoint, Mar. 13, 1968 (New York)
The Joey Bishop Show, July 25, 1968
Dee Time, Apr. 19, 1969
The David Frost Show, July 18, 1969
Number One, Aug. 21, 1969
The Tonight Show with Johnny Carson, Nov. 20, 1969

The 1950s had been a whirlwind of acting and appearances that sent Charlton Heston across the globe to exotic locations and on a blistering schedule of promotional activities. A balm of sorts came when the family finally moved into their new home on the ridge. "Well, we made it at last," Heston recorded in his journal. "Tonight we slept under our own roof on the ridge where I stood dreaming over two years ago." Difficulties remained, not the least was the lack of carpeting, but family friends "brought champagne and bread . . . and we kindled our hearth appropriately."[1]

1 *ALJ*, 84.

Over the years since his first films, the actor had entered the advertising world as a pitchman or spokesperson for various products in conjunction with several of his roles; these ad campaigns frequently reflected his own interests and habits. Now his long recent shoot in Italy and his stature as an established Hollywood star offered him other opportunities for endorsements. "When in Rome, I do as I always do," a campaign for Bank of America opened, as Heston touted the security of saving with the banking institution wherever he happened to be at any given time. "You seem to get around a lot, Mr. Heston," the "us" representing the bank remarked. "Quite a bit," the well-traveled actor replied. "Paris. London. Vienna. Culver City." In each location, he did the "same thing I do in Rome" when it came to financial security and transactions.[2]

Indeed, Heston's recent world travels had included European capitals and sites, but another premiere of *Ben-Hur* took him to the Land of the Rising Sun. The highlight of that trip was the attendance of the Emperor, although the event featured breaks in the film that Heston attributed to the projectionist's "quivering at [the] Imperial presence." Still, the event affected the American as well. "Must say," he noted succinctly after a special audience at intermission, "I was impressed myself." Another day brought him to a dinner with Toshiro Mifune, about whom Heston marveled, "My God, what a presence. If he could act in English, he'd conquer the world."[3]

The new year brought a new level of professional attention to Heston, and also offered an important association for the man, who balanced his innate shyness with a public career. As a card-carrying member of the Screen Actors Guild, Heston affiliated himself as required with an organization that championed the rights of its members. He had often portrayed leaders in his films and in January 1960 he accepted a position on the Guild's board of directors as a replacement for actor James Whitmore. He advanced to the position of third vice president in 1961, served as second vice president from 1962 to 1965, and president in November 1965, serving for six terms. The steady pace of advancement meant that Heston had to share his creative undertakings with his administrative ones in a dynamic tension that remained with him for the rest of his career. One scholar noted that

2 Bank of America advertisement, *LAT*, Mar. 30, 1960.

3 *ALJ*, 91; Michael Fitzmaurice, "Japan's Emperor Goes to the Movies," from *News of the Day*, chronicled the Emperor's arrival and attendance in a rare public appearance. *Ben-Hur*, Collector's Edition DVD; *ALJ*, 91.

this element of his life "consumed more of Heston's time and energy than any of his many other public endeavors."[4]

Involvement at this level in the governance of the most significant entity in his professional life reflected the values Charlton Heston possessed and wanted to project to the world. He appreciated the struggles of those who had gone before him and expected to assume his fair share of responsibility to pave the way for those who would follow. He applied the same formula in every aspect of public life, including service to the nation, and remained proud that when opportunities arose, he often could meet them. Duty and obligation were as strong concepts for him as integrity, professionalism, and heritage, custom, or tradition. He understood well the notion that one could only have a chance to control the continuation of cherished institutions if one joined the race.

Many of the figures he portrayed reflected these concepts. Moses had served as a signature role for Heston as he built upon the success he had obtained in his earlier work under the legendary Cecil B. DeMille, but Judah Ben-Hur promised to place the actor in a rarely equaled stature. Indeed, as the movie continued to generate revenue and attention, it stood poised for Oscar recognition in every major category with eleven nominations.[5]

As the title figure in *Ben-Hur*, Heston received a nomination for Best Actor, placing his name alongside acting tour-de-forces Laurence Harvey, Paul Muni, Jack Lemmon, and James Stewart. Because of a busy schedule that had him returning from Japan just two days before the ceremony, Heston managed to avoid much of the hype associated with the extravaganza. On his "second" April 2, thanks to travel across the international dateline, the actor came back to a house "chaotic and full of relatives," relieved at an improvement in Lydia's mother's health. Though he noted a seeming "drift in the Academy odds slightly in my favor," Heston dismissed the whole phenomenon as "ridiculous."[6]

Amid understandably heightened pressure and attention, the Hestons made their appearance at Pantages Theatre on April 4 for the Thirty-Second Academy Awards. Certainly, competitiveness marked the desire most performers felt about awards in their industry. But Heston recalled that, whatever he might have been thinking, at least one individual was especially gracious on awards night. "I hope

---

4 "Charlton Heston, 1965-1971," SAG-AFTRA, www.sagaftra.org/charlton-heston, accessed Oct. 17, 2018; Raymond, *Cold, Dead Hands*, 89.

5 Solomon, *Ben-Hur*, 786-787; Eliot, *Charlton Heston*, 196-197.

6 *CHA*, 230; *ALJ*, 91.

you win, Chuck, I really mean that," Jimmy Stewart confided quietly as they arrived at the Pantages. "I don't know of another actor alive who would've said such a thing," Heston noted gratefully. "He's an extraordinary man."[7]

Selected for his work in *Anatomy of a Murder*, Stewart may have felt compelled to be positive as he and his wife stood with the Hestons under the glare of the flashbulbs in the lobby, but the fact remained that he could have kept any such sentiments to himself. Heston certainly appreciated the gesture and seemed to recognize in his colleague the key ingredient to success in their shared profession. "He was the quintessential American face," Heston reflected on Stewart after the latter's death. "He loved the work and respected the people who made him a star."[8] This observation was as telling of the man who had made it as it was of the subject of his comments.

Throughout the evening, *Ben-Hur* shattered the competition as one after another of the film's nominees emerged as winners in their respective categories. Then, when Susan Hayward stepped forward, the former co-star of *The President's Lady* had the distinct pleasure of adding Charlton Heston's name to that exclusive list. "I made it," he recorded in the aftermath of the exhausting but exhilarating event. He also enjoyed a moment with the man who had pushed him to a level of undisputed excellence in a performance, and who received yet another Oscar for his own work on this film. "I guess this is old hat to you," he quipped to director William Wyler backstage. "Willy's" reply contained the wisdom of experience and the joy of recognition by one's peers that made all the hard work pay off. "Chuck," he noted, "it never gets old."[9]

Hollywood columnist Louella Parsons recorded the winner's reaction for her readers in the afterglow of the ceremony. "Charlton Heston grabbing on to his wife with one hand and his 'best actor' Oscar with the other, came over to where I was sitting. He was so excited that even while he was eating dinner he kept hold of his Oscar." Another Los Angeles correspondent remarked, "Heston made no attempt to hide his jubilation over his triumph in the motion picture industry's annual decoration ceremony. 'It's sweet, I tell you,' he said. 'It tastes good.'"[10]

---

7 Peter Roberts, "'Oscar' Likes Ben-Hur," *News of the Day*, *Ben-Hur* Collector's Edition DVD; *CHA*, 233.

8 Marc Eliot, *Jimmy Stewart: A Biography* (New York, 2006), 412.

9 "April 1960, 4," *On the Set*; *ALJ*, 91.

10 Louella Parsons, "Brynner Mexico Problem solved," *Los Angeles Examiner*, Apr. 6, 1960, Ben-Hur miscellaneous, Heston Papers, f.50, HL; Jack Smith, "Oscar Winners Rise to Face a Wonderful, Wonderful World," *LAT*, Apr. 6, 1960, HL.

The celebration continued into the night. Walter Seltzer later recalled that a bout with the flu had kept him from attending the ceremony, but that at 2:00 a.m. a knock sounded at his door. A giddy Heston, accompanied by Lydia and a small host of friends and well-wishers, had descended upon the producer's home. Illness faded as the rapturous evening gave way to a dawn of anticipation for a career that now boasted the industry's highest recognition.[11]

Some individuals seemed to believe that the *Ben-Hur* stampede had carried Heston across this particular finish line, just as surely as Yakima Canutt's assurance that his character would win the film's predetermined race. Before he completed a biographical treatment of the actor, writer Marc Eliot produced a volume on James Stewart that was less than laudatory of the 1960 Oscar recipient. "A respectable round of applause followed," he explained of the announcement for Best Actor. "No one in Hollywood ever thought Heston was much of an actor, with his blustery, pompous style and his granite, immovable face. But he was the star of the biggest film of the year and to the voters of the Academy, that mattered."[12]

If he sensed any such sentiment, Charlton Heston could have cared less. He was understandably elated, and dutifully shared as much as he could of the extraordinary moment with his fans in his next newsletter. "I can remember the same kind of happy night, all night long, the night I opened on Broadway for the first time, some years ago," he explained in May. He grasped and appreciated the full sense of the moment, but also felt the nagging element of the fleeting nature of it all. "But life doesn't hold many nights like that," he reflected soberly, before closing genuinely, "I'll never forget this one."[13]

The special night was not three days past when the Screen Actors Guild called on him to assist a negotiating committee. "Flattered to be asked, interested to think I could help," Heston cleared his schedule and "went over." He recalled, "We sat there all day, arguing, caucusing, confronting grimly across long tables." Heston attained useful experience in such professional service engagement but found time to have "shoehorned a Christmas seal film appeal (the only filming in town not struck)," before returning to the negotiations, which eventually produced a deal. "The contract's good, and fair," he concluded, "I'm proud to've helped to get it."[14]

11 *This Is Your Life*, February 26, 1981, 33-34, HL.

12 Eliot, *Jimmy Stewart*, 333.

13 Newsletter, May 1, 1960, HL.

14 *ALJ*, 92.

Interestingly, for an actor who typically shunned the political spotlight, Heston also accepted the title of honorary mayor of Los Angeles. On April 21, he "finally" was "installed" in the honorific post "at a large lunch, much ceremony, and [with] a weighty chain of office." In his short remarks, the actor thought he had "faked a better-than-so-so speech, ad-libbed during dessert." Pulling off the effort effectively on this occasion, he warned himself to avoid a method he dramatically noted was "as dangerous as Russian roulette." He thought he might not be so fortunate on another occasion: "Someday I'll fall right on my ass."[15]

The actor's success brought renewed attention to the man behind the character that had won him the ultimate recognition for acting in film. A *Look* magazine piece featured the Hestons' Coldwater Canyon home in May 1960. He was proud of what the new home meant to him and his family. Now, readers of a popular magazine were allowed to explore the floor plans and photographs of "the house that Ben-Hur built," although that work had preceded the film shoot. Labeled a "showplace" and "one of the finest examples of modern architecture in the U.S.," the $150,000 house incorporated elements from places Heston had seen on location, including a giant doorknob from the movie house of Hur.[16]

Two years later, he was still talking about the house and opening the property to another writer and photographer, this time from *American Home* magazine. The complex included a parking garage, tennis court, open courtyard, and "three-jet fountain" surrounding the glass and stone home. "Before we decided to build, we thought we might buy a big old house and remodel it," Heston explained when he returned home to greet the guests with Fray and Drago, their German Shepherd puppy, in tow. "Now we're glad we didn't." To support the equipment he had wanted for his work, the new house required "eight miles of wiring." The Hestons had allowed the project to develop at its own pace, adding furniture and other accessories as they went, including a dining table the actor designed that friend and fellow performer Milburn Stone constructed. "Our house was finished in February, 1960," he observed. "But because of 'Ben-Hur' I'd actually lived in it less than a month." Though tweaks continued, the actor was enormously satisfied, and looking out over the tree-lined landscape declared, "I almost feel it's my boyhood

---

15 Ibid., 93. Emilie Raymond noted that he referenced Thomas Jefferson and the virtues of limited government in his remarks. See Raymond, *Cold, Dead Hands*, 65.

16 "July 1958," 7 Monday," *On the Set*; Bill Davidson, "The House that Ben-Hur Built," *Look* (May 24, 1960), 56.

home in Michigan." Then, perhaps catching himself, he concluded, "I don't feel transplanted. I feel at home. It's a great feeling."[17]

He recognized that the house, like the person connected with it, could produce extravagant impressions. "I know about the Charlton Heston stories," he once observed wryly, concerning an allegation of near-constant playing of the soundtrack from his Academy Award-winning film in the Coldwater Canyon complex. "But it wasn't the only music, and if you had made as much money as I did from *Ben-Hur*, you'd like to be reminded of it too."[18]

The new home also offered chances to illustrate the Heston humor. In 1960, on a segment of *The Bob Crane Show*, which aired on KNX-CBS Radio, he observed that his downhill neighbors were calling his holdings on top of the ridge "Mount Sinai." With respect to the staff that had provided his Moses with an instrument to perform God's will, he lightheartedly insisted that "[m]y franchise on that stick has run out. I tried to part the swimming pool the other day and it didn't even ripple." Not to be outdone, comedian-host Crane, who later found his own niche on television's *Hogan's Heroes*, responded, "You've actually refused to walk on other people's water when you are swimming in their pools."[19]

Better Homes and Gardens also chose the *Ben-Hur* star to highlight hobby ideas that people could employ for diversion and personal fulfillment. A cover photograph set in the "Heston kitchen" featured the actor preparing the opening course of a meal. "Aside from driving chariots in *Ben-Hur*, Charlton Heston knows his way when it comes to the salad bowl," the caption offered. "Salad making is a good hobby for busy men—even Academy Award winners like Mr. Heston can find time for this at-the-table artistry."[20]

Despite his efforts to appear unchanged to a public that was now more anxious than ever to read and learn more about him, Heston realized that his circumstances were no longer the same. "After *Ben-Hur* won all the Oscars," he wrote later, "I did understand that my situation had altered, radically." He recognized the importance of trying not to saturate the market with similar characterizations, seeing the opportunity he now had to "use the freedom of my contract to work as widely as

17 Jim Liston, "At Home with Charlton Heston," *The American Home* (May 1962), 16, 60–61.

18 Hamill, "Heston: Larger Than Life," 89–90.

19 *The Bob Crane Show*, KNX-CBS Radio, 1960, www.youtube.com/watch?v=8b2tPQ5Cc48, accessed June 11, 2018.

20 *Better Homes and Gardens* (Nov. 1960), cover, 4.

I could, and wanted to get top dollar for the films I chose, trading on my role in the Academy's Best Picture."[21]

He had to adapt to this new situation, taking special care not to succumb to the snares of success. Of course, Lydia was in the best position to help keep him grounded. Still, Charlton Heston could look back on the first year of the new decade with an understandable air of personal satisfaction. "Anyway," he observed in December, "1960 was the year that carried me to several corners of the world, a new house, and the peak of my profession."[22] He had come a long way from Michigan and the cold water flat in New York City and was justifiably proud of what the house on "my ridge" and the Best Actor statuette represented.

From another vantage point, his home became essential to Heston's well-being. When a colleague alluded to a theatrical element, jesting that the actor could use the high ground to repel "invaders," Heston's response revealed more than he might have intended. "You bet. Up here, they can't get me."[23] In many ways, the house on "my ridge" could keep the man and his family at a respectable distance from the people who had helped him put it, and them, there. Conversely, this sense of distance and security also freed him to concentrate on the projects fans now expected from him in order to sustain the career that would continue to make all this possible.

Moses had meant an entrée for Heston in almost any venue, but winning an Academy Award for *Ben-Hur* created a fever pitch of activities for the actor. Between working and promotion, he found little time for anything else. "So far, this has been one of the most travelled years I've ever known," he observed. Opportunities to visit other nations gave him an even greater appreciation for what foreign markets meant to his career and his bottom line. He spent a good portion of his August 1960 newsletter touting the ways in which moviegoers in the Philippines embraced his work.[24]

His sudden, frequent junkets led to an incident that further illustrated the "Heston humor." As he explained, "When I got on the jet on the first leg of my flight to Italy, two days later, the same hostess that had just taken me West met me at the door. 'Mr. Heston,' she giggled, 'here's a script you left in your seat the other

21 *CHA*, 236, 114.

22 *ALJ*, 105.

23 Munn, *Charlton Heston*, 100.

24 Newsletter, August 30, 1960, HL.

day, and I haven't even had a chance to turn it in to Lost and Found yet."[25] Heston did not identify the project or the degree to which its loss would have affected his future endeavors, but he was certainly traveling abroad as often as ever to promote his work.

Returning to the stage was still both a viable option and an outlet. Heston's involvement in an odd play called *The Tumbler* proved short-lived, but it allowed him to work with Laurence Olivier. From the ruins of a prematurely ended cast party, he nevertheless managed to extract lessons from the master. One of the most significant of these insights occurred amidst the gathering's funereal atmosphere. As word filtered into the wrap party concerning how substantially *The Tumbler* had failed with critics in soon-to-be published reviews, the attendees began to drift away. Heston remained behind with Olivier, serving as a companion after the news had doomed the production to a short run. "Well, I suppose you learn to ignore the bad notices," the younger man offered to console his mentor. "Laddie, it's much harder, and much more important," Olivier replied stoically, "to learn to ignore the good ones." Perhaps with this wisdom in mind, Heston explained later, "I got bad notices, but I never believed them."[26]

Beneath Olivier's observation lay a deeper meaning that Heston also came to grasp. "The downside to celebrity is the damage to your character—you start believing your press clippings." It would be hard to determine when Heston came to this conclusion, but Olivier's insight in the context of a bitter theatrical disappointment remained with him. "Still, celebrity is a corrosive condition," the younger man noted, "and I think I was lucky it came to me slowly, so I could adapt."[27]

Another powerful and lasting piece of wisdom from Olivier was an observation that Heston believed he could employ as circumstances dictated future challenges in his own career. "Sometimes the gods inspire a performance, and then the actor can do no wrong, but the actor must also prepare a performance for the night the gods do not attend."[28]

---

25 Newsletter, "Hollywood-on-the-Tiber," Oct. 17, 1961, HL.

26 "October 20th [1988] Thursday USIA Tour Day #2," *BD*, 152; *CHA*, 226. See also a slight variation of the exchange in Donald Spoto, *Laurence Olivier: A Biography* (New York, 1992), 296; Richardson, "Heston," *Esquire* (July 2001), 66.

27 Rader, "If I Ran & Won," 7.

28 Holden, *Laurence Olivier*, 342.

Despite these difficult circumstances, Heston recognized the rare position he held. "I'm the only one who came out of it with any profit," he remarked of his time with the ill-fated play. Others suffered to one degree or another from the fiasco. "But I got out of it precisely what I went in for," he observed, "the chance to work with Olivier." Heston admired the man he considered one of the best practitioners in the business, and was willing to absorb what he could from him. "I learned more from him in six weeks than I ever would have learned otherwise." Interestingly, as a practitioner himself, anxious to improve as much as possible, he concluded that he left the period "a better actor, with more responsibility."[29]

Charlton Heston knew he had to move forward in spite of this setback. The success of *Ben-Hur* buffered him from such temporary reverses and opened new paths for him. He also understood the trade-offs necessary for continued advancement and took the balance between stage and screen, as well as commercial and intellectual properties, in stride. "An actor has to have a commercial success every so often or you don't get other parts," he explained in recognition of his profession's prime directive.[30]

Although the play he had undertaken with Olivier proved disappointing, Heston had the opportunity to see other dynamic leaders at work. One was a colleague from the acting community who had accepted the lead in negotiations on behalf of the Screen Actors Guild. SAG president Ronald Reagan impressed his friend with a deftness in handling the situations the union faced; this prompted Heston to consider Reagan a model for his own future roles in leadership. "Public service—pursuing a group agenda for a common goal—was a new experience for me," he recalled later. As Heston observed, Reagan seemed to possess the necessary traits for the task, having demonstrated himself to be "patient, persistent, moderate, and above all, good-humored, even at three in the morning, going back into caucus to review the same ground yet again." "I saw Ronald Reagan clear in those hours," he observed. Then, when he staggered home exhausted and Lydia asked how the day had gone, Heston replied, "Pretty slow work. But I do believe we've got a leader."[31]

Reagan drew interesting lessons from this period that would apply to Heston as well when the latter became SAG's primary negotiator. Noting that he did not believe his toughness at the table affected his career negatively, Reagan explained,

29 Munn, *Charlton Heston*, 102.

30 Eliot, *Charlton Heston*, 376.

31 D. Erik Felten, ed., *A Shining City: The Legacy of Ronald Reagan* (New York, 1998), 236; *CHA*, 237.

"[Y]ou become typecast in their minds on the basis of what they know about you off screen. They stop thinking of you as an actor." He added, "The image they have of you isn't associated with your last role, but with the guy who sat across the conference table, beefing." Heston likely found this conclusion concerning, given his determination to always be an actor first and foremost. Reagan concluded that such a situation was tantamount to "death," but added, "You develop a sort of aura. People even forget in time how you came to have it. Your name just doesn't come up when parts are being discussed."[32]

On his thirty-seventh birthday, a reflective Heston observed, "I can't complain about a year in which I won the Oscar, but I'd like to have worked more. I must learn to work with this problem, I suppose . . . how to work often enough to satisfy my appetite for acting and still do worthwhile things." Nevertheless, he closed his journal entry on a positive, if tentative, note pertaining to his next project: "Let's hope *El Cid* is that."[33] He had already been at work in Europe on *El Cid* when, at the beginning of February 1961, he let his newsletter readers know the latest inside information on his film. "It'll be hard work and long hours, but I'll have the same advantage I did in that chariot race: I'm bound to win!"[34]

The film centered on Rodrigo Díaz de Vivar, the legendary "Cid" of Spain, in whom Heston found a character of enormous appeal. The Cid had remained loyal to a king who provided him with every provocation to turn against the crown, including holding the warrior's wife and children as prisoners to compel his fealty. Instead, the soldier remained true of his own volition, as Heston noted, "surely one of the outstanding examples of loyalty in history." His final sacrifice came when he succumbed to his battle wounds, but with the help of his wife and associates, rose in lifelessness to ride out in glory and into legend, scattering the enemy troops who had heard rumors of his death and now saw him inexplicably leading his men into the fight against them. Heston's appreciation of these leadership qualities began with the Cid's ability to "inspire men to follow him" and he acceptance of the responsibility for leading them. To the actor, the figure from Spanish history and lore was not unlike Winston Churchill in the "black days" of the battle of Britain or Mahatma Gandhi as a "dauntless warrior," albeit on a far different battleground.[35]

---

32 Ronald Reagan, *An American Life* (New York, 1990), 131.

33 *ALJ*, 101.

34 Newsletter, Feb. 1, 1961, HL.

35 *CHA*, 255; "1961 Vintage Radio Interviews with Charlton Heston," *El Cid*, The Weinstein Corporation, 2008, DVD.

Just as with *Ben-Hur*, this latest motion picture presented Heston with inimitable moments, such as the Cid's ride into immortality. Another instance came when shooting the scene in which Heston's character entered the city of Valencia amidst a horde of supporters shouting their joy at the victory over the oppressive Moors. The adoration reflected the aura that continued to surround the historic figure in a way that the actor did not have to imagine. "You don't have to act that," Heston explained without meaning to exaggerate the effect. "You can't act it. . . . I know, in my bones and blood, what it is to take a city."[36]

Presentation was critical in the creative world Charlton Heston inhabited. How one presented oneself and the degree to which any performer engaged with his audience could make or ruin any performance or shape a career. For Heston this imperative, coupled with the physicality he brought to many of his roles, defined his characters and himself as an actor. Whether rowing a Roman galley, wielding a weapon, or riding a horse in combat, he had to be prepared to take on the physical aspects as well as the associated lines and camera angles to make the bargain with the ticket-buying people in the seats work. "I have to be fit," he explained. "If I wasn't, these parts would almost kill me." This requirement fed his passion for working out, especially by running or playing tennis. In 1963, he observed, "Most of the people I work with know there's always a racquet tucked into my baggage and schedule a match for me when it can be squeezed in." He said the obsession began when he was in his twenties, "too late to learn to do it very well," but insisted in his self-deprecating way that over his lifetime he had still managed to trade volleys "with more great players than any other lousy player in the world."[37]

All this effort was a matter of remaining in good trim, but it was more. "I'm a critical observer of my waistline," he admitted, understanding how important it was for an audience to believe the man they were watching on the screen plausibly filled the physical parameters of the role. "An actor's body is his crucial tool," he observed, "like a concert pianist's Steinway. If it's out of tune, you don't do very well."[38] Even more importantly, any serious lapse would be impossible to hide from discerning viewers, damaging the credibility of the work itself.

---

36 *CHA*, 256. The actor and publicity associated with the film used "Bivar" in preference over "Vivar," ibid. See also "Long Synopsis of Samuel Bronston's 'El Cid,'" and "Interesting Facts about El Cid and His Times," El Cid publicity, Heston Papers, f.74, HL. For Vivar, see William D. Phillips, Jr., and Carla Rahn Phillips, *A Concise History of Spain* (Cambridge, UK, 2010), in which the authors spelled Heston's first name "Charleton," 68.

37 Newsletter, July 18, 1963, "Hollywood, California," HL; *CHA*, 563.

38 Munn, *Charlton Heston*, 107; *CHA*, 396.

The physicality Heston displayed in this film added to the heroic persona he had already established for himself. Indeed, one longtime Hollywood camera operator thought the sword-fighting scenes in *El Cid* impressive. "When this guy gets a sword in his hand, look out. And I don't mean one of them foils Errol Flynn used to use. I mean one of them big, mean, heavy, two-handed jobs."[39]

For all his physical capabilities, training, and focus, Heston's swordplay nearly proved catastrophic when, after a long day of filming a key duel scene, he moved in the wrong direction. "I damn nearly had my head cut off today," he recorded, admitting that he "came home a touch shaken." The expertise of his professional sparring partner, standing in for the opposing actor, prevented anything more resulting from the incident than jangled nerves. Heston tried to treat the moment as routine, but his assessment of another script reflected his continuing disquiet over this incident: "I don't want another swash to buckle now, either."[40]

With respect to *El Cid*, Heston believed he had once more debunked "the old wives' tale, supported for years by cautious film executives, that movie fans do not like to see their favorites die in motion pictures." He felt the record supported numerous individuals who had made careers out of such elements, including his mentor, Laurence Olivier. "As one who has met his end by being trampled into a swamp by Jennifer Jones in *Ruby Gentry*, frozen to death on the moors in *Wuthering Heights*, and squashed under a tiger's cage in *The Greatest Show on Earth*, I can speak with some authority about dying well for my art." Still, he added, as he had done in *El Cid*, "The trick is to die in bed."[41]

The film also provided Heston with unique opportunities for enjoying the culture of modern Spain while promoting the film. He remembered riding one of the two matched stallions that served as his movie warhorse into a bull-fighting venue. "I was to lead the parade around the arena, with much attendant media coverage." Observing that he and the film "were a very hot item that year" Heston delighted the audience by hoisting son Fray from the ground into the saddle "in front of me as we galloped out to wild applause." The screen actor, arena showman, historic personage, and the star's young son combined to leave an indelible

---

39 Hamill, "Heston: Larger Than Life," 88.

40 *ALJ*, 104.

41 "Press Information Department Samuel Bronston Productions, Inc." Release, "Rome, Italy," *El Cid* publicity, HL. In DeMille's circus picture, although the actor felt as if death was a possibility, his character actually survived.

impression upon all who witnessed the scene. "Oh, we were the cat's pajamas," he concluded.[42]

Indeed, this motion picture came to represent something of the transition that Charlton Heston was undergoing as he advanced into superstardom, with its attendant complications. At a restaurant, he noted the gathering of an enthusiastic crowd outside of the area he and the rest of the party occupied. "Now, there's true Spanish courtesy for you," he observed. "Anywhere else, they'd be all over us by now. Here, they wait till we finish eating." Bent upon fulfilling his public role regarding people who were likely to buy tickets to his movie, Heston insisted upon remaining behind while the others left for the vehicles that would whisk them back to their hotel. "I really have to sign autographs for these people," he explained. The gesture illustrated both a conscientiousness and an innocent degree of haughtiness that Heston related with his usual self-deprecating humor. "Of course they ignored me completely," he recalled of the mass of individuals who were not waiting for him after all but had gathered to watch a soccer match just beginning on television. He concluded, dryly, "Ah, fame!"[43]

Celebrity appeared to have a rougher edge when *New York Tribune* writer Marie Tone offered biting observations. "Viewers are becoming accustomed during holy season to the imposing presence of Charlton Heston as he represses the acting urge to give Bible readings on *The Ed Sullivan Show*." For Tone, the actor's choices indicated he had in recent years "contributed more recitations to TV than acting performances." Still, there was no doubt that Heston was progressing in his profession. "My first part on TV twelve years ago paid me $65 and that included two weeks rehearsal," she quoted him as explaining. "My first lead role paid me $125, and that also included two weeks rehearsal." New contracts had since expanded that level of renumeration appreciably.[44]

In the meantime, Heston was in the process of wrapping the long shoot and preparing for the journey back to the United States when he received an unusual invitation. Director Sam Bronston had already showered him with praise for his portrayal and the positive reception the movie was receiving from distributors. "This was my first exposure to the kind of treatment *stars* get," Heston explained. In addition to a Jaguar XKE, however, Bronston wanted the actor and the family

---

42 *CHA*, 255-256.

43 Ibid., 257-258.

44 Marie Tone, "Heston Blames Unions in Part for Poor Shows," *Detroit Tribune*, Apr. 22, 1961 (reprinted from *New York Tribune*, Apr. 4).

to enjoy a final weekend in Rome, "on him, as an extra bonus." The tired performer declined the offer, only to receive a call that elaborated on the matter. One of Bronston's assistants said the vacation was actually an important, grand reception, and it was vital that Heston make an appearance. "I know how ri-sponsif you are to de neets of publicity," the caller prompted. "Mike, I've done at least a hundred interviews and a dozen receptions since we started this film," Heston replied. "When you open it, I'll do several hundred more." With a bit more coaxing, however, Heston agreed to fly over for the event. "So I did, of course," he recalled. "Making movies is a curious business."[45]

Aside from such public appearances, Heston crammed as much family time into his days as circumstances allowed. April saw the end of much of the primary work on *El Cid*. After meeting with film industry folks in Rome and returning to Madrid to rejoin his family, Heston took in the chateaux of the Loire Valley and the Bayeux tapestry before heading to the shores of Normandy. "It was still raining, but it should be when you see the D-day beaches," he noted melodramatically, while contemplating the men who had served under William the Conqueror and Dwight Eisenhower in different moments of historical significance.[46]

He also pondered getting involved in an important movement of the present. At his close friend's request, he agreed to stop in Oklahoma City near the end of May 1961 to take on a different kind of role. "Jolly West wants me to join him tomorrow picketing for desegregation of the restaurants here," Heston wrote in his journal on May 26. "I guess it's time I did something about this kind of thing besides deploring it at cocktail parties." His motivation appeared to be as much personal as it was supporting a meaningful cause. "I can think of no one I'd rather do it with than Jolly."[47]

The next day Heston donned a "sandwich board" and joined the picket line. He chose words from Thomas Jefferson to reflect his views. Deeming it "valuable," he thought the effort more "a triumphal procession than a protest demonstration." Though they "encountered almost no hostility," Heston recognized that those who remained behind stood to risk more than he would from the pressure the situation generated. He said the "warm reception" from members of the African American community, "who have more at stake than I do, seems more than we deserve." News agencies picked up the story of the protest, but Heston felt understandably

45 Ibid., 258-259.

46 *ALJ*, 117.

47 Ibid., 119.

ambivalent concerning the attention he gained from his participation. "I'm comfortable with the moral value of the action," he asserted, "but uncomfortable to think I'll profit from it in publicity terms." Phoenix's *Arizona Sun* informed readers, "Movie Star Leads Demonstrations," and set the total number of participants at eighty persons.[48]

Heston's role in this small but significant real-life drama was not nearly as potentially career damaging for an established star as it might have been for an aspiring one. Whatever ramifications occurred, he had the satisfaction of responding to the call of a friend and satiating a nagging conscience by participating in a good cause. Heston believed his appearance would be worthwhile and recalled, "my public face got us lots of ink and airtime." Scholar Emilie Raymond concluded more circumspectly, "Heston's presence did not draw widespread press coverage so much as mobilize supporters." For all his pride in this and subsequent moments in the civil rights movement, Heston knew enough to put the matter in perspective. "The restaurants we'd demonstrated against soon quietly began to admit blacks, but our little foray made no more than a ripple in the wider world."[49]

Heston's involvement certainly re-energized sagging local spirits, if it did not lead immediately or directly to changing conditions. Clara Luper and other activists in the NAACP Youth Council had been training for and conducting sit-ins and other nonviolent activities to pressure the Oklahoma City community for change, but their efforts took time to produce results. According to Raymond, "Luper and the students had grown weary of the long campaign, but news of Heston's involvement injected them with new energy." Subsequent talks led to dismantling desegregation in a local department store. "It is not clear how much credit Heston should receive for this success," the scholar concluded. "At the very least, the excitement and publicity associated with Heston's visit appears to have hastened the desegregation of Oklahoma City and perhaps marked the turning point there." In another sense, the actor's choice to act on this stage was consequential. "The campaign was actually significant to Heston's public persona."[50]

While the actor pondered the degree to which he would involve himself in this struggle, studio executives admonished him about the potential repercussions.

48 Ibid., 120; "Movie Star Leads Demonstration," *Arizona Sun*, June 8, 1961.

49 *CHA*, 261; Emilie Raymond, *Stars for Freedom: Hollywood, Black Celebrities, and the Civil Rights Movement* (Seattle, 2015), 95-96.

50 Aldon D. Morris, *The Origins of the Civil Rights Movement: Black Communities Organizing for Change* (New York, 1984), 193; Raymond, *Stars for Freedom*, 95-96.

He remembered later, "It's a bad idea, Chuck. You're going to alienate your audience. Keep out of it." Heston maintained that he considered the advice, but rejected it on practical grounds, if no other. "For pete's sake, *Ben-Hur*'s been in the theaters since 1959. Everyone's seen it twice. *El Cid* won't be out for another six months." There seemed to be no reason to worry about a backlash, particularly under the circumstances. "You think they're going to boycott your movie because I'm picketing to let some poor black kids buy lunch in a dime store? If you generate publicity, it will only make people want to watch the chariot race one more time!" On another occasion, he explained that the choice "was easy for me to do because I didn't stand to lose much over it."[51]

Regardless, Chuck Heston considered the moment an important one in bringing him into an expanded arena. "I suppose this small civil rights activism, before it got popular, was a significant milestone for me." The incident also revealed a character element that impelled the shy man to take on greater public roles. "A certain Scots contrariness and a tendency to shoot my mouth off were to involve me in a good many more public sector issues. It was also part of my expanded persona, riding the tiger." He noted at the time, "I'm not deeply involved in the civil rights movement. But every so often you have to stand up and be counted." For Heston, such issues had the tendency to generate excessiveness. "One thing wrong with politics and public movements is that the only people heard from are extremists on both sides." He preferred a reasoned approach that enabled thoughtful response and credible results.[52]

Raymond considered Heston's role in the protest as pivotal beyond the momentary nature of the appearance and the effect it had on local activists. "Heston's work in Oklahoma also marked a milestone in the relationship between Hollywood stars and the civil rights movement." She observed, "He was not the first major white star to speak out on behalf of civil rights, but he was the first to participate in a direct-action campaign."[53] The actor did not see himself as a pioneer in this regard so much as the tangible embodiment of the principles of individual responsibility as a citizen, which he viewed as essential.

A return to Coldwater Canyon and work in California also restored his verve. "Homecoming was never so rich," he wrote as he settled back into his "routine" of workouts and tennis, as well as his usual social and professional activities. Another

---

51 Charlton Heston, *The Courage to Be Free* (Saudade Press, 2000), 10; Crowther, *Epic Presence*, 75.

52 *CHA*, 261-262; Don Alpert, "Heston Scores Extremists," *BSG*, Dec. 19, 1965.

53 Raymond, *Stars for Freedom*, 97.

project was in the offing—a television film—but Heston was uncertain that the effort would offer much outside of another opportunity to "practice my trade."[54]

As his consideration of a television project indicated, in all cases, Heston never strayed far from a desire for balance. A pleasant chore representing the United States State Department at a film festival in Germany was a welcome change. "I must say I like the feeling of taking off on a trip wearing a different hat from an actor's for once," he remarked to his newsletter readers. Other factors were at work as well. "I'm glad to be getting back inside that little magic looking-box, even on a filmed show," as opposed to a live one, in *The Fugitive Eye*. Perhaps most appealing was a shift in apparel to modern clothing. "After eight months in chainmail, THAT'S a switch, for sure."[55]

Serving as an ambassador for his craft meant traveling to Europe to participate in a Berlin Film Festival as an official delegate on behalf of the United States. In the midst of the circuit of conference activities, Heston saw renewed evidence of the divisions that existed in Cold War Germany. He pronounced the tour of "the Eastern sector" as "far more memorable than anything else I've seen here." The proverbial gateway between the peoples of East and West Berlin was about to be closed with the erection of the Berlin Wall, but Heston already felt the sense of desperation and separation that existed. The trip also tapped into an interest in foreign affairs that would hold for the remainder of his life and take on even greater public expressions.[56]

Other considerations held sway as Charlton Heston contemplated his next endeavor. He felt it was critical to venture away from the turf he had traveled so well and so successfully in the most recent phase of his career. In doing so, he would be bucking a time-honored trend. Producers inclined toward repeating successful formulas that could continue to generate business from supportive audiences. Heston knew this formula made sense, but he considered it stifling. "Sam smelled a hit with *El Cid* and wanted to use the unprecedented success of *Ben-Hur* to duplicate both films in one: *El Hur*, or possibly *Ben-Cid*." Heston could make light of the desire, but he preferred to move in another direction. "What I really wanted

54 *ALJ*, 121.

55 Newsletter, June 25, 1961, HL.

56 "Heston Heads Fete Delegates," *NYT*, June 23, 1961. A file on the festival included a certificate from the Department of State as "a Delegate of the United States of America to the Eleventh International Film Festival to be convened in Berlin, Germany, June 23, 1961," and a program listed him as delegate and chairman of the delegation. "Berlin Film Festival," Heston Papers, f.459, HL; *ALJ*, 122.

was something different from what I'd just done." While such a departure might be fraught with peril from an accounting perspective, it was appealing on a personal level. "So I was looking for a comedy, of course," he wrote.[57]

The project was a Paramount production with a quirky title and an unusual genre for an actor seen most often in serious historical or period epics. *Easter Dinner*, which would become *The Pigeon that Took Rome*, provided Heston with a second foray into light comedy. The working titled would have to be jettisoned first. "I hate that title," he admitted at the time, adding later, "Everybody hated that title. Especially with me in the picture, it seemed to suggest a film about the Last Supper."[58]

Heston had done well with the warm and engaging *The Private War of Major Benson*, largely because the part had called for him to be the straight man in a plot that featured youngsters in a military school as his foils. He could not predict how this new feature would turn out, but he was comfortable in the knowledge that whomever the film producers selected as co-stars, he would remain the bankable figure associated with it. "It probably would be best to use new Italian actresses," he maintained, "and trust to me for the marquee weight."[59]

He shared his thoughts on the possibilities with his newsletter readers. "It's a comedy for a change; after that long last winter in armour, it's a pleasure to have wardrobe that bends. Besides, I think it was about time I switched." As his professional stature increased, he tried to calculate the timing and type of work he would undertake to maintain a high level of audience interest. "I have an idea that [the] business of winning races and leading people in and out of cities and Red Seas could begin to wear thin as a standing diet."[60]

Heston was optimistic after filming wrapped. "But the word on it is that it's very good . . . and very funny, which should be a welcome change for audiences." He relished undertaking roles outside those viewers typically expected of him. Heston was willing to take the risk of a negative reaction to alterations in his usual cinematic roles. "My public image was getting a little square and sober, I think."[61] Unfortunately, *The Pigeon that Took Rome* did not fly with critics or patrons. Not

---

57 *CHA*, 264-265.

58 *ALJ*, 124.

59 Ibid., 125.

60 Newsletter, Oct. 17, 1961, "Hollywood-on-the-Tiber," HL.

61 Newsletter, Feb. 8, 1962, HL.

until *The Three Musketeers*, with Heston in the menacing role of Cardinal Richelieu, would he venture into comedy again.

Throughout such introspective periods, the actor analyzed his career in the same manner a golfer would examine his game. The greatest challenge was to be the best that each role allowed him and it to be. He constantly insisted that his goal was to find perfection in every performance. Yet Heston was acutely aware that this motivation was not the only one at play. In a screening of Kirk Douglas's opus *Spartacus*, Heston found himself admiring and envying the result. "Why am I so anxious to *compare?*" he chided himself privately. "This is not a track meet."[62] But he would not have been true to himself or to his work and his audience if he had done any less.

Alternate bouts of doubt and certitude had always marked Charlton Heston's life and career. He was often demanding of himself and others. Yet nothing defined his sense of who he was as clearly as his family, and in the late summer of 1961, he, Lydia, and Fraser were about to expand it by one. "There were various career oddments today," he noted on August 15, "but we're really thinking of little but the baby girl we're getting tomorrow. It'll be strange and wonderful to have an infant in our house again; I can hardly believe it. All of us are happy."[63] Even with a reasonable sense of anxiety about what lay ahead, the Hestons, as new parents once more, were ecstatic at the addition to their family.

"We brought Holly Ann home today," the proud father observed with satisfaction and wonder after the years that had elapsed since he had held baby Fraser. "She seems tinier than I remembered babies could be, certainly smaller than Fray ever was." He was ecumenical in declaring, "We all took to one another at once," since he felt a special warmth for a baby girl, although Fraser proved, at least initially, more ambivalent. Indeed, before he became the protective older brother, he had contemplated putting her up for sale, presumably for the right price.[64]

Heston wanted to ensure the financial security of his growing family in the years to come. "In the twelfth century that meant keeping the swords sharp and the

---

62 *ALJ*, 126.

63 Ibid.

64 Ibid.; *CHA*, 263-264. Biographer Michael Munn noted that Holly Ann Heston was born August 1, 1961: "She was just sixteen days old"; Munn, *Charlton Heston*, 112. In his autobiography, Heston explained, "We brought Holly home on the second day of her life; she was instantly and forever ours"; *CHA*, 264. In his journal, Heston discussed her eleventh birthday party and the failure a showing of the Marx Brothers' classic *A Day at the Races* turned out to be ("August 2, [1972]), and referenced her twelfth birthday the next year on the same date ("August 2, [1973]"); *ALJ*, 392, 414.

horses fed," he asserted colorfully; "for me it meant reading a lot of scripts." He and Herman Citron had collaborated well. As was true with any creative individual, the actor chafed when worthy projects seemed slow to materialize or negotiations appeared to drag on interminably. But the freedom he felt the arrangement offered him blended with his desire for work and creative fulfillment equally. Heston's agent remained a voice the performer trusted, although he had long proven to be his own man in making the final decisions. "It's probably unwise to turn entirely away from the hand that has fed me so often in the past," he recalled a friend advising. Heston had never been afraid to stretch himself creatively and his instincts lay in determining the ways in which he could match with directors on projects that excited him. There was no doubt, however, that he had to consider audience expectations. He might be in a much better position than most of his contemporaries in tackling unusual roles, but Heston still seemed to feel only as good as the response he was getting from his most recent effort. In this instance, "The main thing, of course, is to wait and see what *El Cid* looks like."[65]

As he contemplated participating in an *Old-Fashioned Thanksgiving* for ABC Television, Heston was pleased for the opportunity at a level of performance that connected two passions. One writer in Boston observed, "The star, whose motion picture career has involved him with bigger-than-life characters, wide-screen stories and 'casts of thousands,' will be seen in a role that gives him a unique satisfaction—the role of Charlton Heston, reader." Heston particularly enjoyed the chance to communicate with the listener in an age-old way. "Long before there were plays and actors there were the story and the story teller," the actor informed the interviewer. "I find readings not only a satisfaction, but a challenge. To convey the spirit and intention of a story—and it's all a story whether it's the form of a poem, a psalm or a parable—to convey these with just the voice, that's what intrigues me." This role cast him in the mantle of "the lonely actor," by which he meant carrying out his performance without the usual trappings of stage and film. "In this there's also a great sense of intimacy, of direct communication with a listener," he noted with satisfaction. "It's even stronger than the kind of thing that happens in a stage play. I get this feeling even while making a record. This is really direct discourse—person-to-person, actor to audience."[66]

As a measure of the popular esteem Heston was enjoying at this stage of his career, he also received the honor of immortalizing himself in a popular Hollywood

65 *ALJ*, 126.

66 "Heston Likes Story Telling," *BSG*, Nov. 12, 1961.

tradition. "Charlton Heston will place his footprints and handprints in concrete, in the forecourt of the *Chinese Theatre* . . . tomorrow," a press release touted. "Heston becomes the 139th star to be footprinted at the world-famous site, a leading local tourist attraction. Currently seen in 'El Cid,' he is also the only performer who has starred in three of the ten all-time top box office grossers ('Ben-Hur,' 'The Ten Commandments,' 'The Greatest Show on Earth')." Likewise, the occasion displayed the talents of the other artist in Heston's life, who had developed her own creative niche outside acting. "His wife, Lydia Heston, a professional photographer whose photos have appearances in national magazines, will also be on hand with her camera, to shoot the event."[67]

He seemed less than enthralled by the honor at the time, recording in his journal on January 18, 1962, "I dutifully went through the ancient tribal ritual at Grauman's, putting my feet in wet cement attended by a full complement of photographers and fans." Of course, such exposure ensured that he remained in the forefront of people's minds and even he softened the disdain he seemed to feel for the public occasion with the quip, "So now I'm immortalized, right on top of Marilyn Monroe and Jane Russell. (How many men can make that statement?)" The *Los Angeles Times* presented "Concrete Evidence" of the achievement of the star of *Ben-Hur* and *El Cid* for its readers, noting in the caption of the image, "Charlton Heston makes his mark in cement in the forecourt of Grauman's Chinese Theater, where 138 other stars' handprints and footprints are recorded."[68]

If the event was a relatively nonchalant one for the actor, the fans present were more nonplussed. The photographers requested "just one more" as spectators wondered what would happen to the cement-speckled shoes or clamored for an autograph. "Thanks dear, for coming," the actor called out to his wife endearingly. "I'll be home early." Then, with the chore complete, Heston "leaped into his gallant green racing Jag," as Wanda Henderson of the *Los Angeles Times* wrote, "smiled his it's-a-wonderful-world smile and roared off in a U-turn with the blessing of [police] officer Thompson, sergeant in command."[69]

Heston attempted to assess the meaning of his growing stardom. "I wasn't quite the green Michigan kid who'd come out to make movies a decade before," he noted, but internal debates of how best to proceed on various projects, even at this stage, conflicted him. He wanted to take on a role in a film based on Cornelius

---

67 Press Release, Jan. 16, 1962, *El Cid* publicity, ibid.

68 *ALJ*, 136; "Concrete Evidence," *LAT*, Jan. 19, 1962.

69 Wanda Henderson, "Heston Puts His Foot in It, Makes Lasting Impression," *LAT*, Jan. 25, 1962.

Ryan's book about D-Day, *The Longest Day*, but he had to take time from his Paramount comedy to do it. Heston later termed himself the "six-hundred-pound gorilla" for his desire to exercise his influence in such a manner. But *The Longest Day* became a tonic of another sort for this sense of entitlement when John Wayne wrestled away the role for himself. "The Duke was the *thousand*-pound gorilla, if ever there was one," Heston confessed humbly. The one moment he had for a brief glimpse outside that shadow was when famed director John Ford appeared on the *Diamond Head* set and hinted at a role in one of his future film projects. "What the hell," Heston concluded, "Duke Wayne can't be wearing out yet."[70]

The myriad activities in a very public life now consumed much of Heston's time and energies. In January, he revisited *Ben-Hur* by donning his wardrobe from the chariot race for Milton Berle's show. Time and the elements had rendered the clothing stiff and uncomfortable, reminding Heston of the enormous amount of sweat equity he had put into the role. At the same time, perspiration of another kind accompanied his efforts to secure a deal for the rights to a story that had intrigued him as a possible screenplay and film. The negotiation was only the beginning of a saga involving *The Lovers*, a play that ultimately became *The War Lord*. Heston hoped to turn it into an intimate view of a turbulent historical period rather than a DeMille-sized spectacle. "If we make it, it must not be a huge picture," he asserted. "We should advertise instead 'A Cast of Dozens!?'" He later noted, "It was the first property I ever bought, thus dear to my heart."[71]

Heston's ability to parlay his image for greater good occurred when he traveled to Washington to "lobby for the film unions" in early February. He also had the chance to become acquainted with important power brokers. "Today I met the president, the vice-president, the Speaker of the House, and some twenty or thirty assorted senators and congressman," he noted on the fifth. "Reasonably enough, JFK impressed me most, clearly a very high-powered character." Heston added admiringly, if somewhat cryptically, "His instant assessment of people and situations, coupled with a remarkable store of information on unlikely subjects, was formidable." This journal entry betrayed a star-struck feature that Heston diminished in his autobiography. He clearly enjoyed meeting President John F. Kennedy and was grateful that the politician seemed familiar with his work. He recounted with obvious pleasure the anecdote of a complaint by a White House

70 *CHA*, 270; *ALJ*, 140.

71 Ibid., 136-137; *CHA*, 281.

visitor that Kennedy had insisted on watching *El Cid* for a third time rather than socializing.[72]

If Kennedy had not put much focus "on courting celebrities, or working to bring them into the campaign," as writer Ronald Brownstein maintained, he embraced their presence in the White House through an appreciation of cinema, an additional infusion of glamor, and the opportunities the interactions gave him to demonstrate the expansiveness of his interests and knowledge. He "beguiled the stars" with his personal charm and charisma, as much as by any political or ideological kinship. Charlton Heston certainly would not have agreed with any characterization that he had fallen under the spell of the young leader, even if his private expressions indicated otherwise. Still, as the actor recalled of his chances to make an impact on prominent officials, "Over the years, my public face has made me useful."[73]

Of course, that usefulness continued to depend upon his relevance as a public figure. Heston's personal investment in each of his films included conducting extensive interviews and appearances in support of the releases. Promotion was more than the fulfillment of contractual obligations; he felt that a full commitment to the publicity phase of his work was critical to any motion picture's success and longevity in movie houses. For *El Cid*, the 1962 publicity tour schedule in the United States alone was extensive and intense:

Tuesday 2/13	Los Angeles to Denver
Wednesday 2/14	Denver to Dallas
Thursday 2/15	Dallas to Houston
Friday 2/16	Houston to Oklahoma City
Sunday 2/18	Oklahoma City to Kansas City
Monday 2/19	Kansas City to Minneapolis
Tuesday 2/20	Minneapolis to Buffalo
Wednesday 2/21	Buffalo to Pittsburgh

---

72 *ALJ*, 138.

73 Brownstein, *The Power and the Glitter*, 149, 152-153; *CHA*, 224.

Thursday 2/22	Pittsburgh to Philadelphia
Friday 2/23	Philadelphia to New York City
Sunday 2/25[74]	New York City to Los Angeles

As was so often the case, those responsible for marketing unleashed a barrage of superlatives meant to entice viewers into movie theaters. The hyperbole associated with the distribution seemed to match the sensation the actor had felt in the film itself when capturing cities before adoring crowds. The text of one promotional pamphlet asserted, "The Greatest Romance and Adventure in a Thousand Years! Announcing Global Premieres December, 1961," and laid out the list of "Road Show Engagements" and "International Engagements" with corresponding maps for fans and other interested parties to follow. On the ground came "The Greatest Campaign in the History of the Industry!" with advertising in "36 Magazines" designed to reach "68,479,092 Circulation."[75]

Meanwhile, the actor needed to meet his new film commitments. Location shooting in the Hawaiian Islands for *Diamond Head* occupied March, with the Hestons enjoying an anniversary when Lydia arrived. "Well, we started it," he noted on March 10. "Not stills, not publicity, not riding . . . but actually shooting film. It's a relief to be at it again." In addition to intermittent rains that plagued the filming, other complicating matters arose. "We're inundated with foreign press. They're looming larger each year," the actor noted resignedly, but with a powerful caveat, "of course, you can't overlook their importance."[76] He hoped that coverage in the island paradise would translate into higher box office returns worldwide once the film came out.

Once the shoot ended on one of the remote islands, the actor and his family toured Oahu and took in a polo match. Here, too, Heston's interest in history and his personal experiences intersected as they visited the USS *Arizona* Memorial. He felt "the weight of the bones of the eleven hundred men" interred there and recalled soberly, "Some of them were no older than I was the day they died. While I sat in my room in Wilmette, reading."[77]

---

74 "Charlton Heston Tour for 'El Cid' 1962," *El Cid* publicity, Heston Papers, f.74, HL.

75 Promotional Pamphlet for *El Cid*, ibid.

76 *ALJ*, 139-140.

77 Ibid., 141.

With filming complete in a location in which the demands of the work meant that such "exotic climes are losing almost all their appeal," Charlton Heston was delighted to be back home in Los Angeles, even with SAG duties and more negotiations and additional challenges for *The Lovers* remaining. In the meantime, another massive historically based project loomed. Earlier, Heston, who had a slight sense of guilt over jettisoning his participation in *The Fall of the Roman Empire*, had been susceptible to a new pitch while on a Trans-Atlantic flight. "Chuck . . . we've put *Roman Empire* on hold," came the hook. "Our next picture is *Fifty-five Days at Peking*. We want you to star in it. We *need* you to star in it." The urgent request got the actor's attention. "I was stunned, impressed, and flattered, in about equal measure," Heston asserted at the inference that a film production would be abandoned "simply because I wasn't going to be in it." The actor was aware of the likely exaggeration of the sales effort, but he yielded to it as much as future script and casting approval, and Herman Citron's ability to work out an acceptable deal, permitted.[78]

The setting of the picture was Peking (now Beijing), China, during the Boxer Rebellion of the early 1900s, which marked a rejection of Western imperial intrusion in East Asia. Heston plunged as deeply as ever into "researching marine uniforms for the period so I can do proper sketches," and engaged in his usual spate of "background reading" for his part as a U.S. Marine officer. More troubling was the word that studio executives "want to use Ava Gardner." Although he held script and casting approval, Heston concluded, "I'd better get my ass over there next week and find out what the hell is happening." He later complained, "I'm still convinced Gardner is wrong. I don't see how I got myself into this bind . . . but I hate using muscle in setting up a picture."[79]

Heston's instincts were accurate in this instance, which put to the test his penchant for professionalism, especially regarding his usual business-like approach to his work. Deviations from his expectations left him unwilling to tolerate aberrant behavior by other actors. Often, female co-stars bore the brunt of his displeasure, although he deeply admired several of them. "His favorite actresses are Ingrid Bergman, Judith Anderson, Katharine Cornell, Susan Hayward and Viveca Lindfors," one writer observed, as Heston considered them "[a]ll thoroughgoing professionals—and no nonsense." For others, the verdict differed decidedly. "Sometimes women are not very professional in their attitude in this town. They

78 Ibid., 142; *CHA*, 272-274.

79 *ALJ*, 142, 143.

don't know or care very much about what they are doing." Heston had reason to reach similar conclusions about some of his male co-stars, but concluded singularly, "The industry has created its own monsters and they're all feminine."[80] In *55 Days at Peking*, this attitude led to a bitter assessment of Gardner, who ultimately got the part.

Heston was fortunate to be in the position he was at that point in his career. "By 1963," the actor recalled in his autobiography, "armed with a first-dollar percentage of the gross of my films, a fair degree of creative control, and some fortunate choices, I had more options than I could responsibly sort out, some of them political." By this point, his service to his profession included the presidency of the Screen Actors Guild, "a post, I confess, I was proud to hold." Aside from the sense of obligation he felt to contributing to the state of stage and screen, Heston understood and accepted a larger role: "my worldwide public identity made me an ambassador as well," which he insisted became "useful in other chores, too."[81]

Still, he was not prepared to sacrifice his work to take up a public mantle. He had exercised his franchise, expressed his views, albeit with increasing regularity and vehemence, and taken up causes that aroused his passions, but he was still an actor and content to remain so. That demand was about to take him to another distant location, physically and cinematically, that would require most of his energy and attention.

A long flight to Spain brought the actor into discussions for casting for Sam Bronston's film. Securing the right person for the female lead still presented a daunting challenge that left Heston in "a bearish temper." He admitted, "This casting problem is about to drive me up the walls. I can't believe there aren't a few women you can risk an expensive film on." Yet the indications always seemed to point to Gardner. Only a visit from Jolly West temporarily rescued Heston from the dilemma and made for "a pleasant evening," although he lamented, "It's too damn seldom we have a chance to do this anymore."[82]

Another brief period of rest at his Coldwater Canyon refuge offered "paradise waiting." Holly's adoption was finalized, and in anticipation of traveling overseas for the *55 Days* shoot, Lydia renewed Fraser's passport and obtained one for Holly. "Poor baby girl," Heston noted, "she'll use up a lot of those, with me for a father."

---

80 Steele, "Unmasking Charlton Heston," 52, 74.

81 *CHA*, 308, 310.

82 *ALJ*, 144.

After he conducted some last-minute SAG business, the entourage set out for Europe, via New York, with even Drago the dog in tow.[83]

Heston enjoyed few elements associated with the long, often difficult shoot for *55 Days at Peking*. Happily, one of these was his association with one of his co-stars. Heston recalled, "Working with David Niven was one of the few undiluted pleasures of making *55 Days at Peking*. He's a first-class actor and a lovely, funny man to boot." During one interview, Heston recalled lecturing a journalist about the context of the Boxer Rebellion at one table when he overheard Niven at the next one state simply, "Of course, if we get involved in the politics, we're lost."[84]

The actor also found solace with his family and more visits with Jolly West. When director Nicholas Ray collapsed from exhaustion, progress on the film largely ceased, before resuming under Heston's *Diamond Head* director, Guy Green. In the interim, Heston turned his creative energies to designing a look for John the Baptist in *The Greatest Story Ever Told* with George Stevens. "I'm content with the makeup I've arrived at for the Baptist; at least I got a different effect from Moses, Ben-Hur, and El Cid," he declared in September. As if on cue, Stevens confirmed the work with an effusive cable in which he insisted, "I feel surge of excitement that tells me he will take place beside Moses, Ben-Hur, El Cid, no less in one's memory than those."[85]

Heston had little time to savor such compliments, as the production of *55 Days at Peking* wrapped on October 20, "on schedule, as I said we could." He held out hope that the film could be "cut together" sufficiently to make the finished product worthwhile. "I'm photographed very well," he posited, "and I suppose the chemistry they pay for is there, but my acting is only competent," as he assessed it "from the dailies."[86]

The rest of the year would disappear in a whirl of filming *The Greatest Story Ever Told* for George Stevens, as well as traveling abroad to promote his other work. Heston was always happy to return home. He seemed to find greater contentment in the familiar surroundings and enjoyed new responsibilities, even as *The Lovers* script finally appeared to be emerging. "Long full day of racing around (as always, going-away-time increases my efficiency)," he observed in early January. "I presided

83 Ibid., 145-146.

84 Ibid., 149.

85 Ibid., 152-153, 154.

86 Ibid., 157.

over my first Screen Actors Guild meeting, chairing the negotiating committee for a new contract. A gavel does a lot for your sense of power."[87]

He enjoyed his association with George Stevens, finding the director "as always, available to each suggestion." Heston wanted a hands-on approach to the interpretation of his character, which had not always proven welcome. Much to Heston's delight, the situation was different with Stevens. "The scene went extremely well today," he noted on February 13. "I work at my best with Stevens, partly because of his startling awareness (especially in a film director) of actor's ego." The next day he lamented that filming was coming to a close. "George is quite a man to work for." Stevens even allowed Heston to take the directorial role in some final scenes detailing John the Baptist's capture, which left the actor taken aback. He remembered asking what he should do with the scene and having the director respond, "Whatever you want, Chuck." "So I did," Heston recalled.[88]

He would endure more than his share of jet setting, with "public relations chores" and a royal premiere for *55 Days at Peking*. There was already talk of another project, this time with director Sam Peckinpah. Meanwhile, *The Lovers* remained in the mix and in limbo as Heston searched for improvements in the script and a distributor to take up the project. He even managed to squeeze tennis into his often-tight schedule, providing a release from his other tensions. "There's a marvelous kind of pleasure in totally spending yourself physically like that," he observed.[89]

Despite his presence in so many larger causes, Heston remained a committed member of the Los Angeles community, championing local matters he thought worthy of public attention. One such contribution came with a highly emotional call to halt a "high-rise project for Mulholland Drive" featuring "a highly subjective statement," which he believed "may or may not have any effect." He thought the situation offered him "an interesting experience," and tried to make sense of the jumble of feelings the moment engendered, "swept with emotion and a kind of unease I'd never use in acting a similar scene." Ever the practitioner of his craft, Heston pondered the sensation for future application. "How to trap this for use sometime?"[90]

87 Ibid., 164.

88 Ibid., 165, 166-168.

89 Ibid., 168-174.

90 Ibid., 175.

In the summer of 1963, social reform diverted everyone's attention. The civil rights movement that had taken Heston to a picket line in Oklahoma City now beckoned from the nation's capital as Dr. Martin Luther King, Jr., prepared to undertake a "March on Washington for Jobs and Freedom" to order to exert more direct pressure on behalf of these important causes. The very nature of Heston's involvement illustrated the complexities of the situation. When entertainer and organizer Harry Belafonte reported to Dr. King that he had attracted large numbers of fellow performers to the effort, the religious leader suggested Heston, who had helped as SAG president in a general way to bring King's message to parts of the Hollywood community where doors had been shut. Belafonte was skeptical, but King convinced him that the march, like the movement itself, could not depend solely upon the support of "liberal friends." Individuals from both sides of "the divide" would lend credibility to the affair. "The fact was," Belafonte recalled explaining to Marlon Brando when he broached the idea with him, "Heston knew he wasn't a great actor. Behind those iconic good looks and macho swagger was an insecure guy who yearned for the approval of his peers." The activist thought the task would give Heston personal standing and serve as "a powerful image for mainstream America." Brando acquiesced and Heston accepted readily with the assurance that the press conference/announcement would occur at his home. Belafonte conveyed the news to an elated King. "Now he, too, knew the march would succeed, and lead us where we needed to go. How could it not? We had Moses!" One writer noted with respect to Heston, "By 1963, he was done playing Moses. It was time to be Moses."[91]

News releases spread word of the actor's involvement. Of course, he prepared to join like-minded individuals in promoting the effort, provided it did not stray too dangerously off a course of moderation. A volatile Marlon Brando might see the benefit of a dramatic demonstration; a conservative Charlton Heston did not. These discussions came in his capacity as chair of an "Arts Group," designed to support the civil rights movement and Dr. King. "I suppose I was elected chairman because of the time I put in with SAG," Heston observed, before quipping, "or maybe just because I'd gotten all those folks through the Red Sea."[92]

Not all of Heston's associates thought the idea a good one. Director George Stevens "almost convinced me I was wrong to go," the actor recorded in his journal.

91 Harry Belafonte, with Michael Shnayerson, *My Song: A Memoir* (New York, 2011), 277-278; Ross, *Hollywood Left and Right*, 280.

92 "Actor to Join DC Marchers, *The* [Pascagoula, MS] *Chronicle*, Aug. 2, 1963; *ALJ*, 177.

"Instinctively I share his opposition to group action. I don't like to follow other men's drums; I like to walk by myself, but here I am, ass-deep in a complicated, emotionally charged group action." But while he thought he would do better "to go to Washington by my damn self," he knew that the moment was bigger than that. The independent streak that drove him also required him to demand a more reasoned approach. "We live in a country where we have the right to do this," Heston maintained, "and we're going to do it the way it says in the book."[93]

Heston would come to see Martin Luther King as "a twentieth-century Moses for his people," having already determined by that time that King was impressive and persuasive. The actor's leadership in the Hollywood contingent certainly ensured a more cerebral approach than an emotional one. His "by-the-book" method meant operating amid an unconventional atmosphere in as conventional a manner as possible. Seeing himself, as one scholar observed, as holding "moderate ideas" and serving "as an independent voice of reason," he was prepared to take full advantage of the ways in which his "public face" could be useful in this worthwhile venture.[94]

Lydia accompanied her husband on the trip, but as the moment approached, she had to dismiss efforts by representatives of the FBI to dissuade her from leaving the hotel in order to see events unfold for herself. "Well, that's not the line to take with my girl," Charlton explained. She spent the day in the throng, photographing the march and talking with participants. "I'll bet we had a better time than you big dogs up front," she observed to her husband. "I'll bet she did, too," he concurred.[95]

Belafonte, who had confessed to harboring some anxiety, enjoyed a palpable sense of relief when all went well. He took pleasure as the "posse" he was leading approached the Lincoln Memorial by way of the reflecting pool and everyone shook hands as they passed. "The effect was electrifying," he explained, marveling at the rare moment in history. "I've thought a lot since then about the power of celebrity harnessed to social causes, whether it does any more than give a crowd a thrill and stroke a few stars' egos. Maybe, sometimes," he concluded. "But not that day." He believed that collectively these performers could reach more people than anyone else. "To see us all together, moving as one, saying by our presence here that *segregation would not stand*—that was powerful." In a longer view, Heston insisted that the moment could not be described accurately as "civil disobedience." "The

---

93 Ibid., 178.

94 *CHA*, 314; Raymond, *Cold, Dead Hands*, 73-77.

95 *CHA*, 316-317.

group I went to Washington with . . . broke no local ordinances. It eschewed civil disobedience as a tool." Consequently, he felt the march and their role in it helped to lead to "the passage of the civil rights act—and that's something."[96]

In the immediate aftermath of the march, Heston reflected on his time with Dr. King at the Lincoln Memorial, and felt the exhilaration of the moment. "It was a very stirring day. I'll never forget it, and I'm proud to have been part of it."[97] After he had more time to put the momentous occasion and his place in it into perspective, Heston remained both pleased to have been present and mindful that his role was a relatively small, albeit supportive one. "Our job," he explained in phrasing that matched what he felt he had accomplished in Oklahoma City, "was to get as much ink and TV time as possible." Each member of the artists' group had assignments to maximize media exposure and Heston spoke to a group of "New York people" who were attending the event. Organizers thought writer James Baldwin could best express what Heston should say before the cameras. "I wasn't crazy about the matter," the actor admitted. "Anything that goes out with my name on it, I write." Nevertheless, after reading Baldwin's material, Heston concluded, "the speech he wrote for me . . . [was] very close to what I wanted to say."[98]

Of his moment in the shadow of Dr. King, Heston observed, "We were essentially extras in the event that validated that dream, but we were there. In a long life of activism in support of some good causes, I'm proudest of having stood in the sun behind that man, that morning."[99] Indeed, his participation in the "March on Washington" became a principal element of any discussion he had relating to his activism for the remainder of his life.

According to scholar Emilie Raymond, each of the higher-profile participants understood that this historic event had professional as well as personal consequences. "Individuals such as [Sidney] Poitier, Sammy Davis, Jr., [Harry] Belafonte, [Lena] Horne, [Frank] Sinatra, and Heston had managed to meld their careers and their activism into viable public personas," she explained, "and the March on Washington had helped to solidify their image."[100]

96 Belafonte, *My Song*, 279; Don Alpert, "Heston Scores Extremists," *BSG*, Dec. 19, 1965.

97 *ALJ*, 179.

98 *CHA*, 316.

99 Ibid.

100 Raymond, *Stars for Freedom*, 141.

Stephen Ross captured well the nuanced element of Charlton Heston's carefully cultivated public image. "Throughout his life, Heston's politics remained a jumble of ideological perspectives," Ross observed. Calling the actor "a political maverick—part libertarian, part liberal, part conservative, and part republican in the spirit of the Founding Fathers," Ross recognized that Heston defied conventional labeling in many respects.[101]

The actor's views on important issues aligned him with other high-profile stars. Douglas Brode found commonality between Heston and John Wayne as fellow conservatives on gun issues, but more progressive about censorship. Labeling Wayne "a constitutional conservative, not a moralistic one," he concluded that traditional labels were not enough to describe either man. "Both were libertarians of a civic order, against anyone who would dare to try and tread on them—from the left or the right."[102] Certainly, few matters raised Heston's ire as much as the notion that he, or any other citizen for that matter, should be silent.

Heston often offered his views in letters but believed he could move people with his oratorical skills, too. His "words" had first attracted Lydia, and his ability to provide distinctive narration would long serve him in public settings. Dramatic readings became part of his contribution at important public events. He had the rare ability to make them come alive, as when he gave voice to Abraham Lincoln's iconic expressions for Aaron Copland's *A Lincoln Portrait* with the Utah Symphony, or sampling the works of Robert Frost, Carl Sandburg, Mark Twain, or Ernest Hemingway for various audiences.

Heston had always loved to read and believed that poets and writers offered the best examples of America's artistic and creative strength. In his earliest years as an actor, he brought the same works with him on a tour of Australia, performing special readings for television, usually ending with Frost's "Stopping by Woods on a Snowy Evening." This piece had particular meaning to him, as it evoked memories of his father reading it to him when "I was small," to reciting it for his own son and sharing it with a national audience in a tribute to fallen President John Kennedy.[103]

After returning to Los Angeles from the affirming experience in Washington, Heston settled once more into his routine. "Having finished functioning as a citizen for a while," he noted, "I got back to making a living today with the first

101 Ross, *Hollywood Left and Right*, 281.

102 Douglas Brode, *Dream West: Politics and Religion in Cowboy Movies* (Austin, 2013), 157.

103 "Further and Further Down Under," UCLA archives.

reading on *The Patriots* for Hallmark." He hoped to be able to breathe life into his characterization of a personal hero, Thomas Jefferson, whose name, along with Thomas Paine, remained part of his public and political messaging.[104]

Ever on the lookout for his next project, Heston awaited the script for a Western set during the Civil War. *Major Dundee* remained a work in progress. "There's a lot of good work in it," he remarked, "but I'm a little disappointed. The characters are there, and the bones of the story, but there's a lot of excess mishmash." The usual maneuvering and negotiating for casting followed, with choices ranging from Anthony Quinn and Steve McQueen to Lee Marvin and Omar Sharif.[105]

Once shooting began in a remote location in Mexico, another of those rare moments of verisimilitude emerged that Heston had sensed in special circumstances in other films. This one came as the actors rode into a village before the rest of the modern convoy could join them and Heston as Dundee felt the unsettled gaze of the residents upon the sudden arrivals. They may or may not have known who these riders were, as he surmised, but the chance to imagine how they were feeling intrigued him. "As an actor, I had to use this," he recalled thinking at the time, and believed it helped him "tap into the reality of their reaction." This sensation was the reason he so much enjoyed embodying a host of characters. "I did learn from the experience; I was better in the scenes in the village," he explained. "I think I did well overall finding Dundee," he concluded, "another in the growing gallery of dark, driven men that seemed increasingly to define the fictional characters I played."[106]

Other projects also loomed, including the chance to play another resonating historical figure based upon a popular Irving Stone novel. Regarding *The Agony and the Ecstasy*, Heston knew he had to present a credible portrayal of Michelangelo in order to bring the character off for modern audiences. He never let specific issues limit him, as when he responded philosophically to a query regarding his height for playing the artist. "No, I think I'm too small." Regardless, he plunged into his usual research regimen as he sought to find his character and bring authenticity to the role. One writer noted the commitment the process demanded of the performer. "For one thing, he had to watch some marble sculptors at work to learn the technique of holding chisel and hammer, and he then spent many hours practicing." Heston supplemented the information he gathered about fresco

---

104 *ALJ*, 180.

105 Ibid., 182, 183.

106 *CHA*, 333-334.

painting and his typical historical research with close examinations of the original work itself. "Looking at the real frescoes in the Sistine Chapel, up close," he noted, "gave me the key to understanding the artist. Surely no work of art was ever born out of so much anguish, against such odds."[107]

On the Sistine Chapel set, Heston felt he had a powerful opportunity to give life to Michelangelo and his work. "It was quite an experience," he noted, "to lift a brush to that enormous expanse, and have paint drip down in your eyes and realize what it must have been to do it all . . . alone." As he recalled the process in his newsletter, Heston related, "To even seem to be painting those panels of Genesis is an enormous effort of will." The actor's exertions hardly diminished his appreciation of the original. He considered Michelangelo a "genius who stood taller than any other man but Shakespeare," but getting the person's intangible qualities onto the big screen required special attention and dedication. "If we can get some of this in the film, we'll have something." Yet the frustrations were as real in the actor's time as they had been in those earlier centuries. "Anyway," Heston concluded, "you can see why THE AGONY AND THE ECSTASY is the right title."[108]

Heston was determined to give the production his fullest effort. His regimen of learning as much as possible about his subject and that person's times required his usual method of research; it also meant exploring the medium in which he was to operate in character. A press book for the film touted this preparatory work. "For his role in 'The Agony and the Ecstasy,' Heston, who enjoys amateur standing as a painter, studied the technique of fresco painting with Professor Igino Cupelloni, the expert retained by the Vatican to care for its works of art." The press book also noted that the actor "traveled to see as many of Michelangelo's works as possible and spent long hours in contemplation of the artist's character."[109]

Heston also seemed pleased with the choice of Carol Reed, the man tasked with guiding the process on film. Heston had learned to work with many directorial styles, and preferred the type that had a clear vision for what the film should be and how to shoot it in order to fit that vision. He also appreciated constructive criticism when it was clear that what was happening was good for the project and would make him a better actor. "So far, Carol seems straightforward; he knows what he wants and is pleased with what I give him." The latter point was also

107 Crowther, *Charlton Heston*, 87; Hamill, "Heston: Larger Than Life," 88-89; Heston and Isbouts, *Hollywood*, 146.

108 *ALJ*, 205; Newsletter, "Rome, Italy, August 5th, 1964," HL.

109 "*The Agony and the Ecstasy* Press Book," Heston Papers, HL.

fraught with danger for the perfectionist in the actor, however. "Let him not be too easily pleased."[110]

Heston found satisfaction, at least initially, at the end of the long shoot. "We finally wound it up," he recorded on September 7. The final shot, "showed, appropriately, M/A's last stroke on the ceiling, the finish for both of us." Heston felt he had put some of his best work on celluloid for moviegoers to enjoy. "Four years for him to do it, four months for me to pretend to," he observed. "I don't think I've made a better one, or acted better, either."[111]

When he returned to the United States, he found the eternal verities of nature soothing. "The leaves were yellow, there, too," he remembered of New York, "blowing across our terrace, the full moon over the river hung as it had the night before over the crumbled Roman walls on the Appia Antica. I've always found this comforting, crisscrossing the globe. We move, the earth abides, turning in its seasons, the moon waxing and waning in its own eternal cycle."[112]

The actor and family man, still very much a public person since his appearance in a string of blockbusters, soon had reason to note the benefits that came with his obligations. At the World's Fair in New York, the Hestons and their children moved with relative ease as guests of the Italian embassy. "That's surely the best way to do a vast public attraction," he recalled, adding parenthetically, "(Given my public condition, really the only way)." Their treatment in the Fair's sea of humanity, with the Hestons "cocooned in VIPness," provided a chance for the father to pass along wisdom to his daughter on the world in which they lived. "My message to her was just about what I'd said to him," Heston explained in reference to his earlier advice to Fraser. "Honey, all this stuff with the people and the cameras and yelling is just about Daddy's work. It doesn't have anything to do with you and me and Mommy and Fray . . . it just means they like some of the work I do." Heston wanted his daughter to be unconcerned about the reaction that accompanied his public appearances. "We're glad they do, and we're nice to everybody, and sometimes we get to do fun things and people help us, but the four of us are still the same."[113]

While Chuck Heston tried to assure his family that his success had not changed them, it was clear that as a professional he remained a desired property. The

---

110 *ALJ*, 201.

111 Ibid., 207.

112 *CHA*, 349-350.

113 Ibid., 350.

demand for attaching the star to their various vehicles prompted studios to clamor for his services. After an extended journey, *The War Lord* finally had a home. As a biographer of director Franklin Schaffner noted, "Universal was pleased to have *The War Lord*, principally because of Charlton Heston: he was the most successful star of film spectaculars; he would look good wearing Universal armor."[114]

At the same time, a familiar figure from the past emerged with another prospective job. "I've got a great story which I mean to make and the only man I want for the part is you," Heston's former DeMille costar Henry Wilcoxon offered. "Harry, I'm committed to films for the next three years," the actor explained. "Sorry." Heston then realized he might be in a better position to offer his old friend work than the reverse. "Come here," he asked *War Lord* producer Walter Seltzer, "and see if you think what I do." The two agreed instantly and solved another dilemma by coaxing Wilcoxon back into acting as the Viking leader in their film. The role was certainly not of the same caliber that Wilcoxon had once ensured that Heston would get with Moses, but Heston had his man, who remembered, "I enjoyed every minute of it," with the exception of California's "biggest and most bloodthirsty mosquitos." In October, as he worked to fill the cast for his picture, Heston noted, "Harry Wilcoxon will do the Frisian Prince. It felt odd sitting on the other side of the desk from him, after all those interviews in the De Mille wing."[115]

When not too busy with his personal and professional obligations, Heston tried to find time to respond to requests of various sorts. In a note to his secretary written on *War Lord* stationery for forwarding to one correspondent, Heston suggested an image he felt would suffice to illustrate his views on a subject he deemed of significance to his career as well as his health:

Cora, this is [the] still for a magazine that wanted some item on my athletic activity. Still shows me playing w/Niccola Pietrangeli, Italian amateur champion, during shooting of Agony in Rome this summer. My sports are tennis, riding, plus swimming as a part of my daily workout, which I consider a vital part of my professional preparation. An actor's physical condition is as important to him as an athlete's, and for the same reason. ch[116]

---

114 Erwin Kim, *Franklin J. Schaffner* (Metuchen, NJ, 1985), 197.

115 Marjory Adams, "Producer Gets Caught In Front of Cameras," *BG*, Nov. 2, 1965; *ALJ*, 209.

116 Heston note, Dec. 14, 1964, "Solicitations," Heston Papers, f.481, HL.

As 1964 closed, Heston informed his newsletter readers, "THE WAR LORD brings me to the end of what has been a very full year. As I said, I can't recall a time when I've done three films in one year before . . . surely never films of so much importance to me (and to audiences, too, I hope)." Three films in such close proximity constituted something of an embarrassment of riches for the actor. Just under two decades later, an assessment of his career to that point illustrated the important trends Heston had established, less from any sense of desperation than a desire to remain busy. "So he takes roles in rapid-fire succession—up to two films a year every year since *Dark City*," an interviewer observed. "His long-established routine is to do a play every other year."[117]

The action scenes in *War Lord* gave Heston another chance to work with Joe Canutt, whose father he continued to praise. To Bob Thomas of the *Boston Globe*, he observed, "Ask any four men who was the greatest prizefighter and you're liable to get four different answers. The same is true in any discussion of the greatest author, football player, film director." But he asserted, without deliberate hyperbole, "ask any stunt man who was the greatest in the stunt business and you will get only one answer: Yakima Canutt." The veteran actor thought his talented associate had succeeded because "he reduced stunt work to a science. He could do greater stunts than anyone else because he developed ways of doing them safely." Heston knew that Yakima and Joe had made a profound contribution to his own screen work, including the famous *Ben-Hur* chariot race.[118]

The movie gave rise to another interesting development. Heston had been used to seeing crowds of people on the *Ben-Hur* set to watch the chariot race, but for those scenes filmed on backlots, there was more security and less public intrusion. Yet even as the movie's antagonists battled with each other for control of the tower in *War Lord*, one "determined" outsider "kept infiltrating the set, only to be ejected again." Heston recalled that the director "finally surrendered" to the young man's "persistence and let him watch." The fellow turned out to be a fledgling director named Steven Spielberg.[119]

After a brief timeout for domestic diversions, including Fraser's tenth birthday, Heston flew to New York City for the premiere of *The Greatest Story Ever Told*, where reaction to the film was not as positive as he had hoped. Still, he had little chance to indulge in such concerns, engaging in more chores and tennis before

---

117 Newsletter, December 1, 1964, "Hollywood, California," HL; Plutzik, "Last of the Epic Heroes," 30.

118 Bob Thomas, "Greatest Movie 'Stunter' Makes It a Safe Science," *BG*, Dec. 6, 1964.

119 *CHA*, 354.

heading off to Washington in more conventional attire to carry out SAG business. The issue in this case was the nature of the major television networks' monopoly on programming.[120]

Between his travels, Heston attended the National Conference of Christians and Jews, where he was to receive an award. Another opportunity to hear Martin Luther King, Jr., reminded him of the preacher's formidable oratorical skills. Heston concluded, "[Y]ou couldn't get a better lesson in public speaking." The actor later had a revelation concerning the public perception that actors "should be automatically good at public speaking." He surmised, "Not so. Part of the reason for being an actor is that you have other characters in which to conceal yourself in public." He recognized the transition he had required himself to undertake. "The thought of appearing as myself before an audience appalled me in the beginning. Over the years, I've taught myself, very painfully, a minimal competence as a speaker, but I stand in awe of those who do it well." Of those in his profession who had demonstrated excellence in this regard, he named former Johnson administration figure and acting colleague, Jack Valenti.[121]

Valenti later returned the compliment, noting that when they were preparing to testify before a House committee in Washington, Heston's appearance created quite a stir. "Chuck and I entered this big Rayburn Building Committee Room . . . jam-packed with people . . . and as we came in there was a reverent hush over the audience." Then, someone broke the silence in a "shrill, piping voice saying, 'Holy Smokes, it's Moses!' It brought the house down." Heston recognized this effect and was happy to call upon it as often as needed. "Organizations are eager to have me testify before Congressional committees and the congressmen on those committees are eager to have me do so—because it is likely to get on the six o'clock news," he observed. "That's a contribution I can make that most other people can't."[122]

Heston's "contribution" appeared in the form of testimony he self-deprecatingly declared would offer the "benefits of whatever dubious knowledge I may have pertaining to your debates." He noted the balance between his "Jeffersonian" concern with big government and his appreciation for funding, then reminded his listeners of his role at the hearings. "I am an officer . . . but cannot today speak for the Screen Actors Guild officially." Even so, Senator Jacob Javits observed, "You are a very distinguished artist. We all admire you greatly."

---

120 *ALJ*, 216-217.

121 Ibid., 217-218.

122 "This is Your Life (TV) transcript," 43, HL; Plutzik, "Last of the Epic Heroes," 33.

In the course of his appearance, Heston explained that any artist would welcome financial support provided it included the freedom to act independently. On concerns relating to the question of government subsidies for the arts he observed, "Those who might have misgivings or fears on this subject perhaps could reassure themselves by counting that some of the greatest art in the world was produced under what was, in effect, government subsidy and patronage." He provided another example from the subject of one of his films. "The finest work of Michelangelo, some of the Sistine ceilings, and the like were created under patronage by the Vatican, incidentally, against which Michelangelo rebelled most vigorously. He was an extremely contentious man."[123]

Heston's appearances in Washington represented a level of involvement in political affairs he had not taken often before. He had found John Kennedy personally appealing, and agreed with him generally as president, but it was not until Lyndon B. Johnson's assumption of the office that Heston became, according to one scholar, "a permanent feature on the White House legislative and cultural scene."[124] SAG leadership would do a great deal to elevate his range of political involvement as an advocate and spokesperson for the arts.

The busy actor was soon back in the air, heading for Nigeria via Frankfurt, Germany, on an errand for the State Department as a cultural ambassador. Once in Africa, he planned to attend a special premiere of *Ben-Hur*, "which I hadn't seen in three years or more." The trip had the dual purpose of serving the American administration's desire to reach out to an African government through cultural links as well as a chance for Heston to continue to build his international audience. After adapting to the time and climate changes, he got down to the work at hand. "I did a press conference and some radio interviews this morning," Heston noted on March 6, before managing to squeeze in some tennis.[125]

That evening, Nigerian president Nnamdi Azikiwe held a "command performance" that included "the West African Premiere" of *Ben-Hur* and featured its star in the name of charity. Heston felt pride at the reception of the motion picture. "It's the first time it's been shown here. It was (says he modestly) a smash."

123 Testimony, Joint Hearings Before the Special Subcommittee on Arts and Humanities of the Committee on Labor and Public Welfare, United States Senate and Special Subcommittee on Labor of the Committee on Education and Labor, House of Representatives. Eighty-ninth Congress, First Session, Part I, Feb. 23 and Mar. 5, 1965 (Washington: Government Printing Office, 1965), 56-58.

124 Raymond, *Cold, Dead Hands*, 126.

125 *ALJ*, 218-219; Newsletter, May 1, 1965, "Hollywood, California," HL.

Indeed, *Ben-Hur* continued to pay dividends for Heston's public image. As he speculated later, "Over the years, I do believe I've been to more premieres and grand fund-raisers featuring that film than MGM staged when they first opened the picture."[126]

Subsequently, despite some quiet days at home and the celebration of his anniversary, Heston chafed to get back to work. A request to join Dr. King in Birmingham, Alabama, for another civil rights march came up at this time. Heston approached the matter as he would any other career decision. "I have to decide (A) is it meaningful (to me, to the movement) and (B) is it necessary?" he contemplated. "Yes, I think, on A and B. Now there's C: Can I fit it in?" "C" proved the most difficult challenge. He had to be in New York for a television interview, a commitment that could not be deferred. "I had to drop the trip to Alabama," he rationalized. "There's no way to get there, then to New York by Thursday."[127]

Work continued apace as Heston attended a successful premier for *The Agony and the Ecstasy* in the Midwest, courted director Carol Reed to take the helm of *Khartoum*, flew to New York for an appearance on *The Jack Paar Show*, and considered a script for a part in *Ice Station Zebra*. Reed's withdrawal from the *Khartoum* project left Heston frustrated. "For a script as good as this, we're taking a hell of a long time to get a good director," he complained, before noting that Basil Dearden accepted the assignment several days later.[128]

A frank discussion with Herman Citron reminded about this acceptance of roles in "small films" reminded the actor why he retained the services of "the Iceman." Heston thought Citron was concerned about him taking on projects "independently" on the notion that this "jeopardizes the whole image"; the actor countered that "this is a bit too standardizing for me to go along with. In fact, I think the identification with huge and/or hugely successful films has some drawbacks."[129] Of course, Citron's approach would pay the bills; Heston's would satisfy the artistic cravings. The collaboration had proven successful for both.

On a more pleasant note, Heston maintained a steady dose of tennis that kept him in shape and offered a welcome diversion from other worries. "I'm happy to say that, again today, the best tennis in the world was played on my court," he

---

126 "Programme, First Annual President's Command Performance and the West African Premiere of 'Ben Hur,'" Heston Papers, Ben-Hur miscellaneous, f.50, HL; *ALJ*, 219; *CHA*, 355.

127 *ALJ*, 221.

128 Ibid., 221-223.

129 Ibid., 223-224.

recorded from his home on May 14, 1965. Rod Laver was among his favorite professional opponents. "We all played a bit, of course, but the tennis to watch was when the big boys played together. Fray got to hit a few with Rod Laver, which should be something for his memory book. Quite a day, all in all."[130]

Although he had been reluctant to take on another "epic" role, Heston had found the script for *Khartoum* to be superior. The inclusion of Laurence Olivier as an antagonist made the project that much more appealing. Consequently, he was soon headed back overseas to take on a film that would allow him to yet explore another historical figure for the big screen. The role of Charles "Chinese" Gordon and the ill-fated defense of the Sudanese town of Khartoum offered him another chance to build upon his range of powerful and charismatic leaders. Gordon was a complex personality whose proclivity for the Bible in one hand and a brandy and soda in the other symbolized the Victorian era's contradictions.[131] He would be fascinating to play. Though *Lawrence of Arabia* had been a critical success for Peter O'Toole in 1962, it remained to be seen whether an American audience would embrace a portrayal of another eccentric British military figure.

For *Khartoum*, Heston's determination to "find" his subject through research and wardrobe yielded a fascinating coincidence. A copy of one of Gordon's most ornate tunics had come from a tailor in England; Heston admired his work so completely that he went to the tailor's shop to express his appreciation. "It's amazing how well you copied it from just a photograph," Heston remarked. The tailor said the task had not been as difficult as the actor believed: "You see, we actually made the original for General Gordon. I used the same pattern."[132]

Heston enjoyed the opportunity to explore the character, including the reaction to Gordon's initial appearance in the threatened city. The filming of the scene coincided with the actor's birthday, making for an interesting juxtaposition between the real and the fictional. "We shot Gordon's arrival at Khartoum today. I suppose it's not everyone who can celebrate his birthday with a tumultuous reception by happy thousands greeting the savior of the Nile." The moment reminded him of the Valencia scene from *El Cid*, "only this was a little smaller, and on foot." Heston felt he could count his blessings. "I have no vantage point for

130 Ibid., 226.

131 Heston and Isbouts, *Hollywood*, 150; Lytton Strachey, *Eminent Victorians: Cardinal Manning, Florence Nightingale, Dr. Arnold, General Gordon* (San Diego, 1969), 264-265.

132 Heston and Isbouts, *Hollywood*, 152.

retrospect at the moment," he asserted, "but I seem to be getting where I want to be. I have work, health, happiness, love. What else is there?"[133]

After the initial location shooting, the actor returned to his schedule in California, holding the gavel "for my first regular meeting as SAG president," before heading back to London for studio work on *Khartoum*. Olivier was now available and the chance to work with him as a fellow performer rather than as a director was a thrill for Heston. "Today I began the memorable experience of acting with Olivier," he recorded in his journal on December 14. Several days later, as he returned from the brief work with his mentor, Heston remained enamored. "To work with Olivier was a great experience."[134]

The film itself remained an open question. Biographer Michael Munn thought British audiences embraced the motion picture and its star fully. At the time, Heston maintained, "I've learned not to try and deduce from my own reactions what the public and/or critical response to a film will be. However, I *like* this one." On the way home, he speculated, "I don't know whether it'll be recognized," before adding the telling confession, "This shouldn't matter, you idiot . . . but it does, damn it, it does."[135]

Heston always wanted to get his parts "right" and worked diligently at understanding the roles he was expected to play. Working with Olivier meant that he felt even more internalized pressure to do the part well. The British legend was quite generous in his assessment of his co-star. "Immediately after *Othello*," he wrote in *On Acting*, "I played the Mahdi in *Khartoum*, with Charlton Heston playing Gordon. His seven feet down to my five feet." Olivier described Heston as a "consummate actor who (it is said, and I happily concede) acted me off the screen—not from want of trying on my part."[136]

Another author suggested that Heston's fondness for his role in *Khartoum* stemmed from having "himself surrounded by British actors, with whom he has often felt greater affinity than with Americans." For Jean-Pierre Isbouts, the connection was a deep one. "At his core, Heston is an actor in the Shakespearean mold. His films have always found a warm welcome in England," where he was considered "the consummate actor's actor."[137]

133 *ALJ*, 234.

134 Ibid., 239, 240.

135 Munn, *Charlton Heston*, 136; *ALJ*, 240.

136 Laurence Olivier, *On Acting* (New York, 1986), 322.

137 Heston and Isbouts, *Hollywood*, 151.

Heston related a happy anecdote involving another colleague as they both arrived at Pinewood Studios for the *Khartoum* shoot. The American actor was just exiting his car when the legendary Ralph Richardson drove up in a Bentley. Heston had not met his co-star yet and hesitated to make his acquaintance so informally in the parking lot. Instead, he watched quietly as Richardson patted the hood of his car affectionately: "Goodbye, old fellow, back in a while." The gesture spoke directly to Heston's love of vehicles.[138]

Although Heston admired and enjoyed working with many established British stage and screen figures, decided cultural differences remained between them. "What is that strange substance that Chuck has with his biscuits at tea?" Richardson asked actor Michael Hordern as the cast lunched together between takes. "Peanut butter," Hordern replied, "tried it once—dreadful stuff."[139]

Heston also loved to hone his skills and assert his bona fides on the stage, as he did in a joint run with Lydia in *A Man for All Seasons*. He particularly enjoyed roles which left him free to explore the deeper elements and subtler aspects of character development. This did not always happen in cinema, but in the latter part of the decade, Heston had the opportunity to achieve this goal with his role as weather-beaten cowboy Will Penny. In that picture, Heston was no longer portraying a young, physical Westerner, but a tough, jaded cowhand. One scholar described him as particularly suited for such roles. "Few actors have so strikingly embodied the spirit of rugged individualism as Charlton Heston," he contended.[140]

Many of Heston's roles had reflected traditional figures, but he was not afraid to probe characters in less glamorous or heroic circumstances. In the case of *Will Penny*, one student of the Western genre described the film as "a very different story of the West" that provided "a rare glimpse of the workaday world of the cowboy during the late 1880s." As he explained, "Charlton Heston stars in the title role of an aging cowpuncher who is anything but heroic." *Will Penny*'s promotional campaign featured a narrative that reflected this element. "Everything about this Western stamps it as unusual, except one thing. It takes place in the late 1800's. And that's Heston country."[141]

138 John Miller, *Ralph Richardson: The Authorized Biography* (London, 1995), 200.

139 Ibid., 202-203.

140 Douglas Brode, *Dream West: Politics and Religion in Cowboy Movies* (Austin, TX, 2013), 44.

141 Jay Hyams, *The Life and Times of the Western Movie* (New York, 1983), 169; "Paramount Press Book and Merchandising Manual" for *Will Penny*, 1967, Wills.

Heston captured the essence of a man battling the seasonal nature of an occupation that took him from cattle drives to the routine duties for maintaining vast spreads of territory, and who faced the loneliness that accompanied this life in the saddle. *Will Penny* also meant that as he approached his mid-forties, Heston could explore the challenges of middle age from the relative comfort of another man's perspective.

Ironically, the performer who would embody the character so well initially balked at the script. He was wary of projects that were incomplete as filming approached, but Walter Seltzer's vehemence that he read it anyway convinced him. Seltzer could have predicted the response. "This is one of the best openings I've ever read," Heston observed. The only caveat was that screenwriter Tom Gries wanted to direct the picture himself and, according to Seltzer, had insisted that without this assurance "won't sell us the script." Hoping to put the project in the hands of an experienced director, Heston explained, "I paused . . . maybe eight seconds: 'I just changed my mind.'" If all went well, he would become Will Penny.

In another twist, the initial meeting of actor and writer did not conform to expectations either. Heston envisioned his new collaborator in the form of a younger Yakima Canutt, but instead of a grizzled man from the West, he found Gries to be a Chicagoan who was "the son of a jazz singer." Nevertheless, the writer had found an authentic voice; he and Heston connected immediately. "How could we not?" Heston recalled. "He'd written me one of the great parts of my life."[142]

He was also concerned with accepting a role in another period picture. "For awhile I thought I might sneak my way back into the 20th century, but along came 'Will Penny,'" he explained. "What could I do? It was such a good script. I became a backslider. I couldn't pass up a role like that." Heston never changed his opinion. "It turned out to be one of the best [films] I've made, certainly among my best performances."[143]

Film critics like Leonard Maltin agreed. He called the motion picture "[O]ne of the best films on the cowboy/loner ever to come out of Hollywood. Heston's character is one of great strength." Unfortunately, corporate realities hamstrung the project. It was released in London without fanfare, and consequently gained no traction. What should have been a high point for Heston as a performer in

142 *CHA*, 385.

143 "Seasoned with History," in *Will Penny* "Press Book," 1967, 2, Wills; *CHA*, 391.

a nuanced role that displayed his growth as an actor quickly disappeared from theaters.[144]

Even so, Heston believed he had something special in *Will Penny* and thought others would agree if it were properly promoted. "Walter and I talked a bit about mounting a trade press campaign for Academy nominations on *Will Penny*," he noted in early January 1968. Heston never had difficulty in promoting his work, but admitted that he was "embarrassed at the idea of flacking for a nomination." Fortunately for him, but less so for the motion picture, he was able to shift his attention to other work.[145]

In addition to his screen responsibilities, Charlton Heston undertook his duties as Screen Actors Guild president. On June 20, 1967, he recorded the grueling schedule of "shooting all day, negotiating all night," as his team sought to hammer out a new contract for the members. In a contemporary article for *TV Guide*, Joseph Finnigan highlighted these activities: "Charlton Heston, who has fought cowboys, Indians, Romans, noble knights and raging seas, is sallying forth again, this time to battle television." In this case, Finnigan explained, "He goes armed not with conventional weapons such as swords and guns but with a formidable shield, the powerful and prestigious Screen Actors Guild, whose membership includes all actors who work in movies and TV, from the mighty John Waynes to the most obscure bit players." Heston had learned from Ronald Reagan the effectiveness of employing all the tools, including strikes, to advance an agenda, and knew he had numbers on his side. "One of the more interesting Hollywood spectacles this summer will undoubtedly star Charlton Heston and his army at the gates of network television. Truly a cast of thousands."[146]

In addition to his SAG duties, Heston understood the on-going imperative of reaching the audiences that had been patronizing his films. Twentieth Century Fox brought together several of its stars, including Heston, Julie Andrews, Bette Davis, and Steve McQueen for a short directed by Richard Fleischer. It encouraged people to "Think Twentieth" as they considered their cinematic choices. Fleischer would direct Heston in the science fiction thriller *Soylent Green*.[147]

---

144 Leonard Maltin, *Leonard Maltin's Movie & Video Guide, 2001 Edition* (New York, 2000), 1569; *ALJ*, 284.

145 Ibid., 308.

146 Ibid., 274-275; Joseph Finnigan, "Fighting on Another Front," *TV Guide* (June 17, 1967), 12, 14.

147 "Think Twentieth," Internet Movie Database, Jan. 11, 2019.

Heston had long taken an interest in foreign affairs and remained an advocate for the projection of a strong America in that realm. He was one of a list of prominent actors of film and television who lent their talents to promote the sale of "freedom shares" on behalf of the Treasury Department after President Lyndon Johnson ordered Secretary Henry Fowler to "get some stars" to take up the task. Writer Vera Glaser noted that as a result of the directive, "[t]he department swiftly dispatched an emissary to Hollywood to persuade 15 of the movie colony's biggest names to make 30- and 60-second TV spots." Heston joined Bob Hope, Dean Martin, Dick Van Dyke, Lucille Ball, Andy Griffith, Kirk Douglas, Irene Ryan, Eddie Albert, and Pat Boone in answering the call. "Everybody thought President Kennedy was close to the stars," a Treasury official remarked, "but President Johnson is much closer. He has a greater appreciation of the value of these people on reaching the public."[148]

Will Penny had demonstrated the degree to which Charlton Heston had developed as an actor. *Planet of the Apes* allowed him to expand as one, and to reach new audiences through a powerful science fiction vehicle. He brought to *Apes* a persona that carried his character in ways few other actors could have done. Heston's role as an astronaut thrust into a skewed world where apes had become dominant over humans was a matter of serendipitous casting with contemporary attitudes and movie trends. One writer explained, "I don't think the movie could have been so forceful . . . with anyone else . . . he's an archetype of what makes Americans win." Heston's casting worked because "he represents American power." Another noted that audiences would feel that "if it can happen to Charlton Heston, it can happen to anyone."[149] Of course, the actor maintained that whatever his physical presence might be, if the film succeeded in making moviegoers suspend belief in order to accept the premise, then it was less about him personally than the story itself.

Heston had embraced the physical requirements of each of his previous roles; he was prepared to benefit from a rigid training regimen when necessary and took great pride in maintaining his physique. In *Planet of the Apes*, he played a human who was exposed completely before a tribunal of ape leaders sitting in judgment over him. Allegory aside, for a performer in his mid-forties, such an appearance still

---

148 Vera Glaser, "LBJ Finds Picture He Likes," *BG*, July 1, 1967.

149 Kim, *Schaffner*, 238; Ibid., 239.

elicited appreciation, as when one individual watching the scene unfold gushed, "Hmmm, nice buns."[150]

He also kept his focus on the promotional junkets he knew were crucial to determining the success of his film work. In connection with *Apes*, he appeared on *The Ed Sullivan Show* and did a quick European publicity tour. After a stop in Rome, Heston was in Milan, where he learned that ticket sales for *Planet of the Apes* were already in record-breaking territory for Los Angeles. He later insisted that his interest in such "fiscal gloatings" was similar to "presidents boasting about how many states they carried."[151] Heston was not above such ego-massaging moments, but he knew his continuing viability in his chosen profession depended upon the very success over which he was "gloating."

During the same period, the native Midwesterner also took time to help promote Illinois in a documentary designed to celebrate the sesquicentennial of its statehood. In addition to conducting an interview, Chicago reporter Norma Lee Browning commented on the actor's role in the process. "The taping was scheduled to start at 9:15 a.m. Heston, always meticulously on time, arrived precisely at 9:14." She found him "impeccably attired" for the work and concluded, "Heston isn't the beads-and-turtleneck type." Browning also noted that as the morning proceeded the actor's attire transformed. "First off comes the jacket. Then he loosens his tie, unbuttons his collar, rolls up his sleeves, and paces the floor—rehearsing, rephrasing, reworking, rewriting, and polishing to perfection not only the script he's narrating, but the ring and tone, the flow and inflection of his voice." According to Browning, "Heston is one star who believes sincerely that an actor must never be satisfied with his performance: 'If I ever have the feeling that I cannot better a performance, then it will be time to quit.'" Volunteering on the project "because of love for his home state and his convictions about actors' responsibilities as citizens," the native son "was working as hard" as if he were "being paid his customary $75,000 to $100,000 fee for such an assignment." Heston had to work around scheduling conflicts in order to complete the assignment but thought the project worthwhile. "I like Illinois and I liked the script. It was the kind of thing I could do and wanted to do.' He recognized the value of the work he was

---

150 Champ Clark, "Picks & Pans, talking with . . . Charlton Heston," *People Weekly* (Sept. 7, 1998), 32.

151 *ALJ*, 291-292.

doing for future generations. 'I felt that because of its long-term use in schools and educational projects, it perhaps would be of more lasting value.'[152]

Another welcome connection to the past occurred when *Ben-Hur* raced into re-release in 1969. The selection of Miami for a special showing reflected a concentration on broader appeal. Heston was among the attendees, along with William Wyler, Stephen Boyd, and Yakima Canutt, with a gala event set for February 25. Additional showings followed at venues in major cities in the United States and Canada, including a Washington premiere designed to raise funds for the March of Dimes. These showings only added to the bottom line of a film that was already a giant among box office draws.[153]

Demands on his time persisted as Metro-Goldwyn-Mayer continued to promote its sweeping epic. An "Exhibitor's Campaign Book from MGM" for *Ben-Hur* listed multiple screenings of "The World's Most Honored Motion Picture!" Other articles noted the extraordinary number of the movie's "firsts" and the degree to which it had reached a global audience in 50 different languages. Heston provided an essay devoted to his experiences as a charioteer and numerous photographs offered visual evidence of the splendor and drama of the race settings. Now presented in "Wide Screen," "Stereophonic Sound," and "Metrocolor," Wyler's classic promised to attract new viewers and entice older ones to return. A text for radio spots promised to build upon the film's historic track record: "The most honored motion picture of all-time returns to the screen!"[154]

At home in the "House that Hur built" for his twenty-fifth wedding anniversary on March 17, Heston was both candid and introspective in expressing his appreciation for his wife and companion of so many years. "I remember twenty-five years ago the way she looked, in violet, and how marvelous it seemed to me that she would marry me." They had experienced the difficult and happier times of all couples, "but I know I'm more because I married her than I would ever have been alone."[155]

Tennis remained a welcome diversion, although during another trip to London—"I don't know how many times I've climbed on PAA #120, but I feel as though I've worn a deep trail in the sky, like a boy driving the cows down

152 Norma Lee Browning, "The Spectacular Burden of Being Charlton Heston," "Guggenheim Productions records, Tomorrow is a Day—clippings," f.3235, HL.

153 Solomon, *Ben-Hur*, 789, 791.

154 "Exhibitor's Campaign Book from MGM" for *Ben-Hur*, 1969, Wills.

155 *ALJ*, 310.

through a muddy pasture"—even that release was not always possible due to his demanding schedule. "There was certainly none to play tennis," he observed of the time devoted to other chores, even though he "kept my rackets out of the bag until the last minute." An assistant said to Lydia, "When he dies and knocks on the Pearly Gates, if the Devil taps him on the shoulder and says, 'How about a little tennis?' he'll go.'" Later, while chatting with tennis star Rod Laver, the latter revealed that he was suffering from a case of "tennis elbow, too," to which Heston replied humorously, "It has to be the only thing our games have in common."[156]

Heston undertook a physical role as a veteran National Football League quarterback confronting the downside of his career in *Number One*, a grueling and gritty film. With that picture in the can, he held an informal gathering to review his work and enjoy the associations he had built while engaged in it. One of these included a special screening of *Number One* at what sportswriter John Hall called "the humble Heston shack atop Coldwater Canyon." There the writer joined with several of the coaches, consultants, and players who had helped the actor learn their profession. The attendees included Roosevelt Grier and Mike Henry, both of whom found work in other Heston pictures. "As always, Heston is powerful," Hall concluded, "a very believable member of the violent world." One of the authentic gridiron stars said he had "never seen anybody so dedicated." Hall concurred with the assessment. "Dedication, of course, is the way it's always been with Heston, the unassuming Oscar winner who gets totally involved with everything he does. He drove his own chariot in 'Ben-Hur' and he took all of his own falls and sprawls as the broken cowpoke in 'Will Penny.'" Hall had the last word, however, when he noted how Heston's quarterback assailed sports writers for thinking "they own all of you" for "a hamburger and a beer every Sunday." "Well nobody's perfect," Hall remarked, and "incidentally, I prefer hot dogs."[157]

Heston took additional time away from his film work to perform other duties of professional importance. In November he appeared before lawmakers in Washington in his capacity as president of the Screen Actors Guild. He found a moment to meld his pitch for additional funding for motion pictures with an illustration of the requirements acting asked of those involved in the industry. "Money alone, of course, cannot make good entertainment, but one thing money can buy is time," he explained. "Time to prepare, time to design, time to write,

---

156 Ibid., 314, 315.

157 John Hall, "Welcome to the NFL," *LAT*, July 17, 1969.

time to develop character, time to rehearse and time to learn—learn something new and fresh, something creative."[158]

With his own time at a premium, Heston understood well such demands while remaining focused on his art, although temptations to stray from that path continually emerged. In early December 1969, a group of prominent Democrats "urged" him to run for a seat in the United States Senate. Heston harbored doubts from the start. "I'm pretty sure I don't want to do it, but it's the kind of thing you can't just brush off," he noted in his journal. "I can't deny it's worth doing, but you can't do any job well unless you really *want* to do it. I want to act. I know it's trivial, but there it is."[159]

The next several days found him "mulling over the offer" and polling trusted friends and associates like Jolly West. A round of tennis with Rod Laver and Roy Emerson allowed him a respite from the difficult choice he faced, but a few days before Christmas he still felt the need "to dispose of my nonblooming political career. I talked to Paul Ziffren, who knows as much about it as anyone, and decided what I really felt all along: I don't want to do it enough to do it."[160]

Later, Heston described his initial ambivalence and the sentiment that had guided his final decision most strongly. "When at long last I came back from London, I broached the subject with my most important advisor, Lydia. She knows me better than anyone else, and was best qualified to render advice." Interestingly, she approached the matter indirectly, by posing a question: "But what do you want, Charlie?" The starkness of the question reached him in a way that all the other ruminations had not. "It was as if a light went on," he explained. "Suddenly, I realized that deep down inside, I didn't want to do it. The thought of never being able to act again, go on stage, or wait for the first take was simply unbearable."[161]

In a subsequent interview, he exposed his inner turmoil while rebuffing attempts by California Democrats to draft him into running to take "a highly vulnerable Republican seat here." He suggested he was not closing the door entirely to such a path. "I decided to wait," he observed, "knowing I could run later." Deeper

---

158 Testimony, Hearings Before the Subcommittee on Communication and Power on the Committee on Interstate and Foreign Commerce, House of Representatives, Ninety-first Congress, First Session, November 21, 1969. Re: H.R. 420. To Amend the Communications Act of 1934 so as to Prohibit the Granting of Authority to Broadcast Pay Television Programs (Washington: Government Printing Office, 1969), 141.

159 *ALJ*, 326-327.

160 Ibid., 327, 328.

161 Heston and Isbouts, *Hollywood*, 170-171.

concerns kept him sidelined in such contests, however. "What I've had to face with this Senate thing is if I ran and won—and I think I would—I'd never be able to act again. And that's impossible for me to accept. It means too much to me." With a typical demonstration of humor, he concluded, "I'd rather *play* a Senator than be one."[162] Indeed, if portraying leading historical figures drew him closer to a role in public life outside of the acting sphere, he seemed content for the time being to hold those possibilities at arms' length.

Regarding his calculations on entering politics, Heston also demonstrated an awareness that for all his disdain of a public life as a celebrity, he enjoyed the status it provided and the options for activism it offered. He seemed to understand what one scholar asserted, and Ronald Reagan articulated, in the transition that undertaking political office would require from one realm to another. "Once an entertainer runs for public office," he or she "ceases being a celebrity and begins a career as a politician."[163] As things stood, Heston could have influence in association with politicians and political causes without becoming one himself and sacrificing meaningful elements of his life he considered essential to his wellbeing in the process.

At the beginning of December 1969, such a moment came as he spoke before an audience at the Ambassador Hotel in Los Angeles. The scene of Robert F. Kennedy's assassination was now the venue for honoring the widow of slain civil rights leader Martin Luther King, Jr. Heston's task was to introduce Coretta Scott King and he rose to the occasion with genuine emotion. In tribute to her husband, he quoted William Shakespeare's words, which had been written "more than 400 years ago so he really couldn't have been writing about Martin Luther King, could he? He was, of course, because he was writing about greatness, and great men have much in common." Heston emphasized the cherished theme of roles that individuals could play in shaping history. "I believe in great men. I think most of the important work in the world is done by great men."

"It's good that we do this," observed the actor who took such pride in having marched alongside King in Washington six years earlier. "Good that we gather tonight to mark his memory. Because we need him." Heston believed that "truth" had been a tool in King's hands, and that his words and deeds "became a hammer . . . and it was a tool to make men free." He was fearful that the significance of the issues at stake was already diluting with time. "We are here because the job is

162 Rader, "If I Ran & Won," 4–5.

163 Harvey, *Celebrity Influence*, 20.

not done, and because the tool has been almost forgotten." With the dramatic emphasis of the thespian who had brought Moses to life on the screen, he closed. "I am proud . . . proud to stand here now and say simply, Ladies and Gentlemen . . . Mrs. Coretta Scott King."[164]

The 1960s meant a great deal to the professional life and career of Charlton Heston, with recognition from his peers and striking portrayals that solidified his stature as one of Hollywood's premier stars. One later assessment summarized the circumstances well: "By the mid-1960s," writer Roberta Plutzik asserted in *Horizon*, "Heston commanded more power in the marketplace than most actors."[165] The decade also offered him the chance to accept what he recognized as meaningful off-screen responsibilities as well. He had been able to make a stand for civil rights, which came to define how he saw himself in a moment of crucial national development. A life in the dramatic arts enabled Heston to recognize that challenges remained ahead that even the most stoic figure might find daunting. The track, especially in a turbulent decade, also often became difficult to traverse, and forward momentum proved almost impossible to sustain.

---

164 "Charlton Heston's Speech Introducing Mrs. Coretta Scott King at the Dinner Honoring Her at the Cocoa-Nut Grove, Ambassador Hotel, on December 2nd, 1969," Heston Papers, HL.

165 Plutzik, "Last of the Epic Heroes," 30.

Chapter Six

THE CHALLENGES OF A SLOPPY TRACK
1960s

"Today, surely, we're all faltering."
—Heston on learning of John Kennedy's death, November 22, 1963

"Ben-Hur's Chariot Stolen"
—Theft of Heston's vehicle, 1965

"That's bad news, Jack. Bad for the country."
—Heston's response to Jack Valenti on hearing that
Lyndon Johnson would not seek re-election, 1968

꙳

So much of what Charlton Heston was experiencing in the 1960s reflected the turmoil of the nation. He had reached the pinnacle of his profession with an Academy Award but struggled to maintain control over his career as it progressed. The track had seemed to be laid out well before him, only for him to encounter unexpected hurdles, as had Judah Ben-Hur in the celluloid race that had won esteem for both.

Heston's life was taking on a special intensity as the new decade opened. He had wanted to be in his new home before heading to New York for work on *The Tumbler* and even harbored a brief resentment at the project, "a mood that had better pass before rehearsals begin." But with the house not quite finished and the old apartment awash in "a shamble of boxes and naked parquet" that he now considered "obscene," Heston was finding difficulty maintaining the positivity that he prided himself in exhibiting, regardless of the circumstances.[1]

The junket to Japan for *Ben-Hur*'s premiere initially included Lydia, but her time was cut short by the sudden news that a heart attack had stricken her mother. Charlton noted that she "took" the shocking development "well, even slept, and the day went off as planned, once arrangements had been made for her to fly home tonight." Heston observed at the end of the hectic day, "I got Lydia airborne safely by midnight, standing on the night-breezed observation platform, watching her into the belly of the 707." Their transient life kept them apart for several more days; when he finally returned home, he found "all relieved that Lydia's mother seems past her crisis."[2]

Even the pinnacle of his professional life, when he accepted the Best Actor Oscar for *Ben-Hur*, was not unalloyed. In his zeal to state, for the record, the names of the people he considered essential to the success he and the film had enjoyed, he risked overshadowing the celebration. In addition to his director and the producer, Sam Zimbalist, who had died during filming, the actor mentioned writer Christopher Fry in his acceptance remarks. Heston had come to have a strong feeling for Fry and the contribution he believed Fry had made with a problematic screenplay. This was an opportunity to underscore that appreciation and express his gratitude, whatever anyone else might think. Screenplay contributor Gore Vidal, who had observed caustically that "Chuck has all the charm of a wooden Indian," did not, in Heston's mind, warrant special mention, nor did S. N. Behrman and Maxwell Anderson; Karl Tunberg, meanwhile, had already received sole screen credit.[3]

In the aftermath of that public display, the secretary of the Writers Guild of America, Paul Gangelin, wrote Heston to express his union's outrage over his remarks on the night of the ceremony. "The Board instructed me to express to you our strong protest against what can only be construed as an implied attack on the Guild's procedures which you made in the course of your Academy acceptance speech." Gangelin drew a decided inference concerning the actor's intentions in mentioning Fry's name directly. "By gratuitously interjecting the name of a writer who did not receive screen credit for the picture 'Ben-Hur', you reopened what seems a calculated campaign to detract from the reputation of the man who did in fact receive credit." Even more importantly, from Gangelin's perspective, Heston's

---

1 *ALJ*, 84.

2 "March 1960, 30 Wednesday," *On the Set*; *ALJ*, 91.

3 Eliot, *Charlton Heston*, 166-167, 198-199.

comments "reflected on the repute of the Writers Guild in respect to its credit arbitration function generally, in spite of the fact that this issue regarding 'Ben-Hur' had been resolved long before the time of the broadcast."[4]

The actor took time to reply to what felt was "a ridiculous letter." His April 15 response was itself incredulous. "I am amazed by the amount of meaning you extracted from my rather disjointed remarks . . . the other night; I can only regret that, to you, all of it seemed hostile." He could not contain his displeasure. "In all honesty, it had not occurred to me to get clearance from your organization for my expression of gratitude," he maintained. "I don't see how you can challenge my competence to make this judgment, especially since, while no member of your Guild was in Rome during the filming of Ben Hur, Mr. Wyler, Mr. Fry and I were, of course, there throughout the production." Then in a moment drawn more from the language of *The Ten Commandments* than anything Judah Ben-Hur might say, he questioned: "Is it your intention to expunge Mr. Fry's name from the lips of men?" Heston insisted he "did not invite and do not welcome controversy especially when it comes from a body of men whose craft I respect deeply and whom, as individuals, I have so often found both creative and congenial." Still the matter rankled him too much to let it pass without comment.[5]

Discussion of his Oscars speech spilled over into the Hestons' "first sit-down dinner party in the house." Willy Wyler expressed his pleasure "at the press reaction to the Writers Guild letter to me, plus my reply." Heston thought the issue was "rapidly becoming an entertaining controversy," but the distraction was unsettling. It stayed in his mind for years to come, and was reflected in comments he made twenty years later: "None of this did anything to enhance their position, of course." He felt the Guild "became the laughing stock of the film community" for a time "through a couple of further exchanges, until some wise man wrote back to the executive secretary and said, 'stop writing letters to Chuck Heston.'"[6]

Perhaps nothing represented the mixture of emotions for the actor and his family as much as the permanent home they were establishing on a ridge overlooking the metropolis of Los Angeles. "For months," writer Bill Davidson noted in an article, "while Heston pored over blueprints, Lydia planned closets and kitchen, and Fraser selected such things as checkerboard floor for his playroom." Davidson added, "The Hestons' home took more than a year to build. For young Fraser, the

---

4 "Paul Gangelin to My dear Sir, April 7, 1960," Heston Papers, HL.

5 *ALJ*, 92; "Charlton Heston to Dear Mr. Gangelin, April 15, 1960," Heston Papers, HL.

6 *ALJ*, 92; "Charlton Heston to Dear Jan, August 30, 1980," William Wyler collection, HL.

construction site was a vast playground filled with sand piles and other wondrous things. For Charlton and Lydia Heston, it was an exhilarating but sometimes nightmarish experience." A strike delayed its completion, but the family picnics to bide the time. "It was chaos, but it was fun," Heston observed.[7]

Yet with so much going so well for Heston, signs existed in 1960 that indicated that challenges remained, some of which he would not be able to overcome easily. Undoubtedly, the most bitter of these was the chance to collaborate with one of the profession's most renowned figures in a project that was troubled from the beginning to its ignominious end.

Heston wanted specially to work with Laurence Olivier and accepted an opportunity to do so under his direction. *The Tumbler* was an unlikely vehicle in many respects, not the least because it required an American audience to embrace what one of Olivier's biographers termed "a drama of such distinctively English sensibilities." The plot included an odd twist in which the person accused of murdering the father of a young girl was her stepfather *and* her lover.

Heston also thought the casting another complicating factor, as Olivier initially had turned to a long-standing friend he finally had to fire from the part. Poor notices doomed the play and what should have been a cast party turned into something like a wake. Heston remembered the circumstances through the prism of having worked with Olivier, but the sudden demise of the project was a heavy burden to bear nonetheless. He told Joe Hyams of the *Chicago Sun-Times*, "I'm sorry the play closed. It was a blow to my ego also but none of us thought it would be easy. I figure you can learn more from trying something difficult and failing than trying something easy and making a success of it."[8] For a man who had never shirked his obligations, the point was a meaningful one. He had seen how to handle a very difficult situation that had turned painful at the end by placing the matter in proper perspective. He knew there would be such occasions when, as Olivier had observed eloquently, "the gods do not attend," and he hoped to be as prepared as possible to face that situation with the fortitude, grace, and intelligence he was witnessing now.

He was also considering a new epic film at the time, one that held the promise of building on the momentum from his Oscar-winning performance and would allow the upward trajectory of his career to continue. But Charlton Heston was frustrated that only subpar material seemed to be coming his way, and he had

7 Bill Davidson, "The House that Ben-Hur Built," *Look* (May 24, 1960), 56.

8 Joe Hyams, "Heston Sees Profit in His Stage Flop," *Chicago Sun-Times*, Mar. 6, 1960, Scrapbooks, HL.

serious misgivings about the latest script and his participation in a project that depended on the development of a better one. He also worried that he was falling into a pattern of settling for work based on clauses in contracts for a percentage of the gross, which had "started [him] down the road to whoredom."[9]

The filming of *El Cid* offered exhilarating moments, but also saw its share of challenges that exposed the harder and more demanding side of Heston's professional and personal character. Prime among these was the behavior co-star Sophia Loren often exhibited and his response to it. When her "by now predictably late arrival" sparked his anger, Heston blurted, "I'm not good at this kind of crap, I admit; I hate it so." His assessment that "she's just more star than pro" softened with time, however.[10]

As he returned from Europe, Heston found that the "sybaritic joys" of travel on the *Queen Mary* were not enough to free him from sobering thoughts about the fleeting nature of existence. "I cabled good luck to Coop with chill foreboding," he recorded, having received word that Gary Cooper was gravely ill. As compensation for this sobering reality, Heston turned to other pursuits to power his way through such moments of introspection. "An extra workout failed to wash away awareness of mortality or justify the gluttonous eating habits I inevitably fall into at sea."[11]

These moments seemed to typify the turbulent nature of those days, as pleasant experiences competed with trying ones for the actor. He could not seem to fit in everything, and when he pressed, the result was frustrating. The joys of being back in his native land among friends and family were quickly tempered by "a ghastly lunch press conference," as the man who had worked so diligently to promote his name and career heard an introduction to "'Charles, Chuck Heston,' and it went downhill from there." He noted, "I screwed myself up with an awkward sort of unprepared speech, in a situation completely inappropriate for it." Declaring, "I hate to really blow one like that; it put me in a foul temper for the rest of the day," he fought to regain some semblance of equilibrium by enjoying the view of New York City "from a spectacular restaurant on top of the new Time-Life Building, at dinner with Lydia tonight."[12]

9 *ALJ*, 98.

10 Ibid., 110.

11 Ibid., 117-118.

12 Ibid., 118.

Another lesson in priorities came a few days later with the news that Cooper had died. Heston felt the satisfaction that his friend and fellow traveler in the arts had spent his final moments "safe in the bosom of his church and his family," but could not free himself of the significance of the event. "I'm moved at his death," he admitted. "I'm proud to have known him and worked with him. He's a good man gone, and I sense a sleeve-tug of mortality in it."[13]

Almost symbolically, fire threatened the very sanctuary Heston had established for himself and his family with the proceeds he had gained from *Ben-Hur*. In November 1961, a disastrous blaze spared the Coldwater Canyon house when it ravaged the Bel Air-Brentwood region. After that danger was averted, flames from another fire forced the Hestons to flee and caused significant harm to the roof. One estimate set the damage at $1,000, although the structure remained intact. "Eight Los Angeles fire units quelled the blaze," according to a *Los Angeles Times* report. Heston blamed the situation on faulty ventilation of his steam room and battled the blaze with a garden hose until the professionals could complete the work. "The firemen did well to save as much of the wall and roof there as they did," he recorded, before adding stoically, "It could've been much worse."[14]

Rhetorical fires threatened to consume projects Heston considered during this period. On November 15, he "ran *El Cid* and was very disappointed," although he remained convinced the film "will make a lot of money." As always, he was most critical of his own performance. Four days later came a slight resuscitation of *The Fall of the Roman Empire*, which nevertheless seemed to be going nowhere. "I'm still convinced there is no good reason for me to make the film," he maintained, "since it can do nothing but make me a lot of money."[15]

Curiously, given the Academy Award he had received, Heston remained unsure of how much progress he was making in his profession, but he was less uncertain about the state of his bank account. "*El Cid* put no stars in my crown, but maybe a ruby or two in my pocket." The lessons of *The Tumbler* and the memories of scrambling for work in New York City could not help but temper the relatively recent achievements he might otherwise be willing to embrace. No less a figure than Lydia understood this inner turmoil when she observed, "I would like him to

13 Ibid., 119.

14 "Charlton Heston, Family Flee Fire," *LAT*, Nov. 13, 1961; *ALJ*, 130.

15 Ibid., 131.

work less, and enjoy the success he has more. But he goes into each new film just as if it were his first."[16]

55 Days at Peking was also turning into a difficult chore. After criticizing the project for the lack of a viable working script in his private writings, he shifted, in a public interview, to the unnecessary difficulties he felt co-star Ava Gardner was bringing to the project. "As for Ava—well, I must be careful. But let's say she wasn't the most disciplined or dedicated actress I ever worked with." Gardner's drinking left the cast and crew bewildered and scrambling to continue in her absence. Remembering that Heston had accepted the project as a special favor, filmmaker Philip Yordan observed strongly, "While Heston worked 16 hours a day, she did not, and I not only rewrote most of her scenes, I killed her [character] off early in the picture."[17]

In his journals, Heston vented his anger as best he could in a fashion that allowed him to release the pressure he was feeling toward a production filled with challenges. The usual chores, including a meeting with director George Stevens about John the Baptist for *The Greatest Story Ever Told*, persisted, but the Heston clan was soon on its way back to Madrid, via New York, to spend the summer battling the Boxers. By this point, a contract locked Gardner into the role of a Russian countess; Heston was apprehensive. "I start this picture with more misgivings than I remember about a film since I've had any creative controls," he admitted in early July. He observed that "I haven't worked up the basic enthusiasm you need for this, or any project, yet. The day I make a film without it, I'm a whore."[18]

Heston's admiration of David Niven's deft handling of tricky questions about *55 Days at Peking* by reporters was one of the benefits of watching a talented colleague at work, but he continued to struggle with balancing the vagaries of personality with the necessities of making motion pictures. "This must have been the longest day, and one of the toughest I've shot on the film yet," he noted on August 25. "I'd rather have retaken Valencia, or rerun the chariot race, than whirl through the sixteen bars of the Victorian waltz the scene required." The emotions associated with the film shooting intensified, greatly enhanced by what he viewed as the unprofessional nature of his colleague. By September 1, the pressure had reached a breaking point. "Today marked the worst behavior I've yet seen from the curious breed I make my living opposite," he asserted. "Ava showed up for a

16 "*December 31, Los Angeles*," ibid., 134; Hamill, "Heston: Larger Than Life," 90.

17 Charles Highman, *Ava: A Life Story* (New York, 1974), 211-212.

18 *ALJ*, 147-148.

late call, did one shot (with the usual incredible delay in coming to the set), and then walked off just before lunch." Irritated when an extra took an unauthorized picture of her, Gardner turned the break into a three-hour hiatus that ended just as abruptly not long after she returned to the set. "Great day," Heston observed with a final brush of dismissal. "Poor, sad lady."[19]

On October 4, he noted the mix of emotions that a difficult shoot on a distant location could produce. "At three minutes after midnight, while I was busy defending Peking, they ceased firing long enough to bring me a cake on top of Tartar Wall." The gesture did not allay the sense of drudgery that he felt, but Heston tried to respond to the situation with some degree of equanimity. "I seem to have reached that point in life where you neither feel nor (thank God for my livelihood) look as old as you are. I do begrudge having spent the last months of my thirty-seventh year slaving away at this unresponsive lump of material we still hope to end by calling a film, but that's the way of it." Lydia had presented him with a sword he now saw as an "effective symbol for the rest of this film, the rest of my life. Do what you have to do . . . and cut through the crap." A few days later, he enthusiastically noted the chance to make a brief trip from Spain to New York, "where Lydia could meet me while I narrated a film on Kennedy for the defense department."[20] It was not an exaggeration to say that he clung to her for vital grounding and support in difficult times.

A voracious reader, Heston kept himself as informed as possible about world events. His work for the Department of Defense and his own interests served to direct some of that focus toward foreign affairs. One such set of events was the Soviet Union's involvement in Cuba. President Kennedy's debacle in the Bay of Pigs fiasco and a general sense that he was vulnerable, if not weak, encouraged Premier Nikita Khrushchev to test the administration's resolve in the Western Hemisphere and beyond. At home in California, Heston and his family "sat in a row on the sofa watching JFK on TV, announcing the naval blockade of Cuba." He admitted feeling "scared, and proud" before declaring his support for the action. "It's been a long time since we took any initiative in the world."[21]

In his adult life, especially in entertainment and charity settings, alcohol was usually present. Heston frequently indulged, overdoing it only on occasion. On flights across the Atlantic to and from the overseas settings that required his

19 Ibid., 150-151.

20 Ibid., 155-156.

21 Ibid., 157.

presence, he took the opportunity to catch up on sleep, read scripts, and sip Scotch. "I flew the high thin polar air in a boozy semifuddle," he noted on March 31, "due in equal parts to rich food, rich whiskey, and a remarkably bad action script I read en route." Two months later, he offered the observation, "A long, long flight over, spent rereading the [*War Lord*] script for typos (of which there are too many) . . . and fighting off the extra Scotch they keep pressing on you. This first-class jet travel can turn you into a sot." He had perfected the routine that when by himself, he took the earliest flight, slept briefly after arrival, and lunched before playing some tennis or running "to get my blood circulating, on the theory that I can fall into bed more or less adjusted to European time." Lydia preferred later flights and a long night of sleep to confront the typical traveler's jet lag. Heston noted that he would "always try to schedule any trip, especially overseas, to polish off as many different chores as I can . . . a practice Lydia deplores as excessively Puritan."[22]

Later, as he settled into another extended flight to Europe, Heston continued his ruminations and his travel comforts. In this instance, he was heading to a Dutch royal opening for *55 Days at Peking* and receive the Belgian equivalent of the Best Actor Oscar he had won for *Ben-Hur*. He could not escape feeling vulnerable. "There's something indecent about lolling in liquored luxury seven miles above the ice men scrabbled over, dying for the glory of walking there," he observed as the flight winged its way over Greenland and the polar expanses.[23] Heston did not seem to think that the amount of travel or any of the habits he had formed represented any significant type of difficulty for him at this point. His physical activities, adherence to his professional obligations, and personal pride at doing anything well were enough to keep him going.

His increasingly public role presented him with many challenges, some of which could be perplexing; others were amusing. While in London, the actor took on the role of pitchman for the dairy authority in Britain. Yet on the day after April Fool's Day, the juxtaposition of a shaving accident and a glass of milk made the situation awkward. "This can't have been quite what the Milk Board had in mind," he told his journal.[24] Metaphorically, it must have seemed about right with competing elements defying his efforts to control them.

A rainy Paris compounded the mood, as did continuous interviews between England and France that struck Heston as making things "harder than it is" or

22 Ibid., 169, 171-172.

23 Ibid., 175.

24 Ibid., 169.

"curiously hostile," before his return to the United States. Even a welcome vacation with family and friends in Jamaica proved oddly unsettling. "This kind of day . . . is a little uneasy-making for a country boy from Michigan," he observed. He returned to Los Angeles to find that Columbia had withdrawn from the *War Lord* project. "We've wasted two months while they worked their way back to this position."[25] For Heston, the wheels seemed to be straining for traction, causing momentum to teeter between painful and slow.

Film work again took subordination to promotion, which employed some of Heston's earlier portrayals to generate interest in his latest venture. A publicity booklet for that motion picture used such a comparison to illustrate the star's public cachet as it informed interested moviegoers. "Charlton Heston's role of Major Matt Lewis in *55 Days at Peking* is unlike the star's portrayal of the Spanish warrior hero in the Samuel Bronston production *El Cid*, but it again proves that, as a star who answers the demands of a dominant role in a multi-million-dollar film, he has few equals."[26]

In addition to print materials, a schedule for selling the film promised to be as grueling as ever. An April 1963 press release noted that "Charlton Heston flew from Hollywood to New York yesterday . . . and proceeds to London on Wednesday, to attend the Royal Premiere of Samuel Bronston's '55 Days at Peking.'" From there, the actor would go to France to "attend [the] Paris premiere of the film, returning here May 9."

After a brief stay at home, another release alerted the public that "Heston flew out yesterday . . . for Washington, Pittsburgh and Boston, to promote Samuel Bronston's Allied Artists release, '55 Days at Peking.'" The notice illustrated his hectic schedule. "Star had been at home only over the weekend, after returning late last week from London and Paris premieres. He will cover four more U.S. cities for '55 Days' next week." Audiences might assume that a performer's work ended when the cameras finished rolling, but Heston's itinerary reflected the choreography and precision involved in fulfilling these enormous publicity demands:

Mon. May 13th	Los Angeles	Pittsburgh
Tues. May 14th	Pittsburgh	Washington
Wed. May 15th	Washington	Boston
Thurs. May 16th	Boston	Los Angeles
Mon. May 20th	Los Angeles	New York City

25 Ibid., 170.

26 "Samuel Bronston Presents 55 Days at Peking," *55 Days at Peking* publicity, f.81, Heston Papers, HL.

Wed. May 22nd	Newark	Cleveland
Thurs. May 23rd	Cleveland	Chicago
Sat. May 25th	Chicago	Los Angeles
Sun. May 26th	Los Angeles	San Francisco
Tues. May 28th	San Francisco	New York City[27]

Despite these efforts, mixed word on the box office front and uncertainty over its long-term prospects created tension. Tennis once more served as a release for the actor, but his frustration continued. "So far," he noted on June 1, "nothing has turned up." One studio sent a script, but it seemed to be "more or less like 55 Days at Peking, but smaller"; he concluded, "This is always the way of it. They offer you what you've just done."[28] Of course, movie moguls wanted to maintain successful trends, bringing out sequels until the formula ran dry or tapping into whatever appeared to work before something else came along to take its place. Intellectually, this ran counter to how Heston had sought to arrange his career, even as he understood the imperative itself.

Travel on behalf of Screen Actors Guild duties also supplied diversions, although large gatherings of any kind continued to bemuse and befuddle him. From his perspective, the attendees at such events often seemed mostly interested in promoting themselves. While participating in an international conference of performing unions in Amsterdam, Heston found the bulk of the time consumed by ceremony rather than substance. "They do feed you well," he admitted.[29]

Unfortunately, the feast he had hoped to enjoy—locating funding for *The Lovers*—continued to elude him. "They call it 'Development Hell,'" he later wrote about the exasperating episode, "and it can indeed last, or seem to, for eternity." As usual, timing and luck were critical elements. If the most amenable studio executives were not in position for one reason or another or the political environment did not seem to be right, even a worthy project could languish and die.

Those difficulties appeared to increase with daunting regularity. Heston had finally found a studio to take the work and Franklin Schaffner to direct it when, as they tackled the formidable preproduction matters, a secretary broke into the meeting with the tragic news that someone had apparently shot the president. Heston's travels to Washington had allowed him to interact with individuals in the

---

27 Jack Goldstein to "All Fieldmen Concerned," May 6, 1963, Charlton Heston itinerary, ibid.

28 *ALJ*, 174.

29 *CHA*, 313.

highest levels of government as he advocated for various causes. His admiration for Jack Kennedy was genuine. Then came the shock of events in Dealey Plaza in Dallas, as Lee Harvey Oswald took aim at the presidential motorcade and began squeezing his trigger.

Heston's grief over the slain president was just as heartfelt as his respect for the living figure had been. "It's a blind, brutal pointless act, and because of it we're much less than we were, or might have been," he recorded in his journal as he processed the event that shook both the nation and the security he had felt over his own place in it. Heston contemplated the sudden loss of a dynamic and inspiring leader and the larger ramifications that arose in his mind from it. "If you believe in our system, then you have to believe it won't fail because of this, but it will falter. Today, surely, we're all faltering."[30]

He became involved in the efforts to eulogize the fallen president and celebrate his life and achievements. As he contemplated the impact of the historic day, Heston chose a more stoic assessment that allowed him better perspective as the days following the assassination unfolded. "The program was . . . worth doing, I think," he concluded of his efforts. "It's all we can do." He was grateful to have a method of channeling his emotions in such trying times. He found refuge again on his ridge and in a long ride in the San Fernando Valley with Fraser.[31] They could relax together and bond once more, with Heston freed for the moment from the worldly worries that stood over the next horizon.

Another aspect of the actor's planning had ended with the dissolution of the Russell Lake Corporation upon his assumption of a leadership role in SAG, in order to avoid any appearance of impropriety. But the possibility of film production as a hedge against a diminution in acting opportunities was still attractive. Walter Seltzer thought he had found the solution in an entity tentatively titled Court Productions, which would allow Heston to remain in the background, outside of decision-making that might compromise him, while any projects undertaken by the new entity could generate revenues for all concerned. Later, when he arrived at his Universal Studios office in mid-September 1964 for discussions about *War Lord*, Heston noted a sign on the door that read "Fraser Productions."[32]

---

30 *ALJ*, 184.

31 Ibid; *CHA*, 318-319.

32 Eliot, *Charlton Heston*, 241. Court Productions would be listed along with Universal and Fraser Productions as producers for *The War Lord*; see Internet Movie Data Base, www.imdb.com/title/tt0059896/?ref_=fn_al_tt_1, accessed Dec. 3, 2018; *ALJ*, 207.

For a time, Heston found himself caught between worlds and demands, the whisk of emotion tugging at him while he confronted dragons of one size and shape or another. Fortunately, projects were now in the offing that would keep him occupied with the elements of his craft. He attended a meeting with Sam Peckinpah and Columbia Pictures brass over the possibilities for *Major Dundee*. "The air rings with high protestations of creative integrity," Heston noted in his journal. "Still, this seems like a good chance, using the conflict between the two major characters, both Southerners, one a loyal officer, the other Confederate, to explore the Civil War a little." Then there was "skeptical" word about *The War Lord* and time spent "hack[ing] away at the negotiations" between the American Film Institute and the Motion Picture Producers Association."[33]

In the meantime, Heston closed the year with Christmas Eve high above Coldwater Canyon, which he hoped to make a permanent tradition. He ordered a tree cut from his property in Michigan, and had it shipped and hoisted in their home on the ridge. The family would decorate that night and wait for a visitor from the Northern regions the next morning. At the same time, Heston chafed at the excess he was responsible in large measure for creating: "The day was deluged in gifts. Certainly, too many for one family. Giving is fine, but this much getting verges on gluttony." Even so, he could not resist the happiness the time brought those he loved most. And if a few days later, he lamented, "We're surrounded by food we'll never eat, books we'll never read, clothes we'll never wear," all going against his "Scottish-reared, depression-conditioned sensibilities"; he nevertheless relished knowing that "we're all together, and we love each other."

The end of a turbulent year brought a dampened tone. "This was an odd year, professionally," he noted, with little to show for his career except the always-present chance to grow and learn. He noted a real sense of depression. "For a man in this time, which is not always easy for an actor to keep in focus" he began, "this was a bad year, with many days we'd wipe away if we could. Yet the dark, endless river rolls on, and we're carried with it. Each day you do the best there is to do that day." He felt the need to press on "for an American whose president has been shot, as well as for an actor with a script that won't jell," and took comfort in the family he cherished.[34]

Major Dundee was the next pressing matter. A screening of a Western convinced Heston that its director, Sam Peckinpah, was the proper fit for taking on this film.

---

33 *ALJ*, 174-175.

34 Ibid., 187-188.

The call to bring him into the project left the star and his associates with a feeling of satisfaction—one of "a few undiluted pleasures in the frustrating business of making movies"—that, as with any creative endeavor, was bound to be short-lived. "From that moment on," he explained, "*Dundee* became more complicated. Much more."[35]

Every production in which Charlton Heston was involved had presented challenges and aggravations, but the *Dundee* shoot made these seem miniscule by comparison. The issues started with an unfinished script and the fact that this film represented the first one Peckinpah would be helming for a major studio. As they undertook the collaboration, Heston found himself ensconced in a commodious office with Peckinpah and learned quickly that both worked better when pacing around. This unusual creative dance became problematic until the actor arrived one day to find that the director had used tape to delineate the areas into which each could move without colliding with the other. Heston remembered that the solution, in that instance, "worked fine," but other problems continued to loom between the irascible director and the rest of the cast, crew, and production teams.[36]

Another complication was the remoteness of the location shoot itself. Peckinpah sent the cast and crew deep into Mexico. Heston was not particularly enthused. "Durango is . . . not very much," Heston noted. By the time he typed a descriptive update of his current work to his devoted newsletter readers, he put the matter more positively. "I've never made a film, I think, that moved so far and so often to find food for the cameras." Aside from his hope to make a historically-based movie of *Major Dundee*—"It has to be about the Civil War, I'm convinced"—the history student in Charlton Heston demonstrated an awareness of the conflict by referencing the battles of Gettysburg and Lookout Mountain and generals Ulysses S. Grant, William T. Sherman, Robert E. Lee, and James Longstreet. He also believed the picture would result in important exposure. "Sam Peckinpah will be a name you'll see on a lot of marquees from now on," he predicted, before adding, "I hope you'll come to see it on this one, anyway. And mine, too."[37]

Heston and Peckinpah agreed on some important aspects, including the casting of young Irish actor Richard Harris as a Confederate officer tasked with joining Heston's Maj. Amos Dundee in pursuit of Apache raiders. Harris, however,

---

35 *CHA*, 319.

36 Ibid., 321.

37 *ALJ*, 190, 192; Newsletter, "Jonacatepec, Mar., Mexico, April 11, 1964," HL. Earlier, he had declared that the "new location is marvelous." *ALJ*, 193.

proved contentious from the beginning. The difficult circumstances of the shoot and his disinclination to be awed by Heston's reputation allowed tempers to flare. "The trouble with him is he doesn't think he's just a hired actor, like the rest of us. He thinks he's the entire production," Harris observed of Heston. Harris became particularly disenchanted over his co-star's tendency to insist on promptness. Subsequently, when the Irishman appeared with a large alarm clock strung by a cord around his neck, his colleague was not impressed. "I don't find that amusing," Heston responded, and Harris colorfully informed him how little his opinion mattered to him.[38]

With respect to Heston's professional manner and the testy relationship it created in this instance, biographer Michael Munn noted, "It's true that on film sets his own high standards have not always met with everyone's approval. . . . Richard Harris, for instance, vowed he'd never work with Heston again." Harris thought Heston "the only man who could drop out of a cubic moon—he's so square," which, ironically, would not have come across to the subject of the perceived slight as less than complimentary. Others used similar descriptions for Heston, but without the hostility. One saw him as the "anti-Brando" of his time, "straightforward and earnest and resolutely square," although he added, "at the summit of his career, he was the greater box-office attraction." The author of a *Time* article explained, "It doesn't bother him to be called a square." Indeed, as Heston wryly concurred, "So were Moses and Ben-Hur."[39]

Charlton Heston worked diligently to present a collected persona that reflected the sense of exactitude he brought to all his endeavors, and this irked free-spirited individuals like Richard Harris. But Chuck Heston could become riled, too, particularly when situations went askew. "The familiar characteristics of controlled patience and calming authority were gone," Munn observed about an occasion on which Heston found an item missing during an interview. "He fussed and fumed, clearly upset and annoyed with either himself or someone else for such sloppiness." Waste and carelessness triggered his Scots notion of well-being. "Heston likes everything just *so*," Munn concluded.[40]

One of the ways Heston had learned to succeed in the entertainment business was to pay close attention to almost every aspect of a film's production, including

---

38 Munn, *Charlton Heston*, 123.

39 Ibid., 123, 201; Leibowitz, "Last Stand," 64; "The Graven Image," *Time* (Aug. 12, 1966).

40 Munn, *Charlton Heston*, 10-11.

advertising and promotion. What he saw regarding *Major Dundee* disturbed him to the extent that he strongly expressed his concern to John Flinn of Columbia Pictures while on location in Durango on February 27, 1964. The campaign art seemed all wrong to him and his desire to raise the matter triggered a response that struck him as misguided and unnecessarily defensive. "It is not my letters, or the tactical wisdom of writing them, or of showing me the layout in the first place that is the question here," he explained. "It is the layout itself. John, it is an incredibly bad layout. You KNOW this. I cannot believe that anyone would seriously advance it as the basis for an ad campaign for this film." Heston tried to temper his vehemence. "Now, God knows all men make mistakes. In making a film, we fail a little every day, in every scene." He was anxious to demonstrate his belief that the proper promotion of a project was critical to its success because such failures were endemic to any process. "Why should this not be true selling it too?"[41]

Ever determined to be the professional under all conditions, Heston also appreciated strong, decisive direction, and sought to adhere to instructions when they were clear and understandable. Yet he believed that his history in the industry meant that he should share his views as a fellow collaborator on any film in which he participated. In *Major Dundee* this desire meant that he risked clashing with its headstrong director.

Heston recalled that for a scene in which he was leading his men on horseback, he made a point of asking whether to trot or canter the squad. Peckinpah indicated that a trot was acceptable if they did so while enough light remained to film it. At some point, the director must have thought a canter would look more effective and began to berate his performers for not doing so already. Heston tried to deflect the criticism by reminding Peckinpah that he had told them to trot. The director growled an obscene response, before yelling, "I said canter, you stupid prick." Heston was already returning his men to their line on the ridge as these words echoed in his ears. He turned his horse in an instant and descended on the director, flashing his saber and calling on his men to wipe out their opponents. Peckinpah jumped into a chair on a boom that quickly rose out of the way. "I can't believe I would have actually ridden Sam down, let alone sabered him," Heston recalled, "but I was as angry as I can remember being in my life." He thought there must be some explanation for the indulgence to a temper he kept generally in check,

---

41 "Charlton Heston to Dear Johnny, Durango, February 27, 1964," Peckinpah Papers, *Major Dundee— Correspondence*, HL.

concluding, "A lot of things had piled up, I guess." A calmer Heston rode back and inquired if there was time for "one more" effort, this time "at a canter," and Sam agreed. "So that's what we did," Heston insisted. "Sam printed it, and neither of us ever spoke of it to the other after, in our lives." Peckinpah seemed not to hold the incident against his star. "Heston was superb," he explained of the actor's performance in the film in a post-production interview.[42]

In the meantime, Peckinpah's budget overruns became so worrisome to studio executives and his cantankerous relationship with them so corrosive that the director stood on the verge of having scenes deleted, if not being fired. Heston felt that such drastic actions at this stage would be more than the film could stand and indicated as much to the studio personnel. He explained, "[A]lthough I detest actors who throw their weight around, frankly, I had more muscle than Sam. I found myself using my position to guarantee that we would be able to shoot all the scenes in the script that we hadn't yet shot."[43]

The "guarantee" came in the form of an unprecedented offer to waive his salary to help offset the costs incurred by the extra work. Agent Herman Citron thought the decision a misguided one and did not believe the studio executives' promise to ignore the demonstration as unnecessary. "You're out of your mind, Chuck," he observed. "They'll take it." When word spread that the studio had indeed taken advantage of their star's offer, a reporter asked Heston if he meant to "start a trend with other actors?" "Trend, hell!" the chastened performer replied. "It won't even start a trend with me!"[44]

Under the heading: "Returns $100,000 to Atone for Raising 'Dundee' Cost," a *New York Times* article informed readers that special provisions in contracts sometimes allowed performers input on the film process itself. "The theory is that the actor can thus protect himself against injury to his career that might result from his being put into a poor movie," writer Murray Schumach observed. Of course, no clause could ensure that a film would succeed. The insistence on additional filming on location in Mexico had increased costs, generating "considerable acrimony" according to Heston. He felt that the gesture would lessen the negative financial impact of the project. "I don't think I was being altruistic or idealistic," he noted.

---

42 *CHA*, 330-331. A modified version of the confrontation appeared in Munn, *Charlton Heston*, 123; Kevin J. Hayes, ed., *Sam Peckinpah Interviews* (Jackson, MS, 2008), 58.

43 Rovin, *Films*, 151. Heston explained that despite his gesture, none of the scenes he helped to save made it into the final print, although Peckinpah continued as director of the picture; ibid., 153.

44 *ALJ*, 194-195.

"I was only being responsible. I have always felt that the actor has to have a sense of responsibility toward his pictures." Heston also recognized that, "[I]n effect, I applied the muscle when I did not really have the legal right to do so." Even so, he did not indicate that there was such a motive in this case, that he had made the move to obtain any type of tax relief, or that there was any agreement in place to restore the funds through future projects. "It has never happened to me before and I hope it never happens again."[45]

One trait that surfaced during this film was Heston's desire for fairness, even on matters outside the script or the director's vision and freedom. The shoot in Mexico required that the principals lodge in two different hotels. Michael Anderson, Jr., who played a young trooper in the picture, remembered seeing "Chuck Heston and Jim Hutton and Jim Coburn every night, but the other guys were over at the other hotel." The accommodations of one were superior to those of the other. As one of the men associated with the film noted, "There was the high crew and the crew that couldn't even eat at the tables. Finally, Heston and some of them said, 'If we have tablecloths, they have tablecloths. If we get served, they get served.'"[46]

As the year closed with the contentious shoot finally behind him, Heston found the ghost of Amos Dundee still haunting him in an odd way. From the Dorchester Hotel in London, he wrote Peckinpah to convey Christmas greetings and to pass along word of a review that said Tom Tryon had led a group of "greenhorns" in pursuit of the Sioux. The reviewer noted of the film and its performances, "If I scoff, it is at the direction rather than the writing. Peckinpah's dialogue is composed of ornate courtesies and rhetorical flourishes that need acting deeply marinated in a sense of period if they are to ring true." Not taking direct issue with his misidentification as Tom Tryon or the erroneous description of the object of the command's attentions, Heston observed, "Now that you've been kissed on the lips by such a formidable Establishment critic, I have only one question: Who the hell is Major Dundee?" Taking the blow to his brand and his latest project in stride, the actor closed humorously, "Love the most marinated actor *you* know."[47]

Heston tried not to let inordinate amounts of time pass between projects, not only because he chafed at the relative inactivity, but because he wanted to maintain his presence before audiences on the stage or the screen, large or small.

---

45 Murray Schumach, "Heston Refunds Salary to Studio," *NYT*, May 9, 1964.

46 Susan A. Compo, *Warren Oates: A Wild Life* (Lexington, KY, 2009), 118-119.

47 "Chuck to Sam, The Dorchester, London, Merry Christmas," Peckinpah Papers, *Major Dundee—Correspondence*, HL.

One month after wrapping *Major Dundee*, he jumped into another challenging production: a film about Michelangelo Buonarotti's most significant work as a painter. Based upon a wildly successful Irving Stone novel adapted for the screen by writer Philip Dunne, *The Agony and the Ecstasy* offered both promise and problems. "The Michelangelo script strikes me as possibly the best written that's ever been submitted to me," Heston observed, with an important caveat. "It would be a different part for me, and might be a helluva movie, though whether it can work commercially, I don't know."[48]

When Herman Citron arranged a new deal for *The Agony and the Ecstasy*, Heston's responsibilities increased even as he attended to the needs of the two projects to which he was already committed. The film allowed Citron's client to work with director Carol Reed and fellow star Rex Harrison, a situation the actor deemed "irresistible." The demands of three distinct productions, however, added significantly to the weight that fell on all parties, including Heston. "I don't recommend it," he assessed afterward.[49]

Rex Harrison seemed not to recommend working with his new co-star either. His writings on the film and his relationship with Heston reflected a churlish dismissal. In his 1975 autobiography, he asserted, "I think Charlton Heston was absolutely himself. . . . [The] Pope I knew I was, though the real star was Michelangelo, and Heston very politely and very nicely made me feel that it was extremely kind of me to be supporting him." Harrison then related an unusual contest between the performers. "Heston is an enormously tall man—if I am six foot one, he must be six foot three—and I asked my wardrobe man, as I was wearing long robes, to put a little lift in my shoes, so I could gain a couple of inches, and meet Heston at his own level." Having "congratulated myself that at least he no longer towered above me," Harrison became distressed that as the filming progressed "it seemed to me that he was growing." That actor could not detect the presence of any supplemental devices aiding the other. "Neither of us made any comment," Harrison added, "nor did our wardrobe men—it was a very funny, silent contest."[50]

In another instance, Harrison repeated and elaborated on the story of the unspoken competition of the men to overshadow each other. "Without saying anything, I did the same," he explained of applying the lifts, "so that, day by day,

48 *ALJ*, 181

49 *CHA*, 321-322.

50 Rex Harrison, *Rex: An Autobiography* (New York, 1975), 204-205.

there was the spectacle of two very tall, grown-up men, growing taller and taller." Harrison at least appeared to understand the ludicrous nature of what he was describing, although he apparently felt powerless to break the "juvenile attempt to look down on one another!" Harrison maintained that director Carol Reed was too accommodating to Heston, and argued that his fellow actor was "altogether too wooden to play this great artist." Then, as a final swipe, he offered a faint compliment of Heston's portrayal by observing, "if you crane your neck to see it, his ceiling wasn't half bad, either."[51]

Any latent hostility between the two leads could work well to heighten the testy relationship between the historical artist and pope, but Heston remained unsure of the director's style. "Carol works in terms of praising his actors," Heston related, "which I can't object to, but it makes me a little uneasy." Prone to his own high level of self-evaluation and self-criticism, he was unsure as to how to interpret Reed's gestures: "Why is he praising me? I must be screwing up." In any case, as filming progressed, they clashed only over a couple of matters, with Heston insisting, "He was wrong both times, in fact: about how to block in a figure before painting and how the pulley would react to my fall."[52]

Working long hours in the presence of monumental egos and under conditions that could be unsafe, particularly regarding the scaffolding that let Heston's Michelangelo paint his Sistine Chapel, masterpiece was bound to strain everyone's nerves. Heston always strove to maintain a balance between authenticity and advisability. As he worked on his version of the Sistine ceiling, Heston's Michelangelo lay on the structure as the artist had created it, reinforced only when cameras and crews required it. When not supported, the "pretty rickety affair" could be "a bit spooky." Nevertheless, the focus remained, now as it had done then, on the work. "It makes for good shots, but it's a little shaky," Heston recorded in his journal.[53] Yet in spite of the danger, he did not hesitate to climb it himself.

Heston always felt the finished product was not what it could have been, although his initial reactions were not negative. Critics were less generous, at least of the film and its identification. One scholar noted, "Most British critics regarded *The Agony and the Ecstasy* as a Charlton Heston picture, not the latest in the Reed canon, and the American critics took the same view." Heston remembered that

---

51 Rex Harrison, *A Damned Serious Business* (New York, 1991), 185-186.

52 *ALJ*, 204, 206.

53 Ibid.

the "AGONY notices smarted a bit," although his performance fared better than the film. With some retrospection, he stated, "I think I've learned a little better since then the basic truth involved. You do the work for itself (and for a living, of course). If people don't come to see it, you don't get to do any more, but beyond that, you aim for your own standards, which should be tougher than anyone else cares about, or knows how to set."[54]

The agonizing aspect of the project also seemed to take a toll on his vaunted good humor. Heston attended a wrap party where he spoke briefly with Groucho Marx, whom a writer noted remained a popular guest at such functions despite his "inevitable insults." Perhaps the actor should have been forewarned when he explained how expensive *The Agony and the Ecstasy* had been to make. The screen Michelangelo was not particularly amused when the legendary comedian observed that the producers could have saved a substantial sum by having Heston paint the floor of the Sistine Chapel instead of the ceiling.[55]

Heston continued on this busy streak by taking part in a special program sponsored by the Johnson administration in support of the arts in America. The culmination of this effort was an event held in Washington in the summer of 1965. Numerous individuals from the full range of artistic expression were scheduled to appear. Promotional material hailed the event in grandiose terms. "The largest array of outstanding American artists ever assembled in the White House will perform at the First Festival of American Arts on Monday, June 14 from 10:00 a.m. to 10:00 p.m." Charlton Heston was to take a special role in the section on "The Motion Picture" by narrating a feature highlighting the work of five famed film directors: Alfred Hitchcock, Elia Kazan, George Stevens, William Wyler, and Fred Zinnemann. Unfortunately, rising disaffection with the administration's conduct of the conflict in Vietnam threatened to disrupt what should have been an untrammeled celebration.[56]

An extensive interview for the *Saturday Evening Post* also appeared in the summer of 1965. In it, Heston sought to promote *The Agony and the Ecstasy* and build an audience for its release later that year. Noting the stature of the actor and the man, and the incongruities of a personality that had defied Hollywood's social challenges, interviewer Pete Hamill concluded, "Charlton Heston has established

---

54 Nicholas Wapshott, *The Man Between: A Biography of Carol Reed* (London, 1990), 325; *ALJ*, 237.

55 Charlotte Chandler, *Hello, I Must be Going: Groucho and His Friends* (Garden City, NY, 1978), 37, 310.

56 Press Release and Program, "White House Festival of the Arts, June 14, 1965," Johnson Papers, LBJPL; Raymond, *Cold, Dead Hands*, 148-151.

himself as one of the biggest box-office attractions in the history of motion pictures." But Heston's stature in his profession also resisted easy assessment. "To the bankers and accountants, his astonishing success is an unsolved puzzle, and at times Heston himself wonders about it too." The actor thought it possible that he presented a non-threatening presence on screen to an extended audience, but recognized that some roles would be difficult for him to embody. "I simply don't have a twentieth-century face," he observed. "This just isn't my century." Hamill offered his own explanation: "Heston is indisputably better when he is larger than life."[57]

Though movies demanded his attention, Heston yearned to be back on a stage. Nevertheless, a projected run of *A Man for All Seasons* with Lydia as his co-star seemed destined for difficulty. Work on the Chicago theater that was supposed to serve as the venue for the production was not complete. Construction was still underway when the Hestons returned from Washington to Chicago via Los Angeles, causing no little angst at the loss of valuable rehearsal and technical time. This would be Lydia's first play since appearing with her husband in *State of the Union*. Heston remembered the earlier run favorably—"It went damn well." On July 2, the play opened, and the audience proved receptive. The remainder of the run went well, allowing him to conclude, "I can't put it all to my drawing power, either. I may get them in the house, but the play holds them there."[58]

Between his makeup sessions and tennis matches, the actor's work in London also allowed Heston to indulge in his passion for cars. He had purchased a brand-new Jaguar XKE and navigated it gingerly through the streets of London to and from work sites. One morning, when he called for the vehicle, he was mortified to learn that it was unavailable. Someone had absconded with it, and a solicitous Scotland Yard was convinced that the situation might end badly for the sleek machine. Turning his attention appropriately to his daughter Holly's fourth birthday, Heston purported at the time not to "*care* about the damn car," but his emphasis suggested otherwise. He later admitted, "I did. I loved that car, though it was only a thing." Perhaps more to the point, he confessed, "It smarted a lot to lose it."[59]

News of the theft led to light-hearted jabs at Heston's expense, which played upon his film stature: "Ben-Hur's Chariot Stolen." Not all was lost for the legitimate

57 Hamill, "Heston: Larger Than Life," 88.

58 *ALJ*, 227, 229.

59 Ibid., 231.

owner and driver, however: the authorities located the vehicle intact with only minimal mileage added. The thieves had used it to rob a local gambling club before abandoning it. "I don't usually share the admiration many people feel for the dashing bandit," he observed later in retrospect, "but I had to admire the cool self-possession of the man who stole my car."[60] In the land of Robin Hood, the owner of the purloined machine had gotten off lightly and could turn his attentions to his work and the studio's replacement vehicle to its place in the garage.

After the New York premiere of *The Agony and the Ecstasy*, Heston noted, "With the newspaper strike on, we only got two notices: The *Tribune* hated it, the *Post* loved it." Unsatisfied with this percentage, he added testily, "This is beginning to bug me a bit. I'm good in this film." Heston insisted that if "it doesn't register, there's something bloody wrong somewhere." His travels to Europe to promote the film exposed him to less than stellar reviews from London critics, which sent him into a period of self-reevaluation. "I feel more and more this is a problem of critical backlash centering on me, having to do with my last half-dozen films." For this work, at least, he felt nothing for which to apologize or express remorse. "On careful (agonizing?) reappraisal, I'm still convinced the film's bloody good, and I'm bloody good in it."[61]

This moment of reassessment coincided with his celebration of another birthday. Chuck Heston indulged briefly in a wisp of self-doubt on October 28, when he recorded recent events counterbalanced by his joy in reuniting with his family. "The pleasure of coming home is the surest one I have now; my pleasure in my work is somewhat shaken by developments in the last week. I'm now less sure of my capacity to judge how I'm doing in *Khartoum* or, if it's good, what difference that'll make in how it's received." He observed in almost pro-forma style that the "work should suffice for itself, of course," but seemed anxious to convince himself it was true.[62]

The next day, he felt compelled to list the films he believed both he and the critics admired, those both disliked, and the ones that he felt positively toward despite receiving generally negative reviews. Of the first category, Heston placed *Ben-Hur* and *El Cid* as well as *The Big Country* and *The Wreck of the Mary Deare*. Among those he and the critics thought had fallen short were *The Pigeon That*

---

60 *CHA*, 360; *ALJ*, 231. The authorities subsequently arrested the brazen culprit. Heston repeated his assessment of the crime in *CHA*, 360-361.

61 *ALJ*, 235, 236.

62 Ibid., 236-237.

Took Rome, Diamond Head, 55 Days at Peking, The Buccaneer, and *Major Dundee.* Heston thought his roles as John the Baptist in *The Greatest Story Ever Told* and Michelangelo in *The Agony and The Ecstasy* deserved better treatment from reviewers. His personal assessment took the form of rhetorical questions: "What's created the critical backlash, if it exists? My last ten pictures?" He concluded that while his most recent films had made money, he did not find much to like about either his performances or the quality of the finished products. This was surely a powerful assessment for an artist who always wanted his work to be as close to perfect as possible.

Caught as he often was between current and completed projects with their very different requirements of his energies and attention, Heston found himself less certain of his career trajectory than he wished. A new month saw the actor in his agent's office to take the process to a less introspective level. "I went over the whole thing with Citron," Heston observed, "trying to get a fix on whether I've become too strongly identified with large, highly commercial films." Citron did not think that he had, but Heston was convinced that some other project might be worth pursuing to address the matter. In short order, he referred to a potential film he knew would serve the purpose, even if snags arose to threaten its production. "The *Planet of the Apes* project seems in limbo."[63]

It appeared Heston had much work to do in order to stay ahead of the doldrums, keep the family coffers filled, and meet the many demands being made of him. "A busy morning, doing paper work preparatory to leaving for the *War Lord* tour," Heston recorded on November 8 in Detroit; this was followed by what he termed a "long, hard-sell kind of a day." He concluded, "Not the way I'd lay on publicity for this, or any film, but they're determined this is the best way to do it." He preferred to "bring in people from the outlying cities . . . the ones I can't visit . . . and talk to them instead of to every disc jockey with a portable tape machine."[64]

In Chicago, Heston enjoyed the release of lecturing to critics on the differences between period films and contemporary ones, although he confessed the "schoolteachering impulses ill become me." He then went home to a heavy rain in Los Angeles, which reflected both his mood and the concern he felt over identifying his next project. "Still drifting on choosing work for '66," he lamented.

63 Ibid., 237.

64 Ibid., 238.

"If it's a film, should I do one of the period pieces waiting for me or find something modern?"[65]

By Thanksgiving, Heston was beginning to find sounder emotional footing, and he enjoyed a "quiet sort of holiday." He satisfied his penchant for working by talking to Citron "about various projects cooking on the back burners, but mainly marked time (the healer of all wounds, all jaundiced views . . .) while gnawing moodily on a turkey drumstick." Distinctly omitting any sense of family as a buffer, he concluded, "I'm not really depressed, just adjusting to my situation, which apparently is not quite as rosy as I'd imagined."

A difficult trip to London for technical work on *Khartoum*, during which he "didn't sleep as well on the plane as I usually can," left him in a surly mood. While much his experience during the filming of seemed to go well, there were aspects that did not. "The scenes seemed to play, with some exceptions," he recorded in his journal. "The scenes on the camel with the little girl and with the Bible and (Gordon's servant) Khaleel don't."[66]

Heston might have remembered that during the *Ben-Hur* shoot, his work with camels had left him with a decidedly negative impression of the beasts. "Another day spent almost entirely on camels, & getting on and OFF camels at that," he had noted then. "If Macbeth had camels in it I swear I'd never play the part!" Yet now he was back in the celluloid desert, confronting both Olivier's Mahdi and the occasional camel ride once more. Of course, a sardonic sense of satisfaction must have accompanied the moment he bade farewell to the faithful, humped companion he was sacrificing as the besieged city ran short of foodstuffs. "We ride beneath no more desert stars then. Well, all things must end."[67]

Heston remained in an introspective frame of mind. His carefully designed public persona served many purposes, including allowing him to avoid penetrating too deeply into his own psyche. "If you were to ask me the old question about Who Is the Real Charlton Heston, I wouldn't be able to answer you," he remarked to one interviewer, noting, "but there are few of us who can." He added, "Few of us have the courage or the desire to sit down and find out who they are." Of his journal, he observed, "[E]ven there, in the privacy of those pages, I devote myself to analyzing

65 Ibid.

66 Ibid., 239.

67 "September 1958, 21 Sunday," *On the Set*. Heston, speaking in his role as Gordon in *Khartoum*.

my professional ability. . . . But those deeper questions I prefer to sidestep. I simply like pretending to be other people."[68]

Pretending to be other people did not relieve the actor of an awareness of the world around him. With a nation torn by divided sentiments over a foreign war, the cultural separation between generations, racial injustice, and burgeoning challenges to time-honored values, Heston held firm to his ideals. He was already contemplating a public service tour unlike any other he had undertaken. For his newsletter readers, the actor mused in November, "I'm going to Vietnam for a few weeks." He did not anticipate a typical entertainment junket. "Since I can't sing and can't dance and Bob Hope tells jokes better than I do, I won't be going with a show, so about all I can do is crawl into a few odd corners where there isn't room to send a show, but I'll make certain there're friends in the corners before I crawl in there, believe me!"[69]

One author maintained that Heston was going to the Far East to "assess the situation himself," thereby demonstrating "confidence in his own judgment."[70] But Heston, who made clear his questioning of the conflict before he traveled there, viewed the tour less as confirming a position than supplying the data that would allow him to arrive at one that made sense to him. Just as he applied research techniques to his roles by immersing himself in the wardrobe and setting of those characters, he wanted to see the realities on the ground in Vietnam firsthand so he could understand them better.

Heston ended 1965 on a particularly harsh note regarding himself and the state of his career. "I learned a great deal, much of it not pleasant. I came to realize, for the first time, that I am not exactly the critics' darling. There are two explanations for this dubious phenomenon: that I am in fact not the actor I thought all along I was becoming, or (and this seems at least plausible) a performer who's been in as many popular pieces as I have is not likely to earn critical kudos at the same time." If the latter were true, Heston thought he had "taken steps (or taken steps toward taking steps)" to address the issue. Colorfully, he noted that the lukewarm critical reception to his year's biggest films "amounted to two swift kicks in the balls." In any case, he drew once more on the Bard for wisdom and solace: "Time and the hour run through the roughest day."[71]

---

68 Hamill, "Heston: Larger Than Life," 91.

69 Newsletter, November 24, 1965, HL.

70 Raymond, *Cold, Dead Hands*, 166.

71 *ALJ*, 240-241.

The new year offered the actor time for perspective. Biographer Marc Eliot captured the moment for his subject insightfully. "As for Heston, like every big earner, he always had a healthy paranoia about the sustainability of his career."[72] Charlton Heston wanted to engage in work that would be meaningful for him financially as well as artistically, and his recent films, though lucrative, had not generated the level of critical success he had desired. The moment seemed right for retrospection, which he found in activities with his son Fraser.

His trip to Vietnam might also serve as a public function, which was important to him as a veteran. Such a perspective could allow Heston to recharge and refocus his energies while reminding him that there was more to life than the flicker of the screen or the attraction of klieg lights. Moreover, the trip meant lifting the morale of the service personnel posted far from home, who, as the *Army Times* noted in June 1965, viewed Charlton Heston "as one of the six movie stars American soldiers in Vietnam most wanted to see.[73]

His travels to the war zone offered a contribution that a person who valued public service could embrace. The adrenalin that came from exposing himself to danger was hardly something the actor, husband, and father, or his career, required, but the junket represented an important calling. As he explained later, "I had served in my 'own' war back in the 1940s." Still, he added, "there was simply something that drew me to that place. I just knew I had to go."[74] The young men, many of whom had probably seen his performances in their local theaters, could derive some sense of home by shaking his hand or hearing his distinctive voice in person.

Heston undertook the task with complex feelings. "Like everyone else," he explained in an interview on the conflict, "I had my doubts, misgivings, questions." He felt duty-bound to his country, and believed the men in the jungles and rice paddies deserved support. Yet even in Vietnam, Heston could not escape his image. "Out there Ben-Hur rode a chopper, not a chariot," one front-line reporter quipped. Such modern conveyances were unlike the one that had brought him to cinematic prominence, but it was that stature, and his willingness to use it, that carried the former soldier and veteran actor throughout a grueling schedule. Henry Fonda later noted how a USO representative had used Heston and other actors to persuade him to go to Southeast Asia on one of these "handshake tours." Although

---

72 Eliot, *Charlton Heston*, 274.

73 Ross, *Hollywood Left and Right*, 289.

74 Heston and Isbouts, *Hollywood*, 157.

against the war as a policy, Fonda, like his acting counterpart, thought he should travel to the theater of action for the sake of the men fighting there.[75]

As he had noted in his preparations and despite the public relations nature of his profession, Heston's trip to Vietnam was not designed for entertaining the troops and support personnel in Saigon. He traveled to Danang and Pleiku as well as isolated forward bases. He also ventured into the mountains to make contact with the Montagnards, who were assisting the Green Berets in operations against the Viet Cong.[76]

When he returned to the United States, Heston described the trip for his intrepid newsletter readers. "1966 began for me in Vietnam, where I spent a few weeks visiting the war. It proved to be one of the most learningful and stimulating experiences of my life." The actor noted that he had not traveled blindly. "I flew to the Far East with the misgivings and apprehensions that colour the thinking of every American these days," but he came away transformed. "What I saw there reassured me as to the integrity of our purpose and impressed me beyond measure with the depth of personal commitment on the part of every American in uniform I met." He described his hectic schedule: "So that's what I did, sometimes hitting as many as ten or twenty outposts a day, sometimes only two or three, depending on how easily I could catch a ride, and what was happening wherever I got to."

Whatever his concerns about the state of the country in an unpopular war or his future professional aspects, Heston maintained popularity in his film career. He was also determined to continue to grow as a performer, and in that vein welcomed a theater stint at Miami's Cocoanut Grove Playhouse. "It's good for me to get away from the cameras for awhile, and involve myself in other things . . . especially the stage," he told his newsletter readers in March 1966. "This is actor's country in a sense the screen can never be; you learn things and stretch muscles there that are never needed in front of the cameras."[77]

He reiterated the same theme in an appearance on *The Dick Cavett Show*, where he explained that directors controlled a film's vision in ways actors and writers could not, whereas actors held sway on the stage as directors stepped aside to leave them to their performances. Meanwhile, frustration never seemed far removed from success. *War Lord* had tested Heston's endurance and *Pro*, about a veteran

75 Eliot, *Charlton Heston*, 276; Henry Fonda, *Fonda: My Life as Told to Howard Teichmann* (New York, 1981), 292-293.

76 Wise and Wilderson, *Stars in Khaki*, 134.

77 Newsletter, Mar. 30, 1966, HL.

professional football star facing the end of his career, would do the same. At the end of March, he was still struggling to find a home for the latter picture. "Maybe you're beginning to get the idea of what a long, tortuous, and disheartening process it is to get a film mounted," he observed in his journal during this period.[78]

Even so, Heston benefitted tremendously from his relationship with Herman Citron. He knew the agent could strike deals that would serve both their interests, without sacrificing his own. The actor's instincts also had proven sound, even as negotiations dragged on or productions seemed stalled. "Nothing stirring on PRO," he recorded on April 20. "Citron's quite right to counsel patience, as he did this morning." Waiting might or might not produce results, but it would not betray any sense of anxiousness or desperation to potential producers and distributors. "He also thinks we shouldn't peddle the project. I see his point (that it tarnishes my image as an eminently-in-demand actor), but I still want to move on this, however circumspectly."

Later he provided additional insight. "Herman's point is valid. After an actor reaches a certain point in his career, he's supposed to sit in isolated splendor, selecting from among the offers humbly left at his door" rather than pushing propositions himself. In a profession in which perception was critical, the policy made sense. Heston tempered that point by suggesting that when an actor wanted a project to come to fruition, "the two concepts have to be somehow reconciled."[79]

Charlton Heston seemed to be in a prime position, all things considered. In the future, he would repeat many times a variation of the assertion he made concerning the weight of the figures he had portrayed in *The Agony and the Ecstasy*, *The War Lord*, and a stage version of *A Man for All Seasons*: "That's quite a selection of characters right there: genius, lover, saint."[80] Around this time, a piece in *Time* magazine devoted to Heston and interestingly labeled "The Graven Image," confirmed the complexities of being Charlton Heston. The writer posited that until someone made a film about the life of Lyndon B. Johnson in which the actor could take the lead, he might want to "retire," having played just about every other notable personality, including Moses, John the Baptist, Ben-Hur, El Cid, Macbeth, Michelangelo, Thomas Jefferson, and Andrew Jackson, as well as the off-camera voices of Franklin D. Roosevelt and God. "Of course, the studios would never let him retire. He is, in the trade term, one of the most 'bankable' box-office

---

78 *ALJ*, 250.

79 Ibid., 251.

80 Newsletter, "London, England," Aug. 28, 1965, HL.

stars going." After listing the latest sales statistics for Heston's features, the writer added, "Overseas, Heston is an even bigger favorite." The piece indicated that the "secret" to the actor's prominence seemed to hang upon "his capacity for appearing virile without being lecherous in Olympian roles," ostensibly in terms of greed, sex, or power.[81]

Visits on official State Department tours offered Heston additional non-acting responsibilities. He journeyed to Australia and New Zealand in the summer of 1966. "Exciting as the Australia trip was," he reported for his fans, "it typifies a year in which I've been too busy, doing a multitude of other things that seemed to me important, to make any films." The frustration with being outside the working parts of his craft, even while representing it, could be tempered with the knowledge that a Royal Premiere for *Khartoum* and a reading of *Moby Dick* for university students in Australia nevertheless promoted the arts and engaged new audiences. Of the latter, Heston exulted, "I felt like a Beatle!" Especially with the reception he received in Melbourne, Heston's initial misgivings about the tour dissipated.[82]

In the meantime, one of the problems that surfaced with *The War Lord* was the difference in vision between the intimate film that Heston and Walter Seltzer had in mind and the one the studio executives preferred. Bolstered by his reading of the period and the smaller scale of the events the film would depict, the actor thought the best approach meant a departure from a DeMille or Wyler extravaganza. Such a limited focus might make sense to Heston, but as one writer explained, "This is not the way Universal saw its Charlton Heston epic; it looked like a Universal penny-pinch, bargain basement Charlton Heston epic."[83]

Part of the appeal for Heston was that the film reflected another aspect of his explorations of character. Chrysagon had endured the challenges of his duties and his own foibles only to find himself alone. "It is here, in the ending that Heston's contribution is most keenly felt," a biographer of director Franklin Schaffner asserted. "Still looking physically invincible, he plays a middle-aged man who has been a loner in life, and who, despite his rigorous attention to his duty, feels he has missed something meaningful in his life and is desperately trying to find it." Writer Erwin Kim observed, "This personal theme has influenced Heston's choice of material: it was explored in other films the actor made with Seltzer, most notably

---

81 "The Graven Image," *Time*, Aug. 12, 1966.

82 Newsletter, Mar. 30, 1966, HL. Heston expressed concerns about the programs, not the destinations, and later noted from Melbourne, "This program is working better than I thought it would." *ALJ*, 254, 255.

83 *ALJ*, 137; Kim, *Schaffner*, 199.

Will Penny (1968), in which he played an aging cowboy, and *Number One* (1969), in which he played an aging quarterback."[84]

Unfortunately, age and mortality were not issues for Heston's characters alone. On September 1, 1966, he also lost an important link to his past with the death of his father, Russell Carter.[85] After reconnecting with him, Chuck had utilized Russ to help build the house that became a symbol and a refuge for the aspiring actor and his family. Russ was also a reminder of the pleasant memories of his early youth, although such memories surely rekindled the challenges of his parents' separation and divorce as well.

Yet it was not a character struggling with the loneliness of middle age that offered Heston the greatest challenge in a role. That part came with learning to appear to be believable in his role in the film that became *Counterpoint*. On September 12 he recorded, "I began what's going to be one helluva daunting assignment: learning to pretend to conduct. Unlike, say, charioteering, jousting, or fresco painting, where at least I was familiar with the territory, this is a new line of country entirely." Not knowing how to read music complicated matters, which the conducting consultant handled by creating "a simplified system of musical notation, so I could memorize the scores."[86]

Heston felt he had to be credible in the role for every member of his audience. "Mastering the use of the baton so that it makes sense to musicians and critics who see the finished film is twice as elusive as trying to pick up a globule of mercury, or trying to give the slip to your shadow," he explained to one writer. "This is particularly so in my case, since I play no instrument and can't read a single note." Privately he observed, "I'm up to my ass four hours a day on the opening thirty bars of the Beethoven Fifth, which takes about all I've got." He would remember the effort to master conducting as "the toughest thing I've ever learned for a part," and "one of the most physically exhausting, too."[87]

As the fall of 1966 continued in an election year for California, Heston's multiple commitments appeared to be taking a toll. Constant queries about a potential career in politics prompted him to record testily in his journal, "My current answer is 'Yes, for pope.'" Then on the same day he enjoyed a presentation

84 Ibid., 206.

85 "Charlton Heston's Father Dies," *NYT*, Sept. 3, 1966.

86 *ALJ*, 259.

87 Marjory Adams, "Heston's Toughest Role?" *BG*, July 28, 1967; *ALJ*, 259, 260.

by Governor-elect Ronald Reagan of a SAG award to Barbara Stanwyck, Heston complained of attending an extended roasting of longtime actor and comedian George Jessel, labeling the dinner "damn stupid" and decrying the "four-hour display of the humor of insult, a peculiarly American institution."

In early December, Heston finally stepped onto the conductor's platform on the set of *Counterpoint*. "A bloody frustrating day," he told his journal. "It began well with my first session facing a full orchestra." The experience reminded him of earlier cinematic moments. "Standing in front of a symphony orchestra gives you a great feeling of power, I must say. It's better than parting the Red Sea, since you feel God's less inclined to help."[88]

To his newsletter readers, Heston noted lightly that he had played at conducting in his home while listening to music but had never realized how complicated the actual task of leading an orchestra would prove. Indeed, he became so focused on learning the nuances that he sacrificed virtually all else to the effort. "Even the odd hour on the set between takes that usually finds me sketching, was taken with more sweat over that baton," he confessed in his June 1967 issue. "All in all, it was the most difficult thing I've ever tried to learn for a film, and that includes parting the Red Sea, driving that chariot, and painting the Sistine Ceiling." He had managed to take a few minutes at his typewriter to send the update, before concluding, "Now, back to Beethoven!"[89]

Within a few days of returning to his conducting duties, filming wrapped on *Counterpoint* and Heston immediately prepared to move on from it. "It's odd to have the film behind me," he noted, "though it's strange to be stepping into a new one, with hardly a breathing space between." Yet, before he headed off to the location shoot for *Will Penny*, he had chores to perform in Washington, where he helped dedicate a portrait of Franklin D. Roosevelt with a dramatic reading and was sworn into the National Council on the Arts. Lydia made the second part more palatable by holding a bible for the ceremony, although her husband later professed, "I can't remember what it was we swore to do. Not waste the public money, I hope."[90]

Heston seldom had reason to feel self-conscious in his public roles, but the Roosevelt reading presented an interesting personal challenge. "I was nervous," he professed to one writer, "playing in front of all those Roosevelts!" As things turned

88 *ALJ*, 261.

89 Newsletter, Jan. 20, 1967, HL.

90 *ALJ*, 265, 266.

out, he seemed to do well, although the notoriously opinionated Alice Roosevelt, Theodore's daughter, declared that the family that came out of Oyster Bay "never pronounced the first syllable 'Roos' as in 'rooster' but like the rest of the family they pronounced it 'rose.'"[91]

Lifting a baton creditably in a World War II caper and presenting a dramatic reading in the nation's capital were unlikely to expand the actor's reach, however. The projects that promised to bring Charlton Heston into more nuanced roles and new realms of popularity outside the epics and historically based movies that had established his reputation were the Western *Will Penny* and an unusual science fiction picture entitled *Planet of the Apes*.

Over the next several weeks, the toil associated with shooting *Will Penny* on location seemed to reflect the environment in which the film was being shot. For Heston, it was a strained experience. Even when Lydia agreed to take on a small part, Heston appeared less grateful than aggravated, with him recording at the time, "I don't think she enjoyed it, really." Subsequent issues indicated that Heston did not necessarily agree with his director, asserting at one point that some of Gries's recent efforts were "a waste of our fragile snowfall; we could shoot that scene as easily on a sound stage. Still, I am reluctant to push to a showdown on this with Tom. He has to choose."

Two days later, the star avoided another confrontation by calling producer Walter Seltzer, who served as an intermediary. "I did my shot driving the wagon OK (it's a little easier than a chariot)," he concluded. The sentiment foreshadowed a more pleasant working environment as the exterior locations moved to interior ones and Heston was able to find time to appear at the Academy Awards ceremony. "I looked odd, in full dress and two-week beard, but I was very happy to present the little gold man to Yak Canutt, who received a Special Academy Award." Canutt had helped him master the chariot in *Ben-Hur* and "deserves it," the former Best Actor winner wrote.

The pleasant diversion over, Heston returned to the *Will Penny* set and once more disagreed with the director about their joint work. "I was right," the actor snarled testily in his journal. "After however the hell many films, it's time I knew a little about how it works."[92] He admitted to seeing the director's point, although he might have done better to remember that in different times under

---

91 Betty Beale, "Washington May Never Be the Same Again," *BSG*, Feb. 12, 1967.

92 *ALJ*, 268-271.

other personalities he had maintained that a director only had to tell him what he wanted and he would do it.

With *Will Penny* behind him, Heston was already working on the next picture. In his April 17, 1967, newsletter, the actor offered tantalizing hints that emphasized the secretive nature of the project. Studio executives had gone so far as to insist that lunches be served to the performers on the sets themselves, so that appearances by actors in costume in the commissary would not divulge too much of what was happening prematurely. "Sounds a little wild, doesn't it?" Heston suggested conspiratorially.[93]

Planet of the Apes also represented an experiment in the degree to which makeup could allow an acceptable depiction of nonhuman characters in a science fiction film, including speech and reactions that would be recognizable to moviegoers. One interviewer thought the phenomenon would pose a difficult challenge for the conventional-acting Heston since viewers were certain to focus on the makeup of the "apes." The actor himself professed no such concern. "I would say quite the reverse," Heston explained. "I think the presence of 3 fine actors in those roles was absolutely essential to the success of the piece." He thought the talented performers beneath the makeup gave him the freedom to act in such a way as to let everyone, including himself, "forget that this, after all, has to be make believe."[94]

The filming itself proved enormously challenging. "He has driven a chariot, rowed a slave galley, even parted the Red Sea," one writer observed, before noting Heston's own assessment. "But 'physically, *Planet of the Apes* was the most arduous thing I've ever done.'" The physicality of the role was enormously demanding. "In the first place, I was all but naked through the whole thing, thrashing through the bushes." When not trying to escape capture in the wild, he found himself caged or in pursuit in the ape city as a human specimen on the loose. In that scene, frightened ape residents pelted him with rocks. "And, I'll point out to you," he explained of the props, "even rubber rocks hurt." Heston also observed, "It occurs to me that there's hardly a scene in this bloody film in which I've not been dragged, choked, netted, chased, doused, whipped, poked, shot, gagged, stoned, leaped on, or generally mistreated." Still the vintage humor shone through as he related the comment of his stunt friend Joe Canutt, "You know, Chuck, I can remember when we used to win these things."[95]

93 Newsletter, April 17, 1967, HL.

94 Belmont Interviews, August 1967, 6-7, HL.

95 Champ Clark, "Picks & Pans, talking with . . . Charlton Heston," *People Weekly* (Sept. 7, 1998), 32; *ALJ*, 276.

In one crucial area, the actor did win. In the final scene, a half-buried Statue of Liberty made Heston's astronaut George Taylor realize that he was back on Earth, rather than on some alien planet. Pounding the sand while on his knees in the surf, the stranded astronaut blurts out, "You did it, didn't you . . . you really did it. Goddamn you all to *hell*." To retain the words, including the expletive, Heston observed that Taylor was not cursing arbitrarily or gratuitously. "He's literally calling on God to damn the people who destroyed the world." In retelling the incident in his autobiography, Heston concluded, "We won that one," and the language remained.

The film had potential as a franchise, but Heston thought that he had largely squelched the possibility of an *Apes* sequel until Dick Zanuck came to him with the idea that if he would appear briefly in one, that would be enough. He agreed on the premise that his character perished quickly and the fees that would normally come to him would go to Fraser's private school instead. Heston had to accept that movie imperatives often took actors farther than they wanted to go initially, but concluded, "I'm still comfortable with the way we worked it out." Nevertheless, a nagging fact remained. "My grandson's trust fund," he wrote at the time about Fraser's son, Jack, "would be fatter if I'd taken the path my colleagues did later and done all the sequels myself, but he'll be OK on his own."[96]

In September 1967, he made a second trip to war-torn Vietnam. He found Saigon "at least as crowded as before," but thought his visit to the wounded more difficult. "Hospitals are hard to do . . . the lines and lines of beds, with the young faces lying there." He felt particularly moved by a badly wounded lad who "thanked *me* for coming." On the same day Heston arrived in Southeast Asia, a depiction of his views on the conflict appeared in American newspapers. "I believe Americans are right in fighting in Vietnam . . . if my son were old enough to fight," he noted of twelve-year-old Fraser, "I would have sent him to Vietnam as a soldier."[97]

After leaving Saigon for a return to Pleiku, the actor took off in "stiff new field boots and the starched combat fatigues" to venture across the sprawling complex. "I spent the night in an old C47 (two wars beyond its time, like me)," before settling in with the First Cavalry, "their horses changed now, not to the tanks of WWII, but to choppers." He felt he could detect progress, and found he especially enjoyed "being around fliers." "They're like actors in many ways: an out group with its own standards, similar feeling of informality, professionalism, and concern with

---

96 *CHA*, 398-399.

97 *ALJ*, 279; "Names & Faces In the News," *BG*, Sept. 7, 1967.

talent. I feel at home with them." A few more days of touring, interspersed with more hospital visits, left Heston tired but feeling he had accomplished what he could. He told his journal he was "glad I'm through here, though."

Vietnam continued to be a topic in Heston's conversations with friends and associates like Jack Valenti, as well as with family members of service personnel he had promised to contact when he returned. He found the latter requirements less numerous than before, but concluded, "It's still a tricky chore, but one I wouldn't pass." When he got back, he received a Brotherhood Award from the National Association of Christians and Jews and observed in his self-deprecatory manner, "I can't have them changing their minds."[98]

When the North Koreans fired upon and forced the surrender of the USS *Pueblo* while on a spying mission off the Korean coast on January 23, 1968, holding the craft and its crew in captivity, Heston could not resist expressing his views. Within a couple of days, he sent a telegram to the White House from Beverly Hills, with advice. "Prudence is a virtue but so is a recognition of reality urgently hope you can move to get the Pueblo out of Wonsan Harbor without further delay." National Security Advisor Walt W. Rostow acknowledged receipt of the message on February 1, 1968. "In his statement to the Nation last Friday, the President emphasized the urgency with which we view this critical situation." Promising that the administration would "pursue every avenue that may lead to a quick and peaceful solution," Rostow appended a copy of President Johnson's statement on the matter.[99]

In the meantime, with good news on advance sales for *Planet of the Apes*, the actor had reason to relax from these recent pressures. Heston's resurgence at the box office meant that his staying power continued. He also stayed busy with numerous service initiatives, but the relative hiatus in acting opportunities grated on him. In his May 1968 newsletter, he opened by admitting to being in the "between parts doldrums." All the work and the meaningful time with his family "is well and good, but I'm not acting!" Still, there was much for which to be grateful. "WILL PENNY has gotten the best notices of any Western in some years and APES looks as though it will finally be seen by more people than any film I've

---

98 *ALJ*, 279-280, 281.

99 "Charlton Heston to The President, White House, Beverly Hills Calif Jan 25 [1968]," National Security – Defense (EX ND 19/C) 151), Box 205, Johnson Papers, LBJPL; "W. W. Rostow to Dear Mr. Heston," Feb. 1, 1968, Heston File, Johnson Papers, ibid. The *Pueblo*'s 82 surviving crew members—one was killed in the operation—were finally released from captivity on Dec. 23, 1968.

made since BEN HUR." His new football picture, *Number One*, raised issues that were similar to earlier challenges Heston himself had confronted. "I'll never be the best in the NFL, that's for sure," he quipped. "But, then I don't have to be. . . . I just have to look like it." As for undertaking this physically demanding part, he explained, "I'd put it about half way between having to drive a chariot and learning to conduct Brahms."[100]

Yet even with all these positive developments, Charlton Heston could not insulate himself from the outside world. Stability seemed a rare and precious commodity in 1968, as negative events seemed to occur in quick succession. Often, given his travels, it was up to Lydia to deliver unhappy news when it came. While waiting to travel to Europe for screenings of *Planet of the Apes*, such a call came. Lydia had learned that President Johnson was likely to abandon a run for re-election. Heston had worked with Johnson and supported him avidly. He asked White House insider Jack Valenti if the rumor was true. When his friend confirmed the news, the actor's response came muted with concern: "That's bad news, Jack. Bad for the country," as he left to catch his flight.[101]

Unfortunately, sadder tidings awaited. On April 4, James Earl Ray shot Dr. Martin Luther King, Jr., while the clergyman stood on the balcony of the Lorraine Motel in Memphis, Tennessee. The assassination marked another low point in the nation's recent history. Heston was overseas when Lydia called again to say that the Motion Picture Academy had asked him to seek a postponement in the Oscar telecast out of respect for the fallen civil rights leader's funeral. In response, he noted simply, "I did, then a press conference at the airport, and flew home."[102]

Barely two months later, another tragedy struck. On June 5, Robert F. Kennedy, who had just won the California presidential primary, was felled by an assassin's bullet after finishing a speech before an exuberant gathering of supporters at the Ambassador Hotel in Los Angeles. Heston could not help but be reminded

100 Newsletter, May 8, 1968, HL.

101 *CHA*, 405.

102 *ALJ*, 292. Heston's was hardly the only call for a postponement of the event. Individuals such as Sammy Davis, Jr., Harry Belafonte, Sidney Poitier, Louis Armstrong, and Diahann Carroll, all of whom were scheduled to appear at the ceremony, attended the funeral in Atlanta. "Martin Luther King's Death Postpones Oscars," *Variety*, Apr. 8, 1968, www.variety.com/1968/biz/news/martin-luther-kings-death-postpones-oscars-1201342764/, accessed Dec. 3, 2018; Andy Lewis, "Hollywood Flashback: When the Oscars were Postponed for Martin Luther King, Jr.'s Funeral," *Hollywood Reporter*, Apr. 3, 2018, www.hollywoodreporter.com/news/hollywood-flashback-oscars-were-postponed-martin-luther-king-jrs-funeral-1099031, accessed Dec. 3, 2018.

of the grief he and the nation had endured with the loss of President Kennedy, and most recently, Dr. King. Trying to come to grips with the tragedies that seemed to be enveloping modern American society, Heston turned to his take on the downward spiral of the world as he saw it. "No, I don't think Robert Kennedy's death reveals a hidden core of violence in the American spirit," he posited hopefully. The actor, husband, and father was certain, however, that there were issues lurking beneath the surface of the American psyche that could be revealing. He lamented the fact that an "honorable" sense of "fervor for the protection of dissent as one of the cornerstones of democracy" had led to dangerous excess.[103]

Heston's desire to make a public statement of some kind led him, along with other notable Hollywood figures, to endorse the efforts of President Johnson and members of Congress to confront what Heston labeled "the gun law thing." He worked the telephone to secure the support of actors such as Hugh O'Brian, Gregory Peck, Kirk Douglas, and Jimmy Stewart, all of whom had appeared in Western films and television shows, but he considered himself especially important because of his belief in responsible gun ownership. "I suppose I'll end up making a pitch on TV," he observed, before adding, "I think this law is a good one." Heston understood that the momentum for some level of action existed and clearly thought his involvement would mean a more cautious, thoughtful response, particularly from members of his profession. "I'd rather stand to be counted on it than have some of my colleagues display their emotions on the subject."[104]

On July 17, 1968, Heston joined with O'Brian, Peck, and Douglas in forwarding a statement on the proposed gun legislation to J. Raymond Bell of Columbia Pictures. "We want to add our strongest support to President Johnson's gun control proposal requiring registration of guns, licensing of all gun owners, and prohibition of mail order sale of guns. Please convey our position to your guests on Thursday."[105] A broader statement expounded that "stronger gun control legislation is mandatory." Lest anyone question their credentials, the signatories explained, "The four of us do not speak from ignorance of firearms. We respect the privilege of owning guns as sportsmen or as private citizens." They did not believe the measure would go too far in endangering those rights. "We would like

103 *ALJ*, 295.

104 Ibid., 296.

105 Kirk Douglas, Charlton Heston, High O'Brian, Gregory Peck to J. Raymond Bell (Columbia Pictures), July 17, 1968, "Gun Control," Association of Motion Picture and Television Producers (AMPTP) records, f.167, HL.

to emphasize that the President's proposed strong gun control legislation would not deny any responsible citizen the right to own a gun." For ordinary people, the issue need not be any different than obtaining a driver's license to operate a motor vehicle legally; at the same time, it could prevent purchases by minors or indiscriminate sales across state lines. "We urge you, as a responsible, sensible and concerned citizen, to write or wire your senators and congressmen immediately" they implored, "and demand they support the President's strong gun control bills." The time to act was "now!"[106]

Charlton Heston approached 1969 as busy as ever with public commitments and film projects. He considered *Pro*, as *Number One* was known early on in its odyssey, a special project. "PRO is the first film I've ever made from an *idea* that was mine," he explained. The concept came while jetting overseas on a Pan Am flight and noticing a photograph of a battered and defeated Y. A. Tittle at the end of an NFL game. "I've been carrying it inside me," Heston noted, reflecting his desire to explore the dramatic effect of such a moment in the iconic American game on screen. He had mitigated the loss of another prospect earlier with the thought that "if we had to have one shot out from under us, I'm glad it wasn't *Pro*."

Heston took up the portrayal of a professional football player with the same degree of seriousness he had as a military leader or an artist. He scouted practices at the University of Southern California, deeming the effort "vital for me to understand something of the pressure on these guys." Without saying so explicitly in his journal entries, the quest for perfection was one to which he believed he could relate. "This is part of excelling in anything, maybe, to find how hard you can push yourself."[107]

Shooting would not begin until later that summer, but a foreshadowing of sorts occurred when the actor conducted an interview, "on the significance of male nudity in films." Heston claimed not to be able to fathom how he had become an expert on this subject, but in *Planet of the Apes* he had faced an ape council almost totally unadorned by raiment, and *Number One* would feature locker room scenes in which players appeared in various forms of undress. Indeed, *Photoplay* later ran a piece that highlighted the fact that the movie contained several scenes that were hardly consistent with Heston's usual screen persona. "Not Moses!" screamed the first line, before delving into the interactions Heston's character had with his wife (Jessica Walter) and mistress (Diana Muldaur). Insisting that Kirk Douglas might

106 Ibid.

107 Newsletter, Jan. 17, 1969, Heston Papers, HL; *ALJ*, 293-294.

engage in such screen licentiousness, writer Mike Webb concluded, "Certain actors—to their credit—are just thought of differently: Gregory Peck, Efrem Zimbalist, Jr., Cary Grant and (by all means) Charlton Heston among them." Heston maintained that he "didn't think the love scenes in 'Pro' went too far, even for Moses." Such moments were not included for titillation. "The scenes in this picture are important to the story," he argued, "and, I think, are done with taste." The subject also allowed Heston to remind readers of the magazine, and viewers of the film itself, that his wife, Lydia, did not take the matter personally. "Fortunately, I married an actress. She understands that." Describing their co-star uniformly as "a gentleman," Walter and Muldaur insisted he had been entirely professional throughout the shoot. "So Moses wasn't the wrong man after all for the provocative love scenes in 'Pro,'" Webb observed. "Instead, he was exactly right and anyone of lesser stature would have been wrong." In any case, both writer and actor realized that audiences of the movie would "have the final word" on the matter.[108]

The article suggested the ways in which Heston's character, Ron "Cat" Catlin, compared to the actor who gave him life on the screen. Heston asserted that he related to the football player's personality and found ample means of connecting with him. "There's a great deal of me in Catlin," he explained. "He is, as I am, somewhat reclusive, somewhat obsessed with the disciplines and demands of his profession and there is nothing else that he wants to do with his life than what he does." Heston undoubtedly identified with the fictional quarterback's "only goal," which was "to be as good as he can be."[109]

When not preparing for his role on the screen gridiron, the actor busied himself in other settings. A White House dinner invitation was appealing; being in the capital itself was not. Still, his commitment to the National Council on the Arts brought him back once more. "I'm not an actor anymore, for God's sake," he lamented about a meeting in New York. "I'm an activist." Just as palpable to him and others was his role as gatekeeper to the public trough. "My reputation as a hatchet man on the council must be formidable." He later clarified this position by noting, "I'm against wasting money."

A welcome and diverting trip to London could not delay the inevitable return to his work on the football picture. "I fell back into the harness on the quarterbacking today," he noted on July 12, but he confessed to "lapses" in concentration for the

108 *ALJ*, 295; Mike Webb, "Charlton Heston: The nude love scene that went too far!" *Photoplay* (Mar. 1969), 88, 90.

109 Janet Eastman, "Charlton Heston," *Orange Coast* (Aug. 1980), 13-14.

A glass apple (right) from the estate of Charlton Heston with the inscription "It's Time," encapsulated the spirit the actor used in approaching his life on stage, screen and television. The actor's introduction to Broadway (below) came in Katherine Cornell's production of *Antony and Cleopatra*.

Although Moses in Cecil B. DeMille's classic *The Ten Commandments*, was an iconic role for Charlton Heston, *Ben-Hur* and the fabulous chariot race were indelible parts of his career and reflected the ways in which he worked to establish, develop and promote his "public face."

(top, clockwise) Heston benefitted from his work with legendary and often enigmatic directors including Cecil B. DeMille, William Wyler and Orson Welles.

Heston's first role in a Hollywood production, *Dark City*, brought him recognition as "Mr. Excitement!" and entrée into the world he would inhabit for the rest of his life.

Movie posters and lobby cards helped to promote work like this one *The Naked Jungle*, in which Heston took second billing to co-star Eleanor Parker.

As part of the promotion of his early pictures, Heston offered his image as spokesperson for numerous products. Camels cigarette ad, *Popular Mechanics Magazine* April 1953 and Mayflower Warehouses, *Saturday Evening Post*.

(Top) The actor's rare efforts at comedy worked best when he was the foil for others, as in *The Private War of Major Benson* with Julie Adams and Tim Hovey.

(Above inset) Always viewing his work in theatre as "the actor's country" essential to his development as a performer, Heston starred in many such productions. Stagebill for the Hillsdale Summer Theatre in *Detective Story*.

(Above right) As an actor, Heston took pride in his portrayal of leaders like Andrew Jackson, shown here in *The Buccaneer*.

(Right) *Ben-Hur* has remained one of the two most iconic Charlton Heston performances, and the motion picture that brought him the Academy Award for Best Actor. Left to right: William Wyler, Mary Zimbalist, widow of producer Sam Zimbalist, and Heston.

One method for reaching an audience with *Ben-Hur* was the dissemination of a postcard (above) featuring Heston and the famous race.

The extensive work for promoting *Ben-Hur* included interviews, appearances, print coverage, and an exhibitor's campaign book (left) issued by MGM.

Heston led a Hollywood contingent in "The March on Washington" (seen below with actor Harry Belafonte) and touted his support for Civil Rights for the remainder of his life. *Library of Congress*

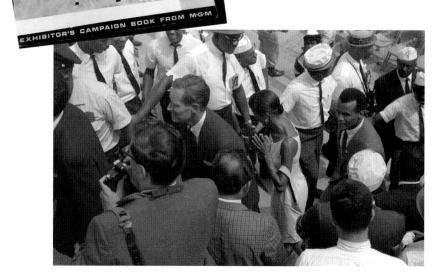

(Right) The relationship with Rex Harrison in *The Agony and the Ecstasy* mirrored the testy connection between the Pope and the artist Michelangelo.

(Right) The actor achieved iconic status with his impression in cement outside Grauman's Chinese Theater in Hollywood, Los Angeles, Ca.

(Below right) As an actor, Heston admired and enjoyed working with Laurence Olivier in *Khartoum*, although their collaborations were not always successful, as the ill-fated play "The Tumbler" demonstrated.

(Bottom) The actor's embodiment of authority figures, such as the legendary Spanish leader El Cid, allowed him to engage in efforts globally on behalf of the arts and other public and charity efforts.

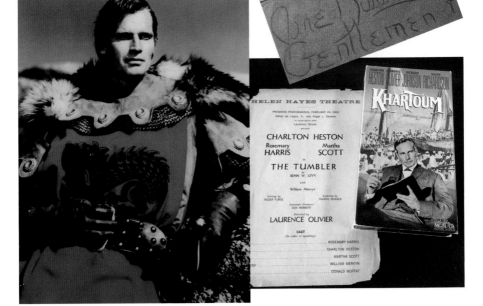

In film, Heston's most contentious moments came with volatile director Sam Peckinpah in the movie *Major Dundee* and with the rollout for *The Mountain Men* (left).

Never afraid to reinvent himself or expand his reach, Heston took on roles that departed from historical and biblical epics, including science fiction projects (below) such as *Planet of the Apes* and the *Omega Man*, as well as disaster movies like *Earthquake*.

Despite his many physical roles, Heston maintained that one of the most daunting was learning to appear to conduct an orchestra in the World War II caper *Counterpoint* (below).

(Below) The stage remained an important refuge. Heston's work on Herman Wouk's "The Caine Mutiny Court-Martial" took him not only to the Kennedy Center in Washington but across the globe to direct a Chinese language version in Beijing.

(Top) The actor often combined his passions with opportunities to support worthy causes (top).

(Above) Heston's later work on television complemented his interest in books. He had read Robert Louis Stevenson's classic *Treasure Island* to his son Fraser as a boy.

(Left) Heston always insisted that he began his political support as a Democrat before shifting to the Republican party, with friend and fellow Screen Actors Guild veteran Ronald Reagan and George H. W. Bush, often lending his "public face" to their campaigns.

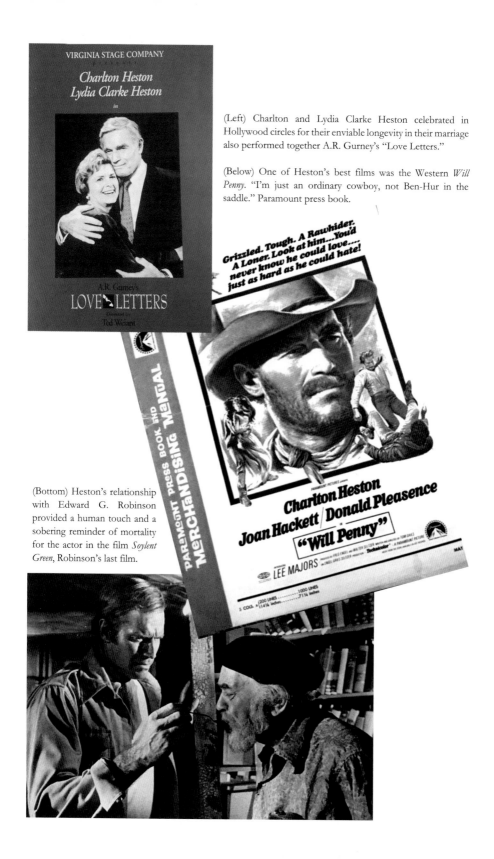

VIRGINIA STAGE COMPANY

Charlton Heston
Lydia Clarke Heston

in

A.R. Gurney's
LOVE LETTERS
Directed by
Ted Weiant

(Left) Charlton and Lydia Clarke Heston celebrated in Hollywood circles for their enviable longevity in their marriage also performed together A.R. Gurney's "Love Letters."

(Below) One of Heston's best films was the Western *Will Penny*. "I'm just an ordinary cowboy, not Ben-Hur in the saddle." Paramount press book.

Grizzled. Tough. A Rawhider.
A Loner. Look at him....You'd
never know he could love....
just as hard as he could hate!

PARAMOUNT PICTURES presents

Charlton Heston
Joan Hackett / Donald Pleasence
"Will Penny"

LEE MAJORS

5 COLS. x 200 LINES .... 1000 LINES
14½ inches .... 71¼ inches

MAT

(Bottom) Heston's relationship with Edward G. Robinson provided a human touch and a sobering reminder of mortality for the actor in the film *Soylent Green*, Robinson's last film.

PARAMOUNT PRESS BOOK AND MERCHANDISING MANUAL

task at hand. "I think we'll be alright," Heston concluded. The complicating factor was always juggling public duties with acting obligations and remaining true to the characters he portrayed and the lives they projected.

Nagging injuries plagued the actor, just as they would the aging professional athlete he was working diligently to present to moviegoers. While traveling to take up the coveted role, he recalled the inspiration for it. "I think back five years to that day on the plane when I saw the photograph of Tittle on his hands and knees that started me into the musing that finally became this script. Now we begin." Ample challenges remained, with Heston worrying whether his teammates would accept him as their screen captain. "I don't mix easily," he admitted, but understood it was "crucial" for him to try to do so in this case. Before he was finished, a good-natured "welcome to the NFL" and a cracked rib provided painful evidence of the player-actors' acceptance, allowing Heston to note legitimately, "Today I bought my ticket to the team."[110]

Number One wrapped in Hollywood on December 19. Heston's quarterbacking days were behind him, except for audiences who would pay to see them on the silver screen. In the exhausting aftermath of filming, a missing Michigan Christmas tree created a crisis for the Hestons, although a forlorn substitute made for a better symbolic ending to a hectic year. As always retrospective as a new year approached, the actor concluded of a party at his director's house, "It was a pleasant evening, I guess, though this is not my favorite holiday. This year, though, is certainly one that counted. We had one film blown out from under us, but I finally made my football picture."[111]

In addition to his acting work, Heston's public face kept him busy off-screen in numerous commitments that wore at his time and energy. "I seem to be involved in a rising tide of public service appearances of one kind or another," he lamented in March 1969. He was glad to participate in some of these, including a reading at a dinner for Helen Keller, whom he remembered from his days acting with Katharine Cornell: "She felt my armor and my face and said, 'Strong. Roman.'"

Other duties seemed more irksome. "I was a little annoyed at having to make still another speech before the ballet tonight, when the president of the bloody group is Joanne Woodward, whose husband [Paul Newman] is a perfectly serviceable public figure, suitable for occasions of this kind." He always disdained

110 *ALJ*, 295, 297, 303.

111 *CHA*, 417-418; *ALJ*, 306.

serving as "a dress-extra" for someone else, observing firmly, "In my own work I do that a great deal."[112]

Whatever feelings his engagements produced, less pleasant affairs seemed to intrude. The theft of Lydia's mink coat in London mitigated the joy Heston normally felt in traveling to England, although a special retrospective on his work made the situation enjoyable. Then, returning to the *Planet of the Apes* sequel, he reemphasized a lingering sense of unhappiness that seemed to permeate the period. "This is the first film . . . first acting . . . I've ever done in my life for which I have no enthusiasm, which is a vital loss." Heston later came to recognize that he was in a generally dark phase. "I did my best during the shooting of the few scenes I had in the *Apes* sequel to keep my mouth shut and do my work, a salutary experience for me. Still, I detect in these entries an excess of self-pity, the worst of human failings."[113]

Once he arrived in Spain for his next project, Heston seemed to be battling recurring problems, starting with taking up quarters "in the same suite, in the same hotel" he had stayed in while filming *55 Days at Peking*. If the "prospects" seemed "somewhat brighter" now, at least initially, various issues quickly hampered the shooting on the new picture, *Julius Caesar*, including obtaining the correct armor for himself, the suitability of Jason Robards as a horseback rider, the quality of the script's Shakespearean writing, and the difficult weather. Heston later compared Robards's attitude to what he had experienced with Ava Gardner years earlier. "He declined to go to the stables and pick a horse," he noted sarcastically, "on the reasonable ground that he was not being paid to ride a horse."[114]

Robards's views on horses, if not his understanding of the need to embrace them for the role, perplexed Heston. He enjoyed riding horses and often took pride in finding suitable animals for roles in his motion picture projects. During a rare break in his work schedule in 1963, Heston remembered "flinging into the Jag to go out to the deep Valley and check a horse someone has recommended as usable in films."[115]

Heston confided his frustration with other factors to his journal. Even in simulated combat, some of the nonprofessionals could not perform their roles.

112 *ALJ*, 310-311; Charlton Heston, "Statement in support of Richard Nixon," UCLA.

113 *ALJ*, 312-313.

114 *ALJ*, 316-317; *CHA*, 420.

115 Newsletter, "Hollywood, California," July 18, 1963, HL.

"A good rule to remember: Extras will not fight. You must use stunt men or soldiers." The next day he "had a quiet solo evening, enjoying a steak tartare and a history of the Roman Imperial Army" better than a larger gathering he might have attended, which he explained was "no reflection" on that party, "just my mood." The work and the darkness continued as Heston headed to Hawaii, a location tourists had long found tantalizing, but in which he had little personal interest. "I'm depressed, and I don't really know why," he noted of the prospect of filming *The Hawaiians*. "I can't pull myself out of these doldrums and into a proper enthusiasm for the part." He had used similar language when doing the *Planet of the Apes* sequel. "*The Hawaiians* is one of the few films in my career I've undertaken less than full-heartedly. I feel very guilty about this and can't really explain it."[116]

Complications from a fall by Lydia and an unusual public moment on one of the beaches also colored the setting in darker hues. In Lydia's case, the situation called for rest, but in the other circumstance, a flash of terror came over the man who had worked so diligently always to appear outwardly composed. Heston had just completed a swim when he noticed "a crowd of fans waiting at the water's edge with cameras." There was no mistaking this uncomfortable situation, which he likened to a scene from his current film in which residents met lepers with clubs as they waded ashore at Molokai in order to steal their few possessions. He turned to swim away, only to notice a few of the more diligent adherents keeping pace on shore. "I felt like an idiot," he recorded, but later assessed the matter more coolly. "Celebrity is to a certain extent a paranoid condition," he explained. "You have to be careful not to surrender to the feeling of being pursued." Cognizant of the individuals who made his career and lifestyle choices possible, Heston concluded, "I take my responsibility to the people who buy the tickets very seriously, but my life has strengthened the reclusive strains in my nature."[117]

Heston might shun unwanted public contacts, but he understood that his celebrity status offered him a platform when he required or wanted one. Only a year before, Heston had been grateful to complete his football movie, but *Number One* had not played that way in the theaters. The movie simultaneously symbolized a decade that held so much promise, but produced mixed results, and a production that represented a dream fulfilled, but ultimately unrealized aspirations. As British biographer Bruce Crowther observed, "It was especially unfortunate for Heston that this film was allowed to disappear, for Catlan was among his best roles and

116 *ALJ*, 317, 320.

117 Ibid., 320, 321.

Heston rises admirably to the opportunity of stretching himself in one of the few non-uniformed twentieth-century roles of his career." Regardless of the challenging circumstances that surrounded his career at the end of the 1960s, Chuck Heston was glad to end the decade as he so often did, in the embrace of family. This was his bedrock in the best and worst, or at least most trying, of times.[118] He would face greater challenges on multiple fronts as a new decade dawned, but could take comfort in knowing that he had weathered a sloppy track and remained on course for the race to continue.

118 Crowther, *Charlton Heston*, 111; *ALJ*, 328.

Chapter Seven

ADAPTING TO THE CONDITIONS
1970s

"[The] Democratic Party moved, I didn't."
—Heston on shifting to the Republican Party

"Professionalism will not necessarily create art, but in film,
it's almost impossible to have art, or even a film, without it."
—Heston, June 4, 1975

"I've been doing interviews for so long, I forget you have to learn how."
—Heston, October 3, 1975

"Actors can be horrible people."
—Heston, August 7, 1976

Performances:
The Merv Griffin Show, June 3, 1970; June 4, 1970; Sept. 9, 1971; Apr. 2, 1974
Julius Caesar, 1970
The Hawaiians, 1970
Beneath the Planet of the Apes, 1970
The Dick Cavett Show, June 18, 1970; Nov. 15, 1971
The David Frost Show, July 8, 1970; June 1, 1972
The Tonight Show Starring Johnny Carson, Oct. 1, 1970; Aug. 18, 1971; May 11, 1972;
Dec. 12, 1972; Mar. 29, 1973; Aug. 23, 1973; Mar. 22, 1974; May 22, 1974; Oct. 25, 1974;
Feb. 5, 1975; Mar. 2, 1976; June 15, 1976; Dec. 10, 1976; Feb. 22, 1977; Sept. 16, 1977; Mar. 14,
1978; Nov. 8, 1978; Feb. 14, 1979; Oct. 18, 1979
The Omega Man, 1971
The Irv Kupcinet Show, Aug. 21, 1971
Parkinson, Dec. 12, 1971
Film Night, Feb. 26, 1972

Skyjacked, 1972

The Crucible, Ahmanson Theatre, Los Angeles, Dec. 5,1972-Jan. 3, 1973

The Mike Douglas Show, June 8, 1972; May 4, 1973; Oct. 23, 1973;
Oct. 15, 1974; Oct. 16, 1974; Nov. 4, 1975; July 23, 1976; Nov. 4, 1976; Feb. 11, 1977;
Feb. 27, 1978; Oct. 10, 1978; Nov. 29, 1978; Mar. 26, 1979

Antony and Cleopatra, 1973

The Call of the Wild, 1973

Soylent Green, 1973

The Three Musketeers, 1973

The Academy Awards, Mar. 27, 1973 (45th, co-host); Apr. 2, 1974 (46th);
Mar. 29, 1976 (48th); Apr. 3, 1978 (50th)

American Film Institute Salute to John Ford, Apr. 2, 1973; *James Cagney*, Mar. 18, 1974;
Orson Welles, Feb. 17, 1975; *William Wyler*, Mar. 14, 1976; *Henry Fonda*, Mar. 15, 1978;
Alfred Hitchcock, Mar. 12, 1979

Today, April 18, 1973

Jack Paar Tonite, Oct. 18, 1973

Dinah's Place, Oct. 23, 1973

ABC's Wide World of Entertainment, May 29, 1974

Earthquake, 1974

Airport 1975, 1974

The Four Musketeers, 1975

Macbeth, Ahmanson Theatre, Jan. 28-March 8, 1975

Dinah! Feb. 14, 1975; May 3, 1976; May 17, 1976; Nov. 18, 1977

Two-Minute Warning, 1976

Midway, 1976

The Last Hard Men, 1976

Long Day's Journey into Night, Ahmanson Theatre, Feb. 18-Apr. 2, 1977

The American Film Institute's 10th Anniversary Special, Nov. 21, 1977

Good Morning America, Nov. 24, 1977; Nov. 25, 1977

Donahue, Dec. 8, 1977

Science Fiction Film Awards, Jan. 21, 1978

America 2-Night, Apr. 10, 1978

Gray Lady Down, 1978

Crossed Swords, 1978

Evening Magazine, Jan. 11, 1979

A Man for All Seasons, Ahmanson Theatre, Feb. 18-Mar. 31, 1979

*The 16th Annual Humanitarian Awards Dinner of National Conference of Christians and
Jews*, Sept. 17, 1979

A sense of unsettlement was already creeping in for Charlton Heston as the 1970s began. Some of the challenges of the previous decade continued to exhibit themselves early in the new one. The family went to Key West for a brief, enjoyable respite of cruising and recreation, but even reflective walks on the beach produced as much opportunity for thinking about the state of his career as moments of relaxation. Biographer Marc Eliot captured the complications of children "growing up too fast," the typical marital "rocky times," and the realities of mid-life. "He remained optimistic, as always, but concerned too about what lay ahead for his acting career moving into the 1970s," and had an understandable focus and desire to generate "both artistic relevance and mainstream popularity in the always fickle and often cruel business of making movies." With difficulty securing both financing and a director for *Antony and Cleopatra*, he had to face the stark reality that "the name 'Charlton Heston' no longer had enough box-office clout to make most A directors jump aboard."[1]

By January 6, Heston was back in Los Angeles experiencing "[m]uch back-and-forthing on *I Am Legend*." Among the chores he had to accept for this project was producing "an outline on what I feel the script should incorporate, and I hate writing." He was also settling back into the demanding public aspects of his career. Looking back on this phase of his life, Heston noted with resignation, "For one thing, my earnest forays into the public sector were beginning to complicate my life more than I'd imagined."[2]

By the end of January, the actor returned to Washington in connection with his obligations for the National Council on the Arts, which held long and often taxing meetings. He found that economic realities were putting a "squeeze" on all the arts and lamented, "Opera, symphony, dance are all on the verge of strangling on it." One scholar noted Heston's "parsimonious ways," as he took his role of protecting limited funds seriously. During these sessions, he felt compelled to take on another difficult aspect of the work. "I performed my classic function as hatchet man," he noted in one instance where he thought funding for one project was out of proportion.[3]

Whether through his personal appearance or his distinctive voice, demands for Heston's help were growing. This was the type of "pro bono work most well-known actors do for various worthwhile groups: breakfasts, luncheons, dinners,

---

1 Eliot, *Charlton Heston*, 325-326.

2 *ALJ*, 330; *CHA*, 406.

3 *ALJ*, 331; Raymond, *Cold, Dead Hands*, 142; *ALJ*.

and receptions; letters, recorded appeals, and instructional materials." He noted, "For me, these range across the spectrum from the Boy Scouts and libraries to the Pentagon and the Department of Energy." Heston's "public face" still sparked interest from those who followed his film career, and he was proud to do what he saw as genuine public service. "I've done appearances, audios, and videos for just about every Cabinet-level department in the federal government." Of all this work, he concluded, "You're glad to do it, obviously, if you weren't you wouldn't. Still, it can wear a bit."[4]

Although he was more than willing to lend his name and voice to public service promotions of all sorts, Heston was not anxious to retire to that type of work exclusively. Television no longer seemed to be an option either, since he believed even commercials offered more substance than did TV series. "I think TV commercials are some of the best films being made anywhere today," he observed, touting the photography in Coca-Cola ads and equating a McDonald's commercial to "a Busby Berkeley musical." He was not prepared yet to enter that world, but thought the production values superior, especially given the amounts of money that was spent on them. Moreover, he observed, "Commercials producers take pains and shoot forever." Still, for a performer who preferred to vary his exposure primarily through theatrical stage appearances, these modern trends seemed disturbing. "But what does a kid do now?" he wondered. "One week he plays a cowboy in Bonanza or a villain in Mannix."[5]

Hints of difficulties also filtered into his reflections on his personal relationships. "Lydia is shaken by the stresses of giving up the apartment . . . which I can understand," he noted on April 6 as they ended a long and important chapter in their lives by leaving their New York living quarters. "We've been here eighteen *years*, for God's sake." After a couple of harried days packing, it was time to go. "We took a last look from the terrace, hurried our bags out through the denuded rooms, and closed the book on our New York identity." Heston tried to justify the transition. "It was lovely to have, but I doubt we spent a total of one year there out of eighteen." He later added, "Like many actors, I'd somehow felt a New York base was necessary to a serious actor." If the "decentralization" of the theater made Broadway seem less important, however, that element had defined their worlds for many years. "Still, it was a fine apartment," he admitted wistfully.[6]

---

4 *CHA*, 407.

5 Haber, "Chuck Heston: A Toga Man in the Jeans Era."

6 *ALJ*, 334-335.

The home "on my ridge" remained the critical refuge. "I unwound readily with a lot of tennis" and time with the family he loved, Heston wrote. "Still there was a darkening swale on the other side of that sunny ridge we lived on," he observed, referencing the migraine headaches that were torturing Lydia with "shattering intensity." If he could admit his difficulties in relating to the excruciating experience—"Blessed with disgusting good health, I tend to be a little inadequate dealing with other people's physical disorders"—he nevertheless recognized that her challenges were his as well.[7]

Still, the darkness he felt during this period did not completely dissipate when he returned to Los Angeles. "A good day for brooding, reassessing the situation," Heston noted on April 10. "It now seems likely I won't make a film this summer . . . any film." Factors beyond his control were dictating the realities. "This is the tightest year for film financing since I came into the business," he asserted. "Still, it is important to keep active, unpressing," although he felt the creeping need to press.

On May 6, after he had written about the sale of items associated with MGM, he asserted, "Everyone's putting great stress on 'being with it,' these days. With what for God's sake?" A few days later, he was strolling along the streets of St. Louis after a National Council on the Arts meeting, noting the nature of the architecture and grounds of homes he felt were "standing for the time they were built . . . when we would live and thrive forever."[8] Amidst these whiffs of nostalgia, there was a clear sense that something important had gone missing, and that he was powerless to do anything about it.

Heston was too busy to indulge his darker moods for too long. He had several projects to consider, any one of which could build on the success he had enjoyed with *Planet of the Apes*. To his newsletter readers, he explained that among the film offers or scripts that he was examining were other science fiction vehicles like *Soylent Green* and *The Omega Man*. Heston wanted to work and was searching for the most appropriate project without necessarily and automatically accepting whatever happened to come along just for the sake of remaining busy. He was also reaching new heights in his ability to help others in causes he felt merited his efforts. "I go to the fund-raisers that stud everyone's calendar out here—that's part of my work," he later observed.[9] Building on his earliest variety appearances with

7 *CHA*, 409.

8 *ALJ*, 335, 337.

9 Newsletter, April 18, 1970, HL; *CHA*, 235.

Ed Sullivan and Steve Allen, he was now becoming a regular guest on *The Tonight Show with Johnny Carson* and many other talk shows with high profile hosts like Jack Paar, Mike Douglas, and Dinah Shore.

Additionally, Heston spent more time testifying before Congress about film and the arts. "I'm beginning to think I should make this my profession," he wrote on May 4 concerning an appearance before the Congressional Committee on Pornography. He supported artistic endeavor and had demonstrated that there were times when something someone might find offensive nevertheless had merit, but he also set boundaries as to the types of material that ought not to appear in film. Still, the frustration continued. A couple of weeks later, when he had to dash once more to the nation's capital to "do my little dance," he sighed, "I've got more work in these free jobs than I can do. I wish I could put something together in my own line, and get paid for it."

Charlton Heston had learned how to employ his skills and his contacts for important causes and concerns. In Washington, he added personal meetings with key congressional figures and a dinner with old friend Jack Valenti in the hopes his presence would obtain "some more Brownie points for us with various [Capitol] Hill and D.C. dignitaries." Of the necessary political courting in which he was involved, the actor concluded, "That's the way the game is played, of course."

At home, he attended to pleasant, routine parental duties that he often missed when traveling. On May 16, he seemed to delight in noting, "A lot of the day went to a parent's prime job: chauffeuring." When business took him away, he felt some satisfaction in knowing that his traveling habits were of some use. In the October 1970 edition of his newsletter, he reminded fans that he benefitted most from an extraordinary ability to handle these matters. "It's amazing how many different balls you can keep in the air as long as you can sleep well on jetliners, and I can."[10]

Heston long maintained an appreciation for the ways in which his star status could be useful personally. One of these was having studios and other agencies provide for travel access and accommodations; another was executive support. For some time, however, the person responsible for arranging his professional affairs had proven difficult to almost everyone else. Finally, while on a trip to London, he reached the point that he no longer could tolerate the situation and the actor sent the troublesome individual back to California, with her telling response ringing in his ears: "Well, we all have the right to our opinions, surely." Upon returning to the United States himself, Heston was overjoyed to learn that she had decided

10 *ALJ*, 336-337; Newsletter, Oct. 28, 1970, HL.

to retire. His new assistant, Carol Lanning, proved to be a significant improvement in this aspect of his professional life. Heston remembered that subsequently, when he traveled, everything he needed was ready for him without complication or concern. "All I need to think about, or what to," he explained, "is the work I have to do when I'm there." Lanning made sure this would be the case. A bulwark and a buffer, she performed her most important duty in allowing him to fulfill his obligations. "It is not true that Carol pins a note to my coat in case I get lost. It is true that she runs my public life with awesome efficiency, but unvarying good humor." He later proclaimed that one of the "few regrets" he had in not entering politics was that "I'd love to have seen Carol Lanning run a senatorial office."[11]

The new decade had started with challenges and its first year ended without significant improvement. As Heston noted in his journal, "Professionally, the worst year [for] films have seen in a long time was more or less reflected in my career. The two films I had released in 1970 were both disappointments, creatively and commercially, though my personal notices were good in both." With studied determination, he assessed the period sharply. "I really think, all things considered, I could've done without 1970."

The new year did not begin promisingly. Lydia had another difficult time, which her husband tentatively accepted; he surmised that most of the pressure on her came "from me, I guess." In early 1971, the fate of the newsletter he had used to remain connected with fans was another fact of reality he had to face. His assistant, Cora Sommer, had decided to retire and Heston had to contemplate how to move forward in her absence. He had once discontinued a fan club and thought he should follow the same course now. "In closing, let me only say that, though I can't manage the Newsletter without Cora, I can still make films. I hope you'll still come to see them." Then, with a characteristic gesture, he typed, "I thank you all," and the "Charlton Heston Newsletter" ceased publication after more than a decade.[12]

Meanwhile, both Hestons felt pressures, with Charlton's coming from anxieties about the prospective *Antony and Cleopatra* and a surprisingly poor script for Jack London's *Call of the Wild*. Heston assessed, "I'm still struggling to decide whether I'm justified in making the sacrifice that must be made to film *Antony*. . . . I'm risking money and reputation." The project still held the possibility of a higher

11 *CHA*, 469-470.

12 *ALJ*, 349, 352; Newsletter, Jan. 26, 1971, HL.

reward, at least artistically. "I should welcome the chance to risk reputation in a part like this," he concluded, "and what else can I buy that I want so much?"

He was concerned about more than just his reputation. "I'm still eating at the *Antony* problem, or it's eating at me," he explained. "For myself, I have no qualms. Still, I have to risk not only money to which my family has a basic right, but also my time, of which they'll be grievously deprived. . . . In a sense this is silly; I've made more money than most men dream of," he concluded. He acknowledged other areas of unease when he added after further reflection, "Another factor in this decision about *Antony* is the amount of energy, both physical and mental, I have to tap for the project."[13]

Just as importantly, he knew that no effort as consuming as this one could work without Lydia's endorsement. She often strained under household and family demands while he traveled to undertake one task or another. Yet, as always, she was there to serve as a sounding board and support. With respect to *Antony and Cleopatra*, Charlton felt she was "committed to the project, willing to sacrifice for it." Complicating matters further, there was also grumbling in the acting community over the fact that the same person advocating for making films in Hollywood was working so frequently abroad in his own projects.[14]

Working through the auspices of the American Film Institute, Heston remained committed to serving his profession in ways outside acting or directing. But at this time, he still felt a nagging sense of how to determine the next creative course he should pursue. The chance for a role in a film called *Deliverance* was appealing, but other commitments prevented him from accepting it; he joked, "[I]t's nice to know they consider me employable." With England and Spain calling, casting and location scouting for *Antony and Cleopatra* progressed, but Heston still struggled to find someone to fill the director's chair. When he ran into friend and associate Franklin Schaffner, Heston dangled the thought of directing himself, "rather diffidently over Scotch." Schaffner, who had directed him in *The War Lord* and *Planet of the Apes*, replied, "Why not! Nothing to it."[15]

Heston had hoped to secure the directing services of either Laurence Olivier or Orson Welles, but both insisted the picture had to have an outstanding Cleopatra in order to work, and neither seemed to think Hildegarde Neil could fill the bill. Heston himself later thought his all-consuming roles had not allowed

13 *ALJ*, 352, 353.

14 Eliot, *Charlton Heston*, 330-331; *ALJ*, 353.

15 *ALJ*, 354-355; Heston and Isbouts, *Hollywood*, 169.

him to provide enough guidance. Lydia insisted that the fault may have rested in more than that. "He made her too soft. He likes his women to be soft, you see." Charlton's retort also illustrated the depth of their connection. "Then how did I wind up marrying you?"[16]

The stress of having to serve in the role of producer revealed more of Heston's personality foibles. He found the requisite demands almost "unbearable" and admitted, "I hate negotiation; I hate the idea of having to persuade, to urge people into doing something." For him, any decision would always involve deep consideration, but after doing due diligence "it always should be something you leap to, or don't do at all."[17]

In the meantime, he saw to the finishing touches for *The Omega Man*. Heston was pleased with the finished product. "This is another of a not very long list of films I have more or less personally conceived, and this may turn out to be the best of them."[18] Of course, box office success would be the surest reflection of where he stood professionally, at least regarding the cinema, and also would help to offset the strain that difficulties with *Antony* posed.

In addition to his various movie projects, Heston held a post that required him to keep his attention on greater issues. As president of the Screen Actors Guild, a meeting with President Richard Nixon and representatives of the film profession led to Heston's involvement in a press conference on matters related to his industry. Nixon later sent him a personal note of gratitude. "There are, of course, no easy solutions for the problems facing the film industry," the president observed, "but the fact that all of us recognize that the industry must take the lead in restoring its own economic vitality is in itself an important step forward." Nixon reiterated his earlier expression of support. "As I noted in San Clemente, I will see to it that the Federal Government makes every reasonable effort to assist you in this difficult task, and needless to say, I greatly appreciate your offer to help on behalf of the Screen Actors Guild."[19]

Though Heston's high-profile public appearances sapped time from his work and family, they allowed him to speak out on issues of importance to him and gave him the opportunity to solidify his connections with the Nixon administration.

16 Heston and Isbouts, *Hollywood*, 167-170.

17 *ALJ*, 356.

18 Ibid., 357.

19 Peter M. Flanigan to "Dear Mayor Yorty," Apr. 9, 1971, and Richard Nixon to "Dear Mr. Heston," Apr. 27, 1971, RNPL.

In the summer of 1971, his ability to mix his passion for tennis also connected him with powerful forces in the nation's capital. On July 7, Nixon assistant Peter Flanigan forwarded a memorandum to the office of White House Chief of Staff H. R. Haldeman. "I understand from Bob that the President gave the tennis court only a one year reprieve," he observed. "That being the case, I think we would lose Charleton [sic] Heston and his friends if we had them put in a new court this year and sow it to salt next year." With an election year pending, there was no need to alienate voices that might otherwise be friendly to the administration, especially over trivial affairs. Of course, "Charleton" Heston would not link his support for the Nixon government or its policies on the basis of the status of the presidential tennis court, but the issue brought to the fore the degree to which the actor had learned to utilize a broad spectrum of skills and assets for his public and political interests.[20]

In reality, "Mr. Heston" was too busy trying to organize *Antony and Cleopatra* to worry about the state of tennis courts in Washington. The dual roles of actor and director, sprinkled with producing concerns, kept him scrambling. He exposed some of this frustration in his journal entries for late March and early April. "For some damn reason, *Antony* won't stay buttoned up. You get one end nailed down and a board curls up at the other corner." At the same time, MGM was refusing to budge on giving Heston access to outtake footage of the naval battles in *Ben-Hur* so he could keep costs down. A deal might yet be struck to the satisfaction of all, but it nevertheless was a distracting complication for the time being.

As spring progressed, the schedule intensified, with casting, rehearsals, and seemingly endless flights, as well as a few remaining chores associated with *The Omega Man*. Then in May, a happy development occurred when Kirk Kerkorian, the new owner of MGM, came through with the *Ben-Hur* footage that Heston wanted, easing concerns about that important element. The actor obviously meant it when he observed, "I'm damn grateful MGM had a change of heart on this."[21]

By the end of May, he recorded with near-relief, "I began it," and even found time to take in an Olivier performance and compare notes together afterward "in his dressing room, [where] he gave me some good whiskey and better advice, about both *Antony* and directing." Still, the schedule was ambitious and grueling,

---

20 Memorandum for Larry Higby from Peter Flanigan, July 7, 1971, ibid.

21 *ALJ*, 357, 359.

with the full range of demands for locations, scenes, characters, bits/extras, and requirements such as animals, furniture, and other set design elements.[22]

Unfortunately, each day seemed to bring new challenges. "A series of disasters today," on June 21; "A brute of a day," on June 28; "We fell behind today," on July 8; "I felt sadly plagued by the gods," on July 12; "Another bitch of a day . . . I'm afraid they're all getting to be that," on July 17; and a day on which he barely made it out of bed from an uncharacteristic stomach illness on July 22. In spite of all these unforeseen or difficult circumstances, Heston found his greatest challenge with Hildegarde Neil as Cleopatra. He wanted to direct and guide without driving her, but one of the issues he feared occurred in one of the principal scenes. "I got my actress snakebit and laid out, not without problems . . . but not the ones I figured." She handled the snake itself well enough. "Our main problem was keeping her from breathing after her death. The poor lady smokes so much she

---

22 *ALJ*, 359; "Antony and Cleopatra schedules," and "Notes on Production—Schedule for 'Antony & Cleopatra,'" Heston Papers, f.37, HL. The scope of Heston's commitment was enormous and included:

Pre-Shooting Schedule
Sunday May 23 8 a.m.   C. Heston arrives London (PA 120)
Monday May 24   Casting Dorchester Hotel
Tuesday May 25 10 a.m.   Reading of script
Rehearsals
Tuesday May 25 2-5 p.m.
Wednesday May 26 10-12 a.m. & 1-5 p.m.
Thursday May 27 10-1 & 2-5
Thursday June 3   C. Heston and H. Neil to Madrid (BEA 180)
Monday June 14   Main Shooting Commences

Art Department, Madrid; March 22nd
Ten weeks shooting in Almeria, May 31st
Shooting studio, Madrid, June 21st . . . to complete July 24th
Rough cut: August 7th
Fine cut in six weeks: Sept. 18th
Dub: Oct. 30th
Deliver answer-print: Dec. 11th
Second Unit scs. Requiring CH as Antony:
                       Inserts fr/Sc 36—Close action on deck of Galley
                       Sc. 54—Close angles fr/Battle on Ridge
                       Sc. 55—Running insert on Horse
                       Sc. 31—CU Antony at sea in Felluca
CH to Madrid for casting: Sunday, May 2nd
" " London for rehearsals: May 9th
"   Back to Almeria for location rehearsals: May 23rd
"   Shoot 2nd Unit w/Antony on galley: May 29th
Joe Canutt to Madrid: May 16th

has little lung capacity. It was really very tough for her. All of it has been, I guess." When location filming wrapped, Heston experienced the understandable mix of emotions, while toasting the cast and "trying to absorb the end of it." He felt an exhausted sense of satisfaction. "I've been looking forward to this for so long," he admitted concerning the project, "and now it's over. I have no way of telling if it's any good at this point. I only know I've done it, and survived."

Reality began to settle in almost immediately, as the production accounting made a budget overrun apparent. After wrangling over how the shortfall had occurred and what might be done about it, Heston went over to the set, then being dismantled. "I can't tell whether my dream of doing it ended there or not," he confessed. "I only know I'm tired . . . as tired as I've ever been. I want to go home."[23] And that was exactly where the Heston entourage headed.

While engaged in his mighty enterprise overseas, he had received a note that reinforced the relationship he was building with the current administration in Washington. Presidential assistant Flanigan now referred to him as "Dear Charlton" and offered his "warmest regards" in the pursuit of their common interests. Once he returned from Europe, Heston renewed this connection at the opening of the new Kennedy Center. Despite describing it as "a very impressive example of the edifice complex," Heston enjoyed being part of the project and the opportunity he had to demonstrate his appreciation of Nixon's support of the arts. A greeting at the Kennedy Center led the actor to reply in kind. "Mr. Heston warmly commends the President for his efforts to improve the lot of the screen actor," a staffer wrote. "Mr. Heston also supports the President's steps to revitalize the economy."[24]

Television interviews for *The Omega Man* and consideration of proposals that would become *Skyjacked*, *Soylent Green*, and *Midway* helped to pass time as Heston tried to offer comfort for Lydia, who was experiencing another barrage of migraines. "No one seems to have any answers as to what causes them, or how to cure them," he noted of his wife's painful circumstances. "I only know I must hang on. Meantime, I have to prod myself into some kind of an active state."

Meanwhile, he awaited the arrival of the rough footage of *Antony* to process. "I go through the motions these days, but I can't hook into them with any enthusiasm. It will pass . . . it will pass. Once the film gets here and I can

---

23 *ALJ*, 362-366.

24 Peter M. Flanigan to "Dear Charlton," June 1, 1971, RNPL; *ALJ*, 368; Memorandum for Leonard Garment from Michael B. Smith, Sept. 24, 1971, RNPL; Peter M. Flanigan to "Dear Charlton," Oct. 23, 1971, ibid.

begin editing, life will look up." Lydia's improvement and a pending interview with Merv Griffin revived his spirits, as did a reunion with Fray from an outdoor excursion and a family discussion "happily (if oddly) of the history of World War II." Unfortunately, this revelry was short-lived. Two days later, "Well, I finally saw my rough assembly . . . and Frank Schaffner was right. It's *terrible*." His friend and associate had warned him of the effect of seeing the raw stock for the first time and advised him not to be discouraged, "but it's disheartening, nonetheless."

Fortuitously, a trip to Washington for an Arts Council gathering required his attention, with meetings in which he lamented the shift in already limited funding toward "social" projects rather than "artistic" ones. In other realms, the actor was willing, even anxious, to exert pressure to send "social" messages in areas he deemed significant. The script for a film relating to a hijacking incident and tentatively called *Hijacked* grabbed his attention for reasons other than performance. "We must sharpen the character of the hijacker, make it utterly clear he deserves no sympathy, that his end is inevitable and just," he noted in October 1971. "I see this as social, not merely dramatic, responsibility." He tamped down disagreement, explaining, "Script approval is a useful tool." In time, he would add context. "I've always felt, given the enormous power film has to shape the way we feel and think about things, that the film maker has a very serious social responsibility, sometimes overriding his creative independence, in the way he treats subjects like terrorism, racism, and a surprising number of other public issues." Whatever statements he hoped to make with his work, Charlton Heston was prepared to step away from one of the venues that had served as a springboard for advancing his profession. "My last SAG meeting was complicated by emotion," he admitted. "An extravagant speech from Vic Jory, and others. I confess to being touched."[25]

As outgoing SAG president, Heston initially felt obliged to remain neutral in the selection of his successor, but that position changed when Bert Freed led a slate of independents against the nominating committee's selections, which were headed by John Gavin. Heston had managed largely to side-step controversies in his six years in leadership. Now, the vocal criticism levied by the Freed slate spurred Heston to support Gavin and condemn the attacks on the SAG's record. "I particularly, bitterly resent this charge," Heston wrote of Freed's argument that the Guild did not represent ethnic minorities sufficiently. Although he focused on the perceived impracticality of the independent slate's platform, he could not help

25 *ALJ*, 367-368, 370-371. The film eventually was titled *Skyjacked*.

but feel that the historically unprecedented challenge of opposition threatened to tarnish his leadership legacy.[26]

Powerful emotions held sway over the election to the leadership of a union that Heston cherished. His personal feelings pushed him to a public display that one scholar maintained "embarrassed him," but it left the actor with an important lesson: in future confrontations, he would try to avoid making statements that called opponents into question regarding possible ties to "any hidden agenda or organization." Whatever his views, Heston seemed to understand that they could be undermined by comments that smacked of a return to the dark days of Hollywood blacklisting.[27]

As it turned out, John Gavin won the election handily by a vote of 6,407-3,237. With this result, the departing president could feel satisfaction that the new leadership would sustain his efforts. In a gesture that reflected his own values, Heston presented Gavin with a gavel and the parting words of advice: "For the Guild's President: To use with all the moderation you find possible, all the wisdom you possess, and all the justice you can discern. Chuck Heston, 1971."[28] He had not assumed the role as a caretaker or placeholder and expected those who followed to be as diligent and vigilant in their service as he had sought to be.

Heston always viewed his SAG tenure with pride, noting that he had served as president "for six terms (longer than anyone else, so far)," during which "my worldwide public identity made me an ambassador as well." He would continue to look for ways to lead in his industry and elsewhere. "That dual role's been useful in other chores, too," he explained.[29] Emilie Raymond observed of the Heston/SAG leadership period, "Despite the controversial issues and the inevitable internal disputes that he faced, Heston enjoyed immense popularity as Guild president because of his talents as an able and competent leader attuned to the actor's needs." She concluded that he had demonstrated himself to be "an able and articulate spokesperson."[30]

---

26 Robert A. Wright, "Screen Actors Guild in Bitter Election," *NYT*, Oct. 20, 1971.

27 David F. Prindle, *The Politics of Glamour: Ideology and Democracy in the Screen Actors Guild* (Madison, WI, 1988), 103.

28 Ibid., 103; "Charlton Heston, 1965-1971," SAG-AFTRA, www.sagaftra.org/charlton-heston, accessed Oct. 17, 2018.

29 *CHA*, 310.

30 Raymond, *Cold, Dead Hands*, 120.

Charlton Heston's career during this period represented the on-going challenge of remaining viable in his profession without succumbing to ego or bowing to pressure from those who thought his name should sell an artistic production. He already had enormous personal capital involved in *Antony and Cleopatra*, but when publicity personnel thought the posters for the project should say, "'Charlton Heston's film of . . . .' I vetoed this." Not only did this run counter to his notion of proper credit—which belonged to the Bard —but he recognized that it would send the wrong message. "I'll be damned if I take a possessive credit on a film Shakespeare wrote every word of." Later, as he reviewed the incident, he concluded, "This was very prudent of me."[31]

As always, choosing the right vehicle could mean reestablishing his relevance to audiences, while sustaining both his family's resources and his career. Unfortunately, some of the worst, or at least most disappointing, film work of Charlton Heston's career occurred during this time, including the Shakespearean feature he had undertaken as a genuine labor of love and another based upon the famous novel *Call of the Wild*.

Before heading to Norway for the Jack London adaptation, Heston took part in *Skyjacked*, a picture that focused on the hijacking of a 707. The acting challenge he faced as the aircraft pilot certainly differed from those associated with his depiction of Mark Antony. Much of his work took place in a cramped cockpit set, with time in a flight simulator allowing him to develop a comfort-level for the space and situation. Heston was generally pleased with the principals, including director John Guillermin, although that mercurial figure nearly caused a difficult moment for his star when he berated co-star and former *Number One* football teammate Mike Henry publicly. Without fanfare or credit, Heston sent word that Guillermin should avoid any such displays in the future or the actor would leave the set. "He never did," Heston recalled.[32]

Publicity for *Skyjacked* focused on Heston's physical regimen, even for what was essentially a sedentary role. One writer noted the actor's running routine as part of his "early morning constitutional," and a "rousing game of tennis" that was so rigorous as to make "ardent Heston fans out of the most cynical disbelievers." The piece featured Heston's own assessment of the importance of these activities. "If I don't run before starting work in the morning, it's a lead-pipe cinch I'm not

---

31 *ALJ*, 372-373.

32 Heston had in mind the example Clark Gable had set while filming *The Misfits* with Marilyn Monroe: "If the King could do it, so by God can I." *CHA*, 465.

going to later at the studio." His focus on fitness was hardly new, but he felt that "without that morning run and the tennis, I would actually be able to watch the pounds go on" courtesy of his "very hearty appetite."[33]

Despite his intense physical preparations for the role, Heston felt oddly "detached" as filming on *Skyjacked* ended. His focus remained on *Antony and Cleopatra*, set to premiere in London. Unfortunately, the news was not pleasant on that front. "Our first notices were not encouraging . . . in fact they were bad," the actor/director observed on March 2; he admitted, "I'm dashed a little, of course, though you learn to be toughened for it." He could see the flaws that had developed a bit more clearly and lamented, "I wish I'd been able to follow through on the whole dub. I wish, I wish."

A day later, after a quick return to Los Angeles, Heston was still absorbing the shock of having the cherished project labeled "a critical disaster," and sought to place the matter in perspective. "Of course I disagree, of course I'm outraged, but it still sticks a little." Edits might still salvage the picture, but the best salve for the actor's bruised ego came with his subsequent arrival in Japan, where throngs of people greeted him. "The Japanese know how to get coverage," he surmised. "Either that or I have a helluva draw in this country. Possibly a little of both. We had a press turnout that staggered me: rows and rows of eyeglasses and notebooks, a platoon of photographers."

Things were looking up elsewhere. *Skyjacked* seemed "surprisingly good, I was relieved to see," and more public service work and tennis provided welcome releases. Herman Citron was keeping the Heston name viable in the industry, with several projects "in the oven, all ripening well, several ready to pop."[34] The actor had learned to take matters in stride and keep driving forward in all phases of his public life; he would need all his reserves to handle what, on the surface, was a promising project.

Indeed, the combinations at work on the next picture seemed virtually guaranteed to produce a winner. Heston had always enjoyed good books, and this movie had the Jack London classic *Call of the Wild* as its base material. He loved dogs, and it incorporated that element as well. He was passionate about the outdoors, and a shoot on location in Norway seemed ideal. Despite a persistent cold and "many reservations" about the script that he nevertheless expected the filming to be able to resolve, Heston embarked on the new assignment with good

33 "Keeping in Trim," MGM Pressbook for *Skyjacked*, 1972, Wills.

34 *ALJ*, 380-381.

humor and optimism. "So another began," he recorded on March 22. "What is it? My fortieth, I think." Whatever could be said of the corpus of his work, it had been meaningful to him. "I've seen a lot of the world and done some remarkable things. I've ridden into captured cities, and won chariot races, and conducted symphony orchestras, and painted the Sistine, and now I've driven a dog sled."

Yet a mixed international team, indifferently trained animals, and a lack of time in which to learn to drive the sled the way he had mastered the chariot for *Ben-Hur* meant that there were too many challenges to overcome for the film to work. Difficulty with language was only one glaring problem. When one of the actors proved "unqualified to act in English," Heston tempered his assessment of the situation before offering the barb, "I know, I couldn't act in French, but then, I wouldn't try."[35]

He remained relentlessly negative toward the cut of the movie the studio decided to release. He took personal responsibility in his published journals, noting editorially, "For the record, it's probably the worst film I ever made. I'm embarrassed to have screwed up Jack London." He later observed, "*Call of the Wild* was an utterly failed film because it was assembled, not created. It was indeed a United Nations of a movie, using actors according to nationality" to fit agreed-upon quotas, "rather than ability." In the end, he implored, "Should you run across it late at night while channel surfing, don't watch it. Please."[36]

The last of his films for that year was a science fiction piece dealing with the issues of overcrowding and planetary adaptation and survival. Despite the messaging implicit in *Planet of the Apes*, Heston later insisted that *Soylent Green* remained "the only film based on social commentary that I've ever made or caused to be made." Interviewers had sought his views on whether *Skyjacked* somehow glorified hijacking airplanes, but Heston thought that except to note the "socially responsible message" that "hijacking is bad for you," the film was "little but a tight suspense story." In MGM's pressbook for the movie, he concluded for potential viewers and critics, "Our hijacker comes to a richly deserved abrupt, unsympathetic end."[37]

Yet even as he considered a role in a film about existential survival in a future world, old issues reappeared that demanded his reaction. From New York

35 *ALJ*, 382, 386. The breakdown of a principal actor under the pressure of the shoot did not help either.

36 *ALJ*, 386; *CHA*, 473-476.

37 Heston, Interview published July 17, 2012; *ALJ*, 387; "Responsible Film Making," MGM Pressbook for *Skyjacked*, 1972, Wills.

City, he noted, "We had a real issue in our press conference on violence today, regrettably. The attempt to shoot Governor [George] Wallace yesterday, while he was campaigning in Maryland, focused attention once again on the degree to which violence is chosen as a solution for the problems of modern life." Heston had confronted the killings of John and Robert Kennedy and Martin Luther King, Jr., with expressions of remorse and condemnation. Now, he demonstrated an evolution in assigning responsibility to "the media" that covered such events and a democratic society that did not know how to respond properly to them. "One of the functions of society is to control these impulses," he noted of the human capacity for violence. Heston did not seem prepared, however, to explain how this might occur and appeared to soften his earlier view on the abuse of weapons by illegitimate parties in such incidents.

This internal discourse about his profession continued for the actor, even as his public roles developed over time. With *Skyjacked* now in theaters he had to be careful not to become too absorbed with numbers. "You can torment yourself to distraction trying to follow too closely something you can't control anyway," he noted. Still, there was the franchise to consider. "If we have a good opening weekend on the film it'll be valuable for me, not only in terms of money, but demonstrating my viability one more time. (You have to keep demonstrating it till it no longer exists, of course.)"[38]

Still, Heston knew he could only do so much outside of his professional endeavors, and even these appeared more troublesome than outsiders might think as he pondered doing *Soylent Green* for MGM. "I wish I weren't going right back into a film for the same studio again, but this is irrational," since actors were no longer tied to studios as they had been in the past.[39] Of course, if MGM executives were pleased enough with *Skyjacked* to take on another Heston property, that could only be positive. Nevertheless, for the man who had started his career with an arrangement that left him free to work as he saw fit on projects that interested him, the issue was one of significance.

Inspired by reading Harry Harrison's *Make Room, Make Room* while on one of his many transatlantic flights, the actor plunged into this next project with gusto. He would play a police officer initially tasked with determining the circumstances of the suspicious death of a wealthy and powerful figure. Detective Robert Thorn finally came to accept the horrifying revelation that the planet's miracle food

---

38 *ALJ*, 387-388.

39 Ibid.

substance, "Soylent Green" did not emanate from sea plankton or some other innocuous source as touted by the authorities.

Heston was excited about acting with Edward G. Robinson again. They had worked together in *The Ten Commandments* and might have in *Planet of the Apes*, except that Robinson had been unable to tolerate the heavy makeup for that motion picture. Now, the aged and as it turned out dying veteran of one hundred and one films gave an outstanding performance as Thorn's friend and researcher. Robinson's Sol Roth, who remembered what life had once been like before the overcrowding and food shortages that plagued the current society, supplied the most powerful scene in the film when he entered a euthanasia center after learning the truth about the composition of the food product "Soylent Green." Heston later insisted, "I believe it is one of my best performances too, and I have often wondered if it was because of some subliminal communication between us, about what he was going through."[40]

Heston's relationship with another colleague, Leigh Taylor-Young, was colder and more reserved by comparison, and reflected Heston's general inability to engage in wider personal interactions with some of his co-workers. Taylor-Young admitted that Heston's reputation and reserve proved intimidating and that her attempts at injecting humor to lighten the atmosphere fell flat. Generationally, he connected more clearly with Joseph Cotten, Chuck Connors, and Brock Peters, although he added Taylor-Young when noting that the cast formed "a pretty formidable group, better than I usually have for company, as far as name value goes, anyway."[41]

Heston hoped the film would have more than purely entertainment value. "No one in *Soylent Green* is terribly upset about the human condition," he noted. "Edward G. Robinson plays a character that laments the lost civilization, but everybody else has a sad sense of acceptance—lethargy—nothing takes on any importance except food and miserable shelter." As he saw it, the movie could serve as the means of combatting such social maladies in the present, thus helping prevent the fiction of the film from becoming fact.[42]

In the meantime, Heston's leadership prompted another indication of support and gratitude from President Nixon. "As you prepare to step down from the National Council on the Arts, I want to thank you for your outstanding service

40 Heston and Isbouts, *Hollywood*, 172.

41 "Commentary by Leigh Taylor-Young and Director Richard Fleischer," *Soylent Green*, Turner Entertainment Co., 2003, DVD; *ALJ*, 393.

42 Rovin, *Films*, 213.

to the nation," Nixon asserted. He also expressed his appreciation for the "great personal sacrifices" Heston had made in the name of public service. "Just as you did when you were President of the Screen Actors Guild, you contributed significantly to the enhancement of the arts in the daily lives of our fellow citizens, and I hope that, in the months and years ahead, we may continue to call upon your help in the Federal arts program."[43]

Even with the changes that stamped this stage of his career, a remarkable degree of symmetry marked Heston's public life in both his film work and his political transition. Work on *Soylent Green* proceeded under the pressure producers felt to build on Heston's other recent work. At the same time, the political campaigning season approached, compelling him to ponder supporting the Democratic nominee for the presidency as he had done in the past or breaking those ties to embrace the Republican candidate.

In mid-July, from Inverlochy Castle in Scotland, Heston composed a thoughtful and candid letter to Richard Nixon. "I've recently reached a decision that's important to me, and, as multiplied by November's electoral millions, to you, too," he observed. "You have my vote, and my support, in the election this Fall." It was not enough to offer this endorsement alone; Heston had to explain his thought process. "All my voting life I've been a registered Independent, on the theory that neither party has a monopoly on able men. I've voted confidently for candidates in both columns of the same ballot, unpersuaded by the rhetoricians of both parties who would [try] to convince me of the malevolent stupidity of the other's candidates." But he admitted, "until now I've always voted for the Democratic candidate for President."

Heston believed the shift came when he assessed Nixon's first term in office and liked what he saw. "As you began your Administration in '69, I watched events with the careful concern of someone who'd voted for the other man. As time went on, though, I've found myself agreeing with your positions on most public questions, and supporting with more and more confidence the harsh choices you made." This evaluation caused Heston to reflect on his past voting pattern. "Now, at the end of what I hope and believe will be only the first half of your Presidency, I think you have done as well as any man could have to guide the country through a most difficult time."[44]

<hr>

43 Richard Nixon to "Dear Mr. Heston," May 3, 1972, RNPL.

44 Charlton Heston to "Dear Mr. President," July 16, 1972, RNPL.

Richard Nixon may have had this support in mind when he sent a short message to Coldwater Canyon that Heston could not fail to find gratifying. "Mrs. Nixon and I saw *Skyjacked* in the White House Theater last night. We agree that it is the best movie we have seen this year." Although he did not specify a category, the politician added, "We hope it wins an Academy Award." Nixon also expressed his gratitude for the actor's political shift. Noting presciently "[t]here are some exciting days ahead," the president wanted Heston to know "I am deeply encouraged by your generous letter of support." With respect to the challenges that lay ahead in a prospective second term, he hoped that by "working together we can make this a time of which America as a nation, and we as Americans, can be truly proud."[45] Certainly, Nixon's was a message that Heston could embrace wholeheartedly, reflecting as it did the theme of national pride in the midst of turbulent times.

At the same time, Heston indulged once more in a public activity that melded service with pleasure. He joined the celebrity side of a tournament with tennis professionals that celebrated Robert F. Kennedy's legacy. Under the circumstances, writer Steve Cady could not help but employ screen references when he noted, "At times, the vine-covered stucco clubhouse looked like a set for an epic film with a tennis background." As he explained, "Charlton Heston, racquet in hand, was standing at the top of the spiral stairs looking down over the courts."[46]

As the election neared, Heston held an impromptu press conference to announce the views he had expressed privately. His public statement affirmed his political transition for his fan base and the world. "I'm a voter, of course, but I've never belonged to either major party," Heston explained. He cherished the notion of being an informed moderate. "Somehow, I've never been able to believe that all the good guys are Democrats or Republicans. And I've always been put off by the way both parties and their supporters tend to make comic strip heavies out of the other side's candidates." He felt that at the bottom of any choice remained a faith in the basic structure of the American system, and elaborated on his thought process:

As an independent voter I have all my voting life cast my ballot for the Democratic candidates for President of the United States, that's starting with Franklin Roosevelt's last election and continuing up until now. I didn't vote for President Nixon in 1960 or in 68. But I'm going to vote

45 Richard Nixon, July 20, 1973, and Nixon to "Dear Mr. Heston," July 25, 1972, RNPL.

46 Steve Cady, "Celebrities Swing With Pros in Kennedy Event," *NYT*, Aug. 27, 1972.

for him this fall. For me that's an important decision. I made it primarily because I think the President has done a better job than I thought any man could do to solve the enormous problems this country faces both here at home and around the world. I agree with the hard decisions he has made in areas I think are vital to our welfare, our security and our future. I think the path he has started us down is the only path that we can walk and I think it is a hard path to find. But, just as important for me is my feeling that the President's direction for this country is affirmative. I agree with that. I am sick to death of the doom watchers and the naysayers. I think this is a good country. I think it offers its citizens and the whole world their best possible chance for peace and happiness and freedom. I know you don't spell America with a k.[47]

"I made a significant change today," Heston noted in his journal on August 3. "After a lifetime of voting for Democratic candidates for president (though often Republican for other offices), I felt impelled to endorse Richard Milhous Nixon for this fall." Heston did not necessarily consider Nixon his favorite choice. "I recognize he's a political animal, but I question whether a man can be anything else in a political job." Despite whatever cynicism his views might reveal, he thought George McGovern too extreme on too many positions to garner his vote. "As I said in the press conference, America is not spelled with a *k*." He was certain that his own political positions had not altered, even as his affiliation underwent a transformation. When he finally registered as a Republican, Heston observed, "[The] Democratic Party moved, I didn't."[48]

Heston could not have the same type of relationship with President Nixon he had known with his Democratic predecessors, or would with most of the Republicans who followed him. Nevertheless, under the headline "Democrats for Nixon" came an "announcement" that the "Co-Vice Chairmen" would include "Charlton Heston, Hollywood, California" and other personalities from entertainment and sports, such as Sammy Davis, Jr., Frank Sinatra, baseball great Mickey Mantle, and football star Sam Huff. Ronald Brownstein, who studied the Hollywood-Washington connection, wrote that these "Nixon celebrities" were "venerable icons." Brownstein concluded, "If there was a mustiness to Nixon's

47 Charlton Heston, Statement in support of Richard Nixon, UCLA.

48 *ALJ*, 392-393; Raymond, *Cold, Dead Hands*, 218.

celebrity entourage (one guest at the San Clemente party called it 'The Hollywood Wax Museum'), there was an undeniable solidity, too."[49]

Nixon's attempts to connect with the acting community hardly reflected the comfortable relationships John Kennedy and Lyndon Johnson had enjoyed with the stars. When he held a gathering of members of the "Entertainment Industry" at San Clemente, California, on August 27, 1972, Nixon turned to the matter of American film. "Now, I am going to say something that Charlton Heston, I know, will appreciate, and also his successor, and all of those who are interested in seeing that this great industry stays alive and remains strong. . . . Any of you who may be reporting this will consider this to be a little bit jingoistic and pro-American. If so, make the most of it." With that caveat, Nixon plunged ahead. "But I like my movies made in Hollywood, made in America." He could "appreciate a good foreign movie, or a foreign movie star or starlet, or whatever the case may be," he added, but there was no substitute in his mind for the homegrown product. "But I think that the motion picture industry—is something that is typically American and it is something that means a lot in presenting America to the world."[50] Of course, President Nixon might have been surprised to note how many "American" films were actually made on "foreign" soil, including many of those starring Charlton Heston.

Robert Semple of the *New York Times* gave readers the impression that the gathering was more political than social or industry-related in nature. "Among the prominent converts to the Nixon cause on hand this evening were Frank Sinatra, who appeared with Vice President [Spiro] Agnew; George Hamilton, a former escort of President Johnson's daughter, Lynda Bird; Charlton Heston, a prominent member of the Democrats for Nixon organization, and Jim Brown, former Cleveland Browns fullback, who is now an actor."[51]

Heston's political transformation continued with his participation in the Republican National Convention in Miami, Florida, and many of its associated events. He recited the Pledge of Allegiance for attendees, but the most significant moment for him involved a different activity: "Tonight I had the moving experience of facing an audience of fifteen thousand and reading a prayer for the POW's," he

49 "Announcement: Democrats for Nixon," *NYT*, Aug. 16, 1972; Brownstein, *The Power and the Glitter*, 245.

50 "Remarks at the Reception for Celebrities of the Entertainment Industry, San Clemente, California, August 27, 1972," *Public Papers of the Presidents of the United States. Richard Nixon* (Washington, 1974), 822. The Hestons were on the guest list for the "Celebrities Reception." RNPL.

51 Robert B. Semple, Jr., "Nixons Entertain Their Hollywood Backers," *NYT*, Aug. 28, 1972.

noted in his journal. "It meant something to me." His emotion was so wrought by the moment that he debated former attorney general Ramsey Clark on the matter when they participated in another event the next day.[52] For the actor, such issues were not about perception or career advancement; they tapped into values he held deeply and, as usual, was not afraid to express.

President Nixon was grateful for the high-profile role Heston was taking with the party. "Your role at the 1972 Republican National Convention . . . held special meaning for me, and added so much to the message we conveyed to the American people—that of concerned, patriotic individuals engaged in the political process." Nixon hoped an electoral victory would further affirm their personal association and forwarded a photograph of the two men greeting each other "as a token of my deep appreciation."[53]

A month later, the president also expressed satisfaction with Heston's support of his administration's policy. "I was deeply pleased to read the full page statement you and your associates placed in the *Times*," he noted. Federal support for the arts would continue. "The next four years can be even more exciting and, if given the opportunity, I will do all I can to merit the confidence you have placed in me."[54]

In spite of his public role on behalf of the Republican ticket, Heston was cryptic in his journal on Election Day. "I voted, with some misgivings but a wholer heart than I'd thought I'd have, for RMN. So, apparently, did almost everyone else." With early results confirming the trends, he "made a ritual appearance at the Reagan suite, which was jammed with happy GOP's." Fraser had been working elsewhere in support of one of the special state propositions. Although both sides won, the father wrote of his son's celebration, "They were having a lot more fun."[55]

Nixon's overwhelming re-election seemed to presage well for the agenda Heston embraced. The exuberant president wired, "The latest Presidential Election results from around the Nation give us good reason for celebration tonight." Nixon thought Heston's assistance had been crucial. "This is a win for all of us, and I know your leadership as National Vice Chairman of Democrats for Nixon has added substantially to our margin of victory." The president signaled his awareness of Heston's personal significance on behalf of his profession. "I am deeply grateful for

---

52 *ALJ*, 394; See also "Picture of Heston at GOP Convention," *New York Times Magazine* (Oct. 1, 1972), 15.

53 Nixon to "Dear Charlton," Sept. 12, 1972, RNPL.

54 Nixon to "Dear Charlton," Oct. 31, 1972, ibid.

55 *ALJ*, 396-397.

the special role you played in taking our message to the entertainment industry."[56] His margin of victory and Heston's help suggested a mandate on behalf of the film industry during his second term.

As the exhilaration of election night subsided, the reflective incumbent repeated his message of thanks to his Hollywood supporter. "As I look back on our victory of November 7," Nixon began in another personal communication, "I realize how very much I owe to those who contributed so selflessly and so generously of their time and talent in helping us roll up a majority of landslide proportions." Again noting his appreciation for Heston's leadership, the president added, "It would be impossible for me to repay you adequately for all the work you did during the campaign." Looking forward, he assured "that I shall do everything possible over the next four years to make a record which will justify your loyal support in the great battle of 1972."[57] Unfortunately for Nixon and his adherents, the battles were only beginning, and they would not end until his presidency imploded.

On a more personal level, October 4 ushered in the last year of Chuck Heston's forties with the degree of perspective that approaching mid-life so often brings. "The major preoccupation of a man as close to fifty as the day brings me should be his adjustment to that watershed date; but I don't find it difficult, somehow." The "somehow" was not actually hard to determine. "I'm in better shape than I was, my tennis is better, I run two miles in fifteen minutes, and still seem eminently employable, in a time when fewer and fewer of my colleagues are." If there was little reason to complain, it was also best not to rest on one's laurels either.[58]

In December Heston happily returned to the stage in *The Crucible*. He felt his performance and the audience's reception were "good," as was the opening day cast party afterward. "I'm back in actor's country," he declared in his journal. "The stage after all is it." He then tempered this view: "That's a little overstated. I'd be sorry to have to give up either medium. Film is the performing medium of this century, and no actor in our time has made an international reputation without it." He had come to realize the connection between the two worlds of performance that had marked his career and the value each gave to the other. "I don't mean to sound presumptuous," he explained in an interview after the precipitous close of *The Tumbler* over a decade earlier, "but as a film star able to make a surplus living

56 Nixon to "Mr. Charlton Heston," Nov. 7, 1972, RNPL.

57 Nixon to "Dear Charlton," Nov. 22, 1972, ibid.

58 *ALJ*, 395.

most of the time, I'm permitted the luxury of trying to improve myself as an actor. I can afford to learn now."[59]

In the meantime, Heston's commitment to public service in the political arena extended to the inauguration. Such symbols reflected the values that the actor found most compelling, especially with respect to patriotism and the democratic process. President Nixon again reached out personally to express his gratitude for Heston's involvement, although the actor's latest film commitment prevented his participation in a state dinner honoring Jordan's King Hussein.[60]

Heston remained ambivalent concerning some of the higher-profile elements that came with his involvement in the public sector. "I did a publicity sort of luncheon," he noted on January 19, 1973, "which I spent largely talking with Bill Graham. Then I went over to the Kennedy Center to check on the music, the lectern height, mike, etc." for a reading of Thomas Jefferson. "I think I should have insisted that Jefferson's words stand alone, without music, but then how do you justify including them in a concert?"

More problematic was a subsequent photo shoot. "I diddled away the evening in white tie and tailcoat being photographed for the cover of *TV Guide*, for God's sake." Less devoted to the exposure this would give him to television audiences than he would have been in the past, Heston concluded almost testily, "It's been a long time since I've gotten so gussied up for so thin a purpose."[61]

The actor was still trying to determine his purpose, in films at least, when director Richard Lester suggested he play one of the three musketeers in an upcoming project. Heston thought the role of Athos only slightly less appealing than the time he would have had to spend overseas doing the extensive and physically demanding work required. "Oh, God, I thought. Four or five months in Spain doing sword fights and horsebacking through the Guarradamas, in winter?" He would hardly have balked at this in the *El Cid* days, but even the lure of working with a good director did not offset the commitment he would have to make. Heston remembered suggesting "a bit" part, "for fun," which seemed very much unlike him.[62]

59 *ALJ*, 397-398; Joe Hyams, "Heston a Wiser Star After a Flop Play," *Herald Tribune*, Feb. 29, 1960, Scrapbooks, HL.

60 Richard Nixon to "Dear Charlton," Feb. 13, 1973, RNPL.

61 *ALJ*, 400-402.

62 *CHA*, 516. Lester tapped Oliver Reed as Athos when Heston agreed to play Cardinal Richelieu instead; *ALJ*, 403.

Remembering this period in his life as "a busy time," Heston embarked on a lucrative run that helped to bankroll his other interests. "As is true for any actor who does both," he explained of stage and screen, "you look to the film work to increase your net worth and maintain your public identity." On the other hand, theater work allowed the performer to keep his "muscles stretched and take an occasional shot at the real man-killers."[63] Heston always viewed such challenges as his opportunity to grow and develop as an actor.

Additionally, Heston's SAG leadership was not entirely over. "Somewhat to my surprise, I found myself back on the SAG Board again, where I never thought I'd be," he noted in March 1973. "It's strange to climb the stairs to that same boardroom, where my picture now hangs among the past presidents, and sit in the same chair at the end of the room where I began, thirteen years ago." This time, he promised, he would maintain "a very low profile." But when the board began to transact business, the old activist in him rose once more. "I finally made a long, complicated motion of censure to be transmitted to them [the Writers Guild], whereupon Walter Pidgeon said from the other end of the table, 'Well, there goes the low profile.'"[64]

As busy as he was with multiple film projects and other activities, Charlton Heston nevertheless continued to be susceptible to the perception of his brand. Professional and exacting, he was as demanding of himself as he could be of others. Such standards could lead to disarming moments and unexpected complications occurred, even on the most public of platforms. For Heston, one of these came on March 27, when he failed to appear as planned for the Academy Awards ceremony at the Dorothy Chandler Pavilion. "It really was one of the outstanding humiliations of my life," he admitted painfully. "To run along the sidewalk by the Music Center, my car abandoned, and hear over the loudspeakers carrying the telecast audio 'Charlton Heston is supposed to be emceeing this part of the show, but.'" An extremely reluctant Clint Eastwood stepped in to cover for him, although material written for Heston as Moses did not work particularly well for his substitute. The incident had been beyond his ability to anticipate or avoid, but a mortified Chuck Heston could not help but observe of the matter, "I've never been late to work in my life, and I have to do it in front of eight million viewers."[65]

63 *CHA*, 516.

64 *ALJ*, 403-404.

65 *ALJ*, 404; Eliot, *Charlton Heston*, 353-355. See also Marc Eliot, *American Rebel: The Life of Clint Eastwood* (New York, 2009), 151-152, and Richard Schickel, *Clint Eastwood: A Biography* (New York,

Marlon Brando's subsequent histrionics in sending a surrogate to make a political statement while accepting the Best Actor Oscar deflected attention from everything else that had happened. Heston nevertheless found it difficult to dismiss the matter of his tardiness. "I'm rebuilding my reputation for punctuality," he recorded. "It'll take me 20 years." Whether anyone actually said something to him or not, he feared snickering asides like, "Where was Moses when the tire blew out?" Brando's clumsy stagecraft should have given him all the cover he required in a ceremony that always ran too long anyway, but he could not help being sensitive. His final journal assessment spoke for itself: "For me, it overshadowed Brando's nonappearance to pick up his Oscar."[66]

The end of March and early April were particularly hectic; a tribute to the work of John Ford by the American Film Institute featured Heston in a special role. "My job consisted largely of introducing the president of the United States, which tends to hold your attention." He was glad Nixon had made the effort and was pleased the AFI could present its Lifetime Achievement Award to the renowned director, whom Heston described as "very old, very sick." "This will be his last appearance, I think," Heston noted. "I'm glad we brought it off."[67]

President Nixon noted his pleasure at being able to attend the tribute, and offered a strong endorsement of Heston's role: "You were the perfect choice as host for the evening, and I want you to know how much I appreciated your gracious introduction when I made the presentation to Mr. Ford." If the politician felt any discomfort over the occasion, he did not betray it. "Mrs. Nixon joins me in sending you our warmest thanks for helping to make March 31 an evening we will long remember."[68]

The actor was back into his public relations mode a few days later in Boston. "The schedules on these tours aren't as tough as I recall they used to be," he observed. "Fewer papers, fewer schlocky things to do (opening dime stores, judging beauty contests). Maybe they think I'm just too grand for all that now." Other elements showed signs of changing as well. "The graying, bibulous Boston movie press has been largely replaced by sharp, shaggy New Journalists," he noted. But he did not

---

1996), 297-298. Both covered Eastwood's awkward moment in relief, although Schickel had Heston shoving his colleague aside to finish the bit, while Eliot had Heston arriving to take the place of "a much-relieved Clint," before starting "from the top as if nothing had happened."

66 Eliot, *Charlton Heston*, 355-356; *ALJ*, 404.

67 *ALJ*, 405.

68 Nixon to "Dear Charlton," Apr. 12, 1973, RNPL.

seem overly concerned by the potentially daunting challenge of relating to a new generation of writers: "Never mind . . . I can play it with them, too."[69]

The message he wanted to send in this instance was that *Soylent Green* had one of its own. "I really wanted very much to make this film because I feel the increasing pressure of population growth is far more of a real danger than a nuclear war." The picture was essentially "a police story" that would provide audiences with a compelling setting for the social context that surrounded it. "The only way you can reach an audience with a message is to entertain it." As always, his touchstone was Shakespeare, "who knew this and has lasted 400 years. Although he had some very profound things to say he knew he had to first entertain the crowd." Already having described his subject as "highly articulate," the interviewer concluded that this "remark may be the clue to Heston's continuous success through 40 films."[70]

He remained confident that his professional stature gave him a cachet that was not available to everyone. As he paused in visits to Philadelphia and Milwaukee, before a trip to Two Rivers, Wisconsin, to assist with the disposition of Lydia's father's home, he assessed his own versatility in handling difficult questions. "That's my main value to any public service group. I can get on more talk shows and do them better." But he still faced the difficult situation regarding his father-in-law, who was "no longer [be] able to live in his own house." Heston concluded, "Even with ample funds, which he has, the final indignity of having to surrender your autonomy like this is demeaning."

It was difficult to know the degree to which circumstances bled into each other to threaten the equilibrium Heston normally felt he brought to his world. The deterioration of Lydia's father's condition put more strain on her and filtered down to him as well. "This must be a heavy time for her," he wrote, trying to convey sympathy. "I only hope she doesn't remember it as horrible." He continued with a grueling series of television interviews in a range of cities and television shows that did not seem to go as well as he wished. "The Cavett show was OK," Heston noted on April 17, but the next day he was decidedly less sanguine. "For some reason, I choked a little on the Today Show. . . . Not that I klutzed it entirely . . . it's just that I didn't have the kind of control I've learned to have over TV interviews."[71]

Lydia's stress manifested itself in terrible migraines, which her husband still felt helpless to address. For this reason, at least, family matters were entering a

---

69 *ALJ*, 405.

70 George McKinnon, "The real Heston strong, but not silent," *BG*, Apr. 22, 1973.

71 *ALJ*, 405-406.

difficult period for the Hestons. The actor's struggles with *Antony and Cleopatra* did not offer refuge, leading him to complain the situation had become "all far too complicated for my simple brain." When he dropped a movie project to which he had already committed himself, he had to admit his distress. "I still feel bad about this, though I'm convinced the decision was correct. It's the only time I've ever withdrawn from a film I said I would do."

Still, the most serious blow was yet to fall. "This turned out to be one of the very worst days of my life," he confessed the next day in his journal. "Everything was wrenched out of joint. For the first time in my life, I believed Lydia would leave me. I spent some bleak hours trying to find some adjustment to it." The couple managed to forge ahead, with Heston turning to work as much as a diversion as anything else. "Still, this is sort of a fallow period," he admitted of the difficult time between projects that struggles with his marriage made worse. Her health challenges and his constant travels added pressure that she seemed to find harder to accept. "It has to do, I fear, with her anxiety at my departures," he surmised as he planned for a trip to London. "They're often marked with really tearing scenes of trauma." After calling from the airport to reassure her, he noted, "I flew overseas calm, though somewhat shaken."[72]

One of the lighter public activities Chuck Heston got to perform during this trying period took place at Universal Studios, where he had the chance to re-create the dramatic scene from *The Ten Commandments* of Moses parting the Red Sea for a studio tour. In this case, "the feat" was part of Universal's "newest attraction." On this occasion, he did not have to rely on screen special effects or divine intervention to "accomplish the miracle though," as a caption writer noted, "there is a lot of electronic help."[73]

As Heston had demonstrated on numerous occasions, he was more than willing to accept his share of public duties. Yet, some of his work commitments took him out of the country when he might have been of service in the United States. A request from the White House for his attendance at a state dinner for visiting Soviet leader Leonid Brezhnev would have had Charlton and Lydia Heston joining Bob Hope, Art Linkletter, Fred MacMurray, and their wives as President Nixon undoubtedly hoped to impress his visitor with the stars of the American entertainment firmament. Completion of his work as Cardinal Richelieu in *The*

72 Ibid., 407-408.

73 "Parting of Waves," *LAT*, May 4, 1973.

Three Musketeers and a visit with Lydia's brother, Bob, who was then stationed in Stuttgart, Germany, precluded the Hestons from attending.[74]

Though he would not have Heston at the White House gala, Nixon would tap once more into his commitment to the individuals who wore the nation's uniform. As a veteran himself, the actor had never shied from that support. In this case, pursuant to his authority as president for making appointments to the United Service Organizations, Nixon informed him, "It is my pleasure to designate you a member thereof for a term of three years expiring in February 1976."[75]

The actor's insertion into the realm of politics was seldom discomfiting, but as circumstances unfolded for the current administration in Washington, the less pleasant aspects of that world began to intrude. "I'm still shaken by Agnew's resignation," Heston recorded of the besieged vice president's recent decision to leave office under scandal in October 1973. "Not because I supported him (I didn't) or because I voted for him (I did), but because it seems a black mark on the system that so clear a crook could rise so high." At the same time, an Arab oil embargo was having an ill effect, even in Coldwater Canyon, where shortages prevailed as they did everywhere else. "We'll survive," the actor observed quietly, "but I'm glad tennis requires no gas."

The world seemed to be taking on an aspect in which art was becoming reality. Unfortunately, in this instance, Heston thought the allusion was not a particularly positive one. "Life is coming closer to *Soylent Green*" he ventured following a particularly grueling flight plagued by limited access to fuel and long delays. The principal issues were not so much cultural as they were economic, but Heston was becoming less optimistic about the future. Things worsened when he "half-crippled" himself, ironically while trying to shoot a "government film" touting running and physical fitness. "I did whirlpool therapy and massage, but it's not much better," he lamented, before turning to a brighter subject. "It did give me a chance to read the giant catastrophe script which Universal feels they need me in as some sort of insurance or talisman or something. The part's not much, which I expected, given a story of this sort. . . . I'm not overjoyed at the prospect of spending my next commitment to it." Two days later, he was still "brooding over possible solutions to the thin character development of the *Earthquake* script for Universal, though I'm still uneasy about it in creative terms."[76]

74 Telegram, "1973 JUN 18," RNPL; *ALJ*, 411-412.

75 Richard Nixon to "Dear Charlton," Aug. 28, 1973, RNPL.

76 *ALJ*, 418-421.

The Hestons returned to the White House for a formal dinner in December, but the past year had seen dark clouds descending over the mansion. The Nixon administration had been in crisis mode over an incident at the Watergate complex in Washington in the summer of 1972. Members of the administration looked widely outside their circles for support. Nixon's faithful personal secretary, Rose Mary Woods, sent out a plea to numerous public figures, including Charlton Heston, which touted the efforts of Tricia Nixon Cox to cast her embattled father in a favorable light in an essay published in *Ladies' Home Journal*. "It is my feeling that you will find Tricia's statement to be an eloquent expression of how a daughter views her father during this particular time," Woods explained concerning the essay. "I know you will feel, like I do, that it is a moving, meaningful article."[77] His journals give no indication of the actor's response, although by the late summer of 1974 the situation had deteriorated to the extent that Nixon faced the choice of resigning from office rather than face impeachment and probable conviction and removal.

The Watergate scandal added to the disconnect between an increasingly besieged president and his would-be supporters. Heston later noted circumspectly, "In the aftermath of Watergate, I'm often asked what I think of my virgin Republican vote." Answering with a humorous but telling reply, he noted, "I feel the way [Maurice] Chevalier said he felt on reaching the age of eighty. 'When you consider the alternative, I feel fine.'" McGovern had been an unacceptable choice in his mind at the time of the election and remained so in retrospect, despite the transgressions that finally forced Nixon from office.

Work continued for Heston whatever the political environment might be. Throughout the spring and summer of 1974, he tried to figure out how to perish selflessly in one disaster film and appear to navigate, or at least help his airline paramour fly, an even bigger plane (747) than he had piloted in *Skyjacked* (707).[78] Heston also understood that though *Airport 1975* was an attempt by movie executives to cash in on the earlier phenomenon of *Airport*, he wanted his character to be worth playing. He could bolster his bank account, if not his critical acclaim, in "disaster" films featuring large casts of stars and impressive special effects.

Heston termed such a picture a "group [or multiple] jeopardy movie" and realized that his earlier roles would make audiences comfortable with the thought

---

77 Guest list, "Dinner at the White House," December 4, 1973, 7:30 p.m., RNPL; Rose Mary Woods to "Dear Mr. Heston," Apr. 8, 1974, RNPL.

78 *ALJ*, 393, 428.

that his character ought to be able to navigate, if not survive, such deadly encounters. Because of the many authority roles he had played over the years, Heston knew his characters could project leadership and calm in the face of on-screen adversity. This allowed movie patrons to identify with these authority figures and the characters around them, who faced fearful odds and life-threatening dilemmas. Heston's screen persona shaped audience perceptions in such instances. "So in this film it isn't necessary to explain that my character will be responsible," he declared, "It's built in."[79]

Ironically, given this public perception of an authority figure saving himself and those surrounding him from danger, one of the higher-grossing action pictures of the early 1970s, *Earthquake*, did not end with Heston's on-screen persona emerging unscathed from the communal trauma. He knew from his *Apes* experience that he did not want his character to survive in this picture and had insisted on it as a contingency for accepting the role. "I had script approval, so in the end, they grudgingly agreed," he explained of his insistence upon his movie demise. Heston harbored no concern that his character's death would have an adverse effect on his future employability. "People always assume the hero has to live. That's not true," he explained. "Take me, for example, I have died at least a dozen times." A desire to avoid meaningless sequels had taught him the utility of dying in a film. Besides, as Lydia observed, "You must understand, he *loves* death scenes." Few moments could be as compelling as those that required the figure on screen to perish, especially in some sacrificial or heroic manner that could evoke sympathy from the audience. "Actors love to play death scenes, of course," he echoed, "and I've played more than my share, surely."[80]

Fortunately, one of the personal aspects that may also have died with the film *Earthquake* was any discomfort he felt toward the star with whom he had known difficulties in an earlier film: Ava Gardner. In this case, Gardner lessened her consumption of alcohol, and according to a biographer, "graciously made up for old differences with Charlton Heston on *Fifty-five Days at Peking*."[81] Heston was ever prepared to be the professional in any project, but it was surely a better situation to have things patched up between them.

---

79 Rovin, *Films*, 218.

80 Heston and Isbouts, *Hollywood*, 180; *ALJ*, 469.

81 Higham, *Ava*, 247. Heston remembered that in this instance, Gardner "gave us no trouble whatever." *CHA*, 471.

Even when the motivation behind his participation in a project was less than artistic, Heston looked for ways to learn new lessons that might be applied elsewhere in his work someday. As both an actor who had worked for some of the industry's greatest practitioners and an occasional director himself, he took pains to observe how each person in that position handled matters. Regarding Mark Robson's treatment of a scene in which Gardner struggled, but the director praised her anyway before sending her back to the dressing room, Heston's puzzled response prompted an observation that he filed away for future use: "Sometimes you have to know when you've gotten all there is."[82]

Heston was acutely aware that in this type of film, he had to imbue his character with some level of layering in order to heighten audience concern about his fate. He confided in his journal he felt he had accomplished this goal through some tinkering with the script. "They've complicated his relationship with his wife, put some texture into his back story, and given him anxieties and misgivings about the girl." Such coloring might not improve the numbers for the motion picture, but because he wanted the role to be as rich as possible and a percentage of the gross meant that the better the movie did the better he would do, Heston was prepared to do whatever he could to stand out in what he termed the "crowded canvas" of the disaster genre. He recognized that his motivation for accepting the role was a potential impediment to creativity. "This one, I guess, is done at least partly for the money," he admitted, which he knew was "a lousy reason to do a film."[83]

Charlton Heston was not the only bankable star accepting such roles and receiving significant remuneration in spite of limited screen time. "Making these films meant, of course, that most of the major actors were playing smaller parts than they had in years, though still getting their standard salaries." He was being "compensated in first-dollar gross percentiles," and the effort required work for "no more than a few days for seven-figure paychecks."[84]

Economic well-being remained on the actor's mind during this period. On March 18, 1974, he recorded, "Good news on the dollar front . . . from several quarters, as a matter of fact." He had sunk much emotional, professional, and financial capital into *Antony and Cleopatra* and was relieved to learn the IRS had approved his request to deduct the financial losses he had incurred on the project.

82 *CHA*, 471.

83 *ALJ*, 424-425.

84 *CHA*, 470-471.

Furthermore, the reports of foreign receipts for *Soylent Green* and *Skyjacked* were quite good. His initial assessment of *Skyjacked*'s earning potential two years earlier had taken this possibility into account. "I won't get any kudos for this job," he observed, "but I'll earn some money. That's necessary, too." But with a lingering level of uncertainty nagging at him, especially for a person who prided himself on frugality and the responsibility he held for supporting his family through his work, Heston was not trying to be facetious when he observed, "All in all, I'm not in immediate danger of starving."[85]

After a period of doubt, the actor seemed to be finding his footing once more in his profession. Marc Eliot observed that *Skyjacked* "would do for disaster films what *Planet of the Apes* did for science fiction movies, giving Heston the opportunity to kick-start another dominant genre." To another writer, he appeared to be "thriving on disaster movies."[86] As was his wont, however, Heston was also prepared to work to promote these films and to assist fully in generating as much publicity as possible to increase their chances for box office success.

He was already feeling the effects of his hectic schedule while on an East Coast leg of the publicity tour. "I started damn early (one drawback to this sort of tour)," he noted while in New York, "some of the best TV talk shows get you up at bloody dawn to do them." He had also reached the point where the shadows that followed him were made up of more than just the roles he had played. "I spent much of the day feeling stabs of déjà vu," he admitted. "There are so many places in this town where I've done so many things . . . and I go through the day remembering them."[87]

To Richard Dyer of the *Boston Globe*, he pondered the current themes of his career. "I make movies for a living," he explained of his efforts on behalf of *Airport 1975* and *Earthquake*. "I'm beating the drum with each hand for these two pictures." Heston felt that for such expensive "multiple jeopardy" films, the producers "want security blankets in them, and I am a security blanket." Dyer offered a different take. "Charlton Heston is not simply a security-blanket actor. He is in a position to assure, sometimes, that a picture ought to be made." Still, if his box office clout was indeed critical, he wanted his work to have the ring of authenticity. "I need to be around someone who is expert in ways I'm not," he

85 *ALJ*, 381, 425.

86 Eliot, *Charlton Heston*, 339; Richard Dyer, "Charlton Heston thriving on disaster movies," *BG*, Oct. 14, 1974.

87 *ALJ*, 435.

noted, remarking that at the end of the scene in an airplane cockpit he had the tendency to look at the consulting pilot rather than the director.[88]

These lucrative films were keeping him viable, but he had the itch to return to the traditional theater and another opportunity to tackle William Shakespeare. "I think I may do it," he insisted of one proposed stage appearance, "if only as a creative balance to these nonacting roles." Time on the boards would also remind him that he could work with female co-stars, including those with whom he had little in common outside of acting. In the case of *Macbeth*, he would be performing with Vanessa Redgrave.

While in London, he had enjoyed "an exploratory meal" with Redgrave. "Each of us [was] equally anxious to explore the other, no doubt," he concluded. He set aside any concerns with characteristic humor. "She seemed to've taken some pains for the meeting . . . neatly dressed, hair, makeup, rather nontypical of her Trotskyite image, one would think (although one might be quite wrong, of course)." When the play ran, the actors found additional reason for tension. Heston thought the original could use some adaptation, while Redgrave felt the text should remain unchanged. It helped that other differences did not intrude. "Obviously I disagree with her politics," he explained later; "she makes Jane Fonda look like Herbert Hoover. But she never forced anything down my throat. I think she thought I was a lost cause."[89]

At the end of November, he was back in the United States. "I did the ABC *Morning Show*, speaking another of my little pieces on behalf of another of my constituencies," he noted stoically. "I hardly know which hat I'm putting on these days, but none of them's an acting hat." A month later these musings continued. "As for my work, I didn't do anything remarkable creatively. . . . I did make two enormously successful films, which means I can still feed my family doing the work I still love."[90]

Heston's leadership roles in his industry and his willingness to embark on public endeavors led him once again to the halls of Congress. In his role as chairman of the board of trustees for the American Film Institute, he joined friend and film associate George Stevens, Jr., before a House committee that was considering a bill to make the AFI an independent agency. In his opening statement, the actor noted

---

88 Dyer, "Charlton Heston thriving on disaster movies."

89 *ALJ*, 428, 435; Crowther, *Epic Presence*, 132.

90 *ALJ*, 438, 440.

the importance of film as "the art of the 20th Century; it is also the American art." He concluded his initial remarks with a flourish. "Art fills the soul as surely as meat fills the belly," he maintained, employing an allusion he felt could reach "Great Society" legislators, before completing the image. "And if art fills the soul, then film is the bread and butter that is part of every meal our citizens take at the table." Stevens noted that for AFI programming, figures from Hollywood such as "Mr. Heston, Frank Sinatra, George C. Scott, Cicely Tyson, donate their services. They appear on that show for no remuneration. This is an asset we have." Furthermore, the AFI director explained, "Mr. Heston travels throughout the country on our behalf. He flew in on the Red Eye last night to be here for this hearing this morning," getting only an hour's sleep in the back of the Stevens family station wagon before he had to be on Capitol Hill.[91]

The supporting material presented for the hearing emphasized both Heston's leadership in AFI and the mission of the organization to promote and conserve the work product of the country's cinema. Repeating his assertion of film as a distinctive American art form in an article provided for the committee, Heston indicated an understanding of the power of film, and by association, his own reach. "It speaks more loudly than the most persuasive of ambassadors." The audience was indeed extensive among the more developed societies. "They all go to the movies, they all have television," he explained. "Film is the most generalized democratic art form of all."[92]

Heston continued to play the role of cultural ambassador in other settings as well. For a luncheon in Los Angeles to host Emperor Hirohito of Japan, he joined "Duke Wayne (who) seemed to be the only other actor around." Applying his characteristic humor to the situation, Heston thought the visual effect noticeable. "I wonder why the mayor invited two of the tallest actors in town to lunch for a short emperor? Anyway, it was fun."

One of the other "hats" Heston enjoyed wearing was an outdoors one, although a mishap very nearly had an adverse effect on his literal "public face" in a way he had not experienced since a long-ago football collision had broken his nose. In this instance, while traversing the unruly Salmon River in Idaho with close friend Jolly

---

91 Testimony, Hearings Before the Special Subcommittee on Arts and Humanities of the Committee on Labor and Public Welfare, United States Senate. Ninety-third Congress, Second Session on H.R. 17504, December 11, 1974 (Washington: Government Printing Office, 1975), 6, 14, 45.

92 Dodie Gust, "The American Film Institute," *Hollywood Reporter 44th Anniversary Edition*, Nov. 29, 1974, in ibid., 34, 38.

West and son Fraser, he recorded, "We lost a kayak, and I got clipped on the head trying to rescue it while we were running a rapid. (I will undoubtedly live)."[93]

West remembered the incident on "the River of No Return" differently. He recalled that when the kayak they were carrying began to slide off their raft, "He dives half over to grab it and the kayak carried by the water w[h]acks him right across the bridge of the nose and I thought, 'Oh, boy, there goes America's Number One Face' . . . [blood was] streaming down." The actor seemed less concerned than the doctor. "He pulls it in, he never would let go of it. Meanwhile, he's covered in blood." West ministered to the wound as best he could, with tape as a substitute for stitches. "Meanwhile we rinse it off with river water and by the time the three days are gone, we're to the mouth [of the Salmon], it's all healed up. . . . And . . . he doesn't even have a scar there anymore."[94]

Heston did not need to worry about his famous countenance after tangling with wild river rapids, but he remained sensitive to the quirks of his business. The strenuous demands of *Macbeth* were resulting in a reassessment of his capabilities. "I'm getting a little long in the tooth for a broadsword fight after four acts of *Macbeth*," he admitted. On the other hand, he thought the lessons he continued to learn made the effort worthwhile. He particularly appreciated director Peter Wood's ability to "dig deeper and deeper into the play." This was especially the case, when Wood brought his attention to a different sort of challenge. "Your problem with the part, Chuck," he remembered the director telling him, "is that you feel any man must be in agony to have done what Macbeth has done. You must learn not only to accept it, but to *embrace* it." Of course, what was true for "any man" might not be the case for Macbeth, and it would be up to each performer to determine the motivation for himself. Still, Heston appreciated the insight. "That's bloody good," he decided. "He's right, about me, and about Macbeth."

While he sought to understand Macbeth better, Heston also wanted a clearer sense of the state his career. Meeting with his agent for lunch, he contemplated his longevity. "It's something of a mystery to me why I'm all but the sole survivor of my generation of stars, when I never seemed to quite top the list in anything but the overall grosses of my films. I suppose this is part of it." Even so, he believed there was a reasonable explanation. "Professionalism will not necessarily create

---

93 *ALJ*, 455, 431.

94 "This is Your Life (TV) transcript," 38-39, HL.

art," he observed, "but in film, it's almost impossible to have art, or even a film, without it."[95]

As he aged, physical fitness also remained crucial in his mind. Tennis was an enjoyable part of that regime, and it provided an outlet for his excess energies. Just as significantly, he employed the sport as a means of supporting various causes through celebrity and pro-am charity events. For these efforts, Heston called upon friends and entertainment associates for assistance, "corralling" on one occasion a number of celebrity figures, including Clint Eastwood, Jim Brown, James Franciscus, and Michael Landon, to participate in a tournament to benefit Youth Tennis of Southern California.[96]

During an appearance in apartheid-ridden South Africa to publicize his film work, Heston turned to tennis to promote the social values he considered important. African American tennis star Arthur Ashe had recently won a singles world championship in the United States, but as one writer noted, "according to actor Charlton Heston, Ashe is doing even more spectacular things in a much less publicized manner halfway around the world—in South Africa." Heston touted Ashe's efforts after only two years of being allowed to enter the country, noting "both the draw and the audience were integrated . . . I believe for the first time." The actor had taken pride in his civil rights activities, and now saw a chance to use the game he loved and a player he respected to further that cause on an international scale. Heston said his participation in an exhibition and Ashe's in the pro tournament, which raised "a good sum for the Black Tennis Foundation," represented "far more constructive acts than picketing the South African Davis Cup team as some had advocated."[97]

Charlton Heston understood the multi-faceted aspects of his public life. He had to maintain an audience for his work, and this required him to remain aware of the expectations of those who attended his films and theatrical productions. This level of patronage offered both the freedom of continuing to work productively and the restriction that came with the public's identification as that work progressed.

95 *ALJ*, 442, 444, 452.

96 See for example, "Heston Team Wins Celebrity Tennis Title" (*LAT*, Mar. 29, 1971), in Lake Havasu City, Arizona, to benefit the Colorado River Indian Handicapped Children's Fund; Christy Fox, "Keeping the Ball Bouncing," *LAT*, Sept. 6, 1971; and "Pro-Celebrity Tennis to Raise Political Funds" (*LAT*, Sept. 26, 1974), at which Heston served as the featured amateur in the Alphonzo Bell Pro-Celebrity Tennis Tournament that raised funds for Bell's Congressional re-election campaign and the Jack Kramer Club's Junior Tennis Development Program.

97 Dwight Chapin, "As Barriers Fall," *LAT*, May 19, 1975; *ALJ*, 448.

"After an actor becomes established in the public mind," he observed, "you become followed throughout your career by the lengthening shadow of the parts you've played." He realized that this circumstance "blocks you out of certain things, but it makes you credible by just standing there." Because his viewers could point to the types of projects he had undertaken, they could feel comfortable in accepting him in the new ones that came along. "I'm usually accepted in whatever I try," he concluded.[98]

Heston employed the same descriptive quality in explaining how he enjoyed this phenomenon. "No matter how versatile an actor may be or how he strives to widen his range, he must deal with his shadow," he maintained. "And my shadow has been Moses, El Cid, and Michelangelo, not to mention a president or two." Particularly when the part called for an authoritative figure, he felt confident that film audiences and ostensibly producers of such projects would "think of me."[99]

There was no doubt that he had achieved a level of comfort in his public role that overcame his innate preference for privacy. He often kept busily engaged in routine interviews that he had learned to streamline effectively. So much of what Heston now experienced was part of a long-standing repertoire. Yet he still found his patience tested when others struggled with the same routines that were habitual for him. "I've been doing interviews for so long, I forget you have to learn how," Heston observed after seeing his young interviewer toil at the practice while promoting *Airport 1975*.

In June 1976, the process went even more smoothly for him. "The filmed interviews went predictably," he observed while in New York City, "and one assumes the value to the film will be well worth the energy invested." Indeed, investment was how he saw the matter. Time involved here would translate to business at the box office, or at least exposure for himself and his work. "Maybe that's why I'm still around when so many of my peers are doing TV commercials . . . or nothing," he speculated. "Still, I'm as much of a salesman as Willy Loman ever was. It's just that life is considerably easier . . . and I know the territory." Of course, given his knowledge of *Death of a Salesman*, the choice of comparison between himself and the fictional protagonist who ultimately ends his life for an insurance payment was interesting.

In virtually every instance, Charlton Heston continued to be mindful of the image he projected in public. These moments need not occur on stage or set.

---

98 Eliot, *Charlton Heston*, 376-377.

99 Rovin, *Films*, 218.

Often, they could happen in those ancillary instances when he made appearances or conducted the ordinary affairs of a public life. Witnessing what amounted to a tantrum by another celebrity participant in a tennis match, Heston observed, "Actors can be horrible people."[100] He was determined not to be that type of individual, especially in public.

Harsh assessments could come from both colleagues and critics, some of whom saw a stiff and imperious presence they could not penetrate. But behind the scenes, and not just with family, Charlton Heston could be extraordinarily generous and thoughtful through heartfelt gestures that took the feelings of others into account. Susan Hayward had presented the golden statuette to him when Heston won his Academy Award for *Ben-Hur* in 1959. Fifteen years later, he demonstrated a sense of compassion and genuine affection at the Forty-Sixth Annual Awards when he escorted the gravely ill Hayward onto the stage at the Dorothy Chandler Pavilion to present the award for Best Actress. "Easy, girl," he said as she moved gingerly in the wings, his steady arm assuring that Hayward would be able to make her presentation. "He did it at the right moment," she recalled. "I was shaking so bad." Hayward died of cancer less than a year later.[101]

Meanwhile, he strove to remain busy in his work. With the nation's bicentennial in full swing, he had a role, albeit fictional, in *Midway*, which depicted the great turning point in the Pacific Theater during World War II. Roles for acting stalwarts like Henry Fonda, Robert Mitchum, and Glenn Ford put him in good company. Shooting aboard the USS *Lexington* and employing actual color footage of the battle provided by the U.S. Navy offered crucial advantages, which Heston thought would have been "impossible to duplicate." The majesty of the ocean setting and of the *Lexington* impressed him. "The rest, I suppose, is up to us."[102] The "rest" involved, as it always did, more than acting, writing, and directing; it meant selling and promoting.

In one sense, the promotional task was easier because of its timing. "It certainly is a good time to show something, historically, that we did [and that] we can be proud of," director Jack Smight asserted. Smight had overseen Heston's salvation of a crippled jet liner in *Airport 1975*, and the gross on that film ensured that *Midway* would be another "big picture." For this purely fictional role, Heston practiced the same habit he would undertake for portraying a historical person—he created

---

100 *ALJ*, 455, 470, 474.

101 Linet, *Susan Hayward*, 3-4.

102 *ALJ*, 450.

an elaborate biography for his character. Like setting and wardrobe, this level of detail supplied a comfortable context. The nature of shooting on the bridge of a heavy cruiser and Heston's own cinematic history also proved powerful to the participants. "This ship will be alright," one of the crew remarked, "Moses is steering."[103]

By the end of 1975, Heston was working on another Western, a genre he particularly enjoyed. This one, however, featured troubling tones of brutality and retribution. His character, a retired law officer in pursuit of escaped criminals who had kidnapped his daughter, had to endure her sexual assault before he could save her. In his journal, Heston added, "Later, when the company came in, I asked Morgan Paul[l] (who plays the vilest of my daughter's despoilers) if they'd killed him off yet. 'Oh no,' he said, 'When you rape Chuck Heston's daughter, you don't die easily.'"[104]

The Last Hard Men did not see wide distribution for two years, although when it opened in Los Angeles, critic Kevin Thomas of the *Times* deemed it "admirable," and considered Heston's work noteworthy. "So often ensconced—and perhaps immured—in the heroic mold, Heston is the kind of star one too easily takes for granted (which in a way is a kind of backhanded compliment for reliable professionalism). Heston here is ever the hero, to be sure, but is rendered more human by the frailties of age." The movie's trailer likened it to *High Noon*, although this film was decidedly more intense in its violence and Heston's Sam Burgade, the protagonist dedicated to hunting the prison escapees down, was much grittier than Gary Cooper's Marshal Will Kane.[105]

Heston was as anxious as ever to focus on his work on stage and screen, but both he and Lydia remained committed to many public interest and charity programs. They served as national honorary chairpersons of the National Retinitis Pigmentosa Foundation in June and presided over a dinner-dance that raised funds for that cause. He also had participated in Jane Wyman's 19th Annual "Stop Arthritis Telethon" a few years earlier.[106]

103 Patrick McGilligan, "Hollywood's Bicentennial Salvo: Battle of Midway," *Boston Sunday Globe*, July 20, 1975.

104 *ALJ*, 458.

105 Kevin Thomas, "'Last Hard Men' Here at Last," *LAT*, Sept. 28, 1977. The trailer's narration places the film is "in the classic tradition of *High Noon*." www.imdb.com/title/tt0074776/videoplayer/vi3015225369?ref_=tt_ov_vi.

106 "Retinitis Foundation Dinner," *LAT*, May 24, 1976; *LAT*, Feb. 2, 1974.

Such efforts built on the host of causes both the couple and the actor himself championed and continued to endorse out of the sense of responsibility Heston felt due to his public stature. In an insightful interview with writer Don Alpert, he noted how the walls individuals constructed for themselves served only to contain them. According to Alpert, "The authority for this is Charlton Heston, who long ago sacrificed his privacy for what might be called a public-public life." To Heston, claims of encroachment on the performer's private life made little sense. "An actor cannot claim a right to a private life. I look with a jaundiced eye at actors who lament the loss of privacy." This view was particularly the case where he was concerned. "I'm fortunate," Heston explained. "I make more than a living." As a result, he did not have to labor for the sake of scratching out an existence. "The time I might have spent doing something else, that's the time I use to help others." To be sure, he enjoyed his lifestyle, but Heston recognized a sense of obligation that came with his privilege. "Seems to me I should put something back in."[107]

During the bicentennial summer, Heston undertook an extensive press tour for *Midway* that included interviews, briefings, and wide-ranging travel. Work for the Pentagon and an appearance on the *Donahue* talk show preceded a trip across the same vast Pacific he had defended on film (and in real life) to Japan, the Philippines, Hong Kong, and Australia. In his first stop in Tokyo, he was grateful that going from studio to studio was no longer necessary in order to obtain the same wide level of coverage. "The video tape recorder's a great blessing for actors doing public relations tours," he concluded. "I did all the things I've learned so well, their value never clearer than here in Japan." An appearance by movie nemesis Toshiro Mifune added to the attention. "We got a formidable chunk of space, plus TV time," Heston noted. The pace and language barrier were beginning to wear on his admittedly "strained" patience, although the seasoned professional understood the significance of what he was doing. "Still this is a major audience for me. . . . I must hang in. I *am* hanging in."

The hectic pace continued in Manila and Hong Kong, where interpreters and delayed flights gave way to a welcome escape in Sydney and "a cold can of Foster's [beer]." "The schedule (eight interviews and a cocktail reception), speaks for itself," he observed, before recalling the genuine attempt of one interviewer to try to be different, only to "proceed to ask exactly the same questions everyone else has asked, of course." Of the promotional blitz and travel extravaganza, the glazed Heston wrote, "Once you've done three or four thousand miles, you don't feel any

107 Don Alpert, "Heston Scores Extremists," *Boston Sunday Globe*, Dec. 19, 1965.

more tired, no matter how far you go. Still, I was damn glad to put my head down on my pillow tonight."[108]

He was also proud that *Midway* brought attention to an important aspect from the period through its attempt to humanize the impact of the removal of people of Japanese descent from the coastline areas of the United States. "How quickly people forget," the actor explained in one interview of the peremptory action that took place in the emotional aftermath of the attack on Pearl Harbor. "It is one of the most unfortunate things in our history."[109]

Heston's appreciation of American history did not confine itself to his cinematic endeavors or the promotion of them. With the nation celebrating its bicentennial, he returned from overseas to take part in activities in Philadelphia after a brief stopover in Los Angeles. Addled a bit by the travel schedule, he initially agreed to step away from a duty he would typically have embraced. "I was so tired that I accepted with weary docility Mayor [Frank] Rizzo's decision to take over my introduction of the president tomorrow," he noted on July 3. "I don't like controversies where my ego might seem involved." Lydia then prevailed on him to step up to the task he had accepted. "I called them back and said I really preferred to either do what they had invited me to fly from Australia for, or go home. I will introduce the president."[110]

The next day, July 4, 1976, an ostensibly freshened Heston assumed the role as "master of ceremonies for the Bicentennial proceedings" and introduced President Gerald R. Ford. He felt satisfied at the occasion, terming the day "glorious" and concluding the event represented "a proper two hundredth birthday party" for the nation. "I did what I was supposed to do, and I was proud to be there," he observed quietly, adding, "as a performer and as a citizen."[111]

Heston had built up tremendous good will with the Department of Defense and the various military services with his portrayals and public support. For another picture, *Gray Lady Down*, Heston took a role under the seas as opposed to above them as he had done in *Midway*, playing a submarine commander closing out

---

108 *ALJ*, 471-472.

109 Vincent, "Security, Asheville Almost Got Him." The film employed the issue as one of the story lines involving Heston's character and his son regarding a romantic interest of Japanese American descent.

110 *ALJ*, 473.

111 Ibid.; "Remarks of Gerald R. Ford in Philadelphia, Pennsylvania (Bicentennial Celebration)" July 4, 1976, Public Papers of the President of the United States: Gerald R. Ford, 1976-1977 (Washington, United States Government Printing Office), 1966 and 1971.

his active career whose craft has a catastrophic collision with a freighter that was approaching a port in a thick fog. The film also tapped into the disaster genre that had worked so well for him and with audiences in recent years, although as one reviewer noted, the formula flipped the usual situation he occupied. "It is strange to see Charlton Heston, his square jaw covered with a mod beard, in the position of needing rescue," Mal Vincent of Norfolk's *Virginian-Pilot* observed. "He usually is in the business of rescuing."[112]

To prepare for this part, Heston carried out his typical research agenda. As a result, he learned both that members of the contemporary Navy could grow beards, and that a modern nuclear submarine was less claustrophobic and friendlier to a landsman than he had imagined. The role once again allowed the actor to play an authority figure, albeit one who faced the challenges and anxieties of a crisis as his vessel awaited rescue. Heston did not know if the formula would result in box office success this time, but in the course of the project, he received an award "for making fifty films, which they claim have grossed a billion dollars." He was not sure if "this is true, but it's nice to hear, anyway."[113]

He took pride in knowing when his work found the mark of success, but realized as much as anyone else when he missed on a film that turned out to achieve the same status without him. In at least two pictures that generated enormous box office revenues, *Jaws* and *The Omen*, he had either taken himself out of consideration with his contractual requirements or chosen not to participate. For *Jaws*, Herman Citron's insistence on a percentage of the gross for his client led executives to offer the role of Chief Martin Brody to Roy Scheider instead. With regard to *The Omen*, Heston explained, "Greg Peck did it, and it's now the only film this year doing better than *Midway*. It's a better film, too. Greg is just right, at least as good as I would've been." He had little reason to regret his choices, but concluded of this one, "On balance, I suppose I should have done it. On the other hand, it would be downright obscene to be in the two biggest hits of the year."[114]

Heston had passed on *The Omen* after consulting with Lydia, rationalizing, "You have to be skeptical . . . I do, anyway . . . of accepting an offer just to reassure yourself you're employable." Actually, various factors from timing to family and the realistic potential that the film would be made poorly, kept him away from it. Later, when he addressed the missed opportunity in his memoirs, the actor

---

112 Mal Vincent, "'Gray Lady' Above Average," *VP*, Mar. 17, 1978.

113 *ALJ*, 478.

114 Eliot, *Charlton Heston*, 361; *ALJ*, 478-479.

insisted, "I remember being irritated with myself for not being in both of the summer smashes, which was not only greedy but foolish of me." In addition, the circumstances surrounding yet another foreign shoot had not made the project as appealing at the time.[115]

He had reached the point in his life and career when the past dictated his reactions to much of what was happening to him professionally. "Up until *Ben-Hur*, I had made almost all of my films at Paramount, so it was a very nostalgic experience going back today, where I've not been since *Will Penny*." He could look at virtually any part of the sets and see his own history before him. "We shot on the stage where de Mille wrecked the circus train in *The Greatest Show on Earth*, where Fray floated in the bulrushes in *The Ten Commandments* (and where I made bricks for the pharaoh, entered his palace in triumph, and was led out in chains)."[116]

Charlton Heston had also arrived at a place in his career where deference was a part of his usual encounters with others. He loved the benefits of his work and knew how they compared with earlier times when he was struggling hard just to establish his footing in the industry. "An old Paramount crewman came up to me while we were waiting and said cheerfully, 'Just like old times with de Mille, eh, Chuck?'" Rather than reinforce the feeling of nostalgia, Heston responded, "No, sir, de Mille would've had five guys' heads on stakes by now." Of course, the actor was probably right about the director, but of the chance to re-connect with a man who had worked in the studio those many years ago, all Heston could think of now was of the money being lost in wasted production time. "If the film fails," Heston insisted, sounding like his old boss, "it's my failure, not some sloppy crewman who can't do his job right."

At the same time he was involving himself in various arenas of entertainment, or at least Lew Wasserman was on his behalf. When the NFL's Los Angeles Rams failed to sell a certain number of tickets, Heston's agent purchased them on the requirement that the network grant a halftime interview to the star to promote the thriller *Two-Minute Warning*, which featured Los Angeles Memorial Coliseum threatened by a sniper while filled with spectators watching a championship game. "Lew is no fool, as I've observed before now," Heston concluded, knowing that the interview would reach the audience that ought to be the most receptive to the film. Nevertheless, the initial word on the action movie was disappointing. "I've been spoiled, I guess," Heston postulated, "of my last twelve pictures all but

115 *ALJ*, 453; *CHA*, 310-311.

116 *ALJ*, 479.

three have been hits (and none of the failing three had a full release). That's an unusual record," he admitted, "but I've come to expect it." The failure did not affect Heston's finances adversely, although it seemed to put a dent in his theatrical armor. "My interview with the accountants reveals that I seem to have managed to make a fortune acting for pay," he noted. "I can't resist recording the boast here, but I also feel apologetic." In many ways, he remained the Michigan boy who had managed to make good, and he recognized the luck and timing that had propelled him to financial security.

For all his commercial success, Heston maintained a view that he had to believe the premise of a story in order to accept it. In one instance, with Seltzer pressing him to accept, he turned down a project because he did not like the message it sent of the U.S. Army as an insane asylum pitted against the outside world. "In this time in the twentieth century, given the realities of the world, I don't care to make that point. I don't believe it, and besides, the part's not that good."[117]

In November 1976, *Newsweek* ran a critical assessment of several well-known performers. The feature examined the state of "stars of the 1950s" who were now facing "a Hollywood mid-life crisis." The writers focused first on Gregory Peck, who was about to bring the flamboyant Gen. Douglas MacArthur to the screen and who had recently enjoyed renewed box office success in *The Omen*. Noting the exertions of Burt Lancaster, Robert Mitchum, and Kirk Douglas in developing their roles, the writers cited Heston's observation that "[o]nce an actor is known, it's an agent's job to make the deals, not get the parts." Nevertheless Heston, whose career had also lasted since the early 1950s, was an exception. "The one box-office idol who has managed to remain regularly on top is Charlton Heston, 52, who takes pains to refer to himself as a contemporary of Paul Newman." The writers considered his formula for identifying projects as part of the reason for this success and his longevity in the profession. "By not asking for too much up front (his standard fee is $250,000 plus 10 per cent of the gross), by carefully selecting scripts, and by ingratiating himself with studios through a willingness to promote his films at no extra cost, he has managed to work steadily and make more money than any other star in Hollywood."[118]

One scholar suggested that he chose parts that "conveyed his own bourgeois ethics and principles" and rejected offers that "violated them."[119] Certainly,

117 *ALJ*, 479-481.

118 Betsy Carter and Martin Kasindorf, "The Over-the-Hill Gang," *Newsweek* (Nov. 15, 1976), 106.

119 Raymond, *Cold, Dead Hands*, 164.

Charlton Heston was aware of how any given film project presented him to the audience and how that movie might generate the box office success that he desired. Yet he had proven willing to accept or decline roles based upon their worthiness as meaningful parts. It was easier for him to portray characters with values he held personally, but if that were not the case, he was willing to consider the role regardless of this variance.

The stage remained "actor's country" for Charlton Heston, and he pushed himself to prepare for *Long Day's Journey into Night*, turning to famed accent guru Robert Easton to assist. "I've been neglecting this kind of training when I do a play, and that's stupid," he lamented. Within days, he had corrected the oversight and felt he was on his way to preparing for his portrayal of James Tyrone in the Eugene O'Neill drama.

For Christmas 1976, Heston continued to ground himself in his family's traditions, especially with a tree brought in from Michigan. "With our friends, we got it up, tall and thick as the dark, deep woods of my boyhood," he explained. "This party is our own tradition, and I love it," although on this occasion Lydia unfortunately missed the festivities with a migraine.[120]

As a dispassionate businessperson, he understood the bottom-line in his profession and worked to secure the best arrangements he could for his participation in every project he undertook. This had driven him, through his agent, to require percentages in his films in addition to a salary. Heston also accepted roles as a pitchman or spokesperson for companies that knew his voice would resonate with potential customers. But this work was not without drawbacks. A *Newsweek* article touting the efforts of an angry citizen to stem the tide of telephone solicitations included a glancing shot at Heston. "One common technique involves . . . a recorded message from a celebrity," such as baseball legend Mickey Mantle. "Other well-known telephone hucksters include Charlton Heston (for cable television)."[121] Even so, the actor did not view activities of this sort as potentially detrimental to his subsequent work.

The "public face" of a well-established actor who happened to be involved in high-profile pictures gave anyone who wished to employ Heston's name the kind of exposure they hoped that awareness would ensure. When geologists and others sought to raise attention to the real dangers of a powerful earthquake along

---

120 *ALJ*, 480-481.

121 Tom Nicholson, Pamela Abramson, and Janet Huck, "For Whom the Bell?" *Newsweek* (Oct. 17, 1977), 89.

California's volatile San Andreas Fault, they were not shy to exploit the actor's recent screen activity. Thus when the Goddard Space Flight Center in Maryland released a study that addressed potentially concerning movements of the tectonic plates along the fault line, public reaction was indifferent at best. The writers of a short piece in *Newsweek* concluded, "During the week after the findings were released, the San Francisco emergency-services office, which is usually first to record tremors of public concern, reported not a single anxious citizen had called—not even Charlton Heston."[122] The actor's name might garner additional attention and keep the cause prominently displayed in the public consciousness.

His influence would always be dependent upon continuing to build on his career and reach an ever-changing audience. In 1976, he still seemed to be hitting his stride in a vast range of areas. "In the last seven weeks, I've visited eighteen cities in five countries . . . six if you count Hong Kong," he recorded in his journal that July. "I've made part of one picture, sold the hell out of another one; played in two tennis tournaments, raising considerable money for the Muscular Dystrophy Fund; and introduced a president." Not without pride in the achievement, he concluded, "So much for a quiet summer."[123]

Charlton Heston moved through the mid-1970s with the satisfaction that he was making films that audiences wanted to see, even if they were not presenting him with the challenges that Shakespearean productions offered. In his 1976 short biographical history of Heston and his work, writer Michael Druxman noted that four of the actor's recent releases had proven to be "major box-office hits," and concluded that this circumstance paid important dividends. "Heston's 'bankability' with film investors has increased and more lucrative offers have rolled in."[124]

Around this time, Northwestern University, the institution that had helped establish the foundation of his career, welcomed back its famous alumnus. "It's odd to come back to the campus where so much began for me," Heston noted in his journal. He was there to aid in shaping plans for a new performance venue as chair of the committee to raise the requisite funds. "They needed a new theater when I tried to learn to act here in 1941," he explained. Narrating a filmed campaign effort in fall 1975 and returning to the campus for the groundbreaking ceremonies in June 1978, the celebrity chair led the slow but steady progress on the project, with a formal dedication program two years later. In addition to the groundbreaking

---

122 Jean Seligmann, Sharon Begley, and Michael Reese, "Tracking the Fault," *Newsweek* (July 10, 1978), 62.

123 *ALJ*, 473.

124 Druxman, *Charlton Heston*, 136.

for the theatre center, Heston served as commencement speaker for his alma mater in 1978.[125]

Given all his acclaim, Heston recognized that his place in the strata of film stars put him in an unusually powerful position regarding future projects. At the end of November 1976, he assessed his role in a modern crime thriller by noting his wife's disdain. "Lydia's unimpressed with *Two-Minute Warning*, for which I can't blame her." Yet he still saw the benefit of the producers' determination to include him on his own terms, or at least those of his agent. "Again, they're meeting Herman's very tough deal for me to play a relatively small part in a film in which I'm regarded as an insurance policy."[126] This was hardly a ringing endorsement of the part or the project, but it was a reality the actor knew came with his stature in the profession.

Heston took all these matters in stride, telling Jeff Rovin, who authored a compendium of his films during this period, "My only obligation to the public is to perform." This form of work meant "making a living" for Heston. On the other hand, his "obligation to them as a public person is to do my work and respond, in some way, to my public identity, and what their concept of their needs from it are."[127]

The chance to act in the theater was always a welcome diversion for the performer who seemed to be more often engaged in other activities. During this period, Shakespeare gave way to Eugene O'Neill, which brought an issue to the forefront that Heston had not confronted in some time. He wanted Deborah Kerr to join him in *Long Day's Journey into Night*, but she insisted upon being billed first. "That hasn't happened to me since *Naked Jungle*, with Eleanor Parker," he recalled. "I find it irritating, but it's nonsense, really." Of course, it "really" was not "nonsense" to either star. Nevertheless, Heston's age and history encouraged him to look at the matter in circumspect. "We want her in the part, we'll give her the billing."[128]

Subsequently, when he made his return to the stage at the Ahmanson Theatre as James Tyrone in the O'Neill classic, which ran from February 18 to April 2, 1977, this "journey" continued to evoke a mixture of emotions. A *Los Angeles Times* review by Dan Sullivan tempered the joy of acting for him and again exposed a normally latent sense of insecurity that drove him toward the ever-elusive perfect performance. "He has Charlton Heston here and it is a big step down," Sullivan

---

125 *ALJ*, 390; Karen Werling, "Appreciation: Charlton Heston's life as a Wildcat," *North by Northwestern* (April 16, 2008), www.northbynorthwestern.com/story/heston-at-northwestern.

126 *ALJ*, 457.

127 Rovin, *Films*, 23.

128 *ALJ*, 473.

noted, "but it wouldn't be fair to say that Heston's the major problem in this production." For Sullivan, "The flatness is universal." Heston's response carried a telling postscript: "I DO agree with you on one point. I'm a big step down from Olivier. But then, who isn't?"

Sullivan's critique had struck a nerve with Heston. "In the time-worn phrase, you're entitled to your opinion," he began in a response. "Forgive me. I have the advantage of you: you've seen the play, several times, no doubt. I *know* the play." Still, the actor could not resist reminding the critic, "Happily, if the current indications hold true, we will break the house record we set with MACBETH. I know that distresses you, but I'm sure you can understand that we take pride in filling a 2100 seat house for Shakespeare and O'Neill."[129]

Another reviewer phrased his comments differently, although still in a manner intended to be more damning than not. "But for once, in his third appearance on stage here, Charlton Heston's courage as an actor is exceeded by his talent." Ray Loynd asserted. "That's good news, hopefully burying Heston's 'Macbeth' (or rather those who won't let him forget it) once and for all." The *Los Angeles Herald-Examiner* critic added, "Heston is a nice surprise. I really forgot I was watching Heston."[130]

Charlton Heston placed any Shakespearean production at the highest point to which any serious performer could aspire. He offered a modern-day allusion to solidify his point to one interviewer. "Shakespeare is the real Super Bowl of acting. Thousands of years from now, if they are still acting, they will be acting Shakespeare." He did not explain whether he thought anyone who performed well in any of these parts would enjoy the same longevity of reputation as the Bard, but clearly, he thought the work sustainable.

While focused on the stage production in Los Angeles, Heston also looked for opportunities to share his experiences and expertise with younger generations of aspiring actors. He agreed to a special luncheon and coaching session with students. An expression of thanks for the gesture reflected the star's personality: "Your generosity is exceeded only by your stamina." That stamina included the physical demands that he still brought to his films on his own terms rather than cede all the action to stunt doubles. Citing the fighting scenes from *The Last Hard*

129 Dan Sullivan, "O'Neill's 'Journey' at Ahmanson," *L.A. Times View*, Feb. 21, 1977; "Chuck Heston to Dear Mr. Sullivan, February 21, 1977," "*Long Day's Journey into Night* (Ahmanson Theatre, 1977)," f.400, Heston Papers, HL.

130 Ray Loynd, "Heston, Kerr in O'Neill's 'Journey,'" *Los Angeles Herald-Examiner*, Feb. 21, 1977, HL.

Men, one writer concluded, "No man at virtually any age could look any more tough and fit and trim than Charlton Heston at 53."[131]

Heston sought another method of identifying with his audience by turning from the stage and screen to the pen, or more appropriately, the typewriter. Approached with the idea of a biography, or possibly a ghost-authored autobiography, the actor balked at letting anyone else take his words and extract them in order to speak on his behalf. He did need someone to organize and synthesize what he had written, but his would remain the voice. The result was *The Actor's Life: Journals 1956-1976*, which presented the story Heston wanted to tell the way he wanted to tell it, using his journal entries. As he forwarded material to the compiler, Hollis Alpert, he told him, "'I don't want you to make any cuts in the material. Just cut out days at a time.' I'm very touchy about somebody writing something and putting my name on it."[132]

In this book, Heston tackled many aspects of his life and profession with candid assessments. One example dealt with his position on President Lyndon Johnson's gun control measure a decade earlier. In the notes accompanying the corresponding entry in his published *Journals* and well before the actor assumed a larger leadership role on the issue of gun rights, Heston remarked, "For the record, what I regard as a moderate position on gun control does not include either registering or confiscating all the firearms in private hands. I grant I'm prejudiced; I've used guns all my life. Also, in my view, the Constitution establishes certain rights in this area not granted to citizens of other countries."[133]

The publication of *The Actor's Life* meant another extensive publicity tour for the new author. A program for the book tour included press releases and a photo by Dutton News, along with a full schedule that featured an opportunity to meet Heston at the iconic Windows on the World restaurant atop the World Trade Center in New York on Monday, November 13:

Houston	November 2
Dallas/Ft. Worth	November 3, 4, 5
Los Angeles	November 6, 7, 8
Pasadena	November 9

---

131 "James H. Hansen to Dear Mr. Heston, February 25, 1977, and March 14, 1977"; Kevin Thomas, "'Last Hard Men' Here at Last," *LAT*, Sept. 28, 1977.

132 Carol Schwalberg, "Bookviews Talks to Charlton Heston," *Bookviews* (Nov. 1978), 16-18.

133 *ALJ*, 296.

New York	November 10, 11, 12, 13, 14
Toronto	November 15
Chicago	November 16, 17, 18, 19
Cleveland	November 20
Minneapolis	November 21, 22
San Diego	November 27, 28
Seattle	November 29, 30
San Francisco	December 1, 2[134]

One writer prompted a thoughtful response when he asked if Heston intended to publish additional work. "I suppose when I get another 10 years down the road, I might publish a sequel," Heston noted. "I still keep my working journals. If you had come in a little later, you would have found me at a typewriter. I've got the pages for the last weekend in my briefcase."

Should such a publication occur, the writer wondered what the actor thought it might include. "Ideally, I would have done Macbeth one more time in London's West End, making me the fourth American actor to play Shakespeare in London at all." Heston continued to speculate on the potential highlights. "I would, let's say, have five huge successes in films and two or three interesting failures and maybe found a new play I liked well enough to do." Fittingly, he added a thought concerning his children. "And my son would have written some successful films and my daughter would have finished school and found what she wants to do with her life and someone she wants to do it with."[135]

In another interview that covered the release of *The Actor's Life*, Carol Schwalberg of *Bookviews* traveled to the offices of the American Film Institute in Beverly Hills. Heston proved comfortable in discussing the project and offered his views on a wide range of topics, including his screen work. Schwalberg was interrupted by an inadvertent alarm from Heston's watch. Wondering if the incident showed that the time had not gone well, the interviewer learned otherwise. "Oh no," his publicist insisted, "He enjoyed it." How would one be able to tell, Schwalberg wanted to know. "I don't know why that alarm sounded, but he never once looked at his watch."[136]

---

134 "Program, *The Actor's Life*," Heston Papers, "*The Actor's Life*—publicity," f.452, HL.

135 Dann Gire, "Life and peanut butter suit Heston fine," *The Sunday Herald*, Nov. 18, 1979, HL.

136 Carol Schwalberg, "Bookviews Talks to Charlton Heston," 19.

Despite Heston's inherent shyness and a desire for privacy, he professed not to mind letting the public through this window into his life. "I wonder if one ever writes a journal just for oneself," he responded to a query on the matter. Then, seeming to draw almost instinctively on his early days in the Michigan woods, he stated, "You don't carve initials on a tree just for yourself, but for someone else to see." Yet he could be contradictory in his expressions on the same subject, as when he answered another question about some of his more stinging remarks about fellow performers. "That was because they were never written for anyone else but me to read," he maintained, despite knowing readers would be seeing those comments as well.[137]

Whatever Charlton Heston might think about others in his profession, the members of the Academy were prepared to bestow one of the highest honors on their colleague in the form of the Jean Hersholt Humanitarian Award. Slated as part of the April 3, 1978, Oscar ceremony, the presenter was the caustic Bette Davis, who had not always been laudatory in earlier remarks about the recipient. On this evening, however, she stayed on script to describe in glowing terms Heston's professional and personal activities, ranging from his six terms as Screen Actors Guild president and his work on the National Council on the Arts and with the American Film Institute, to his support for the Center Theatre Group in Los Angeles and the Motion Picture and Television Fund. In the larger public sector, his fundraising efforts on behalf of Planned Parenthood, Muscular Dystrophy, the Heart Fund, and the American Cancer Society also highlighted a truly humanitarian spirit. "Chuck Heston has not done any of these things for recognition or credit," Davis intoned. "It's just the way he is, a man of conscience. And to boot, a darn good tennis player, who turns even that hobby into charity."

Heston responded with graciousness and genuine gratitude. "When Bette Davis says it," he began, "you figure it must be true, but really, I think I won this award for doing the kind of chores a whole lot of other people do, but because I'm an actor, when I do them they take my picture." This was a position he had long taken regarding the utility of his "public face," although he was no less appreciative because the recognition came at the hands of his colleagues. "Like all the awards given tonight, it represents the good opinion of the men and women you do your work with, and always, for all of us, that's the best praise of all."[138]

137 Schwalberg, "Bookviews," 18; Munn, *Charlton Heston*, 186.

138 "Charlton Heston Receives the Jean Hersholt Humanitarian Award: 1978 Oscars," www.youtube.com/watch?v=Vd4y2PiwU7w.

The 1970s represented a productive and profitable period for Charlton Heston, who had seen something of a rebirth of his career. The *Planet of the Apes* phenomenon and his other science fiction vehicles, *The Omega Man* and *Soylent Green*, won him new fans and indicated his continuing box office clout. Yet the actor had not been content to remain in that formula and found additional success in the disaster films that marked the middle and latter stages of the decade. Between these productions, he returned to historical dramas and Westerns, served as the foil for gallivanting French musketeers, and tried to bring a trapped crew from a sunken submarine, although the great disappointments were his cherished directing and acting project, *Antony and Cleopatra*, and the forgettable *Call of the Wild*.

When not engaged in this work and the promotional requirements demanded for each project, he remained active in professional and public service and leadership ventures, as well as the welcome diversions of family, stage productions, and tennis. Each piece of his life represented another departure from the shy young Michigan boy who had found a career and meaning on the stage and the screen, married his college sweetheart, and raised a family. The release of his published account of his performances and achievements in the journals that he had kept for twenty years reflected these myriad priorities. Like his life and career, however, Heston's book also suggested a work in progress as he continued to strive to adjust in his chosen course. The race was set to move into the final stretch, but the actor was determined to keep the pace and finish strong.

Chapter Eight

TURNING FOR HOME
1980s

"You just can't overestimate the importance of an audience's perception of a performer."
—Heston's assessment of his public image

"I guess I'm sort of the official conservative spokesman. I didn't seek it out, but there it is."
—Heston on his evolution as a celebrity in politics

"I'm the NRA."
—Advertising slogan for the National Rifle Association

Performances:
The Awakening, 1980
The Mountain Men, 1980
The Academy Awards, (52nd) Apr. 14, 1980, (55th) Apr. 11, 1983
The Tonight Show Starring Johnny Carson, Apr. 30, 1980; July 24, 1980; Nov. 7, 1980; Dec. 15, 1980; Feb. 23, 1981; Dec. 4, 1985; Sept. 21, 1987; Mar. 20, 1989; Aug. 2, 1989
The John Davidson Show, July 8, 1980; Nov. 3, 1980; Dec. 11, 1980; Mar. 19, 1981
All-Star Inaugural Gala, Jan. 19, 1981
The Mike Douglas Show, July 14, 1980
Crucifer of Blood, Ahmanson Theatre, Dec. 5, 1980-Jan. 17, 1981
This is Your Life: 30th Anniversary Special, Feb. 26, 1981
Let Poland Be Poland, Jan. 31, 1982
All-Star Birthday Party at Annapolis, May 25, 1982
Mother Lode, 1982
Chiefs, 1983
Once upon a Murder, 1983
The Stars Salute the U.S. Olympic Team, Jan. 29, 1984
Detective Story, Ahmanson Theatre, Feb. 4-Mar. 31, 1984
Nairobi Affair, 1984

Aspel & Company, Jan. 12, 1985

50th Presidential Inaugural Gala, Jan. 19, 1985

The Caine Mutiny Court-Martial, London, 1985

Bob Hope's Happy Birthday Homecoming (London Royal Gala), May 28, 1985

Television's Vietnam, June 26, 1985

Dynasty, Oct. 9, Oct. 16, and Nov. 13, 1985

All-Star Party for "Dutch" Reagan, Dec. 8, 1985

The Moviemakers: George Stevens: The Man & His Movies, 1985

The Fantasy Film Worlds of George Pal, 1985

The Colbys, Nov. 20, 1985-Mar. 26, 1987

An All-Star Celebration Honoring Martin Luther King, Jr., Jan. 20, 1986

The Starlight Annual Foundation Benefit, Feb. 14, 1986

The People's Choice Awards, Mar. 11, 1986 (12th); Aug. 23, 1989 (15th)

Good Morning America, Apr. 3, 1986

American Masters: Directed by William Wyler, May 1, 1986

Liberty Weekend, July 3, 1986

All-Star Tribute to General Jimmy Doolittle, Aug. 1986

Regis Philbin's Lifestyles, Sept. 9, 1986

Walt Disney World's 15th Anniversary Celebration, Nov. 9, 1986

The Lou Rawls Parade of Stars, Dec. 27, 1986

The 44th Annual Golden Globe Awards, Jan. 31, 1987

Saturday Night Live, Mar. 28, 1987; Sept. 24, 1989 (15th Anniversary)

Happy 100th Birthday, Hollywood, May 18, 1987

The USA Today's 5th Anniversary Gala, Sept. 10, 1987

Proud Men, Oct. 1, 1987

The Annual Thalians Ball, Oct. 17, 1987, (32nd); Oct. 28, 1989 (34th)

The Dame Edna Experience, Oct. 10, 1987

Wogan, Nov. 9, 1987; May 19, 1989

Christmas Night with the Two Ronnies, Dec. 25, 1987

The World's Greatest Stunts: A Tribute to Hollywood Stuntmen, 1988

America's Tribute to Bob Hope, Mar. 5, 1988

A Man for All Seasons, Dec. 21, 1988

Talking Pictures, 1988

The Pat Sajak Show, Jan. 30, 1989; July 17, 1989

Original Sin, Feb. 20, 1989

The Arsenio Hall Show, Mar. 16, 1989

Later with Bob Costas, June 1, 1989

The London Programme Saving Rose Theatre, June 2, 1989

The 7th Annual Golden Boots Award, Aug. 5, 1989

Call from Space, 1989

Nineteen eighty was an election year. Former actor and California governor Ronald Wilson Reagan challenged incumbent Jimmy Carter and third-party maverick John Anderson for the presidency. The Carter administration had proven turbulent enough to concern any individual who cherished a firm hand at the tiller and an even-keel for the ship of state. Charlton Heston was such a person; he had grown increasingly disgruntled with the state of the union and prepared to take an active role in support of Reagan's candidacy. His utility on the hustings would become significant at rallies and campaign events across the country, helping to draw crowds and aid fundraising for the Reagan-George H. W. Bush ticket.[1]

Part of the incentive for these efforts came from Heston's view of the current state of affairs in the country. In a moment of candor, he observed, "I'm not very sanguine about the human condition." Heston felt that neither he nor others in public positions could do much to affect larger circumstances, but thought that in those rare exceptions, individuals rather than humankind writ large stood the best chance to make a difference. "My admiration for man is in terms of the extraordinary individual rather than man in the mass, who I think falls infinitely short of what God must have had in mind."[2]

Ronald Reagan appeared to be such a person. Heston's connection with Reagan was multifaceted and of longstanding. One writer speculated, "It is possible that Heston was a bit starstruck by Reagan."[3] This admiration still did not prompt him to want to participate directly in the political arena other than in a supporting role. The notion that at least some people thought Heston could be an ideal candidate continued to produce frequent queries along those lines. "The first time I heard about the senate thing I was flattered by the idea," he explained in 1980, "but I remember thinking it through very carefully and examining myself very closely about it." Admitting that he was more connected with the "exterior me," which he deemed "my favorite of the two," Heston realized the fundamental truth remained for him: "I didn't want to run." Acting might not result in a high level of performance each time, as he always hoped it would, but when he fell short

---

1 Heston made several appearances with Reagan outside of California, including at a rally in Cincinnati alongside Bob Hope and former President Gerald Ford on Nov. 2, 1980.
www.video.search.yahoo.com/search/video?fr=yfp-t-s&p=President+Ford+Charlton+Heston#id=1&vid=1f16eea59f3b030150450c5598c5a536&action=click.

2 Rovin, *Films*, 21.

3 Raymond, *Cold, Dead Hands*, 218.

of perfection the lapse would not have consequences more serious than personal disappointment or limited ticket sales. In the end, at this point in his life and career he felt he could not "act as a moral or intellectual arbiter for somebody else's life; I have troubles enough of my own." As long as acting opportunities came, he was content. "Fortunately, as you get older," he explained, "the parts that are right for an actor begin to change, and I find that process to be constant and interesting." As far as political office was concerned, his exposure to the world of Washington had left him with the sense that even when someone thought he had achieved something worthwhile, nothing of substance appeared to take place. "If I had to spend the rest of my life dealing in the corridors of power and dealing thus every day with that kind of inertia, I don't think I'd be a very happy human being."

In his own craft, Heston remained as aware as ever of the significance of the public's acceptance of his work. In an interview, he asserted, "You just can't overestimate the importance of an audience's perception of a performer," and noted that deviations from these norms often came at a cost. "My point is, what an audience remembers seeing you do predisposes it to accept you in a certain way."[4] Unspoken was the understanding that the same people might reject the performer if that individual deviated too greatly from those expectations.

Yet Heston cherished his freedom of expression as a citizen and felt that whatever movie and theatergoers thought of his screen representations, he should support the causes he wished. When Reagan secured the Republican nomination, Heston saw his course in support of his old friend and colleague as clear. In the days that followed, former President Gerald Ford remembered that working for the ticket took on greater urgency. "Almost immediately after the convention they asked me to participate in the campaign." Ford joined Ronald and Nancy Reagan in Michigan and Ohio before heading to the West Coast. "When it looked like the election was going to depend on California, they got Charlton Heston and me to spend a whole day campaigning all over the state." Heston added star-power and Ford national political heft to the lineup, the latter in spite of having lost out to George H. W. Bush for the vice-presidential slot on the ticket.[5] One writer noted of the developing relationship Heston was forming with his friend, "[B]y the time of Reagan's election he was the first star conservatives called when they needed a flash of glamour." Heston's assessment was simple: "I guess I'm sort of the official

4 Linderman, "Charlton Heston Interview," 108, 110-112.

5 Deborah Hart Strober and Gerald S. Strober, *Reagan: The Man and His Presidency* (Boston, 1998), 28.

conservative spokesman. I didn't seek it out, but there it is."[6] Politicians like Reagan and Ford understood that someone like Charlton Heston had broad appeal.

Heston also believed important societal changes had affected his profession and compelled him to accept a more active role outside of it. "I really think the difference is that Hollywood is now making movies about victims," he asserted. Ascribing these new sensitivities to "an anxiety, a loss of confidence, a feeling of inadequacy, that we can probably attribute to a post-Watergate, post-Vietnam pessimism," Heston understood that this new reality existed for him as a performer as well. Even so, he hoped to avoid becoming too "marked" by this new trend. He observed wistfully, "But I believe in the hero." Most importantly, Heston still believed, as he had once remarked of the legendary figure El Cid, that a great leader must also accept "responsibility for the things that happen to everyone else."[7]

Heston thought he was witnessing a tide that threatened to engulf modern society and sought both to warn about the dire effects to come and to attempt to limit the damage inflicted. In *The Unreality Industry*, Ian I. Mitroff and Warren Bennis described the ways in which they identified the social unraveling that engendered such fears. "Once traditional boundaries are no longer sacred," they maintained, the resulting "boundary warping" undermined leaders who sought to confront problems directly in favor of those who developed popular images and offered platitudes, trading serious work for celebrity. Heston's increasing focus on the role of individual leaders with a passion for improving society over egocentrism and ambition mirrored this view. He recognized and lamented the passing of an older order based on heroic individuals who embodied what he considered immutable public values and virtues that served as models for others. In answer to an earlier query about Fraser, he explained, "I must teach my son what things in the world really have value. He must teach himself how to reach them."[8]

He was not always successful in motivating others to join his causes, however. When performers appeared to suffer from loss of revenue from cable screenings and home videos of their theatrical films, the Screen Actors Guild attempted to encourage some of the more high-profile members to join picket lines in protest.

---

6 Brownstein, *The Power and the Glitter*, 287.

7 Linderman, "Charlton Heston Interview," 176; "1961 Vintage Radio Interviews with Charlton Heston," *El Cid*, The Weinstein Corporation, DVD, 2008.

8 Ian I. Mitroff and Warren Bennis, *The Unreality Industry: The Deliberate Manufacturing of Falsehood and What it is Doing to our Lives* (New York, 1993), 18, 44; "Interview with Charlton Heston, 11-9-64," "*The Agony and the Ecstasy* publicity," f.2, Heston Papers, HL.

"Gregory Peck has picketed; Jane Fonda and Shirley MacLaine have promised to," Heston noted of his attempts to rally support. "But Robert Redford, Paul Newman, and George C. Scott haven't returned my calls." He thought that at any rate, SAG might have to suspend its efforts, since the strike had created unintended collateral damage with a "ripple effect" that in impacting the industry also affected "the entire community."[9]

Heston thought he had a chance to utilize the familiar heroic formula through his portrayal of the trapper Bill Tyler in *The Mountain Men*, although not so much in the mold of Moses, El Cid and Charles "Chinese" Gordon as in the sense of men who struggled to endure in a transitioning and dangerous world. He insisted that neither his character nor his friend and associate, Henry Frappe (Brian Keith), really were exceptional in terms of rank or position. "Playing Bill Tyler was different for me," he explained in one interview. "I have often played extraordinary men—presidents, leaders, geniuses, saints. But mountain men? They weren't heroes. They were only survivors." But if Tyler and his compatriot had to endure the changes besetting their world, audiences could at least celebrate their tenacity and resolve in the face of these challenges.

The Mountain Men offered another form of welcome collaboration. Fraser Heston had grown up in the movies with his father. After his debut as the infant Moses, his time on sets came as family support for the star. His development as an outdoor adventurer and writer brought his own perspective to his work. By the 1980s, that included working on screenplays and eventually assuming the roles of producer and director. Fraser had written *Wind River*, the novel that served as the basis for this film, although another difficult lesson for father and son was the degree to which the original work failed to determine the final product that audiences would see on the big screen.

To promote this project, Charlton and Fraser attended a modern frontier "rendezvous" with a film crew from the popular television program *The American Sportsman*. Pitting their skills at marksmanship against and trading stories with the participants gave the two Hestons an entertaining equivalent to the tale found in the film. Father and son attributed much of the authenticity of the screen work to the types of re-enactors who added color and accuracy to the portrayals and settings. It was also clear that the two men genuinely enjoyed the camaraderie of fellow students of this unique form of frontier history.[10]

9 Marilyn Beck, "Star Pickets Hard to Find," *RTD*, Sept. 15, 1980.

10 "Mountain Man episode," *The American Sportsman*, UCLA.

Heston later expressed exasperation over the finished product, but a press junket to the camp suggested a man who was taking enormous delight in his work. After marching the outsiders through a gauntlet of characters who greeted him warmly, and occasionally wrangled an autograph, the actor took his visitors to a tent and began to expostulate on the men and the times they were depicting. "They struggled hard, but each was his own man, in control of his own destiny," at least as much as outside forces permitted. Then, adding in a way that implied as much about himself as these historical figures, Heston remarked, "That aspect, to me, is most important—greater than money, success, or celebrity." Feeling an uncommon level of comfort in these surroundings, he asserted, "I love mountain people. It's the only large group I can walk freely amongst. Basically I'm a shy man and don't like getting mobbed by crowds. Here, they leave me alone; I can be my own man."[11]

Of course, potential life lessons could only be imparted if moviegoers came to the theater to see the film, and Heston was troubled that his own timing would prove problematic in that regard. "I am concerned because '*The Mountain Men*' is in release in Europe at the same time as '*The Awakening*,'" he noted of a thriller with supernatural undertones he had just completed. "I shouldn't have two films out at the same time."[12]

The process of making the historically based film became intensely dissatisfying to the elder Heston. In a flurry of reactions to the situation, he vented his anger in anticipation of a meeting with studio executives. "Shocked to realize this month is my 30th anniversary in films," he began. "Made 55 films in that time . . . for all the studios [and] lucky enough to work with some great filmmakers, & almost always w/good, decent professionals." Taking aim at himself first—"God knows made share of bad films—thank God a few good ones as well," Heston turned to the matter at hand. "Never had so miserable an experience, never has my judgement, my creative opinions been dismissed so highhandedly, with such arrogant disdain for what I hope I've learned about the business we all love." Filmgoers would never get a hint of the serious degree of dissatisfaction the actor had with this project and his place in it, but it was very real for him. "Not Wyler, not Stevens, not DeMille, not Welles . . . not even, God save the mark, Sam Peckinpah ever displayed anything like the clear contempt for my instincts [as] an artist," he typed in his note, adding in handwriting "[& professional,] as I faced throughout [every step of] this film."

11 Robert Kerwin, "Safe Conduct as Heston Parts the Mountain Men," *LAT*, Aug. 10, 1980.

12 Carole Kass, "Heston: Many Faces Mark His Varied Career," *RTD*, Sept. 7, 1980.

I am humiliated to realise [sic] I was lied to, deceived, cheated [from the beginning] . . . second unit, title xchange, staffing and editing.

Mind you, not bad fil[m]. I've made many wrose [sic], maybe not all that many better. But this one could have been SO much better. I don't think I've ever made a film that fell so far below what it might have been . . . if the people who made it had cared, or tried, a little more.

Still, bottom line is the film works for an audience. In the end, that's what counts, and I suppose what should count. Audiences like it; if you get lucky and make some good decisions, you may make a lot of money I honestly hope so.

Determined to remain professional in the face of what he saw as almost unendurable treatment during the filming, Heston insisted, "I also want to tell you I will proceed with Colu[m]bia's plans for me to tour with the picture." He would not do so because he expected to enhance his share of the gross receipts the film might achieve, should anyone wish to question his motivations. "I will tour because you gentlemen (at the top of the organization) have always dealt honestly and decently with me and made your plans on the assumption I would tour, and because I told you I would <u>tour</u>."[13]

Though he managed to suppress most of his anger over *Mountain Men* publicly for years, Heston remained bitter over the project for which he initially had cherished such high hopes, but that was undermined by the Hollywood system. He allowed his sentiments to spill onto the pages of his autobiography when it appeared. "The print ads were worse, featuring cartoon drawings of Brian [Keith] and me running away from some pretty ridiculous Indians." But deeper, more troubling flaws still existed in his mind. "The ads were an appalling surprise, the editing was a shocking violation of assurances [Martin] Ransohoff had given me." The litany of transgressions aggravated still fresh wounds. "It was my first and to this day the most outrageous encounter in this town with that kind of behavior. *Mountain Men* remains a bitter memory of what could've been a fine film."[14] Heston had faced disappointment before and knew there was little he could do except express his views to the appropriate parties and attempt to steel himself against similar situations in the future. In the meantime, he could accept roles in which he might still make a difference.

13 Typed note card, "*The Mountain Man* miscellaneous," f.111, HL.

14 Ibid., 524.

Despite the disappointing realities of working in an industry whose commercial imperatives often clashed with creative ones, the younger and elder Hestons found additional ways to work together. They created Agamemnon Films in 1981 as a framework for generating motion pictures or television dramas. The result would be a string of productions that reflected their shared interest in history, literature, and the stage and that offered both men meaningful creative outlets.[15]

The Awakening, which Heston had worried might crowd his other work, symbolized the constant struggle of trying to identify projects that resonated with new audiences. The 1970s had witnessed the rise of the star-filled disaster film genre that the actor tapped into successfully, but it also produced occult/horror classics like *The Exorcist* (1973), *The Omen* (1976), and various spin-offs. Having missed out on *The Omen*, he hoped to make his own mark in this dramatic formula and *The Awakening* seemed to hit that mark. The story involved a British archeologist who unwittingly opened the way for the malevolent spirit of a departed Egyptian royal to inhabit his modern-day daughter (Stephanie Zimbalist). Heston's earnest attempt to crack into this genre demonstrated once again that he was willing to defy the heroic roles that had largely defined him, and illustrated the degree to which success well in popular trend would be difficult for him to duplicate.

Because Ronald Reagan was in the White House, Heston's public roles were not limited to his work in film or on the stage. In May 1981, Reagan tapped him to co-chair the Presidential Task Force on the National Endowment for the Arts and Humanities alongside Hanna Gray, president of the University of Chicago. They were to have a broad mandate to assess arts programs across the country and how, in the face of budget cuts, they could be maintained or streamlined. Writer Jack Slater thought Heston was an excellent choice for such a leadership role. "The air of the quintessential man of action always seems to surround Charlton Heston," Slater observed. "As Moses, he led the children of Israel out of slavery. As Ben Hur, he reasserted his sense of manhood against the forces of evil. In the role of El Cid, he drove the Moors from Spain." Now, as the man charged with leading this effort, he once again appeared appropriate to be well cast. "Identified in celluloid as a man who gets things done, it is only natural that that identity should follow him into the real world." Heston understood the responsibility that confronted him and his associates. "It's been a busy summer," he remarked as the group prepared for a report to be issued in September. "When the President asks you to do something,

---

15 Fraser is listed as the president and CEO of Agamemnon Films on its website, www.agamemnon.com/about.php.

you're supposed to do it, if at all possible," he noted of the diversion from the work he would rather be doing. "I'm an actor," he reminded the reporter. "And I want to act."[16]

Heston's association with President Reagan continued both professionally and personally into the summer months as the task force conducted its work. During fact-finding tours, the actor thought he spent too much time and energy deflecting the notion that he "had been appointed Lord High Executioner" for some modern version of the Spanish Inquisition. "I spent almost as much time doing interviews denying this as I did chairing meetings," he remembered. On Monday, June 15, Reagan recorded in his diary a meeting with Heston and other "members of the Task Force on Arts and Humanities."[17] Heston supported his friend and former SAG colleague strongly, seeing him not only as the right person to guide the country, but as a leader in promoting the arts as well.

When the task force assembled for a White House luncheon, Heston was away on location filming. Even so, he sent a message of support. "I regret that the film I'm shooting in British Columbia keeps me from joining you to second the convictions I know Hanna will express. I've been preaching the independence and perseverance of the artist all summer. Now, I'm trying to practice it." He closed, "My thoughts are very much with you. I am grateful for your trust in us." [18]

Around this time, the recognition of Charlton Heston's life and career culminated in a pleasant surprise. For the thirtieth anniversary of *This is Your Life*, a helicopter appeared over the tennis court on the actor's ridge. Setting the scene, the voiceover explained, "Charlton Heston, full-time tennis player, part-time actor . . . this is your life." Key participants in his progression from Michigan to Hollywood and beyond, ranging from his family to his friends and close associates appeared on the program. Lilla, Lydia, Fraser, Holly, and Jolly West offered personal stories and insights, while David Bradley, Orson Welles, Laurence Olivier, Walter Seltzer, and Yakima Canutt provided glimpses into his show business and performing worlds. Jack Valenti brought the actor's experiences into the political and broader public arenas as well. In assessing this aspect of Heston's persona, Valenti opined, "I think in Texas we would say that Chuck is a 'can-do' man. . . . He's always there

16 "Announcement of the Establishment of the Presidential Task Force on the Arts and Humanities," May 6, 1981, in *Public Papers of the Presidents of the United States. Ronald Reagan. Containing the Public Messages, Speeches, and Statements of the President: 1981* (Washington: Government Printing Office), 407; Jack Slater, "Arts Task Force: Heston's New Role," *LAT*, Aug. 26, 1981.

17 *CHA*, 529; Douglas Brinkley, ed., *The Reagan Diaries* (New York, 2007), 25.

18 "Remarks at a White House Luncheon for Members of the Presidential Task Force on the Arts and Humanities," October 14, 1981, *Reagan Presidential Papers: 1981*, 925-927.

when you need him." He detailed a catalog of public contributions, asserting, "this fellow not only served his industry, but people don't know how much he served his country. He travelled around the world for the State Department, and the Voice of America, National Council of the Arts, Trustee, Board of the Academy, a driving force behind the American Film Industry." Finally, with a nod to another famous actor who had moved on to the White House, Valenti added, "And he served, in fact, six terms, as president of the Screen Actors Guild, and you know where that job leads to."

Heston found the retrospective humbling and exhilarating. As the show drew toward its conclusion, he noted his appreciation at being "one of that lucky minority of men who can make a living doing what we would really do for free." His was "a marvelous, marvelous life," alongside Lydia, without whom "none of it would have happened." Saving a salacious moment until the last, the host proclaimed, "but finally, Chuck, we couldn't let this end without revealing fearlessly to the world, the one tragic addiction that you have fought but failed to overcome . . . peanut butter."

Indeed, as Valenti had pointed out, Charlton Heston had remained active in causes he found worthy of his attention and would continue to do so as a vital part of the "public face" he had developed over a long career. In September 1981, the actor became involved in a documentary about farm exports entitled *We Can Turn the Tide*. The Agriculture Council of America made the announcement of his participation as part of its promotional effort, "U.S. Farm Export Education Program." Heston donated his services for the narration of the film and in a series of public service announcements set to appear as television spots.[19]

Exposure was certainly something he had cultivated in many different forms throughout his career. He had played a glamor role in *Lucy Gallant* in 1955 and had served as a spokesperson for products using that film in mutual promotions. By the early 1980s, he took a prominent part in a Rolex watch campaign that noted the "extraordinary" features of both the timepiece and the spokesperson. Like the cufflinks he had once seen adorn the shirts of actors, Rolexes marked important symbols of success for Heston. The stylish and expensive accessory was also a significant advance over the earlier products he had advocated, and foreshadowed his role as wealthy entrepreneur Jason Colby in the popular television serial *Dynasty* and its spinoff, *The Colbys*. Heston always seemed to miss not being able to play the type of character Cary Grant had embodied so frequently, observing that Grant

19 "Heston helping farmers," *RTD*, Sept. 1981.

"was without peer in films where he stood around in beautiful rooms wearing beautiful clothes and saying beautiful things to beautiful women."[20]

All his achievements in film and the stage could not buffer Heston from the vagaries of time. Changing dynamics in the leadership of the Screen Actors Guild and its mission mirrored the actor's concern about the shifting nature of a society that he no longer felt he recognized. In 1980, Heston had opposed SAG president William Schallert's use of a strike as a means of exerting leverage over rights associated with pay television and work disseminated on videocassettes. Using the Reagan model of negotiation he had employed successfully during his own tenure as SAG president, Heston expressed his views accordingly. Unfortunately, some of the critics in SAG felt that Schallert had not done enough, rather than going too far, and began to champion popular television and film actor Edward Asner as a replacement.

More than internal politics was at work in this battle over SAG leadership. The fight seemed to be against those embracing liberal or progressive ideals and those who adhered to conservative ones. "Ronald Reagan's victory put Moses and Lou Grant on their collision course," an observer of the Hollywood/Washington phenomenon explained colorfully. A Democratic pollster asserted, "We've heard people in focus groups talk about the fact that Charlton Heston says something on television and you believe it because it's Charlton Heston."[21]

Asner wanted to move the discussion and the philosophy that shaped SAG to a different level. Asner, who had played a cantankerous figure on *The Mary Tyler Moore Show* and the title character in its spinoff, *Lou Grant*, was determined to take SAG in a more activist and partisan direction. Ronald Brownstein termed Asner's approach "pugilistic liberalism," and labeled the entire matter a "muscular view of blue-collar solidarity" that appealed to those who wanted to put the organization into the mainstream of progressive unionism.[22] For Heston and similar-minded members, this approach represented an unmerited and unwise alteration in the focus of the leadership and the Guild itself, which threatened to shift the union's purpose away from advancing the interests of their acting peers by imposing divisive political positions onto the membership.

---

20 *CHA*, 227. Heston noted enviously that while in London for a play, he dined with Prime Minister Margret Thatcher, while Lydia sat next to Cary Grant. "That says it all," he observed; ibid.

21 Brownstein, *The Power and the Glitter*, 287-288.

22 *The Mary Tyler Moore Show* ran from 1970 to 1977 and *Lou Grant* from 1977 to 1982; IMDB; Brownstein, *The Power and the Glitter*, 288.

One aspect of this change in SAG priorities came in its support of the brief strike by and its condemnation of the August 1981 firing of members of the Professional Air Traffic Controllers Organization (PATCO). When SAG's information director, Kim Fellner, took the unprecedented step of alerting members that Ronald Reagan was the leading contender for a "Life Achievement" award and encouraging its executive committee to rebuff the choice of the awards committee as a message of solidarity with the air traffic controllers, she was subjected to internal criticism. Unfortunately, Fellner heightened the pressure by making the matter public.[23]

Externalizing the disagreement was the least of Heston's worries, as he expressed in a letter to Dean Santoro, a copy of which Santoro forwarded to President Reagan. Insisting that Santoro had been the sole individual among "dozens" who expressed themselves negatively to Heston's position, he noted, "You are distressed by my comments on the clumsy bungling of the SAG Award, and Kim Fellner's role in this. The incident was important only for the embarrassment it brought the Guild and what it revealed of Miss Fellner's concept of her responsibilities as an employee." Heston tried to deny any special interest before observing, "What does concern me, very deeply, is the metamorphosis of the SAG Board into an aggressively partisan political body, inserting itself into a variety of issues unrelated to the employment of actors." He insisted that he had no political agenda himself:

> For the record, I have never belonged to either political party, always voting as an independent. Perhaps this is one reason why it wasn't hard for me to maintain the Guild's historic non-partisan stance during my tenure as President. I think the radical change of direction undertaken by the current Board not only fails to reflect the wishes of the membership, but is grievously unresponsive to their needs. As such, it demands the fullest possible debate. That's why I've spoken out. I'm sorry you feel my action is inappropriate, but as a member you'll concede it's my right. As a former president, I think it's my duty.

He felt it was important that SAG leadership avoid the trap of venturing outside the traditional parameters. "It's very heady stuff to sit in a board room and debate world issues, to issue bulletins on national events, to endorse this candidate and oppose that one," Heston remarked, "but it's an indulgence our priorities cannot justify." Worse was the use of "hard-to-come-by dues" to provide "$5,000

---

23 Raymond, *Cold, Dead Hands*, 227-228.

to striking air controllers who make ten times what they do." SAG president Asner might claim that he "doesn't have all that much to do with" the board's actions, but Heston believed his colleague bore responsibility anyway by virtue of his position. "We have a right to expect our Board and our President to focus on the problems of actors, not air controllers," he closed, adding the salutation, "Fraternally."[24]

President Reagan had expressed himself on the matter to veteran actress Marie Windsor, who had served as director of SAG for 25 years and was a friend of Heston. In early 1982, both she and Heston communicated with Reagan to note their mutual concerns about the current state of the organization. The president replied that he had known little about what was going on "except Chuck Heston's letter." As the information she provided added to what he learned, he remarked, "Now I know a lot more about the whole affair." The former SAG official admitted, "Marie I've been upset by what's happened to our Guild for some time." The proudest part of SAG membership, Reagan observed, was its nonpartisan stance, "because we respected the fact that our members were not of one party or political persuasion." He recalled that in his time, before SAG representatives embarked on any negotiations they held "a little reminder session," which emphasized the objectives of pursuing what was "good for actors, fair to the other fellow and good for the industry." Reagan lamented that those days appeared to be over.[25]

President Reagan's and Heston's prior service with SAG in the same position that Asner held currently made the present involvement of the organization doubly annoying to both men. Reagan offered support to his friend. "I hope you know how much I valued your call," Heston noted in a lengthy message to the White House. "It meant a great deal to me, not only that you were aware of what I'd said, but that you'd take the time to communicate your approval." Noting that the bulk of the other messages he had received were also positive toward his stance, Heston added, "I'm trying to keep as much heat on the current SAG leadership as I can." The actor requested that the president not "bother to reply to this; keep your eye on the country instead," and cited Winston Churchill's soaring call during World War II, "Never give up," to his politician friend.[26]

---

24 "Charlton Heston to Dear Mr. Santoro, January 13, 1982," in "Presidential Telephone Calls (052000-061999)," WHORM Files, PR Public Relations, PR007-02, Box 2, RRPL.

25 "Ron to Dear Marie," Jan. 12, 1982, in Kiron K. Skinner, Annelise Anderson, and Martin Anderson, eds., *Reagan: A Life in Letters* (New York, 2003), 152-153.

26 "Chuck to Dear Mr. President," Jan. 18, 1982, WHORM Files, RRPL.

Not surprisingly, major news outlets such as the *New York Times* covered the dispute. The next day, the paper trumpeted the struggle over SAG leadership extensively. "It's the stuff that motion picture and television dramas are made of—Ben-Hur vs. Lou Grant—but the battle is not Hollywood make-believe," one such article began. Asner's assertion that he considered his personal positions distinguishable from those of the organization did not convince Heston, although the latter opposed a recall effort and vehemently condemned threats against the SAG president. "I would suggest that the serious professionals in the Screen Actors Guild would not want the guild to take positions on El Salvador or solar energy, but on acting," Heston insisted. The former SAG president thought Asner was "carelessly derelict in his responsibility" in giving the impression that he was speaking for the whole membership rather than himself.[27]

Additional coverage in *Newsweek* reflected the critical dichotomy. "A rally against Asner's union leadership in North Hollywood with Heston as keynote speaker attracted 250 upset guild members," the writer noted, "and claimed the support of prominent personalities such as Jimmy Stewart and Clint Eastwood." Another account noted that Heston had joined with "a few hundred stunt men, and an elite corps of actors" to stand against "the proposed merger of SAG with the 5,100-member Screen Extras Guild."[28]

Writer Pete Hamill provided his readership with a sense of Heston's importance in this clash of wills and policies. "Asner's critics have rallied round the figure of Charlton Heston," explaining that the latter was the "six-time former president of the union, [and] a big man in the American Film Institute." Hamill incorrectly noted that Heston "once walked a civil-rights picket line with Martin Luther King," but added accurately that he "ended up" supporting Republican presidential candidates Richard Nixon and Ronald Reagan.[29]

The war of words escalated between the opposing camps and their most prominent supporters into a contest widely labeled as "Star Wars." Asner described Heston as "Reagan's stooge" and referred to him as a "scumbag," to which the latter responded, "There are a lot of circles where you get hit in the mouth for that." Fortunately, the rhetoric marked the only aggressiveness, although Heston's

---

27 "Heston Awaits Asner's Reaction to Protest," *NYT*, Feb. 23, 1982; "Heston-Asner Struggle Is Splitting Entertainers," *NYT*, Feb. 24, 1982.

28 Mark Starr with Ron LaBrecque, "Asner the Activist," *Newsweek* (Mar. 8, 1982), 23; Pete Hamill, "What Does Lou Grant Know About El Salvador?" *New York Magazine* (Mar. 15, 1982), 25.

29 "What does Lou Grant know about El Salvador?"

descriptions were hardly decorous either, as when he observed that Asner wielded power "like some Mafia don." Robert Conrad joined in the criticism, but Heston remained the principal verbal pugilist. "I don't know him well," Heston insisted of Asner. "But he seems an extremely angry and short-tempered man." Calling him "enormously sensitive" toward those who disagreed with his position, Heston concluded of Asner, "That may be his personal style, but I suggest it will not serve the Guild well in the office he holds."[30]

Publicly, Heston professed not to care what causes Asner might as a private citizen endorse, but he was livid that observers should connect SAG itself with them. "I've been fielding calls" Heston explained, citing anger and confusion over Asner's inability, if not outright refusal, to "make it clear he wasn't speaking for the [Guild]." Both men thought better of their abilities to handle media coverage, if not actually shape it, than may have been possible. "Over time," Ronald Brownstein concluded, "these two men so proud of their skill at manipulating the media appeared trapped in the roles they had scripted for themselves." More significantly, according to Brownstein, "most sophisticated Hollywood observers" saw the "Asner-Heston struggle" as a "frightening parable of how the reduction of people into symbols—the very process that at a fundamental level provided stars with their political platform—exaggerated and polarized political conflict."[31]

At about the same time, President Reagan reiterated his angst to Marie Windsor "about what's happening to our Guild." He professed that attacks on him had not phased him. "I don't mind being a target for loud mouth Asner personally, but I sure do resent what he's doing to an organization we all put a lot into, including love and loyalty." If SAG had once been a "force for good in the motion picture industry," he was not certain that this was the case any longer.[32]

In his defense, Asner suggested that his SAG colleague's engagement might be attributable more to advancing Heston's career than revealing his positions on the issues. "On one level," he observed, "this is a wonderful way to drum up interest in the name Charlton Heston for a movie that he has coming out." Asner did not indicate which project the effort was supposed to benefit, but added, "It's a drumroll for Heston to acquire new friends, new partisans."[33]

30 Brownstein, *The Power and the Glitter*, 285, 291; Mark Starr, with Ron LaBrecque, Martin Kasindorf, and Janet Huck, "Ed Asner's Star Wars," *Newsweek* (Mar. 22, 1982), 90.

31 Raymond, *Cold, Dead Hands*, 230-231; Brownstein, *The Power and the Glitter*, 291-292.

32 "Ron to Dear Marie," Mar. 11, 1982, in *Reagan: A Life in Letters*, 153.

33 Hamill, "What Does Lou Grant Know About El Salvador?", 25.

Charlton Heston knew that even with the high profile of his "public face," and the assistance of other prominent figures in the industry, the best way to fight would be to organize as well. Consequently, he and several associates created Actors Working for an Actors Guild (AWAG) to counteract Asner's position in SAG. The group emerged from disgruntled conservative SAG members and was not intended to be mere showmanship, but to engage actively in order to obtain real results. Heston served as one of the designated spokespersons. On June 13, 1982, an official meeting located symbolically at the same venue at which SAG had been formed brought together key figures, who then made their intentions clear in the press.[34]

This battle between the performing stars and their associates reflected the powerful juxtaposition that marked the intersection of art and politics. "Both men treasured their ability to focus the media on their causes," Ronald Brownstein explained. They were certain that whether appropriately or not, they could and should command the necessary public attention to make their points. Civilized discourse became the first casualty. Actor John Forsythe, who had connections to both antagonists, noted glumly, "With the heightened visibility of everybody, there comes a heightened antagonism in confrontations. The Asner-Heston thing is a perfect example. God, they abused each other terribly."[35]

Despite the battle that was unfolding in full view, Heston remained convinced that good work could still be done on important issues. A powerful intersection of cinematic history and public advocacy occurred in the summer of 1982 when Heston appeared in a Senate hearing room in Washington to seek Congressional assistance for motion picture performers. Jack Valenti, president of the Motion Picture Association of America, wanted a royalty for sales of videocassette recorders and the raw tapes that consumers could feed into them to add to Hollywood coffers. As one scholar wrote, "His lead warrior and prime witness was none other than Charlton Heston." Howard Kurtz of the *Washington Post* drew the comparison with the headline "Chariot for Hire," and offered readers an image of the star from *Ben-Hur*'s iconic race. "At the witness table sits the star of the occasion, and for a change in Washington it is a real star: Charlton Heston," he explained, "whose roles in 'Ben-Hur' and 'The Ten Commandments' prepared him well for this assignment. Now he is a front man in the Ben-Hur of Washington lobbying extravaganzas." Ironies reigned supreme as Heston criticized Japanese control of

34 Raymond, *Cold, Dead Hands*, 232-233; Prindle, *The Politics of Glamour*, 150-151.

35 Brownstein, *The Power and the Glitter*, 291-292.

the American market, when *Ben-Hur* had been among the top-grossing films in Japan and its star remained popular with Japanese audiences.[36]

While he carried out his Washington chores for the industry, Heston also made time to travel to India to participate in a film "on the problems of providing relief for refugees," according to one wire report. Even in India, Heston was unable to escape the pervasive questions on his own interests in emulating President Reagan and running for political office. Once more deploying his argument that he had already been president "three times," he informed a gathering in New Delhi that his SAG leadership was "enough" for him.[37]

Elsewhere, the actor and his impressive body of work were enjoying special forms of recognition, further enhancing his public standing. The Deauville American Film Festival in France featured ten of Heston's films, and he planned to make an appearance. He was then scheduled to continue to Paris, where, by one account, he would attend "the unveiling of his likeness at the wax museum, Musée Grevin."[38]

Happily, these travels were not all Charlton Heston looked forward to experiencing. Fraser had pitched one possible project to his father, with an intriguing twist: he wanted him to play twins, at least one of which had homicidal tendencies. The elder Heston was required to tackle a complex dual role in *Mother Lode* by portraying a poacher who menaced Kim Basinger and Nick Mancuso as they searched for a lost friend. In addition, Heston directed the picture. The filming offered challenges of its own, including a lack of chemistry between two of the principal actors. Heston described his efforts to bring the scenes off in the framework of the personal antagonism between Basinger and Mancuso. "I cleared the set—the only time I have ever done that as a director—and threw everybody out." Then, he explained to Basinger that she would have to collect herself and proceed, regardless of her personal feelings for her co-star: "They call it acting."[39]

Promoting the film as he had done so often and so effectively for other rollouts over a long career gave the actor an additional audience to enthrall. Biographer Michael Munn watched Heston work his magic in London and enjoyed the opportunity to meet the rest of his family. "A press conference was arranged

---

36 Solomon, *Ben-Hur*, 788, 789, 830. For the actor's personal appeal in Japan and his assessment of it, see *CHA*, 229, 300-301.

37 Ben Welter, "Heston says he'll stay out of politics," *VP*, July 4, 1982.

38 "Honors ahead," *RTD*, Aug. 13, 1982.

39 Heston and Isbouts, *Hollywood*, 175.

for their arrival which was where I got to meet them all and discover just how differently Heston performs for a crowd of journalists as opposed to one. He seemed to thoroughly enjoy himself, moving from one group of interviewers to another." Indeed, when Fraser tried to hurry his father along, the elder Heston demurred in order to convey the rest of a story about Vanessa Redgrave. "But Fray could see that his dad was tired, as I had noticed too." Yet if Heston's indomitable energy had new limits that came with age, Munn noted, "I think, however, he was more tired than old." Then, the writer unwittingly revealed the secret to the actor's appeal: "He performed magnificently, just for us."[40]

Back in Hollywood, Asner continued to take a dim view of the Reagan administration's policies regarding anti-Communist positions in regard to Central America. Heston would have found little to quarrel with the basic premise emanating from the White House, which insisted that the "Contras" who opposed the Sandinista regime of Daniel Ortega in Nicaragua were equivalent to "the freedom fighters who led the American Revolution." Stark versions of good versus evil always played better than the nuanced realities of shading. Indeed, Heston forwarded his support for President Reagan's speech before a joint session of Congress on the matter, calling it "superb" and arguing that the message "addressed eloquently one of the major issues facing the West." The actor remained enthralled by Reagan's communication skills. "Of course it goes without saying (but I'll say it anyway), your delivery was masterful. I can't wait to see you debate [Walter] Mondale, (or [Gary] Hart, or [Alan] Cranston, or whoever. Would that it could be [Ted] Kennedy!) Congratulations . . . and thanks."[41]

In reply, Reagan wrote, "Just a line (somewhat tardy) to thank you for your letter and kind words. I'm most grateful. The battle goes on and there will be a struggle to win approval in the House of any meaningful help in Central America." As far as the president was concerned, the issue reflected the inability of some to be able to identify a "a threat from the left," rather than only those "from the right and you don't have to be very far right." Of course, Reagan knew he had no need to worry about his friend, who recognized the threats as he wished them to be understood. Brownstein observed that Heston, whose career was "slowing somewhat anyway in its later stages, suffered no apparent damage" from his struggle with Asner and his

---

40 Munn, *Charlton Heston*, 199-200.

41 Reagan, *An American Life*, 477; "Chuck to Dear Mr. President," Apr. 28, 1983, SP283-22, 133557-141177, WHORM Files, SP-Speeches, Box 82, RRPL.

allies, although he appeared to be defending conservative ground in such a public fashion as a singular yet "effective" conservative voice in Hollywood.[42]

As was his wont, Heston did not wait for government action to accomplish what he thought was necessary. He became a board member for a private initiative called the "Nicaraguan Freedom Fund," headed by former Secretary of the Treasury William Simon. The group, which had raised significant funds, sent a first installment of $50,000 to assist the Contras and prepared to make additional disbursements pending Congressional legislation.[43]

Charlton Heston was taking on public debates in ever-increasing amounts. Public calls for a nuclear arms freeze ensured that Ed Asner was not the only acting colleague with whom he would collide on issues he deemed important. Paul Newman was anxious to make his voice heard on the matter, and Heston's differing position meant that he would do the same on the opposite side of the equation. The two men had worked together during the civil rights movement, but any sense of that camaraderie dissipated quickly and decisively under the blistering engagement over California's Proposition 12.

As was so often the case, Heston considered the issue more than a passing fad or a harmless affectation; an attempt to freeze nuclear weapons would, in his opinion, only make America more vulnerable. He derided those who spoke on the matter as a "gut" issue. "You don't decide important questions with your guts, you do it with your mind. And you can only use your mind if you inform it." Heston felt so passionately about the question that he brought writers and reporters to his Coldwater Canyon home for a press conference. "We have what seems like unfair access to a public forum. Nonetheless, we have that access," he reminded them. Then, he concluded of his fellow performer, "Paul is a good man and a good actor, but if he is going to speak out, he has a responsibility to check the facts first." Heston understood the obvious. "There are any number of people far more qualified to speak out on this issue. But when the headline begins 'Paul Newman' or 'Chuck Heston,' it gets more space."[44]

---

42 "Ron to Dear Chuck," May 10, 1983, ibid. Brownstein noted that Asner, at least, believed the controversy had impacted his career adversely, at least on the short term; see *The Power and the Glitter*, 292.

43 "Freedom Fund may fold if contra aid is approved," *AC*, June 16, 1985.

44 Chase, "Between Scenes with Charlton Heston," 44; Lee Dembart, "Heston, in Political Role, Hits Newman's Pro-Freeze Stance," *LAT*, Oct. 15, 1982. See also "Heston Nuclear Freeze Press Conference," UCLA Media.

Prepared to expend considerable personal capital, the actor embarked on what amounted to a crusade, complete with television commercials and appearances to state his case, including time on the Christian Broadcasting Network's *The 700 Club* with conservative host Pat Robertson and Sen. Strom Thurmond. Heston answered public calls by Newman for a bilateral freeze with the Soviet Union by insisting, equally publicly, that such an arrangement could not work because the other party to it could not be trusted. On ABC's news program *The Last Word*, the two stars renewed their fervent discussion. One scholar labeled the program "one of the strangest media events of the decade" and argued that the "bizarre" Heston-Newman confrontation left puzzled observers "temporarily wondering whether the trend toward the use of stars as mouthpieces for complex issues had gone too far."[45]

With a little time for perspective, Heston felt the situation that had developed between the men was regrettable. "Although Paul and I have never been close," he told an interviewer, "I've always respected him. He's a Democrat. I'm an Independent." Yet he liked Newman's work and considered their earlier interactions "amicable." In the aftermath of the public encounters, Heston professed himself to be "shocked when I went in to do the debate and he wouldn't shake hands with me." Indeed, brushing off a pleasantry, Newman remarked, "I hate this personal shit you've been doing." With respect to his position on such critical issues, Heston insisted that he remained "hurt" that Newman "would take personal offense at that."[46]

As with the Asner-Heston *contretemps*, critics found the use of celebrities on either side of such public issues fascinating. Howard Rosenberg labeled the latest square off first as "Moses" against "Butch Cassidy," and then as "the Bible" versus "Cool Hand Luke." The writer denigrated this departure from the professional arena for both antagonists. "I'm not doubting the sincerity of either actor," Rosenberg explained, although he thought Newman "the better actor" and Heston "the better debater." For him, "The problem with professional performers is that they tend to perform." Yet he also viewed the significance of the phenomenon as running more deeply than it appeared. "The deification of Heston and Newman as spokesmen on the nuclear issue seems almost a natural outgrowth of TV's merging of news and entertainment." Rosenberg concluded, "We place enormous faith and trust in celebrities because of the camera personae they always carry with them. Too much faith and trust." The fact remained that the insertion of celebrities into

45 Raymond, *Cold, Dead Hands*, 220-221; Brownstein, *The Power and the Glitter*, 285.

46 David Resin, "20 Questions: Charlton Heston," *Playboy* (May 1983), 139.

any discussion brought public awareness that might not otherwise exist, or at least to the extent that it did. According to Ronald Brownstein, "Stars were essential for both raising money and attracting attention."[47]

Heston was under no illusions that his willingness to speak out, his ability to garner attention, and the soundness of his arguments and positions would change the world he inhabited personally and professionally. "The Hollywood community is probably as liberal as any community outside the university faculty. I certainly wasn't able to change that. Nor did I imagine it was a doable thing." Yet he believed it was critical to express himself as a concerned citizen, and he assumed a stance that he considered straightforward. "We live—God knows we always have—in an infinitely dangerous world. We'll never get out of it alive. But while we're here, surely reason must tell us to put the infinite treasure of the peace of the world in the hands of those we trust, not those we fear." The Soviet Union would only respond to strength if the United States was prepared to demonstrate it, much as it had done at the end of the Second World War. "I, too, was scheduled as part of the Eleventh Air Force, to take part in Operation Coronet," he replied to a question on the matter, with substantial casualties projected for both sides in a potential invasion of the home islands of Japan. In his view, ending the war as speedily as possible was the only sane measure. "Whether we did it by destroying Hiroshima or could have done it by a demonstration over Tokyo, unquestionably the atomic bomb ended World War II. And I am bloody glad it did." The actor liked to cite a Churchill story from 1934, when the British leader was asked why he was so adamant about convincing his people that Adolf Hitler was a dangerous man. "If I do not succeed, madam," he noted Churchill as explaining, "I'm afraid you will find out."[48]

Author Emilie Raymond insisted that Heston's development of a "new persona" starting in the late 1970s represented an effort on his part to "strengthen the steadily growing Right." Yet if the actor felt "useless and ideologically outcast," he was casting about less for firm political ground on which to stand than for an audience to hear his messages and help him maintain his artistic viability.[49] The same individual who could talk comfortably before *700 Club* viewers could also

---

47 Howard Rosenberg, "Nuclear Policy a Bomb in the Hands of Actors," *LAT*, Nov. 2, 1982; Brownstein, *The Power and the Glitter*, 285.

48 Brownstein, *The Power and the Glitter*, 292; "The Nuclear Arms Freeze. Proceedings of a Roundtable Discussion February 14, 1983," Strom Thurmond Institute, Heston Papers, f.482, HL.

49 Raymond, *Cold, Dead Hands*, 201, 203, 211.

tout the heritage of brewing beer for Anheuser-Busch and advocate environmental awareness and sensitivity for the forestry service.

Heston's public service led him to engage in other controversies from which he could not entirely detach his opinions or himself. As an observer for the State Department at the UNESCO World Conference on Cultural Affairs in Mexico City, the actor found an unfriendly atmosphere regarding American film. He attempted to deflect the matter by insisting that politicians should not interfere with the arts.[50]

Heston took on a new challenge that had public utility and personal fulfillment. *When Will the Dying Stop?* brought the story of relief for destitute regions to documentary viewers. Lydia lent her photographic expertise to the project as teams ventured to Thailand, Mali, and Bangladesh to record efforts being undertaken by a humanitarian group called "World Relief." "As we traveled in Africa and Asia with the film crew," Heston explained, "and saw how this organization is bringing permanent self-sufficiency to people who formerly had no hope at all, we grew passionately committed to the work of World Relief." Most significantly, awareness brought satisfaction; "It became for us a very personal project."[51]

In the meantime, Heston continued to work diligently at reminding potential viewers of his professional career by delving in personal matters. In May 1983, he submitted answers to the "20 Questions" feature of the men's magazine *Playboy*. Buttressed by a photograph of the actor in his preferred attire—tennis shirt and sweatbands—while spreading Skippy Super Peanut Butter lavishly on a slice of bread, the actor clearly hoped to bring a degree of his personality to the readership. Contributing editor David Resin traveled to the Coldwater Canyon home to pose his queries and began with the actor's reaction to media coverage. "I've taken fairly exposed positions for some time now, back to the civil rights days. But I have never felt myself terribly ill used by journalists," Heston responded. He realized that expressing himself openly on subjects of importance, while possibly beneficial, required him to develop a thick skin. "If you can't handle it so that it comes out reasonably supportive, then it's your fault."[52]

The interview allowed another glimpse into the actor's approach to his public persona. When asked how he compared himself to Robert De Niro, for whom

---

50 Crowther, *Epic Presence*, 161.

51 "Heston special on WJKW-TV8 shows World Relief in action," *TV Sun Stations* (Cleveland, Jan. 20-26, 1983), inside cover.

52 David Resin, "20 Questions: Charlton Heston," *Playboy* (May 1983), 139.

he had expressed admiration, Heston responded candidly. "There are parts I can play that De Niro couldn't. And vice versa. But acting is not competition." For Heston, the motivation continued to be striving toward perfection in every role he undertook. "Every actor should set standards for himself that are higher than those anyone else will set."

As for Heston's physical attributes, Resin maintained, "You probably have the major franchise on presence." But then Resin inquired if he felt any of that stature "slipping away" as he grew older? "Well, obviously, it happens as you age," the fifty-nine-year-old actor replied. "I suppose that up to a certain point, the face I have improves with age." Then, noting his daughter's recent comment on his physical attractiveness in earlier times in one of his films, he added, "I laughed of course. But my face is, perhaps, more useful now than it was 30 years ago."[53]

Work may have been slowing from the pace he had set during his prime years, but Heston had another chance to play a prominent figure in *Chiefs*, a miniseries set in a fictional town in the deep South. He touted his return to television as being possible because the miniseries format meant the limits of a typical show would not be in effect. "What attracted me to this was I realized that with the long-form—I'm not comfortable with the term miniseries, because it sounds like little teeny-weeny actors in teeny-weeny sets—you get to do something you can't do in a theatrical movie and you can't do on the stage, and that is to tell a story that takes more than three or four hours." Heston was also drawn to *Chiefs* because of the ways in which his character, Hugh Holmes, reminded him of the uncle he had lived with briefly and visited in Georgia during his youth. "My memories of him were very valuable to me in this role," he explained.[54]

Heston, who played the part of a leading citizen of the community, did not depend upon his memories of the brief time he had spent in Georgia to develop his accent for the part. As he had done with Robert Easton when acting required accents, he turned to individuals who could help with regional variations. Subsequently, some reviewers derided the effort, with one witty critic remarking, "Let's just say it's a good thing Heston never tackled 'Cat on a Hot Tin Roof.'" Another writer with the same paper, however, noted that the actor had employed recordings of Georgian James S. Peters, supplied by author Stuart Woods, in order to obtain the proper intonation. "While Woods insists that Heston has captured

---

53 Ibid., 206.

54 Bill King, "*Chiefs*: An Unusual Portrayal of the South and an Unusual Role for Heston," *AJC*, Nov. 11, 1983, 4-5.

Peters' diction," columnist Frederick Allen explained, "men of good will can easily disagree." Still, Allen applauded the effort, noting, "to the extent that Charlton Heston as an actor always speaks with the authority of a born leader of good conscience, he has captured the essence of Mr. Jim."[55]

While filming for the "long-form" drama in South Carolina, Heston's mother Lilla visited the set to watch the process unfold. Observing that she "just likes movie sets," the performer explained, "She sits in my chair in the corner and seems very content." He did not mind her presence and insisted, "It's very supportive," then added, "It's nice to have your mommy there. You know she's going to like what you do."[56]

Heston continued his publicity blitz for the miniseries with an interview for *TV Guide*, although its audience was not always a receptive one. A thinly disguised scoffing piece "from the *Chiefs* set" carrying the unusual title, "Thou Shalt Not Whine," appeared to be constructed with Heston's public rifts with Ed Asner and Paul Newman in mind. Writer Joyce Wadler insisted that "Charlton Heston doesn't whine." Tapping into his epic film persona, she maintained, "Heston wringing his hands publicly would be like Ben-Hur whining that the Romans were not equal-opportunity employers." The actor deflected Wadler's barb by taking the broader view: "I think one of the worst flaws of modern society is the reluctance to take responsibility for your own life." For him, these choices were his to accept. "No actor is universally admired for a given part." Then, with another glancing shot at his recent antagonist, he added, "To say, 'Why didn't I get this part, I really wanted that part' . . . that sounds like Ed Asner when they canceled his TV show." Still, Wadler observed, even if Heston had no television program to be canceled himself, the actor might feel justified in expressing remorse. "Of late the crown has slipped" she argued, noting *Time* magazine's description of him as "a tired act" and one of his recent pictures as "a tired movie." The writer found the actor imperious, sitting between takes in his own handmade and elaborate leather chair, built for him to direct *Antony and Cleopatra*. "It's a lotta chair," she explains. "Likewise, Heston is a lotta actor." In her assessment, even as he avoided the "psychobabble" of many of his current colleagues, "Heston has his own conversational tic: Actor Babble." The face and voice continued to sustain the aura of authority and his return to television, and what he preferred to call "the long form" provided him with the

---

55 John Carmen, "'Chiefs' dodges locale identity," *AC*, Nov. 11, 1983; Frederick Allen, "Mr. Heston, Mr. Jim, and Georgia's schools," *AC*, Nov. 15, 1983.

56 "Heston's mother visits set," *AC*, Oct. 12, 1983.

work and the creative freedom he desired. The writer asked, "Is there anyone out there missing the fact that this guy is dead serious about his work?"

Heston's *Chiefs* costars reached the same initial impression as they watched and interacted with him on the sets and locations. Paul Sorvino thought his colleague exhibited "the impression of being formal to the point of difficulty," but then "saw a lighter side that suggested more." Both he and co-star Stephen Collins found Heston accessible. "Because he does have this image as Moses," Collins explained, "he did seem stiffer in person. But when he felt relaxed and let his guard down, he could spin wonderful stories." Wadler seemed annoyed at what she termed Heston's often "pedantic tone," perhaps as much out of frustration for not finding "a chink in the armor" she could exploit. Even so, there was a grudging admiration. "Not that on the set he is ever the spoiled superstar. He is in control."[57]

Heston returned to Georgia in October 1983 to attend the Atlanta premiere of the astronaut picture *The Right Stuff*. He had not appeared in the production but admired the type of fortitude that had sent Americans into space. The American Film Institute sponsored the event, along with two other premieres in Washington and Chicago, with Heston's appearance coming in his capacity as the AFI's chairman. The evening also provided an opportunity for media mogul Ted Turner to introduce Heston with a local twist. "It's one thing to play the Dodgers," he drawled, referencing his Atlanta Braves. "It's another to stand next to Moses."[58]

Heston continued to demonstrate interest in the public causes that had meaning to him. A life-long advocate of responsible gun ownership, the actor, hunter, and sportsman had briefly sided with attempts by the Johnson administration at gun control in the wake of the assassination of President Kennedy. His views on the matter were hardly rigid, however, particularly when it came to draconian measures that threatened legitimate owners' rights. Such an effort appeared in California, as he saw it, in the form of Proposition 15, which called for registration of firearms; the banning of sales after April 1983 except to replace previously registered guns; a ban on such weapons for new arrivals to the state; and a mandatory six-month sentence for anyone convicted of carrying an unregistered concealed handgun. Heston and popular cowboy star Roy Rogers took strong positions against the measure, prompting one wag to say the two were performing "a sort of 'Praise the

57 Joyce Wadler, "Thou Shalt Not Whine," *TV Guide* (Nov. 12, 1983), 35-36, 38, 39. Heston said he borrowed the application "long form" from British expressions for the style, believing the more dignified term was "surely the proper usage," while disdaining "miniseries" as "tacky and silly," and adding dismissively, "I don't like it." Ibid., 38.

58 Paula Crouch, "2,500 See 'Right Stuff' Lift Off Here," *AC*, Oct. 18, 1983; "Cheers Ring Out for a Local Guy," *AC*, Oct. 19, 1983.

Lord and pass the ammunition' number." The same writer observed the mixed results of at least part of the endeavor. "Charlton Heston taped a 28-minute commercial against Prop 15 last month, but then the campaign had trouble finding stations willing to sell such a long segment of air time." More importantly to his future endeavors, it was during this period that Heston also became associated with Wayne LaPierre of the National Rifle Association.[59]

Advocating for protecting responsible gun ownership was not the only matter that allowed the actor to combine personal and public interest. The melding of his passion for cars and public service caused Heston to make a statement in support of conservation through the donation of a specialized Corvette to benefit the Solar Lobby in Washington. He hoped to draw attention to the use of renewable energy resources. The organization indicated that it planned to make the vehicle available "for public education events to show how alternative fuels can be used." A press release on the event stated that "Heston, a strong advocate of alternative energy, converted his Corvette to methanol in 1981." This endeavor tapped into his concerns for the nation's energy vulnerabilities, and he saw it as a tangible way to bring attention to the need for "lifting American dependence on oil, which he feels has eroded our country's security."[60]

Heston also harbored a long-standing concern for the people who endured the dangers of military postings abroad. He had traveled twice to Vietnam, venturing to distant outposts rather than contenting himself with viewing actions from safer venues. In volatile, civil war-ridden Beirut, Lebanon, after explosions decimated the Marine barracks on October 23, 1983, killing 241 American and 58 French personnel, Heston chose to visit the location in person to support the troops and their peacekeeping mission. He arrived for New Year's Eve and began to mingle with many of the 1,200 men stationed in the region. According to a Marine Corps spokesperson, "He came because he wanted to come. It was all set up in 48 hours." Major Dennis Brooks noted, "Three days ago most of the kids here hadn't even heard of Heston. Now there isn't one Marine who doesn't know him." The actor signed autographs and tried to lighten the mood with quips about his role as Moses, demonstrating an element his Marine hosts had not expected. Brooks labeled him a "very funny man despite all the dramatic roles he played in the movies." The most sobering moment came at a wreath-laying ceremony for the victims of the bombing. That his visit had achieved its chief purpose became clear

59 "California's Gun Battle," *Newsweek*, Nov. 1, 1982, 98; Eliot, *Charlton Heston*, 421.

60 "Charlton Heston Presents the Methanol Car," Oct. 18, 1983, "Solar Lobby," Heston Papers, f.480, HL; "Charlton Heston Dramatizes Need for Renewable Energy," Oct. 18, 1983, ibid.

with an assessment that "He's done an awful lot to boost morale." Heston could not have wanted a better outcome from what had proven to be a very receptive audience.[61]

His appearance in the Beirut war zone garnered widespread attention. A wire report account at the beginning of the new year noted that while visiting the troops, Heston "spent the night on a U.S. 6th Fleet warship offshore, [and] signed autographs before leaving." Heston wanted these service personnel to know they had not been forgotten while deployed in difficult and dangerous circumstances away from their homes and families, especially during the holiday season.[62]

As his visit to Lebanon demonstrated, Charlton Heston was used to employing his "public face" for causes he championed. Another issue involved indications that, although the Vietnam War had ended, possibly as many as twenty-five hundred Americans remained behind in Southeast Asia. The actor felt an affinity for these missing service members and their families. During the conflict itself, Heston had gathered notes and personal communications to bring family members when he returned to the United States. He had visited the wounded in hospitals and marveled at the sacrifice these soldiers were willing to make. He had worn a bracelet of support, as did many other sympathetic Americans. Now, the possibility that some of them, perhaps a significant number, were unaccounted for, motivated him to become involved once more.

Along with former U.S. Congressman John LeBoutillier, he solicited support for the "Skyhook II Project." In a personal appeal included in the print campaign, the actor explained, "Many of our men were held behind, and they're still held there to this day. Locked in bamboo cages in the jungles, in caves in the mountains, some of our men are used as slaves, forced to drag plows in rice paddies. . . . Well, I can't forget them. I hope you can't either. In fact, America can't forget these men. We have to try to bring them home, all of them." Convinced of the veracity of such reports, he maintained, "They're ours, and they're heroes, real heroes." With enough contributions, the resources dedicated to this mission might mean finally bringing them back home. Clearly, LeBoutillier thought "the active support of Charlton Heston" could make a difference.[63]

---

61 Heston in Beirut,
www.upi.com/Archives/1984/01/01/Charlton-Heston-visits-Marines-in-Beirut/7493441781200/.

62 "Blasts open year in Lebanon," *AC*, Jan. 2, 1984.

63 "Dear Fellow Citizen" from John LeBoutillier, with "An urgent message for you from Charlton Heston," Skyhook II Project," n.d., Wills. See also Michael J. Allen, *Until the Last Man Comes Home:*

The reputation Heston had earned in his iconic films ensured that he still got attention in important circles. As Jack Valenti noted in an appearance before a Congressional hearing to discuss copyright laws, the actor's presence meant that even popular lawmakers took notice. On this occasion, one organizer noted, "We had 40 members of Congress lined up to get their pictures taken with Charlton Heston. It was like Moses was in the hall."[64]

Heston's work continued to resonate on the small screen with impressive numbers for audience share and the viewership this represented. In April 1984, *USA Today* placed a short piece entitled "It's the 8th 'Commandment'" in connection with the eighth television broadcast of *The Ten Commandments* "since its 1973 debut." Spikes of a 40-or-over share four times during the period indicated respectable viewership in the other years, including twice when the film was aired in two parts.[65] Heston's staying power as Moses had received important support from both returning audiences and new ones that emerged over that decade of the movie's annual appearance on television.

Though his screen confrontations with Pharaoh remained, Heston's public tiff with Ed Asner finally subsided. "Our delegation was received with great courtesy and we all shook hands," Heston observed of the effort to arrange "peace talks" between the factions of competing SAG interests. "But," he added, "that's about all." Still, the "truce on name-calling" represented an improvement over the language that had so frequently characterized their prior exchanges, which brought no credit to either side.[66]

The presidential election of 1984 also meant that public attentions would shift to new battle grounds. Once more, Heston planned to hit the road in order to provide his "face" in the effort to elect Republican candidates. President Reagan joined Heston and singer/actor Pat Boone in an appearance in Peoria, Illinois. One newspaper quipped that "Charlton Heston is making waves again—instead of parting them," one newspaper writer quipped, citing the actor's television work for Sen. Jesse Helms of North Carolina. This race provided a heated contest and

POWs, MIAs, and the Unending Vietnam War (Chapel Hill, 2009), 57, 246. According to the Defense POW/MIA Accounting Agency, as of October 14, 2020: "Of the 1,996 firsthand reports received since 1975, 1,941 (97.24%) reports are resolved." Vietnam-Era Statistical Report, www.dpaa.mil/Portals/85/Statistics%20as%20of%20October%2014.pdf.

64 "Arts lobby mixes show biz and politics," *AC*, June 10, 1984.

65 "It's the 8th 'Commandment,'" *USA Today*, Apr. 13, 1984.

66 "Calling halt to name-calling," *AJC*, May 28, 1984.

ample room for celebrity endorsements on both sides as Gov. Jim Hunt took on Helms. In addition to Heston, the incumbent's supporters included the fictional sheriff of Mayberry Andy Griffith.[67]

In August, Heston delivered the Pledge of Allegiance at the Republican National Convention in Dallas prior to Wayne Newton's performance of "The Star-Spangled Banner" and Rev. Jerry Falwell's benediction. The highlight of the evening consisted of a tribute to Nancy Reagan, an appearance by Sen. Barry Goldwater, and the roll call of the states for their nominees.[68] Goldwater's inclusion in the process appealed to the conservative wing of the party; according to Heston, it also underscored the focus that reflected the shift in his political thinking and allegiance.

The actor insisted late in his political journey that while traveling on a California roadway from a *War Lord* location shoot, the slow pace of traffic caused him to pay closer attention to a billboard advertising Goldwater's slogan for his 1964 campaign against Lyndon Johnson: "IN YOUR HEART YOU KNOW HE'S RIGHT." The catchy phrase did not seem to reflect Heston's connections to the Johnson administration or his earlier support for national Democrats from Adlai Stevenson to John F. Kennedy. Yet as he remembered the transformative moment, while stopped at an intersection, he claimed he suddenly realized that Goldwater's assertion was valid for him, too. "As we waited, I experienced a true revelation, almost an epiphany, like St. Paul on the road to Damascus," he insisted. Focusing on Heston's later assertion, writer Ed Leibowitz labelled the conversion tale "[t]oo mythic to be true." Biographer Marc Eliot termed the recollection "interesting, obviously apocryphal, but effective." Perhaps Heston would have been better served by remembering what he maintained was the salient feature of his journals when he published selections of them: "It's not always the way you remember it was."[69]

Heston had enjoyed his earliest interactions at Republican events and rallies. One writer noted that as an "avowed independent, he likes to tell audiences at party fundraisers: 'I'm the only one who's not a Republican in the room.'" When the listeners booed in response, he quickly and mischievously added in reference

67 Brinkley, ed., *Reagan Diaries*, 107; "Heston making waves," *AC*, July 18, 1984; William A. Link, *Righteous Warrior: Jesse Helms and the Rise of Modern Conservatism* (New York, 2008), 298.

68 "Wednesday's schedule," *AC*, Aug. 22, 1984.

69 *CHA*, 353-354; Ed Leibowitz, "Charlton Heston's Last Stand," *Los Angeles*, 148; Eliot, *Charlton Heston*, 259; *ALJ*, xi.

to their shared work for the Screen Actors Guild, "But I voted for Ronald Reagan before you could." At the same time, Heston speculated that he "was one of the first Hollywood stars to have become actively involved in politics."[70]

By the 1980s, Charlton Heston's shift in political affiliation was complete. News features during the 1984 election cycle noted the presence of Hollywood figures on both sides of the spectrum, with Heston joining Frank Sinatra, Jimmy Stewart, Helen Hayes, Dorothy Lamour, Dean Martin, Cary Grant, Mickey Rooney, Bob Hope, and Arnold Schwarzenegger to support the Reagan-Bush ticket. Campaigning as often as his extensive travel and commitments permitted, Heston once more earned the "heartfelt" appreciation of the president and first lady. "I know something of the schedule you've been keeping on my behalf," Reagan noted at the end of October, "and just want you to know I'm more grateful than I can say." The president felt renewed by the reception he had gotten, particularly from young audiences. "I've been on several campuses these past few days and can't get over the enthusiasm of young America. They are so gung-ho I get a lump in my throat. They are a far cry from those flag burners in the '60s."[71]

Heston's efforts on behalf of Reagan and other candidates for higher office also represented a shift in his thinking. In the latter part of the 1960s he had asserted, "I think actors have both the right and the responsibility to function as conscientious citizens." For him, this meant, "If the state department asks you to go to Nigeria, for instance, personally I feel a responsibility to go." His sense of civic obligation did not go much past that point, however. "But I think an actor's role in public life is most usually looked on as a responsibility to turn out in support of political candidates he admires. And this I believe is the *least* important part of his role as a conscientious citizen. . . . In fact, I take a rather dim view of this myself." He did not think it was in the performer's best interests "because it reduces the actor to a sort of dress-extra. And secondly, because the undue dimensions and the unrealistic public images of the actor give a disproportionate weight to any political endorsement he might make." Still, Heston did not advocate avoiding the duties of citizenship as he identified them. "I don't mean that an actor has no right to support the candidate of his choice but I don't believe he should make public endorsements or actively campaign for anyone," he explained. For actors who were better known than the candidates they supported, this concern was particularly

70 Julianne Hastings, "Do two roles make Heston a born-again TV star?" *AJC*, Oct. 13, 1984.

71 "Celebrities of Tinsel City light up for political favorites," *AC*, Nov. 1, 1984; "Ron to Dear Chuck, Circa October 26, 1984," in Skinner, Anderson, and Anderson, eds., *Reagan: A Life in Letters*, 562.

manifest. "They know they can influence votes. But I don't believe this is part of their responsibility as citizens."[72]

In this new, more politically active era, the degree to which these high-profile personalities translated their support into votes for their respective candidates was impossible to measure. Republican Buddy Ebsen observed, "An actor or a public figure cannot deliver votes." A spokesperson for the campaign of Democrat Walter Mondale maintained, "A celebrity endorsement doesn't bring votes with it, but there certainly is an attraction."[73] Few persons knew better than Charlton Heston about the effect a star could have in drawing crowds and generating enthusiasm, and he was willing to do what he could to serve in that role for candidates like Ronald Reagan and George H. W. Bush.

Heston continued to balk at any temptation to go beyond this type of political activity himself. When Reagan ran for re-election, the opportunity to see the incumbent on the campaign trail once more left Heston marveling at his friend's stamina. As a close acquaintance of both "Ronnie" and Nancy Reagan—"I've known Nancy longer than *he* has"—Heston had close access during the 1984 campaign, including a flight aboard Air Force One. Noting that Reagan "feeds" on "politics," Heston was reminded why he would not be following the president's example in running for public office. "I think I decided not to go for it that day on Air Force One," Heston remarked of a possible U.S. Senate run of his own. "I looked at the President and thought: I don't have it in my belly, the fire there." Where Reagan seemed to grow stronger, Heston could detect for himself only weaker moments. "I get tired. I do publicity tours and get pretty damn exhausted." The comparison caused him to admit, to himself as much as to anyone else, "If I had to do that in politics, I'd think: God, I'd rather be playing Shakespeare somewhere."

Even as he grappled with renewed interest in his potential candidacy for elective office, Charlton Heston seemed to indicate a deeper source for his ambivalence. "I think politics is an Irish talent," he noted, citing the Kennedy brothers and others. "That fire burned in each of them. But with us Scots, it's a different thing. We do things out of a dour Calvinistic sense of duty." Perhaps most tellingly he revealed, "We take no pleasure in it."

He recognized better than most that as a political figure he would be subjected to stresses and strains not required of a thespian. "I think many actors are shy," he

---

72 Browning, "The Spectacular Burden of Being Charlton Heston," "Guggenheim Productions records, Tomorrow is a Day—clippings," f.3235, HL.

73 "Celebrities of Tinsel City light up for political favorites," *AC*, Nov. 1, 1984.

observed as he had done numerous times in the past. "People think of actors as extroverts. They're not." The "fourth wall" between performers and their audiences could serve as important protective buffers. Asserting himself into the public sphere as a political entity would pierce that wall and open the inner person to a degree of exposure that could no longer be avoided. Despite his well-known screen persona, Heston preferred at this point not to indulge any latent desire on his part that might crave a different role that necessitated such incessant and intense scrutiny.[74]

Of course, Charlton Heston was not the only actor to be considered for high-level office; various individuals bandied Gregory Peck's name about for the same purpose. Later, a jesting piece compared Heston's potential presidential appeal to Peck's. Writer Neil Postman of *The Nation* suggested that the former's refusal to stand for a Senate seat had been a gambit for higher stakes. "No doubt the arguments for Heston's considering a run for the Senate were that a Presidential candidate needs to know something about current issues and have a political record." Instead, by appearing in a spinoff from the hit series *Dynasty*, "Heston realized that it would be more useful to his Presidential bid to be seen on television every week than to be buried for two years in the Senate." Postman argued that in any case, Moses, Ben-Hur, Michelangelo, and Andrew Jackson would give the Republican Heston strength among certain demographics that a Democrat like Peck could not match. "However, Heston is not without his political liabilities. He not only failed to do as well as he might have against a group of monkeys (*Planet of the Apes*) but in the same movie bared his rear end. Nudity does not go down well with the folks from Sioux Falls." A Peck biographer's explanation for his subject's reluctance fit Heston's personality as well. "For a man as ferociously private as Greg, who recoiled from strangers invading his personal space . . . [for] a man who insisted on controlling how he was perceived by the public, life in the White House fishbowl would have been pure hell."[75]

In any case, Heston was busy plying his trade as well as expanding his sphere of influence. He often traveled to exotic locations for film shoots that also allowed him to absorb local culture and learn directly about the conditions of the region. The television film *Nairobi Affair* brought the actor and the cameras to Kenya, where filming wildlife added color to the story and placed a spotlight on the scourge of poaching. This feature offered Heston an opportunity to underscore the

---

74 Rader, "If I Ran & Won," 4-5.

75 Neil Postman, "President Heston," *The Nation* (Oct. 5, 1985), 300-301; Lynn Haney, *Gregory Peck: A Charmed Life* (New York, 2004), 345.

unintended consequences of the regulation of hunting. "The Kenyan government thought they could preserve the animal population by banning hunting, but it proved opposite," he observed. Employing an explanation on the "Darwinian" role of "professionals" who "kept the poachers out," he glossed over the longstanding activities of amateurs and sport hunters who had been part of the equation as well. Still, his focus on illicit behavior was important. "Now you have poachers going after ivory with machine guns and hand grenades. The thrust of the story is about ivory poaching."[76]

Overseas locations also drew the attention of many Americans, Charlton Heston included, to other desperate situations. Famine had struck the Horn of Africa with a vengeance, exacerbated by vicious in-fighting among competing factions in civil wars that tended to employ innocent civilians as pawns. The actor had taken interest in Africa with his earlier film work and during the Johnson administration with a state department-sponsored tour to Nigeria, but his trip to Ethiopia struck a different chord. He was not inclined to be pessimistic or cynical, even in the face of such widespread deprivation, but he could see enormous need and felt a duty to help turn public attention to it. Heston agreed to join former NFL star Mel Blount in a Red Cross-sponsored venture, and tried to keep the tone of the announcement on a difficult subject as light as the circumstances allowed by observing, "It is not true I promised to part the Red Sea when I get there."[77]

Despite the attempt at levity, the actor took the effort very seriously, embarking on an eight-day mission that crossed a wide-expanse of territory. The effort represented a shift from traveling to promote a film or to perform a government function to advocating for a special humanitarian cause. He believed the United States had the power and the moral authority to play an important role wherever trouble occurred. That he might be a factor in assisting a vital aid program was not alien to him either, although more skeptical voices questioned the roles of high-profile personalities in such ventures. Indeed, author Susan Moeller observed of the phenomenon, "By December, with Christmas coming, Ethiopia soon became the place to be." She dismissed the very genuine efforts Heston and others like him were making in the crisis. "By the first week of December actors Charlton Heston and Cliff Robertson had come, made charity films, and gone," Moeller asserted.[78]

76 Julianne Hastings, "Do two roles make Heston a born-again TV star?" *AJC*, Oct. 13, 1984.

77 Blount played for the Pittsburgh Steelers. "Heston, Mel Blount touring Africa," *AC*, Dec. 3, 1984.

78 "Famine's 'walking skeletons' touch student," *AC*, Dec. 11, 1984; Susan D. Moeller, *Compassion Fatigue: How the Media Sell Disease, Famine, War, and Death* (New York, 2002), 118.

Heston took such work to heart. He brought the matter graphically to the White House, where President Reagan recorded, "A Red Cross delegation including Chuck Heston reported in on their trip to Ethiopia. Chuck who is a very fine sketch artist had sketched an 11 yr. old boy—a famine victim who only weighed 16 pounds." The effort seemed to obtain the intended result. The president concluded, "I need to remind our people the Red Cross can use donations directed to the famine in Africa." For his part, the actor's role appeared significant and meaningful. "The fact that he was Charlton Heston, giving a press conference at every airport, helped us get through," CNN reporter Peter Arnett explained. Without hyperbole, the correspondent added, "The Ethiopians had seen his movies and knew he parted the Red Sea." Of course, this celebrity had a double edge. A focus on the star meant less on other aspects. "They said that everyone wanted to talk to Heston and brief him, leaving less time for them to cover the story."[79]

More to the point than his role as a public advocate, Heston felt the responsibility of his place as a recorder of events. "I see my function as one of bearing witness, in the biblical sense," he explained, "and later conveying that witness back to the American people." Sketching what he saw and reporting on it were legitimate contributions the Hollywood star believed he could make to a horrific situation. *Los Angeles Times* writer Don Shannon noted, "Actor Charlton Heston, another member of the group, said only three doctors and six nurses are available to help the 16,000 famine victims" at one Ethiopian station. Tellingly, he observed, there were substantially more gravediggers at the location than health care professionals. Perhaps reflective of his director's eye for detail, he recalled how a single water faucet "glistens in the sun because it is constantly being polished by hundreds of hands."[80]

Heston's public service efforts took a more personal route when he accepted roles in antismoking television spots. The one-time purveyor of Camel cigarettes was now appearing on behalf of the American Cancer Society and Action on Smoking on Health (ASH). As a parent he had the welfare of his children to consider, insisting that "growing evidence [demonstrated] that smokers endanger not only their own health, but the health of others, which puts another adjustment on it." He also maintained that at least part of his motivation stemmed from another significant, adverse family connection to the use of tobacco: "My father

79 "Monday, December 10, [1984]," Brinkley, ed., *Reagan Diaries*, 285-286; Howard Rosenberg, "CNN Reporter Connects with Ethiopian Famine," *LAT*, Dec. 14, 1984.

80 "'Celebrity Glut' May Be Near, *LAT*, Dec. 3, 1984; Don Shannon, "Red Cross Begins Africa Famine Drive," *LAT*, Dec. 11, 1984.

was killed by smoking cigarettes." In 1992, he participated in the documentary *Dying for a Smoke*.[81]

Meanwhile, issues over leadership in the Screen Actors Guild continued to build, even as its membership sought to move past the Heston-Asner imbroglio. In 1985 the conservative figure Ed Nelson lost an election to Patty Duke, who had received Asner's endorsement, thwarting the efforts of Heston and others to return the organization to the philosophy it had once held. Heston remained adamant that a merger between SAG and SEG would result in membership defections and warned Duke not to "defy our members and inhale the extras." Once again, it would take a little while for tempers to settle, but by 1986, Heston felt free to tell conservative talk show host Laura Ingraham, "Miss Duke has proved excellent; she's disavowed the social agenda which upset so many."[82]

Heston found another challenge to his views closer to home. Lilla Heston had always been one of the strongest-willed personalities in his life, from the mother who gave him a new name as a young child to the parent who continued to critique him in later years. By the mid-1980s, as the actor looked back at sixty years of life, he found her disputing parts of this narrative. Concerning his cherished memory of freelancing in the Michigan woodlands while "hunting rabbits," she asserted, "He never hunted a rabbit in his life!" Then, with respect to the notion that she directed his education to include the sciences, Lilla retorted, "Why would I advise him to take chemistry? I have no interest in it." Her dismissal of such a position meant that he could not possibly have held it himself. "He had no interest in it. He was interested in becoming an actor." While he agreed with the sentiment that his first love was acting, Heston found his mother disputing a final, crucial element of his life's story. Of his connection to rural roots, she explained that he was hardly the "shy little country boy" he maintained himself to be. "We lived in Wilmette," in the Chicago suburbs.[83]

Disputes of memory did not displace the importance of this narrative for Heston or prevent him from insisting that he had spent his lifetime overcoming his innate shyness. His interests and activities remained as widespread as ever in 1986, as did his political connections. On February 12, President Reagan dashed off a message to his friend in California. "Just a note to thank you for your letter

81 Chase, "Between Scenes with Charlton Heston," 45; *Dying for a Smoke*, Jan. 1, 1992, IMDB.

82 "Patty Duke Wins SAG Election," *TV Guide*, 1985; Eliot, *Charlton Heston*, 424; Raymond, *Cold, Dead Hands*, 235.

83 John Stark, "Chatter," *People* (Aug. 19, 1985), 110.

and kind words," he opened in a now familiar pattern. "Also to let you know I ran a TV tape last night and saw you in another stellar role: you were narrating a one-hour exposé of how television distorted the war in Vietnam. It was just great and is something all Americans should see—but then we know TV will never help them see it."[84]

Heston had also established an increasingly friendly relationship with Vice President George Bush, reflected in a note sent from Bush's office on February 21, 1986. "I just wanted you to know that I received your personal message about the event in Los Angeles. It was thoughtful of you to check in," Bush observed. The vice president knew that he and the star would likely cross paths again. "Bar and I would loved to have seen you, but please remember, the Heston memorial guest room—with full access to the V.P. tennis court—is ready for you whenever you get back to Washington."[85]

As Bush knew, tennis remained important to Charlton Heston. The actor also saw the sport, on the international stage at least, as symbolic of the United States, for better or worse. In the case of volatile young star John McEnroe's histrionics on the court, he was certain it was for the worse. "Tennis," Heston explained to one interviewer, "which is a sport to which I am passionately devoted," risked having any traditional sense of decorum diminished over public displays of tantrums over calls a player deemed incorrect. "I hardly watch any more because of John McEnroe. It just offends me to the soul, his whining, his complaining, his outrageous assaults."[86]

Heston's disdain increased as he traveled to London to direct and star in a production of *The Caine Mutiny Court Martial*, whose dates happened to coincide with the Wimbledon tournament, and a chance for the actor to sit in the Royal Box. "I simply don't want to sit in that wonderful place and risk the embarrassment, as an American, of seeing an American disgrace our country," he explained. The biting assessment continued. "McEnroe is a great player. He's also an insufferable boor who demeans the game that made him a millionaire." Heston believed McEnroe's behavior had consequences to the game he loved. "For many of us he has ruined tennis as a spectator sport. The damage his attitude is doing to young players everywhere is appalling." McEnroe's antics had already prompted

---

84 "Ron to Dear Chuck," Feb. 12, 1986, in Skinner, Anderson, and Anderson, eds., *Reagan: A Life in Letters*, 113.

85 "George to Dear Charlton," Feb. 21, 1986, Name Files, Vice President George Bush, GBPL.

86 Wadler, "Thou Shalt Not Whine," 39.

Heston to suggest to American Davis Cup coach Arthur Ashe that the team leave the star at home.[87]

The actor was much happier being in Great Britain on his own account for *The Caine Mutiny Court-Martial.* "If you haven't acted on stage in London, you haven't acted on the stage," he insisted. Although reviews for his London stage debut were mixed, "You don't do it for the critics," he maintained. "If the critics like you, you think how marvelous they are. If they don't, you think. 'What do they know?'" In any case, he was convinced he had accomplished a significant performing milepost. "I feel I've acted. I've had my passport stamped."[88]

By the end of June 1985, the constant rain and dreariness of London began to strain the actor's enthusiasm. "It has been rewarding," Heston insisted, even after the run had to be extended while Lydia remained in a London hospital for back surgery. With her recovery and the expiration of his work permit, the time had come, after a formal dinner at the ambassador's residence to welcome Vice President Bush, for them to "hotfoot it for home."[89]

Although an Anglophile in many ways, Heston was an unabashed American, which was also an essential part of the persona he sought to maintain. A *Good Housekeeping* interview covered the actor's early life and entry into show business, via stage and live television, before turning to his marriage and family life. The anecdotes revealed a humorous but private man, as well as a dedicated professional and family patriarch, devoted to his wife, his children, tennis, and peanut butter. Even so, Vernon Scott observed, "Charlton Heston is not an easy man to know. At first, he appears aloof, even distant. Despite the polished social graces he has attained over the years, he remains essentially a shy, retiring man who guards his privacy and is inclined to intellectual pursuits." Heston continued to insist that he had no intention to enter politics: "I will not seek public office." Still, Scott was skeptical that the actor could resist the allure of a different stage and audience. "Others have said this and didn't mean it." Then, in a moment that captured the parameters of Heston's public face, the writer ventured, "But would Moses lie?"[90]

As the 1980s progressed, Heston's profile included involvement in a spin-off of the popular series *Dynasty* that would put him in a part similar to the one John Forsythe played in the original. This role represented a departure from the stance

---

87 "Holy Moses! Heston blasts McEnroe," *AC*, June 26, 1985.

88 "Heston's London debut," *AC*, Jan. 9, 1985; "Mixed reviews for Heston," ibid., Mar. 22, 1985.

89 Roderick Mann, "Heston's Queeg to Steer for Home," *LAT*, June 29, 1985.

90 Vernon Scott, "Charlton Heston's Life Story," *GH*, 130, 247-248, 250.

he had once taken toward such projects. In late 1957, he had struggled with an offer for a television series that would have proven very lucrative. "I had a difficult lunch," he noted at the time, "weighing MCA's offer for Cimarron, the TV series they insist would net me at least a million in keeping money. I don't know. Do I *want* a million? To do a TV *series*?"[91] At the time, it seemed to violate the very freedom he had gained by not being tied to an exclusive studio contract. Now, he could afford to jettison such qualms in search of a new audience and a chance to continue working.

According to *TV Guide* writer Bill Davidson, "Heston knew exactly what he was doing" in becoming affiliated with the new series. "As my agent said," Heston explained, "'Last year they were making films for 20-year-olds by 25-year-olds. This year they're making films for 14-year-olds by 14-year-olds.'" Heston recognized that modern demographics were working against him. He concluded, "I'm damned if I'd end up playing the father of a teen-age computer genius in Encino. So, for better or worse, here I am back on the little tube."

The producers of *The Colbys* noted Heston's initial disinterest in the project, but when an overture to Burt Lancaster fizzled, co-producer Esther Shapiro decided to travel to London, where she knew Heston was appearing on stage. She persuaded him to have lunch and made a successful pitch. "I convinced Chuck that this would be an extension of all the authority roles he had ever played—prophets, presidents, cardinals, lawgivers—and when he asked me who else was going to be in the series, I said I was going to try for Barbara Stanwyck, though I hadn't even approached her as yet." Heston had long admired Stanwyck and also became intrigued with the project when Shapiro likened it to the popular and critically acclaimed production *I, Claudius*. "This is a much challenged comparison made many times in the past by [Esther] Shapiro," Davidson noted, "but it hit the spot with Heston." Ironically, Stanwyck agreed to join the show when she learned that Heston had signed on as the patriarchal figure.

Davidson noted that during the production the actor was supposedly as difficult as his fictional portrayal was regarding his prerogatives. "There have been rumors that Heston has been throwing his weight around and causing trouble," the *TV Guide* reporter maintained. "The show's producers deny this." He reported that producer Robert Pollack had insisted, "We don't consider what Chuck is doing to be in the category of causing trouble. On the contrary, he is making great contributions in the development of this Jason Colby entrepreneur character."

Heston's insistence upon script approval was sacrosanct to him in providing creative collaboration and maintaining what he saw as character integrity. Of course, such intervention could be detrimental. "He keeps coming in with line changes that strengthen the character," Pollack observed. "No writer likes to think that an actor can do it better, but we all accept the major proportion of his suggestions. Not once has he asked for a change in story, only character." Unlike in his *Mountain Men* experience, Heston's prominence brought him a degree of deference on this occasion. "To someone unknowledgeable listening to this on the set," Pollack concluded diplomatically, "it may sound like trouble, but it isn't."[92]

Heston was clear concerning his fictional character, without appearing to feel beholden to the writers who were part of the process as well. "Jason Colby as I have invented him," he explained to one interviewer, "shares the capacity to focus on a single objective, shares the pleasure in using his energy and power for affirmative goals." For a figure who had acted in the fashion that would further his ends by any means to add to his wealth and family status, the comparison was a curious one. Still, Charlton Heston may have seen something of himself in the observation, "He is a man who likes to walk through the front door justified."[93]

The actor did not hesitate to insert himself where he thought his presence could be useful. He was also pleased to continue to support causes he deemed significant. In the latter part of 1985, the biggest issue he felt merited his involvement was national security. Heston lent his name and voice to the advocacy of a "Peace Shield." Deploying the same sense of the special "access to a public forum" that came with his status as a performer, he demonstrated that he was still not afraid to employ it. In this critical matter, he called on fans and supporters, "I want to invite you personally to join with me."[94]

Heston's profile meant that wherever his work might lead, he remained in the public eye. Organizations and institutions sought his help to promote their agendas by having him provide remarks, host events, or make spots on radio or television. Because of this activity, he received the Responsible Citizen Award for 1986 and a congratulatory telegram from Ronald Reagan. "I can speak with full authority about the many ways in which you have served your nation and your

---

92 Bill Davidson, "The Possibilities of More Lust, Power, and Intrigue Seemed Endless," *TV Guide* (Nov. 16, 1985), 35, 38-39. See also David Zurawik, "New series 'The Colbys' mirrors life at White House," *AC*, Nov. 29, 1985.

93 Robin Leach, "Fame, Fortune, and Romance," UCLA.

94 "Heston Nuclear Freeze," and "Heston 85 American Security Council," Political Spots, UCLA.

fellowman," Reagan noted. "You are deservedly admired by all who know you for your dedication to the principles which formed and nurtured this great country."[95]

As his work on the "Peace Shield" illustrated, Heston remained an advocate of a strong defense. In September 1986, he traveled to Norfolk, Virginia, to participate in the launching of the U.S. Navy's newest nuclear submarine, USS *Chicago*. Rear Admiral Malcolm MacKinnon, III, could not resist commenting on the actor's most identifiable role when he told the audience, "With a little help from Mr. Heston, we could figure out how to part the waters where Soviet submarines are. They might be easier to find." Heston provided remarks and a benediction for the occasion. As a Chicago-area native, along with his mother, Lilla, who was present as well, he offered the lines of Carl Sandburg's poem "Chicago," before concluding, "This will do for this ship, too."[96]

Heston's involvement in political events remained at a high level as summer gave way to fall in 1986. He threw his support behind Congressman Ed Zschau's effort to unseat Alan Cranston in his bid for re-election to the U.S. Senate. In addition to his Democratic Party affiliation, Cranston was a vocal adherent to the nuclear arms freeze movement that Heston opposed. In a television appeal, the actor began by noting that he had once voted for John F. Kennedy, but that this year, in the age of Ronald Reagan, the choice should be a different one. "This November," Heston admonished his fellow Californians, "join me in voting for a strong America. Support President Reagan, defeat Alan Cranston." In an attempt to remain upbeat, the actor's script for a thirty second spot sounded almost lyrical. Zschau was "like a fresh breeze over our political landscape, bringing new energy, new opportunities, new ideas, most of all new hope."[97]

The actor immersed himself fully in opposing Cranston, but others thought he would be more successful as the Republican candidate and attempted to cajole him once more into the fight. Even at social occasions with the Reagans, Heston maintained that he had already been president of the United States "three times," and that he saw no reason to try again at this point in his life.[98] Had he aspired to

---

95 "Program: Thomas Jefferson Research Center, 23rd Anniversary Banquet, April 9, 1986," and "Telegram from Ronald Regan for 1986 Responsible Citizen Award," Correspondence, f.466, HL.

96 "Called tops in technology, the *Chicago* commissioned," *VPLS*, Sept. 28, 1986.

97 "Heston, Californians for a Strong America Defeat Cranston Project 9-29-86," UCLA. Cranston defeated Congressman Ed Zschau in a close contest, 49.3% to 47.9%, with both candidates receiving over 3.5 million votes. See www.ourcampaigns.com/RaceDetail.html?RaceID=3657; John Balzar and Keith Love, "Cranston, Zschau Shift Gears, Opt for 'Going Positive' as Voting Nears," *LAT*, Nov. 1, 1986.

98 Frances Spatz Leighton, *The Search of the Real Nancy Reagan* (New York, 1987), 304.

leadership opportunities outside his own profession, this was another time for him to act on them; he chose not to do so.

Heston's interests expanded beyond political campaigns to embrace policy issues that reflected his views. He supported an effort to uphold a right-to-work law in Idaho against a referendum designed to challenge it. In television spots, such as one entitled, "America is Watching," the actor/activist implored viewers to "Strike a blow for freedom." Then, when SAG president Patty Duke endorsed overturning the statute and promised to campaign on its behalf at the request of the Idaho AFL-CIO, Heston countered with his own press conference at his home in Beverly Hills. He maintained that the division between SAG and the Actors Working for an Actors Guild was actually between "those who want us as a small, very poor union, to concentrate on the problems of film actors, and those on the board who want to pursue a broad social agenda." When asked about the contradiction for the conservative group campaigning for a "broad social agenda" in Idaho, he retorted that he was no longer on the SAG board and "was spending my own money on this."[99]

For the time being there was to be no united front regarding the organization that Charlton Heston had led for six years. One member wanted to rescind Heston's lifetime membership, in an effort that failed to gain wider support. At the subsequent December meeting, however, a significant portion of Screen Actors Guild members voted to forward a motion to censure their colleague for his actions, deeming them "anti-union." Heston remained stoic, declaring that those individuals had taken the step because they disagreed with him.[100]

Whatever his fellow actors might think of him, Heston's public image still elicited interest. A May 1986 promotion featured him and several other celebrities, including former President Ford, as "peanut butter nuts" who "have let their love for peanut butter spread into their adult lives." The Peanut Advisory Board, representing farmers in Georgia, Florida, and Alabama but based in New York, reflected the degree to which modern American consumers, including Heston, loved peanuts and their various by-products. Heston's culinary tastes were not new. "My own taste runs to English muffins and peanut butter," he had recorded almost two decades earlier. Indeed, one writer noted the actor's predilection, as well as

---

99 Heston Television Spots, "Right to Work" and "America is Watching," May 29, 1986, UCLA; Prindle, *The Politics of Glamour*, 176; Henry Weinstein, "Actors Guild Divided Over Right to Work," *LAT*, Sept. 12, 1986.

100 Prindle, *The Politics of Glamour*, 176; "Actors denounce Heston for supporting non-union hiring,"*AC*, Dec. 10, 1986.

an ancillary complaint. "One of the hardest things to do on a tour, especially overseas," Heston explained at the time, "is to keep a serious peanut butter habit supplied."[101]

Because of his high profile, interest in intimate aspects of Charlton Heston's personal life remained high. In November 1986, *Parade Magazine* featured a question from a native of Biloxi, Mississippi, who asked about the ages of the stars of *The Colbys* and also made a personal commentary on Heston's coiffure. The answer put Barbara Stanwyck's age at 79 and her male co-star's at 62, then noted, "Some heads are easier to fit with hairpieces than others." Just as with fellow film superstar John Wayne, Charlton Heston preferred to maintain the public visual appearance of an earlier stage in his life.[102]

In his first decade in motion pictures, Heston had served as product spokesperson in print advertising to promote his roles and films, but soon expressed wariness over such endorsements after he had established himself in major motion pictures. Now, the actor turned again to the medium for that purpose. The viability of the Heston brand exhibited itself in a series of television commercials for the communications giant ConTel. Touting the company's ability to meet the needs of modern business interests, he pronounced the tagline, "For ConTel, I'm Charlton Heston." One of the segments of the campaign ran during Super Bowl XXI on January 25, 1987. With a halftime salute to Hollywood's 100th Anniversary for a game played in the Rose Bowl, Heston's appearance also made sense for reaching the nearly ninety million viewers that tuned in to the contest.[103]

Heston's interest in gun ownership and Hollywood's centennial celebration brought him back to the pages of *TV Guide* in the spring of 1987. A feature article listed numerous stories from the "Hollywood beat," including a situation in which Los Angeles police "almost gunned down Charlton Heston." The actor had appeared outside his home in response to reports of an armed man in the neighborhood, carrying his own pistol and prepared to defend his home as circumstances dictated. Unfortunately, when the police reached the scene, they could only see an armed figure in the darkness, but Heston's compliance with their commands and a hesitation on their part to be certain of the apparent perpetrator's

---

101 "They're peanut butter nuts," *AC*, May 13, 1986; *ALJ*, 218; Dann Gire, "Life and peanut butter suit Heston fine," *The Sunday Herald*, Nov. 18, 1979, Heston Papers, "*The Actor's Life*—publicity," f.452, HL. Gire had first noticed the habit when he saw the actor in Nov. 18, 1978; ibid.

102 *Parade Magazine*, Nov. 23, 1986.

103 The New York Giants defeated the Denver Broncos 39-20 in the game.

identification prevented a tragedy. Later, Heston was on safer ground when he joined approximately 150 other stars for the "birthday extravaganza."[104]

At the same time, the actor inaugurated the "Charlton Heston Celebrity Shoot," a gathering for friends and associates from the Hollywood community who wanted to demonstrate their skills with firearms and socialize with like-minded persons. From an initial 40 participants, it grew into a large event that featured stars of motion pictures and television.[105]

Television was providing Heston with opportunities he had not enjoyed for decades, including the chance to engage in live comedy in a popular series. While preparing to host NBC's *Saturday Night Live*, Heston spent time with the writers, sharing his experiences from an era in which the format thrived. "In the 50s I did Sid Caesar's show about eight times when it was really much the same kind of show." Heston reminisced about working with the likes of Neil Simon, Mel Brooks, and Carl Reiner to get the material *SNL's* writers would use.[106]

Heston's next foray into television was in *Proud Men* as a rich cattle rancher fighting a different kind of war with his estranged son (Peter Strauss) over the young man's conscientious objection to serving in Vietnam. Columnist Mal Vincent of Norfolk's *Virginian-Pilot* pronounced Heston as being "Back in the Saddle," and maintained, "'Actor-of-the-ages' Heston does himself proud in TV movie." In conducting that interview, Vincent observed in a reference to Heston's epic portrayals, "One was tempted to bow and ask for either a blessing or protection from the spear-waving infidels who had to be storming the gates outside." Alluding specifically to *Ben-Hur*, he noted, "It was he who escaped from the galley slaves to beat out the heavily favored Roman team in the chariot race." In addition to a survey of Heston's career and the plot of his latest film, Vincent noted that the actor "has had to endure all those Moses jokes," including one in which Moses gets confused with Heston himself. "It is clear that Charlton Heston would probably like to be 'one of the guys,'" the writer concluded, but even in contemporary clothing, "there is still something epic" about him.[107]

---

104 Patricia Klein, "The Day the L.A. Police Almost Gunned Down Charlton Heston," *TV Guide* (May 16-22, 1987), 4, 6; "A 100th Birthday Extravaganza," ibid., A60-62.

105 David Freed, "Hollywood's Shooting, and Not Just Films: Firearms: Show business turns to guns for recreation and security. 'I would feel very naked,' without one, says Charlton Heston," *LAT*, May 21, 1992, www.articles.latimes.com/1992-05-21/news/mn-358_1_charlton-heston.

106 Kathryn Baker, "Heston Jokes on NBC; Philips on HBO," *LAT*, Mar. 27, 1987.

107 Mal Vincent, "Back in the Saddle," *VP*, Sept. 28, 1987.

Despite his appearances on television, the stage remained "actor's country" for Heston and an opportunity to revisit Sir Thomas More, this time in Great Britain, was irresistible. Even when harsh weather threatened to prove troublesome, Heston was pleased to note strong attendance at the performances. Buttressed by good notices, he felt even greater validation when playwright Robert Bolt offered his approval. Subsequent showings indicated that his name still held powerful attraction with theater patrons. "It is nice to go on in the stage door and see SOLD OUT pasted over the posters."[108]

Charlton Heston had long enjoyed connections with friends and colleagues who were less conservative than he was, and refused to shy away from associations with other public figures who held opposing political views when a mutual cause of significance existed. Jolly West had prompted his involvement in the civil rights movement and Vanessa Redgrave was a welcome colleague on stage and screen. For a campaign to promote the environmental impact of the space program for the U.S. Space Foundation, he collaborated with feminist activist Gloria Steinem. "We probably disagree on most things," he remarked in the spot, with Steinem agreeing in a good-natured banter as reflected in the script: "Heston: But when they asked us to talk about how the peaceful exploration of space benefits *all* men. Steinem: All *people*. Heston: We agreed."[109]

His "public face" also continued to have utility for government agencies. In a 1988 campaign for the U.S. Forest Service, he accepted a role that put him in the great outdoors in a cowboy hat and jeans. "I really love these forests," he observed in versions cut into spots that ranged from ten to sixty seconds long. "Charlton Heston for America's National Forests" tapped into his memories of the Michigan wilderness of his youth and the vast outdoors that he felt allowed everyone "elbow room when the city starts squeezing you in."[110]

During this same period, the publication of a history of the Screen Actors Guild allowed Heston to restate his belief that the beloved organization, of which he had served as president, had drifted from its path. In a blurb endorsing David F. Pringle's work, the actor hailed the book as "the first serious history" of SAG,

108 *CHA*, 504-505.

109 "U.S. Space Foundation Environmental Impact, May 22, 1987," "Miscellaneous ads, scripts, etc. – miscellaneous," f.354, HL.

110 "Forest Service—USDA, 5/5/88," UCLA.

before adding, "With meticulous objectivity, he's documented the radicalization of one of the last of the true craft guilds."[111]

One of Heston's more enthralling stage ventures occurred in the fall of 1988, when he and Lydia traveled to Beijing to oversee an all-Chinese production of Herman Wouk's *The Caine Mutiny Court-Martial*. Their packing for the extended trip also illustrated their priorities, with "sixteen bags full of both needs and wants" that included "peanut butter, rehearsal Reeboks, and drawing pens." Lydia took her camera to capture the Orient as she saw it, while the couple "were hand-carried" through their time abroad, a practice the actor admitted, "I've come, irrationally, to count on."[112]

Heston determined to accept the challenge, made at the behest of the Chinese Ministry of Culture, of directing a cast that would rehearse and act entirely in Mandarin. This would be done through an interpreter, though Heston had the comfort of understanding the play explicitly, having acted and directed it himself repeatedly. The subsequent publication of his *Beijing Diary* chronicled the production process and reflected his views on the project and its participants.

These cultural "exchanges" were not always confined to the arts or the upcoming stage performances. A meeting with his Chinese hosts turned to other topics of mutual interest. "In the bar, we talked mostly about beer," Heston noted, "exchanging our experience of it in different countries." The American actor/director pointed out that his ranged "from Argentina to Australia, Bangladesh to Norway, Scotland to South Africa." He concluded, "A clear consensus emerged: Perhaps alone among the works of man, almost all countries make a pretty good beer."[113]

While abroad, Heston also appreciated the relative "pleasures of anonymity" he could enjoy in China when not working on the play. "I'd forgotten what it felt like to be a private man," he observed, "even in public." While recognizing that celebrity had more advantages than disadvantages ("I can get a table at a restaurant or tickets to a show or a seat on a plane"), the only place he encountered any deviation from this relative "anonymity" was when he had to dodge the American tourists who crowded the Sheraton lobby or waited outside for their buses. He solved that problem by walking "fast" and catching a car to the theater "on the street corner, beyond the hotel entrance."[114]

---

111 Pringle, *The Politics of Glamour*, back cover.

112 *BD*, 25.

113 Ibid., 26-27.

114 Ibid., 70.

Even from China the actor kept abreast of the course of election year politics at home. He reiterated his feeling that he and "millions of other Americans" were justified in moving away from a Democratic Party he believed "had changed, drifting steadily leftward." Of course, his focus was on the play and the cultural exchange it represented, but he considered it "my pleasure in reading today that George Bush was judged to have won the presidential debate last night, leaving him with his lead intact. Let's hope so."[115]

Having established a warm relationship with Vice President Bush and wanting to see the work of Ronald Reagan continue unabated, the actor pledged his support. "Dear Chuck," Bush wrote on May 2, 1988, "Just a quick note to thank you for your most generous offer to help out in the fall. I am delighted." The politician knew his actor friend could be beneficial in many ways, despite a busy schedule that would take Heston across the globe. "Have a great and productive time in London and China," Bush added. "I'm sure I'll see you at the New Orleans convention, and that makes Barbara and me happy." The vice president repeated his appreciation and offered a pledge of his own. "Many, many thanks again for your generous offer of support. I'm going to work my heart out for this one, and believe I can make it." Bush closed with his "[w]armest regards."[116]

Bush also sent his appreciation in a personal, hand-written, note, in August, to "Dear Chuck." "Thanks so much for coming to Tuesday's L.A. event. With all your travel plans—that appearance was 'beyond the call'—But there you were—with us—and it helps a lot." Bush knew that Heston was involved with the *Caine* project. "I hope your Chinese venture is a huge success," the one-time United Nations ambassador and envoy to that country noted. "You'll love the Chinese people and they'll love you."[117]

The blend of American politics, Chinese theater, and a sprinkling of tennis occupied Heston's time. He marveled at being able to watch the last Bush-Dukakis debate on live television and reacted to the performances of the principals as much as to their messages. Michael Dukakis was "still tight," and he thought an advisor ought to "talk to him about his rapid pace, the down-stresses at the end of each sentence, constantly accented by double hand chops." Bush did "better" in his evaluation. "That's a professional judgment of performance . . . what I do for

---

115 Ibid., 69.

116 "George to Dear Chuck," May 2, 1988, Name Files, Vice President George Bush, GBPL.

117 "George to Dear Chuck," Aug. 15, 1988, GBPL.

a living. Never doubt that political leadership, particularly at that level, requires performance."[118]

To Heston's enormous satisfaction, the election went to George Bush and Dan Quayle handily, with wins in both popular and electoral votes over Michael Dukakis and Lloyd Bentsen. California's 47 electoral votes went into the GOP column as well, although the popular tally separation in the state was less than five percent. A formal letter to "Dear Charleton" [sic] followed in December. "Barbara and I would like to extend our heartfelt thanks for all of your efforts on our behalf," he noted. "All the best, and thanks again for your loyal and effective support."[119] The victory ensured that Heston would continue to have a friend in the White House and that his role as public advocate for the arts and many other issues would continue.

As the rehearsals progressed in Beijing, Heston assisted his new actors as best he could in finding their characters while making cuts to this version of their play. As much as time permitted, the Hestons also absorbed Chinese culture. Inside the hotel, when he "stepped out of the lobby and back into celebrity," he good-naturedly endured the cameras and videorecorders while responding to well-intentioned queries from individuals who occasionally confused him with Burt Lancaster and his work. "I agreed it was a hard question, but I was careful not to point out that I wasn't in either [of Lancaster's films]."

While dining out on one of the rare occasions, the Americans found themselves alone with another couple from Japan. Communicating primitively out of politeness, Heston recalled, "I kept drawing little pictures, which gets the idea across, but of course there had to be autographs, which I don't mind, and those damned little instant cameras, which I do." Revealing a phobia related to the public image he continued to craft, he added, "When I think of the millions of lousy photographs of me that lie curling in bureau drawers all over the world. . . . Never mind."[120] Whatever he might profess about the challenges of stardom, the Beijing episode gave Heston another chance to confront the logic of a life in lights and the meaning it held for him.

Back at home, his special relationship with the fellow actor and Republican Party standard-bearer reached another dimension when he attended the

---

118 *BD*, 121.

119 The GOP ticket won by seven million popular votes and 426 to 111 electoral votes; "George to Dear Charleton," Dec. 9, 1988, Name Files, Vice President George Bush, GBPL.

120 *BD*, 72, 83.

groundbreaking for the Ronald Reagan Presidential Library and Center for Public Affairs in Simi Valley, California, on November 21, 1988. Reagan had served as a role model from the days of the Screen Actors Guild, and the connection between the Reagans and Hestons remained through the White House years and beyond. Humor as well as pragmatism had long marked the bond between the men, as illustrated when Reagan quipped, "And thank you, Chuck, I hope everyone here is suitably honored by your presence. After all, it's not often that you get Moses to lead you in the Pledge of Allegiance." The honoree, who never shied away from joking about his age, added with respect to Moses, "I should know . . . when I knew him he didn't even speak English."[121]

Heston was also finding his footing with the organization that would define him, for good or ill, for the remainder of his days. By the end of the decade, he was ready to take his support for the National Rifle Association to a new level. In April 1989, he lent his considerable presence to its advertising campaign, maintaining that he had "always spoken out on issues I feel strongly about. Voting, civil rights, defense, the environment. Also, the Bill of Rights. Why am I comfortable as a member of the NRA? Because I'm comfortable with the Bill of Rights."[122]

His new higher profile with the NRA attracted much of the attention he received as a public figure, but Heston continued to be active in areas he deemed worthy of support that did not always gain such widespread notice. In one endeavor, he joined with actors Earl Holliman and Laraine Newman in volunteering to serve Thanksgiving meals at the Los Angeles Mission. The effort expected to provide meals to as many as 5,000 homeless individuals and fit into his notions of the responsibility he felt public figures owed to their larger communities.[123]

Charlton Heston had long supported political candidates and causes of his choosing without concern for what his public positions might mean to those who would decide whether to employ his services or support his work. The actor was as determined as ever to chart his own course. Asserting independence as a personal trademark, Heston understood that his television roles and NRA leadership offered him the audiences that allowed him to find self-fulfillment and continued purpose.

121 "Remarks at the Groundbreaking Ceremony for the Ronald Reagan Presidential Library and Center for Public Affairs in Simi Valley, California, November 21, 1988," *Public Papers of the Presidents of the United States. Containing the Public Messages, Speeches, and Statements of the President. Ronald Reagan. 1988*, (Washington, 1989), 1565.

122 *Newsweek*, Apr. 10, 1989.

123 "The Holiday Spirit," *LAT*, Nov. 22, 1989.

His latest project, a televised version of *Treasure Island*, also provided a bridge from the past in which a favorite book was part of a child's imagination (his and Fraser's) and the present, where the adult could continue his acting career with a meaningful character.[124]

During the filming of the Robert Louis Stevenson classic, Heston devoted his full capacity to his role as the nefarious pirate leader, Long John Silver. Crossing the uneven territory of a ship's deck or an island location while using a crutch to support himself as well as participating in action sequences, Heston found himself increasingly taxed physically. On one occasion, as Lillia visited the set, the 90-year-old mother thought the work too much for her son. "I can still *do* these fights," he remembered telling her. "I just need a hand up afterward."[125]

Another film, the science fiction venture *Solar Crisis*, included numerous stars, but Heston almost was not one of them. He was unsettled by the fate of his character, a Navy admiral. "When I read the script," he observed, "I said 'The only thing wrong is that my character lives.'" Partly as a result of his distasteful experience in *Beneath the Planet of the Apes*, he observed, "I was raised in the era when sequels were considered sort of tacky." Yet the producers were clear that this was the very reason they had wanted to keep their options open if the space thriller enjoyed success.[126]

During these years, Heston's support for Republican candidates remained unwavering. Traveling to Houston in December 1989 to assist in fundraising activities for Sen. Phil Gramm, he found the worlds of acting and politics combining once more. President Bush referred to the iconic role that had come to define the actor. "You know, the only thing better than being introduced by Phil Gramm," Bush remarked, "is having Phil Gramm being introduced by Moses." The president turned his attention to Heston specifically, touting the actor's latest work in bringing the classic novel *Treasure Island* to the small screen. "And Chuck, it's a great pleasure to see you again, 'Long John Silver,'—that'll be a tremendous success, I know."[127]

---

124 Heston noted his delight at reading from the novel to Fraser, "our third trip to that durable archipelago"; *ALJ*, 132.

125 *CHA*, 541.

126 "Thinking Ahead," *AJ*, Oct. 31, 1989.

127 "Remarks at a Fundraising Dinner for Senator Phil Gramm in Houston, Texas, December 7, 1989," *Public Papers of the Presidents of the United States. Containing the Public Messages, Speeches, and Statements of the President. George Bush. 1989* (Washington, 1990), 1665.

The next day, Heston appeared before a crowd in Denver in support of U.S. Senate candidate Hank Brown. President Bush did not repeat the Moses reference in Colorado but recognized the actor's presence in clear terms. "And I also want to say hello to Charlton Heston," he noted, "who came out here today from Houston last night, a real trooper, a true patriot—having him here today is just wonderful."[128]

The nature of Heston's work for Senator Gramm exposed the degree to which the actor could both benefit from public perceptions and be vulnerable because of them. Heston had not been afraid to tout the work of the Founding Fathers, often referring to them as "those wise old dead white guys who invented this country." For some audiences this terminology was an appealing reminder of the past; for others they represented a jarring dismissal of the changes wrought in the nation since that time and the degree to which such references were not only outmoded and outdated, but demeaning. Heston remained defensive toward such criticisms and felt that the results validated his views. "I campaigned in fourteen states, on behalf of twenty-four candidates for both the Senate and the House," he explained later in his memoir. "As a foot soldier in the revolution (if it proves to have been that), I'm proud that in the states we visited, we won nineteen of the seats contested." Phil Gramm had been among the victors.[129]

Through the 1980s, Charlton Heston had worked to remain relevant in a changing world, personally, professionally, and politically. The next decade would determine the degree to which the actor was successful in transitioning to supporting roles rather than as the headliner, or as a spokesperson for products and public or government causes. He was no longer called upon to carry a film as its star, but his name still held cachet among older ticket buyers especially. Charlton Heston was still Moses or a victorious Judah Ben-Hur to many. He had once derided those in his profession whom time or circumstance had relegated to producing such public endorsements, but his voice and stature with film aficionados meant the same course would be likely for him as he entered the final stretch of his long and productive career.

128 "Remarks at a Fundraising Luncheon for Senatorial Candidate Hank Brown in Denver, Colorado, December 8, 1989," ibid., 1668.

129 *CHA*, 575-576.

Chapter Nine

DOWN THE BACKSTRETCH
1990s

"This was just me and Time Warner."
— Heston on lobbying against offensive rap music lyrics

"If Americans believed in political correctness, we'd still be King George's boys."
— Heston before an NRA meeting, 1996

"If the big screen didn't exist, they would have to invent it for Charlton Heston."
— President William J. Clinton, Kennedy Honoree Reception, 1997

Performances:

Entertainment Tonight, Jan. 10, 1990
The Tonight Show Starring Johnny Carson, Jan. 12, 1990
Treasure Island, Jan. 22, 1990
With Orson Welles: Stories from a Life in Film, Feb. 5, 1990
The Academy Awards, Mar. 26, 1990 (62nd); Mar. 23, 1998 (70th)
Solar Crisis, 1990
The Little Kidnappers, Aug. 17, 1990
Almost An Angel, 1990
A Night on Mount Edna, Dec. 15, 1990
The Hollywood Road to Oz, 1990
Korea: The Unknown War, Aug. 1990
Air Force One: The Plane and the Presidents, 1991
The Man Who Saw Tomorrow, Feb. 20, 1991
All-Star Salute to Our Troops, Apr. 3, 1991
The Crucifer of Blood, Nov. 4, 1991
Reflections on the Silver Screen, 1991
One on One with John Tesh, Nov. 22, 1991
Dying for a Smoke, Jan. 1, 1992

MGM: When the Lion Roared, 1992
Crash Landing: The Rescue of Flight 232, Feb. 24, 1992
The 18th Annual People's Choice Awards, Mar. 17, 1992
Noel, Dec. 1, 1992
Symphony for the Spire, 1993
The 14th Annual CableACE Awards, Jan. 17, 1993
The Bold and the Beautiful, 1993
Wayne's World 2, 1993
Tombstone, 1993
The Mystery of the Sphinx, Nov. 10, 1993
All Aboard: Riding the Rails of American Film, Dec. 2, 1993
Late Night with Conan O'Brien, Dec. 3, 1993; June 3, 1997; Oct. 8, 1998
Saturday Night Live, Dec. 4, 1993
The Golden Globe Awards, Jan. 22, 1994 (51st); Jan. 21, 1995 (52nd)
This is Your Life, Apr. 13, 1994
SeaQuest DSV, May 1, 1994
Wyatt Earp: Walk with a Legend, 1994
The Bible According to Hollywood, 1994
A Century in Cinema, 1994
1994 MTV Awards, June 4, 1994
The Tonight Show with Jay Leno, June 13, 1994, Aug. 22, 1996
True Lies, 1994
In the Mouth of Madness, 1994
The Great Battles of the Civil War, Dec. 26, 1994
America: A Call to Greatness, 1995
The Avenging Angel, Jan. 22, 1995
Biography: Charlton Heston, Mar. 20, 1995; *Edward G. Robinson*, Oct. 2, 1996;
Sophia Loren, Mar. 17, 1997; *Barbara Stanwyck*, May 12, 1997;
Jimmy Stewart, Dec. 22, 1997; *John Wayne*, Mar. 15, 1998; *Rex Harrison*, Aug. 13, 1998;
Roddy McDowall, Oct. 8, 1998; *Susan Hayward*, Dec. 2, 1998
Texas, Apr. 16, 1995
Bob Hope: Memories of World War II, Aug. 5, 1995
The Late Show with David Letterman, Sept. 6, 1995
Clive Anderson Talks Back, Nov. 17, 1995
Corazón, corazón, Dec. 2, 1995; Dec. 2. 1996
The Mysterious Origins of Man, Mar. 25, 1996
Andersonville Diaries, Feb. 28, 1996
The Dark Mist, 1996
Alaska, 1996
Hamlet, 1996
The Daily Show, Aug. 15, 1996
Ben Johnson: Third Cowboy on the Right, Sept. 1, 1996

Dennis Miller Live, Jan. 17, 1997

I Am Your Child, Apr. 28, 1997

The Rosie O'Donnell Show, June 4, 1997

Big Guns Talk: The Story of the Western, July 27, 1997

Hercules, 1997

Hollywood Aliens & Monsters, Nov. 9, 1997

Charlton Heston Presents The Bible, Dec. 1, 1997

Space Ghost Coast to Coast, 1997

The Kennedy Center Honors: A Celebration of the Performing Arts, Dec. 26, 1997

Friends, Feb. 5, 1998

Gary Cooper: The Face of a Hero, Mar. 17, 1998

Alaska: Spirit of the Wild, June 1, 1998

AFI's 100 Years . . . 100 Movies: America's Greatest Movies, June 16, 1998; *In Search Of*, July 1998

The Best of Hollywood, 1998

Armageddon, 1998

Gideon, 1998

Private Screenings, 1998

Behind the Planet of the Apes, Sept. 6, 1998

The Roseanne Show, Oct. 20, 1998

60 Minutes, Dec. 20, 1998

Sworn to Secrecy: Secrets of War, 1998-2002

The Howard Stern Radio Show, May 8, 1999

The 20th Century: Yesterday's Tomorrows, 1999

Television: The First Fifty Years, 1999

Forever Hollywood, 1999

Any Given Sunday, 1999

Town & Country, 1999

As Charlton Heston approached the backstretch of his career, he had the benefit of a new source of entertainment that would allow him to reclaim his earlier cinematic magic and tap into another generation of potential consumers of his work. Individuals who had seen the disaster movies of the 1970s as children and teenagers were now parents who sought to take advantage of entertainment venues built around the Universal films of the era for their family vacations. In the summer of 1990, Universal Studios opened a theme park in Florida that featured a special-effects driven ride based on Heston's movie *Earthquake*, with narration by the star and the promise that participants could experience "the big one" as they moved through a recreated subway system while being subjected to a catastrophic natural disaster.[1]

At the same time, Heston and President George H. W. Bush continued to develop the rapport they had established during the Reagan administration. The actor shared his pleasure at learning that the Bushes wanted to view *Treasure Island* and promised to send a print. "Given Barbara's focus on literacy, she'll be interested in the film's roots," he explained. "When Fray was about five, I decided he was too old for the kid's books I'd been reading him and introduced him to Stevenson's masterpiece, a chapter a night." The reading thrilled Fraser, who asked his father to do it again. "I read it four more times, till he could do it himself," the proud dad recalled. "That turned him into a book nut and, thirty years later, impelled him to write and direct what we feel is a definitive version."[2]

In May Heston covered a range of subjects with the chief executive, particularly noting his opinions on Bush's recent positions on Lithuania and the Soviet Union. The actor observed, "Believe me, sir, I know how hard you're striving for peace and stability in a harsh and changing world." He drew upon his knowledge of history to explain, "I'm sure [Neville] Chamberlain felt the same at Munich and [Franklin] Roosevelt at Yalta. Let's pray your choice here is wiser than theirs."

Their correspondence shifted to lighter tones, as when they discussed the president's public statements concerning his indifference toward broccoli as a food choice. "I want you to know I'm with you all the way on the Broccoli Policy," Heston chimed in after the news spread of Bush's disdain for the vegetable. Borrowing from the rhetorical style of John Kennedy, he added his intent to "go anywhere, bear any burden, pay any price to reduce the finite permanent supply of broccoli drifting around the United States, re-heated, re-served, and ignored night after night." Heston then appended a handwritten post-script that revealed the extent of comfort he had with the Bushes when he said of protests against Barbara Bush's commencement appearance at Wellesley College: "Please tell Barbara I think those Wellesley girls are idiots. (I know you can't say that, so I did)."[3]

---

1 Opened on June 7, 1990, the park's attractions included the shark from *Jaws* and King Kong. In order to continue to generate interest, the *Earthquake* ride expanded to the broader "Disaster!" before finally closing and shifting to a *Fast & Furious* theme to attract the new generation of fans of that franchise.

2 "Chuck to Dear Mr. President," Feb. 14, 1990, WHORM files, GBPL.

3 "Chuck to Dear Mr. President," May 3, 1990, C0091-Lithuania, ibid.

In response, President Bush promised that, regarding Lithuania, he and his advisors were "monitoring the situation carefully." He also wanted Heston to accept "[m]any thanks for your support on the broccoli issue." In his post-script, a delighted Bush noted, "Your support on broccoli rates the attached—wear it with pride!" and included a specially designed T-shirt for Heston to enjoy.[4]

Even with such new venues for displaying his "public face" emerging and a light-hearted exchange with the new president, the 1990s were already proving to be difficult years for the aging star. His attempt to re-enter the science fiction realm fell short in *Solar Crisis*, a joint U.S.-Japanese production. Heston had enjoyed enormous popularity in the Far East and had some success there with *Solar Crisis* as well. But American interest failed to pique, and the actor had to recognize that his name was not enough to sustain a picture in a new era of film.[5]

A shaky motion picture's box office was not the only matter that caused Heston angst during this period. When British actor Jonathan Pryce found himself barred from a part in *Miss Saigon* when it came to Broadway from London because he was not of Eurasian descent, Heston reacted strongly. He crafted a letter of resignation from Actors Equity in protest. "Actors Equity was the first union I joined," he explained. "Until now, I've always been proud of my membership. I'm now deeply ashamed." Terming the act as "obscenely racist," he declared his revulsion at the decision. "As actor and director, I thought the idea was to get the best actor for the part, no matter what color, religion, or politics," he argued.[6]

Two days later, the union reversed its position and agreed to let Pryce play the role in New York. Heston refused to budge on his decision. "I objected to what they did," he proclaimed. "Now they have stopped doing it. But they still did it." The reversal of their decision had only occurred in answer to outcries and public pressure. "We're talking about artistic freedom here."[7] He knew that some of his best roles, including Moses and Ben Hur, might not have been available to him had such thinking applied when he was being considered for them.

4 "George Bush to Dear Chuck," May 17, 1990, ibid.

5 Heston and Isbouts, *Hollywood*, 200.

6 "Heston Resigns From Actors Equity Over 'Saigon,'" *LAT*, Aug. 15, 1990; "Heston quits actors union over 'Miss Saigon' action," *VP*, Aug. 16, 1990. The actor sent a copy of the full letter to President Bush; see "Heston to the President and Board of the Actors Equity Association of America," Aug. 14, 1990, GBPL.

7 Kari Granville and Don Shirley, "Actors' Equity Says White Can Portray Eurasian," *LAT*, Aug. 17, 1990.

Subsequently, Heston shared his sentiments with President Bush, thanking him for additional personal time. "Access is coinage to be spent sparingly," he observed. Then, he broached the matter involving Actor's Equity. "After 43 years in Equity, I rebelled." The restrictions would have prevented Laurence Olivier from offering "his all-time, all-world performance as Othello." He added emphatically, "This is not what I marched with Dr. King for."[8]

Similarly, his stance with the NRA was drawing increased criticism from some circles. What impact this perception might have on future castings was unclear. Yet as one biographer observed, Heston was willing to "pay the price" for his public expressions among peers who did not embrace his politics or positions. Whatever the costs in the parts he no longer received or the bigger paychecks that would have accompanied them, he still enjoyed the benefits accrued over a long career. "By the '90s, when he became president of the NRA," Marc Eliot observed, "he had already made his name in movies, won his Oscar, raised his children, and banked a sizable sum." Eliot insisted that Heston "cared more about being a voice for freedom and a defender of the Second Amendment than having the approving roar of the crowd or hearing the ongoing jingle of the cash register," which was true in many respects. Yet, Heston knew he had found an audience that signaled its unqualified and enthusiastic support for him. Campaign-style NRA buttons that proclaimed "Charlton Heston is my President" allowed the actor to have his own Reaganesque appeal to people for whom that figure also continued to have resonance. For Eliot, at this stage in his life, "Charlton Heston" might be Chuck Heston's "best character," and the actor maintained a meaningful connection with "those audiences eager to see him perform it."[9]

Heston was still quite willing to parlay his celebrity status into public service projects. For the U.S. Department of State's "'Heroes' Campaign," this image fit the purpose perfectly. He began with a reintroduction of himself before shifting to the theme he was promoting. "I'm Charlton Heston. In the movies I usually play a hero, but I know that real life heroes are ordinary people who do extraordinary things for their fellow man." He had portrayed the pilot of a hijacked airliner who saved his passengers, but with bombing campaigns and other incidents remaining in the headlines, he was happy to advocate vigilance. "If you have any information about an act of terrorism, you can be a hero by saving innocent lives. Now, the U.S. government, along with the pilots and airlines, are offering up to four million

---

8 "Chuck to Dear Mr. President," Oct. 3, 1990, WHORM files, GBPL.

9 Eliot, *Charlton Heston*, xvi.

dollars for this information, confidentially, and protection can be assured for these heroic people. Are you the next hero? Please contact the authorities or the U.S. Embassy."[10]

Heston's public service endeavors also reflected his love of the outdoors and a desire to do what it took to pass along important natural resources to future generations. Work on behalf of the National Arbor Day Foundation's "Trees for America" campaign occupied two days and produced spots that featured the actor noting the lasting benefits of one "little pine seedling . . . that makes things better for everybody," set against music by popular singer and environmental advocate John Denver. Marked through with his own edits, as was his wont when approving any script he used, he ended with an identifying tagline. "I'm Charlton Heston, for the National Arbor Day Foundation. Hey, why don't you plant a tree, too? Please."[11]

In a more traditional vein, his work also included cameos and narrations in film and television projects. In an offbeat comedy featuring *Crocodile Dundee* star Paul Hogan, Heston assumed the role of "God" in a brief appearance in *Almost an Angel*. Through the rest of the decade, he supplied the narration for a documentary on cults, a history of bagpipes, for the films *Texas* and *Armageddon*, as well as the voice of Abraham Lincoln for the Smithsonian's *Great Battles of the Civil War* series.

At the same time, the actor refused to contain his points of view on matters he deemed important. He had long championed freedom and independence, including supporting right-to-work laws, yet he remained an inveterate observer of national events. Harkening back to his days as SAG president, Heston had exerted untiring pressure for workers' rights with respect to the requirement of union membership dues. He had long pushed for this in SAG in order to allow members to focus on the issues he believed the Guild should promote and protect. Heston saw the Supreme Court's earlier decision in *Communications Workers of America v. Beck* as a means of exerting pressure on the Bush administration to allow workers to claim "financial core status" in order to avoid union dues from going toward political causes they did not support. Heston wrote to Secretary of Labor Elizabeth Dole, encouraging her to use her office to inform workers of their rights under the ruling. He felt that connecting the Republican government to these laborers would broaden their reach and "diminish" the power of unions on

10 "Jacques Guerin to Dear Mr. Heston," Oct. 9, 1990, Heston Papers, Miscellaneous ads, scripts, etc.—miscellaneous, f.354, HL.

11 "Greg Smith to Dear Carol," Sept. 4, 1990, ibid.

behalf of the Democratic Party to a degree that "would alter the political landscape overnight." In a second letter to Dole he reiterated that *Beck* was a political issue the administration could not afford to ignore.[12] This appeal fell into the glacial flow of Washington politics and would not be acted upon for another two years, adding to the actor's frustration over the inability of even a favorable administration to get things done.

Heston expressed his views to audiences wherever they might be found, including by debating current issues on news programs. In one instance, the tone devolved into insult. As a result, he received widespread support, including from some highly placed individuals. On February 12, 1991, he sent a message to President and First Lady Bush. "I hope you know already how pleased I was that you took the trouble to phone me about my encounter with Christopher Hitchens the other day." The actor and the sitting president had enjoyed an amiable connection, but he was not alone. "Curiously, former President Nixon wrote a note expressing similar sentiments, as did former President Reagan and Nancy in person at his birthday dinner," Heston noted with pleasure of the Republican leadership's response. "I guess you call that the hat trick." However, he could not resist a dig at others. "Former President Carter and Saddam Hussein have yet to be heard from." He invited the president to watch another debate, with former governor of California Jerry Brown, "on the same issue on the Phil Donahue Show on NBC Wednesday afternoon should you be inclined to tune in."[13]

Ten days later, President Bush sent a short reply, explaining that he had missed the Donahue program, "but no doubt it was another ringer." Bush wanted the actor to know that he had used a quote from the Revolutionary voice of conscience, Thomas Paine, which Heston had suggested. Then, in a handwritten note, Bush replied humorously to Heston's reference to silent voices on the matter: "Don't hold your breath waiting to hear from Saddam."[14]

In the meantime, as he had tried so often to do, he found theatrical work to complement his efforts in cinema and television. For Heston, this meant appearances in diverse productions that ranged from Shakespeare to Eugene O'Neill. He approached each of these performances professionally, always seeking a better interpretation as an actor, or on rare occasions as a director. Even so,

12 "Heston to Elizabeth Dole," Mar. 13, 1990, GBPL. Emilie Raymond covered this issue effectively in *Cold, Dead Hands*, 237-240; "Heston to Dole," Aug. 27, 1990, GBPL.

13 "Heston to Dear Mr. President and Barbara," Feb. 12, 1991, ibid.

14 "George to Dear Chuck," Feb. 22, 1991, ibid.

his views on current events managed to enter the picture as well, such as at the conclusion of A. R. Gurney's play, *Love Letters*, when he responded to a query about the Gulf War. "President Johnson made the grave mistake of trying to control the Vietnam War from the Oval Office and we were bogged down for years," he asserted. "President Bush, by leaving tactical decisions up to the professionals, is allowing the military to win."[15]

In the late summer of 1991, an opportunity came for Heston to take on the role of real-life pilot hero Al Haynes, who had saved 184 of the 296 passengers entrusted to him during a horrific plane crash. Television news coverage had captured Haynes's United Airlines DC-10 cartwheeling dramatically during an emergency landing on July 19, 1989, in Sioux City, Iowa, before settling into flaming wreckage in a nearby cornfield. The project based upon that incident, originally entitled, *A Thousand Heroes*, received a significant boost with Heston's addition to the cast. "He represents the kind of heroic man Al Haynes is," the producer noted. "We're thrilled at the opportunity to be working with him."[16] Joining Heston in the project that came to be known as *Crash Landing: The Rescue of Flight 232* were James Coburn and Richard Thomas.

Portraying a living individual presented interesting challenges. Although Heston corresponded with Haynes, who served as a consultant for the film and for whom the actor expressed both admiration for his "skill and courage" and gratitude "for a good part," he decided to delay meeting his subject while filming interior scenes in Los Angeles. "Acting comes from creative imagination," he observed. Reality nevertheless crept into the process. Heston learned that during the rescue scenes, two of the extras in the film had provided the same function for Captain Haynes. "The genuine emotion was palpable," he noted.[17]

On a troubling personal note, Lydia was dealing with more than migraines during this period. At Holly's insistence, she had agreed to a physical examination, which located breast cancer that required surgery. The circumstances compelled her husband to refocus on the person who had been his companion and bulwark for so long in order to provide as much comfort and support as he could while

---

15 "In Hollywood," "Actor Charlton Heston," *LAT*, Jan. 22, 1991.

16 "Heston to play pilot in upcoming TV movie based on real life," *Statesboro* [GA] *Herald*, Aug. 12, 1991.

17 "Heston to play airline pilot," *Statesboro Herald*, Oct. 1, 1991; "Crash Landing: The Rescue of Flight 232," *Statesboro Herald TV Week*, Feb. 22-Feb. 28, 1992.

she endured the surgery and recovery. A busy schedule often obscured his deep devotion, but such elemental experiences reminded him of it and reinforced it.[18]

Two critical events for Heston occurred on November 4, 1991. The first was the TNT premier of the Sherlock Holmes drama *Crucifer of Blood*. That same day, he participated in the dedication of the Ronald Reagan Presidential Library in Simi Valley. With the five living presidents—Richard Nixon, Gerald Ford, Jimmy Carter, Ronald Reagan, and George H. W. Bush—in attendance, Heston offered a perspective on those leaders who represented "America . . . and Americans." As he left the proceedings to hasten back to Lydia's side, he recalled, "Five presidents sent their good wishes to my girl."[19]

That autumn, Heston appeared once again in several showings of *Love Letters* with former *Colbys* co-star Stephanie Beacham as part of a celebrity couples participation in the one-year anniversary of the play. He also traveled to Virginia, where he was "the guest of honor at the fourth annual Virginia Festival of American Film" with "a gala showing of 'Ben-Hur.'" He returned to another familiar role, albeit after more than thirty years, when he accepted the post of grand marshal for the 60th Annual Hollywood Christmas Parade in Los Angeles.[20]

At the same time, the "Charlton Heston Celebrity Shoot" took on greater prominence among acting circles for those performers who supported gun ownership and sportsmanship. A *Los Angeles Times* feature noted the attendance of 130 stars who divided into teams for demonstrating their prowess with handguns and shotguns in competitive rounds. "When the celebrity shoot was first held in 1987, only one woman participated," writer Kathryn Bold remarked. "This year 25% of the competitors were women." The event was part of a national campaign that raised $9 million for the rifle team expected to compete in the Olympic Games in Barcelona, Spain in 1992.[21]

A bound volume provided biographical sketches of an eclectic range of film and television star participants in the shoot, including Ned Beatty, Gary Collins, Robert Conrad, Charles Durning, Susan Howard, Dean Jones, Steve Kanaly, Vicki

18 *CHA*, 549.

19 C-Span captured Heston's remarks; see www.c-span.org/video/?c4582655/charlton-heston-speech; *CHA*, 549.

20 "'Love' Couples," *LAT*, Mar. 20, 1991; "Love Letters," *LAT*, Nov. 17, 1991; Howard Pousner, "Heston is guest for UVA film fest," *AJC*, Oct. 20, 1991; "Heston to Lead Christmas Parade," *LAT*, Oct. 30, 1991; "Hooray for Hollywood—Sunday is Parade Day," Nov. 28, 1991, ibid.; "Charlton Heston to be grand marshal," *Statesboro Herald*, Oct. 31, 1991.

21 Kathryn Bold, "Shooting Stars Come Out for NRA Gala," *LAT*, July 16, 1992, www.articles.latimes.com/1992-07-16/news/vw-3455_1_u-s-shooting-team.

Lawrence, Michael Learned, Geoffrey Lewis, Patrick Macnee, Joe Mantegna, Jerry Mathers, Christopher Noth, George Peppard, Suzanne Pleshette, Richard Roundtree, Stan Shaw, Paul Sorvino, Robert Stack, and Dub Taylor, as well as sports personalities Dave Butz and Bob Lilly. Heston's foreword touted the event's growth along with its focus on gun safety and its role as an inspiration for "young people to 'shoot for the stars' as they work to be a part of our United States Shooting Team." The actor was more determined than ever to highlight the broad spectrum of personalities that supported the gathering and its agenda.[22]

Charlton and Lydia Heston continued to grace stages and find ways to demonstrate appreciation to communities that had special meaning for them. A return to Asheville in 1992, where community theater had provided an important early foundation for their work, allowed the couple to present *Love Letters* and dedicate an auditorium in the theater in which they had once co-directed that would now bear their names. *Love Letters* also brought the couple back to Northwestern University in March 1993.[23]

Heston took time away from the stage to enjoy the fruits of the lobbying effort he had undertaken with the Bush administration. On April 13, 1992, he was in the Rose Garden for a signing ceremony in connection with an Executive Order by President Bush relating to the requirement of federal contractors to advise their employees of their rights to limit dues payments to nonpolitical matters. The president introduced his guest with a familiar reference. "And fresh from parting the Red Sea yet again on TV last night, an old friend, Charlton Heston." Bush, however, was not content with merely a cultural identification. Heston had been too integral behind the scenes as a champion for the cause. Consequently, Bush labeled the actor "[o]ne of America's most intrepid fighters for individual rights" asserting, "He's given much of himself to put collective bargaining rights into practice. And he's been equally committed to saying that no company or organization may infringe a worker's individual freedom of conscience." Delighted that the man who had also joined Republican Party campaign efforts had "traveled all across the country as a crusader for individual rights," Bush concluded, "You are most welcome."[24]

---

22 *Charlton Heston Celebrity Shoot*, n.p., n.d., although inclusion of a page on the NRA under President Robert K. Corbin would place the event in 1991-92.

23 Karen Werling, "Appreciation: Charlton Heston's Life as a Wildcat" *North by Northwestern* (April 16, 2008).

24 Raymond, *Cold, Dead Hands*, 237-240; "Remarks on signing the Executive Order on Employee Rights Concerning Union Dues, April 13, 1992," *Bush Papers, 1992-93*, 593-594.

Author Emilie Raymond thought the Heston-Bush relationship was "every bit as warm as the one Heston shared with President Reagan, if not more so."[25] Certainly, the cordiality demonstrated through their interactions indicated as much, as their light-hearted exchange about broccoli underscored. Yet his connection with George Bush was never as deep or as longstanding as his personal and professional ties to Ronald Reagan.

If such public moments seemed to validate his determined stance on matters of freedom, they did nothing to advance his career. Of course, Charlton Heston did not necessarily want or need to reinvent himself, but he felt he had to reintroduce, and in some cases, introduce himself to potential viewers of his work. Among his more inventive efforts was an appearance on *The Whoopi Goldberg Show*. Slated to take advantage of the host's energetic personality, the opening show featured Elizabeth Taylor, as well as other entertainment figures. If Heston did not seem right for the setting, his appearance demonstrated that Whoopi had a genuine interest in his work and an affection for him as an iconic Hollywood star. Whatever viewers might have anticipated, the conversation never turned antagonistic, and when Goldberg inquired about any wariness concerning Heston's intimacy with African American co-star Rosalind Cash in *The Omega Man*, he responded with a demonstration of the kiss that Goldberg was obviously thrilled to receive.[26]

An affinity for Westerns had led to some of Heston's best work in film in *The Big Country*, *Will Penny*, and more recently, *The Last Hard Men*. On November 7, 1992, this connection led to the actor's selection for the "seventh presentation of the Hollywood Westerner Hall of Fame Award," along with recognition for the legacy of Gary Cooper. On the day before the announcement, President Bush sent a message for the gathering of the President Reagan Award Luncheon. "Congratulations to my very good friend Charlton Heston and to the family of Gary Cooper." Bush added that "Heston has also ensured lasting acclaim for his achievements as an actor, and as one who has had the honor of his friendship, I know, firsthand, of his very deep respect for our history."[27]

Governor Pete Wilson of California added his congratulations in a message that reiterated the impact he felt the actor had made in the entertainment industry. "For decades, audiences young and old have enjoyed your wide range of performances,

---

25 Raymond, *Cold, Dead Hands*, 240.

26 *The Whoopi Goldberg Show* lasted one season, 1992-93; James Robert Parish, *Whoopi Goldberg: Her Journey From Poverty to Megastardom* (Secaucus, NJ, 1997), 258-260.

27 George Bush, Nov. 6, 1992, Bush Papers, GBPL.

spanning the dramatic spectrum of television and the cinema. Your remarkable performances in such classic films as 'The Ten Commandments,' 'Ben Hur,' 'Major Dundee,' and 'Khartoum' have delighted many, and your extraordinary skill has made you one of America's most notable actors. Millions still enjoy your work on the stage and screen, and I am confident that you will remain a constant force in the performing arts for many years to come."[28]

About this time, Heston turned once more to his connections with religious imagery in an ambitious project for Agamemnon Films that melded drama and dramatic reading: *Charlton Heston Presents The Bible*. Filmed on location at various sites in the Holy Land, the actor drew upon his narrative skills and directorial experience, connecting the famed voice with the sites and stories that occasionally had served as the settings for his films. Subsequently, when the series switched to a new format, a writer for *Billboard* magazine noted grandiosely, "Holy Cyberspace! A biblical CD-ROM," and declared, "Parting the Waters—Charlton Heston will become the first Academy Award winner to enter the interactive promised land via his performance in his forthcoming CD-ROM, 'Charlton Heston's Voyage Through the Bible.'"[29]

As part of the project's initial rollout, Heston guested on Robert H. Schuller's popular television program *Hour of Power* and provided the voice narration for Schuller's upcoming Christmas extravaganza. Subsequently, a family-oriented companion volume included a personal statement from Heston that tied his present and past efforts together. "Ever since playing Moses in *The Ten Commandments*, I've felt a deep, personal connection with the Bible, which remains as vivid and vital today." Noting his role as "a storyteller, not a scholar," Heston observed, "In my own quest to understand the Bible, I have discovered that its reach extends far beyond the realm of religion, and want to share with you more than just a reading of the Scriptures." To demonstrate the ecumenical nature of the project, which included a combination of video and audio cassettes, the producers included a certificate of endorsement from a rabbi and a priest.[30]

The actor's forays into politics enabled him to reiterate his public positions and make the political contribution he believed continued to resonate. He threw his support behind Virginia Republican gubernatorial candidate George Allen,

---

28 "Governor Pete Wilson to Heston," Nov. 7, 1992, Correspondence, f.466, HL.

29 Eliot, *Charlton Heston*, 435; Marilyn A. Gillen, "Holy Cyberspace! A Biblical CD-ROM," *Billboard*, Nov. 5, 1994, 96.

30 Charlton Heston, *Charlton Heston Presents The Bible: A Companion for Families* (New York, 1997).

working his way across the commonwealth at various appearances, although he and Allen were not personally acquainted. Noting that Heston had "offered through the Republican National Committee to come down and help George's campaign," the candidate's press secretary noted, "we were glad to accept. He's a very vocal Republican supporter. Mr. Heston believes in George's positions and very strongly supports George and wants him to be elected."[31]

The actor lent his talents to other efforts as well. In early December 1993, Heston combined his love of reading with a different endeavor when he sat before 150 children at the Los Angeles Mission to offer dramatic renderings of "A Visit from St. Nicholas" and other selections. "They did well," he observed of his young audience. "They can be restless, little children especially." Lydia joined her husband at the event and participated in the singing that also marked the festive occasion.[32]

Having lived through the changes wrought in his industry over the decades he had spent treading the boards or appearing on screens large and small, Heston was also aware that he had to repurpose his career choices to appeal to new audiences. Cameos in the 1993 films *Wayne's World 2* and *Tombstone* kept his face before the moviegoers of another generation as he sought to connect with younger viewers or remind older ones of his continued presence. He no longer had to sustain a picture or work the interminable hours required of him in earlier times, but his desire to find receptive audiences remained unabated.

Interestingly, one author found Henry Hooker, Heston's *Tombstone* character, remarkable, given the film's "values" concerning guns. Douglas Brode felt the actor's agreement to appear as an ally of the Earps, who were dedicated to keeping weapons off the streets of Tombstone, to be counter to the advocate's position that owning weapons was a matter of individual choice, affirmed by the Constitution. Brode thought Heston ought more appropriately to be connected with the Clanton-McLaury faction than Wyatt Earp and his associates. Heston had indicated in the past that performance was not dependent upon aligning with personal choices and had undertaken projects with social undertones of varying positions. At this stage of his career, however, he obviously was less interested in making a statement regarding gun control than he was at securing a part in a motion picture that had all the hallmarks of achieving box-office success and consequent longevity on movie screens. Any stance the actor/activist took on social issues certainly would not require a fictional film character to convey a message to his audience. He

---

31 Martha J. Milner, "Film star to visit Abingdon," *BHC*, Oct. 28, 1993.

32 "Heston reads to children," *BHC*, Dec. 13, 1993.

remained unequivocal in what he viewed as the moral decay of the presidency, and was robust in his criticism of Bill Clinton's administration and the chief executive personally. Emilie Raymond noted that Heston apologized for applying a negative term to the president out of respect for the office and his desire to display decorum in his public expressions. Nevertheless, the actor thought the many transgressions he observed meant that Clinton was untrustworthy on numerous social issues. Heston felt little need to restrain his scorn openly, remarking to one group that the Clinton White House brought to mind figures from the classic film *The Wizard of Oz*, although he preferred for his listeners to determine for themselves which individuals in Washington fit which characters.[33]

The *Tombstone* work had amounted to only a few days, with some of the shots using a stand-in once Heston had left the set. Yet, the actor's brief appearance made a powerful impression on his colleagues. Though Henry Hooker was initially supposed to be a passive figure, Heston's signing meant "the character's persona changed significantly," according to author John Farkis. "Naturally, the actor's resonating, distinctive voice, chiseled jaw, broad shoulders, and larger-than-life commanding appearances in films such as *The Ten Commandments*, *El Cid*, *Ben-Hur* and *Khartoum* wouldn't jive" with the initial visualization. "As a result, Heston played the role as . . . Heston."

Bent with age and infirmities, Heston consistently defied the expectations of younger actors, and "as the total pro," rose to his fullest capacity when filming his scenes. "Between takes, Heston would sit on the ranch porch, regaling extras with his stories from his fabled life and sharing pearls of wisdom." Confronted with the well-meaning suggestion of retiring to his trailer, the veteran actor would insist, "No. I'm holding court here."

On other occasions, he wanted to demonstrate that he was no different than any of the other performers. "Despite his prestige and mystique, Heston, from his very first day on the set, just wanted to be one of the guys," Farkis noted. "Surprisingly, Heston had a wicked sense of humor," When one of the crew sat in his chair, the actor insisted he remain. "I'm going to sit in Kurt Russell's chair. It'll drive him crazy." At lunch he would take his place in the line and decline assistance. Then, after the shooting, when others watched the NBA Finals on

33 Brode, *Dream West*, 45-46; Raymond, *Cold Dead Hands*, 273 and 352, note 53; "So, who's Dorothy? Hillary or Chelsea?" *VP*, Mar. 31, 1998.

television, Heston would make his way down to the bar, "have three Scotches, and go back to his room: very nonchalant, very unpretentious."[34]

Between his features and other activities, Heston turned to yet another platform in order to locate new avenues for professional involvement. Observing of his appearance on the daytime soap opera "*The Bold and the Beautiful*, he explained, "I've made a lot of movies that were not seen by 35 million people and this show is seen by that many people around the world."[35] Heston knew he was likely not the primary incentive for those millions who tuned in, but his observation as to the exposure it would bring was valid. Chuck Heston understood he had to be content to "be Charlton Heston" when executives called on him for roles he would have rejected earlier in his career.

The actor also located other outlets that allowed him to reach wider audiences. A brief feature in the May 1993 issue of *Playboy* put him in company with outspoken National Basketball Association star Charles Barkley and a popular model from the game show *The Price Is Right*. For readers of the "Video" section of the magazine, Heston touted *Citizen Kane* as the "greatest film of all time," and recommended Laurence Olivier's *Henry V* and Merchant-Ivory's *Howard's End* for contemporary video viewing. Obviously, there was the collateral belief that consumers would also choose *Ben-Hur* or *Planet of the Apes* while they patronized their local video entertainment outlets.[36]

Continued public exposure meant Heston could still employ his persona to advance special causes. In 1993, this meant venturing into another dangerous war zone when he went to Somalia to support peacekeepers defending international humanitarian aid operations in a country wracked by starvation and warlord violence. He shared time with Army and Marine units, as well as Australian troops, and visited an orphanage. In the transition from the administration of George H. W. Bush to that of Bill Clinton, Heston found the constant to be the American soldiers who answered their country's call to duty and accepted the important, if often uncertain nature of their missions.[37]

The actor had also reached the stage in his life and career where his focus could turn increasingly to his legacy. Under the auspices of the Screen Actors Guild,

---

34 John Farkis, *The Making of Tombstone: Behind the Scenes of the Classic Modern Western* (Jefferson, NC, 2019), 78-82.

35 Eliot, *Charlton Heston*, 439.

36 Susan Karlin, "Guest Shot," *Playboy* (May 1993), 28.

37 Wise and Wildman, *Stars in Khaki*, 134. See also "Thumbs Up," *BHC*, Feb. 20, 1993.

he gave an interview ranging from his earliest days in the Michigan woodlands and Northwestern University to his present superstar status. He understandably devoted a good portion of the retrospective to his work with SAG, revealing his most pressing concerns and influences. He had found Ronald Reagan an "effective negotiator" and accepted an invitation to board membership at his behest. "I did and still do object strongly to the politicization of the board," he asserted. With respect to his own political expressions, he affirmed, "I revere Thomas Jefferson." Though his efforts in support of Republican candidates of various stripes suggested otherwise, he maintained, "I've always thought of myself as a political independent." In terms of his other roles as an endorser or spokesman, Heston observed, "As a public face, I've had access." This role particularly suited his desire to remain as active as possible. "It's something that I can do that is useful."[38] For Charlton Heston, such were the hallmarks outside of acting that he championed, and that he hoped others would identify in him: leadership in his profession, historical awareness, political independence, and public advocacy and involvement.

Another Heston hallmark was the longevity of his marriage to Lydia Clarke. The couple marked their fiftieth anniversary with an elaborate dinner-dance that included toasts and roasts from friends and close associates. One account noted, "It was a far bigger affair than the Hestons' wedding, witnessed by two strangers." Among the reminiscences was one attendee's recognition of "a couple currently appearing in the longest-running marriage in town." "May there be many curtain calls." Lydia had maintained early in her husband's career that she "enjoyed the entire adventure." At the same time, he acknowledged the "sacrifice" of her own acting career to support him and their family.[39]

The Second World War had provided the backdrop for the Hestons' nuptials, and in the month after their golden anniversary celebration, the conflict was once again a factor in the actor's public life. The former Air Force staff sergeant joined with other luminaries to welcome Prince Andrew, Duke of York, to a gala event in Beverly Hills to generate funds in support of the American Air Museum in Great Britain. Raising nearly $250,000 for the project, the ceremony included special honoree Bob Hope and remarks by Heston. Hope and Heston appeared again in a special entitled *Memories of World War II* in 1995.[40]

38 "Screen Actors Guild Interview—Legacy, June 1994," UCLA.

39 "Hestons Mark 50 Years of 'Symbiosis,'" *LAT*, Mar. 21, 1994; "1961 Vintage Radio Interviews with Charlton Heston and Lydia Heston," *El Cid*, The Weinstein Corporation, 2008, DVD.

40 Hillary Johnson, "Royalty Stars as Old Allies Reunite," *LAT*, Apr. 11, 1994; *Bob Hope: Memories of World War II*, Aug. 5, 1995, IMDB, accessed Jan. 11, 2019.

The actor spent a portion of the summer months as he had so often done, supporting Republican candidates and broader social causes. He combined his interest in sport-shooting with campaigning for U.S. Senate candidate and actor Fred Thompson.[41] At a campaign event in East Tennessee, Heston insisted that Thompson had better prove successful in a first bid for public office so that "a string of Heston endorsements of winning Republicans in Texas, Georgia, and Virginia—including Virginia Gov. George Allen—remains unbroken," according to journalist Rick Wagner. "I'm on kind of a roll," Heston observed, noting that he had explained to one aspirant for office, "You'd better not lose. It'll ruin my reputation," citing the effort as "a high priority" for him to undertake on the candidate's behalf.

Heston's humorous aside downplayed the nuanced nature of his commitment to GOP causes. Responding to a question about his potential support for Republican nominee Oliver North for a senate seat from Virginia, the actor noted, "I don't make all my own choices on campaign matters. I frankly don't do a lot of this." Always sensitive to his independent stance, he argued, "I am not at the beck and call of the Republican Party." Still, Heston admitted, "I am advised by Phil Gramm's office and others in the Republican Party."[42]

As it had with Ronald Reagan, Heston's connection with Fred Thompson represented the ways in which the arenas of acting and politics intersected. "Politics is partly a performance art," he explained at a press conference. "You are in effect leading people, persuading people. That is performance." The Thompson campaign also allowed Heston to tap once more into his appreciation for his favorite leaders in history to make his point by citing Winston Churchill's inspiring messages to the British people at the height of their struggles against Nazi Germany.[43]

Encomiums for the actor's own career continued with a tribute held by the Friars Club of Beverly Hills. Among those who offered remarks was former President Reagan, who termed Heston "an individual Nancy and I hold especially dear." Reagan provided context for a film montage that he maintained "will remind all of us why we've always felt safe when Charlton Heston has been around—this hero bigger than life, this actor supreme." The actor-turned-politician recognized

41 "Heston to shoot at Big Springs," *BHC*, June 16, 1994; "Heston campaigning for Thompson," ibid., June 17, 1994.

42 Rick Wagner, "Heston touts fellow actor," *BHC*, June 25, 1994.

43 Alan Weston, "Charlton Heston backs Thompson for Senate," *Kingsport* [TN] *Times-News*, June 25, 1994.

the qualities of his friend on screen and off. "His magnificent screen performances aside, it's the way Chuck has always conducted his life that especially makes him a hero in my eyes." For Reagan, Heston was "a singularly dedicated person of the highest moral caliber," who was "never been afraid to speak his mind or stand up for what he believes in."[44]

The degree to which professional curtain calls remained was an unspoken factor in another personal milestone for the film celebrity and his wife. Accepting the realities of his own age and lengthy career, Heston recognized that he could not play the roles he had once undertaken. His persona nevertheless ensured that some roles were his if he desired them. One of these came in the form of the director of a CIA-style agency in the Arnold Schwarzenegger vehicle *True Lies* in 1994. As Spencer Trilby, he was supposed to be able to keep the subordinate and his freewheeling associates in line. "I need a guy who can plausibly intimidate Arnold," director James Cameron maintained. "If I can intimidate the Pharaoh of Egypt, I can intimidate Arnold," the star replied, referencing one of the roles that stamped his cinematic persona.[45]

In the mid-1990s, as he entered his seventh decade, Charlton Heston took stock of his life and career in a memoir that highlighted his journey from the Michigan backwoods to Coldwater Canyon. The autobiography, *In the Arena*, represented something of a self-generated Rorschach test for Heston. It capitalized on the elements he felt had brought him the most success professionally and reflected his admiration of figures in history from whom he drew inspiration. Like a modern-day Theodore Roosevelt, Heston felt he had entered the arena and offered his best effort at advancing causes he was convinced would benefit a flailing society.

Perhaps most tellingly was a revelation about his assessment of a Roman emperor. "I'm an admirer of the Emperor Hadrian," Heston began. "Of all the thousands of clowns and tyrants, good men and bad, who've governed other men through all the centuries, he seems to have done as well as any." The actor considered some of Hadrian's writings "the most penetratingly honest comment on the human condition I've ever read from a head of state." The Roman had insisted that he did not despise men and could not rule over them if he had. "I *know* men," he had observed, citing all of the qualities that made them "capable of almost anything for the sake of their own profit, or increasing their own esteem . . . or even

44 "Remarks at a Friars Club Tribute to Charlton Heston, Beverly Hilton Hotel, Beverly Hills, California, July 29, 1994," D. Erik Felten, ed., *A Shining City: The Legacy of Ronald Reagan* (New York, 1998), 238.

45 Heston and Isbouts, *Hollywood*, 201.

simply for the avoidance of their own suffering." From this beginning, the actor shifted the focus to the realm in which he felt most comfortable. "Never having played Hadrian, I'm afraid I'm not enormously well-read on him, but it occurs to me he was like Michelangelo and Jefferson and Richelieu and several other great men I *have* played, in that he was lonely." Heston concluded, "It might well be true that such men are usually *separate* men, cut off a little from the rest of us by their capacities and perceptions. . . . I've played a lot of these guys. Believe me, they are *not* like you and me."[46]

Reaction to the autobiography was generally positive. "When actor Charlton Heston appeared on the Family Channel's '700 Club' in Virginia Beach last week, all he had to do to get a prolonged standing ovation was show up," guest columnist Bill Ruehlmann explained in *The Virginian-Pilot*. The "70-year-old actor with the Mount Rushmore mug [who] seemed to have grown into the living image of his most famous role, Moses," was in town to promote the book. "It still works," he observed to host Ben Kinchlow, of the prop staff from the film he had brought to the show. "I can part the pool with it," he said, adding quickly that he was "kidding." Reuhlmann liked the stories that Heston included in the volume and found the book "substantial and straightforward" like its author.[47]

Heston also continued to build on his authoritative brand in unique formats. In early 1995, he headlined a "Success 1995" program, touted as "California's Most Popular Business Seminar," alongside motivational maven Zig Ziglar and Debbi Fields, founder of Mrs. Fields Cookies. Each panelist offered techniques and advice for participants from their own experiences, presented "live and in person." In addition to inspiring the audience "by recalling the tradition of excellence exhibited by America throughout history," the actor offered an "extraordinary session" with the themes: "How to step beyond what you think you can achieve" and "Why great men are an endangered species."[48]

A role as another dynamic cinematic figure emerged in 1995 when he took a supporting part as Mormon leader Brigham Young for a television production. Although not the central figure in the project, his presence nevertheless reminded everyone that Heston remained a recognizable star. The actor's penchant for research and tangible, physical elements such as wardrobe as vehicles for embodying roles

---

46 *CHA*, 348.

47 Bill Ruehlmann, "Like Heston, memoir is substantial, straightforward," *VP*, Sept. 17, 1995

48 "Success 1995," *LAT*, Jan. 15, 1995.

benefitted him once more as he approached the role of the charismatic Mormon church president. He felt he could draw upon his previous work as Moses to find this character—"I know this guy. I've seen him before."—yet the TNT production, *The Avenging Angel*, offered him an even greater resource. "I went to Salt Lake City," Heston explained, where he was able to explore the landscape the leader had inhabited. Visiting Young's house and perusing his possessions, the actor extracted meaningful context. "The plate he ate off is there." This opportunity gave Heston an immediacy to his subject that he thought was rare. "This is the first experience I've had playing someone of whom there's such a complete personal record."[49]

In his own time and world, Heston did not find much in culture to recommend itself, preferring books and symphonies to more modern expressions of artistic creativity. These questions were not simply matters of taste, but threats to civility and decency that he could not abide or ignore. Never afraid to tackle issues on which he felt strongly, the actor engaged with one of those dangerous cultural elements, in his estimation, when he spoke out against Time Warner's release of rapper Ice-T's *Cop Killer* album. Heston found the lyrics that included anti-police sentiments and its cover imagery profoundly offensive. He considered this crusade was comparable to the work he had done for civil rights three decades earlier, although on a different scale. "Then we were following Dr. King," he remarked of his place in that effort. "This was just me and Time Warner."[50] The fight with the media giant reflected the continued transition for the actor from an earlier period in which he felt performers were better served not taking public stands to a time in which he now believed it was essential to use his platform to advocate for values he felt were under attack and worth defending.

Later, when television producer Dick Wolf made his intention known of hiring the rapper for the popular *Law & Order* franchise, Heston dashed off a letter to the editors of the *Los Angeles Times* to explain how he had worked to have Time-Warner remove *Cop Killer* from its playlist. "Aside from my work on civil rights with Martin Luther King in the early '60s, before it got fashionable, there is no public sector activity of which I'm more proud." Left unsaid was the specific action he wished to encourage the producer to take. "Do well, Mr. Wolf. You're a gifted man. Ice-T, I wish you well, too. Be a better man."[51]

49 Bernard Weinraub, "Holy Moses! Now Charlton Heston's Playing Brigham Young," *TV Guide* (Jan. 21, 1995), 26-27.

50 Raymond, *Cold, Dead Hands*, 260.

51 "Ice-T's Opportunity," *LAT*, Aug. 17, 1996.

Heston enjoyed other connections to various communities. When gridiron success for his alma mater led to an appearance in the Rose Bowl after the 1995 season, he responded with gusto. Greeting the Northwestern team at Universal Studios personally, he brought the Moses staff out of retirement once more to wave in encouragement and inspiration. "Fear not, oh Wildcats," he called out to them, "I shall not abandon thee." *Los Angeles Times* staff writer David Wharton described the actor as in "giddy delirium" over the team's 10-0 regular season, noting that he "gave it his best Moses as the waters—dyed Northwestern purple—parted by way of special effects pumps, allowing the team to roll through on a tram." To assure that no temporal element was overlooked, Heston also presented the squad with tablets containing only one commandment: "Thou Shall Not Lose."[52] Unfortunately, the enthusiasm and theatrics did not prove enough for the game, as the University of Southern California Trojans prevailed 41-32 over their Midwestern opponents.

If the outcome prompted Wildcat supporters to indulge in libations to assuage their disappointment, Heston would not have been completely averse to joining them, as he had recently started appearing in a series of advertisements for Anheuser Busch. "The Good Life" allowed Heston to exhibit his interest in American history with references to the *Mayflower* and Thanksgiving, the Continental Congress and the Founding Fathers, as well as ancient history with connections to the Egyptians and "Ancient Art," all while extolling the virtues of the liquid refreshment for "80 million responsible consumers."

In *Pledge and Promise* he narrated various segments aimed at appealing to the broader population, as well as to consumers. Heston reminded viewers that finite natural resources must be protected. "We don't inherit the Earth, we borrow it from the next generation," he noted in one clip. In another, featuring a sea lion named George and calling for wildlife preservation, he presented a similar argument. "Why do we do this? Because we believe the world we share is only given to us in trust." Arguing for a corporate citizenship that mattered, he observed, "The continuing Anheuser-Busch commitment to preserving wildlife. That's our pledge and promise to you. And to the Georges of the world."[53]

The unique Anheuser Busch Bud Light beer campaign featuring the tagline "I love you, man!" aired in conjunction with Super Bowl XXX in January 1996. In

---

52 David Wharton, "Team Gets Star Treatment," *LAT*, Dec. 29, 1995; "Promised Land Didn't Have 'Waterworld,'" ibid.

53 "Commercials," UCLA; "Anheuser-Busch 'Pledge and Promise' 1-30-91" and "George/Wildlife Preservation 1-30-91." Heston also shot "Twins/Ecology," featuring elk in Montana; Heston Papers, HL.

one ad, Heston is shown at a cocktail party regaling listeners with his chariot story from *Ben-Hur*. Suddenly, he finds himself face to face with a fan who expresses his admiration for "that chariot thing you did" and "the water stuff" he had performed as Moses. "You're not getting my Bud Light," Heston responds with a degree of firmness that holds the admirer at bay, before offering a more epic rendition of "I love you man!" and having a fresh beer thrust into his hand.

In a *Los Angeles Times* article entitled, "Prophets, Presidents—and the King of Beer," Elaine Dutka offered a "Sermon on the Malt" that featured the popular sales pitch. "On Super Bowl Sunday, Charlton Heston became the fourth target of Johnny, a character who achieved cult figure status in Budweiser Light's fabulously successful 'I love you man' advertising campaign." Dutka noted the actor's awareness of the ways in which the effort could prove beneficial to him. "After years of playing presidents, generals, prophets and kings, Heston said it was a chance to show new colors." Like the attempts he had made to shift to comedy at other points in his career, he seemed unconcerned that the effort might appear beneath the dignity of the roles that had made him famous. "A lighthearted ad like this provided some balance in that I allowed the audience to laugh at me," he maintained. As in other instances, he obtained "creative control" so that nothing he felt was detrimental would make it into the ad. "Public image notwithstanding, Heston says he felt little conflict signing on." In the final analysis, he considered the experience a positive one. "But I'm an actor, for heaven's sake. You have to compartmentalize. And, as long as the product is inoffensive, the stigma of doing TV ads decreases as the price escalates. They spent a bundle on this Super Bowl ad—well into the six figures. I don't come cheap and neither do the networks."[54]

While repeating his chariot race story for beer-drinkers and fans, Heston also had to relive a troubling but persistent tale from *Ben-Hur*. A report that Gore Vidal's work on the William Wyler classic ventured not only into more substantial authorship of the script, but also contained latent homosexual themes, merited Heston's attention. "What are we to make of Gore Vidal?" he wondered, before noting that the writer had only "produced a scene of several pages which Wyler rejected after a read-through with Steve Boyd and me. Vidal left the next day." As for the assertion of including subliminal messaging concerning the relationship between the one-time friends, he explained, "Vidal's claim that he slipped in a

---

54 Actor Rob Roy Fitzgerald, whom Elaine Dutka described as "a sad soul going to any lengths to get a Bud Light," was Heston's foil in the commercial. The game was played on Jan. 28, 1996, with the Dallas Cowboys defeating the Pittsburgh Steelers, 27-17; Elaine Dutka, "Prophets, Presidents—and the King of Beers," *LAT*, Mar. 31, 1996.

scene implying a homosexual relationship between the two men insults Willy Wyler, and I have to say, irritates the hell out of me." One correspondent observed, "Whether he's acting or campaigning, Heston always seems to have time to write letters. He's become known as an inveterate writer of letters to newspapers."[55]

At least one individual found this Heston letter-writing trend irritating. Ephraim "Eph" Moxon called an earlier missive "rambling" and described it as "nothing more than a study in name-dropping. Better yet, nickname-dropping." The actor was proud of his past associations, but some of these appeared to be wearing thin. "Other than telling us about Yak, Willy, Dick and Joe, the letter didn't tell me anything I didn't already know. One does not need to be a genius or a 'legend' to know that a mistaken stunt can cost money or a life." Moxon implored, "Please don't print letters simply because of star recognition."[56] Of course, Heston had no intention of stifling his expressions or curtailing his actions to suit a disgruntled editorial page reader. He would say something if he believed he had something to say that was worth hearing.

While he reasserted the liberty of expressing himself wherever he was located, Heston turned to work that was still taking him to extraordinary locations. In this case the story was set in Alaska, as seen through the film substitute of British Columbia, with Fraser Heston directing and Charlton Heston starring as a villainous poacher menacing a father, two children, and an orphaned polar bear cub. Aside from the chance to make a movie in a stunning setting, Heston had the opportunity to play a villain, which he found a welcome departure from his usual heroic roles.[57] Despite this, the film failed to find much traction at the box office.

Yet if good screen roles were harder to come by, the need for an audience still existed for him. He found one when he took on a leadership position in the National Rifle Association. At the time, the NRA was grappling with divisions between those who wanted "responsible" gun ownership and those who saw any challenge at any level as indicative of the eminent destruction of Second Amendment rights. Always a hunter, gun collector, and defender of the Constitution as he understood it, Heston cherished the right to own guns, but nevertheless placed himself in the first category. In this context, he worked his way onto the NRA board and then

---

55 Charlton Heston, letter, "Equal Billing," *LAT*, Mar. 17, 1996; Carla Hall, "Conservative actor Charlton Heston has a long history of activism. Now, the screen icon hopes to help lead the NRA to a better place," *LAT*, May 27, 1997.

56 Ephraim (Eph) Moxon, letter, "Equal Billing," *LAT*, Mar. 17, 1996.

57 Heston and Isbouts, *Hollywood*, 204-205.

ran for the first vice presidency of the organization. Internal divisions virtually guaranteed that despite his stature, the actor would not win easily, much less automatically. The final tally was astonishingly close—a four vote margin—but Heston won. The position offered him the chance to mold the NRA according to his views.[58]

As *Vanity Fair* contributor Sarah Ellison, observed, "In the 1990s, the N.R.A. found its most potent spokesperson: the actor Charlton Heston."[59] Caricature was never far removed from the organization's most dynamic figure. Moses with a gun rather than a bible could lead new followers to their own version of a promised land, but he risked conflating entertainment with the complexities of serious issues such as gun violence. Still, Heston had celebrity stature; everyone around him knew it and prepared to exploit it one way or another.

The actor was ready to take on the perceived cultural threat when he attended the NRA's annual meeting in Dallas. Standing before the gathering, he encouraged the members to follow the examples of "great men" who had accomplished so much in history. "I know there are great women, too, but I don't get to play them," he added with characteristic Heston humor. Nevertheless, his message was meant to be taken seriously. "If my Creator endowed me with the talent to entertain you, the gift to connect you with the habits and minds of these great men. . . . Then I choose to use that same gift now, to reconnect you with a greatness of purpose that already resides in you." Following a history lesson meant to extol American values and virtues, Heston stressed gunowners' ability to feel "the warm breath of freedom" through "the majesty of the Second Amendment." The actor considered the NRA essential to this most significant of Constitutional rights and challenged any notions to the contrary. "If Americans believed in political correctness," he maintained, "we'd still be King George's boys." On the strength of such a performance, Heston seemed a logical choice to serve as the public face of the organization as its first vice president. "He's Moses to our people," executive vice president Wayne LaPierre exclaimed, before adding quickly, "I'm serious!"[60]

Heston began to see his purpose, outside his priorities of family and acting, in his role with the NRA. One scholar asserted that the timing was critical for both

58 Raymond, *Cold, Dead Hands*, 263.

59 Sarah Ellison, "The Civil War that Could Doom the N.R.A.," *Vanity Fair*, June 27, 2016.

60 "Remarks before the 125th Annual Meeting of Members of the National Rifle Association, March 30, 1996, Dallas, TX," Heston, *The Courage to be Free*, 164-168; *Newsweek*, May 19, 1997; Eliot, *Charlton Heston*, 442.

the performer and the entity he had decided to embrace. "Heston's assumption of the first vice presidency could not have been more fortuitous for either him or the NRA," Emilie Raymond observed. "The flailing organization desperately needed a strong and charismatic central figure to reunite and revitalize its membership and improve the organization's public reputation."[61]

The NRA's signature publication, *American Rifleman*, had already introduced the actor to the membership. The July 1997 issue featured Heston alongside Marion Hammer, the organization's president, and LaPierre, with a statement regarding his principles to appear the following month. The September issue's cover showed the actor surrounded by children and the notation, "Charlton Heston's Crusade to Save the Second Amendment." The NRA demonstrated that it had found a new champion. Both LaPierre, in his advocacy piece, "Standing Guard," and President Hammer, in her "Pass the Torch" column, explained to readers why they were thrilled to turn to Heston for a leadership role. A full-page statement by "Charlton Heston, NRA first vice president," put out a call to members: "Let's Save the Second Amendment." He maintained "It wasn't an easy decision for me to become first vice president of this Association. At 72, I'd rather be playing in blanket spaceships and tepees with my grandson, Jack." Then, using a different definition for the word that characterized his work, he added, "But sometimes history leaves you no choice but to act." He was quick to reference his willingness to answer the call in the past with military service and activism in such causes as civil rights. Another full page with the actor at center stage, sitting before a blackboard and an American flag in a classroom setting, offered a précis that anyone could "clip and save," touting, "The Second Amendment: What Every Kid Should Know."[62]

In one photograph of Heston, sprinkled amidst the advertising pages and showing him in a hat and vest and with an open shotgun, the actor offered his views on gun rights. "As the twenty-first century approaches, I won't stand by and watch the Second Amendment die. Wayne LaPierre has asked me to come back to the arena. It's my time—and your time—to serve." Heston reiterated that concerns for his grandson's future had prompted him to accept the challenge, as so many had done at Concord, Gettysburg, Okinawa, and Vietnam. "Real liberty demands action based on conviction. And that is why, at 72 years of age, I am returning to the arena one more time." An accompanying campaign queried, "Charlton

---

61 Raymond, *Cold, Dead Hands*, 263-264.

62 *American Rifleman* (July 1997; Aug. 1997); Various elements, *American Rifleman* (Sept. 1997), cover, 7, 12, 22, 24.

Heston Said Yes. Will you?" It noted that with a "three-year mission membership," a member would receive Heston's video, *The Torch with No Flame*.[63]

"Once again, it's Charlton Heston into the breach," writer Carla Hall maintained as he assumed his new role with the NRA. In order to do so, Heston had to bypass Ned Knox, who had been in line for the same office. Knox's wife observed, "Mr. Knox feels very flattered that they had to bring in Moses, the voice of God, and Ben Hur to knock him out of his chair." Nevertheless, for Heston, the choice made perfect sense. "I have a public face. I know how to do interviews," he explained in one of them. "In the case of the NRA, one of the most useful things I can do is have access to just about any office on [Capitol] Hill. I've done this for years for many causes." Hall observed, "Heston has made his activism into a systematic part of his life," and also explained the ways in which the actor drew upon the organizing principles he had learned over the years and had already used effectively. "Through his ArenaPAC, which permits him to contribute his time and services . . . he made appearances in 21 states on behalf of 54 candidates for federal offices . . . in the 1996 election." Congressman Robert Barr of Georgia observed, "He can make sure that the NRA is a mainstream organization . . . and deflect some of this criticism that the NRA represents the fringe elements of society. Charlton Heston is not a fringe person." Heston, however, was a performer first and insisted that he was never going to be able to give the organization total commitment if work in his profession arose. "If I have a movie I want to do, I'll do it. But I think I can give you useful time."[64]

Among the other programs that sought to feature the actor's prominent visage was one catering to viewers interested in knowing more about successful figures in American society. Robin Leach, the self-styled promoter of the rich and famous, thrived in this element of depicting the world of the stars, and Charlton Heston was more than willing to oblige. In the course of showcasing the Heston home and its resident to his viewers, Leach inquired as to the effect of popularity on the actor's personal life. "Celebrity is a condition of my life," Heston responded. Yet he believed he had benefitted by working to achieve his status rather than having it thrust upon him suddenly. "The fact that success and the attendant celebrity that came with it were a fairly steady and gradual process for me extending over a period of several years" helped make the adjustment easier.[65]

63 Heston, "My Crusade to Save the Second Amendment," and advertisement, ibid., 30-34.

64 Carla Hall, "Conservative actor Charlton Heston has a long history of activism. Now, the screen icon hopes to help lead the NRA to a better place," *LAT*, May 27, 1997.

65 Robin Leach, "Fame, Fortune and Romance," UCLA.

Appreciation for the actor's work extended beyond his typical orbits. In December 1997 the White House released its list of Kennedy Center honorees, which included Lauren Bacall, Bob Dylan, and Charlton Heston. In his remarks for the prestigious occasion, President Bill Clinton noted that while he could not "thank him for campaigning . . . I do have a lot to thank him for." Recalling his youth in Arkansas, Clinton noted, "Charlton Heston showed me how to part the Red Sea, drive a Roman chariot," and "guided millions of movie lovers through nearly every great era of Western civilization." The president concluded of the honoree, "If the big screen didn't exist, they would have to invent it for Charlton Heston."[66]

The clout of Heston's film characters still held in other circles as well. In a BBC interview, Tim Sebastian sensed an air of awe in the audience, and heard someone say that "God is here" when Heston arrived in the studio for his show. "How do you take to the fame?" he queried. The actor replied, "I've had a public face for a long time now. It's part of yourself. You have to learn to be a public person and you learn it after a while." Then, in the course of their conversation, Heston answered a question about how his career had affected him: "I think I have certainly not emerged unscathed, but I've never been deeply wounded, and I feel I'm still the man I've tried to be from the beginning." He recognized the benefits. "You get so used to being hand carried. . . . Not fawning, just someone there." Then, when asked if he liked the special attention his status provided, he explained, "You get used to it, of course. Who wouldn't like it, you know?"

Still, Heston realized there was a level of personality presence that offered a certain perspective: "It isn't as though I'm a rock star." As an illustration, he told the story of being in London for the *Khartoum* premiere when, after dinner, he planned to race for the car scheduled to pick him up. He inadvertently jumped into the wrong vehicle, prompting the understandable query from the occupant, "What are you doing in my car?" For Heston, location also determined the degree of recognition. "Depends on where you are," he noted of a celebrity's chance for anonymity. "In Hollywood you can [go out], because people are more used to actors . . . they're underfoot all the time."

Sebastian then asked if fame had changed him in any meaningful way. Heston pondered, "Well you must learn early on, and I think I did learn it early on, largely by watching people like Jimmy Stewart, and Hank Fonda, and Gary Cooper, with whom I had the good fortune to work, when I was still very green. And you learn

66 "President Clinton Speaks at Kennedy Center Honors Reception," December 7, 1997, www.clintonwhitehouse4.archives.gov/WH/New/html/19971208-2814.html, accessed June 17, 2019.

how to behave, not acting, that you have to do yourself." The distinction was important in the environment of his profession beyond the camera or the stage. "But you learn how to behave, again, as a public face. Also you learn you must never take yourself as seriously as other people are prepared to take you." Always sensitive to the perceptions of others, Heston struggled to avoid appearances that he had a loftier status than the actors with whom he worked unless he was in the director's chair, "Don't call me last," to come to the set he had insisted as he strove to avoid the appearance of being treated differently.

On a practical level, Heston understood that his physical attributes were often the key elements of any production and that while he wanted to participate as fully in every performance as possible, there were times when common sense had to prevail. "The actor who tells you he does his own stunts is either an idiot or a liar." He had learned to ask the appropriate question of professionals like Yakima Canutt. "Can I do this shot? You shouldn't do this one, Chuck. OK." In fact, the iconic race sequence in *Ben-Hur* had compelled just such a practical assessment. "Actually, once I learned to drive the chariot it was kind of fun."[67]

Heston's reputation meant that public expectations remained high. "You are an exemplar," he explained. "You owe them quite a debt." His desire to achieve perfection in every performance also left him open to regret when negative criticism occurred. In other aspects of public life, the actor was prepared to take a stand: "I'm an activist myself." He particularly targeted trends he thought dangerous. "I hate political correctness. It's ridiculous. It's insane." The current political climate reminded him of the fictional world created by author George Orwell in *1984*.[68]

The extended interview then moved from current public interest matters to Heston's background and early years, before proceeding to his thoughts on aging in his profession. "I don't get the same parts I got, but you still get parts," he noted. Sebastian wondered, "Do you worry about image, about appearance?" Heston replied, "Every actor knows what he looks like. He has to know what he looks like." Were there parts still out there that he hoped to bring to life? "The Duke of Wellington," he answered.[69]

67 HARDtalk, BBC Interview with Tim Sebastian, 1997, part 1, www.youtube.com/watch?v=KnsDeAZtJbE, accessed June 11, 2018.

68 HARDtalk, BBC Interview with Tim Sebastian, 1997, part 2, www.youtube.com/watch?v=0MhfXt-2LTc, accessed June 11, 2018.

69 HARDtalk, BBC Interview with Tim Sebastian, 1997, part 3, www.youtube.com/watch?v=LkhLjPnjyYQ, accessed June 11, 2018.

The American actor might never be able to embody on film the famed British leader who successfully challenged Napoleon, but his ascendancy in the NRA continued. Calls for unity did not prevent a mixed slate of candidates for the organization's annual election, but Heston's public persona stood him in good stead. When *American Hunter* sent out ballots in its March 1998 edition, a stirring image of Charlton Heston gripping a musket graced a cover that boasted, "Armed with Pride." The slogan was also a theme embedded prominently in an interview between LaPierre and the first vice president that amounted to a campaign statement to promote Heston to the presidency. "I feel confident we can defeat this enemy," Heston explained of the advocates of modified gun control, "because there truly is a new feeling of energy within the NRA. We're back in the arena, focused on the future, and filled with pride to defend what's right."[70]

"An Urgent Message for NRA Voting Members," seeded in front of the 1998 NRA ballot, informed prospective voters which candidates to support and which to oppose. Hammer, Heston, and LaPierre stood alongside Second Vice President Kayne B. Robinson, actor Susan Howard, singer Ted Nugent, Congressman Bob Barr, and Oliver North, among others, as acceptable choices. Another advertisement aimed at defeating an amendment to the NRA's by-laws bookended the ballot and contained a strong statement by First Vice President Heston against "censorship," however "artfully disguised."[71]

In this framework, the actor and activist appeared before the participants at the 127th Annual Meeting of the NRA in Philadelphia on May 22, 1998. He still marveled at the "bunch of amazing guys" who had met to create a country and the debt he felt that everyone owed the Founding Fathers for their work. "Freedom has only one enemy it cannot defeat," Heston warned, "and that is negligence." Grasping the significance of the setting, he observed, "Of all man's works beneath the Heavens, none shines brighter than our Constitution." Yet even if the great figures of "Jefferson and Paine, Adams, Madison, Mason, [and] Franklin" were watching over them, it would still be up to vigilant members to "stand with me." Heston swept the crowd up in his soaring rhetoric, calling on the members to embrace the Second Amendment as "America's First Freedom" and the means that "makes all freedoms defensible, possible, the one that protects all the others." He might no longer be able to part the Red Sea for Cecil B. DeMille, but he would be, as LaPierre had remarked, the NRA's Moses. "I came here today because, like you

---

70 "NRA: Armed with Pride," *American Hunter* (Mar. 1998), 28, 31.

71 *American Hunter* (Mar. 1998).

and those great men that travelled here two and a quarter centuries ago . . . we have freedom's business to attend to." He would do so as the organization's president for at least a one-year term. "The great thing about Charlton Heston is that he becomes the megaphone to get our message out," LaPierre asserted, noting that until the actor arrived the NRA's was "a message that is not being heard."

Individuals outside the NRA, including those reporting on it, recognized the role the actor was supposed to play. *New York Times* coverage noted that a new advertising campaign and other high-profile voices, such as former Seattle Seahawks wide receiver and current Oklahoma Congressman Steve Largent, were meant to help as well. "But in the end," writer Michael Janofsky observed, "the association seems to be counting on Mr. Heston more than anything else to provide a new profile for gun owners."[72]

Indeed, as NRA president from 1998 to 2003, Charlton Heston became the organization's critical lodestone, and it gave him meaning and purpose as the final furlongs of his own race approached. He found a receptive audience for his message, as well as the power of a membership that he represented across the country and in the halls of political leadership. Within a short time, he appeared before a subcommittee of the powerful Senate Judiciary Committee, chaired by John Ashcroft of Missouri. The venue offered another opportunity to make the organization's case for the critical status of "the right to keep and bear arms."[73]

Of course, Heston's assumption of a larger public role with the NRA did not curtail his craving for acting opportunities or his ability to obtain work. Stars aligned on both sides of the volatile gun-rights matter, just as they would on any hot-button social issue. Gregory Peck was one of the actors that gun control advocates counted on to champion their cause. Heston's friendship with the Pecks complicated things among those who thought it might compromise the larger framework regarding gun control. James Brady, one-time member of Ronald Reagan's administration who had suffered debilitating injuries when a deranged John Hinckley attempted to assassinate the president in 1981, pointed out this incongruity to his acting friend. "We're colleagues, rather than friends," Peck

---

72 "Remarks before the 127th Annual Meeting of the Members of the National Rifle Association, May 22, 1998, Philadelphia, PA," in Heston, *The Courage to be Free*, 190-192; Michael Janofsky, "N.R.A. Tries to Improve Image, with Charlton Heston in Lead," *NYT*, June 8, 1998.

73 "'The Right of the People to Keep and Bear Arms,' Oral Statement of Charlton Heston, President, National Rifle Association of America, Hearings of the Second Amendment Subcommittee on the Constitution Committee of the Judiciary, United States Senate, September 23, 1998, Washington, D.C.," in Heston, *The Courage to be Free*, 193-195.

insisted of his one-time co-star. "We're civil to each other when we meet. I, of course, disagree vehemently with him on gun control."[74]

Among his generation of acting colleagues, Heston seldom seemed to feel any sense of disparagement, or project it openly on those with whom he differed. He had long admired Peck and presented his former *Big Country* co-star with an award for "outstanding achievement" from the Screen Actors Guild in 1970. In March 1989, he participated in a tribute for a Lifetime Achievement Award the American Film Institute gave Peck. When his colleague began a program to support the Los Angeles Public Library through a series of readings named in Peck's honor, Charlton Heston was among those who responded readily.[75]

Heston's ability to meld such worlds together was less a testament to his talents for rousing support for a cause than to the personal connections he and Lydia had made through the years. One individual explained, "He has a lot of friends and a lot of respect in Hollywood. He and Lydia are liked personally." Individuals such as Peck could remain friends and acting compatriots without letting their public discourse interfere with that relationship.[76]

That summer, the actor remained busy off the stage and screen in other ways. In a letter to a reporter in Fargo, North Dakota, Heston expressed thanks for a "collection of movie memorabilia," some of which he had not seen. Then, he turned to politics. "I'm sorry we didn't have a chance to meet at Senator Gramm's event," he explained; "I just may be through North Dakota again this fall on behalf of Bob Dole. Maybe we can shake hands then."[77]

The same year offered Heston the irresistible chance to return to Shakespeare under a dynamic actor and director who had established himself as a modern interpreter of the Bard's works. Kenneth Branagh hoped to bring an element of the star-laden epic to the project by enlisting numerous prominent figures to join the cast, including Derek Jacobi, John Gielgud, Richard Attenborough, Jack Lemmon, and Julie Christie, as well as younger performers such as Kate Winslet, Billy Crystal, and Robin Williams. Branagh understood that he needed a veteran Shakespearian to take on the role of the "Player King" and looked to Heston to fill the bill.

---

74 Haney, *Gregory Peck*, 410-411.

75 Fishgall, *Gregory Peck*, 263, 322, 336-337.

76 Haney, *Gregory Peck*, 411.

77 Heston to Daniel Hillstrom, June 20, 1996, Heston Papers, Wills.

Heston suggested his own redaction of the text and promised to send the results for Branagh's reaction. Perhaps the actor failed to detect hesitation on the director's part for the idea, but Heston proceeded. "So Kenneth hangs up," he explained, "and I am left with the impression that he's agreed to this approach." When Heston heard nothing after sending the work to Branagh, he contacted the director. "Chuck, I should've called you sooner," the voice on the other end of the receiver observed, "I really, really want to use the full text. I should've made that clear in the beginning." In the conscientious mindset of a professional, Heston had memorized the part as he had written it in the shortened version. Now, he had to return to the part, discard the text from which he had been working, and start all over again with little notice. "Well, he was under a lot of stress," Heston concluded generously. "He was also the director, so I didn't press the issue. But the hardest thing was to go back and memorize a text that was similar but different from the one I had redacted, in such a short period of time."

Heston could have insisted upon following the agreement he thought he had reached with Branagh, but in so doing would have violated the rule to which he had adhered for a career of following the director's vision and desires. Flashes of DeMille and Wyler, and perhaps more appropriately Welles and Peckinpah, must have crossed in his mind, but the work remained. For the actor, the inconvenience faded as the shooting began. "It was great to be at Pinewood [Studios] once again and play in this magnificent production," he observed. Without any sense of rancor, the veteran recalled of his young leader, "Ken empathizes wonderfully with his actors. He knows where he's going and how to get there. He prods and pushes—and I like directors who demand a lot."[78]

In all areas of his life, Heston remained committed to the values he believed that significant individuals represented. On Abraham Lincoln's birthday, he read the Gettysburg Address at a gathering at Los Angeles National Cemetery. He admired the wisdom of the homespun president who had guided the United States through the trauma of a war that also had helped to reshape the nation. Terming the Address "the finest speech ever given by an American," Heston also took a few moments to ponder the scene where veterans rested after their own lifetimes of service to their country.[79]

Though he had lived through enormous changes in the structure and culture of Hollywood, adapting to some and resisting others, even Charlton Heston could

---

78 Heston and Isbouts, *Hollywood*, 207-208.

79 "Heston Delivers Gettysburg Address at Cemetery," *LAT*, Feb. 13, 1996.

not respond to every emergency. When fire struck a barn at the Hollywood Studio Museum in Los Angeles that had served as a studio for the first feature-length film and now contained his chariot from *Ben-Hur*, the "irreplaceable" contents nearly fell victim to the flames. Fortunately, firefighters managed to extinguish them, covering the iconic vehicle with a tarp to prevent water damage as they did so.[80]

Despite such threats to his temporal screen legacy, at this phase in his life Heston found himself once more buoyed by the warm embrace of family. These intimate connections remained central to him. He wanted the people who had followed his work, on the screen and stage and in writing, to know that side of him. In a classically patriarchal manner, he took pride in the achievements of his children even as he gave deference to the role of Lydia and the marriage that had sustained all over the many years. From his refuge in Coldwater Canyon, he turned his focus to the youngest generation. Writing a short volume entitled, *To Be a Man: Letters to My Grandson*, Heston sought to provide a lasting connection with his grandchild, John Alexander Clarke, and impart wisdom to both Jack and all those who read the book. In addition to a few letters and personal stories, Heston sprinkled the book with stories of the individuals who had affected him. He concluded that the most valuable lesson he had learned about raising children (or a grandchild in this instance) was to maximize the time you could spend with them. "Beyond any other measure, the best thing you can give your child is your time." Remembering the challenges of his early life with a missing father and his own harried efforts with Fray and Holly, Heston observed, "It's often not easy, sometimes not doable, but it's time you *must* find somehow, and seize, whether you're a senator or a street cleaner." If the actor sought to make another attempt to "seize time" with his family, he was doubly determined to do as much as possible with his grandson Jack while he was able. Just as he had imparted to his children, he wanted his grandson to know his cardinal rules: "[D]o your best and keep your promises, be fair, but never give up," and with a nod to tennis, advised him to face life's challenges with "something like a backhand volley." He also urged Jack "to *read* and some day grow into a good man."

Heston also confronted his own mortality. Using the child's nickname for him, "Ba," he quoted the lad as asking him "[A]re you old?" Heston replied, "Yeah, Jack, I'm pretty old." The actor could not be sure how much precious time remained to him and wanted to grasp as much of it as possible. He also knew this book would reach new audiences as well as the fans who had followed him through the decades.

---

80 Duke Helfand, "Hollywood Artifacts Rescued From Blaze," and "Hollywood Memorabilia Rescued From Flames," *LAT*, Sept. 19, 1996.

Even so, he could not resist the temptation to aim a parenthetical blast at his political adversaries. "(Excuse me, Mrs. Clinton, but you're dead wrong: It doesn't 'take a village to raise a child.') It takes a family."[81]

Heston's disavowal of what he felt the Clintons symbolized did not remain in the pages of a book. Appearing before the Conservative Political Action Conference (CPAC) in Washington on January 25, 1997, the actor recounted what he saw as the deficiencies of the Clinton administration and encouraged involvement from his listeners. "We are in the arena, and we are right," he asserted. Reiterating his twin motivations of family and history by referencing his grandson and employing the words of Samuel Adams, he observed, "For my Jack, and for yours, have the courage now to 'Be yourselves, O Americans.'"[82]

Heston found a similarly receptive audience for his message at CPAC's 1998 meeting in Alexandria, Virginia. "Thank you for that very kind introduction," he began, before turning to an allusion he knew would resonate with his listeners. "Some day I'll arrive at one of these events in a chariot just to live up to your expectations." More importantly, he wanted the people seated before him to know that he was issuing a call to action, which he hoped would lift them from reticence or complacency when it came to engaging in the modern "cultural wars." "This is why I've formed ARENA PAC," he explained, "my own political action committee." The actor felt he could speak out when others might feel more constrained. "But it's a job I can do better than most, because most can't." The argument was based not so much on personal capabilities as on the freedom his career had given him to "go on the road—catching redeye flights, speaking at rallies in Seattle and eating pancakes in Peoria and eating rubber chicken in Des Moines," to bring his message to individuals across the country. "Moses led his people through the Wilderness, but he never made it to the Promised Land—not even when I played him," he added, employing another element of his public persona. "But he did do his job— he pointed his people in the right direction."[83]

As the end of another decade approached, Charlton Heston faced the close of an incredibly productive and personally profitable period of his life, but he was also confronting the twilight of that career and issues of health that challenged the approach he took with his personal life and fitness. A routine check-up in

81 Heston, *To Be a Man*, 51, 22, 20.

82 "'Be Yourselves, O Americans,' Remarks before the Conservative Political Action Conference, January 25, 1997, Washington, D.C.," in Heston, *The Courage to be Free*, 170, 174.

83 "'Armed with Pride,' Remarks Before the Conservative Political Action Conference, January 27, 1998, Alexandria, Va.," ibid., 182, 184-185.

June 1998 led to the discovery of prostate cancer, and he was advised to address it as quickly as possible. This led to "six to seven weeks" of "intense radiation treatments." In January 1999, the actor was pleased to announce, "It's not totally gone but it's on the path to it. Happily, I seemed to have survived. It's very good news."[84]

On a more positive note, that month *George* magazine named him "[t]he celebrity whose political views we take most seriously" as part of its "Editors' Picks" for 1998. The short article featured a smiling Heston with the caption "Sweetest Celebrity," and touted him as "the real thing: a straight shooter who's been to the mountaintop and keeps on climbing." The editors noted of Heston's ascendance to leadership in the National Rifle Association, "Not many actors cap off their career by heading one of the country's most powerful lobbying groups. But then, the man who played Moses has never been gun-shy about taking on large roles."[85]

George provided another venue for Heston to assert himself in his NRA role. With an advertisement featuring Wayne LaPierre clutching a vintage weapon, both men promoted the NRA's National Firearms Museum. Noting the extensiveness of the museum's collection, Heston said it told "the story of human freedom and the American experience through compelling exhibits." The actor often chose the words for texts and scripts for such ads himself, and the emphasis on values he recognized as time-honored was unmistakable. "Make it a rewarding and educational stop on your next visit to the nation's Capital," the NRA president explained, reflecting the multi-faceted aspects of history and education that he held closely.[86]

Clearly, Charlton Heston continued to be unafraid to promote causes he felt deeply about or to confront his own challenges publicly. In addition to revealing his recent health issues for the newspapers, he took his story before readers of *TV Guide* in an interview that appeared in February 1999. He first addressed his recent diagnosis and treatment. The actor displayed stoicism in describing himself as "the poster boy for prostate cancer" and explained his studied approach to the issue. "It was not my favorite piece of news," he confessed, but it was not nearly as disruptive or unnerving as his service in World War II had been. Not wishing to compromise his professional obligations to the production of *Town and Country*, which he was filming with Warren Beatty, he had spent mornings getting radiation treatments

---

84 "Charlton Heston treated for cancer," *BG*, Jan. 2, 1999.

85 "Editors' Picks, 1998," *George* (Jan. 1999), 93.

86 "I'm the NRA," advertisement, *George* (June 1999), 29.

before shooting his scenes in the afternoon. These treatment sessions allowed him to continue working, and he declared that the disease was in remission. [87] His ability to keep occupied in the craft he loved certainly served as a welcome diversion from other concerns.

In the same interview, contributor Mary Murphy turned the discussion to his time on television, from his earliest years to his most recent experiences. Of the latter, she noted Heston's "guest appearance on one of the hottest shows on TV—*Friends*." The veteran performer replied, "I loved doing that," although he had been skeptical initially. "What is *Friends*? Whose friends?" The desire to tackle the role, however, received a considerable boost by the level of compensation he would obtain for playing it: "They paid me an obscene amount of money." Still, the effect of expanding his audience to new viewers was consequential. "And I get a lot of mail," he noted proudly after the first show aired. NBC thought enough of his appearance on the program to make the segment part of the February 1998 "sweeps" for its "Must-See TV" campaign. [88]

Heston's referral to his compensation was not intended to be braggadocio. He had long maintained that his increased salary structure provided him with more choices and control over the path his career took, even if some of the roles were less consequential. "Doing rather less challenging parts in huge commercial successes gives me the freedom to do the things I love," he insisted, including "play[ing] the real giants on the stage." [89] Even so, supporting roles such as the professional football league commissioner in *Any Given Sunday* gave him the type of authority role that audiences would expect, including scenes of the famed chariot race.

Whatever the screen or stage roles, Heston's work with the NRA generated the most attention. The affiliation produced additional friends, but also enemies for the outspoken advocate. Working diligently to dismantle obstacles to gun ownership wherever they might be found, he made multiple trips to Missouri to support a ballot initiative that would lift a ban on concealed weapons if passed. Employing references to the Revolutionary War and supporting the pro-gun efforts with substantial sums to pass Proposition B in the state, the NRA sought, with Heston

---

87 Mary Murphy, "Prime Chuck," *TV Guide* (Feb. 20-26, 1999), 32.

88 "Today," *LAT*, Feb. 5, 1998. Heston confronted Matt LeBlanc when the young actor arrived on the set after a fishing trip and borrowed the star's dressing room shower. "Put some pants on kid, so I can kick your butt." "Charlton Heston,"
www.imdb.com/title/tt0583525/?ref_=nm_flmg_act_16, accessed Jan. 11, 2019.

89 Heston and Isbouts, *Hollywood*, 196.

as its most visible standard-bearer, to appeal to rural voters and suburbanites afraid of violent crime. Yet when the tally came, Proposition B went down to defeat by a vote of 52 to 48 percent, with the urban votes in St. Louis and Kansas City going significantly against the measure. Watching the drama unfold from Boston, correspondent Derrick Z. Jackson employed imagery from Heston's film career to illustrate the blow to him as well as to the NRA. "This week Heston was Rameses," he observed, rather than Moses. "Heston found out this week that it takes more than being a god on the silver screen to make people slaves to handguns," the writer declared with cinematic flair. "No longer can Heston show up and assume that just because he has played Moses, the sea will part on his command."[90]

The actor recognized the challenges and responded to them with a mixture of humor and resolve. "1998 was a great year for me," he told attendees at CPAC's 1999 conference in Washington. His first reference suggested the positive: "I did three films." His second indicated more troubling aspects: "and had dual hip surgeries." Still, he maintained, "that was nothing. I survived *Time Magazine* and *60 Minutes*, in that order." His reference to an interview with the intrepid Mike Wallace did not reflect the degree to which the *60 Minutes* correspondent had managed to hammer the actor's association with the NRA. So much now appeared to hinge on Heston's willingness to serve as a conservative lightning rod. The more he spoke, the more heat he took. "In fact, I can sense my agent and my publicist bracing themselves now."[91] Even so, unlike the television news magazine's viewership, this was a receptive rather than a resistant one. He could have his say here and feel secure.

In spite of the circumstances that now seemed so frequently to prevail, Heston entered more battlegrounds to wage war against what he saw as increasing social dysfunction. He continued to make speeches at conferences and other gatherings and supported issues and candidates that reflected his political views and social standards. He recognized that his positions might have a deleterious effect— "I'll never be offered another film by Warner, or get a good review from *Time* magazine."—but he felt the imperative of speaking out. To the Yale Political Union, he insisted on April 16, 1999, "My life has always been a life of activism," and he took pleasure in pressing boundaries. "The thought police do not frighten me. I hope I frighten them."[92]

90 Derrick Z. Jackson, "Missouri smites 'Moses,'" *BG*, Apr. 9, 1999.

91 "'Conservative Challenge for a New Millennium,' Remarks Before the Conservative Political Action Conference, January 1999, Washington, D.C.," Heston, *The Courage to be Free*, 209-210.

92 "'Truth and Consequences,' Remarks Before the Yale Political Union, April 16, 1999, New Haven, Connecticut," ibid., 221.

Though Heston decried a world in which the norms he accepted seemed violated, he did not appear to appreciate that his tone had turned more ominous and strained. He had once described his home in America as "Heaven" to an interviewer, although he may have been thinking of his "home" on the ridge rather than of the nation as a whole.[93] Still, the term did not apply to his current descriptions of a society in peril. To be sure, he loved his country, but the danger was that for a man who had so often displayed optimism, darker hues were descending that threatened the message he sought to convey. If the voice became too shrill, the warnings of the elder statesman of Hollywood too angry, the power even of a modern Moses could be squandered and lost, defeating the purpose of sounding the tocsin in the first place.

Indeed, a sudden and tragic event called Heston's strongest activist expressions into question. A horrific mass shooting at Columbine High School in Littleton, Colorado, on April 20, 1999, shocked the nation. The NRA was scheduled to hold its annual meeting in Denver less than two weeks later, but under the circumstances scaled back its activities to only a business session. If the leadership thought the gesture would quell reaction from outside the organization, however, they were mistaken. As the *Chicago Tribune* noted, the public reception for the NRA cooled decidedly, and the billboards that had featured Heston calling on members to "Join Me" came down.[94]

Nevertheless, the actor and NRA president braved protestors to tell the attendees that they were as justified in expressing their horror and grief as anyone else at what had taken place at Columbine. Heston's opening remarks struck a defensive tone toward demands that the entire conference be cancelled. He reminded Mayor Wellington Webb that he had responded to his nation's call during the Second World War. "Since then, I've run small errands for my country from Nigeria to Vietnam." Furthermore, he and the NRA membership "have the same right as all other citizens to be here . . . to help shoulder the grief . . . to share our sorrow . . . and to offer our respectful, reasoned voice to the national discourse that has erupted around this tragedy."[95]

93 "Interview with Charlton Heston, 11-9-64," "*The Agony and the Ecstasy* publicity," Heston Papers, f.2, HL.

94 "NRA Subdued After Columbine Shootings," *Chicago Tribune*, May 2, 1999. www.articles.chicagotribune.com/1999-05-02/news/9905020283_1_gun-debate-gun-control-nra-leader, accessed Mar. 7, 2019.

95 "Remarks Before the 128th Annual Meeting of the Members of the National Rifle Association, May 1, 1999, Denver Colorado," Heston, *The Courage to be Free*, 228-229.

When the members reassembled after their business session ended, Heston returned to the podium to offer more extensive and even stronger remarks, reminding listeners that he had marched with Martin Luther King and now felt compelled to speak out against a new "harvest of hatred." He lamented "the two camps" into which so many fellow citizens had fallen and warned, "Somewhere right now, evil people are scheming evil things." If to some the NRA had become "a villain" conjured for "political gain and media ratings," the membership must also realize that they were the defenders of the Constitution and the Bill of Rights. "Let's go from this place renewed in spirit and dedicated against hatred," he insisted, adding dramatically, "when the sun sets on Denver tonight and forevermore, let it always set on we the people . . . secure in our land of the free and home of the brave." Sounding much like a modern Moses exhorting his people to follow his example, he repeated a familiar refrain, "I, for one, will do my part."[96]

As the most prominent public face of the NRA, the actor insisted, "We're often cast as the villain. That's not our role in American society and we will not be forced to play it." He recognized the tenor of the debate as reflected by the number of protesters who had assembled, and the bad optics of signs being televised that condemned the organization and its membership as the "Pushers of Child Killer Machines." "We cannot, we must not let tragedy lay waste to the most rare, hard-won right in history."[97]

The next morning, Heston followed his NRA address with an appearance on *Good Morning America*, the ABC talk show, that he thought would allow him to speak to the protests and respond to the reactions from the victims' families. Without the sympathetic audience present to buttress his stance, the actor had to appeal to a viewership filtered by the medium that gave him access to it. His arguments rang hollow to a nation still raw with emotion and made him and his members appear less sympathetic to the trauma that was happening around them.[98]

Some of the criticism the NRA champion received exposed the complications regarding the positions he had taken so publicly and so strongly. "Even the best actor can fluff his lines," an editorial for London's *The Economist* asserted. Noting the actor/activist's appearance before a university audience, it observed, "To their

---

96 Ibid., 230-234.

97 "NRA takes defiant stand during convention," *KTN*, May 2, 1999; "NRA takes defiant stand during Denver convention," *BHC*, May 2, 1999.

98 Eliot, *Charlton Heston*, 450-451.

parents, Mr. Heston is an American icon, somehow embodying the heroism of his film roles of yesteryear. Ben Hur in his Roman chariot, Moses bearing aloft God's ten commandments, El Cid defying the Moorish hordes." The stentorian voice could still reach across the generational divide; the impact of the speaker remained unmistakable. "But when they listen, they hear one of America's most inspiring voices, achieving all the atavistic longing, felt even by the young, for a simpler, better nation." Heston eagerly employed the image he expected to resonate: "Here I am still in the chariot."[99]

More often now, "his chariot" in film work meant utilizing his immense narrative skills or recalling Hollywood's bygone days. The actor long realized that he occupied multiple public spaces, and understood as well as anyone that he could use one level of exposure he had in the artistic universe to support the rest. He remained poised to answer critiques in writing, which allowed him to craft his words as he wished before sending them out into the public sphere. Thus, when director Spike Lee blurted a statement at the Cannes Film Festival that suggested Heston should be shot, the actor replied by reiterating his earlier associations. "When Lee was still in diapers," Heston reminded the young director and the wider world, "I was working with Dr. Martin Luther King to break down the racist code in the Hollywood technical unions that denied blacks any place behind the cameras, paving the way for young filmmakers like Lee." The actor purported to seek no apology, insisting, "my character speaks for itself," and wished the young director well on his next project.[100]

A decade of acting and activism was increasingly giving way to reflection. To attendees of a speech at Penn State University in September 1999, Heston observed, "In the business of being someone you're not, my 'people' have included kings, presidents, prophets, crusaders. Plus a cowboy or two, even some saints." But he knew those characterizations could only take him so far; "when those stage lights dim you gotta go back to the real world, the same way everybody else does."[101]

99 "Charlton Heston's Tablets of Stone," *The Economist*, May 1, 1999, 30.

100 "Lee's Gun Gaffe," *LAT*, June 7, 1999. See also "Low Noon," *LAT*, May 29, 1999.

101 "Freshmen, Fads, and Freedom: Remarks at Penn State University, September 21, 1999, State College, PA," Heston, *The Courage to be Free*, 243.

Chapter Ten

FINISHING THE RACE
2000s

"I want to say those fighting words for everyone within the sound of my voice to hear and to heed, and especially for you, Mr. Gore: 'From my cold, dead hands!'"
—Heston, NRA meeting, May 20, 2000

"I can part the Red Sea, but I can't part with you."
"I'm neither giving up nor giving in."
—Heston addressing his future facing Alzheimer's disease

"Our revels now are ended."
—William Shakespeare, Prospero, *The Tempest* Act 4, Scene 1

Performances:
Heston of the Apes, May 12, 2000
When the Pipers Play, June 1, 2000
The Outer Limits, Sept. 3, 2000
Legendary Hollywood Homes 2, Sept. 17, 2000
The Weber Show, 2000
Hollywood at Your Feet, 2000
E! Mysteries & Scandals: Hedy Lamarr, Dec. 12, 2000; *Vincent Price*, Mar. 5, 2001
AFI's 100 Years . . . 100 Thrills: America's Most Heart-Pounding Movies, June 12, 2001
The Gun Deadlock, June 18, 2001
Planet of the Apes: Rule the Planet, July 25, 2001
Larry & Vivien: The Oliviers in Love, Sept. 13, 2001
The Making of 'Midway', Oct. 30, 2001
MADtv, Nov. 24, 2001
Eco Challenge: US Armed Forces Championship, Dec. 5, 2001
Intimate Portrait: Shirley Jones, 2001
Cats & Dogs, 2001

Planet of the Apes, 2001
The Order, 2001
My Father, Rua Alguem 5555, 2001
Bowling for Columbine, 2001
2002 ABC World Stunt Awards, May 19, 2002
Gala Paramount Pictures Celebrates 90th Anniversary with 90 Stars for 90 Years, July 14, 2002
Biography: Jennifer Jones, Aug. 18, 2002
The Face of Evil: Reinhard Heydrich, Oct. 10, 2002
20/20, Dec. 20, 2002
Hollywood History, 2002
Lasting Love, Feb. 6, 2003
Cecil B. DeMille: American Epic, Apr. 4, 2004
The People's President, Feb. 20, 2006
Genghis Khan: The Story of a Lifetime, 2010
Cameraman: The Life and Work of Jack Cardiff, May 13, 2011
Cooper & Hemingway: The True Gen, Sept. 27, 2013

As the year 2000 arrived, Charlton Heston entered more firmly into a turn in his life and career marked as much by recollection as by acting. Part of this renewed focus came of necessity as age limited the roles he could play, and the available audiences steered him to performances that catered to their changing demands. Heston had long demonstrated himself to be a thoughtful individual, plunging into research for roles and looking for insights among the collected wisdom of historical personalities. One of the reasons he had such an ease in portraying those who belonged to the past was that he was comfortable in their presence. He also enjoyed distilling life's lessons through quotations from historical and literary personages he respected. He could capture the essence of virtually every aspect of life from individuals such as Thomas Jefferson, Abraham Lincoln, Theodore Roosevelt, and William Shakespeare. Now, these expressions helped him to make sense of a world he found more difficult to fathom than ever before.

His work often reminded the actor of what mattered most to him as an individual. Narrating a documentary on bagpiping appealed to his Scots roots, while another on the history of the Chinese Theatre in Hollywood reminded everyone of the heady days when the cement that encased his hands, feet, and signature was still wet. An on-going series, *Sworn to Secrecy*, enabled audiences to hear his voice imploring them to learn the "secrets of war," while a project called *Lasting Love* offered insights into the secrets of long marriages such as his and Lydia's. As they had in the previous decade, galas and celebrations underscored his long career and appreciation for long-departed colleagues like Cecil B. DeMille. There were glories to be remembered, and, he hoped, work left to do.

Heston had always demonstrated a sense of self-deprecating humor that buffered him from much of the criticism of others. He had already faced more than his share of barbs and witticisms thrown his way, and took pride in responding with professional diffidence, if not outright graciousness. Comedian Jay Leno took a particularly creative approach to the on-going feud between Heston supporters and the Clinton administration. "It's tough taking sides in an argument between Charlton Heston and Bill Clinton," Leno maintained, because "on one side you got a classic actor trained to fake emotion for the camera, trained to win you over with a well-rehearsed script, and then on the other side you have Charlton Heston."[1]

The leadership of the National Rifle Association was determined to do what was necessary to retain its most important celebrity spokesperson as efforts to amend its by-laws to allow Heston to "run for an unprecedented third term as president" gathered steam. The actor had worked tirelessly to promote the organization's agenda and to defend its executive vice president, Wayne LaPierre, including insisting on NBC's *Today* morning show, "You guys owe Wayne an apology. He was right and you guys were wrong." An election of officers was set to occur at the annual convention, to be held in Charlotte, North Carolina, on May 19-21.[2]

Heston's importance to the NRA and his power as a representative had reached well beyond acting or gun control settings. *Boston Globe* sportswriter and analyst Norman Chad departed from his prognostications on NFL contests to offer a cultural allusion in relation to Al Groh as head coach of the New York Jets. "Following Bill Parcells on an NFL sideline," Chad observed mischievously, "is like following Charlton Heston at an NRA fundraiser," as he offered advice to the Jets' upcoming opponent, the Green Bay Packers.[3]

An appearance before the opening session of the Arizona State Legislature provided the actor a moment of both personal consideration and political advocacy regarding the positions he held dear. Heston called upon the lawmakers to continue

---

1 "Laugh Lines," *LAT*, March 16, 2000.

2 "NRA Changing Rules So That Heston Can Seek 3rd Term," *LAT*, May 4, 2000.

3 Norman Chad, "Root for Redskins? Not if Snyder paid me," *BG*, Sept. 1, 2000.

the "generally thankless job of managing the people's business" and commended them for seeking to "leave the future better than you found the present." He felt that in order to achieve that "noble" goal, however, they must demonstrate "the courage to be unpopular." He had been around politicians at every level for so long that he knew the initial reaction to this rallying cry would be muted at best, but he wanted the legislators to know that bold stances would not often be met by public acclaim. "Having portrayed dozens of historic people—and having lived a few years myself—I can tell you this: popularity is history's pocket change. Courage is the true currency of history." And it was history, he believed, that would vindicate their course, especially if undertaken in difficult times and against long odds. The Bill of Rights should be the guidepost and must remain inviolate.[4]

Of course, his cherished view came as a result of his interpretation of that document. Interestingly, for a student of history, Heston allowed his soaring rhetoric to carry him away. He defined the Bill of Rights as "those sacred personal freedoms granted not by government but by God," diminishing the role of the leaders who had gathered in Philadelphia to hammer out a workable solution to their government through compromise after the version of it based upon the Articles of Confederation had failed so conspicuously. Additional condemnation of those who were inclined to question the original also neglected the device found in the Constitution for amending it. Having earlier invoked the name and legacy of Dr. King, Heston did so once more in closing with the civil rights icon's prayer for "leaders" from a "freedom rally" speech in 1957.[5]

In remarks at Brandeis University, the actor continued his assessment of public trends and his determination to challenge them. He had often presented readings to such audiences with positive reactions, but now found the attendees challenging given his position on the Second Amendment. Although still popular among segments of the group he stood before, his views remained anathema to many others. Heston tried to mitigate negativity with references to his own son and to his work with Martin Luther King. He believed there was a defense to be made of his stance and an argument that this effort was illustrative of the courage required in difficult times not to remain silent.[6]

---

4 "Remarks Upon the Opening Session of the Arizona State Legislature, January 8, 2000, Phoenix, AZ," Heston, *The Courage to be Free*, 266-267.

5 Ibid., 267-268.

6 "Remarks at Brandeis University, March 28, 2000, Waltham, MA," Heston, *The Courage to be Free*, 269; Jarnel E. Watson, "Heston brings gun debate to Brandeis," *BG*, Mar. 29, 2000.

Heston's interest in promoting a pro-Second Amendment stance also took him to Canada. British Columbia reminded him of the natural beauty that marked the Michigan forests of his youth. He lamented that his chance to enjoy "the unfettered freedom to be part of God's green earth," was no longer as possible for him as it once had been. "But I still cherish it. It is part of my heritage, part of a grand and wonderful tradition." In a few words, he encapsulated the energy that continued to drive him, and he proceeded to link Canadian and United States citizens' rights. "We're of the same sturdy pioneer stock, cut from the same frontier cloth," he asserted as he closed. "Freedom is a North American legacy, and our governments had better never forget it."[7]

Aside from these presentations, Heston spent part of the first year of the new decade exorcizing personal demons. In May, he checked himself into a Utah treatment facility for help in regulating the alcohol consumption that had long been part of his social and professional life. According to his publicist, Lisa DeMatteo, the actor "thought he needed to take care of something that could possibly become a huge problem." The three-week program allowed him to take steps to address the matter on his own terms. "He's actually back at work," DeMatteo observed, "taking care of himself, and feeling great." Although she added rather incongruously, "I think it was overwork. He keeps a horrendous travel schedule, and he's 76 years old."[8]

Despite these challenges, Heston continued his work as circumstances allowed. He took a voice role as "The Mastiff" in a comedy that centered on a battle between pets in *Cats & Dogs*, and played Professor Walt Finley in the Jean-Claude Van Damme thriller *The Order*, in which he was reunited with screen and stage performer Ben Cross.

The actor also felt he had more to say through his writings. Just as he had tried to do in the brief volume to his grandson Jack about applying life's lessons, he wanted *The Courage to Be Free* to serve as a guide to traversing the murky waters of modern society. The book included a compendium of the arguments found in his speeches as well as samples of the transcripts from many of his most recent ones.

---

7 "Remarks Before the British Columbia Wildlife Federation, March 11, 2000, Prince George, British Columbia, Canada," Heston, *The Courage to be Free*, 276.

8 "Heston's Rehab Confirmed," *LAT*, Aug. 1, 2000. See also Michael Saunders and Jim Sullivan, "Heston dried out,." "Names & Faces," *BG*, Aug. 1, 2000. Heston's *Journals* contain references to drinking that occasionally transitioned into something more significant. On May 24, 1973, he recorded that "a drink in the bar, which developed into several drinks at the bar, with Oliver Reed . . . and his entourage" caused Heston to miss dinner. See *ALJ*, 218, 320, 366, 389, 409.

Much of the volume's content reflected a combination of nostalgic retrospection and sincere concern for current conditions as he saw them. Coupled with a respect for the Founding Fathers who had crafted the Bill of Rights and established the nation after wrenching free from British control was a disdain for those who now seemed unwilling or unable to guide it effectively. Chuck Heston preferred to rest his confidence on that earlier generation of leaders, while charging the latest one to respond to the challenge themselves.[9]

Aside from reflecting the philosophical and cultural musings of its author, *Courage* also served as a paean to the Second Amendment and the recreational and social importance of owning firearms. Wayne LaPierre provided a foreword to the volume that extolled the virtues of the NRA's leading public face. "While others of equal fame bask undisturbed in the glory of their personal accomplishments," LaPierre observed, "Charlton Heston actively and eagerly continues to seek new stages and new roles." The actor who had built his brand depicting the lives and impacts of leading historical figures now stood prepared to serve in such a capacity himself. "Today he is as much a prophet and an integral part of America's public conscience as he is a great actor," LaPierre continued. "The voice remains strong, the vision remains clear." For the NRA chief, who had watched the organization reach new heights of popularity and steered an effort to change the by-laws to allow Heston to assume a third term as president, this was an enduring example to be appreciated and followed. "And the nation has been made better off because he was born among us, a relentless and gifted patriot, a one-of-a-kind American, a lesson in what it means to be a legend, and a model for living life with the courage to be free." The role of its star was definitely more than symbolic for a membership that had doubled from 2.9 million under Heston's watch.

As the last decade had indicated, change was inevitable for the actor, personally and professionally. He had always relied on key individuals to help guide his affairs. His "Iceman" Herman Citron had kept the focus on projects that could advance the performer's career. Now, public relations guru Tony Makris led Heston's NRA reinvention. The desire to continue acting presented challenges to the Makris method. "The damn acting thing gets in my way," Makris observed, hoping to get the message to the man who had insisted that his disavowal of seeking public office had existed because he did not wish to sacrifice his craft. "You may not ever

---

9 Heston, *The Courage to be Free*, 9, 125.

understand this," Makris argued to his client, "but your last great role may be political."[10]

A new decade also presented Heston with an opportunity for reasserting his presence on the national stage of gun rights with a stirring visual image and a slogan that would be long remembered. As he stood before the NRA gathering in Charlotte on May 20, 2000, anticipating another contentious election year, the actor/activist took the matter firmly in hand. He strongly believed that in the wake of lifting the NRA to greater prominence in membership and donations that one mission remained: "Winning in November. That's why I'm staying on for a third tour of duty." Then, noting that Democratic forces were likely to disparage those who advocated gun rights, he hoisted a reproduction of a vintage musket over his head and called out the "five unscripted words" he had used before to rally the faithful: "I want to say those fighting words for everyone within the sound of my voice to hear and to heed, and especially for you, Mr. Gore: 'From my cold dead hands!'" One newspaper writer declared, "Move over Bill Clinton; The National Rifle Association, which has made the president a personal target in its campaign for gun rights, has selected a new enemy, and it is [vice president and presumptive Democratic nominee] Al Gore."[11]

As he demonstrated well in this context, Heston understood the power of his rhetoric and grand theatrical gestures. Once done the first time, his audiences came to expect it, again and again, almost ritualistically. Son Fraser thought the "bit" was overly dramatic. "I wondered why he did that myself," he observed when asked, before recognizing the most convincing explanation. "But the fact that we're talking about it . . . may be the point." Still, his father's most frequent and undeniably popular reference remained tied to his award-winning performance: "So, again, I tell you ladies and gentlemen, stay in the damned chariot."[12]

For at least one writer, Heston's efforts in this political arena constituted a "last stand." Ed Leibowitz's analysis, published in the aftermath of the 2000 election, featured Heston's whirlwind of appearances on behalf of Republican nominee George W. Bush. Remarking that the actor had spent a morning in Roanoke,

---

10 Heston, *The Courage to be Free*, xvi; Ed Leibowitz, "Charlton Heston's Last Stand," *Los Angeles* (February 2001), 148.

11 "Remarks Before the 129th Annual Meeting of Members of the National Rifle Association, May 20, 2000, Charlotte, N.C.," Heston, *The Courage to be Free*, 282–286; Susan Milligan, "NRA's top brass aims for Gore," *BSG*, May 21, 2000.

12 John H. Richardson, "Heston," *Esquire* (July 2001), 136.

Virginia, after two days in Grand Rapids and Flint, Michigan, and stops in Pennsylvania, he noted that Heston ended the day in Richmond. "Hip-replacement surgery and old age have dampened the fabled dynamism," Leibowitz concluded before adding, "no more battles with broadswords, no more chariot races for him." Yet if Heston approached the platform more gingerly, he still commanded attention and a message calculated to appeal to the would-be voters before him. He discovered an unusual legacy among the adoring crowds: members of the younger generation named after him. "So many of these Southerners and Midwesterners saw *The Ten Commandments* in church when they were four, five, six," the writer noted. "In their earliest recollections, Heston's is the face of the prophet who spoke directly to God." He added, "His career as a heroic leading man—as Moses, as Ben-Hur, as El Cid—has given him matchless reserves of political capital." For Leibowitz, characters of lesser stature would have prevented Heston from having as large an effect as he had enjoyed on the crowds that still came to see him. Additionally, the actor had cashed in on that political capital most effectively. Leibowitz confessed that the "thunderous ovation he drew not just in Chesapeake and Richmond but across West Virginia, Tennessee, and Arkansas in the closing weeks of the election" seemed to have "tipped the balance in Clinton's and Gore's home states toward Bush." In a tightly contested race that was ultimately decided by the Supreme Court over "hanging chads" in Florida, Heston avowed that NRA voters had made the difference.

Of any continuing role in NRA leadership, Leibowitz speculated, "Had Al Gore prevailed, Heston might be more inclined to consider a fourth term. But with a Bush presidency finally assured, he feels less urgency." Still, Chuck Heston seemed to be uncertain as to how to process the reception that Charlton Heston was now so often receiving. "I've never seen anything like it," the actor noted; he offered the best comparison he could make: "It's opening night of an enormous hit." Leibowitz found Heston's appearance before a raucous crowd at the Oxford Union emblematic of the star's limits and capabilities. A "thunderous ovation" for 'Moses himself! Mr. Charlton Heston!'" devolved into moments that might have panicked another man. "Before NRA audiences," he observed, "Heston had been so robust. But now, what with the malfunctioning TelePrompTer, an unfamiliar script, and an audience whose mood swings from loud approval to jeers on the turn of a phrase, he appears befuddled." Leibowitz wrote that "[f]or once, the public Heston seems an elderly man." As disaster seemed imminent, however, he reverted to familiar material and "begins to win it back with stories of Hollywood, burnished and honed through years of retelling." Finally, when a single individual remained intractable, Heston knew that he had the device he needed to win the audience over. "I always hope for a heckler," the actor maintained, before relaxing to tell the story of the time when a similar situation confronted playwriter George Bernard Shaw after a London presentation when he received a rare standing ovation, with one exception. "To the sole critic who loudly declared the production 'rubbish,' Heston offered the retort Shaw made, employing an Irish brogue and pausing for dramatic effect, 'I'd be inclined to agree with you, my friend. But what are we two against so many?'"[13]

The combination of the NRA and the distinguished actor proved powerful in the political arena. Robert Dreyfuss of *Rolling Stone* noted the prominence of both at a subsequent CPAC convention that featured both Vice President Dick Cheney and "Moses himself." Quoting NRA chief LaPierre, Dreyfuss explained that during the recent election, appearances by Heston on the hustings outdrew candidate Al Gore in states where the latter should have enjoyed widespread support "when the two appeared simultaneously."[14] Without specific poll numbers to determine the extent to which the results could be attributed to Heston's appearances, there was nevertheless ample anecdotal evidence to suggest that he had motivated supporters of the winning Republican ticket.

Heston left no avenue closed for advancing his messaging on guns and gun safety. In a letter to advice maven Ann Landers, he noted being "a frequent reader of your column" before agreeing with her concerning the advice to store guns properly and keep them out of the reach of children. "You will be pleased to know that the NRA spends $1 million a year (far more than any other organization in the country) visiting hundreds of schools to teach proper gun safety to children." For her part, Landers responded succinctly, but firmly. "Never thought I'd live to see the day I would give space to someone touting the National Rifle Assn. But fair is fair, and here's your letter. I appreciate your taking the time to write."[15]

An extensive interview in *Esquire* also allowed the performer to reach more readers in an article that displayed his wit and wisdom. John Richardson noticed the same troubled gait but witnessed Heston's ability to laugh at himself and

---

13 Leibowitz, "Last Stand," 61-62, 65, 149.

14 Robert Dreyfuss, "Bush's Concealed Weapon," *Rolling Stone* (Mar. 21, 2001), 35-36.

15 Ann Landers, "Teach Kids About Gun Safety," *LAT*, Sept. 27, 2001. Previously, Heston's proclivity for writing included a short note to "Dear Abby" concerning the nature of outdoorsmen to use all the facilities at their disposal for relieving themselves. "All Men Mark Territory," Dear Abby, *LAT*, Oct. 22, 1998.

charm an audience. At one appearance, a few protesters were present, donning ape masks and carrying signs with anti-gun slogans. Heston awaited his summons affably, then strode to the stage and declared, "Take your stinking paws off of me, you damned dirty apes!" The homage to *Planet of the Apes*, made possible by the students themselves, produced the reaction he had sought. "The fellows in the ape masks were a gift that got him the laugh," Richardson explained. "After that he had them."

Heston also displayed a self-deprecating humor that had more sting than the audience realized as he launched into a story of a time when someone approached another famous actor to say how much they had enjoyed his performance in *Ben-Hur*. "But that wasn't me. That was another fella," Heston had the individual responding. Nonplussed, the fan simply replied, "Well, if you aren't Burt Lancaster, then who are you?"[16]

At the same time, however, Heston's work in the profession that had guided his life and career was clearly in decline. Although he appeared in an episode of *Outer Limits* as a chief justice figure, he knew his chances to find opportunities on screen were fading. Still, a special uncredited cameo allowed him to revisit one of his most successful films. Director Tim Burton's remake of *Planet of the Apes* placed the recognizable face inside the visage of a dying elder in the ape community who warned his son of the dangers of a human intruder into their world. In a scene between Heston's Zaius and Tim Roth's General Thade, the truth of the threat came in the form of a pistol, kept hidden as a reminder for future generations of apes. In a moment reminiscent of Heston's 1968 character, the stranded astronaut Taylor, learning of the destruction of Earth, Zaius exclaimed with his dying breath of these humans, "Damn them . . . damn them all to Hell." The makeup that left only the voice recognizable to those who had seen the original took four hours to apply.[17]

In the scene, Heston's character employed the human-made handgun as a symbol of the depravation and danger mankind posed to the fictional ape society.

16 One account has the actor in question as Jeff Chandler and another as Kirk Douglas. See Crowther, *Epic Presence*, 64 and Richardson, "Heston," *Esquire* (July 2001), 67-68.

17 Scene from *Planet of the Apes* (2001); Eliot, *Charlton Heston*, 458. Costar Tim Roth later insisted he would not have taken the role if he had known about Heston's involvement, given his own passionate feelings about gun control and the veteran performer's association with the NRA. "Roth's Fury at 'Monster' Heston" www.contactmusic.com/tim-roth/news/roth.s-fury-at-.monster.-heston, accessed Jan. 11, 2019; "Tim Roth and Charlton Heston's Opposing Gun Views," July 27, 2001, www.imdb.com/news/ni0051586/#:~:text=Tim%20Roth%20And%20Charlton%20Heston%27s%20 Opposing%20Gun%20Views.,pair%20had%20to%20work%20together%20in%20the%20movie, accessed Jan. 11, 2019.

Boston Globe correspondent Tom Russo apparently thought that symbolism meant the actor was confusing his on-screen and off-screen personas with contradictory signals on guns and gun control: "Talk about your mixed messages." Yet if he could agree that irresponsible gun ownership was problematic in the real world, Heston was using the Zaius character to connect back to the frustrated human figure he had played in the earlier version rather than as a statement on modern conditions.

It is hard to document the degree to which the roles Heston accepted at this stage represented anything more significant than chances to work. "I've been a lucky man. I have no regrets," he told one interviewer. There were still roles he hoped to play, and "much I want to do." He might yet be the insecure boy that melded into the images of other figures he could embody, but something more satisfying characterized him. "And, inside, I still feel like a young man full of optimism and wonder."[18] That sense of wonder would become more imperative as he faced his most serious personal challenge.

In August 2002, the actor released a statement to "My Dear Friends, Colleagues and Fans." He shared the news that his doctors had determined he "may have a neurological disorder whose symptoms are consistent with Alzheimer's disease." Always health conscious and determined to remain as fit as possible for as long as he could, Heston recognized the difficulty he faced with this struggle. "So . . . I wanted to prepare a few words for you now, because when the time comes, I may not be able to."

Charlton Heston had always stressed at critical points that any words published under his name needed to be consistent with his sentiments. In this instance especially, they had to match the depth of the sense of gratitude he felt for his career and those who had helped to make it possible. "I've lived my whole life on the stage and screen before you. I've found purpose and meaning in your response. For an actor there's no greater loss than the loss of his audience. I can part the Red Sea, but I can't part with you."

Chuck Heston was determined to wage this new war on his own terms, with a sternness of purpose and a sense of humor. "I'll insist on work when I can; the doctors will insist on rest when I must. If you see a little less spring in my step, if your name fails to leap to my lips, you'll know why. And if I tell you a funny story for the second time, please laugh anyway." Regardless, he wanted to affirm, "I'm neither giving up nor giving in." He also harkened back to the figures with whom he had battled on behalf of issues of social import through much of his life, insisting that defeat was not an option he would accept. "I believe I'm still

18 Rader, "If I Ran & Won," 7.

the fighter that Dr. King and JFK and Ronald Reagan knew, but it's a fight I must someday call a draw."

Heston's love of family shone through brightly as he closed his statement. Beloved grandchildren Jack, Ridley, and Charlie would allow him to "touch immortality," as would his work in film and television and his abiding love of William Shakespeare. He used the Bard's words from *The Tempest* to mark his closing: "Be Cheerful, sir. Our revels now are ended. . . . We are such stuff as dreams are made on; and our life is rounded with a sleep." Film critic Roger Ebert may have summed up the sentiment of many of those who knew and admired Heston's work, if not necessarily his latter-day politics. "It is always tragic when someone suffers from Alzheimer's," Ebert observed, "but his bravery and grace in publicly acknowledging his illness was dignified and touching."[19]

The actor's spokesperson explained that he had chosen the videotaped method as a way of ensuring that his message came across as he intended. "It is very emotional and personal," Lisa Powers noted. "He wanted to deliver the statement appropriately and in its entirety." In the means that he chose to convey his prerecorded remarks, Heston could put into practice a lifetime of experience in presentation, with the intonation and wording that he preferred for the viewers to see and hear.[20]

Many accounts, including one that appeared in the *Los Angeles Times*, approached the issue sympathetically, but without becoming maudlin. "The world is a tough place. You're never going to get out of it alive," the *Times* article quoted him as saying in the "first interview" since the actor had sent out his video-taped announcement of his condition. "Heston faces his illness squarely," writer Robert W. Welkos maintained. "He appears rather frail and walks at a slower pace," but he also seemed "quick-witted and delivers vivid recollections of his early years in Hollywood as he looks ahead, he hopes, to years of acting before the curtain finally comes down on his acting career." Although candid concerning his long-term prognosis, Heston hedged in admitting he already had the degenerative disease. When he insisted, "I can say for certain that I don't have it now," son Fraser

---

19 "Charlton Heston's Alzheimer's Announcement and Goodbye," www.junebergalzheimers.com/charlton-hestons-alzheimers-announcement-and-goodbye, accessed Nov. 18, 2018; "Heston says he has symptoms of Alzheimer's," *KTN*, Aug. 10, 2002; Roger Ebert, "Charlton Heston, Richard Widmark: Tough Guys, Strong Presences," April 10, 2008, www.rogerebert.com/interviews/charlton-heston-richard-widmark-tough-guys-strong-presences, accessed June 7, 2019.

20 Susan King, "Heston Tells of Disease," *LAT*, Aug. 10, 2002.

intervened almost clinically. "Well, I wouldn't say that is correct, Chuck. That is not quite what they told you. They are as certain as they are going to be."

He had always faced problems stoically and privately, if he could. This new challenge had left him with no real alternative but to go public if he wished to exert any measure of control about how the news came out. "Heston says he chose to make public his private medical condition because he feared that it would leak out eventually, and then it could appear that he was hiding something," Welkos explained. Almost immediately, well-wishes came in from many sources, including Nancy Reagan, gun-control advocate Sarah Brady, and President George H. W. Bush. Bush had offered his best wishes and expressed his pride in "what I had done for my country." Heston deflected the compliment with characteristic humor as "perhaps, overstating it a little." In the meantime, he looked forward to an animated version of *Ben-Hur* that he was working on because "no one has ever done it," and expected his faith and family to sustain him. "I go to church," he remarked, before admitting, "I don't go as often as I should. But I believe in God, and I think the things that have happened to me would not have happened without his consent." Those elements included his work, his children and grandchildren, and most importantly his marriage to Lydia: "I couldn't imagine being married to anyone else."[21]

Lydia Heston remained the critical foundation and bulwark for her husband. He had depended upon her for the support that allowed him to be himself and to pursue a career that had furnished the capacity for making their lifestyles and life choices possible for an expanding family. Heston was never shy in attributing this role to his wife and stressed the importance it played for the sustainability of their long-standing marriage in a professional and personal environment that never ceased to present challenges to them. She would continue to stand by him as they faced the last furlongs of his race together.

Such moments of intense introspection aside, Heston was set to demonstrate that he was not ready to surrender to the signs of mortality that beset him. In October 2002, newspaper notices reported, "Actor and National Rifle Association president Charlton Heston is headed to New Hampshire" in support of candidates "who will fight for the right to bear arms." His presence alone would entice fans and ensure wider news coverage. Accounts suggested that despite his personal challenges, the actor expected to maintain a hectic schedule, which included "a dozen states between now and election day."[22]

---

21 Robert W. Welkos, "Heston Faces His Illness Squarely," *LAT*, Aug. 18, 2002.

22 "Charlton Heston going to N.H. rally," *BG*, Oct. 15, 2002.

While his personal struggle continued, Heston's involvement with the NRA exposed him to an awkward situation when documentarian Michael Moore ventured to the "ridge" to interview the actor for *Bowling for Columbine*. Attempting to underscore the power of the gun culture in the consciousness of the nation as incidents of shootings appeared to be on the rise, Moore disclosed his own NRA membership to his subject before shifting to question the organization's actions in the wake of the death of a young girl in Michigan and the Columbine killings. Building on the actor's increasing discomfort, Moore continued to drive his points relentlessly until Heston rose to exit the interview. As he left the property himself, the filmmaker placed a picture of the Michigan victim dramatically on a column to speak for itself.

Moore's ultimately award-winning effort revealed the degree to which a man who had prided himself on winning such debates could no longer do so. Whether a victim of an unexpected line of questioning—Heston biographer Marc Eliot termed the incident a "tasteless 'ambush'" and assistant Carol Lanning thought it "cruel" and "both unfair and manipulative"—or a result of the effects of his neurological condition, the actor appeared at a loss as to how to respond to Moore's aggressive line of questioning. Nevertheless, he handled the matter with quiet dignity when he realized nothing further could be gained through the one-sided discussion and stepped away. One writer concluded of the unsettling confrontation, "Whether one agrees on the political issue, the last scene . . . is perhaps the most moving. Bowed by arthritis, Heston walked silently away from the screaming filmmaker—shaking his head in confusion—back into his home."[23]

Contemporary accounts suggested one motivation for the encounter. "Crusading documentary filmmaker Michael Moore and screen-legend-turned-NRA stumper Charlton Heston might not be a match made in Second Amendment heaven," newspaper correspondent Tom Russo observed, "but there's no question that, thrown together, this odd couple makes for provocative viewing." Russo noted the actor's critical role as foil. "Heston serves as a lead antagonist throughout 'Bowling for Columbine,' Moore's Oscar-winning examination of gun control and America's culture of violence." Yet the writer thought the "climactic showdown with Heston—some might say ambush of him—turns uncomfortable fast."[24]

---

23 Eliot, *Charlton Heston*, 467; Mal Vincent, "In the nick of time came a rock-jawed hero," *VP*, Apr. 8, 2008.

24 Tom Russo, "Opposites Attract," *BG*, Aug. 21, 2003.

Despite such moments, as Heston had explained candidly in his Alzheimer's statement, he planned to continue to work as his condition and circumstances permitted. He also looked, as he had always done, for roles that challenged him. Although he had created his public image by inhabiting the lives of numerous great figures of history, Charlton Heston never shrank from accepting the challenges of portraying men of less savory character. Just at a time when he might have avoided such a depiction, he took up the role of the notorious Nazi doctor Josef Mengele. His was not the primary character in *My Father, Rua Alguem 5555*, released in 2003, but Heston's was the most provocative. An exile haunted by the constant possibility of discovery, this Mengele had reached an advanced stage in life, still embracing the notion that he had done no more than his duty required and harboring fond if distant memories of his homeland. Mengele's son came to confront his father and learn the truth of his activities in such heinous venues as Auschwitz, allowing the war criminal to present his logic in defense of the indefensible.

Biographer Eliot passed off the performance in a note as little more than an extended cameo.[25] Yet Heston's part in the production was essential and included compelling dialogue. In one of the more poignant scenes the aged Mengele grabbed a walking stick and gingerly led his son through a maze of jungle he compared to the Black Forest of Germany. For the practitioner of his craft for well over half a century, the gangling boy of *Peer Gynt* had become the frail and reclusive figure living at 5555 Rua Alguem. Even so, Charlton Heston remained dedicated to exploring a character whose qualities Chuck Heston would never have embraced otherwise.

The performer's film career and personal interests seemed to converge when sculptor Blair Buswell brought him into his studio to pose for a statue of screen cowboy Will Penny, destined for display at the National Cowboy and Western Heritage Museum in Oklahoma City. The artist found his subject compatible. "He was real good, real easy to be around, cordial - he had some great stories, of course. It was a lot of fun." Buswell noted that he had to take age into account in crafting the work of the figure of the weather-beaten cowboy but concluded that Heston's personal charisma assisted in the effort. "He just really has a presence about him."[26]

On his other stage, Heston's unprecedented five-term presidency of the NRA ended in 2003. His involvement with that organization often overshadowed his

---

25 Eliot, *Charlton Heston*, note, 468.

26 "Heston to Attend Statue Unveiling at Cowboy and Western Museum," *Oklahoman*, Sept. 25, 2002, www.newsok.com/article/2808486, accessed Nov. 18, 2018.

lifetime of artistic achievement in some circles. In others, he remained an iconic figure. Important accolades continued to come his way. On July 18, 2003, President George W. Bush announced that the actor would receive the Presidential Medal of Freedom. The ceremony took place on July 23, with Heston in attendance. The audience heard once again of his lifetime of achievements in acting and in public service. Citing a few of his most celebrated roles, the recognition read: "In the process, Charlton Heston himself has become one of the great names in film history."[27]

Even in the face of some disgruntlement in Hollywood circles over Heston's political and gun rights stances, the leadership of the American Film Institute, under director and CEO Jean Picker Firstenberg, moved forward with the creation of the Charlton Heston Award to honor its chair emeritus for his "distinguished contributions to both the film and television communities and to the American Film Institute." The actor had jested that he had only received the chairmanship while he had excused himself during a meeting, but he took enormous pride in this association, serving as chairman of the AFI Board of Trustees from 1971 to 1982 and as president from 1983 to 2002. Current chair Howard Stringer acknowledged Heston's considerable imprint. "For decades, he has been a major presence in movies and television around the world and his strong spirit of commitment to AFI lives on through this honor." To bestow the recognition, Jack Valenti, an AFI founding trustee and a longtime associate of the actor joined Stringer and Firstenberg at Heston's Coldwater Canyon home on September 23, 2003 for a private ceremony.[28] The two accolades, coming during the closing furlongs of his race, represented a form of appreciation of the service and entertainment Heston's life and career had illustrated.

Yet he remained a mysterious iconoclastic figure to many. A humorous article highlighting a "mini-fest" of double-bills of Heston's films at Boston's Brattle Theatre also sought an explanation for his shift in political alignment "from left to right." Writer Mark Feeney thought the transition in "Heston's ideological journey

---

27 "Remarks on Presenting the Presidential Medal of Freedom, July 23, 2003," George W. Bush, *Public Papers of the Presidents of the United States. Containing the Public Messages, Speeches, and Statements of the President. George W. Bush. 2003.* (Washington: Government Printing Office, 2004), 910-913.

28 "AFI Establishes Charlton Heston Award, Distinguished Actor to Receive First Honor," Sept. 24, 2003. Valenti received the award the following year. "Jack Valenti Receives Charlton Heston Award, AFI Board of Trustees Salute Legendary Film Statesman," Feb. 26, 2004. www.afi.com/Docs/about/press/hestonaward.pdf, accessed Nov. 18, 2018. See also Heston and Isbouts, *Hollywood*, 193, and the bittersweet family reaction in Eliot, *Heston*, 468-470.

is all the more striking for the fact that several of his movies can be read in overtly liberal terms." Feeney's conclusion, however, drew more on lighthearted whimsy than serious assessment: Heston "had his reasons" for accepting his screen roles in *Planet of the Apes*, *The Omega Man*, and *Soylent Green*. "It's enough to make even the most progressive person appreciate the virtues of the Second Amendment—or at least reach for a Bud Light."[29]

Of course, this view and the sense of humor Heston himself possessed belied the fact that the actor/activist had a reputation for seriousness in his views and in his profession. He was determined to represent positions whatever reaction they might engender, and understood that as a "public face" he bore both a responsibility and the exposure that came with that visibility. "One of the reasons I'm useful in jobs like this," he explained of his numerous public advocacy positions, "is my high visibility."[30] Heston could not accept what he believed to be unsubstantiated attacks on his work or issues of public import that mattered to him, but he always insisted upon the right of such critics to express themselves as freely as he felt should be in reacting to them.

Heston's political fires remained stoked when he deemed portrayals of his positions on public issues misrepresented in the political arena. He had touted the success of a program in Richmond, Virginia, called "Project Exile," to combat gun violence, but considered Virginia Democratic gubernatorial candidate and former Richmond mayor Tim Kaine's emphasis of this support as suggestive of an endorsement of Kaine the Republican Heston disputed. "To my knowledge, Mr. Heston has never met the man," the actor's spokesperson asserted.[31]

Despite playing the voice of God on Mount Horeb for Cecil B. DeMille, a celestial figure in a modern Paul Hogan comedy, or appearing on *Saturday Night Live*, Heston never deluded himself into thinking he had command over his mortality. He had remained as fit and active as his health allowed and embraced his personal demons with the aplomb of one his screen personas, but he saw the sun setting, even as he authored his autobiography in 1995. Heston closed that work as he would others, with quotations from the individuals he admired most and whose principles he had striven so mightily to apply to his own life. "I can't do better here than to leave you with the words of these Americans: Martin Luther King, Jr., F. Scott Fitzgerald, Tom Paine, Samuel Eliot Morrison, William Faulkner, Thomas

---

29 Mark Feeney, "Brattle mini-fest shows actor's wide political spectrum," *BG*, Aug. 17, 2007.

30 Plutzik, "Last of the Epic Heroes, 33.

31 Michael Sluss, "NRA takes aim at Tim Kaine," *Roanoke Times*, June 17, 2005.

Wolfe . . . and Abraham Lincoln." In the mix of these voices, he had found his own. "I believe that says it all. Thanks. It's been a pleasure."[32]

In this same context, Charlton Heston ran his final furlong quietly and finished his race in the bosom of family and friends. He was no longer able to travel and had long ceased doing the appearances and performances that provided fuel to his life and career. Although he had once thought it would be best to reach the end of his run in a dressing room or on a movie or theater set, he met his personal finish line, most appropriately, on his ridge in Coldwater Canyon on April 5, 2008, several months shy of his eighty-fifth birthday.[33]

---

32 *CHA*, 577.

33 *ALJ*, 4; Eliot, *Charlton Heston*, 471, 473-474.

CONCLUSION
"A Great Run"

"Sooner or later, the man with the scythe comes along and says, 'It's time.' When that time comes I'll say, 'OK, I had a great run.'"
— Heston to his son Fraser

"I have fought a good fight, I have finished the course, I have kept the faith."
— II Timothy 4:7

"An Epic Life."
— *Entertainment Weekly* title for a Heston retrospective

Whenever Chuck Heston confronted the most significant challenges of his life, he repeated the habit he had often employed at such moments of introspection of assessing his status in his work. Often, his own judgments were more difficult than those anyone else would have made, laced with the disappointments of critical or personal shortfalls. While doing this near the end of a productive career, the actor and family man implied that he was coming to a point of acceptance for the body of work he had produced, the public services he had rendered, and the ways in which he had tried to support his loved ones. A writer noted the actor's words as he was coming to grips with his mortality while simultaneously contemplating his legacy. "Sooner or later, the man with the scythe comes along and says, 'It's time.' Heston says that, when that time comes, he would like to say, 'OK, I had a great run.'"[1]

---

1 Welkos, "Heston Faces His Illness Squarely."

Virginian-Pilot writer Mal Vincent, who had covered Heston's career in film, noted his passing in an "appreciation" that "Charlton Heston came along at just the right time," when the country needed a "movie hero." Vincent explained to those who had asked if he knew the actor, "Yes, Moses once walked among us." Heston's preference to discuss matters other than his latest cinematic endeavors and his recent positions with the NRA could prove perplexing, but the writer believed, "movie fans tend to see film in theaters, not on newspaper pages. His place stands." Heston's last publicist noted, "If Hollywood had a Mt. Rushmore, Heston's face would be on it."[2]

Following Heston's death, one of the more interesting reflections on his life and career came from *Los Angeles Times* columnist Al Martinez, which he entitled, "Learning more about the man known as Moses." Though Martinez carried a genuine aversion to the actor's role as NRA president and his advocacy for gun ownership, he learned that he had worked with fellow actor Peter Dennis, who had lost a son to gun violence, to give voice to the beloved A. A. Milne figures Winnie the Pooh and friends. Dennis observed, "I saw the man the way he was. Being at his home with family and friends, I got to know people who knew and loved him, and through them I got to know him." Spending time with Heston as the latter declined in the final months of his life, Dennis detected a smile when he whispered that their fictional friend was also there in spirit. "No one could love the little bear and his friends . . . as Heston loved them and be evil," he concluded. As Martinez pondered that sentiment, he agreed there was more to the man and his legacy than any single element.[3]

Martinez's tribute underscored the nuance of being "Chuck Heston" beneath the trappings of a well-known public figure. A complicated life and complex personality marked the individual who had risen to prominence in his craft and eventually to international superstardom. His profession had sent him across the globe and into theaters and living rooms throughout it. He had met with figures of renown and royalty and had portrayed others for audiences that embraced his performances. His refuge remained the "House that Hur built," and he involved his formerly estranged father in its construction. Heston's face and voice stayed recognizable, foremost among those who had watched his work for decades,

2 Vincent, "In the nick of time came a rock-jawed hero," *VP*, April 8, 2008; "Charlton Heston, Oscar winner, film legend, dies," *BHC*, Apr. 7, 2008.

3 Al Martinez, "Learning more about the man known as Moses," *LAT*, Apr. 21, 2008. Martinez also noted that Heston had gladly assisted the English-born Dennis in obtaining a green card to work in the United States.

but also to younger generations who caught only a relative glimpse of them. An astounding résumé that included work on stage and screen, in documentaries, and as a spokesperson, marked his long career. Popular critic Roger Ebert maintained at the time of the actor's death that "Heston made at least three movies that almost everybody eventually sees: '*Ben-Hur*,' '*The Ten Commandments*,' and '*Planet of the Apes*' (1968)."[4]

An effort to highlight the numerous Hollywood connections for Kanab, Utah, with a "Walk of Fame" of its own included a marker for Charlton Heston that mentioned his role in *Planet of the Apes*. Though the outdoor shots for the 1968 version of *Apes* were filmed elsewhere, Kanab served as the location for numerous other Westerns and television programs, including the 2001 *Planet of the Apes* remake. The marker fittingly depicted Heston in his role as Buffalo Bill Cody from *Pony Express*.[5]

Heston's contributions have remained prevalent in the prodigious amount of stage and screen work he created, and his "public face" allowed him to extend that influence in leadership roles in his profession. Yet Chuck Heston did not have the opportunity for the kind of send-off he remembered for co-star and acting legend Edward G. Robinson after filming for *Soylent Green* had wrapped. The men shared a powerful scene when Robinson's character Sol went to a euthanasia center and Heston's Thorn forced his way into the observation chamber. Thorn gazed in amazement at an enormous screen of stunningly filmed views from the natural world the aged and dying man had once known and the younger man had never experienced. "For us, he was finishing in the film," Heston recalled years later of a final gathering for his esteemed colleague. "For Eddie, he was finishing as an actor, standing for the last time on a sound stage, where he'd lived so richly, for so much of his life." He would have to wait to cherish such moments in retrospect since no one knew the end that Robinson was facing: "Twelve days later he was dead," Heston observed, before adding a wistful note. "No actor could ask for a better way to go." Earlier in his career, he had remarked, "The important thing to me is that I'm a working actor. I'll settle for that on my tombstone."[6]

When family and friends gathered to remember his life at a service that took place on a lovely, wooded canyon that overlooked Pacific Palisades, there was a

---

4 Ebert, "Charlton Heston, Richard Widmark: Tough Guys, Strong Presences."

5 "Charlton Heston - Utah's Little Hollywood," The Historical Marker Database, www.hmdb.org/m.asp?m=41318, accessed Oct. 23, 2018.

6 *CHA*, 478; Finnigan, "Charlton Heston Is Proud of Being a Working Actor."

sense of appreciation for the man and the artist. Reverend Michael Scott Seiler noted Heston's pew in St. Matthew's Episcopal Church, and other speakers called upon the mourners to ponder the life of the devoted family man and patriot. Writer Bob Thomas described the actor as "one of the last lions of Old Hollywood" who presented "an imposing figure both in his politics and on the big screen." In addition to his wife and children, longtime friends like Nancy Reagan and actors Arnold Schwarzenegger, Tom Selleck, Keith Carradine, Pat Boone, and Olivia DeHavilland were among the individuals who came to pay their final respects. "I never knew a finer man," Fraser Clarke Heston reflected; "I will never know a finer man." Thomas offered a retrospective that summarized the professional aspects of a longstanding career, concluding that "Heston was one of the biggest box-office draws of the 1950s, '60s, and '70s, often playing legendary leaders or ordinary men thrown into heroic struggles."[7]

Like Judah Ben-Hur, Heston had overcome obstacles early in life, and had endured. He remained a force in his craft and "a public face" that those who followed his work would long remember. His efforts on behalf of organizations like the American Film Institute and the National Rifle Association ensured that he would have an impact after he was gone. Likewise, his willingness to represent the country through cultural and governmental endeavors were significant contributions. "Politics/public service has been a fixture of my career all along," he explained in his later years, "and if I have contributed something that helped people in the process, for that I am grateful."[8]

But his place in the entertainment industry through his film and television work were his most enduring legacy. Charlton Heston would always be as young and real as the character on the screen for moviegoers and television audiences. In homage to his career, the United States Postal Service added his image to its "Legends of Hollywood" series as the eighteenth person so honored. Unveiled in a "First Day of Issue" ceremony on April 11, 2014, the stamp setting featured Heston as Ben-Hur. Co-presented by Turner Classic Movies, the event included a video tribute and comments from SAG-AFTRA President Ken Howard and President-Emerita Jean Firstenberg, as well as from Fraser Heston. "With his chiseled jaw, compelling baritone voice and muscular physique, Heston seemed perfectly at home leading a cast of thousands," the text of the commemorative program explained. Highlighting his Academy Award-winning performance in *Ben-Hur* it

7 Bob Thomas, "Hollywood luminaries gather to pay last respects to Heston," *BSG*, Apr. 13, 2008.

8 Heston and Isbouts, *Hollywood*, 193.

added, "In one of the most famous action sequences ever filmed, Heston raced a chariot and thundering team of four horses in a spectacular contest against his Roman rival."[9]

Two years later, in March 2016, Bonhams offered an auction of items from the Heston estate. "The Charlton Heston Collection" featured household furniture and personal memorabilia. Turner Classic Movies host Robert Osborne provided a preface that included an assessment of the man: "Meeting Chuck in person made you realize immediately he was the kind of guy you hoped he would be—a straight-shooter, a thinking man, sturdy, dependable and professional." Osborne also took note of the actor's "shyness." "But even he admitted the very nature of his work made people look up to him in a way that reflected the impact of the characters he played—rather than the real Chuck Heston." Osborne thought the assessment "a little too self-effacing," adding, "Thankfully, we'll always have his films to remember him by."[10] But the man understood the essence of performance longevity. Once, while waiting in a line with others to take their seats in a restaurant, a friend asked why Heston did not simply tell the *maitre'd* who he was. "If he doesn't know who I am, I'm nobody," the actor replied.[11]

Writer Bruce Crowther described Charlton Heston as the "epic presence," who embodied many memorable screen personas. "Yet, like it or not, while he and careful students of his work will remember him for his stage appearances and for such film roles as Andrew Jackson, Mike Vargas, Amos Dundee, Chrysagon, General Gordon, Ron Catlan, Mark Antony, and Will Penny, he will be remembered by the great mass of the movie-going public for Moses and Ben-Hur." Crowther concluded that this reality irritated Heston, "but considering the lifestyle he has enjoyed, and the fame and the acclamation which follow him wherever he goes, it cannot have been too big a price to pay."[12]

Indeed, Charlton Heston would have been less likely to emerge as an international cinematic star had it not been for these iconic roles. Robert Osborne employed a circus allusion when he observed, "The name of Charlton Heston has become as identified with massive film epics as Barnum with Bailey." He also noted

---

9 "Charlton Heston Limited Edition Stamp, First-Day-of-Issue Ceremony," program, April 2014.

10 "The Charlton Heston Collection, Tuesday Mar. 22, 2016, Los Angeles, Bonhams," 3. The next page featured Chuck and Lydia Heston on the chariot from *Ben-Hur*, and the cover photo was a still of Heston as Judah Ben-Hur holding the garland of victory from the race; ibid., cover, 4.

11 Barney Glazer, "Spitz wise in quitting Oscar show," *BG*, Feb. 27, 1973.

12 Crowther, *Epic Presence*, 176.

that these films had tended to "stand among the biggest moneymakers in U.S. film history," and "made corpulent pots of money."[13] Chuck Heston would have been the first to explain that much of the credit went to direction, technical support, and other factors, yet would have been hard pressed to deny that his acting had played a large role in this success.

While most moviegoers thought of him as Judah Ben-Hur or Moses, Heston remained attached to the loner Will Penny, who allowed him to depart successfully and meaningfully from those epic figures. "It's one of my favorite roles, because it is real, you see, and not all faked up to make it nice. It even has an unhappy ending," he explained to Roger Ebert about the motion picture. "That's one nice thing about 'Will Penny,'" the actor concluded. "I'm just an ordinary cowboy, not Ben-Hur in the saddle."[14]

As the nature of his most popular movie roles suggested, one of the most interesting components of his work was his public association with religious elements. Heston's recordings of biblical passages and well-documented travels to the Holy Land built upon this perception. He could be plainspoken and earthy in his language and more than a little titillating in his image as a man, but in a life devoted to family and professional and public service, he presented a dedication that rivaled the legendary Judah Ben-Hur, and this helped him achieve lasting fame and star status. True to his perception of his own values and ideals, Heston remained determined to make as much a difference in the world around him as his stature would allow. In this regard, in his personal race, he very much embodied the notion expressed in the scriptural passage of II Timothy: "I have fought a good fight, I have finished the course, I have kept the faith."

To so many, Charlton Heston became the embodiment of morality on the screen that suggested deep religious convictions in the man. Yet, Lydia Heston observed of her husband, "Chuck was never an extremely religious person, in the generally accepted sense." Still, she felt that his work, especially with regard to his role as Moses, represented for him "a profound insight into human behavior." Her assessment provided useful context for an answer he gave to an Italian interviewer when *The Agony and Ecstasy* was released concerning how he imagined Hell. For Heston, it would be "a place where there was no work and no challenge: exactly what some people, in fact, imagine to be heaven. A place where everything you

---

13 Robert Osborne, *Academy Awards Illustrated: A Complete History of Hollywood's Academy Awards in Words and Pictures* (LaHabra, CA, 1966), 245.

14 Ebert, "Charlton Heston, Richard Widmark: Tough Guys, Strong Presences."

tried worked perfectly, from your concept of Macbeth to your tennis backhand; where both your wife and your horse did exactly what you wanted them to do." Heston seemed to lament the notion of eternal perfection in Heaven, concluding, "Man is the only animal whose reach exceeds his grasp. If he never fails, he is never challenged."[15]

The actor delighted in observing that he had "[l]earned to be a public person" before admitting, "But I suppose that too, is a role I play." Indeed, over a long career, Charlton Heston enjoyed "a great run." One scholar of the actor's place in American politics employed the final race for Judah Ben-Hur in her assessment of Chuck Heston the man. "He won that race," Emilie Raymond observed. "He also won the race of life. Not only did he boast a closely knit family and an accomplished film career, but he also emerged as the most influential celebrity activist of his time."[16] Although the power of his influence could be debated, few could dispute that he played a role as impactful as anyone else did in the causes for which he lent his considerable physical and professional stature.

The man who sampled acting in his earliest years and dedicated himself to the training and practice of the profession for the remainder of them, worked diligently to make himself relevant in his time. He continued to seek an audience, often refurbishing his "brand" for that purpose, and cherished the freedom and security his work offered. A long marriage and devotion to family marked the other important aspects of his life. Had circumstances allowed, he would have preferred to exit the stage or the studio only after finally achieving as close to the perfect performance as he was capable.

Although he had portrayed impressive figures in film and on stage and television, Heston knew better than to think he had somehow become them. "It's fun to talk about how you get inside a character and go home and act like him— but I don't think you do, at least, *I* don't, and I don't think it's healthy to do it," he observed in an interview. "I mean, when you play Macbeth you are *not* Macbeth. And if you are, then you're in trouble." He once asserted, "I can never stop being Charlton Heston, and I can never wholly become Michelangelo, or Macbeth, or Moses. Every man has within him the raw materials that make up all men. From

---

15 Hyatt Downing, "Hollywood's Moses," 4, "*The Ten Commandments* publicity," Heston Papers, HL; "Interview with Charlton Heston, 11-9-64," "*The Agony and the Ecstasy* publicity," Heston Papers, HL.

16 *The Mike Walsh Show*, UCLA; Raymond, *Cold, Dead Hands*, 319.

mad men to prophets. The actor's job is to try to put the pieces together in the right order."[17]

Certainly, Chuck Heston's identification with his work, public service, and family was crucial to who he was in any meaningful sense; it shaped his persona and his legacy. "Is Charlton Heston his stage name or his real name?" someone in a crowd assembled to watch *Soylent Green* inquired. "It's my name," came the simple, certain reply.[18] And so it was.

17 Linderman, "Charlton Heston Interview," 108; Raymond, *Cold, Dead Hands*, 13.

18 Richardson, "Heston," *Esquire* (July 2001), 136.

BIBLIOGRAPHY

Primary Sources:
Archives:
> George H. W. Bush Presidential Library and Museum, College Station, TX
> LBJ Presidential Library, Austin, TX
> Margaret Herrick Library, Beverly Hills, CA
>> DeMille, Cecil B. Collection
>> Heston, Charlton. Clipping Files
>> Heston, Charlton. Papers
>> Hopper, Hedda Papers
>> Peckinpah, Sam. Papers
>> Wyler, William. Collection (Compiled by Jan Herman)
> Richard Milhous Nixon Presidential Library and Museum, Yorba Linda, CA
> Ronald Wilson Reagan Presidential Library, Simi Valley, CA
> Brian Steel Wills Collection, Wise, VA
>> Charlton Heston Papers

Government Documents:
Defense POW/MIA Accounting Agency, Vietnam-Era Statistical Report
www.dpaa.mil/Portals/85/Statistics%20as%20of%20October%2014.pdf
Heston, Charlton. Testimony, Joint Hearings Before the Special Subcommittee on Arts and Humanities of the Committee on Labor and Public Welfare, United States Senate and Special Subcommittee on Labor of the Committee on Education and Labor, House of Representatives. Eighty-ninth Congress, First Session, Part I, February 23 and March 5, 1965 (Washington: Government Printing Office, 1965), 56-58.
———. Testimony, Hearings Before the Subcommittee on Communication and Power on the Committee on Interstate and Foreign Commerce, House of Representatives, Ninety-first Congress, First Session, November 21, 1969. Re H.R. Res. 420. To Amend the Communications Act of 1934 so as to Prohibit the Granting of Authority to Broadcast Pay Television Programs. Washington: Government Printing Office, 1969, 141.
———. Testimony, Hearings Before the Special Subcommittee on Arts and Humanities of the Committee on Labor and Public Welfare, United States Senate. Ninety-third Congress, Second Session on H.R. 17504, December 11, 1974 (Washington: Government Printing Office, 1975), 6, 14, 45.

Newspapers:
[Phoenix] *Arizona Sun*
Atlanta Journal Constitution
Boston Globe
The [Pascagoula, MS] *Chronicle*
Detroit Tribune
[Washington, DC] *Evening Star*
New York Times
Parade Magazine
Richmond Times-Dispatch
Statesboro [GA] *Herald.*
Virginian-Pilot and Ledger-Star

Books:

Belafonte, Harry, with Michael Shnayerson, *My Song: A Memoir*. New York: Alfred A. Knopf, 2011.

Bush, George H. W. *Public Papers of the Presidents of the United States. Containing the Public Messages, Speeches, and Statements of the President*. Washington: United States Government Printing Office.

Bush, George W. *Public Papers of the Presidents of the United States. Containing the Public Messages, Speeches, and Statements of the President*. Washington: United States Government Printing Office.

DeMille, Cecil B. *The Autobiography of Cecil B. DeMille*. Edited by Donald Haynie. Englewood Cliffs, NJ: Prentice-Hall, 1959.

Dern, Bruce, with Christopher Fryer and Robert Crane. *Things I've Said, but Probably Shouldn't Have*. Hoboken, NJ: John Wiley & Sons, 2007.

Douglas, Kirk. *The Ragman's Son: An Autobiography*. New York: Simon and Schuster, 1988.

Felten, D. Erik, ed. *A Shining City: The Legacy of Ronald Reagan*. New York: Simon & Schuster, 1998.

Fonda, Henry. *Fonda: My Life as Told to Howard Teichmann*. New York: NAL Books, 1981.

Harrison, Rex. *A Damned Serious Business*. New York: Bantam Books, 1991.

———. *Rex: An Autobiography*. New York: William Morrow, 1975.

Heston, Charlton. *The Actor's Life: Journals 1956-1976*. Edited by Hollis Alpert. New York: E.P. Dutton, 1976.

———. *Beijing Diary*. New York: Simon & Schuster, 1990.

———. *Charlton Heston Presents the Bible: A Companion for Families*. New York: GT Publishing, 1997.

———. *In the Arena: An Autobiography*. New York: Simon & Schuster, 1995.

———. *To Be a Man: Letters to My Grandson*. New York: Simon & Schuster, 1997.

———. *The Courage to Be Free*. Saudade Press, 2000.

Heston, Charlton, and Jean-Pierre Isbouts. *Charlton Heston's Hollywood: 50 Years in American Film*. New York: GT Publishing, 1998.

Leyda, Jay, ed. *Voices of Film Experience: 1894 to the Present.* New York: Macmillan Publishing Co., 1977.

Olivier, Laurence. *Confessions of an Actor.* New York: Simon & Schuster, 1982.

———. *On Acting.* New York: Simon and Schuster, 1986.

Reagan, Ronald. *Public Papers of the Presidents of the United States. Containing the Public Messages, Speeches, and Statements of the President.* Washington: U.S. Government Printing Office.

———. *Reagan: A Life in Letters.* Edited by Kiron K. Skinner, Annelise Anderson and Martin Anderson. New York: Free Press, 2003.

———. *Ronald Reagan: An American Life.* New York: Simon and Schuster, 1990.

———. *The Reagan Diaries.* Edited by Douglas Brinkley. New York: Harper Collins, 2007.

Skinner, Kiron K., Annelise Anderson, and Martin Anderson, eds. *Reagan: A Life in Letters.* New York: Free Press, 2003.

Welles, Orson and Peter Bogdanovich. *This is Orson Welles.* New York: Da Capo Press, 1998.

Articles:

"All Men Mark Their Territory," Dear Abby, *Los Angeles Times*, Oct. 22, 1998.

"Ben-Hur Rides Again," *Look* (December 8, 1959), 62-63.

Delson, James. "Heston on Welles," *Take One* (Vol. 3:5), 7-9.

———. "Heston on Welles," in Comito, Terry, ed., *Touch of Evil, Orson Welles, Director.* (New Brunswick, NJ: Rutgers University Press, 1985), 213-222.

Ford, Gerald R. Public Papers of the President of the United States: Gerald R. Ford, 1976-1977. Washington: U.S. Government Printing Office.

Hamill, Pete. "Heston: Larger Than Life," *Saturday Evening Post* (July 3, 1965), 87-91.

———. "What Does Lou Grant Know About El Salvador?" *New York Magazine* (March 15, 1982), 24-30.

Henderson, Wanda. "Heston Puts His Foot in It, Makes Lasting Impression," *Los Angeles Times*, Jan. 25, 1962.

Heston, Charlton. "Camels" advertisement, *Popular Mechanics Magazine* (April 1953), Back Cover.

———. "Charlton Heston's Alzheimer's Announcement and Goodbye." www.junebergalzheimers.com/charlton-hestons-alzheimers-announcement-and-goodbye.

———. "Charlton Heston 'Ben Hur' Diaries," *Cinema* (July 1964), 10-13, 29, 34.

———. "Front Row Center," *Atlanta Weekly*, August 11, 1985.

———. "Heston to Attend Statue Unveiling at Cowboy and Western Museum," *Oklahoman*, September 25, 2002, www.newsok.com/article/2808486

———. "Jervis Antiseptic Hair Tonic" advertisement, *Look* (April 7, 1953), 6.

———. "Van Heusen Century Shirts" advertisement, *Life* (September 7, 1953), 115.

Johnson, Lyndon B. *Public Papers of the President of the United States. Containing the Public Messages, Speeches, and Statements of the President.* Washington: United States Government Printing Office.

Klein, Patricia. "The Day the L.A. Police Almost Gunned Down Charlton Heston," *TV Guide* (May 16-22, 1987), 4-8.

Landers, Ann. "Teach Kids About Gun Safety," *Los Angeles Times*, Sept. 27, 2001.

Linderman, Lawrence. "Charlton Heston Interview," *Penthouse Magazine* (August 1980), 106-112, 174-176.

Martin, Pete. "I Call on Ben-Hur, *Saturday Evening Post*, August 20, 1963, 20-21, 40, 42-43.

Murphy, Mary. "Prime Chuck," *TV Guide* (February 20-26, 1999), 32-33.

Nixon, Richard. *Public Papers of the Presidents of the United States. Containing the Public Messages, Speeches, and Statements of the President.* Washington: United States Government Printing Office.

Rader, Dotson. "If I Ran & Won, I'd Never Be Able to Act Again," *Parade Magazine* (March 9, 1986), 4-7.

Rensin, David. "20 Questions: Charlton Heston," *Playboy* (May 1983), 139 and 205-206.

Schwalberg, Carol. "Bookviews Talks to Charlton Heston," *Bookviews* (November 1978), 16-19.

Scott, Vernon. "Charlton Heston's Life Story," *Good Housekeeping* (May 1986), 128-130, 247-250.

Vincent, Mal. "Security, Asheville Almost Got Him," *Virginian-Pilot*.

DVDs:

"Commentary by Leigh Taylor-Young and Director Richard Fleischer," *Soylent Green*, Turner Entertainment Co., 2003.

Fitzmaurice, Michael. "West Coast Welcomes Ben-Hur," *News of the Day*, *Ben-Hur*, Collector's Edition, 2011.

———. "Japan's Emperor Goes to the Movies," *News of the Day*, *Ben-Hur*, Collector's Edition.

Roberts, Peter. "Costliest Film Makes Screen History," *News of the Day*, *Ben-Hur*, Collector's Edition.

———. "'Oscar' Likes Ben-Hur," *News of the Day*, *Ben-Hur*, Collector's Edition.

———. "'VIP' Opening: Capital Welcome for Ben-Hur," *News of the Day*, *Ben-Hur*, Collector's Edition.

"1961 Vintage Radio Interviews with Charlton Heston," and "Charlton and Lydia Heston," *El Cid*, The Weinstein Corporation, 2008.

Websites:

The Bob Crane Show, KNX-CBS Radio, 1960, www.youtube.com/watch?v=8b2tPQ5Cc48

"Charlton Heston: Utah's Little Hollywood," The Historical Marker Database, www.hmdb.org/m.asp?m=41318, 8.

Charlton Heston, *What's My Line?* October 28, 1956, www.youtube.com/watch?v=ZavJcwBIlrU.

"F.O.E. Ten Commandment Monuments in North Dakota (6),"
www.eaglesmonuments.com/states/North_Dakota.html.
"HARDtalk, BBC Interview with Tim Sebastian, 1997," part 1,
www.youtube.com/watch?v=KnsDeAZtJbE
"HARDtalk, BBC Interview with Tim Sebastian, 1997," part 2,
www.youtube.com/watch?v=0MhfXt-2LTc
"HARDtalk, BBC Interview with Tim Sebastian, 1997," part 3,
www.youtube.com/watch?v=LkhLjPnjyYQ
"La Jolla Playhouse, California," www.lajollaplayhouse.org.
"Reagan Rally, Cincinnati, Ohio, November 2, 1980."
www.video.search.yahoo.com/search/video?fr=yfp-t-s&p=President+Ford+Charlton+
Heston#id=1&vid=1f16eea59f3b030150450c5598c5a536&action=click
Trailer, *The Last Hard Men*,
www.imdb.com/title/tt0074776/videoplayer/vi3015225369?ref_=tt_ov_vi.

Secondary Sources:
Books:
Allen, Michael J. *Until the Last Man Comes Home: POWs, MIAs, and the Unending Vietnam War.* Chapel Hill: University of North Carolina Press, 2009.
Birchard, Robert S. *Cecil B. DeMille's Hollywood.* Lexington: University Press of Kentucky, 2004.
Brode, Douglas. *Dream West: Politics and Religion in Cowboy Movies.* Austin: University of Texas Press, 2013.
Brownstein, Ronald. *The Power and the Glitter: The Hollywood-Washington Connection.* New York: Pantheon Books, 1990.
Bruck, Connie. *When Hollywood had a King: The Reign of Lew Wasserman, Who Leveraged Talent into Power and Influence.* New York: Random House, 2003.
Carroll, Linda, and David Rosner. *Duel for the Crown: Affirmed, Alydar, and Racing's Greatest Rivalry.* New York: Gallery Books, 2014.
Chandler, Charlotte. *Hello, I Must be Going: Groucho and His Friends.* Garden City, NY: Doubleday & Co., Inc., 1978.
Charlton Heston Celebrity Shoot, n.p., n.d.
Cohan, Steven. *Masked Men: Masculinity and the Movies in the Fifties.* Bloomington: Indiana State University Press, 1997.
Compo, Susan A. *Warren Oates: A Wild Life.* Lexington: University of Kentucky Press, 2009.
Crowther, Bruce. *Charlton Heston: The Epic Presence.* London: Columbus Books, 1986.
Druxman, Michael B. *Charlton Heston: A Pyramid Illustrated History of the Movies.* New York: Pyramid Communications, 1976.
Eliot, Marc. *American Rebel: The Life of Clint Eastwood.* New York: Harmony Books, 2009.
———. *Charlton Heston: Hollywood's Last Icon.* New York: HarperCollins, 2017.
———. *Jimmy Stewart: A Biography.* New York: Harmony Books, 2006.

Farkis, John. *The Making of Tombstone: Behind the Scenes of the Classic Modern Western*. Jefferson, NC: McFarland & Co., 2019.

Fishgall, Gary. *Gregory Peck: A Biography*. New York: Scribner, 2002.

Freese, Gene. *Classic Movie Fight Scenes: 75 Years of Bare Knuckle Brawls, 1914-1989*. Jefferson, NC: McFarland & Company, 2017.

Haney, Lynn. *Gregory Peck: A Charmed Life*. New York: Carroll & Graff, 2004.

Harvey, Mark. *Celebrity Influence: Politics, Persuasion, and Issue-Based Advocacy*. Lawrence: University Press of Kansas, 2017.

Higham, Charles. *Ava: A Life Story*. New York: Delacourt Press, 1974.

Hirsch, Foster. *The Hollywood Epic*. South Brunswick, NJ: A. S. Barnes, 1978.

Holden, Anthony. *Laurence Olivier: A Biography*. New York: Athenaeum, 1988.

Hyams, Jay. *The Life and Times of the Western Movie*. New York: Gallery Books, 1983.

Linet, Beverly. *Susan Hayward: Portrait of a Survivor*. New York: Athenaeum, 1980.

Link, William A., *Righteous Warrior: Jesse Helms and the Rise of Modern Conservatism*. New York: St. Martin's Press, 2008.

Kim, Erwin. *Franklin Schaffner*. Metuchen, NJ: Scarecrow Press, 1985.

Koury, Phil A. *Yes, Mr. DeMille*. New York: G. P. Putnam's Sons, 1959.

Leighton, Frances Spatz. *The Search for the Real Nancy Reagan*. New York: Macmillan Publishing Co., 1987.

Madsen, Axel. *William Wyler: The Authorized Biography*. New York: Thomas Y. Crowell, 1973.

Maltin, Leonard. *Leonard Maltin's Movie & Video Guide, 2001 Edition*. New York: Signet Books, 2000.

McGilligan, Patrick. *Clint: The Life and Legend*. New York: St. Martin's Press, 1999.

Michaud, Michael Gregg. *Sal Mineo: A Biography*. New York: Crown, 2010.

Miller, John. *Ralph Richardson: The Authorized Biography*. London: Sidgwick & Jackson, 1995.

Mitroff, Ian I. and Warren Bennis. *The Unreality Industry: The Deliberate Manufacturing of Falsehood and What it is Doing to our Lives*. New York: Oxford University Press, 1993.

Morris, Aldon D. *The Origins of the Civil Rights Movement: Black Communities Organizing for Change*. New York: Free Press, 1984.

Munn, Michael. *Charlton Heston: A Biography*. New York: St. Martin's, 1986.

———. *John Wayne: The Man Behind the Myth*. London: Robson Books, 2003.

Osborne, Robert. *Academy Awards Illustrated: A Complete History of Hollywood's Academy Awards in Words and Pictures*. LaHabra, CA: Ernest E. Schworck, 1966.

Parish, James Robert. *Whoopi Goldberg: Her Journey From Poverty to Megastardom*. Secaucus, NJ: Birch Lane Press, 1997.

Paul, Joanna. *Film and the Classical Epic Tradition*. Oxford, UK: Oxford University Press, 2013.

Peretti, Burton W. *The Leading Man: Hollywood and the Presidential Image*. New Brunswick, NJ: Rutgers University Press, 2012.

Phillips, Gene D. *Out of the Shadows: Expanding the Canon of Classic Film Noir*. Lanham, MD: Scarecrow Press, 2012.

Phillips, Jr., William D. and Carla Rahn Phillips. *A Concise History of Spain.* Cambridge: Cambridge University Press, 2010.

Prindle, David F. *The Politics of Glamour: Ideology and Democracy in the Screen Actors Guild.* Madison: University of Wisconsin Press, 1988.

Raymond, Emilie. *From My Cold, Dead Hands: Charlton Heston and American Politics.* Lexington: University Press of Kentucky, 2006.

———. *Stars for Freedom: Hollywood, Black Celebrities, and the Civil Rights Movement.* Seattle: University of Washington Press, 2015.

Ross, Steven J. *Hollywood Left and Right: How Movie Stars Shaped American Politics.* New York: Oxford University Press, 2011.

Rovin, Jeff. *The Films of Charlton Heston.* Secaucus, NJ: Citadel, 1997.

Russell, James. *The Historical Epic and Contemporary Hollywood: From* Dances with Wolves *to* Gladiator. New York: Continuum, 2007.

Schickel, Richard. *Clint Eastwood: A Biography.* New York: Alfred A. Knopf, 1996.

Solomon, Jon. *Ben-Hur: The Original Blockbuster.* Edinburgh: Edinburgh University Press, 2016.

Spoto, Donald. *Laurence Olivier: A Biography.* New York: Harper Collins, 1992.

The Story of the Making of Ben-Hur: A Tale of the Christ. New York: Random House, 1959.

Strachey, Lytton. *Eminent Victorians: Cardinal Manning, Florence Nightingale, Dr. Arnold, General Gordon.* San Diego, Harvest.

Strober, Deborah Hart and Gerald S. Strober. *Reagan: The Man and His Presidency.* Boston: Houghton Mifflin, 1998.

Wapshott, Nicholas. *The Man Between: A Biography of Carol Reed.* London: Chatto & Windus, 1990.

Wills, Brian Steel. *Gone with the Glory: The Civil War in Cinema.* Lanham, MD: Roman & Littlefield Publishers, Inc., 2007.

Wills, Garry. *John Wayne's America.* New York: Touchstone Books, 1998.

Wise, James E., Jr., and Paul W. Wilderson, III. *Stars in Khaki: Movie Actors in the Army and the Air Services.* Annapolis, MD: Naval Institute Press, 2000.

Articles:

Alpert, Don. "Heston Scores Extremists," *Boston Sunday Globe*, Dec. 19, 1965.

Adams, Marjory. "Charlton Heston/A hero for all roles," *Boston Globe*, Oct. 20, 1970.

———. "Charlton Heston Visits Boston, Gives Lucky Girls Orchids," *Boston Daily Globe*, March 26, 1954.

———. "Film Producers Want Actors Not Charmers, 'Hot' Star Says," *Boston Daily Globe*, August 8, 1950.

———. "Heston (as Moses) Nearly Lost His Own Son in the Bulrushes," *Boston Daily Globe*, Nov. 16, 1956.

———. "Heston's Toughest Role?" *Boston Globe*, July 28, 1967.

———. "Producer Gets Caught In Front of Cameras," *Boston Globe*, Nov. 2, 1965.

———. "'10 Commandments' Filming in Egypt Described by Heston," *Boston Sunday Globe*, Dec. 19, 1954.

Allen, Frederick. "Mr. Heston, Mr. Jim, and Georgia's schools," *Atlanta Constitution*, Nov. 15, 1983.

Ames, Walter. "Bergen, Charlie McCarthy in TV Debut Today; Heston Says Movies Tougher Than Video," *Los Angeles Times*, Nov. 23, 1950.

Bacon, James. "Heroic Heston Wants to Do Comic Next," *Boston Daily Globe*, April 19, 1960.

Baker, Kathryn. "Heston Jokes on NBC; Philips on HBO," *Los Angeles Times*, Mar. 27, 1987.

Balzar, John and Keith Love. "Cranston, Zschau Shift Gears, Opt for 'Going Positive' as Voting Nears," *Los Angeles Times*, Nov. 1, 1986.

Beale, Betty. "Washington May Never Be the Same Again," *Boston Sunday Globe*, Feb. 12, 1967.

Beck, Marilyn. "Star Pickets Hard to Find," *Richmond Times-Dispatch*, Sept. 15, 1980.

Biekelhaupt, Susan. "Before he was Moses," Names & Faces, *Boston Globe*, Feb 13, 1995.

Blowen, Michael. "Bearer of Bad Tidings," *Boston Globe*, Aug. 21, 1980.

———. "For Heston the key is resilience," *Boston Globe*, July 21, 1980.

———. "Heston's desert career continues," *Boston Globe*, Sept. 6, 1981.

Blume, Mary. "Donald Pleasance—Proud of His Wicked Film Ways," *Los Angeles Times*, July 21, 1968.

Bold, Kathryn. "Shooting Stars Come Out for NRA Gala," *Los Angeles Times*, July 16, 1992, www.articles.latimes.com/1992-07-16/news/vw-3455_1_u-s-shooting-team.

Burr, Ty. "It was always clear where the actor stood," *Boston Globe*, Apr. 7, 2008.

Carmen, John. "'Chiefs' dodges locale identity," *Atlanta Constitution*, Nov. 11, 1983.

Carmody, Jay. "Newest of Male Film Stars Dreams of a Stage Role," [Washington, DC] *Evening Star*, August 14, 1950.

Carter, Betsy, and Martin Kasindorf. "The Over-the-Hill Gang," *Newsweek*, November 15, 1976.

Chad, Norman. "Root for Redskins? Not if Snyder paid me,"·*Boston Globe*, Sept. 1, 2000.

Chapin, Dwight. "As Barriers Fall," *Los Angeles Times*, May 19, 1975.

"Charlton Heston going to N.H. rally," *Boston Globe*, Oct. 15, 2002.

"Charlton Heston's Tablets of Stone," *The Economist*, May 1, 1999.

"Charlton Heston treated for cancer," *Boston Globe*, Jan. 2, 1999.

Chase, Donald. "Between Scenes with Charlton Heston," *Saturday Evening Post*, November 1983, 42.

Davidson, Bill. "The House That Ben-Hur Built," *Look* (May 24, 1960).

———. "The Possibilities of More Lust, Power, and Intrigue Seemed Endless," *TV Guide* (November 16, 1985).

Dreyfuss, Robert. "Bush's Concealed Weapon," *Rolling Stone* (March 21, 2001).

Dutka, Elaine. "Prophets, Presidents—and the King of Beers," *Los Angeles Times*, March 31, 1996.

Dyer, Richard. "Charlton Heston thriving on disaster movies," *Boston Globe*, Oct. 14, 1974.

Eastman, Janet. "Charlton Heston," *Orange Coast*, August 1980.

Ellison, Sarah. "The Civil War that Could Doom the N.R.A.," *Vanity Fair*, June 27, 2016.

Feeney, Mark. "Charlton Heston: going from left to right," *Boston Globe*, Aug. 17, 2007.

Finnigan, Joseph. "Charlton Heston is Proud of Being a Working Actor," *Boston Sunday Globe*, July 1, 1962.

———. "Fighting on Another Front," *TV Guide* (June 17, 1967).

Fox, Christy. "Keeping the Ball Bouncing," *Los Angeles Times*, Sept. 6, 1971.

Freed, David. "Hollywood's Shooting, and Not Just Films: Firearms: Show business turns to guns for recreation and security. 'I would feel very naked,' without one, says Charlton Heston," *Los Angeles Times*, May 21, 1992.

Gertson, Jill. "Living in the shadow of a famous husband," *Boston Globe*, Apr. 5, 1980.

Gillen, Marilyn A. "Holy Cyberspace! A Biblical CD-ROM," *Billboard*, Nov. 5, 1994.

Glaser, Vera. "LBJ Finds Picture He Likes," *Boston Globe*, July 1, 1967.

Graham, Sheilah. "Hollywood Diary," *Evening Star*, Feb. 20, 1952.

———. "'One Night I Was on TV, and the Next Day I signed a Movie Contract,'" *Boston Sunday Globe*, July 17, 1955.

Granville, Kari and Don Shirley. "Actors' Equity Says White Can Portray Eurasian," *Los Angeles Times*, Aug. 17, 1990.

"The Graven Image," *Time*, August 12, 1966.

Gust, Dodie. "The American Film Institute," *Hollywood Reporter 44th Anniversary Edition*, Nov. 29, 1974.

Haber, Joyce. "Chuck Heston: A Toga Man in the Jeans Era," *Los Angeles Times*, December 3, 1972.

Hall, Carla. "Conservative actor Charlton Heston has a long history of activism. Now, the screen icon hopes to help lead the NRA to a better place," *Los Angeles Times*, May 27, 1997.

Hall, John. "Welcome to the NFL," *Los Angeles Times*, July 17, 1969.

Hastings, Julianne. "Do two roles make Heston a born-again TV star?" *Atlanta Journal/Constitution*, October 13, 1984.

Helfand, Duke. "Hollywood Artifacts Rescued From Blaze," *Los Angeles Times*, Sept. 19, 1996.

———. "Hollywood Memorabilia Rescued From Flames," *Los Angeles Times*, Sept. 19, 1996.

"Heston sees cassettes actors' savior," Names and Faces in the News, *Boston Globe*, Nov. 23, 1970.

"Heston special on WJKW-TV8 shows World Relief in action," *TV Sun Stations*, Cleveland, OH, January 20-26, 1983.

Hirshon, Paul. "But would he say the same to the BSO?" Names and Faces, *Boston Globe*, June 3, 1990.

Hopper, Hedda. "Charlton Heston Set for Billy Wilder Film," *Los Angeles Times*, Oct. 11, 1951.

———. "Glenn Ford, Eleanor Film Globe-Trotters," *Los Angeles Times*, March 10, 1950.

———. "Heston Believes in Hard Work," *This World San Francisco Chronicle*, April 6, 1953.

————. "Local and Imported Discoveries Project Elusive 'Movie Presence,'" *Los Angeles Times*, Dec. 31, 1950.

————. "Phyllis Kirk to Star in 'Come on, Texas,'" *Los Angeles Times*, July 29, 1952.

————. "Pidgeon Winning Good Role of Legal Eagle," *Los Angeles Times*, Dec. 1, 1950.

————. "Second Story Bought for Robert Merrill," *Los Angeles Times*, Sept. 27, 1950.

Jackson, Derrick Z. "Missouri smites 'Moses'" *Boston Globe*, Apr. 9, 1999.

Jancovich, Mark. "'Charlton Heston is an Axiom': Spectacle and Performance in the Development of the Blockbuster," in Willis, Andy, ed., *Film Stars: Hollywood and Beyond*. New York: Manchester University Press, 2004.

Janofsky, Michael. "N.R.A. Tries to Improve Image, with Charlton Heston in Lead," *New York Times*, June 8, 1998.

Kass, Carole. "Heston: Many Faces Mark His Varied Career," *Richmond Times Dispatch*, September 7, 1980.

Kelly, Kevin. "What Charlton Heston Regrets About 'Ben Hur,'" *Boston Daily Globe*, Nov. 5, 1959.

Kern, Rusty and Kathy Kern. *Playset Magazine* (Nov./Dec. 2006).

Kerwin, Robert. "Safe Conduct as Heston Parts the Mountain Men," *Los Angeles Times*, Aug. 10, 1980.

King, Bill. "*Chiefs*: An Unusual Portrayal of the South and an Unusual Role for Heston," *Atlanta Journal/Constitution*, Nov. 11, 1983.

King, Susan. "Heston Tells of Disease," *Los Angeles Times*, Aug. 10, 2002.

Kirkpatrick. William S. "A Dark Corner of U.S. History," 1957.

Leibowitz, Ed. "Charlton Heston's Last Stand," *Los Angeles* (February 2001).

Lewis, Andy. "Hollywood Flashback: When the Oscars were Postponed for Martin Luther King, Jr.'s Funeral," *Hollywood Reporter*, April 3, 2018.

Limke, Helen. "Bringing Up Baby," *Photoplay* (October 1955).

Linet, Beverly. "I Was There," *Photoplay* (June 1952).

Liston, Jim. "At Home with Charlton Heston," *The American Home* (May 1962).

Mann, Roderick. "Heston's Queeg to Steer for Home," *Los Angeles Times*, June 29, 1985.

"Martin Luther King's Death Postpones Oscars," *Variety*, April 8, 1968.

Martin, Pete. "I Call on Ben-Hur," *Saturday Evening Post*, August 20, 1960.

Martinez, Al. "Learning more about the man known as Moses," *Los Angeles Times*, April 21, 2008.

Marton, Andrew. "Ben-Hur's Chariot Race," *Films in Review* (January 1960).

McCabe, Bruce. "Puffery, trifles, politics, glitter," *Boston Evening Globe*.

McGilligan, Patrick. "Hollywood's Bicentennial salvo: Midway," *Boston Sunday Globe*, July 20, 1975.

McKinnon, George. "Movies/Heston as 'failure,'" *Boston Globe*, June 21, 1970.

Nashawaty, Chris. "An Epic Life," *Entertainment Weekly*, April 18, 2008.

Nason, Jerry. "Graham Makes Actor of Heston," *Boston Globe*, Nov. 4, 1959.

Nicholson, Tom, Pamela Abramson, and Janet Huck. "For Whom the Bell?" *Newsweek*, October 17, 1977.

Nowell, Paul. "NRA elects Heston president for 3d term," *Boston Globe*, May 23, 2000.

"NRA: Armed with Pride," *American Hunter* (March 1998).

"NRA elects a movie hero with mainstream appeal," *Boston Globe*, June 9, 1998.

Plutzik, Roberta. "Last of the Epic Heroes," *Horizon* (March 1980).

Postman, Neil. "President Heston," *The Nation* (October 5, 1985).

Pousner, Howard. "Heston is guest for UVA film fest," *Atlanta Journal/Constitution*, Oct. 20, 1991.

Ribadeneira, Diego. "Venerable Heston still goes by the Book" The Spiritual Life, *Boston Globe*, Nov. 29, 1997.

Richardson, John H. "Heston," *Esquire* (July 2001).

Rosenberg, Howard. "CNN Reporter Connects with Ethiopian Famine," *Los Angeles Times*, Dec. 14, 1984.

———. "Nuclear Policy a Bomb in the Hands of Actors," *Los Angeles Times*, Nov. 2, 1982.

"Roth's Fury at 'Monster' Heston"
    www.contactmusic.com/tim-roth/news/roth.s-fury-at-.monster.-heston

Ruehlmann, Bill. "Like Heston, memoir is substantial, straightforward," *Virginian-Pilot*.

Russo, Tom. "Opposites Attract," *Boston Globe*, Aug. 21, 2003.

Saunders, Michael and Jim Sullivan. "Heston dried out," Names & Faces, *Boston Globe*, Aug. 1, 2000.

Schallert, Edwin. "Charlton Heston Eager for Capt. Cook Break; Cooper Forms Company," *Los Angeles Times*, Sept. 22, 1954.

———. "Charlton Heston Plans Varied Activities," *Los Angeles Times*, Oct. 11, 1956.

———. "Hal Wallis to Spend $19,500,000 on Pictures; Marlowe Joins 'Mister,'" *Los Angeles Times*, June 9, 1950.

———. "Heston-Romulus Deal in Negotiation; Noah Beery Stirs Up Indians," *Los Angeles Times*, March 6, 1954.

———. "Lupino Again to Star Tod Andrews; 'Cities' Features Ann Vernon," *Los Angeles Times*. April 1, 1950.

———. "Wechsler Will Produce 'Anne'; Heston and Wife Named Play Principals," *Los Angeles Times*, June 23, 1951.

Scheuer, Philip K. "Brando's Neither 'Slob' Nor Best Actor, Critic Argues," *Los Angeles Times*, Dec. 5, 1954.

———. "'Dark City' Introduces Charlton Heston, Promising Rugged Type," *Los Angeles Times*, Feb. 5, 1951.

Schumach, Murray. "Heston Refunds Salary to Studio," *New York Times*, May 9, 1964.

Scott, Vernon. "Charlton Heston Gets Ready for New Epic Film," *Boston Globe*, Aug. 30, 1960.

———. "Asner denies Heston's charges," *Boston Globe*, Jan. 26, 1982.

Seligmann, Jean, Sharon Begley, and Michael Reese. "Tracking the Fault," *Newsweek*, July 10, 1978.

Shannon, Don. "Red Cross Begins Africa Famine Drive," *Los Angeles Times*, Dec. 11, 1984.

Sherman, Marjorie W. "A Boston Tribute to the United Nations," *Boston Globe*, March 12, 1965.

Slater, Jack. "Arts Task Force: Heston's New Role," *Los Angeles Times*, Aug. 26, 1981.

Sluss, Michael. "NRA takes aim at Tim Kaine," *Roanoke Times*, June 17, 2005.

Stark, John. "Chatter," *People* (August 19, 1985).

Starr, Mark, and with Ron LaBrecque. "Asner the Activist," *Newsweek*, March 8, 1982.

———, with Ron LaBrecque, Martin Kasindorf, and Janet Huck. "Ed Asner's Star Wars," *Newsweek*, March 22, 1982.

Steele, Joseph Henry, "Unmasking Charlton Heston," *Photoplay* (January 1958).

Stoddard, Maynard Good, and Cory SerVaas. "Charlton Heston: He'd Rather Pretend Than Be President," *Saturday Evening Post*, Sept. 1984.

Sullivan, Elizabeth L. "Heston in Bible Verses Tonight—Comedy Thursday," *Boston Sunday Globe*, May 1, 1960.

Thomas, Bob. "Greatest Movie 'Stunter' Makes It a Safe Science," *Boston Sunday Globe*, Dec. 6, 1964.

———. "Hollywood luminaries gather to pay last respects to Heston," *Boston Sunday Globe*, April 13, 2008.

Thomas, Kevin. "'Last Hard Men' Here at Last," *Los Angeles Times*, Sept. 28, 1977.

Thomsen, Ian. "Trojan tradition: ancient history?" *Boston Globe*, Sept. 18, 1987.

"Tim Roth and Charlton Heston's Opposing Gun Views," July 27, 2001, www.imdb.com/news/ni0051586/#:~:text=Tim%20Roth%20And%20 Charlton%20Heston%27s%20Opposing%20Gun%20Views.,pair%20had%20 to%20work%20together%20in%20the%20movie.

Tizon, Tomas Alex. "Suit Pans Director's Publicity Stunt," *Los Angeles Times*, July 27, 2003.

Van Slyke, Helen. "From 'Moses' to 'Midway,' Charlton Heston is Larger Than Life," *Saturday Evening Post*, Jan./Feb. 1976.

Vincent, Mal. "Back in the Saddle," *Virginian-Pilot*, September 28, 1987.

———. "'Gray Lady' Above Average," *Virginian-Pilot*, Mar. 17, 1978.

———. "In the nick of time came a rock-jawed hero," April 8, 2008.

Wadler, Joyce. "Thou Shalt Not Whine," *TV Guide* (November 12, 1983).

Waterbury, Ruth. "Charlton Loves Lydia," *Photoplay* (June 1953).

Watson, Jarnel E. "Heston brings gun debate to Brandeis," *Boston Globe*, Mar. 29, 2000.

Webb, Mike. "Charlton Heston: The Nude love scene that went too far!" *Photoplay*. (March 1969).

Weinraub, Bernard. "Holy Moses! Now Charlton Heston's Playing Brigham Young," *TV Guide*, January 21, 1995.

Weinstein, Henry. "Actors Guild Divided Over Right to Work," *Los Angeles Times*, Sept. 12, 1986.

Welkos, Robert W. "Heston Faces His Illness Squarely," *Los Angeles Times*, Aug. 18, 2002.

——— and Susan King. "Charlton Heston, 84; Actor was larger than life, on screen and off," *Boston Globe*, Apr. 6, 2008.

Welter, Ben. "Heston says he'll stay out of politics," *Virginian-Pilot*, July 4, 1982.

Werling, Karen. "Appreciation: Charlton Heston's Life as a Wildcat," *North by Northwestern* (April 16, 2008), www.northbynorthwestern.com/story/heston-at-northwestern/.

Wharton, David. "Team Gets Star Treatment," *Los Angeles Times*, Dec. 29, 1995.

Wright, Robert A. "Screen Actors Guild in Bitter Election," *New York Times*, October 20, 1971.

Ziegler, Philip. *Olivier*. New York: MacLehose Press, 2013.

Index

About the Author

Brian Steel Wills is the Director of the Center for the Study of the Civil War Era and Professor of History at Kennesaw State University in Kennesaw, Ga. In addition to leading tours, offering lectures, and conducting programs, Dr. Wills is the award-winning author of numerous works relating to the American Civil War, including biographies of Confederate generals Nathan Bedford Forrest and William Dorsey Pender and Union general George Henry Thomas. He has also written about the Civil War in Virginia and in the movies, as well as a volume that focuses on non-combat deaths in the Civil War. A graduate of the University of Richmond, Va., and the University of Georgia, he spends time on his farm in Virginia when not teaching and working in Kennesaw.